Social Simulation:
Technologies, Advances, and New Discoveries

Bruce Edmonds
Manchester Metropolitan University, UK

Cesáreo Hernández
University of Valladolid, Spain

Klaus G. Troitzsch
Universität Koblenz–Landau, Germany

INFORMATION SCIENCE REFERENCE

Hershey · New York

Acquisitions Editor:	Kristin Klinger
Development Editor:	Kristin Roth
Senior Managing Editor:	Jennifer Neidig
Managing Editor:	Sara Reed
Copy Editor:	Michael Goldberg
Typesetter:	Jamie Snavely
Cover Design:	Lisa Tosheff
Printed at:	Yurchak Printing Inc.

Published in the United States of America by
Information Science Reference (an imprint of IGI Global)
701 E. Chocolate Avenue, Suite 200
Hershey PA 17033
Tel: 717-533-8845
Fax: 717-533-8661
E-mail: cust@igi-global.com
Web site: http://www.igi-pub.com/reference

and in the United Kingdom by
Information Science Reference (an imprint of IGI Global)
3 Henrietta Street
Covent Garden
London WC2E 8LU
Tel: 44 20 7240 0856
Fax: 44 20 7379 0609
Web site: http://www.eurospanonline.com

Library of Congress Cataloging-in-Publication Data

Social simulation : technologies, advances and new discoveries / Bruce Edmonds, Cesareo Hernandez & Klaus G. Troitzsch, editors.

p. cm.

Summary: "This book, a reference survey of social simulation work comprehensively collects the most exciting developments in the field. Drawing research contributions from a vibrant community of experts on social simulation, it provides a set of unique and innovative approaches, ranging from agent-based modeling to empirically based simulations, as well as applications in business, governmental, scientific, and other contexts"--Provided by publisher.

Includes bibliographical references and index.

ISBN-13: 978-1-59904-522-1 (hardcover)

ISBN-13: 978-1-59904-524-5 (ebook)

1. Social sciences--Computer simulation. 2. Social interaction--Simulation methods. 3. Social exchange--Simulation methods. I. Edmonds, Bruce. II. Hernandez, Cesareo. III. Troitzsch, Klaus G.

H61.3.S625 2008

300.1'13--dc22

British Cataloguing in Publication Data
A Cataloguing in Publication record for this book is available from the British Library.

All work contributed to this book set is new, previously-unpublished material. The views expressed in this book are those of the authors, but not necessarily of the publisher.

Table of Contents

Section II
The Empirically-Oriented

Detailed Table of Contents

Section I
The Model-Oriented

Chapter I

Conditional cooperation is a prominent explanation of reciprocal cooperation in repeated exchange. However, empirical evidence for commitment behavior indicates that people tend to build long-term cooperative relationships characterized by largely unconditional cooperation. Using an agent-based ecological model, earlier work showed that in competitive environments commitment can be a more successful strategy than fair reciprocity. We move further in two respects. First, we add the possibility of randomly mutating strategies under evolutionary pressures. Our results show the lack of evolutionary stable strategies but we also find that commitment strategies still outperform fairness strategies on average. Our second extension introduces inequality in individual capabilities. We find that inequality shifts the balance from commitment towards fairness strategies. Our explanation is that under inequality, strategies benefit from changing interaction partners from time to time because this gives more agents access to strong partners.

Chapter II

This chapter describes the development of a prototype multi-agent based model—the Tax Compliance Simulator (TCS)—designed to help tax administrators think about ways to reduce tax evasion. TCS allows the user to define unique behavioral, income, and tax enforcement characteristics for one or two distinctive taxpayer populations. The capabilities of the model are demonstrated in a simulation of the deterrent effects of taxpayer audits. The simulation finds that a significant portion of audit-based deterrence may depend on the influence of taxpayers' social networks rather than the probability of detection or penalty for underreporting as indicated by economic theory (Allingham & Sandmo, 1972).

What are the principles underlying social differentiation? Socioeconomic models generally consider agents that pursue some particular ends a given, prior to their social activity. In this chapter we propose an alternative in the framework of metamimetic games. We claim that the distribution of ends in a population is the outcome of social interactions and not only what drives them. We take the example of the prisoner's dilemma in spatial games to illustrate how cultural co-evolution can lead to a spontaneous differentiation of ends in a population with a high level of cooperation. From this perspective, the question is not the traditional: "How can altruists 'survive' in a selfish world?" but rather to understand how heterogeneous ends can reinforce or limit each other to collectively entail the emergence of a social cooperative order.

This chapter studies continuous opinion models with extremists, and we use probability distribution models which approximate the behaviour of agent-based models in order to explain their attractor patterns. The probability distribution is defined on a discrete grid in the opinion / uncertainty space. We compute the equations of probability flows between each of the sites of the grid for different variants of the opinion influence model (bounded confidence, relative agreement, and two others). The simulations show that the probability distribution models yield attractor patterns very similar to those obtained with the agent-based models. Moreover, a study of the probability distribution evolution helps to better understand the process of convergence to single and double extreme attractors observed in agent-based models.

Chapter V

Science is important, not only in the knowledge it gives us, but also as an example of effective distributed problem solving that results in complex and compound solutions. This chapter presents a model of some of the social interactions in science, namely those between the body of published knowledge and the scientists' individual knowledge. The structure of knowledge is modelled by a formal Hilbert system for a classical propositional logic. Individuals have limited selections of the total knowledge available which they use to derive new knowledge, and may submit to the central journal to be published. This model shows how difficult it is to achieve the accumulation of knowledge as in science and also that publishing more does not necessarily lead to more important knowledge being discovered.

Chapter VI

Since Holland (1993) introduced the concept of tags, a number of tag models with intriguing and potentially very useful, properties have been advanced. However, there is currently little understanding as to the exact mechanisms that produce these results. Specifically, it is not known what (if any) are the necessary conditions for tag systems to produce high levels of cooperation in social dilemmas. In this chapter, by comparing existing tag models to formulate a hypothesis and then using simulation, we identify what appears be a necessary condition for high cooperation. Previous tag models implicitly contained the condition but authors did not identify the significance of it.

Chapter VII

This chapter explores the effects of a more realistic agent-based land exchange mechanism on the relative competitive success of innovative and imitative strategies for selecting land uses, using the FEARLUS-ELMM model. A key question in our investigation is whether land use decision strategies can be studied in isolation from land-market exchange decision strategies. Results derived via computational experiments show that land-market modelling decisions do affect outcomes, improving to an extent the relative success of innovators. We also conclude that further additions are needed to our model, and finally, we question whether a "big bang" strategy may have been more effective than our step-by-step evolution to the land-market model, which was chosen to facilitate comparison to results derived from the original FEARLUS.

Chapter VIII

In this chapter, the authors perturb a Minority Game (MG) with some sociological issues, first by implementing a social network among the involved agents, through which they can somehow communicate their decision to a group of "friends," a local subset of those participating the game. Thus, the emergent aggregate behaviour will be very far from that of the original MG; the stress here is on the possibility of an agent changing his or her own decision, after getting the information from other n agents. Two different communication protocols among the agents will be examined: a synchronous one and the more realistic asynchronous one. Additionally, in some experiments, a memory is introduced, acting as a selection mechanism. Last, some special agents (Opinion Leaders) whose influence over the others is higher than normal, in order are implemented in order to study how this can change the aggregate results.

Chapter IX

The analysis of relations between different levels of a system is a key issue in social science simulation. Here, I discuss the contribution of different modelling methodologies relative to this. Special emphasis is given to the formalism of "Probabilistic Graphical Models," or "Bayesian Networks," which are both advantageous for level transitory inference and integration of empirical data. Furthermore, issues of practicability and area of application are considered. The argumentation is exemplified by the demonstration of a toy-application for which explicit level-transitory statements are inferred.

Chapter X

Evolutionary studies account for cooperation under the shadow of the future. But how can altruism spread without direct reciprocity? Learning from punishment, including criticism, is impossible in harsh environments, where agents do not survive the rejections received. Imitation is indispensable, but what to imitate? Frequent behaviors are not necessarily socially desirable, nor is their fitness observable. In this chapter, agents meeting with infrequent but lethal food scarcity survive thanks to food sharing. Saving recipients from certain death, donations reduce altruists' lifespans. Results show that prudent donors, helping only when [who are]above the starvation point, are exploited by cheaters and are soon extinguished. The same happens with agents taking reciprocity into account, and helping only when their credits are turned off. Instead, agents endowed with dynamic goals (survival versus giving help) learn even the most unconditioned form of altruism, thus avoiding extinction. Tentative conclusions are discussed. Among others, dynamic goal-directed agents are autonomous entities learning even the most generous forms of altruism. Moreover, prudence is not necessarily more adaptive than unconditioned altruism; indeed, it may be self-defeating under the given conditions.

Chapter XI

This chapter presents the purpose, basic concepts, implementation, and a scenario run of the agent-based part of a large Decision Support System for the water resources management of the Upper Danube basin, Western Europe. Sixteen process models from 11 disciplines in the natural and social sciences are integrated in the system. They use common spatial and temporal concepts to communicate with each other at run time. A variety of agents based on large scale empirical evidence serves to model the drinking water use of households. An example scenario run under global warming conditions shows the interplay between modelled water supply companies, households, climate, and groundwater resources.

Section II
The Empirically-Oriented

In this chapter, we present a multi-agent system that models and simulates the dynamics of intra-urban mobility through the automated formation and evolution of both groups of households and groups of housing-units. We consider global rules of evolution instead of individual events to represent the evolution of both the population and the housing-stock. The moving mechanism is modelled by interactions between groups and urban-sector agents in a simulated housing market. We have tested this system on the basis of several census datasets of Bogotá city. The evolution of groups has been simulated over 20 years and compared to real data. The results of group formation and evolution mechanisms have been compared to classes produced by classical classification methods. Very good correlations have been found. The simulated population has been compared to real distributions of several Bogotá districts and appears to be close for an important number of them.

In this chapter we show how agent-based social simulation helps us to improve some of the traditional models and theories in financial economics. In particular, we explore the links between the microbehaviour of investors and the aggregated behaviour of stock markets. First, we build an agent based model of an artificial financial market, populated only with rational investors. We observe that the statistical features of this market are in agreement with the theoretical markets suggested by mainstream financial economics, but far away from the features shown by real financial markets, like the Spanish Ibex-35, the Spanish Stock Market main Index. In order to fill the gap, we introduce heterogeneity in the model. We add psychological investors, as suggested by Kahnemen and Tversky (1979), and we are able to reproduce non-normality, excess kurtosis, excess volatility, and volatility clustering. Then, we introduce technical traders, and we also get higher levels of excess volatility and unit roots from the model. In other words, psychological dealers seem to be responsible for volatility clustering, whereas technical traders trend to introduce unit roots into the process. All these "financial patterns" are a common feature not only for Spanish Ibex-35, but also the most important stock markets. We conclude that agent based social simulation helps us to fill the gap between economic theory and real markets, as we explain the statistical features of financial time series from the bottom-up.

In this chapter the authors demonstrate with three relevant issues that agent based modelling (ABM) is very useful to design emissions permits auctions and to forecast emission permits prices. They argue that ABM offers a more efficient approach to auction design than the usual mechanistic models. The authors set up the essential components of any market institution far beyond supply and demand. They build an ABM for the emissions permits auction of the Environment Protection Agency (EPA) and demonstrate why the EPA failed. In the second experiment they show that in a competitive and efficient auction, the Continuous Double Auction, there is room for traders' learning and strategic behavior, thus clearing the perfect market paradox. In the third experiment they build an ABM of the Spanish electricity market to get CO_2 emissions price forecasts that are more accurate than those obtained with econometric or mechanistic models.

Concession behavior is typically seen in bargaining processes, e.g., in intergovernmental negotiations. In traditional bargaining theory, especially in game-theoretic models, concessions to opponents are interpreted as actions in which the conceding party loses face. In this chapter, we propose a new approach to bargaining: peer coordination. Rather than losing face on conceding to opponents, focal governments will increase their reputation among peers when adjusting to the present positions of the peers. Relying on a data set on the EU Intergovernmental Conference of 1996 which led to the Amsterdam treaty, we test and corroborate the hypothesis that a peer coordination model which assumes peer coordination in intergovernmental policy networks makes better predictions for negotiation outcomes than a random model which we interpret as a kind of null model.

Following the traditional approach to decision theory it is very difficult to obtain policy hints for complex systems. On the other hand, the study of complex systems supplies powerful instruments that capture useful information on the behaviour of economic systems. This difficulty is enhanced when we are interested in differential regional effects. In fact, for complex systems, even for aggregate analysis, results will differ deeply for each simulation. The literature has shown how we could obtain policy hints for these kinds of systems. Here, we will extend this methodology to the case of differential regional effects. The analysis will be based on a New-Keynesian microfoundated model with Heterogeneous Agents proposed by Salzano (2005). It will be developed in two directions: (a) obtaining better models of differential regional policy effect; (b) obtaining policy suggestions for differential regional effects. We will compare the results of our scheme against traditional results.

This chapter develops an agent-based model to analyze microscopic and macroscopic links between investor behaviors and price fluctuations in a financial market. This analysis focuses on the effects of Passive Investment Strategy in a financial market. From the extensive analyses, we have found that (1) Passive Investment Strategy is valid in a realistic efficient market, however, it could have bad influences such as market instability and inadequate asset pricing deviations, and (2) under certain assumptions, Passive Investment Strategy and Active Investment Strategy could coexist in a Financial Market.

In a collective action, people act together with the intention of producing public goods. Public, or collective, goods are states or objects that benefit the many but only emerge if a sufficient number of persons make contributions. The present study explains the dynamics of participation in collective action campaigns by considering the interaction of different processes. With the resulting model it is possible to determine the optimal combination of diffusion measures for such a campaign. Before using the model for experimenting, we calibrate its parameters using data from a real world collective action. We find this to be a most important step in order to demonstrate that the model can be grounded empirically and to demonstrate the practical usefulness of simulation for consulting and design of real world processes. Finally, some "what if" scenarios reveal the model's power of explanation and prediction.

This chapter presents an agent-based computational model of the emergence of money. It is based on classical economic theories of money, advocating that money is a symbol of credibility. The most interesting and mysterious feature of money is a departure of its face value from its intrinsic value. People accept and appreciate a piece of paper because it is believed as money. The model examines how such belief creates money in a society. Further more, by incorporating spatial activities of agents into the simulations, the model can examine various hypotheses which were difficult to examine in previous approaches. The simulation results show that parameters such as credibility and communication between agents will affect the outcomes. The model not only provides the foundation for a more generalized theory of money, but also demonstrates that agent-based modelling can be an effective tool to examine various hypotheses of social sciences.

Section III
The Participant and Experimentally-Oriented

Chapter XX

Starting from a simple gaming-simulation experiment about the management of a common resource, two modelling experiments were conducted in different settings. In the first experiment, the game was played by farmers and the modeller subsequently inferred a model from behaviour observed during the game. In order to address the validation problems underlying this type of modelling, a new experiment was conducted, in which computer science students played the game and then "self-modelled" their behaviour. We shall present, compare, and discuss both these modelling processes. We show that self-modelling facilitated a better understanding of the players' behaviours, although it is not a complete solution.

Chapter XXI

When selecting work team members several behavioral components concur. In this chapter we are interested in investigating the effects of these components in terms of team selection, agent aggregation and performance of groups. A computational model, together with a theoretical approach and the results of two human experiments where subjects interact in a similar game, allow us to identify some of the most important determinants. Our results suggest that the occurrence of two factors is crucial: the presence of leaders as aggregators of knowledge and agents being able to expand and improve their higher profit projects. It is particularly evident that leaders have a threefold role. First, they increase the social network of other agents making possible projects otherwise impossible. Second, they state the pace of a balanced growth in terms of social network, while taming the otherwise combinatorial explosion. Finally, they help in selecting one of the theoretically possible equilibria.

Chapter XXII

This chapter introduces a formal model of a complex knowledge integration process named "thinking along." Here the firm is modelled as a working environment consisting of agents arranged into work-practices, which provide the context for their interactions. The objective of the simulations reported here is to compare two different practice structures and test their effectiveness for solving problems by thinking along. To do so we will also introduce the notion of problem complexity as the basis for different experiments. From such a comparison it emerged that complex problems are better tackled when practices group together agents with disparate skills (i.e., divisional practices) whereas simple problems can be more effectively addressed by organisational practices composed of agents with similar skills (i.e. functional practices). In either case, the simulated knowledge integration process played the dominant role.

This chapter describes a multi-agent model of a double-auction market in which simulations are led. In our market study we focus on information processing and hence make assumptions about the cognitive use that agents make of this information. For some years now, experiments have been used to study auctions and now resulting data are used to make hypotheses about learning. We propose simulations here that are organised on the same model as experiments, as a succession of auction sessions where each agent is either seller or buyer and has to exchange before the end. Communication is made of bids and asks that can be accepted by the others and lead to transactions. Our main result is the fact that we actually obtain convergence although agents have no knowledge of others' limit prices and only interact through a completely impersonal market. This corresponds to experimental data, which is a positive result in our search of the representation for economic rationality and is discussed methodologically in the chapter.

This chapter discusses qualitative and quantitative approaches to informing and validating ABMs. Research is introduced which addresses the question of how new e-commerce technology is leading to the restructuring of value chains. A case study was undertaken within a major international organisation, focusing on exploring those issues identified as interesting and important by a small stakeholder group working in the company and actively participating in the research. A central theme of this chapter is the interaction and relationship with stakeholders during the project, regarding the development of the ABM. The chapter concludes that a multi-methodological approach is appropriate to simulation-based projects, and identifies stakeholder participation as being useful in several ways, in particular because it facilitates model validation.

Preface

INTRODUCTION

Social simulation is *the* "killer application" of multi-agent systems. Our world is populated with complex independent entities which interact in complex ways, be they humans, institutions, animals, computers, or even machines. In many cases the interactions between these cannot be satisfactorily modelled without including a lot of the detail of the individuals and their individual interactions (Granovetter, 1985). When you include these individuals and their interactions in a model, one has an individual-based model. Most such models of this kind do not admit to analytic solutions and are instead explored and used in computational forms. Thus, computational models dominate this kind of modelling, with analytic techniques tending to perform supporting and complementary roles.

Human and animal societies are the richest source of analogies and conceptual models for understanding such models. When such societal interpretations are used to guide and understand such individual-based models, you have a social simulation. Thus social simulation can be seen as a natural consequence of a more detailed modelling of phenomena that is usefully divided into separate but interacting chunks (Edmonds, 2003). This explains the interest and applicability of the field of social simulation to researchers across a wide variety of fields, including (but not limited to): sociology, economics, archaeology, computer science, artificial intelligence, artificial life, visualisation, philosophy, robotics, and psychology.

As Turkle has documented, computers and computational entities (such as agents), are natural objects to take as a model for the self. For this reason it is natural to interpret the individuals in many individual-based models as having some sort of cognition that we can recognise as being analogous with our cognition—what Dennett calls "the intentional stance" (Dennett IS) with respect to the intentions/ goals subset of our cognition. Indeed, it has been argued that it is part of our human social nature that we use others around us as models for our own cognition as well as projecting our cognitive processes upon other candidate entities. When we can usefully interpret the individuals in our models as cognitive entities, we have an agent-based social simulation. A software "agent" is no more and no less than a computational entity that is usefully thought of as a having some sort of cognition.

For the above reasons, multiagent-based simulation (MABS) has become a popular tool with which to theorise about distributed but interacting phenomena. You will see that agent-based simulation dominates this volume of chapters, with almost all describing such a model. The above also explains many of this technique's advantages and disadvantages. Such MABS can provide a good half-way house between some complex phenomena and our understanding, "mediating" (Morgan & Morrison, 1999) between the two. They represent a step towards a more descriptive manner of modelling, because the entities in the model separately represent the entities in what is observed and the interactions in the model represent the observed interactions—the model is structured in a way that mirrors the known structure of the phenomena. However, their complexity means that it is usually impossible to completely understand the model—the relationship between the set-up of the model and the results from the model is typically very complex. Thus, we necessarily have to have theories about the behaviour of our model—a model of our model.

Since a computational model is completely open to our inspection and easily modifiable in a controlled manner, it is ideally designed for experimentation. Thus, unlike most social modelling, we can use MABS to perform extensive experimentation upon the entity to test and develop our understanding of the mechanism or behaviour involved. We view social simulation with MABS as laboratories where we can *grow* from micromechanisms to macroscopic social structures that match observed signatures or have desirable properties. Thus, the use of social simulation is not restricted to predict unknown futures in the same way as a theory in physics, but allows a better understanding (and hence explanation) of microbehaviour and agent interactions.

Even at a minimum, MABS models of social phenomena involve several different kinds of models. There is the computational model itself, of course this is often in the foreground of the description of such work. However, there are typically the following other "models." Note that the word "model" has many distinct meanings, all subtly different (Wartofsky, 1979):

- There is the conceptual model that the modeller has of the phenomena of interest.
- Separately, there is the conceptual or mental model of the MABS model, the theories that the modeller has as to how the MABS model works—this is usually described but is often left somewhat implicit—this is usually less complex than the conceptual model that the modeller has of the phenomena of interest, since it is usually impractical to include all of what one thinks happens in a single model.
- Often one finds that researchers conflate their mental model of their MABS model with their conceptual model of the target phenomena—they get so used to *thinking* about their object of study *using* their model that they come to identify the two completely. This can be seen as the ultimate kind of "theoretical spectacles" that Kuhn talked about. Thus, in many descriptions of social simulations the same words are used to refer to entities or properties of the target phenomena, and the objects and their attributes of the MABS model that more properly only represent such real-world entities and their properties, respectively.
- If the results of the model are going to be compared with recorded observations, for example time-series data, then the data itself are a kind of model—a data model. It can be important to clearly distinguish data from the phenomena it derives from, because it relies upon the process and assumptions used in obtaining it (which, in turn, can often involve other models or theories of measurement, for instance). This is especially so when such observations are deliberately abstracted and processed, for example: to show power laws, as social networks, or to "stylised facts." It is almost never the case that the results from a MABS model *exactly* match those in such data models and the reasons that a mismatch is acceptable are often found in the nature of the data model (as well as the gap between the conceptual model of the MABS model and the conceptual model of the phenomena). Many models do not use any sort of data model to partially validate their model, relying instead on purely conceptual links to what they are studying. Such models can be interesting and informative, but have no independent guarantee that the model has *anything* to do with the phenomena it is claimed to be about.

In addition to the above, much work seeks to formalise conceptual models. Thus, one might have mathematical models that abstract the behaviour of the MABS model, often by simplifying it using assumptions and/or approximations, or by taking simple subcases. Such models have the advantage of being analytically tractable and are potentially completely transparent to our understanding; they sit "above" the MABS model in terms of a level of abstraction. The great advantage here of using a MABS model is that it serves to stage the abstraction from observation to mathematical theory, preserving more of the reference in the model and making it more open to criticism and improvement. When someone asks why this formula is specified in this way, a definite (and checkable!) answer can be given in terms of the observed behaviour of the MABS model, which can, in turn, be potentially checked against data series (which could be checked against actual observations).

This contrasts strongly with what might be called "over-ambitious" analytic modelling of complex phenomena which apparently seeks to "leap-frog" such tedious descriptive modelling stages and, by use of clever assumptions, go straight to a useful but tractable theory. With such theory one often has to rely upon a considerable level of interpretation to get the theory to fit any actual observations, they act more as a sort of theoretical analogy than anything else—a way of expressing *how* a person thinks about something rather than a verifiable or otherwise useful theory *of* the target.

In any case, in all the work described in this book, there is not only one model being used but more of a closely-related hierarchy of models, from those that are more directly derived from observations up to the most abstract conceptualisations of behaviour: from data model, through a MABS model, up to a theory of MABS model (formalised or otherwise, implicit or explicit). More than this, hopefully, clusters of such models (as explicated within) may be emerging that, together, form the nearest thing we have to a theory of social phenomena. The models that accompany the foreground MABS model are essential to fully understanding the significance and scope of such work.

Of course, the *purpose* of any model is also important to its understanding.. Some models are meant mainly to *illustrate* a process, whilst others are meant to *describe* a particular case study. In this book some of the models are not primarily meant as a *representation* at all, but more of a *tool* to facilitate some interaction between people. Thus, in some work in this area the involvement of participants and stakeholders is of utmost importance—not just their involvement at the beginning and end of the modelling process, but during the process. In this way, *users* of the model can begin to *own* the model by being more intimately involved in its *control*. This is a matter of degree: In order for a model to be a good *tool* it usually has to accurately *represent* something (if only the users' perceptions of the target), and to *represent* social phenomena it is often the case that experts' and stakeholders' feedback on using the model as a *tool* is sought as a way of checking or improving a model.

THE CHAPTERS

The above account should make the organisation of the book (and indeed each chapter) easy to understand. The book is divided into three sections, which *very roughly* categorise the chapters as to their type. These divisions separate: those chapters which are *more* concerned with exploring a model that is suggested by the modeller's understanding of some social phenomena (the "Model-Oriented" section); those which seek *more* to describe or explain observations of phenomena by comparing the behaviour of the model with sets of recorded observations (the "Empirically-Oriented" section); and those which seek to involve other people in the model development *more* directly, through participatory approaches and experiments (the "Participant and Experimentally-Oriented" section). We cannot emphasise enough that this is a rather *ad-hoc* division in many cases, but we felt that some division would help the reader to navigate through this volume. Within each division the ordering is purely arbitrary, being determined by the alphabetic ordering of the surname of the first author of each chapter.

It must be said that the distinction between these kinds of work are not always clear-cut. When investigating the behaviour of a model, most authors will have in mind a certain class of social phenomena. They will select the range of model behaviour that is explored as that which are compatible with and interesting for understanding this target. Thus, in that kind of work there is almost always an *implicit* filtering and selection process: The focus is on the behaviour of the model but the work is filtered through the authors' understanding of what the model represents. Likewise, modelling work that seeks primarily to describe or explain observations will also include some exploration of the model. It is almost always the case that not all aspects of the model are intended to be representational of what is observed, for example, the exact nature of random-number generators used. To check that the behaviour of the model corresponds with that of the observed process in those aspects that are *intentionally representative* it is necessary to vary the other aspects to see if the processes that are claimed as representing those observed remain. So some model exploration is necessary to check this, even though the main aim is description and/or representation of observed processes.

Likewise, there is not a clear-cut distinction between work that seeks to involve stakeholders in a participatory manner and those which seek to match their models against recorded data in a more traditional manner. Even when the model development is being driven by the views of stakeholders, the credibility is (implicitly or otherwise) judged against what is observed. In the more traditional style of modelling where stakeholders are not directly involved in the model development, intuitions will still be important in determining (or at least framing) the specification of the individual's behaviour in the model. These intuitions will almost always be ultimately derived from accounts of such behaviour given by people (even if it is only the modellers themselves). It is a major advantage of individual-based simulation that it can include such accounts in its design and validation—this allows a whole new world of evidence to be used in the formulation of formal models, and can make the models more accessible and more comprehensible for nonexperts.

The chapters in all the sections of this book, cover a wide range of approaches, purposes, techniques and subject matter. They are a good snap-shot of the best current work in social simulation. There are, however, certain themes and topics that run through many of them. In the rest of this preface we will use these themes to introduce the various chapters.

Section I: The Model-Oriented. Axelrod (1984) and his colleagues used an abstract game, the "prisoner's dilemma" (PD), to represent social dilemmas within an individual-based model. In this model, the individuals would play each other, often many times. In this game, each player has the choice of either cooperating with the other or not. The essence of this structure is that those who manage to coordinate their action so they both cooperate get a positive outcome but if one "cheats" when the other is cooperating, the cheater does slightly better at a huge cost to the cooperating one. The point is that everybody does better on average if all cooperate, but if some try for a slightly better outcome for themselves, the average benefit drops sharply. Indeed, in many set-ups all the individuals quickly adapt so that no one cooperates (the situation with no coordination/trust) and all do very badly indeed. When this game is played several times with the same partner, this is called the "Iterated Prisoner's Dilemma" (IPD). There is now vast literature on this game and the simulations that use it to represent social-dilemma situations in an abstract way (Axelrod & D'Ambrosio, 1994). The advantage of this is that it has resulted in a large body of work that is strongly interrelated. The downside is that, sometimes, those involved forget that this is an abstract and contrived representation and *assume* that their conclusions can tell us about real social situations.

Three chapters use the IPD in their models to represent the interaction between agents. Chapter I by Back and Flache extends the classic Axelrod IPD, with commitment or fair reciprocity. They try adding the evolution of strategies and then an inequality between partner strengths. They find no evolutionary stable strategies but runs with commitment seem to do better than those with fair reciprocity; the balance shifts towards fair reciprocity when fair reciprocity is enforced. In Chapter III by Chavalarias, it is shown how cultural co-evolution on IPD games can lead to spontaneous differentiation of ends in a population with a high level of cooperation. This is because the spreading of imitation rules can lead to a spontaneous diversity in the population where the heterogeneous ends reinforce or limit each other collectively within the metamimetic framework set up. Meanwhile, Hales in Chapter VI examines a whole family of simulations based around the PD game where individuals are biased towards interacting with those that have similar tags as their own. He identifies what appears be a necessary condition for high cooperation (namely for tag-based systems to support high levels of cooperation, tags must mutate faster than strategies) and also states a "mini-theory" to explain this.

Chapter X by Di Tosto, Paolucci, and Conte looks at a similar situation to the PD, but based on the interaction between vampire bats. These bats survive infrequent but lethal food scarcity by sharing food. The chapter shows that unlike either prudent donors (helping only when above the starvation point) or those taking reciprocity into account; agents with dynamic goals can learn even the most unconditioned form of altruism, thus avoiding extinction.

A similar sort of motivation underlies the work in Chapter VIII by Remondino and Cappellini, but this time it is based around a different game: the "minority game." This game was first brought to prominence by Brian Arthur as the "El Farol Bar problem" [B. Arthur], but this was later rechristened to the "minority game" by subsequent researchers. The idea here is that one wins the game by being different from the majority of other players. This chapter looks at some social extensions of this set-up, investigating the effect of: explicit social networks, the difference between synchronous and asynchronous regimes, agent memory, and the presence of opinion leaders. The consequences of social networks are also investigated in Chapter II.

Chapters II, IV, V, VII, and X are less abstract, being motivated by more specific sets of cases. However the reported work is concerned more with how the model works rather than whether the model can be validated against observations of the modelling target. Thus, these models are only suggestive of what is happening in the real world cases and are closer to computational analogies—ways of thinking about the target phenomena—rather than being *representations* of them.

Bloomquist, in Chapter II, views a model of tax-evasion, examining the deterrent effects of taxpayer audits therein. He finds that a significant portion of audit-based deterrence may depend on the influence of taxpayers' social networks rather than the probability of detection or penalty for underreporting.

Deffuant and Weisbuch continue a series of papers examining opinion-dynamics models in Chapter IV. The target of this investigation is a family of continuous opinion-dynamics models, where individuals have an opinion represented by a floating point number in the [-1, 1] interval. Individuals can also have a similar uncertainty concerning their opinion. The model shows a drift to either one or two extremes by the whole population, given some initial certain extremists, and only occasionally a convergence to a moderate opinion. This chapter is of particular interest because it combines the use of an individual-based simulation with a mathematical approximation (via a master equation) which is thennumerically calculated and used to explain the dynamics of the individual-based model.

Edmonds in Chapter V uses a process of distributed theorem-proving as a model for some of the knowledge-sharing processes that may occur in science or mathematics. Knowledge here is a set of theorems in a formal logic. Individuals generate new knowledge by proving new theorems, given their limited knowledge, which may then enter the public domain by publication in a journal. He finds that publishing more does not necessarily result in more important knowledge being collectively discovered. It is interesting to compare the representation of knowledge here with that in Chapter XXII.

In Chapter VII, Polhill, Parker, and Gotts look at the effects of changing the process of going bankrupt and selling off land in a model of land-use change. They show that land market modelling decisions do affect outcomes, improving to an extent the relative success of innovators when a market-based selling mechanism is introduced. They note that what they call "decision ecologies" may evolve, so as to ensure stability or long-run survival at the scale of the rural system.

Schwenk's chapter (Chapter IX) is very different from the others in this section. It is more philosophical in inclination. It argues that we should formally separate out a model into different causally-connected levels. He suggests a way of doing this using probibilistic networks at each level. He argues that this is necessary since the comprehension of complex processes is always accompanied by the introduction of functional higher levels. He shows how graphical models of processes can be supplied with a precise interpretation which allows exactly for this. This is an ambitious but highly abstract chapter which points the way to a radically different way of modelling complex social phenomena.

Section II: The Empirically-Oriented. The chapters in this section all have at their core a concern to *represent* some observed social phenomena. Each of these are related to the observed world to greater or lesser extents and each then uses the model either to explore some of the possibilities that might be found by varying some of the setup, or to produce explanations of parts of the processes that are hidden. Of course, even if no exploration of the model occurs, one still has a useful computational *description* of some observed phenomena—a description that captures some of the dynamics of the situation. It is often forgotten that description is a useful and valid scientific activity, all too often by-passed in the rush for a general theory. Financial markets have continued to fascinate modellers for a host of reasons: First, they *seem* to be simple enough to be able to make some progress, second, there is a lot of aggregate data about them in the form of time-series (but much less of other kinds of evidence, such as ethnographic studies or social network studies, etc.), and third, they are important social institutions with a potentially large impact upon society in general. Since the classic paper by Palmer et al. (baron) on the artificial stock market, there have been a host of papers using the power of individual-based simulation to try and understand them. This book has two of these.

The first is Chapter XIII by Pascual and Pajares on the role of risk aversion and technical trading in Spanish financial markets. Here they explore the links between the microbehaviour of investors and the aggregated behaviour there. They expand the Palmer et al. model to include psychological investors whose risk aversion changes over time depending on their previous performance in the market as well as technical traders who go for short-term gain. They find that more psychological investors leads to greater kurtosis in the resultant time series while more technical traders result in unit roots (showing the trend to be stochastic). In other words, the psychological dealers are related to the emergence of bubbles, and technical trading makes the system stationary. The time-series derived from the Spanish Stock Market exhibits both kurtosis and unit roots suggesting that (if the model is correct) there are both psychological investors and technical traders present.

The second individual-based simulation is Chapter XVII by Takahashi, Takahashi, and Terano. This examines possible links between investor behaviour and price fluctuations in a financial market. It focusses on the effects of passive investment strategy in such markets, and that introducing such strategies is realistic but can cause instability of market and inadequate asset pricing deviations. They conclude that under certain assumptions, Passive Investment Strategy and Active Investment Strategy could coexist in a Financial Market.

Two other chapters deal with markets of other kinds, one in this section and one in the next (Chapter XIV). Thus, Posada, Hernández, and López-Paredes model an emissions permits auction, and show that in a competitive and efficient auction there is room for traders learning and strategic behaviour, thus dealing with the perfect market paradox. Then they show that an agent-based model accurately predicts prices for CO_2 emissions for the Spanish electricity market.

Yamadera in Chapter XIX are also concerned with economic phenomena, namely seeking to explain how money might emerge. This is based upon classical economic theories of money, advocating that money is a symbol of credibility. In the model, a number of items are traded for each other such that their face value it not necessarily the same as their intrinsic value. The idea is that people accept and appreciate a piece of paper because it is *believed* to be money. The model in this chapter examines how this kind of belief creates money in the society. By incorporating spatial activities of the agents into the simulations, the model examines various hypotheses, showing that parameters such as credibility, spatial constraints, and communication between agents will affect the outcome of the emergence of money.

The remaining four chapters in this section are of noneconomic social phenomena, showing how formal modelling is allowing a range of ideas and evidence to be brought into the scientific discourse. I will deal with these in the order that they appear.

Ernst, Schulz, Schwarz, and Janisch, in Chapter XI, describe an agent-based part of a large Decision Support System for the water resources management of the Upper Danube basin. Sixteen different process models from 11 disciplines in the natural and the social sciences are integrated into this system, using common spatial and temporal concepts to communicate with each other at run time. The model is used to explore the scenario of rising temperatures, reduced precipitation, and shrinking groundwater aquifers. They conclude that if this scenario may be Danube's tomorrow, then it is necessary to have more precise ideas about the interplay between natural and social factors in the water cycle. This sort of negative conclusion is quite common in social simulation as the complexity of the subject matter has not been eliminated by assumption (as in statistical or analytic approaches). It is a huge advantage; you may not get *an answer* but that may just reflect the reality that for this system there is not any such single answer, rather the way forward can suggest further avenues for investigation and understanding of the target system.

In Chapter XII, Gil-Quijano, Piron, and Drogoul exhibit a model of the co-evolution of population and housing stock in the city of Bogotá. In this model, intra-urban mobility is achieved through the automated formation and evolution of both groups of households and housing-units, and the moving mechanism is modelled by interactions between these groups and urban-sectors agents in a simulated housing market. The model has been tested against several datasets derived from censuses of Bogotá city.

Saam and Sumpter describe an ambitious model of peer coordination in intergovernmental negotiations in Chapter XV. Their theory is that rather than losing face in conceding to opponents, governments will try to increase their reputation among peers when adjusting their present positions. They compare the results with a data set on the EU Intergovernmental Conference of 1996 showing its superiority to a null model.

In Chapter XVI Salzano offers a model of differing regional policies within a geographic area. They showed that the effect of regional policy tools (public expenditure in this example) is strongly modified if we take into account the interactions of individuals. The conclusion is that one cannot leave out their heterogeneity or their interaction safely.

Tobias and Mosler in Chapter XVIII describe a diffusion and social network model of participation in collective action campaigns. They use data that were collected in the Swiss municipality of Muensingen near Bern to validate the model. They then used the model to explore a number of factors, including: number of diffusion events, number of participants, and the participants' intention to participate. They draw tentative conclusions pointing towards the importance of when to end a campaign.

Section III: The Participant and Experimentally-Oriented. The last section gathers together the chapters which involve on-line interaction with participants in some way, and not only via abstracted "data models" of outcomes. The techniques concerning how to do this in the best and most productive way are still very much an open topic, one in which there has been significant development over the past few years. Here, a range of such techniques and approaches are represented—they do not give a complete picture of this area but they do give a good flavour of this rapidly developing and exciting work. We will deal with these in the order in which they appear in the book.

In the first chapter in this section (Chapter XX), Boissau, Sempé, Boucher, Drogoul, and Bousquent describe two gaming-simulation experiments, both concerned with the management of a common resource. This innovative work uses simulations between humans as a core tool. Playing games between people (whether mediated by computers or boards and pieces) can give huge insight into the social processes involved and the thinking of stakeholders, as well being as a mediating tool between the stakeholders. This completely breaks the abstract simulation and compare cycle of traditional simulation approaches and can give the stakeholders some real, interactive control over model development. Here, a board game concerning grazing and resources was played between farmers, informing a model of their behaviour for the modeller. In the second experiment, computer science students played the game and then "self-modelled" their behaviour. The authors present, compare, and discuss both these modelling processes, showing that self-modelling facilitated a better understanding of the players' behaviours, although not a complete solution.

The next two chapters illustrate how individual-based models can escape the confines of numerically-based simulation when this is appropriate, allowing structure to play a key role. Dal Forno and Merlone describe a model of co-worker selection and their networks in Chapter XXI. This was based upon an empirical study on group composition. What is lovely here is to see the *development* of social structure in different cases.

In Chapter XXII, Morone and Taylor model knowledge production and integration in working environments, based upon the findings of an ethnographic study. Here, appropriately enough, knowledge is not represented as an *amount*, but in relation to other knowledge in an intricate structure. The development of links between firms comes as a result of the interaction of firms, their knowledge, and the way the various pieces of knowledge relate. They tentatively conclude that if a firm is normally confronted by predictable, focused problems, the most effective arrangement might be functional, whereas if challenged by unpredictable, complex problems, divisional might be better.

Rouchier and Robin investigate a model of double-auction market in Chapter XXIII, in particular the cognitive use of information by the participating agents. They obtain convergence to a final market price although agents have no knowledge of others' limit prices and only interact through a completely impersonal market. This corresponds to data and accounts gained form experiments with people. As a result of this data, they structure the individual decision-making process around two elements: reservation price and stress, defined as the time-pressure that is perceived by the agent. It expresses the fact that the agents know they have to exchange before the end of the market period.

Finally, in Chapter XXIV, Taylor describes a model which illustrates the integration of qualitative data to inform a model of e-commerce value chains. It uses stakeholder opinion and qualitative interview data to help validate the model in an integrated manner.

REFERENCES

Arthur, B. (1994). Inductive reasoning and bounded rationality. *American Economic Association Papers*, *84*, 406-411.

Arthur, W.B., Holland, J. H., LeBaron, B., Palmer, R., & Taylor, P. (1994). Artificial economic life: A simple model of a stock market. *Physica D 7,* 264-274.

Axelrod, R. (1984). *The evolution of cooperation*. New York: Basic Books.

Axelrod, R., & D'Ambrosio, L. (1994). *Annotated bibliography on the evolution of cooperation.* Retrieved from http://www.cscs.umich.edu/research/Publications/Evol_of_Coop_Bibliography.html

Dennett, D. (1989). *The intentional stance*. MIT Press; reprint edition.

Edmonds, B. (2003). Against: A priori theory For: Descriptively adequate computational modelling. In E. Fullbrook (Ed.), *The crisis in economics: The post-autistic economics movement: The first 600 days* (pp. 175-179). Routledge.

Granovetter, M. (1985). Economic-action and social-structure: The problem of embeddedness. *American Journal of Sociology*, *91*(3), 481-510.

Giere, R.N. (1988). Explaining science: A cognitive approach. *Science and its conceptual foundations series*. Chicago; London: University of Chicago Press.

Kuhn, T.S. (1962). The structure of scientific revolutions. Chicago: University of Chicago Press.

Morgan, M., & Morrison, M. (Eds.). (1999). *Models as mediators: Perspectives on natural and social science*. Cambridge: CUP

Suppes, P. (1962). Models of data Logic. In E. Nagel, P. Suppes, & A. Tarski (Eds.), *Methodology and the philosophy of science: Proceedings of the 1960 international congress* (pp. 252-261). Palo Alto, CA: Stanford University Press. Retrieved from http://suppes-corpus.stanford.edu/article.html?id=41

Turkle, S. (1984). The second self, computers and the human spirit. London: Granada.

Wartofsky, M. W. (1979). *Models*. Boston Studies in the Philosophy of Science, Vol. 129. Dordrecht: Reidel.

Section I
The Model–Oriented

Chapter I
Fairness, Commitment, and Inequality

István Back
University of Groningen (RuG), The Netherlands

Andreas Flache
University of Groningen (RuG), The Netherlands

ABSTRACT

Conditional cooperation is a prominent explanation of reciprocal cooperation in repeated exchange. However, empirical evidence for commitment behavior indicates that people tend to build long-term cooperative relationships characterized by largely unconditional cooperation. Using an agent-based ecological model, earlier work showed that in competitive environments, commitment can be a more successful strategy than fair reciprocity. We move further in two respects. First, we add the possibility of randomly mutating strategies under evolutionary pressures. Our results show the lack of evolutionary stable strategies but we also find that commitment strategies still outperform fairness strategies on average. Our second extension introduces inequality in individual capabilities. We find that inequality shifts the balance from commitment towards fairness strategies. Our explanation is that under inequality, strategies benefit from changing interaction partners from time to time because this gives more agents access to strong partners.

INTRODUCTION

Endogenous cooperation in durable relationships is often explained by reciprocity under a sufficient "shadow of the future" (Axelrod, 1984; Friedman, 1971). Evolutionary game theory has demonstrated that cheaters are outperformed by reciprocators if exchange relations persist long enough. However, empirical studies of cooperative behavior, in particular in interpersonal relationships, indicate that often reciprocity may be much less strict than this argument suggests. People have a tendency to build long-term cooperative relationships based on largely unconditional cooperation, and are inclined to hold on to them even in situations where this does not appear to be in line with their narrow self-interest (see, e.g., Wieselquist, et al., 1999). Experiments with exchange situations (Kollock, 1994; Lawler & Yoon, 1993, 1996) point to ongoing exchanges with the same partner even if more valuable (or less costly) alternatives are available. This commitment also implies forgiveness and gift-giving without any explicit demand for reciprocation (Lawler, 2001; Lawler & Yoon, 1993).

A range of computational studies following the seminal work of Axelrod suggest explanations of commitment based on evolutionary game theory. Computational analyses of exit effects (Schüssler, 1989; Vanberg & Congleton, 1992; Schüssler & Sandten, 2000) highlight the importance of commitment between cooperators for the viability of cooperation, because this mechanism implies the exclusion of defectors from interactions with cooperative partners. Other computational studies that include partner selection are, for example, Yamagishi, et al. (1994) or Hegselmann (1996, 1998)(cf. Flache & Hegselmann, 1999a, 1999b; Flache, 2001). Yet other works link reputation and norms with emergent relationships between agents, modelling partner selection explicitly as a result of agents' cognitive representations of their interdependencies with others and thus their need for interaction and collaboration (Conte & Castelfranchi, 1995; Sabater, et al., 2006).

While this previous work demonstrated the viability of relaxed accounting and commitment under certain conditions, it does not explain the deeply rooted emotions and behaviors related to interpersonal commitment. De Vos and collaborators (de Vos, Smaniotto, & Elsas, 2001; Zeggelink, de Vos, & Elsas, 2000; de Vos, & Zeggelink, 1997)

used evolutionary psychology (Cosmides, 1989; Cosmides & Tooby, 1993) to provide an answer. According to evolutionary psychologists, the way our mind functions today is the result of a long evolutionary process during which our ancestors were subject to a relatively stable (social) environment. Individual preferences for various outcomes in typical social dilemmas stabilized in this ancestral environment and still influence the way we behave in similar situations today.

Building on this work, Back and Flache (2006) showed that strategies following some form of commitment behavior are highly successful under a wide range of conditions, outcompeting fair, reciprocating strategies. In the current chapter, we move further and relax two key simplifications, putting the evolutionary explanation of commitment to a better test. First, we introduce random mutation of strategies under evolutionary pressures. This imposes the additional pressure of attacks from "smart cheaters" upon commitment players and, more generally, gives a larger coverage of an infinite strategy space. Second, we introduce variation in individual capabilities. Earlier studies based on fairness strategies (Hegselmann, 1996, 1998; Flache & Hegselmann, 1999b, 1999a; Flache, 2001) suggested that individual differences may give rise to core-periphery network structures in which the strongest members of the population exchange help with each other, driving weaker actors to the margin of the network. However, we may expect that commitment strategies reduce the exclusion of weak members from exchange networks, because commitment strategies bind themselves to "old helping partners" irrespective of the balance of exchanges.

In Section 2, we motivate and describe our model. In Section 3, we formulate conjectures based on previous work. In Section 4, we report results from computational experiments. Finally, Section 5 contains conclusions and a discussion of our findings.

MODEL

We use the delayed exchange dilemma (DED), an extension of the repeated prisoner's dilemma (see de Vos, et al., 2001; Back & Flache, 2006). The DED models the problem of cooperation in a sequential exchange perspective, and at the same time presents agents with a dilemma to choose interaction partners (see also, e.g., Hayashi & Yamagishi, 1998).

The DED is played by n agents in successive rounds. Initially, agents are endowed with f_i points. In the beginning of each round, Nature puts each agent with a given individually independent probability P_d in need of help from other agents. Needy agents are the initiators of interactions. Each asks another agent for help which is either provided or not. Providing help costs f_h points for the donor. Moreover, each agent may provide help only once during one round and only agents who are not distressed themselves may provide help. If a help request is turned down, the distressed agent may ask at most m further agents within the same round. If an agent does not get help before the end of the round, it experiences f_d loss in points. If the points of an agent fall below a critical threshold f_c, the agent dies.

To implement differences in individual capabilities, we introduce random variation in agents' effectiveness to help. We assign to each agent a fixed, random capability value from the [0,1] interval that describes how much help the given agent is able to provide to help-seekers. More precisely, the amount of points a distressed agent a_i loses when help is provided by agent a_j is equal to $f_d \cdot (1-\gamma_j)$, where γ_j is the helping capability parameter of agent a_j.

We assume moreover that helping capability, unlike social preferences, is not an inheritable property of agents, but purely phenotypic. An agent's helping capability, γ, is randomly assigned at birth and is unrelated to its ancestors' γ value. In this way we disentangle evolutionary pressures that operate directly on agents' capacity to help, from those pressures that operate on social preferences for discriminating between strong and weak exchange partners.

To study the viability of social preferences, we assume four types of preferences that determine agents' behavior. The first preference is to be generally cooperative, to help whenever asked. The second preference is to be fair: Do not help or ask agent a more often than agent a has helped or asked one to help. In other words, fairness introduces conditionality into cooperativeness. The third preference is to build long-term relationships, to interact with the same agent repeatedly (commitment). Note that this preference takes into account the absolute number of interactions between agent a and b, and not the relative proportions of cooperative and defective interactions, as in the case of fairness. Finally, the last preference is to interact with the most capable others.

Each agent has a combination of hypothetical genes that describe the strength of each of these preferences. Whenever an agent a_i has to make a choice between others, these preferences determine which other agent, if any, agent a_i will interact with. The genes are inherited and are subject to mutation[1] from generation to generation. This leads to huge variation in possible preferences, and thus in behavior over time.

Agents may face two different types of decisions in the DED. (1) They have to select an interaction partner to ask help from. And, (2) when asked to provide help they need to decide whether to provide it and in case of multiple requests whom to provide it to. In both cases, agents order possible interaction partners according to the overall attractiveness of interacting with them. Attractiveness is based on the individual preferences agents have with regard to past interaction histories.

The attractiveness of agent a_j for *giving help to*, calculated by agent a_i, is formalized as:

$$U_{ij}^G = comm_i^G \cdot INTFREQ_{ij} + fair_i^G \cdot INTBAL_{ij} + capa_i^G \cdot \gamma_j + coop_i,$$

where $comm_i^G$ is the preference for commitment in giving, $fair_i^G$ is the preference for fairness in giving, $capa_i^G$ is the preference for giving to the most capable others (γ_j is the help-seeker's capability here), and $coop_i$ is the preference for general cooperativeness. $INTFREQ_{ij}$ is the proportion of cooperative interactions[2] a_i had with a_j compared to the total number of cooperative interactions a_i had. $INTBAL_{ij}$ is the standardized interaction balance between agents a_i and a_j, calculated by adding the number of times a_i received help or refused to give help to a_j, subtracting the times a_j received help or refused to give help to a_i, and dividing this by the total number of interactions they had.

In the actual implementation of our model, every time an agent has to make a decision, there is a small probability that the agent will choose randomly from the set of available decisions, each being equally likely. This random error models noise in communication, misperception of the situation or simply miscalculation of the utility by the agent. Taking this random error into account increases the robustness of our results to noise. The attractiveness of agent a_j for *asking help from* is defined in a similar way, the differences being that agents may put different weights on the two history-specific decision parameters and that there is no general cooperativeness parameter[3]:

$$U_{ij}^A = comm_i^A \cdot INTFREQ_{ij} + fair_i^A \cdot INTBAL_{ij} + capa_i^A \cdot \gamma_j.$$

Note that in this case, γ_j denotes the capability parameter of the *donor*.

Before agents make a decision, they calculate the corresponding attractiveness respectively for each agent who asked for help (U^G), or for each other agent in the population (U^A). In the case of help giving, they choose a partner with the highest attractiveness, if that attractiveness is above an agent-specific threshold u_i^t. Notice that $INTFREQ_{ij}$ and $INTBAL_{ij}$ are always smaller than or equal to 1 in absolute value. We allow $comm_i$,

$fair_i$, $capa_i$, and $coop_i$ to take values from [-1;1]. Thus, we allow the attractiveness threshold to take values from [-4;4].

If the attractiveness of all possible agents is below the threshold, no help is given to anyone. Otherwise, if there is more than one other agent with highest attractiveness[4], the agent selects one randomly. In help seeking, agents also choose a partner with the highest attractiveness but there is no threshold, i.e., agents in distress always ask someone for help.

Definition 1 (Strategy) *A strategy is a combination of five genes for help giving behavior ($comm^G$, $fair^G$, $capa^G$, $coop$, and u^t) and three genes for help asking behavior ($comm^A$, $fair^A$, and $capa^A$).*

The evolutionary dynamic of our model captures *random mutation* of strategies and *selection* of objectively successful ones based on the replicator dynamics (Taylor & Jonker, 1978). Broadly, the replicator dynamics dictate that more successful strategies replicate at a higher rate.

We implement the evolutionary dynamic as follows: To keep the size of the population constant, at the end of each round we count how many agents have died and replace them with new agents in the next round. Each new agent a has the same strategy as a randomly selected other agent b, currently present in the population who has reached a minimum age n (measured in the number of interactions it had). The probability of choosing this other agent b is proportionate to the share of points b holds within the total number of points held by the group older than n. Before a is added to the population, with probability P_{mut}, its strategy undergoes mutation. Mutation may occur in exactly one, randomly chosen gene, with equal probabilities for all genes, thus $P=1/9$ for each gene. The new value of the gene is a uniformly distributed random value from the interval [-4;4] for the attractiveness threshold, and from [-1;1] for all other genes.

CONJECTURES

To guide the simulation experiments, we formulate a number of conjectures derived from previous work.

Definition 2 (Stability) *Stability of a strategy* s *is equal to the number of consecutive rounds* s *existed in a population in a given simulation run, counting from the first round it appeared until the round in which it became extinct. A strategy* s *is infinitely stable if it does not become extinct.*

Generalizing from analytical results about the evolutionary stability of strategies in repeated games that are simpler than the DED (cf. Bendor & Swistak, 2001), we expect that there is no single strategy that is superior to all others in the dilemma we study. In other words, for every incumbent strategy there exists another (mutant) strategy that can take advantage of the incumbent's weakness.

Conjecture 1. *There is no infinitely stable strategy in an infinitely played game of DED.*

Nevertheless, the length of time a strategy exists (stability) carries an important message about its viability. Therefore, stability of a strategy will be one of the indicators of its viability[5]. The other measure is typical longevity within a strategy (variable LONGEVITY, the average age at death of agents belonging to a strategy). Note that in our model, there is no upper age limit on reproducibility. Based on previous studies (e.g., Back & Flache, 2006), we expect:

Conjecture 2. *Individual preferences for interpersonal commitment and fairness have a positive effect on the viability of a strategy.*

Earlier studies based on fairness strategies (Hegselmann, 1996; Flache & Hegselmann, 1999b) suggested that individual differences in capabilities may give rise to core-periphery network structures in which the strongest population members exchange help with each other, driving weaker actors to the margin of the network. However, we believe that the evolutionary advantages of discrimination will actually be relatively small in our framework. The key reason is that we focus on differences in capability that are unrelated to the genetic makeup of agents. In such a world, agents who discriminate against the weak would harm their genetically related but weak "siblings" just as much as they would benefit genetically from unrelated but strong others. Accordingly:

Conjecture 3. *Preferences for commitment and fairness are more important for the viability of the strategy than a preference for capability.*

While we expect that both commitment and fairness tend to preclude exclusion of the weak, we also think that there will be important differences between these two strategy types in terms of their viability in a heterogeneous population. Commitment segregates the population into closed cliques (especially dyads), which could produce inefficient distribution of help. This is because the superior helping potential of the most capable agents will only benefit their fixed interaction partners and not the entire population, a problem that fairness strategies largely avoid. Hence, we posit:

Conjecture 4. *Variation in capability reduces the degree to which preferences for commitment foster viability and increases the degree to which preferences for fairness sustain viability.*

RESULTS

We conducted two sets of experiments. In the first set, we assumed equal helping capabilities. Correspondingly, in this set of experiments we used strategies without the two traits *capa*^{G} and

5

$capa^A$. In the second set, individual variation in capability was introduced.

We ran more than a hundred replications in both experiments, each time with the initial strategy randomly chosen from the strategy space. We did not find any significant effects of what the initial starting strategy was. Soon after the initial rounds, mutation ensured a large variety of different strategies in the population. Simulation runs ended with either the extinction of all agents[6] or after an arbitrarily chosen large number of rounds (10 million). We then repeated the simulation run with another, randomly generated initial population.

During each simulation run we recorded all strategies and their key characteristics that have ever appeared through random mutations. These characteristics include, on the individual-level, the genes describing a strategy ($comm^G$, $fair^G$, $coop$, u^t, $comm^A$, $fair^A$, and in the second set of simulations also $capa^G$ and $capa^A$) and on the strategy-level, average longevity measured in rounds of game play.

Initial Parameters

To preserve comparability of our results, we started our simulations with the same initial parameters (where applicable) that were used in earlier work. These are $P_d = 0.2$, $f_h = 1$, $f_d = 20$, $f_i = 100$, $f_c = 0$, $N = 25$, $P_e = 0.05$, and $m = 2$. These parameters impose a set of conditions under which, for strictly instrumental agents, the choice between purposeful defection and cooperation is as difficult as possible (see Back & Flache, 2006). We refer to this setting as the baseline condition. After obtaining results for the baseline condition, we vary interesting parameters of the model in additional runs.

Stability

In support of Conjecture 1, we found no infinitely stable strategy for both sets of experiments and all initial parameter settings. We simulated 300 runs altogether, during which almost ten million different strategies were generated. However, no strategy existed longer than 500,000 rounds, and most lasted only few hundreds of rounds. This shows that for each strategy there exists a better response that takes advantage of the strategy's weakness. Figure 1 illustrates these dynamics for average age at death and helping behavior, using a typical simulation run. The upper part of the figure shows how the average age at death (measured in interactions) changes over time within one simula-

Figure 1. Age at death and cooperation (single run, initial 1 million rounds)

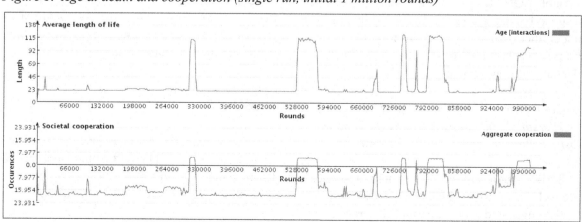

tion round. Compare this figure with the level of cooperation, generated for the same simulation run, in the lower part of the figure: Periods of high refusal rates coincide with short lives.

The Importance of Interpersonal Commitment

To test Conjectures 2 and 3, we compared the relative importance of the genes with a linear regression analysis of average longevity as the dependent variable. Model A (see Table 1) is based on the dataset obtained in the first set of simulation experiments, conducted *without* variation in helping capability. Models B1 and B2 were created for the second set of experiments, which contained individual differences in capability. To filter "random noise" from the strategy set, we excluded highly unstable strategies (stability<500 rounds).

In Model A (N=34,143) the effects of preferences for commitment and for fairness in giving are both positive but larger for commitment, as

expected (Conjecture 2). The cooperation preference has a very large effect. Preferences in asking are negative but for fairness the coefficient is larger in absolute value. This suggests that strategies that restrict their partner search too much either to old partners or to partners with balanced exchange ratios are disadvantaged because their search space is overly reduced. The attractiveness threshold u^t has a large negative effect, because high thresholds make it difficult to bind future helping partners or establish mutually cooperative balanced exchange relationships.

The Relative Importance of Fairness, Commitment, and Capability

In the second set of experiments (corresponding to Models B1 and B2 on Table 1, N=344,778) all conditions were kept equal to the first set, except that we now assumed variation in γ and, accordingly, included the traits of $capa^G$ and $capa^A$ in the genetic makeup of the agents.

Table 1.

	Model A (equality)		Model B1 (inequality)		Model B2 (inequality)	
	Unstandardized Coefficients		Unstandardized Coefficients		Unstandardized Coefficients	
	B	Std. Error	B	Std. Error	B	Std. Error
(Constant)	97.035**	(0.088)	53.793**	(0.068)	53.805**	(0.068)
$comm^G$	1.754**	(0.128)	3.016**	(0.089)	2.926**	(0.089)
$fair^G$	1.393**	(0.134)	6.217**	(0.090)	6.179**	(0.090)
$coop$	5.625**	(0.126)	4.843**	(0.089)	4.792**	(0.089)
$comm^A$	-0.754**	(0.129)	1.740**	(0.089)	1.651**	(0.089)
$fair^A$	-4.340**	(0.135)	-1.077**	(0.090)	-1.056**	(0.089)
u^t	-6.798**	(0.051)	-6.442**	(0.029)	-6.423**	(0.029)
$capa^G$					1.031**	(0.090)
$capa^A$					2.426**	(0.090)
	R	R²-adj.	R	R²-adj.	R	R²-adj.
	.670	.448	.158	.158	.160	.160

We find a remarkable effect of variation in capability on the relative importance of social preferences. For heterogeneous populations, the effect of being fair (*fair^G*) and cooperative (*coop*) when giving are the largest, followed by being committed (*comm^G*), whereas the effect of commitment was stronger than that of fairness in homogenous populations. Model B1 is a *ceteris paribus* replication of the regression analyses we conducted for the homogenous case. Model B2 demonstrates that the difference is robust even when additional effects are included in the regression. The fact that fairness is more important under inequality than commitment both supports our Conjecture 4 and contradicts earlier findings (Back & Flache, 2006). A possible explanation follows.

If capabilities are not inherited, a group with widespread preferences (or norms) for helping weak members will fare better. Both commitment and fairness are such preferences. Commitment leads to stable friendships, in which capabilities do not matter, while fairness leads to uniformly equal shares of help among all members. The disadvantage of commitment comes from the fact that once a strong member binds itself to another agent, its superior capability to provide help will no longer benefit the rest of the group. Whereas in the case of fairness, this superior agent will distribute its help equally among all members of the group. Interestingly, this suggests that the relative disadvantage of commitment vis-à-vis fairness in a heterogenous population is based on the same mechanism that Back and Flache (2006) identified as the explanation of the success of commitment in a homogenous population. In a homogenous population, the tendency of fairness to change partners inevitably produces a higher rate of collision of help requests than commitment would produce. Accordingly, fairness strategies are more likely to run out of help givers and to suffer a loss of points. But in a heterogenous population this turns into an advantage, because strong members' help is distributed more efficiently in the population.

The results also support Conjecture 3. As expected, the importance of giving to the most capable partner (*capa^G*) for longevity is significantly smaller than the importance of commitment and fairness. The picture is somewhat different for asking. The effect of being fair on longevity when searching for help (*fair^A*) is negative, suggesting that it is harmful to distribute help requests in a uniform manner. The effect of commitment (*comm^A*) is only marginally significant, and the difference between fairness and commitment is probably due to the coordination advantage of commitment over fairness (Back & Flache, 2006). Most beneficial here is *capa^A*, showing that it is helpful to turn to the most capable helpers. However, the importance of this preference is still far below that of fairness in giving (*fair^G*).

To test our results for sensitivity, we repeated our simulations for a range of parameter settings. While qualitative results remain robust under a large range of conditions, we also found that higher environmental harshness (f_a, the cost of not getting help) amplifies the importance of commitment relative to other preferences, consistent with findings of de Vos et al. (2001).

DISCUSSION

In this chapter we examined the evolutionary arms race between three social preferences. These preferences are fairness or reciprocity (cf. Axelrod, 1984), commitment (cf. de Vos et al., 2001), and the preference for capable interaction partners. The idea behind conditional cooperation is: "Be cooperative but retaliate against those who cheated on you before." In contrast, commitment implies: "Be generally cooperative but always favor long-term exchange partners." The preference for capability is an elitist striving: "Try to interact with partners who have the highest capability to provide help." Previous computational modelling studies of the evolution of commitment—including our own work—have neglected individual differences in capability. In this chapter, we have filled this gap.

The current study moves beyond previous research in another important way as well. Previous work has pointed to the evolutionary advantages of commitment in the human ancestral environment. In this chapter, we allowed for the random mutation of competing strategies and thus implemented a much tougher evolutionary selection. Our results for homogenous populations still point to certain evolutionary advantages of interpersonal commitment but the findings also highlight weaknesses of commitment and put results of earlier research into perspective.

The overall advantage of commitment in the evolutionary competition with fairness disappeared when we relaxed the assumption of homogeneity in capability. Contrary to previous work, we found that fairness is more important than commitment once heterogeneity is allowed for. In heterogenous populations, commitment's advantage to avoid colliding help requests entails a graver disadvantage, the exclusion of most population members from the benefit of being helped by the strongest players at least once in a while.

Our study has both supported and refined evolutionary accounts of interpersonal commitment, as well as studies of the effects of heterogeneity on help exchange networks. At the same time, this work has its potential limitations which point to a need for future research.

On the theoretical side, one of the most interesting extensions to explore in future research is a combination of two sources of variation in helping capability—genetic sources and nonheritable sources. Genetically more capable strategies can be expected to have an advantage but only if they combine this with discrimination against the weak. We believe that testing this intuition in further computational experiments may provide a fruitful avenue towards establishing a theoreti-cal relationship between social preferences and genetic traits of genotypes.

A more obvious limitation of our work is the lack of a direct empirical test. Previous empirical work supports the importance of commitment (e.g., Kollock, 1994; Lawler & Yoon, 1993, 1996; Lawler, 2001; Smaniotto, 2004). But all these results do not allow us to disentangle conclusively rational commitment and our indirect evolutionary explanation that posits "irrational" emotions as a proximate mechanism driving commitment. Future work should devise laboratory experiments that allow one to distinguish between these competing explanations of commitment.

ACKNOWLEDGMENT

We wish to thank Henk de Vos, Tom Snijders, and an anonymous reviewer for their inspiring and helpful comments. István Back's research was financially supported by the Ubbo Emmius fund of the University of Groningen and a Reisbeurs grant from the Netherlands Organization for Scientific Research (NWO). The research of Andreas Flache was made possible by the Netherlands Organization for Scientific Research (NWO), under the Innovational Research Incentives Scheme.

REFERENCES

Axelrod, R. (1984). *The evolution of cooperation.* Basic Books: New York.

Back, I., & Flache, A. (2006). The viability of cooperation based on interpersonal commitment. *Journal of Artificial Societies and Social Simulation, 9*(1) 12. http://www.soc.surrey.ac.uk./JASSS/

Bendor, J., & Swistak, P. (2001). The evolution of norms. *American Journal of Sociology, 106,* 1493-545.

Conte, R., & Castelfranchi, C. (1995). Simulating multi-agent interdependencies. A two-way approach to the micro-macro link. In K.G.Troitzsch, U. Mueller, G.N. Gilbert, & J. Doran (Eds.), *Social science microsimulation* (pp. 394-415). Springer.

Cosmides, L. (1989). The logic of social exchange: Has natural section shaped how humans reason? Studies with the Watson selection task. *Cognition, 31*, 187-276.

Cosmides, L., & Tooby, J. (1993). Cognitive adaptations for social exchange. In J.H. Barkow, L. Cosmides, & J. Tooby (Eds.), *The adapted mind: Evolutionary psychology and the generation of culture* (pp. 163-228).

de Vos, H., Smaniotto, R., & Elsas, D.A. (2001). Reciprocal altruism under conditions of partner selection. *Rationality and Society, 13*(2), 139-183.

de Vos, H., & Zeggelink, E.P.H. (1997). Reciprocal altruism in human social evolution: The viability of reciprocal altruism with a preference for 'old-helping-partners.' *Evolution and Human Behavior, 18*, 261-78.

Flache, A. (2001). Individual risk preferences and collective outcomes in the evolution of exchange networks. *Rationality and Society, 13*(3), 304-348.

Flache, A., & Hegselmann, R. (1999a). Altruism vs. self-interest in social support. computer simulations of social support networks in cellular worlds. *Advances in Group Processes, 16*, 61-97.

Flache, A., & Hegselmann, R. (1999b). Rationality vs. learning in the evolution of solidarity networks: A theoretical comparison. *Computational and Mathematical Organization Theory, 5*(2), 97-127.

Friedman, J. (1971). A non-cooperative equilibrium for supergames. *Review of Economic Studies, 38*, 1-12.

Hayashi, N., & Yamagishi, T. (1998). Selective play: Choosing partners in an uncertain world. *Personality and Social Psychology Review, 2*,276-289.

Hegselmann, R. (1996). Solidarität unter ungleichen. In R. Hegselmann & H.-O. Peitgen (Eds.), *Modelle sozialer dynamiken—Ordnung, chaos und komplexität* (pp. 105-128). Wein: Hölder–Pichler–Tempsky.

Hegselmann, R. (1998). Experimental ethics–A computer simulation of classes, cliques and solidarity. In C. Fehige & U. Wessels (Eds.), *Preferences* (pp. 298-320). Berlin: De Gruyter.

Kollock, P. (1994). The emergence of exchange structures: An experimental study of uncertainty, commitment, and trust. *American Journal of Sociology, 100*(2), 313-45.

Lawler, E., & Yoon, J. (1993). Power and the emergence of commitment behavior in negotiated exchange. *American Sociological Review, 58*(4), 465-481.

Lawler, E., & Yoon, J. (1996). Commitment in exchange relations: Test of a theory of relational cohesion. *American Sociological Review, 61*(1), 89-108.

Lawler, E.J. (2001). An affect theory of social exchange. *American Journal of Sociology, 107*(2), 321-52.

Sabater, J., Paolucci, M., & Conte, R. (2006). Repage: Reputation and image among limited autonomous partners. *Journal of Artificial Societies and Social Simulation, 9*(2), 3.

Schüssler, R. (1989). Exit threats and cooperation under anonimity. *The Journal of Conflict Resolution, 33*, 728-749.

Schüssler, R., & Sandten, U. (2000). Exit, anonymity and the chances of egoistical cooperation. *Analyse & Kritik, 22*(1), 114-129.

Smaniotto, R.C. (2004). *"You scratch my back and I scratch yours" versus "love thy neighbour": Two proximate mechanisms of reciprocal altruism*. PhD thesis, ICS/University of Groningen. Available online at http://irs.ub.rug.nl/ppn/269506969

Taylor, P.D., & Jonker, L.B. (1978). Evolutionary stable strategies and game dynamics. *Mathematical Biosciences, 40*, 145-156.

Vanberg, V., & Congleton, R. (1992). Rationality, morality and exit. *American Political Science Review, 86*, 418-431.

Wieselquist, J., Rusbult, C., Agnew, C., Foster, C., & Agnew, C. (1999). Commitment, pro-relationship behavior, and trust in close relationships. *Journal of Personality and Social Psychology, 77*(5), 942-66.

Yamagishi, T., Hayashi, N., & Jin, N. (1994). Prisoner's dilemma networks: Selection strategy versus action strategy. In U. Schulz, W. Albers, & U. Mueller (Eds.), *Social dilemmas and cooperation* (pp. 311-326). Heidelberg: Springer.

Zeggelink, E., de Vos, H., & Elsas, D. (2000). Reciprocal altruism and group formation: The degree of segmentation of reciprocal altruists who prefer old-helping-partners. *Journal of Artificial Societies and Social Simulation, 3*(3). http://www.soc.surrey.ac.uk/JASSS/3/3/1.html

ENDNOTES

[1] Mutation in this case can be seen as either genetic or cultural.

[2] Interactions take place always between exactly two agents. Possible interactions are giving help (cooperation) and refusing to help (defection). Asking for help is always followed by one of these.

[3] A general cooperativeness parameter would not make sense in the case of *asking* for help.

[4] This is unlikely, as the preference parameters are high precision real values and interaction histories tend to differ with time.

[5] We will not use here stability concepts from the evolutionary game theory literature (e.g., evolutionary stability or asymptotic stability) because they do not allow to express relative stability of strategies.

[6] Extinction is possible if all agents die within one round and thus there is no basis for the distribution of strategies in the next generation.

APPENDIX A: PARAMETER VALUES USED IN THE SIMULATION

probability of distress (P_d) = 0.1, 0.2, 0.4
probability of decision making error (P_{err}) = 0.05
cost of helping (f_h, measured in points) = 1
cost of not getting help (f_d, measured in points) = 5, 10, 20, 30
initial points (f_i) = 50,100
critical points (f_c) = 0
group size (N) = 25,50
length of simulation runs = 10,000,000 rounds
number of help-seeking subrounds in a round (m) = 1,2,3
evolution frequency min. childbearing age (measured in interactions) = 20
mutation probability (P_{mut}) = 0.05

Chapter II
Taxpayer Compliance Simulation:
A Multi-Agent Based Approach

Kim M. Bloomquist*
United States Internal Revenue Service, USA

ABSTRACT

This chapter describes the development of a prototype multi-agent based model—the tax compliance simulator (TCS)—designed to help tax administrators think about ways to reduce tax evasion. TCS allows the user to define unique behavioral, income, and tax enforcement characteristics for one or two distinctive taxpayer populations. The capabilities of the model are demonstrated in a simulation of the deterrent effects of taxpayer audits. The simulation finds that a significant portion of audit-based deterrence may depend on the influence of taxpayers' social networks rather than the probability of detection or penalty for underreporting as indicated by economic theory (Allingham & Sandmo, 1972).

INTRODUCTION

Tax evasion is the deliberate failure to pay taxes lawfully owed to the government. In recent years, many governments have become concerned about an apparent rise in the level of evasion. Some have linked this presumed increase to a growing tax burden that provides firms and individuals with an incentive to conduct business in the underground or nonobserved economy where

detection is harder (Schneider & Enste, 2002). An alternative explanation offered by Bloomquist (2003a) sees higher evasion resulting from the trend of widening economic inequality that has taken place in many developed and developing countries in the last 30 years. One characteristic of this trend is a shift in the composition of income away from wages and salaries, which are more easily detected by tax authorities, to less visible sources, such as commercial transactions and investments. Unfortunately, the lack of reliable time-series evasion measures hampers efforts to resolve the debate one way or the other.

Regardless of evasion trends, many countries are facing serious fiscal challenges in the years ahead. Perhaps the best-known and most urgent of these challenges is the graying of the post-World War II "Baby Boom" generation. In many countries, a growing retirement-age population is expected to demand a greater share of government outlays in the form of pensions and health care. One measure that has been proposed to expand the tax base in order to meet this need is to permit more immigration. However, new immigrants also require substantial public investment in affordable housing and schools as well as training in language and workforce skills to help them assimilate into the national economy. Therefore, faced with the prospect of significant growth in public expenditures on aging and immigrant populations, many governments are looking for ways to increase revenues, preferably without raising the tax burden. Reducing tax evasion is seen by many politicians as an acceptable solution.

This chapter describes the development of a prototype multi-agent based model—the tax compliance simulator (TCS)—designed to help tax administrators think about how best to reduce the level of tax evasion. According to Taber and Timpone (1996, p. 11), computational models are most useful in social science applications when "some lower threshold of process theory exists but mathematical and statistical methods are intractable, where measurement seems less direct, and where one wishes to gather theoretical pieces into an integrative whole." All of these conditions aptly describe our present state of knowledge about tax evasion which, I believe, makes this topic ideally suited for agent-based modelling.

The next section reviews earlier efforts to develop agent-based models of income tax evasion. This is followed by an overview of major design features of TCS. In the fourth section, TCS is used to analyze the deterrent effects of taxpayer audits.

Finally, the last section summarizes main points and outlines topics for future research.

PRIOR AGENT-BASED MODELS OF INCOME TAX EVASION[1]

Constructing computational models for tax compliance research is a relatively new development. Mittone and Patelli (2000) were the first to develop a multi-agent based simulation (MABS) model of income tax evasion. Building on the theoretical work of Myles and Naylor (1996), Mittone and Patelli assume the existence of three classes of taxpayers: honest, imitative, and free riders. Each taxpayer category has a unique utility function that describes its behavior. Honest taxpayers derive additional utility by conforming to the social norm of compliance (with utility being proportional to the percentage of honest taxpayers in the population). Free riders derive maximum utility from paying as little in taxes as possible. Imitative taxpayers maximize their utility by paying what other taxpayers pay (population mean). All three groups also derive utility from public sector goods and services supported by voluntary and enforced tax contributions. Individual behavior is influenced indirectly by the group via the level of utility derived from public goods and services.

In each time period during the simulation, taxpayer agents must decide whether to evade more, less, or the same as in the preceding period. The decision is stochastic, but the choice probabilities depend on whether calculated utility decreased, increased, or was unchanged from last time. Decision probabilities are updated each time period based on the change in total utility associated with the previous round's compliance decision.

Mittone and Patelli use their model to examine how aggregate evasion behavior varies with different starting mixes of taxpayers. They find that even when all taxpayers are initially honest, the absence of taxpayer audits causes revenues eventually to fall to zero (except for the occasional random tax payment). This outcome results as random dips in tax payments induce otherwise compliant taxpayers to reduce their support for public goods, thus producing a self-reinforcing negative feedback cycle that discourages voluntary tax payments.

When audits are introduced, the additional enforcement revenue increases the quantity of public goods and taxpayers' utility. The tax agency also informs taxpayers about the average amount of tax paid and the proportion of "honest" (fully compliant) taxpayers so that imitative and honest agents can correctly calculate their utility. The authors test two different audit strategies: uniform and tail auditing. Uniform auditing implies a fixed random probability of selection. Tail auditing means audits are performed only on taxpayers who report the least amount of tax (although the article does not specify the cutoff point used). As one might expect, tail auditing is found to have a weaker deterrent effect than uniform auditing.

Mittone and Patelli programmed their model in SWARM, one of several publicly-available freeware packages designed to promote the development of agent-based applications. Others include: RePast, Ascape, NetLogo, and MASON.[2]

Davis, Hecht, and Perkins (2003) construct a MABS model using *Mathematica* software to test the hypothesis that the diffusion of tax evasion exhibits "tipping point" behavior similar to the propagation of a disease epidemic. Tipping point behavior refers to a population that undergoes a sudden transition from one state or condition to another for a small change in the environment. In their model, the authors want to identify the audit rate at which a predominantly honest population starts evading or the reverse case where a group of evaders suddenly begins to comply.

Davis, Hecht, and Perkins also assume the existence of three classes of taxpayers: honest, susceptible, and evader. First, they develop a representative agent mathematical model and determine its solutions in equilibrium. They find stable equilibria both at high and low levels of enforcement. However, the transition from one state to the other is both nonlinear and asymmetric. In other words, when the population is initially honest audit rates must fall to some extremely low level to trigger widespread evasion. Conversely, if the initial population is comprised of evaders, the audit rate must be raised to a different (and higher) level before taxpayers suddenly become honest.

Next, the authors develop a MABS approach to determine if the solution derived analytically using a representative agent model is true for heterogeneous agents as well. In their MABS model, taxpayers start out either as honest or evading. An evading taxpayer reverts to being honest only if audited. Honest taxpayers become susceptible if they observe someone in their social network evade without being audited. The authors do not specify how agents learn about each other's evasion success, but assume information is transmitted through direct observation. Once taxpayers become susceptible, they will evade if either the audit rate or the proportion of their acquaintances that are compliant falls below some pre-determined (random) threshold. Evaders who are audited by the tax agency revert to being honest until the next time they observe an acquaintance evading.

Davis, Hecht, and Perkins find that their simulation results support the hypothesis that tax evasion exhibits tipping point behavior. However, this conclusion remains in doubt due to their model's lack of parallelism with real world conditions. For example, the authors assume only evaders are audited whereas about one in four audited taxpayers receive a refund or owe no additional tax (IRS, 1996). Also, results from their agent-based simulation show taxpayers becoming 100 percent compliant for audit rates as low as 0.03. This finding is not supported by IRS random audit studies that show little variation in the overall noncompliance rate in the last forty years despite audit rates ranging from less than 0.01 at present to 0.05 during the 1960s (Christian, 1994).

DESIGN AND DEVELOPMENT OF TCS

Drawing on these pioneering efforts, Bloomquist (2004a, 2004b) developed a prototype MABS model of taxpayer compliance behavior known as the tax compliance simulator (TCS). TCS is written in the NetLogo simulation language (Wilensky, 1999). Compared to other agent-based modelling languages that require previous knowledge of C++ or Java, NetLogo is relatively easy to learn and, therefore, well-suited for prototyping. A large collection of sample programs written by an active NetLogo user community also is available for new users to study.

TCS allows users to define one or two distinct taxpayer subpopulations having unique behavioral, income, and tax enforcement characteristics. This option permits greater parallelism with the naturally occurring world where the opportunity to evade may vary considerably from one group of taxpayers to another (e.g., wage earners versus sole proprietors). Taxpayers are represented as software agents each having 29 potentially unique characteristics, including income level, fraction of income visible to the tax authority, age, life span, memory, a static list of acquaintances, perception of enforcement activity, etc.

TCS enables the user to separately estimate the induced, direct, and indirect effects of taxpayer audits (Bloomquist, 2003b). The induced effect of taxpayer audits is the increase in voluntary reporting compliance due to the existence of a program of taxpayer audits. Direct effects refer to the additional tax revenue identified by auditors from examination of taxpayers' tax returns. Indirect effects are mainly of two kinds: subsequent period effects and social network effects.

Subsequent period effects refer to the increase in voluntary compliance by those taxpayers who were audited in a previous time period. The social network effect is the additional voluntary compliance that results from knowledge of a tax audit of someone personally known by the taxpayer. In a compliance context, social network effects are a form of induced effects stemming from an enhanced awareness of enforcement activity.

Taxpayer Reporting Decision

TCS enables the user to declare a percentage of each taxpayer's income to be "visible" to the tax authorities. By default, the model assumes all such income is fully reported. This feature is used as a way to include such institutional arrangements as information reporting and withholding that empirical studies have shown to be positively correlated with levels of reporting compliance. For example, the 1988 Taxpayer Compliance Measurement Program (TCMP) study found over 99 percent of wage and salary income was reported to the IRS (IRS, 1996). However, what taxpayers perceive as "visible" income need not be restricted to explicit reporting mechanisms, but could also encompass implicit forms of visibility, such as might be the case for licensed businesses whose existence is known to government officials.

For income that is not declared "visible," TCS assumes taxpayers adopt the approach of standard microeconomic theory (Allingham & Sandmo, 1972) which says that a risk neutral taxpayer will evade whenever the perceived audit rate (p) and penalty rate (f) take on values that make the following expression true:

$$p < \frac{1}{(1+f)}, \quad \text{where } f \geq 0 \qquad (1)$$

Bloomquist (2003b) argues that taxpayers with high compliance opportunity costs (high discount rate) are more likely to evade, ceteris paribus, than other taxpayers. In order to account for this behavior, TCS modifies the taxpayer's reporting decision by incorporating variables to account for the time lag between an act of evasion and its detection and the taxpayer's discount rate. A third variable is included that represents an auditor's ability to detect evasion. With these modifications, the taxpayer's income reporting decision becomes:

$$p < \frac{1}{(1+g)}, \quad \text{where } g = (f \times d) \big/ (1 + r_i)^t \quad (2)$$

In expression 2, t = number of time periods between evasion and detection, d = auditor detection rate ($0.0 \leq d \leq 1.0$), and r_i = discount rate for taxpayer i ($r_i \sim N(r, s)$, $r_i \geq 0$, with r and s determined by the user). Expression 2 implies that the present value cost of evasion is inversely related as an exponent to the length of time between an act of evasion and its detection. Finally, internal IRS studies find that auditors detect only one of every three dollars of unreported income not covered by information reporting (IRS, 1996). TCS enables a user to vary the level of auditor efficiency (d) to determine how this parameter influences taxpayer behavior.

How much tax is voluntarily reported by the taxpayer is calculated using equation (3), which takes into account reporting of both visible and nonvisible income components.

$$T_r = \tau(Y_v + \omega Y_{nv}), \quad \text{where } \omega = \begin{cases} 1 & \text{if } p \geq \dfrac{1}{(1+g)} \\ 0 & \text{otherwise} \end{cases}$$

$$(3)$$

In equation (3), T_r is the reported tax amount, Y_v is visible income, Y_{nv} is nonvisible income, and τ is the tax rate. The current version of TCS assumes a single, flat tax rate for all reported income. It is anticipated that a future version of TCS will incorporate actual tax rate schedules.

Audit Risk Perception

Andreoni, Erard, and Feinstein (1998), among others, have pointed out that the observed level of compliance is far higher than predicted by expected utility (EU) theory. Given the low audit and penalty rates in most countries, theory

Figure 1. Relationship of EU and RDEU weighting functions for audit probability

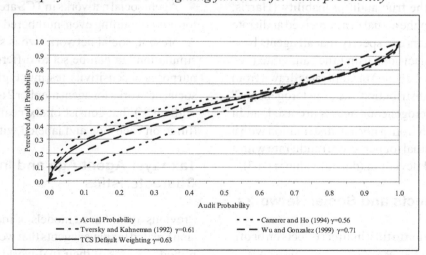

suggests virtually all taxpayers should evade the maximum amount. One explanation for higher than expected levels of compliance is the tendency of people to overweight low probability events (Neilson, 2003). Bernasconi (1998) shows that if audit probabilities are transformed using an empirically-derived weighting function based on rank dependent expected utility (RDEU) theory, one obtains predicted compliance close to observed levels.

In TCS, users may select either unweighted (EU) or weighted (RDEU) audit probabilities. In the latter case, default values are calculated using a single parameter RDEU transformation function with a shape parameter that is the mean of three independently estimated values for an identically-specified function (Tversky & Kahneman, 1992; Camerer & Ho, 1994; Wu & Gonzalez, 1999). Figure 1 displays for comparison the default RDEU weighting function used in TCS (solid line), the three weighting functions from which it is derived, and the EU (linear) probability function.

In addition to weighting of audit probabilities, taxpayer agents are allowed to perceive a mean audit rate that is higher or lower than the actual audit rate. This might be an appropriate assumption if it is thought that taxpayers tend to overestimate the true audit probability (Harris, 1988). Whether the actual or a perceived audit rate is assumed, users can specify that all agents base their evasion decisions using the same rate (i.e., "representative" agents) or audit rates drawn from a probability distribution (i.e., "heterogeneous" agents). If heterogeneous agents are used, audit rates are drawn from a normal distribution with a mean of the actual (or perceived) audit rate with a fixed standard deviation (default value = 0.03).

Indirect Effects and Social Networks

TCS has an option to turn indirect effects on or off. When activated, users must specify the range of values that indicate how much audit risk perception increases when an agent is audited or when they learn that someone in their social network has been audited. Two options are available: +*Random0-20* and +*Random0-N*. The first option tells TCS to add a random value in the range of zero and 20 percentage points to each taxpayer's perceived audit rate when indirect effects are activated. This value is fixed throughout each agent's life span. Specifying the second option requires the user to enter an additional value between one and 100 at set-up time to indicate the maximum value for the indirect effect. Two other optional parameters related to indirect effects are the *NETWORKSIZE* and *TIMEAFFECTED*. The *NETWORKSIZE* slider (a separate slider for each of the two agent population subgroups) is used to set the size of each agent's social network. If a value of zero is selected, only subsequent period effects for audited agents are modeled. If *NETWORKSIZE* is set to some positive and even value (say, six), then each agent's social network consists of exactly six other taxpayers. When one member of the social network is audited, the other members are assumed to hear about it and become subject to indirect effects. The *TIMEAFFECTED* slider (again, one for each population subgroup) is used to indicate the duration (number of time periods) of indirect effects.

Agent social networks in TCS are configured as toroids containing even-numbered sets of agents. At present, social network size is static during a simulation but can be set to different values for purposes of sensitivity testing. Figure 2 displays social networks for agent number 2 and 10 (labeled with an *X*) that consist of six nearest neighbors (three on each side and labeled with an *n*).

Taxpayer Agent Age and Income Characteristics

Previous agent-based models of income tax evasion created taxpayer agents that were highly simplified versions of their real-world counterparts. For example, both Mittone and Patelli (2000) and Davis, Hecht, and Perkins (2003) assume taxpayer

Figure 2. Two social networks in TCS

Agent	0	1	2	3	4	5	6	7	8	9	10	11
2	n	n	X	n	n	n						n
10	n	n						n	n	n	X	n

agents live forever and have constant incomes. In contrast, taxpayer agents in TCS have finite life spans (minimum age of 16 and maximum age of 100). When an agent dies it is replaced by another agent having characteristics drawn from the same population subgroup as the deceased agent. Furthermore, agent incomes in TCS follow a typical earnings lifecycle with a peak occurring between ages 45 and 55. An agent's maximum lifetime earnings are determined by a random draw from a triangular distribution with maximum and mode specified by the user. For every time period, each agent's income is calculated as a percentage of lifetime maximum annual earnings based on the agent's current age. The relationship between an

agent's age and maximum lifetime earnings is derived from data compiled by the U.S. Bureau of the Census.[3]

Running a Simulation and Agent Visualization

The TCS user interface screen (Figure 3) enables users to easily change many key model parameters through the use of sliders, switches, and choice buttons. Simulations can be run in interactive mode with full graphics display or in "batch" mode using a NetLogo option called BehaviorSpace. At first, users may want to run the model in interac-

Figure 3. TCS user interface screen

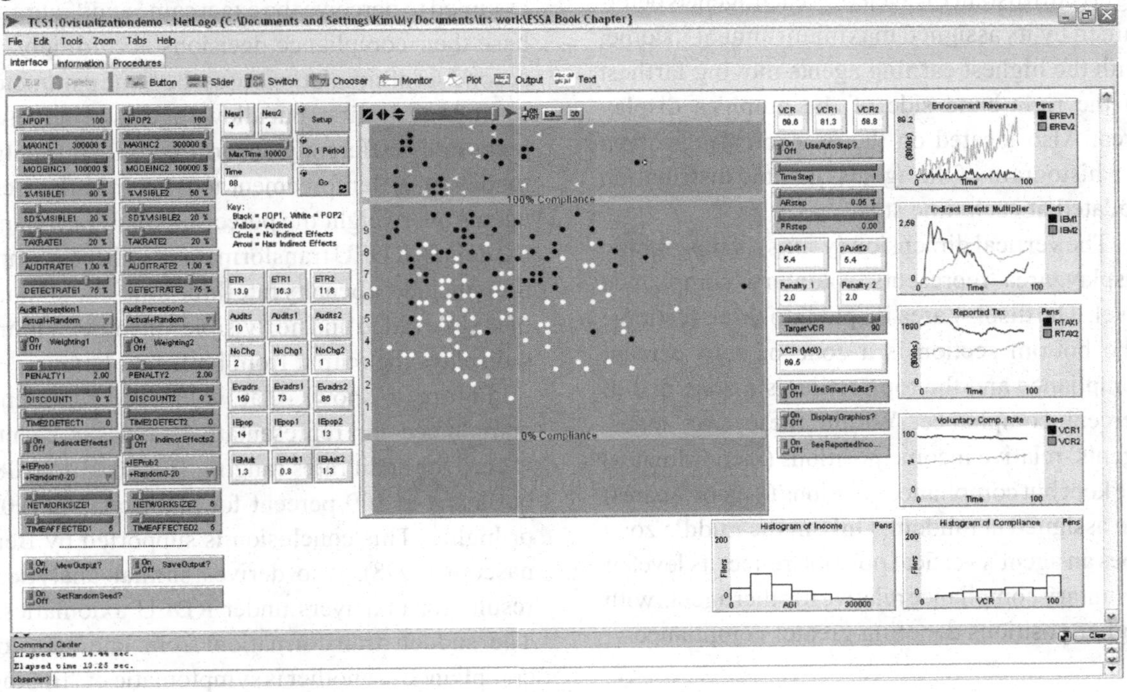

tive mode to set up and validate a simulation, then switch to batch mode to carry out the analysis. Users can set a target voluntary compliance rate (VCR) and gradually increment the audit and penalty rates to identify threshold values that achieve the desired level of compliance (given the model's assumptions about taxpayer behavior). An option is available to seed the random number generator with a system-supplied value or a value supplied by the user. This option is useful to examine the output for possible anomalous behavior and to ensure consistency when porting the model to a new computing environment.

By default, agents are depicted as black or white dots (if two population subgroups are used). Agents subject to indirect effects change shape to an arrow but retain their original color. When agents are audited, their color changes temporarily to yellow.

During an interactive session, agents move from left to right in the graphic display area (grey region in the center of the screen) as they approach middle age and earn more income and from right to left as they exit their peak earning years. The rightward distance traveled by each agent is determined by its assigned maximum annual income, with the highest earning agents moving farthest to the right-hand side of the graphics display area. Also located on the user interface screen is a histogram of the agents' income distribution updated at each time step.

The vertical dimension (y-axis) of the graphic display area represents voluntary compliance level. The display area is split into three sections: The bottom section is a zone of zero percent compliance and the top section is a zone of 100 percent compliance. Within these two zones, agents' relative income positions (x-coordinates) are kept but compliance positions (y-coordinates) are assigned at random. Only in the middle zone does an agent's vertical position reflect its level of voluntary compliance relative to other agents with higher positions denoting greater compliance.

SIMULATING THE DETERRENT EFFECTS OF TAXPAYER AUDITS

This section presents a hypothetical example using TCS to estimate the deterrent effects of taxpayer audits. The first set of simulations illustrates how different assumptions for audit rate perception (representative agents versus heterogeneous agents) influence the simulation output. This is followed by an analysis of the deterrent effects for taxpayers with different proportions of "visible" income. A third group of simulations explores the relationship between social network size and deterrence. Finally, all three of these influences are combined to assess the relative magnitude of deterrence from induced versus indirect effects.

Representative vs. Heterogeneous Agents

In this first example, TCS simulates the compliance behavior for a population of 300 taxpayers over 300 time periods for audit rates from 0.01 to 0.10. In one set of simulations, all agents are assumed to perceive the exact same audit rate and base their compliance decisions accordingly. A second set of simulations uses the same parameter settings as the first, but allows agents to perceive audit rates differently according to their mental models of IRS enforcement activity. In both cases, agents overweight the perceived audit rate using the default RDEU transformation. Other assumptions include: a penalty rate three times the amount of taxes evaded and no "visible" income.[4] Figure 4 displays the output from both simulations.

Figure 4 shows that voluntary reporting compliance for representative taxpayer agents is zero for audit rates ranging from 0.01 to 0.08, but leaps to 100 percent for audit rates of 0.09 or higher. This conclusion is supported by Bernasconi (1998), who derives similar analytical results for taxpayers under RDEU axiomatics.[5] The sudden transformation from one state of compliance to another is symptomatic of "tipping

Figure 4. Voluntary compliance rate (VCR) by audit rate and agent type

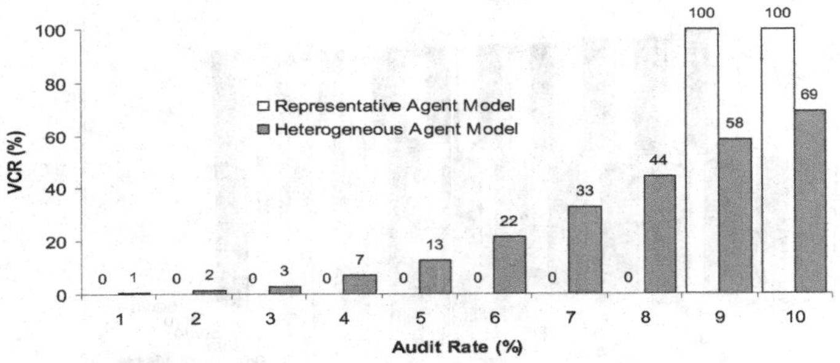

Simulation parameters: RDEU transformation of audit probabilities (overweighting), 3x penalty rate, no visible income, 300 agents, and 300 time periods.

point" behavior, which is the focus of the paper by Davis, Hecht, and Perkins (2003). However, such an abrupt transition from zero to 100 percent compliance does not correspond to observed taxpayer behavior.

When heterogeneous agents are used, voluntary compliance is seen to rise with each increment in the audit rate, although the marginal impact is greatest for audit rates between 0.06 and 0.09. This outcome is intuitively more appealing than the off/on compliance behavior of the representative agent model. Note that while the representative agent model predicts 100 percent compliance when the audit rate equals 0.10, the heterogeneous agent model predicts that taxpayers will only report $.70 of each $1 of tax due. This "tax gap" reflects taxpayers' different mental models of audit risk.

Income Visibility

The second group of simulations illustrates the deterrent effect of audits when different proportions of income are visible to the tax authority. As previously mentioned, TCS assumes such "visible" income is fully reported to the tax agency similar to the observed reporting compliance for wage and salary income. Therefore, increasing

the percentage of visible income will shift the voluntary compliance rate upward by a constant amount.

Five groups of simulations were run for audit rates ranging from 0.01 to 0.10. In Figure 5 and Table 1, the simulation labeled "0/0" is identical to the previous simulation using heterogeneous agents. In this case, "0/0" refers to zero percent visible income and a standard deviation of zero percentage points. The simulations labeled "50/0" and "90/0" assume all taxpayer agents have exactly 50 percent and 90 percent of their income visible to the tax authority. The two simulations labeled "50/20" and "90/20" denote where the proportion of visible income assigned to taxpayers is drawn from a normal distribution with mean 0.50 (or 0.90) and a standard deviation of 0.20. This option is included to improve parallelism with real world conditions where the proportion of income subject to information reporting varies from taxpayer to taxpayer.

Table 1 and Figure 5 show that increasing the audit rate improves compliance for all taxpayers but has a much greater marginal impact on taxpayers with no visible income and the smallest impact on taxpayers with 90 percent visible income. For this hypothetical case study, Table 1 shows that raising the audit rate from 0.01 to 0.05

Figure 5. Voluntary compliance rate by audit rate and percent visible income

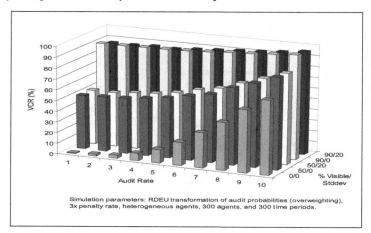

Simulation parameters: RDEU transformation of audit probabilities (overweighting), 3x penalty rate, heterogeneous agents, 300 agents, and 300 time periods.

Table 1. Voluntary compliance rates by income visibility and audit rate: Simulation results

% Visible/	Audit Rate									
Stddev	1	2	3	4	5	6	7	8	9	10
0/0	1	2	3	7	13	22	33	44	58	69
50/0	50	51	52	53	56	60	63	72	78	85
50/20	51	50	52	54	57	61	65	72	78	85
90/0	90	90	90	91	91	92	93	94	96	97
90/20	87	86	87	87	88	89	91	92	93	95

Source: Calculated by author using TCS.

increases voluntary compliance by 12 percentage points for taxpayers with no visible income but only one point for those with 90 percent visible income. The data in Table 1 also reveal an apparent anomaly where the VCR is seen to fall below the mean visible income level when agent values are drawn from a probability distribution. This phenomenon is evident in the lower audit rates for the simulation labeled "90/20" and is due to the fact that income visibility cannot exceed 100 percent but can be as low as three (or more) standard deviations from the mean in the opposite direction. In this example, an agent three standard deviations from a mean value of 90 would have 30 percent of income visible to tax authorities. Therefore, the disparity between the calculated

VCR and mean visible income level will widen with higher levels of visible income.

Social Network Size

The next simulations look at the impact of social network size on voluntary reporting compliance. In order to perform this analysis in TCS it is necessary to first flip the *IndirectEffects?* switch to the "on" position. This activates a choice parameter *+IEProb[1/2]* and two sliders: *NETWORKSIZE[1/2]* and *TIMEAFFECTED[1/2]*. For these simulations, each taxpayer's probability of audit was incremented by a random number between 0 and 0.20 (using the *+Random0-20* option for *+IEProb1*) and *TIMEAFFECTED1* was assigned a value of 5. These settings imply that when a taxpayer is audited or discovers that someone in his/her social network has been audited, their perception of audit risk increases (by a random number between 0 and 0.20) and that this condition of elevated risk perception lasts for exactly five time periods. In addition, all simulations were executed using heterogeneous agents and assume a mean 50 percent visible income with a standard deviation of 20 percentage points ("50/20"). Finally, separate simulations were executed for agent social networks of size 0 (self only), 4, 8, 12, 16, and 20. The results are displayed graphically in Figure 6 with numerical output shown in Table 2.

From Table 2, we see the expected finding that deterrent effects increase with social network size. However, we also note that the marginal impact is greatest going from a social network size of zero to four. This suggests that a taxpayer's audit status need only be known by a small group of close friends (who also then act on the information) in order for sizable indirect effects to be realized.

SUMMARY AND FUTURE RESEARCH

The purpose of this chapter was to describe the development of TCS, a prototype model devel-

Figure 6. Voluntary compliance rate by audit rate and social network size

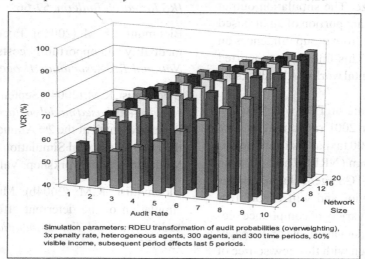

Simulation parameters: RDEU transformation of audit probabilities (overweighting), 3x penalty rate, heterogeneous agents, 300 agents, and 300 time periods, 50% visible income, subsequent period effects last 5 periods.

Table 2. Voluntary compliance rates by social network size and audit rate: Simulation results

Social Network Size	Audit Rate									
	1	2	3	4	5	6	7	8	9	10
Self Only	51	54	56	59	63	68	73	80	85	90
4	56	61	67	70	75	80	84	87	92	94
8	59	66	70	75	79	83	87	91	93	95
12	61	67	73	77	81	84	88	91	94	96
16	63	70	76	78	83	85	89	91	95	96
20	66	72	75	80	83	86	89	92	94	96

Source: Calculated by author using TCS.

Source: Calculated by author using TCS.

oped by the IRS to estimate the deterrent effects of tax compliance alternatives. Along the way we discussed the scope and causes of income tax evasion. Although official estimates of tax evasion are only available for the U.S., it is likely that many of the same factors and behaviors observed in the U.S. apply in Europe and other OECD countries as well.

TCS incorporates a number of parameters identified as evasion determinants. These are: audit rate, audit risk perception, penalty rate, transaction visibility, social networks, timeliness of audits, and auditor effectiveness. A hypothetical case study was presented that demonstrated the model's capability to estimate deterrence resulting from different assumptions regarding taxpayers' perceptions of audit probability, the proportion of income visible to tax authorities, and social network size. The simulation output suggests that a significant portion of audit-based deterrence could come from group influences on compliance behavior. This finding is supported by the recent experimental work of Alm, Jackson, and McKee (2004).

Future enhancements of TCS will focus on incorporating tax year 2001 random audit data on approximately 46,000 taxpayers from the National Research Program (NRP). The NRP data will be used to define TCS agent characteristics and compliance behavior and will enable IRS researchers to model a variety of compliance scenarios using the latest data available on taxpayer behavior. However, even with this new source of information, we will still lack critical knowledge about the cause and effect relationship between enforcement activity and taxpayer behavior. For the foreseeable future, tax administrators will continue to rely on the scientific tools of research such as field studies and laboratory experiments, along with agent-based computer simulation, to inform their thinking on ways to improve taxpayer compliance.

REFERENCES

Allingham, M.G., & Sandmo, A. (1994). Income tax evasion: A theoretical analysis. *Journal of Public Economics, 1*, 323-338.

Alm, J., Jackson, B.R., & McKee, M. (2004). The effects of communication among taxpayers on compliance. *The IRS Research Bulletin*, 37-48.

Andreoni, J., Erard, B., & Feinstein, J.S. (1998). Tax compliance. *Journal of Economic Literature, 36*, 818-860.

Bernasconi, M. (1998). Tax evasion and orders of risk aversion. *Journal of Public Economics, 67*, 123-134.

Bloomquist, K.M. (2003a). Trends as changes in variance: The case of tax noncompliance. *The IRS Research Bulletin*, 59-66.

Bloomquist, K.M. (2003b). Tax evasion, income inequality and opportunity costs of compliance. *National Tax Association Proceedings*, 91-104.

Bloomquist, K.M. (2004a, September). *A comparison of agent-based models of income tax evasion*. Paper presented at the 2nd Annual Conference of the European Social Simulation Association and Model-to-Model Workshop, Valladolid, Spain.

Bloomquist, K.M. (2004b). Multi-agent based simulation of the deterrent effects of taxpayer audits. *National Tax Association Proceedings*, 159-173.

Camerer, C.F., & Ho, T.H. (1994). Violations of the betweenness axiom and nonlinearity in probability. *Journal of Risk and Uncertainty, 8*, 167-196.

Christian, C. (1993/1994). Voluntary compliance with the individual income tax: Results from the 1988 TCMP study. *The IRS Research Bulletin*, 35-42.

Davis, J.S., Hecht, G., & Perkins, J.D. (2003). Social behaviors, enforcement and tax compliance dynamics. *The Accounting Review, 78*(1), 39-69.

Harris, Louis and Associates, Inc. (1988). *Taxpayer opinion survey.* Internal Revenue Service Document 7292 (1-88).

Internal Revenue Service. (1996). *Federal tax compliance research: Individual income tax gap estimates for 1985, 1988, and 1992.* IRS Publication 1415 (Rev. 4-96), Washington, DC.

Mittone, L., & Patelli, P. (2000). Imitative behaviour in tax evasion. In B. Stefansson & F. Luna (Eds.), *Economic modelling with swarm.* Amsterdam: Kluwer.

Myles, G.D., & Naylor, R.A. (1996). A model of tax evasion with group conformity and social customs. *European Journal of Political Economy, 12*, 49-66.

Neilson, W. S. (2003). Probability transformations in the study of behavior toward risk. *Synthese, 135*, 171-192.

Schneider, F., & Enste, D.H. (2000). Shadow economies: Size, causes, and consequences. *Journal of Economic Literature, 38*(1), 77-114.

Tversky, A., & Kahneman, D. (1992). Advances in prospect theory: Cumulative representation of uncertainty. *Journal of Risk and Uncertainty, 5*, 297-323.

Wilensky, U. (1999). *NetLogo.* Center for Connected Learning and Computer-Based Modeling, Northwestern University. Evanston, IL.

Wu, G., & Gonzalez, R. (1996). Curvature of the probability weighting function. *Management Science, 42*, 1676-1690.

ENDNOTES

[1] The material in this section and the next draws heavily from Bloomquist (2004a, 2004b).

[2] Links to sites for these and many other software packages for agent-based modelling can be found at: http://wiki.swarm. org/wiki/Tools_for_Agent-Based_Modelling

[3] See http://www.census.gov/statab/www/

[4] The following additional assumptions also apply for all simulations: Maximum possible lifetime annual earnings of $300,000 and modal lifetime annual earnings of $100,000.

[5] Bernasconi (1998) finds 100 percent compliance occurs for a penalty rate of 2.10 and an audit rate equal to 0.09. However, he uses an RDEU transformation function with a shape parameter of 0.56 from Camerer and Ho (1994), unlike TCS which uses a shape parameter value of 0.63 that is the mean of three independent estimates (see text). The larger shape parameter value in TCS necessitates a higher penalty before full compliance is reached.

NOTE

[*] **Disclaimer:** The views expressed here are those of the author and should not be interpreted as those of the U.S. Internal Revenue Service (IRS).

Chapter III
Cooperation as the Outcome of a Social Differentiation Process in Metamimetic Games

David Chavalarias
CREA, Ecole Polytechnique, France

ABSTRACT

What are the principles underlying social differentiation? Socioeconomic models generally consider agents that pursue some particular ends a given, prior to their social activity. In this chapter we propose an alternative in the framework of metamimetic games. We claim that the distribution of ends in a population is the outcome of social interactions and not only what drives them. We take the example of the prisoner's dilemma in spatial games to illustrate how cultural co-evolution can lead to a spontaneous differentiation of ends in a population with a high level of cooperation. From this perspective, the question is not the traditional: "How can altruists 'survive' in a selfish world?" but rather to understand how heterogeneous ends can reinforce or limit each other to collectively entail the emergence of a social cooperative order.

INTRODUCTION

What are the principles underlying social differentiation? Socioeconomic models generally consider agents that pursue some particular ends which are given top-down by the modeler. Standard game theory, for example, grounds agents' decisions on maximization of material payoffs. In most modelling frameworks, agent's ends share the following characteristics:

- They are assigned to the agents prior to their social activity and are immutable thereafter.
- In theory these ends could be heterogeneous but in practice they are often all the same,

i.e., all the agents share the same payoffs' functions or these payoffs functions evolve under the same selection pressure (which is formally equivalent).

Hidden behind most models we find something equivalent to a social teleology (everybody wants to maximize the same function or the whole system wants to minimize a given potential function) which is paradoxically close to the adhesion to a holistic principle. In this line of thought, social differentiation is a mere differentiation of means serving more or less the same ends.

This bias is understandable since socioeconomic modelling has been largely influenced by game theory and rational choice theory were orginally normative disciplines stating how people should behave if they wish to achieve certain ends (Luce & Raiffa, 1957). However, when it comes to understanding or reconstructing stylized facts relative to socioeconomic dynamics, this bias is questionable. What are these ends that everybody should pursue? There is no reason to think that particular ends exist relative to which all the others could be considered as means. Think, for example, to a person who buys a car. Has he or she worked to be able to buy this car or does he or she buy this car to be able to go to work? Indeed, it could be none of these reasons. The issue of teleology was already raised by Hayek in economic modelling (1978):

I now find somewhat misleading the definition of the science of economy as 'the study of the disposal of scarce means towards the realization of given ends' ...the reason is that the ends which a Catallaxy[1] serves are not given in their totality to anyone, that is, are not known either to any individual participant in the process or to the scientist studying it.

This remark changes radically the perspective of social system modelling. If ends are multiple and cannot be listed, what can models say about social dynamics? How can we speak about social dynamics if the distribution of ends that drives them cannot be identified clearly? This issue was addressed more than a century ago by an eminent sociologist, Gabriel Tarde (1898), who suggested that rather than assuming the existence of an end relative to which all the others would be means, we should assume that there is an infinite number of possible ends trying to take advantage of one another. This "ecology of ends" and the parameters that influence its dynamics should be studied with the same investment than the classical problem of end-means derivation.

This second issue yields an epistemological shift in social systems modelling. From this perspective, the guidelines for the understanding of social dynamics are the different modes of internal consistency of a given distribution of ends in a population. Ends are no more immutable traits that could be assigned to the agents prior to their social activity, they evolve all along the agents' lives as their interact with their social environment. This entails the production of diversity with emergence of social groups, which is the opposite of the optimization of adaptation. From this perspective, external constraints (like economical constraints or biological ones) act as border conditions on the extent of the diversity of possible ends. They do not determine the dynamics *per se*. This view, in line with Varela's notion of *operational closure* (Varela, 1989), suggests that social differentiation is in the first place, the self-organization of possible ends rather than a mechanistic equilibrium between a diversity of means serving more or less the same end. This article will provide a simple example of such a differentiation process.

The modalities of this kind of self-organization raise some tricky issues, in particular because they require some kind of self-reference in the definition of the dynamics. We explored this problem in previous work with *metamimetic games* (Chavalarias, 2004). This formal framework builds on the fact that human metacognition and reflexivity can be introduced as features in formal models so that imitation rules can be their own metarules. We can then build on this property to propose models based on a mimetic principle where the distribution of agents' ends in a population is endogenous. The resulting social dynamics are self-referential in the sense that driven by agents' ends they determine their distribution. This distribution becomes the outcome of a social differentiation in a cultural co-evolution process.

In this chapter, we illustrate this kind of differentiation with a spatial prisoner's dilemma as a case study. The aim is to illustrate the epistemological shift for social systems modelling associated with this approach. In passing, we will see how this approach renews the perspectives on the well-known paradox of large-scale cooperation in human societies. Before presenting this case study, we will first briefly review the main features of metamimetic games. For a more detailed description, see Chavalarias (2006).

METAMIMETIC GAMES

Human beings build their identity through individual and social learning. One of the most important aspects of social learning, and apparently the first in ontogeny, is learning by imitation. This learning skill is exceptionally developed in human beings compared to what exists in other animal species. Human imitation takes several forms, from automatic imitation that is present from birth and seems to persist thereafter in some kind of conformism, to rational imitation where pros and cons are carefully evaluated, what Tarde (1890) called *logical imitation*.

Metamimetic games address this last form of imitation, although it might be the case that some kinds of automatic imitation also rely on similar mechanisms. The advantage of metamimetic games is to provide a way to reflect on the properties of enfogenous dynamics of ends within population of agents.

To understand how ends are represented in metamimetic models we will start with a general definition of *imitation rule*:

Definition: Imitation Rule

Given an agent A and its neighborhood Γ_A, an imitation rule is a process that:

1. Assigns a value $v(B,\Gamma_A) \in \mathfrak{R}$ to the situation of each agent B in Γ_A. v is called a *valuation function*.
2. Selects some traits to be copied from best agent(s) and defines the copying process.

For example, in the classical payoff-biased imitation, the value assigned to each neighbor's situation is its payoffs. The agent has then to infer which of the traits of the most successful neighbor(s) are responsible for this success and try to copy these traits. This process of inference involves beliefs about other agents, but for clarity we will discard this dimension in the following. The valuation function above plays a role analogous to the utility function in game theory. The difference here is that it is subjective and it evolves through ongoing social dynamics. In the following, this valuation function will stand for the expression of the ends of the agents. Two agents can have different valuation functions, and the diversity of valuation functions in a population reflects the diversity of ends[2].

To summarize the above definition, we can say that in step one, potential models are selected whereas step 2 determines which of these potential models are going to actually influence the agent's behavior and how.

From this definition, the general sketch for metamimetic games is the following: Agents are defined by the actions they undertake in the world plus their rules for decision-making (in our case, imitation rules). These rules for decision-making can be organized hierarchically in levels and metalevels according to which one serves the ends of the other and which one is able to modify the other. These hierarchies of rules define what we called *metamimetic chains,* which are an equivalent notion to strategies in game theory. For example, in a financial market, an agent might have as a first goal profit maximization. To achieve this end, he or she might decide to be temporarily a conformist (try to buy what the majority buys) because it is the rule for decision-making that proves to be the most efficient in the current environment. This hierarchy of strategies evolves as the agents update the different levels according to the rules of the above levels (it might happen that since the environment changed, it is more profitable to be in the minority of buyers and consequently a payoffs-maximizer agent will start to play minority games with other agents).

The three assumptions defining a metamimetic game are the following:

1. **Bounded rationality:** The number k of metalevels in metamimetic chains is finite and bounded for each agent by its cognitive bound c_B, $(k < c_B)$.

2. **Metacognition:** At all levels in a metamimetic chain, imitation rules are modifiable traits. They can be changed for other rules if it is judged relevant by the application of the rule(s) of the above level.

3. **Reflexivity:** Imitation rules can update reflexively, changing the length of the metamimetic chain in the limit of the cognitive bound of the agents. When the cognitive bound is reached, imitation rules might update themselves.

To give an example illustrating these three assumptions, consider a payoffs-maximizer agent that has only two opportunities of action, C and D. If after reflection he or she concludes that a conformist behavior is the most successful in terms of material payoffs, he or she might decide to change strategy by changing the length of the metamimetic chain as described in Figure 1.

Figure 1. Endogenous variation in the length of metamimetic chains

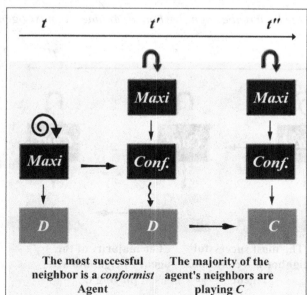

But, if the cognitive bound of the agent does not allow him or her to keep in mind the two distinct ends ($C_B=1$), they might then revise strategy and drop the main end, as described in Figure 2.

At time t, a maxi-agent A has a conformist neighbor that is strictly more successful than all other neighbors. If A infers that this success is due to the conformist rule, he or she might adopt this rule as a first level. Since $C_B=1$, this simply replaces the original maxi-rule. Thereafter, it might be that according to this new rule, the current behavior is not the best one and has to be changed.

This is not the place to discuss the relevance of these kind of transitions (see Chavalarias, 2006 for more details). Let us just mention three kinds of relations between goals and subgoals that can be stylized by these transitions:

- The agent adopts a new end and progressively forgets (for any reason) its old end.
- The new end is so time-consuming that although the old end is still present in mind, it is never taken into account in subsequent decisions.

- The agent enjoys the activities associated to the new end more than those associated to the old one and progressively adopts the new one as his or her main end.

In all cases, the salient feature is that new ends are adopted because they are consistent with old ones at the moment they are the focus of attention. At any moment, the set of current ends constrains the way this set will evolve.

Now, if we consider a population of artificial metamimetic agents with a given set of possible ends, the principles outlined above define the internal dynamics of the artificial social system (described mathematically in previous works by the Markov chain P^0). These dynamics have some stable states, *metamimetic equilibria,* that are *counterfactually stable states, i.e.,* states such that *no agent can find itself better off when it imagines itself in the place of one of its neighbors.* More frequently, we encounter stable sets of states, *metamimetic attractors.*

Figure 2. Reflexive update at the limit of the cognitive bound. At time t, a maxi-agent A has a conformist

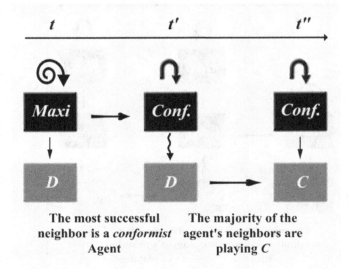

The most successful neighbor is a *conformist* Agent

The majority of the agent's neighbors are playing C

Since agents make errors at the different levels of decision-making process (inference, reasoning, and action implementation) and because their environment is noisy, the right object to study *in fine* is a perturbed Markov process $P\varepsilon^0$ in the framework of stochastic evolutionary game theory (Foster & Young, 1990). However, in this chapter, we will mainly focus on the internal dynamics (P^0).

After these preliminaries, we are now able to give an example of a social differentiation process by cultural co-evolution.

THE SPATIAL METAMIMETIC PRISONER'S DILEMMA GAME

The Model

Following Nowak and May (1992), we will consider a spatial model for evolution of cooperation. We choose this particular model as first example for three reasons: First, the PD game and evolution of cooperation is a scientific puzzle in the consequentialist view of human decision-making. Second, rules for decision-making in the original model of Nowak and May can be interpreted as payoffs-biased mimetic rules which simplify the comparison with the model presented here. Third, the properties and limits of this original model are well known and can be summarized as follows (see, for example, Hauert, 2001):

1. Cooperation is possible in some areas of the parameters' space where there is a coexistence of zones of cooperation and defection, constantly evolving with time.
2. These areas of the parameters' space are nevertheless very tiny and correspond to weak social dilemmas. Consequently, cooperation is not sustainable most of the time.

The model can be described as follows: Agents are displayed at the nodes of a two-dimensional toric grid. Agents play a prisoner's dilemma game (PD game) each period of time with each of their neighbors, choosing between two simple actions: cooperate (C) or defect (D). The actions used in the games with different neighbors are the same for a given period. Neighborhoods of players are composed of the eight adjacent cells. When two agents play together, they receive a payoff of R if both cooperate (C) and P if both defect (D). In case their strategies are different, the one who played D receives a payoff of T and the other receives S (*cf.* Table 1). This game is a PD game if:

1. $T > R > P > S$: Defection is always more advantageous from the individual point of view.
2. $T+S < 2.R$: Mutual cooperation is strictly the best you can do collectively.

At the end of each period, the payoffs of each agent are summed and agents update their strategies on the basis of the available information on the last period.

The Set of Strategies

We will consider agents with $C_B=1$. Their metamimetic chain will thus be described by a behavior and an imitation rule for decision-making: $s=(b,r)$. Although $C_B=1$ is not a realistic assumption[3], this will be sufficient to illustrate our purpose. For simplicity, we will also assume that the second step in an imitation process is just pure copying of the trait.

Table 1. The matrix of the prisoner's dilemma game

Player A	Player B	
	C	D
C	(R,R)	(S,T)
D	(T,S)	(P,P)

The set of rules for imitation should represent all the possible ends that agents can imagine from what they perceive. Consequently, it's important that this set is generated from what the agents can perceive and what kind of processing the agents can do regarding these perceptions[4]. For this reason, we define the set of imitation rules as the outcome of a combination of different kinds of cognitive operators: operators for the selection of a particular dimension in the perception space and operators for computation on this selection. We thus have the following scheme:

PERCEPTION→PROCESSING→
IMITATION RULES

Here, we will assume that:

As for the perception, agents can perceive:

- Material-payoffs of their neighbors
- The last action (C or D) of their neighbors
- The imitation rules of their neighbors

Here, perceptions are "exact," and agents are somehow mind-readers. The issue of errors in perception and inference is addressed in Chavalarias (2004) but is outside the scope of this article. *As for computation, agents can:*

- Compute the proportions of different behaviors and rules in their neighborhood.
- Compare two real numbers and take the max (max of payoffs, max of proportions).
- Multiply a real number by *1* (if agents can imagine a sorting of a set of issues, they can also imagine the opposite sorting, or to say it differently, if they can compute the max of two numbers, they can also compute the min).

Moreover, we will assume that the agents have zero memory: They can only build a rule from the

information on last period's outcome[5]. This generates four valuation functions and consequently four imitation rules (cf. Table 2):

1. **Maxi:** "Copy the most successful agent in your neighborhood in terms of material payoffs."
2. **Mini:** "Copy the less successful agent in your neighborhood."
3. **Conformism:** "Copy the trait (behavior or rule) used by the majority of agents."
4. **Anti-conformism:** "Copy the trait (behavior or rule) used by the minority of agents."

In the computational study presented here, each period proceeds with parallel updating as follows[6] (see the detailed algorithm in Appendix):

1. Each agent looks at the situation of its neighbors (payoffs, rules, and behavior).
2. For any agent A, if according to A's valuation function some agents in Γ_A are better off than A, and if all these neighbors have a valuation function different from A's, then A imitates the rule of an agent taken at random among its most successful neighbors.
3. If according to its (eventually new) valuation function A is not among the more successful agents in Γ_A, then A chooses one of its most wealthy neighbors at random and copies its behavior (C or D).
4. For each agent, the scores of the eight PD games with its neighbors are computed and the sum is the new material payoffs of the agent.

Table 2. The four imitation rules

Operator	Perceived dimension	
	Densities	Payoffs
max	*Conformist*	*Maxi*
min	*Anti-conformists*	*Mini*

Note that an agent will be satisfied with its own situation and will not engage in an imitation process if it does not have a neighbor with a better situation. It will just stick to its former strategy.

We will now see with some social simulations what metamimetic attractors look like and illustrate our view on social differentiation. The results presented in next section are qualitatively unchanged in case of asynchronous updating, even with endogenous time constants (Chavalarias, 2004).

SELF-ORGANIZATION OF RULES AND STABILITY OF COOPERATION

We will study the influence of the strength of the social dilemma (parameter p) and of the initial propensity of the population for cooperation (*Inicoop*, i.e., rate of cooperator at the beginning of the simulations). The initial state for all the following simulations is a uniform distribution on the four imitation rules.

We will adopt the following exposition plan:

1. A detailed study for the "historical" settings of the PD game (Axelrod, 1984): $T=5$, $R=3$, $P=1$, and $S=0$, and an initial rate of cooperation of *30 percent*.
2. An extensive study of the influence of p and *Inicoop*: stability of the qualitative properties of the attractors found in 1.

Emergence of Social Groups and Cooperation

Let's begin with a study for a particular set of parameters: $T=5$, $R=3$, $P=1$ and $S=0$, and an initial rate of cooperation of 30 percent (Figure 3). We report here a study on 50 independent multi-agent simulations with a population of 10,000 agents each. The spatial distribution of the different kinds of rules was uniform, according to the initial proportions (25 percent of each type).

The first noticeable facts are that in all simulations, the system quickly reaches a *heterogeneous* attractor while the rate of cooperation *increases*[7]. This attractor is mostly static (only a few oscillators remaining). This means that at the attractor, most agents are counterfactually stable even if almost all possible ends are represented in the population. The attractor is heterogeneous at both behaviors and rules' levels. The emerging patterns make sense relatively to the ends of the socially embedded agents and an external observer could even guess who is who in Figure 3: Conformists are clustered in large areas where they are in the majority, anti-conformists are scattered throughout the territory and are locally in the minority; maxi and mini agents have interlaced populations, the former "exploiting" the others which enjoy.

The interpretation of these emerging structures is that the structure of the attractor reflects the constraints imposed by the self-consistency of the rules: They are the projections at the collective level of the *elementary virtualities* contained in each agent.

At the behavioral level, we found a structured heterogeneous population with plain clusters of cooperators and defectors, interlaced areas, and scattered exceptions. These structures can be explained only if we look above at the rule level. For example, *mini*-agents exclusively cooperate because it is actually the best way to minimize one's payoffs. It should be emphasized that most agents change both their behavior and imitation rule during their lives, sometimes several times. The original assignment of rules at first period only weakly determines what agents will be in their social life. An agent stops changing its strategy when it finally finds a rule and a behavior such that the behavior is consistent with its social environment relative to its rule. It is this multitude of agents looking for their identity that collectively produce a global stable order. This process is what we call *social cognition* (Chavalarias, 2007).

Figure 3. Each small square represents an agent. This configuration is globally stable (only a few oscillators remain at the attractor). Legend: Upper part—white: conformists, black: anti-conformists, light grey: mini, dark grey: maxi. Lower part—light grey: cooperators, dark grey: defectors.

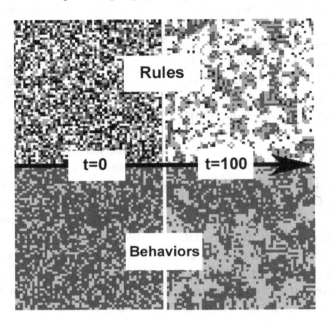

Now, if we run different simulations with same initial settings and look at the path toward the attractor, we can see that (Figure 4):

1. All populations reach their attractors very quickly.
2. These attractors are statistically and qualitatively similar, as are the trajectories to reach them (the variance on the distribution of distributions is quite small).

This suggests that the kind of structure an artificial society reaches is well constrained by the internal cognitive structure of the agents (the perception and computation operators), the initial statistical distribution of rules and behaviors, and the PD game matrix. We will now study the dependence of this structure toward these last parameters.

The Influence of Environmental Constraints

To study the influence of the initial rate of cooperators and the strength of social dilemma on the dynamics, it is more convenient to consider a PD matrix parametrized by only one parameter. Two parameters suffice to describe the whole set of distinct games. The issue now is to select a subset of this 2D space that would nevertheless generate all the interesting dynamics. For this purpose, we will take a parametrization frequently used in the social dilemma literature (*cf.* Table 3). Here p measures the strength of the dilemma: The higher p, the stronger the dilemma.

We will assume that $0 < p < 0.5$ so that the condition $T > R > P > R$ is satisfied. The condition $T+S < 2R$ is violated (we have equality) but it doesn't have noticeable consequences on the dynamics[8].

Figure 4. Left: evolution of the distribution of imitation rules. Here T=5, R=3, P=1, and S=0, and the statistics have been computed on 50 runs, 10,000 agents each. In all runs, the attractor is composed of about 48 percent conformists, 27 percent max, 20 percent mini, and 5 percent anti-conformists. Right: Statistics on the evolution of cooperation. The rate of cooperators increases from 30 percent to a proportion of 44 percent of cooperators.

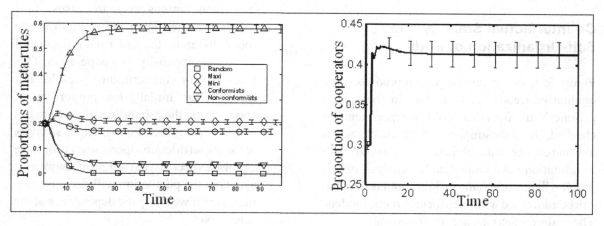

Table 3. A parametrization of the PD game matrix

Player A	Player B	
	C	D
C	$(\bar{I}p, \bar{I}p)$	$(0,1)$
D	$(1,0)$	(p,p)

Studies here are similar to the case presented in previous section for the initial rate of cooperation (*Ini Coop*) varying between five and 95 percent and *p* varying between 0.1 and 0.4. The same qualitative properties were observed concerning the attractors (cf. Figure 5).

Behavioral Level

The rate of cooperation at the attractor is plotted in Figure 5a. This rate is always above 9.5 percent and above 40 percent in the majority of the cases. Attractors at the behavioral level depend heavily on *IniCoop* for low *p* but are almost independent of *IniCoop* for *p>0.2*. On the contrary, *p* has always had a great influence on these attractors. Even if it

is not the point here, it is noteworthy that the high level of cooperation for most of the parameters' range is a very interesting result by the perspective of the emergence of cooperation.

Metarules Level

Inicoop has less influence on the metarules than it has on behaviors. The proportions of conformist agents decrease when *p* increases to the benefit of *maxi* and *mini*-agents. Conformist agents are always the population with the highest density, but there is a significant proportion of *maxi*- and *mini*-agents when *p>0.2* (more than 20 percent for each population). On the contrary, the proportion of nonconformists is not sensitive to *p* and is almost constant along both axes (it seems to be a function of the social network's topology). At the attractor, most agents perform repetitive behavior. However, few agents at the border of clusters keep oscillating between the two rules of two behaviors.

Each point represents the mean rate of cooperation (on 10 independent runs) at the attractor for the couple *(p,IniCoop)* considered. The rate of cooperation is always above 9.5 percent. Co-operation is sustainable under all the conditions studied. The line represents the set of simulations corresponding to the area of parameters used in the right figure.

Counterfactual Stability and Self-Organization of Ends

Figure 5a is interesting because it predicts some qualitative trends for behaviors in the spatial prisoner's dilemma that could be experimentally checked. Given the simplicity of the model, there is a strong chance that such verification would result in refutation but a more detailed analysis of this graph will provide some insight about issues that can be addressed with such metamimetic models. The main predictions are the following:

1. **Influence of the initial rate of cooperation:** The initial rate of cooperation has a positive influence on the rate of cooperation at the attractor. For a given p, this dependence has a S shape along the *IniCoop* axis, which is the well-known signature of conformist

social learning. We can thus expect that this shape is due to some kind of conformist behavior.

2. **Influence of the strength of the social dilemma:** As we can see, the surface of the graph flattens as p increases. This means that the higher the strength of the social dilemma, the lower the influence of the initial propensity for cooperation. This leads to very counterintuitive results. For example, for initially low proportions of cooperators, the proportion of cooperators at the attractor increases when the strength of the social dilemma increases. From 1, we can also expect that the weight of conformist agents in the population will decrease as p increases if we study the dependence at the rules' level.

To explain these qualitative results, we actually have to look at the rules' level (Figure 5a). We can observe that the distribution of rules for imitation varies as p increases from an almost all-conformist society to a mixed population of conformists, *maxi*, and *mini-agents*. For low p,

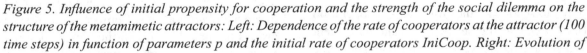

Figure 5. Influence of initial propensity for cooperation and the strength of the social dilemma on the structure of the metamimetic attractors: Left: Dependence of the rate of cooperators at the attractor (100 time steps) in function of parameters p and the initial rate of cooperators IniCoop. Right: Evolution of

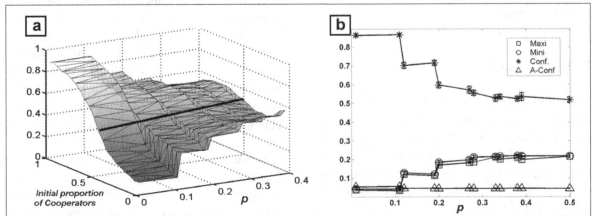

the dynamics are thus close to a game between conformist agents: Initial conditions matter and the higher the initial rate of cooperation, the higher the rate of cooperation at the attractor. For high p, populations of *maxi* and *mini* are sufficiently important to influence the behavior of conformist agents. Since these two populations are in equivalent proportions, and since they tend to adopt opposite behaviors (C for *mini* and D for *maxi*), these two behaviors will be roughly equally distributed in the conformist population. This accounts for the high rate of cooperation in the whole population.

This qualitatively explains the particular structure of the behavioral level at the attractor. In models where ends are given top-down, turning these intuitions into analytical results would be the end of the story, but here, the stakes are quite different. We have to explain why the rules' level behaves like this. The distribution of rules at the attractor depends endogenously on the initial values of p and *IniCoop*. Can we account qualitatively for this dependence? This explanation requires that we enter in the internal logics of the diverse rules. Because of the high complexity of these systems, we will not provide exact analytic results here but only qualitative intuitions.

Conformists and *anti-conformists* don't care about material payoffs *per se*. Consequently, they should not be influenced in their choices at the rule level by variations in p. Since in this case rule update is only dependent on the rule's distribution, variation in *IniCoop* should not directly influence their proportions. This means that situations with strong social dilemmas favor an evolution toward preferences indexed on material payoffs. On the contrary, the behavior of *maxi* and *mini* depends heavily on payoffs. Since this dependence is relative and not absolute, the crucial factor is the way p influences the disparities of payoffs.

To understand this, we have to enter into the logic of these types of agents. What is it to be in the skin of a *maxi* agent? At the beginning of the game you have to find the strategy that will give

you the best payoffs in your neighborhood. But the environment is changing quickly in these first periods, each of your neighbors is looking for an identity, imitating those they think to be the best. In particular, the configurations of behaviors and consequently configurations of payoffs are fluctuating. As *maxi*, there is little chance that you will keep playing C for a long time, because if you happen to do so you will soon have a neighbor playing D that will beat you. So unless you drop your rule for another one, you will quickly adopt to D. Still, there are some cases where you can be supplanted by one of your lucky neighbors (more neighbors playing C). If this neighbor is not a maxi-agent, you will be tempted to copy its rule. The counterfactual stability of maxi-agents will thus be positively correlated with the probability for an agent playing D to be disappointed when it compares its material payoffs with one of its neighbors. We can give an estimation of this probability in a function of p and the initial propensity of the population for cooperation.

- Given p and *IniCoop*, the probability for a given agent A to have k neighbors playing C is : $w(k) = C_8^k \, IniCoop^k \, (1^- Inicoop)^{(8^- k)}$.
- The corresponding payoffs are $g_C(k) = k.(1^- p)$ if A is playing C and $g_D(k) = k + (8^- k).p$ A is playing D.
- The distribution of payoffs in the population has thus for modes $g_D(k)$ and $g_C(k)$ with weights $(1^- IniCoop).w(k)$ and $IniCoop.w(k)$ respectively. Let F be the cumulative distribution of these payoffs.

To have a more precise idea of what happens, we can plot the distribution of payoffs relative to the behavior of the agents (Figure 6).

The degree of overlapping between two plots for a given p indicates the degree of *dominance* of D on C ; the variance of these distributions indicates the *uncertainty* for a maxi-biased agent when playing D.

We see that there are two issues. The first is that in some spatial configurations, an agent playing D can have lower payoffs than one of its neighbors playing C. This is the degree of dominance of D on C in the space of spatial configurations. The second is that an agent playing D can still have a neighbor playing D with higher payoffs. This is linked to the variance of the payoffs' distribution for each action C and D and will have the consequence that a maxi-agent (and symmetrically a mini-agent) will have a higher probability to question the relevance of its rule when this variance is high. An increase in p both reduces this variance and increases the degree of dominance of D on C. Consequently, we might expect that the higher the p, the more counterfactually stable are mini- and maxi-agents.

From the above, the probability for a defecting maxi-agent to be disappointed when it compares itself to one of its neighbors can be approximated by an index of counterfactual instability for *maxi*:

$$I_{maxi} = \sum_{k=0...8} w(k).(1-F(g_D(k)))$$

The plot of this counterfactual instability index enables to predict two main qualitative traits relative to the influence of p and *IniCoop* on the *maxi* rule distribution (Figure 7). First, this index decreases with some discontinuities[9] as p increases: the higher the strength of the social dilemma, the higher the counterfactual stability of *maxi*-agents. Second, this index has an inverted U-shape along the *IniCoop* axis and the U gets distorted as the strength of the social dilemma increases: *maxi*-agents are relatively more counterfactually stable when the initial propensity for cooperation is high than when it is low. A similar analysis holds for *mini*-agents.

These predictions are corroborated by the multi-agent simulations (Figure 8). Moreover, we can deduce from the above the evolution of conformism in function of the strength of the social dilemma (p) and the initial propensity of the population for cooperation. The conformist group

Figure 6. Plot of the distribution of payoffs as a function of the behavior of the agent (C: stars ; D: circles) for IniCoop=50 percent . p=0.1— black line ; p=0.4—gray line.

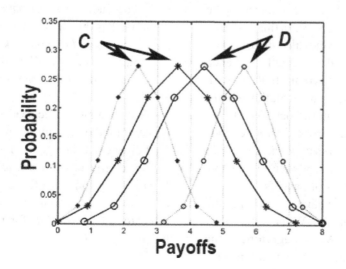

will benefit from the counterfactual instability of *maxi* and *mini*. Consequently, their proportions should be positively correlated with the quantity $1^-(1^-I_{maxi}) \cdot (1^-I_{mini})$. This is exactly what we can observe when we compare the proportion of conformists with the variations of this index.

The index is inversely proportional to the mean proportions of maxi. It has thus been multiplied by 1^- and translated to ease the comparison with the simulation's results. The small figure in the upper right corner is the index without any transformation. *Left:* The evolution of conformism in function of the strength of the social dilemma and the initial propensity of the population for cooperation plotted against the index $1^-(1^-I_{maxi})$. We can see that variations of this index are a well correlated with the variations of proportions of conformist agents.

With this qualitative insight, we can better understand the shape of the surface plotted in Figure 5a and the dependence of the level of cooperation on the strength of the social dilemma and the initial propensity of the population for cooperation. Moreover, this insight concerns all

the parameter space for this given initial uniform distribution of imitation rules. From this study, the two critical factors are:

- The spatial dominance of the different behaviors (here D and C) relative to the different valuation functions. Spatial dominance of a behavior A on a behavior B relative to a valuation function can be defined as the proportion of spatial configurations on behaviors such that payoffs associated to A behavior according this valuation function is higher than payoffs associated to B.

- The *residual uncertainty*: This is related to the variance of payoffs on spatial configurations of neighbors and second neighbors for a given behavior. Even in the case where there are some behaviors that spatially strictly dominate the others, two players with the same behavior can have different payoffs because they have different opportunities with their own neighbors. This could lead to the counterfactual instability of an agent.

Figure 7. Evolutions of the distribution of rules in function of the strength of the social dilemma (p) and the initial propensity of the population for cooperation (IniCoop). Left: On the same plot the mean proportions of maxi-agents at the attractor and the index of counterfactual instability I_{maxi}.

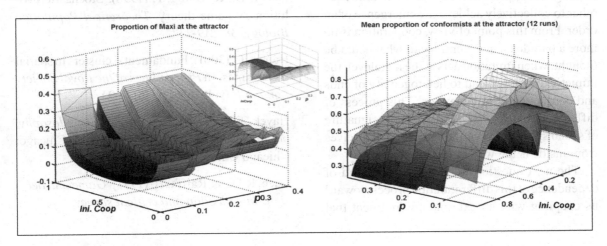

CONCLUSION: OPTIMIZATION VERSUS INTERNAL DYNAMICS

-Well mister A., I am afraid you lose! You are in the minority.
- But that's exactly what I was looking for, I'm anti-conformist!

This short dialog illustrates the impossibility to interpret all socioeconomic behaviors in terms of an optimization process, especially if this does not take into account the diversity of ends. In a previous chapter (Chavalarias, 2006), we outlined a formalism for social systems modelling designed to take into account the self-organization of a multiplicity of ends. The distinction has to be made between the internal dynamics of a social system (P^0) and its coupling with the environment (P_ε^0). We gave here an illustration of what internal dynamics look like with a case study on a spatial prisoner's dilemma.

Contrary to most models explaining cooperation in social systems as the output of an optimization process, we have introduced a metamimetic principle and explained cooperation as the outcome of a spontaneous differentiation process under cultural co-evolution. In this framework, the question is not the traditional: "How can altruists 'survive' in a selfish world?" Rather, in line with Tarde (1890), the main issue is to understand how heterogeneous ends can reinforce or limit each other to collectively achieve the emergence of an order. From this point of view, cooperation is no more a paradox since, contrary to what could be thought, when imitation acts at the metalevel, the mimetic dynamics lead to heterogeneity of ends and consequently of behaviors. This process of differentiation, *social cognition*, is the signature of social systems for which changing themselves from inside is the way of functioning.

The next question to address is the kind of dependence of this differentiation process toward its coupling with an external environment that imposes viability constraints and introduces noise into its internal dynamics.

ACKNOWLEDGMENT

I would like to thank the Ecole Polytechnique—Paris for material support. This chapter benefited from numerous discussions at the CREA. All my gratefulness goes to its members.

REFERENCES

Axelrod, R. (1984). *The evolution of cooperation.* NY: Basic Books.

Chavalarias, D. (2004). *Métadynamiques en cognition sociale–Quelle définition de meilleur est la meilleure?* Unpublished doctoral dissertation, Ecole Polytechnique, Paris, France.

Chavalarias, D. (2006). Metamimetic games: Modeling metadynamics in social cognition. *Journal of Artificial Societies and Social Simulations, 9*(2).

Chavalarias, D. (2007). La part mimetique des dynamiques de congition sociale: cle pour penser l' auto-transformation du social. *Novuvelles Perspectives en Sciences Sociales, 2*(2).

Foster, D., & Young, P. (1990). Stochastic evolutionary game theory. *Theoretical Population Biology,* 38, 219-232.

Hauert, C. (2001). Fundamental clusters in spatial 2×2 games. In *Proceedings of the Royal Society London B* (vol. 268, pp. 761-769.)

Hayek, F.A. (1978). *New studies in philosophy, politics, economics and history of ideas.* Chicago: Chicago University Press.

Luce, R.D., & Raiffa, H. (1957). *Game and decision: Introduction and critical survey.*

Nowak, M., & May, R.M. (1992). Evolutionary games and spatial chaos. *Nature,* 359, 826-829.

Tarde, G. (1890). *Les lois de l'imitation.* Jean-Marie Tremblay (Ed.), Les classiques des Sciences Sociales.

Tarde, G. (1898). *Les lois sociales.* Esquisse d'une sociologie. Jean-Marie Tremblay (Ed.), Les classiques des Sciences Sociales.

Varela, F.J. (1989). *Autonomie et connaissance.* Seuil.

ENDNOTES

1   Hayek distinguishes the notions of *Cosmos*, which is a spontaneous order with no purpose, and *Taxis*, which is an order that relies on prior ends. *Catallaxy* is the kind of economic arrangement within a *Cosmos*, whereas Economy is the kind of economic arrangement within a *Taxis*.

2   Several terms are used in the literature to define the principles grounding the agents' decisions and actions: ends, goals, aims, motivations, preferences, utility function, values. Although there is undoubtedly a distinction between these terms, at the level of details considered in our simple example, they are subsumed under the generic notion of ends. A more accurate model would require to introduce several time scales. For example; Hayek (1978) distinguishes ends and values from their proper time scale. A first study in that direction can be found in (Chavalarias, 2004) where these time scales are properties of the aims considered and depend endogenously on the levels at which their appear in the hierarchical organization of ends.

3   Neurobiological studies seems to indicate that for the 'now and here' we have something like $C_B=2$ (Etienne Koeklin, personal communication).

4   Note that in social systems, this is already a cultural construction.

5   See Chavalarias (2004) for a study of the influence of memory.

6   In the following we say "it" for agents since now we are dealing with artificial agents.

7   Should we remind the reader that in the original model of Nowak and May, the rate of cooperation would have collapse down to zero with such parameters?

8   Actually, this condition is often discarded in models.

9   The discontinuities are well-known consequences of the fact that payoffs are discrete.

10   We remind that the parallel update do not generate artifacts (Chavalarias, 2004).

APPENDIX

The algorithm used for the simulations is the following:

Set up of the game:
- Give a value for p, $0 < p < 0.5$.
- Agents are displayed on a toric grid, their neighborhood is composed by the eight adjacent cells.

Initial conditions:
- Give the spatial distribution of imitation rules. In our examples, we considered four rules. For each agent, we assigned one of these rules randomly, with a probability $1/4$
- Give the spatial distribution of behaviors. Here, for each agent, we assigned the behavior C, with a probability *IniCoop* and D otherwise.

At each period, for each agent, with parallel update at the population level[10]:
- For each agent, the scores of the eight PD games with its neighbors are computed and the sum is the new material payoffs of the agent.
- Each agent looks at the current situation of its neighbors (payoffs, rules, and behavior).
- For any agent A, if according to A's valuation function there are some agents in Γ_A which are better off than A, and if all these neighbors have a valuation function different from A's, then A imitates the rule of one of these agents taken randomly.
- if according to its (eventually new) valuation function, A is not among the more successful agents in Γ_A, then A chooses at random one of its neighbors in the better situation and copies its behavior (C or D).

Chapter IV
Probability Distribution Dynamics Explaining Agent Model Convergence to Extremism

Guillaume Deffuant
Laboratoire d'Ingénierie des Systèmes Complexes, France

Gérard Weisbuch
Laboratoire de Physique Statistique, France

ABSTRACT

This chapter studies continuous opinion models with extremists, and we use probability distribution models which approximate the behaviour of agent-based models in order to explain their attractor patterns. The probability distribution is defined on a discrete grid in the opinion/uncertainty space. We compute the equations of probability flows between each of the sites of the grid for different variants of the opinion influence model (bounded confidence, relative agreement, and two others). The simulations show that the probability distribution models yield attractor patterns very similar to those obtained with the agent-based models. Moreover, a study of the probability distribution evolution helps to better understand the process of convergence to single and double extreme attractors observed in agent-based models.

INTRODUCTION

In recent years, we proposed several models of opinion dynamics to model the influence of individuals with an extreme opinion in a population of moderate agents (Deffuant et al., 2002; Amblard & Deffuant, 2004; Weisbuch et al., 2004). These models rely on several general hypotheses about the agent behaviour:

- Agents opinions vary continuously between some bounds.

- An agent might change its own opinion under the influence of other agents with opinions which are not too far from its own opinion.
- There are extremist agents, that are very convinced of their opinion (they do not change easily), and their opinion is extreme (at the bounds or very close to the bounds).

Deffuant (2006) performed a systematic comparison between model variants, on several network topologies:

- Bounded confidence model (BC) (Hegselman & Krause, 2002; Deffuant et al., 2000; Weisbuch et al., 2002; Urbig, 2003; Urbig & Lorenz, 2004). In this model, each agent has a threshold in addition to its opinion (sometimes interpreted as an uncertainty), which limits the range of opinions of those agents it interacts with. The extremists are initialised with an opinion equal to one of the bounds, and a very low uncertainty. In this model, each agent has a threshold in addition to its opinion (sometimes interpreted as an uncertainty), which limits the range of opinions of those agents it interacts with. The extremists are initialised with an opinion equal to one of the bounds, and a very low uncertainty.
- Gaussian bounded confidence (GBC), in which the opinion and uncertainty influence depend on a Gaussian function of the difference of opinions.
- Relative agreement (RA) model (Deffuant et al., 2002), in which the influence takes into account the interlocutor uncertainty compared with the overlap between both segments of opinions.

- Gaussian bounded confidence model (GBCU), in which we multiply the influence by a Gaussian function of the interlocutor uncertainty.

The objective of this chapter is to integrate the corresponding master equations for the probability distribution, thus gaining some insight into the behaviour of the agent-based models. This approach can sometimes be seen as an alternative to agent-based models, as practiced in sociodynamics (Weidlich & Haag, 1999). However, in several cases it can be used as a complement to agent-based models, in order to give a more precise and systematic understanding of their behaviour; this was particularly the case for binary or discrete states models (Edwards et al., 2003; Deffuant & Huet, 2006), but also for the bounded confidence model with continuous opinion (Ben Naim et al., 2003). In the latter case, the master equation approach requires one to discretise the continuous opinion. It can be also considered as a distribution model of the discrete opinion version proposed by Stauffer et al. (2004). In the present chapter, after checking that the distribution model gives a good prediction of the agent-based model attractor, we study in more detail the convergence process of the distribution model. This allows us to draw some conclusions about this process, which are also valid for the agent-based model.

In Section 2 we recall the definitions of the different agent-based models and their convergence types. In Section 3 we derive the master equations for the probability distribution and apply them to our particular case. In Section 4 we compare patterns of attractors of the distribution in the parameter space with those obtained from the agent-based models. In Section 5 we study more closely the evolution of the distribution in single and double extreme convergences in order to better understand these dynamics. The final section provides some points of discussion and conclusions.

THE AGENT-BASED MODELS

Common Features

The considered models share the following aspects:

- The population includes N individuals, each having a continuous opinion and a continuous uncertainty.
- The moderate agents are initialised with opinions uniformly distributed between -1 and $+1$, with uncertainty U.
- The population includes a proportion p_e of extremists. Half of the extremists are initialised with opinion -1, and the other half with opinion $+1$, all with uncertainty u_e.
- The interactions take place in randomly chosen pairs of connected individuals.

Moreover, for all the models, when an individual with opinion x and uncertainty u meets another individual of opinion x' and uncertainty u', the modifications of the individuals' uncertainties and opinions follow a common scheme. They depend on a kernel function of x, x', u, and u'. Let k be this function:

$$x := x + \mu.k(x,x',u,u').(x'-x)$$
$$x' := x' + \mu.k(x',x,u',u).(x-x') \qquad (1)$$

$$u := u + \mu.k(x,x',u,u').(u'-u)$$
$$u' := u' + \mu.k(x',x,u',u).(u-u') \qquad (2)$$

In the next paragraph, we list the variants of the models corresponding to different choices for k.

Variants of the Kernel Function

Bounded Confidence (BC)

The initial bounded confidence model including only equations (1) was modified, for instance in Weisbuch et al.(2005), to include equations (2) on the uncertainties. In this case, the kernel function is independent of u', it is a Heaviside function of the difference in opinions:

$$k(x-x',u) = 1 \quad \text{if } |x\text{-}x'| < u$$
$$k(x-x',u) = 0 \quad \text{otherwise} \qquad (3)$$

Gaussian Bounded Confidence (GBC)

In this case, the kernel function has the form of a Gaussian function, and is also independent of u':

$$k(x-x',u) = \exp\left(-\left(\frac{x-x'}{u}\right)^2\right) \qquad (4)$$

Relative Agreement (RA)

The relative agreement was proposed in Deffuant et al. (2002), and it introduces a new assumption: individuals take into account the uncertainty of their interlocutor, such that interlocutors with a low uncertainty (high confidence) tend to be more influential than those with a high uncertainty. The rules use v, the size of the overlap between segments $[x-u, x+u]$ and $[x'-u',x'+u']$.

$$v = \min(x+u, x'+u') - \max(x-u, x'-u')$$

$$k(x,x',u,u') = \frac{v}{2u'} \quad \text{if } v > 0$$

$$k(x,x',u,u') = 0 \text{ otherwise} \qquad (5)$$

The value of this function is 1 when the segment $[x'-u',x'+u']$ is totally included in the segment $[x-u, x+u]$, otherwise, it is lower than 1.

Gaussian Bounded Confidence with Influence of Uncertainty (GBCU)

This model expresses the same assumption as the RA model, considering that low uncertainty

Figure 1. The three attractors. Time plot of the agents opinion for N = 50, 2 extremists at +1 and −1, ue = 0.01 (extremist opinions are represented in grey). Top: U = 0.3, RA model. Central attractor. Middle: U = 0.9, RA model. Double extreme attractor. Bottom: U = 1.3, GBCU model. Single extreme attractor.

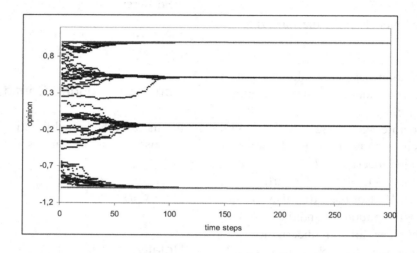

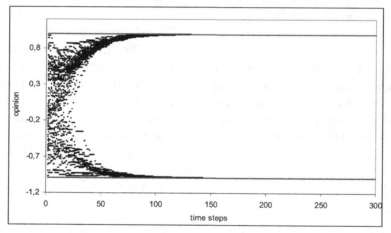

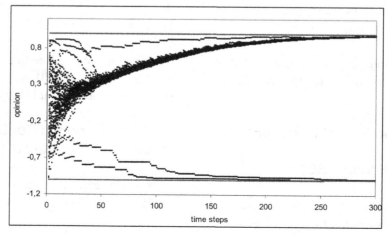

gives more influence than high uncertainty. This is expressed as follows:

$$k(x-x',u,u') = \exp\left(-\left(\frac{x-x'}{u}\right)^2\right).\exp\left(-\left(\frac{u}{u'}\right)^2\right)$$

(6)

With this kernel, if u is much smaller than u', then the change is necessarily small.

Attractor Types

These attractors depend upon the values of the parameters and we would like to compare the patterns of attractor in the parameter space for the different variants of the model.

THE PROBABILITY DISTRIBUTION MODEL

Initialisation of the Distribution

Rather than following individual opinion trajectories, we use the master equation describing the evolution of the joint probability distribution of opinion and uncertainty. We here generalize the approach taken by Ben Naim et al. (2003) by taking into account the uncertainties. Therefore, we consider a probability distribution on a grid defined on the compact $[-1,+1] \times [u_e, U]$. We thus cut the opinion and uncertainty intervals into pieces of size δx, by discretising the opinion and uncertainty segments:

$$x(i) = -1 + i.\delta x, \quad \text{for} \quad i = 0,...,i_m.$$
$$u(j) = u_e + j\delta x, \quad \text{for} \quad j = 0,...,j_m. \quad (7)$$

The integer values i_m and j_m are the maximum indices, given the value of δx.

The probability distribution $\rho(i,j)$ represents the probability that an agent of the population has its opinion x and its uncertainty u such that:

$$x \in [(x(i) - \frac{\delta x}{2}, x(i) + \frac{\delta x}{2}]$$

(8)

$$u \in [(u(j) - \frac{\delta x}{2}, u(j) + \frac{\delta x}{2}]$$

(9)

Distribution ρ is initialized with:

$$\rho(0,0) = (1 + \Delta)\frac{p_e}{2}, \rho(i_m, 0) = (1 - \Delta)\frac{p_e}{2}$$

$$\rho(i, j_m) = (1 - p_e)/(i_m - 1), \quad \text{for} \quad i = 1,...,i_m - 1$$

$$\rho(i, j) = 0, \quad \text{otherwise.}$$

(10)

Parameter Δ allows us to introduce a small asymmetry in the initial distribution, giving, e.g., a higher initial density to the negative extreme.

Computation of the Master Equation

The principle of the model's dynamics is to compute the flows of distribution from one site (i,j) to any other site (k,l), and to sum them up to compute the distribution change (the update of the distribution is parallel).

More precisely, for each site (i,j), we consider all the other sites (i',j'), and we compute the interaction between both sites. An interaction takes place only if $\lfloor a \rfloor$ means the integer part of number a):

$$di = \lfloor \mu k_{u(j)}(x(i), x(i'), u(j')).(i'-i) \rfloor \neq 0$$

(11)

$$dj = \lfloor \mu k_{u(j)}(x(i), x(i'), u(j')).(j'-j) \rfloor \neq 0$$

(12)

Indeed, in this case the agents belonging to site (i',j') have an influence on agents belonging to site (i,j). This influence adds di to the opinion and dj to the uncertainty. The probability of encounter between agents of site (i',j') and agents of site (i',j') is proportional to the product $\rho(i,j)\rho(i',j')$. Therefore, the influence of agents of site (i',j') on agents of

Figure 2. 3D representation of the initial probability distribution on a grid in the space x × u. The moderate uncertainty is 1.7 (line on the top), and the extremist uncertainty of 0.05 (the two bottom peaks), with a global density of extremists of 0.05 (0.2625 on the negative extreme, 0.2375 on the positive extreme). The discretisation includes 1,591 sites.

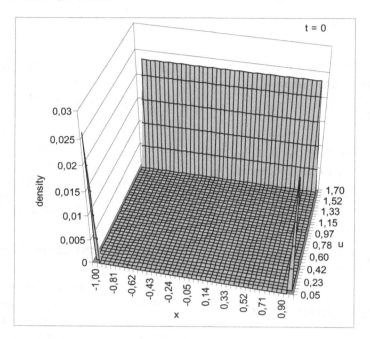

site (i,j) will induce an increase of $\rho(i + di, j + dj)$, and a decrease of $\rho(i, j)$, λ is the kinetic parameter of the algorithm:

$$\rho(i + di, j + dj) := \rho(i + di, j + dj) + \lambda\rho(i, j)\rho(i', j')$$
$$\rho(i, j) := \rho(i, j) - \lambda\rho(i, j)\rho(i', j') \qquad (13)$$

Actually, because the change is made in parallel, we define $d\rho(i, j)$ as the distribution of the changes of $\rho(i,j)$. At each time step, we initialise $d\rho(i, j)$ with only 0 values. Then, we fill its values by computing the flow of distribution from one site (i,j) to another site (k,l). The computation is as follows:

Computation of $d\rho$
For $(i, j) \in \{0, ..., i_m\} \times \{0, ..., j_m\}$ do:
    For $(i', j') \in \{0, ..., i_m\} \times \{0, ..., j_m\}$ do:

If $di = \lfloor \mu k_{u(j)}(x(i), x(i'), u(j')).(i'-i) \rfloor \neq 0$
or
$dj = \lfloor \mu k_{u(j)}(x(i), x(i'), u(j')).(j'- j) \rfloor \neq 0$
$d\rho(i + di, j + dj) := d\rho(i + di, j + dj) + \lambda\rho(i, j)\rho(i', j')$
$d\rho(i, j) := d\rho(i, j) - \lambda\rho(i, j)\rho(i', j')$
    end if
  end for
end for

Global Algorithm

After the initialisation, we repeat the modification of ρ until changes become negligible. The stopping criterion is obtained by comparing the norm of $d\rho(i,j)$ (noted $|d\rho|$) with a threshold ε. Therefore, the global algorithm is the following:

Evolution of ρ:

Initialise ρ

Repeat

        Compute $d\rho$

        For $(i,j) \in \{0,...,i_m\} \times \{0,...,j_m\}$

$\rho(i,j) := \rho(i,j) + d\rho(i,j)$

While ($\rho > \epsilon d$)

In the following simulations we chose ϵ = 0.0001.

Example

Figure 3 shows a few steps of evolution of the distribution shown on Figure 2, according to the BC model.

Comparing the Distribution Dynamics with Agent-Based Simulations

We now compare attractor patterns provided by both dynamics. We focus on the variation of two parameters: U, the initial uncertainty of the moderates, and p_e, the initial proportion of extremists, keeping constant the other parameters, $\mu = 0.3$ (the kinetic parameter) and $u_e = 0.05$ (the uncertainty of the extremists). For the agent-based model, we consider the results of Deffuant (2006): We take 51 values of U between 0.2 and 2, and 51 values between 0.01 and 0.21 for p_e, and N = 400 (number of individuals). For the distribution model, we take 21 values of U between 0.2 and 2, and 21 values between 0.01 and 0.21 for p_e,

Figure 3. First steps (iteration 10 and 20) of probability distribution evolution for the BC model, with a proportion of extremists p_e = 0.05, (Δ = 0.05, i.e., on the negative extreme, the initial density is 0.02625, on the positive extreme, it is 0.02375), uncertainty of extremists: u_e = 0.05, initial uncertainty of the moderates U = 1.3, μ = 0.3 (kinetic parameter of the opinion dynamics), λ = 0.5 (kinetic parameter of distribution update). We note that in this case the distribution concentrates quite rapidly.

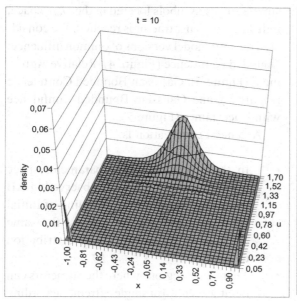 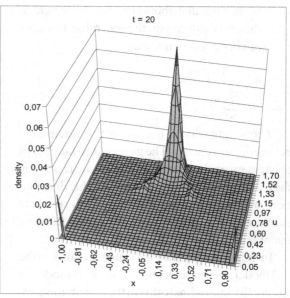

because the simulations are longer, and there is no need to evaluate the random variations since the model is deterministic. The other parameters of the distribution model are: $\lambda = 0.5$ (kinetic parameter of distribution update), size of the uncertainty/opinion grid: 1500, $\Delta = 0.05$ (asymmetry between negative and positive extremists).

Characterisation of the Attractors

To characterise the attractor of a simulation, we consider the distribution at convergence, and we combine two indicators (the same as in Deffuant, 2006):

- The average of the absolute value of the opinions, noted X, which indicates how extreme the population is:

$$X = \sum_{i,j} \rho(i,j) |x(i,j)| \qquad (14)$$

- The generalised number of clusters, noted n, which is a smooth number of clusters obtained following the method defined in Derrida and Flyvbjerg (1986). Considering a final state of the distribution involving k clusters of average opinion x_i, of weight w_i, in the total distribution minus the weight of the initial extremists, the generalised number of clusters is defined by:

$$n = \frac{1}{\displaystyle\sum_{i=1}^{k} w_i} \qquad (15)$$

The weight w_i is the fraction of the distribution belonging to a cluster. The generalised number of clusters gives the exact number of clusters when they all include the same part of the distribution, and intermediate values for intermediate situations. The rationale is that small clusters count less.

In the computation of indicators defined on the AB model, we consider only the initially moderate agents. To approximate this in the distribution, we subtracted the initial values of the extremes from the final distribution. This approximation relies on the assumption that the initial extremists do not move much, which generally holds as long as the uncertainty of the extremists is low enough.

We combine the two indicators to compute the attractor type, with the following rules:

- If $X < 0.8$, then attractor = "central".
- If $X > 0.8$
  - If $n < 1.25$, then: attractor = "single extreme".
  - If $n > 1.66$, then: attractor = "double extreme".
  - If $1.25 < n < 1.66$, then: attractor = "intermediate between single and double extreme".

These attractors have a higher peak in the negative extreme, but the peak at the positive extreme is not negligible.

Patterns of Attractors in the Parameter Space

The next figures, for both the agent-based and the distribution models, represent the result of a simulation by symbols located in the U, p_e space, indicating which attractor is reached. We considered the four model versions of opinion influence: Bounded confidence (Figure 4), Relative Agreement (Figure 5), Gaussian Bounded Confidence (Figure 6), and Gaussian Bounded Confidence with Uncertainty (Figure 7).

A general observation is:

- In those regions in the parameter space when only one attractor is observed in AB dynamics whatever the sampling of initial conditions and coupled agents, the same attractor is obtained by the distribution dynamics.
- There exist regions where the attractors can be either central or single extreme, according

Figure 4. BC model. Left: AB model in total connection. Right: distribution model. Each symbol represents one simulation and the shape codes for the attractor (central, single extreme, intermediate between single and double extreme, and double extreme)

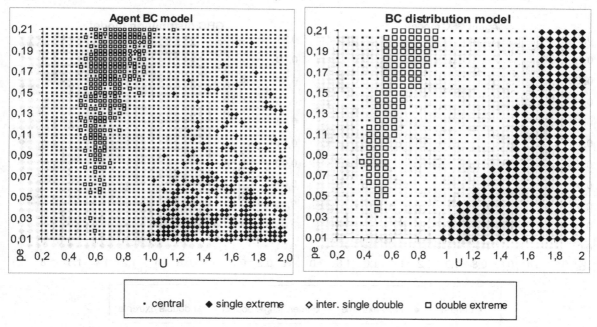

Figure 5. RA model. Left: AB model in total connection. Right: distribution model. Each symbol represents one simulation and the shape codes for the attractor (central, single extreme, intermediate between single and double extreme, and double extreme).

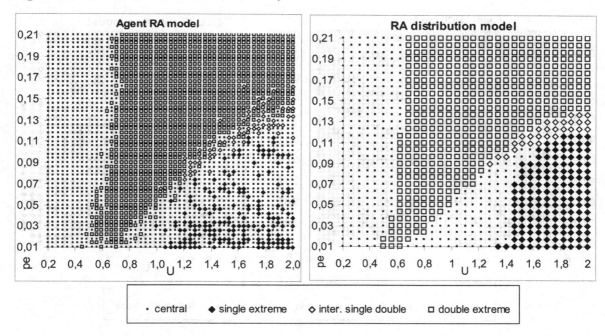

Figure 6. GBC model. Left: AB model in total connection. Right: distribution model. Each symbol represents one simulation and the shape codes for the attractor (central, single extreme, intermediate between single and double extreme, and double extreme).

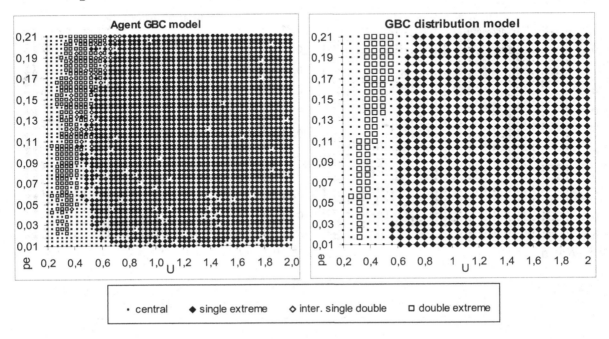

Figure 7. GBCU model. Left: AB model in total connection. Right: distribution model. Each symbol represents one simulation and the shape codes for the attractor (central, single extreme, intermediate between single and double extreme, and double extreme).

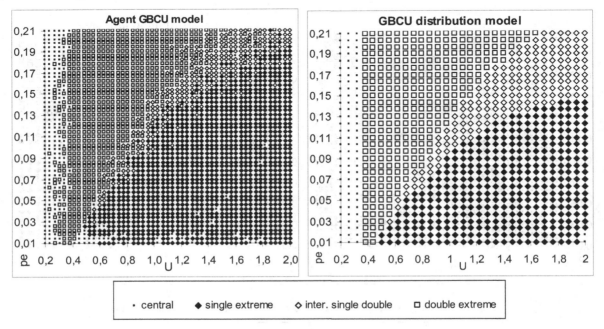

to the sampling of initial conditions and of coupled agents in AB dynamics, for the same values of the parameters. In these regions, the distribution dynamics always yield the same attractor for the same parameters because it is deterministic. The boundaries between the attractor regions depend upon the magnitude of the asymmetry parameter.

STUDY OF THE EXTREME ATTRACTOR IN THE DISTRIBUTION MODEL

In order to better understand the process of convergence, a particularly useful tool is to visualise the influence zones of the extremists on the grid. We distinguish four zones which are represented in Figure 8. By having an influence, we mean that the extremes will induce a flow from the sites located in the zone. From the equations of the models, one can derive for both the RA and BC models:

- The condition for site (x, u) to be influenced by the negative extreme: $x - u < -1$.
- The condition for site (x, u) to be influenced by the positive extreme: $x + u > +1$.

We focus first on the BC and RA models, because they use sharp boundaries of the influence zone.

Figure 8 visualises these conditions.

These zones will be particularly useful to understand the evolution of the distribution when double or single extreme attractors take place.

Single Extreme Attractor

Figure 9 shows some pictures of the evolution of the distribution in a case of convergence to a single extreme attractor for the BC model, and Figure 10 shows a convergence to a central attractor. The comparison between these cases helps to understand the convergence to a single extreme attractor.

Figure 8. The influence of the extremes on the grid opinion/uncertainty. The black lines show the limit of the influence of positive and negative extremes, and define four zones. In the bottom triangle the extremes have no influence, in the left triangle only the negative extreme has an influence, in the right triangle only the positive extreme has an influence, and in the top triangle both extremes have an influence.

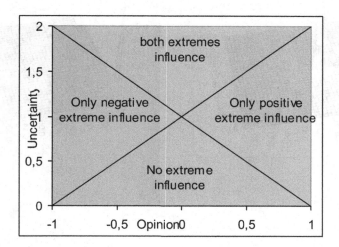

Figure 9. Pictures of distribution evolution for a single extreme attractor with the BC model. U = 1.7, ue= 0.05 size of the grid: 1500, μ = 0.3, l = 0.5. The initial density of extremists is 0.05, on the negative extreme: 0.02625, on the positive extreme: 0.02375.

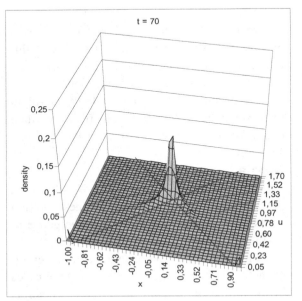
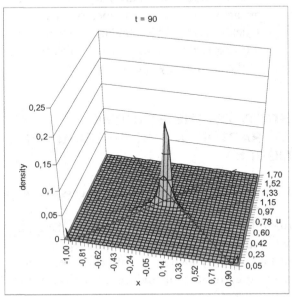
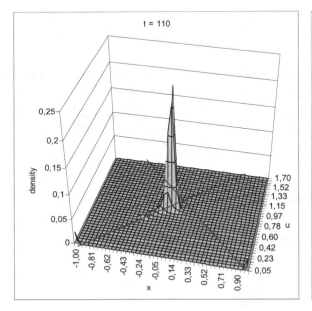
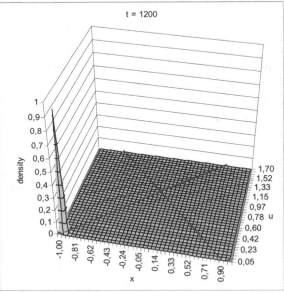

The value t on top of each graph is the number of iterations. When the distribution goes down through the intersection of the extreme influence zone limits (black lines) it is already concentrated, and the maximum of the distribution is located in the negative extreme influence zone (see at $t = 90$). This enhances the dissymmetry of the distribution ($t = 110$), which keeps an important part in the negative extreme influence zone. However, the density maximum lies in the zone where the extremes have no influence, which explains why the convergence is generally quite slow. The process continues until the single extreme convergence: More than 90 percent of the initial distribution is finally at the negative extreme (after around 1,200 time steps).

The importance of these zones relies on the fact that the convergence occurs in two time scales:

- First the moderates' cloud converges in the neighbourhood of the centre of gravity of the initial distribution, with a fast decrease of uncertainty (the vertical axis). This process takes place because the cloud is located in the influence zone of both extremes (above the intersection of the lines).

- The crucial moment which determines if the attractor will be single extreme or central is when the distribution crosses the intersection of the lines separating the influence zones:

  ◦ If the distribution is very concentrated (as in Figure 9), a major part of the distribution tends to go into the zone where only the negative extreme is influent because this extreme is slightly more influent from the beginning, and only a small deviation tends to have the maximum of the distribution inside the negative extreme influence zone (see Figure 9, $t = 90$). The asymmetry of the distribution tends then to keep a significant part inside the negative extreme influence zone. This part of

the distribution pulls the rest (which remains in the zone of no extreme influence) slowly toward the negative extreme. The whole process leads to the convergence to a single extreme.

  ◦ If the distribution is not concentrated (as in Figure 10), the difference between the part of the distribution which goes into the positive influence zone and into the negative influence zone is much lower. Indeed, at $t = 30$, for instance, there is a significant part of the density in the positive extreme influence zone (which is never the case in Figure 9). Therefore, the asymmetry is not enhanced as in Figure 9. The distribution lies mainly in the triangle where the extremes have no influence, which leads to the convergence to a central attractor.

It appears that the critical moment which decides between moderate and single extreme convergence is when the distribution goes through the intersection of the limits of the extreme influence zones, and the concentration or the dispersion of the distribution at this moment is particularly important.

Double Extreme Attractor

The same type of study can be done in order to better understand the convergence to a double extreme attractor. In the next figures, we compare the evolution of the distribution, with the same parameters, for the BC and RA models. The BC model yields a central attractor, whereas the RA model yields a double extreme attractor.

On Figure 11 (RA model), at $t = 50$, there is a larger part of the distribution located in the extreme influence zones (above the black lines), which leads to a reinforcement of the attraction to the extremes (visible at $t = 70, 100$). On the contrary, on Figure 12 (BC model), at $t = 40$, there

Figure 10. Pictures of distribution evolution for central attractor with the BC model. U = 1.2, u_e = 0.05, size of the grid: 1500, μ = 0.3, λ = 0.5. The initial density of extremists is 0.1, on the negative extreme: 0.0525, on the positive extreme: 0.0475. The value t at the top of each graph is the number of iterations. When the distribution goes down through the intersection of the extreme influence zones, limits (t = 30), it is much less concentrated than in Figure 9. Therefore, the dissymmetry is not so much enhanced (t = 40). The distribution is globally attracted down into the zone where extremes have no (direct) influence, which leads to a concentration of the distribution at an opinion close to 0 (t = 50), which will continue until the distribution is completely in the zone where extremists have no influence (for t = 460).

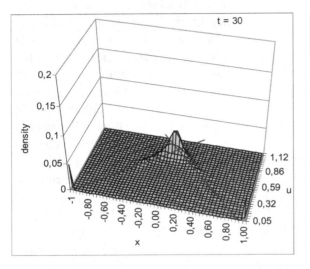

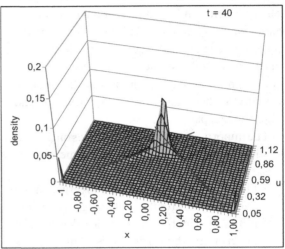

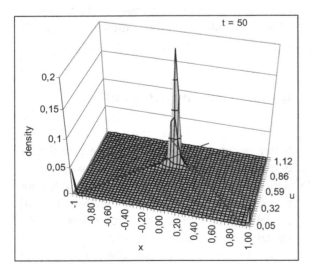

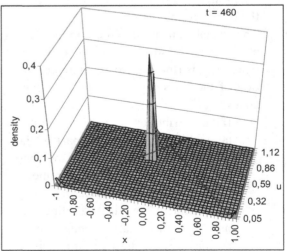

Figure 11. Views of convergence to double extreme attractor with the RA model. U = 1.0, ue= 0.05 size of the grid: 1500, μ = 0.3, l = 0.5. The initial density of extremists is 0.1, on the negative extreme: 0.0525, on the positive extreme: 0.0475. We note that at t = 50, the concentration tends to be higher in the extreme influence zones (above the black lines). This leads to the formation of two peaks, one at each extreme (double extreme convergence). The final attractor (double extreme) is reached at t = 390.

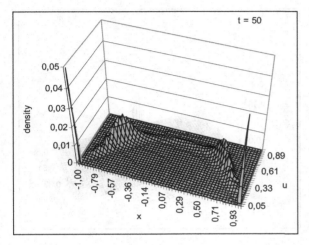

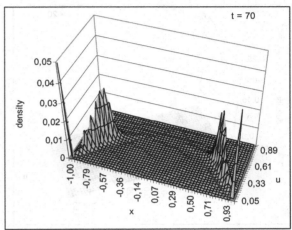

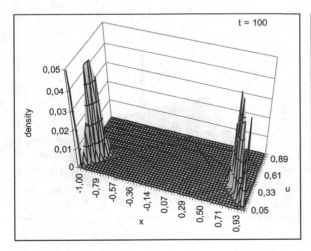

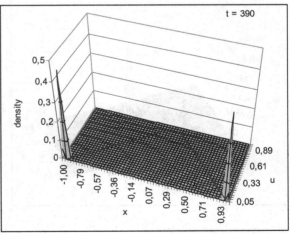

is a larger part of the distribution which is located in the zone where the extremes have no (direct) influence, which leads to a concentration of the distribution at an opinion close to 0 and a high uncertainty (visible at *t* = 50 and at convergence at *t* = 580).

The difference is due to the fact that the RA model gives relatively more influence to the ex-

Figure 12. Views of moderate convergence with the BC model, with the same parameters as in figure 11. U = 1.0, ue= 0.05, size of the grid: 1500, μ = 0.3, l = 0.5. The initial density of extremists is 0.1, on the negative extreme: 0.0525, on the positive extreme: 0.0475. We note that at t = 20, there is already a higher concentration in the centre, in the zone where the extremes have no influence (under the black lines). This leads to the formation of a peak located at an opinion which is close to 0, and with an uncertainty remaining high, as shown at t = 40 and t = 50. The final distribution (after around 600 time steps) is classified as central by our rules.

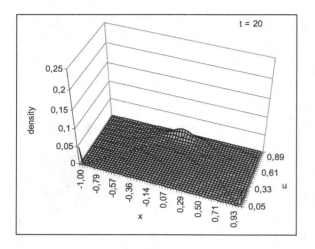

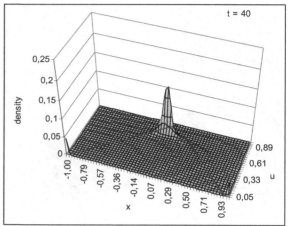

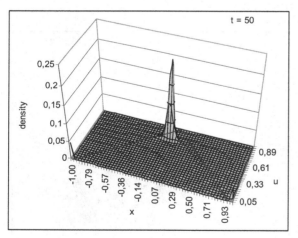

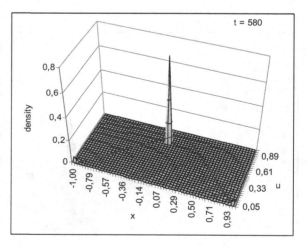

tremists, which attract the initial distribution to the extremes more quickly than the BC model. The double-extreme convergence takes place when the distribution splits into two almost equal parts, each located in the influence zone of one extreme.

DISCUSSION–CONCLUSION

We have shown that distribution dynamics, similar to that proposed in Ben Naim et al. (2003), yields attractor patterns in the parameter space which are similar to the ones obtained with the agent-based model for different variants of the influence model

(BC, RA, GBC, and GBCU). This result opened the possibility to study the distribution model in order to understand the process of convergence taking place in AB simulations.

We then studied the single and double extreme convergence, for BC and RA models. We observed the distribution in the extreme zones of influence. The observation is particularly relevant for the single-extreme convergence because it reveals that the shape of the distribution when going through the intersection of the extreme influence zones limits is crucial. Indeed, if the distribution is concentrated at this moment, it has very likely to enhance any small asymmetry very strongly. The same type of observations can be done for the other variants of the social influence models (GBC and GBCU), although the limits of the influence zones are not strict.

The interpretation of this observation in terms of collective social behaviour would be that the convergence to a single extreme is much facilitated in groups with a strong tendency to uniformity. There is a moment when the group uncertainty decreases to a threshold which makes it vulnerable to one extreme because it became indifferent to the other extreme. The process requires that the uncertainty of agents decreases when it interacts with both extremes (otherwise the central cloud would remain above the uncertainty threshold) which is certainly a questionable assumption.

Beyond the discussion about the realism of the model, we would like to stress the interest of deriving an aggregated model from an agent-based model. Of course, a similar study could have been done with AB models. However, the interpretation of the observed process is easier with the distribution model; the shape of this distribution appears crucial in the process. Therefore, in this example, the aggregated model helped to explain why the AB model converges to one or the other attractor.

REFERENCES

Amblard F., & Deffuant, G. (2004). The role of network topology on extremism propagation with relative agreement opinion dynamics. *Physica A., 343*, 725-738.

Ben-Naim, E., Krapivsky, P.L.,Vazquez, F., & Redner, S. (2003). Unity and discord in opinion dynamics. *Physica A., 330*(1-2), 99-106

Deffuant, G., Neau, D., Amblard, F., & Weisbuch, G. (2001). Mixing beliefs among interacting agents. *Advances in Complex Systems*, 3, 87-98.

Deffuant, G., Amblard, F., Weisbuch, G., & Faure, T. (2002). How can extremism prevail? A study based on the relative agreement interaction model. *Journal of Artificial Societies and Social Simulation, 5,4.* http://jasss.soc.surrey.ac.uk/5/4/1.html

Deffuant, G. (2006). Comparing extremism propagation patterns in continuous opinion models. *Journal of Artificial Societies and Social Simulation*, *9*(3). http://jasss.soc.surrey.ac.uk/9/3/8.html

Deffuant G., & Huet, S. (2006). Collective reinforcement of first impression bias. *Proceedings of the 1st World Conference on Social Simulation*. Kyoto.

Derrida, B., & Flyvbjerg, H. (1986). Multivalley structure in Kauffman's model: Analogy with spin glasses. *J. Phys. A*19, L1003-L1008.

Edwards M., Huet, S., Goreaud F., &Deffuant, G. (2003). Comparing an individual-based model of behaviour diffusion with its mean field aggregate approximation. *Journal of Artificial Societies and Social Simulation*, *6*(40).

Hegselmann, R., & Krause, U. (2002). Opinion dynamics and bounded confidence models, analysis and simulation. *Journal of Artificial Societies and Social Simulation, 5*(3). http://jasss.soc.surrey. ac.uk/5/3/2.html

Stauffer, D., Sousa, A., & Schulze, C. (2004). Discretized opinion dynamics of the Deffuant model on scale-free networks. *Journal of Artificial Societies and Social Simulation, 7*(3). http://jasss. soc.surrey.ac.uk/7/3/7.html

Urbig, D. (2003). Attitude dynamics with limited verbalisation capabilities. *Journal of Artificial Societies and Social Simulation, 6*(1). http://jasss. soc.surrey.ac.uk/6/1/2.html

Urbig, D., & Lorenz J. (2004, September 16-19). Communication regimes in opinion dynamics: Changing the number of communicating agents. In *Proceedings of the Second Conference of the European Social Simulation Association (ESSA)*, Valladolid, Spain.

Weidlich, W., & Haag, G.(1999). *An integrated model of transport and urban evolution.* Springer.

Weisbuch, G., Deffuant, G., Amblard, F., & Nadal, J.P. (2002). Meet, discuss and segregate! *Complexity, 7*(3), 55-63.

Chapter V
Artificial Science:
A Simulation to Study the Social Processes of Science

Bruce Edmonds
Manchester Metropolitan University, UK

ABSTRACT

Science is important, not only in the knowledge it gives us, but also as an example of effective distributed problem solving that results in complex and compound solutions. This chapter presents a model of some of the social interactions in science, namely those between the body of published knowledge and the scientists' individual knowledge. The structure of knowledge is modelled by a formal Hilbert system for a classical propositional logic. Individuals have limited selections of the total knowledge available, which they use to derive new knowledge, and may submit to the central journal to be published. This model shows how difficult it is to achieve the accumulation of knowledge, as in science, and also that publishing more does not necessarily lead to more important knowledge being discovered.

INTRODUCTION

Science is a collective enterprise—it is not simply the aggregated efforts of individuals. In fact, some writers (e.g., Longino, 1990) go so far as to claim that the social processes particular to science are the *only* thing that distinguishes it from other activities. In any case, the social processes are critical to the success and character of what we know of as science. Here I exhibit a simulation that explores some of these.

Traditionally, there is the "building-block" picture of science (Hempel, 1966), where knowledge is slowly built up, brick-by-brick, as a result of reliable contributions to knowledge—each contribution standing upon its predecessors. Here, as long as each contribution is checked as completely reliable, the process can continue until an indefinitely high edifice of interdependent knowledge has been constructed. However, other pictures have been proposed. Kuhn(1962) suggested that often science progresses not gradually but in revolutions, where past structures are torn down and completely new ones built.

Despite the importance of the social processes in science to society, they are relatively little studied. The philosophy of science has debated, at some length, the epistemological aspects of science—how knowledge is created and checked "at the coal face of the individual." Social processes have been introduced mainly by critics of science—to point out that because science progresses through social processes it is "only" a social construction, and thus has no special status or unique reliability.

Here I take a neutral view that is it is likely that there are many different social processes occurring in different parts of science and at different times, and that these processes will impact upon the nature, quality, and quantity of the knowledge that is produced. It seems clear to me that sometimes the social processes act to increase the reliability of knowledge (such as when there is a tradition of independently reproducing experiments) but sometimes does the opposite (when a closed clique acts to perpetuate itself by reducing opportunity for criticism). Simulation can perform a valuable role here by providing and refining possible linkages between the kinds of social processes and their results in terms of knowledge. Earlier simulations of this sort include Gilbert et al. (2001). The simulation described herein aims to progress this work with a more structural and descriptive approach, that relates what is done by individuals and journals and what collectively results in terms of the overall process.

THE SIMULATION

The General Structure

The simulation involves a fixed number of agents (representing individual or closely-collaborating teams of scientists) and a journal (only one in the present simulation) which includes the set of formal sentences representing the knowledge that is discovered and published. Each agent has a private store of knowledge which may or may not be public (i.e., an axiom or published)—this store is their working knowledge. In order to use a public item of knowledge to produce new items, it must be added to their private store.. They submit some of this knowledge to the journal which selects (according to some criteria) a subset which is then published and becomes available to others. The whole set-up is illustrated in Figure 1.

Figure 1. An illustration of the set-up with two agents (circles are items of knowledge, rectangles are agents)

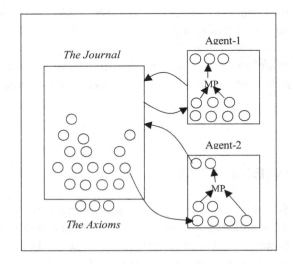

The Environment and Task

Science continually progresses into the unknown. In science, sometimes the end points are known—for example, when it is known that a certain disease is passed on genetically, then the genes that are responsible may be sought. Often, however, scientific discoveries are a surprise to their discoverers. Thus, it is often the case that scientists do not know exactly what it is they are searching for. This is in contrast to engineering, where it is usual to know the problem for which an answer is sought. This poses a problem for a would-be simulator of the social and cognitive processes that contribute to science—*How can one simulate creative discovery of the unknown*?

The answer I have chosen is to use a formal system (logic) as the representation of knowledge, so that the agents work on the logical structures to produce new structures (theorems in the logical sense), but where it is impossible to know in advance how useful these will be. This decision has distinct consequences both in terms of the possibilities and limitations of the model and in terms of the assumptions on which it relies. These will be discussed later. This can be seen as following Langley et al. (1987).

Thus, the universe of knowledge that the agents will explore in this simulation is the set of inferable formal sentences derivable from a given set of initial axioms. For ease of implementation, I have restricted myself to logics formalisable as Hilbert Systems (that is, ones with a set of axioms and a single rule of inference, Modus Ponens, which is recursively applied (see an introduction to logic, e.g., Copi (). The agents can produce new sentences by applying existing sentences to other sentences using Modus Ponens (MP). The form of this is: if you know A and you know $A{\rightarrow}B$, then you can also conclude B (written $A, A{\rightarrow}B{\vDash}B$). An example of this is: When A is $(a{\rightarrow}a){\rightarrow}(a{\rightarrow}a)$ and B is $(a{\rightarrow}a)$, from $(a{\rightarrow}a){\rightarrow}(a{\rightarrow}a)$ and $(a{\rightarrow}a){\rightarrow}b){\rightarrow}b$ we can infer $(a{\rightarrow}a)$. This is illustrated in Figure 2.

The agents thus have the task of discovering new formal sentences. The advantages of this structure are that: (1) future developments from any item of knowledge are not known in advance; (2) knowledge is not only useful as an end in itself but can be used as a tool to act upon other knowledge to produce new knowledge (as the major premise in MP, the A in Figure 2); (3) the programmer of the simulation does not necessarily know how one gets to any given theorem of the system, which reduces the temptation to bias the simulation to get specific results; (4) the task is suitably hard, as the development of automatic theorem-provers shows.

In order to set up the field of knowledge that the agents will collectively explore, the simulator needs to list the symbols being used and the axioms of the relevant logic. Optionally, the simulator can also list a number of known theorems that are considered important by logicians and give them a value, though *how* one derives these does not need to be specified (this is for the agents to find out). These "target theorems" are unknown to the agents until they discover them. They represent (in the loosest possible way) useful technologies that may come out of science. Counting how many of these have been discovered (and the total value of their "worth") is an indication of the effectiveness of the collective discovery effort, and can be a better measure than simply counting how many new sentences have been discovered, since it is

Figure 2. An illustration of the working of MP

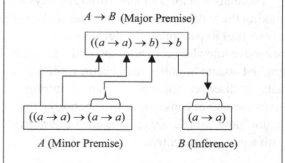

easy to develop trivial elaborations of already known sentences.

The Agents

In this simulation the agents have a very simple-minded approach to the production of new knowledge: Agents select two items in their own store of knowledge and apply the MP rule to it, which may or may not result in a new item of knowledge which is added to their store. Each agent has two private stores of knowledge: *first*, a store of formal sentences that are candidates for the minor premises for the MP rule and *second*, a store composed of candidates for the major premises. The former roughly correspond to the primary knowledge of a scientist and the second as the set of techniques of the agent, since it determines which transformations can be applied to which items and what can be produced.

Each time period the agent does the following:

1. Decide what new items of knowledge (both major and minor) to add to its private store from the published set, also which to drop.
2. Decide which major premise and what set of minor premises it will try with the MP rule and add any results to its (minor) store.
3. Decide which of its private knowledge (that is not already public) it will submit to the journal.

There are obviously many different ways of making these decisions. Each of these will have a (varying) impact upon the development of the collective knowledge. In addition to the above, a gradual update of policy may occur: If the agent fails to discover any new sentences during a given number of consecutive time periods it may "panic" and completely replace one of its stores with a new set of sentences.

Key parameters and setting of the agent are as follows. For each of its private knowledge stores (minor and major) the update policy includes the following: size, the rate at which it adds or drops knowledge from this store, *how* it does either the addition, the dropping, or the panic replacement (at random/probabilistically the best/the best judge either on raw past fertility or past fertility with a bias towards simplicity), whether it panics and how long it endures lack of success before panicking, which to try (the best/probabilistically the best/untried/random), and how it judges what it knows (personal fertility/lack of failure to produce new knowledge).

Also key is its submission policy: whether it submits all novel (i.e., unpublished) sentences to the journal or only the simplest/best ones.

The Journal

The journal (*The Journal of Artificial Sentences and Successful Syllogisms*) is the gatekeeper to the repository of public knowledge. The key aspect of the journal is the criteria it uses for assessing the items submitted to it, so as to decide what (if any) it will publish. This occurs in three basic stages: the short-listing of those that met basic criteria, the evaluation of those short listed, and their ranking. The journal then publishes a selection of the top *n* in the ranking (if there were more than *n* short listed), otherwise all of them. This final selection could be the best (from the top) probabilistically on the weighted score (the higher the score the more likely it is to be selected), randomly, or simply all of them. The evaluation of the submissions is done as a weighted sum of scores for a number of aspects: the number of variables in the sentence, its brevity, the extent to which it shortens sentences when used in MP, and the past success of the author. The weights and selection policies can be set by the programmer.

Methods of Evaluation

Key to many of the decisions made by the agents or the journal is the evaluation of existing knowledge. Ultimately this can be considered as a guess at the future usefulness of that knowledge, in terms of either: its productivity in producing new knowledge, reaching the hidden "target theorems," or in getting published. This may be done in a number of ways. One way is by looking at the historical record of how productive the sentence has been in the past in resulting in new published knowledge (this can be done in a recursive way to value sentences that have produced productive sentences, etc.). Another way is to look at the most published agents and see what knowledge they have used (in published work). Other ways include considering features of the sentences themselves, for example, measures of their simplicity (how many variables they have, how long they are, to what extent the sentence results in a shortening of sentences when applied using MP, etc.).

Preliminary Results

At the time of this writing, only preliminary results are available, which explore only a very small proportion of the possibilities inherent in this model. By the time the full paper is due, I expect to have a better feel for the nature of some of the results and the deeper limitations of the model structure. However a summary of the indications so far obtained follows.

Many of the settings do affect the outcomes to a significant degree. However many which increase the short-term success (measured in a number of different ways) of the scientific progress also have the effect of reducing the longer-term maintenance of new results. Thus, for example, adding new sentences *at random* to an agent's private knowledge (i.e., regardless of the agent's evaluation of sentences) decreased the short-term level of discovery markedly, but then that level of discovery lasted a longer time. In contrast, where agents followed other agents closely (preferentially adding sentences used successfully by others) results followed much more quickly to begin with but then petered out to zero after 40-60 time periods (only then deviating from zero when an agent panicked and was lucky with its new set of knowledge). Such a result would indicate that a process of fairly frequent, but collective revolution was one of the most efficient collective modes of discovery.

In general, most of the targeted sentences were either discovered very soon, or never. This suggests that "deep" sentences (those difficult to reach in this collective but individually stupid manner) require guidance from a deeper knowledge of the individual logics concerned, and are not so amenable to a generic approach (collective or otherwise).

DISCUSSION

The Possibility of Limited Validation

Following Gilbert et al. (2001), it may be possible to compare the structure of the published knowledge that results in this simulation (i.e., which authors/items are derived from which previous items by which authors) might be compared with the structure found in citation indexes such ISI, using a number of measures, statistics, or structural comparisons. Unfortunately, negotiations with ISI indicate that they are only prepared to part with the structural information of their databases (suitably anonymised) for rather large quantities of money (i.e., around \$30,000). If anyone knows of an alternative source, please contact the author.

Limitation and Extensions

Clearly, many of the limitations in this simulation are arbitrary, thus I list a few possible extensions as examples:

- Decision methods of arbitrary complexity can be implemented in agents (indeed these methods could themselves be evolved by GP).
- There could be many journals so that the prestige of a journal, its impacts, and the quality of its submissions could be allowed to develop with the simulation.
- Instead of inferring new knowledge, the agents could hypothesise and test candidate sentences by performing tests on the logical semantics (e.g., a row of truth tables as in classical logic).
- a peer review system could be implemented whereby reviewers are selected depending on their past publishing success and impact. They could use their own experience of what is useful as their criteria for judging entries and their own tests, and items could be selected resultant on the votes of reviewers.
- informal social networks could be introduced to pass knowledge from agent to agent rather than via official journals.
- agents could be allowed to reproduce in terms of the students they teach and retire after a suitable time (or if they are spectacularly unsuccessful).

More fundamentally, the present structure of the simulation assumes that there *is* some independent "correct" knowledge to be discovered and that it is checkable. This could be corrected by providing a database of atomic facts (e.g., the linkage structure of part of the Web) and then hypotheses about these could be induced (as in inductive data-mining techniques). The journal (or journals) would not be able to check the veracity of any knowledge 100 percent but have to rely on some fallible process to come to a judgement upon the knowledge. However, a disadvantage of such an approach is that it would lack the tight inter-dependency of knowledge that seems to be such a characteristic of some sciences[1].

Relationship with Distributed Theorem Proving (DTP)

The simulation *is* a forward-chaining theorem prover, and can be seen as an answer to Fisher and Wooldridge (1977), since it could be truly distributed. However, it is a very inefficient one—it is deliberately *generic* in that it has not been "tuned" for performance (by using deep properties of the particular logic being investigated), since this is not its goal. Despite this, lessons learned in this simulation do have potential in terms of informing the design of distributed theorem provers and *vice versa* from what is discovered about efficient DTP in this simulation (and potentially science itself[2]).

OTTER (Wos et al., 1984), a particular and quite successful theorem prover is quite close to how a single agent works in the above simulation. It has a list of candidate minor and major premises and works on these to extend the set of known sentences until it reaches the target theorems. It allows for a large range of techniques in re-writing formulas, guiding search, and applying rules that are not touched upon here.

CONCLUSION

I hope to have shown how it is possible to capture some aspects of the social processes that contribute to the construction of science. Such modelling has the potential to intermediate between observations concerning how science works and areas of distributed knowledge discovery in computer science, e.g., automated theorem proving. It could help sort out the roles of the different processes in science confirming or disconfirming philosophical speculations, such as Edmonds (2000).

REFERENCES

Longino, H. (1990). *Science as social knowledge.* Princeton: Princeton University Press.

Hempel, C. G. (1966). *Philosophy of natural science.* Englewood Cliffs, NJ: Prentice-Hall.

Kuhn, T. S. (1962). *The structure of scientific revolutions.* Chicago: University of Chicago Press.

Ahrweiler, P., Gilbert, N., & Pyka, A. (2001). Innovation networks—A simulation approach. *Journal of Artificial Societies and Social Simulation, 4*(3). <http://www.soc.surrey.ac.uk/JASSS/4/3/8.html>

Bradshaw, G.G., Langley, P., Simon, H.A., & Zytkow, J.M. (1987). *Scientific discovery: Computational explorations of the creative processes.* MIT Press.

Fisher, M., & Wooldridge, M. (1977). Distributed problem-solving as concurrent theorem-proving. In Boman & van de Velde (Eds.), *Multi-agent rationality.* Springer-Verlag.

Boyle, J., Lusk, E., Overleed, R., & Wos, L. (1984). *Automated reasoning: Introduction and applications.* Englewood Cliffs, NJ: Prentice-Hall.

Edmonds, B. (2000). *The purpose and place of formal systems in the development of science.* CPM Report 00-75, MMU, UK. (http://cfpm.org/cpmrep75.html)

ENDNOTES

[1] Of course it *may* be that this *is* more appropriate for the social sciences.

[2] One can but dream!

Chapter VI
Understanding Tag Systems by Comparing Tag Models[1]

David Hales
University of Bologna, Italy

ABSTRACT

Since Holland (1993) introduced the concept of tags, a number of tag models with intriguing, and potentially very useful, properties have been advanced. However, there is currently little understanding as to the exact mechanisms that produce these results. Specifically, it is not known what (if any) are the necessary conditions for tag systems to produce high levels of cooperation in social dilemmas. In this chapter, by comparing existing tag models to formulate a hypothesis and then using simulation, we identify what appears be a necessary condition for high cooperation. Previous tag models implicitly contained the condition but authors did not identify the significance of it.

INTRODUCTION

Tags are markings or social cues that are attached to individuals (agents) and are observable by others (Holland, 1993). They evolve like any other trait in a given evolutionary model. The key point is that the tags have no direct behavioral implication for the individuals that carry them. Through indirect effects, however, they can evolve from initially random values into complex, everchang-ing patterns that serve to structure interactions between individuals.

Riolo (1997) showed how tags could boost cooperation in a scenario involving agents playing the iterated prisoners dilemma (IPD). Agents bias their game playing towards individuals with similar tags (the indirect effect). In these studies, tags were represented by a single real number attached to each agent.

Subsequently, Hales (2000) advanced a model, using binary tag strings, that demonstrated the evolution of cooperative interactions in the single round Prisoners Dilemma (PD). Further work (Riolo et al., 2001) showed the emergence of altruistic giving behavior and the evolution of cooperation and specialization (Hales, 2002)[2].

These latter models are important because they advance a novel mechanism for evolving coordinated and cooperative interactions between unrelated agents that have no knowledge of each other and have never met previously (i.e., strangers). This obviates the need for repeated interactions (Trivers, 1971), "genetic" relatedness (Hamilton, 1964), "image scoring," (Nowak & Sigmund, 1998) or strict spatial relationships (Nowak & Sigmund, 1992) in the production of cooperation. Tag mechanisms therefore have potential engineering applications where these other methods are not applicable (Hales & Edmonds, 2003).

Although the general mechanism by which tags produce these results appears to be the result of a dynamic group formation and dissolution process (Hales, 2000; Riolo et al., 2001; Sigmund & Nowak, 2001) with selection at the group-level, there has been little analytical or empirical exploration of this hypothesis. Indeed, it is not even currently understood what the necessary and/or sufficient conditions might be to produce tag systems that give rise to these properties of interest (other than the specific existence proofs of the simulation results presented). In this chapter we begin this process.

PAPER OUTLINE

In this chapter we identify what appears to be a necessary condition that all previous models implicitly contained. In each case the authors had not identified this property as significant, yet without it the phenomena of interest disappears.

We report the results of computational simulations that demonstrate the necessity of the condition and begin to sketch out a way towards analytically capturing the condition.

The necessary condition is that the mutation rate of the tag must be much higher than the mutation rate applied to any behavioral traits. In this way cooperative "groups" (agents sharing the same or similar tags and interacting cooperatively with each other) can be "cloned" before being invaded by exploitative mutants that "kill" or "dissolve" the group. We demonstrate this by varying a parameter (the tag/action trait mutation ratio) over many runs of a simulation model and measure cooperation. The result is a (nonlinear) sigmoid-like relationship, indicating a transition threshold for the relative mutation rate in a given system.

Since recent work (Hales & Edmonds, 2003 and in press) has indicated how tag mechanisms might be applied to the solution of complex engineering problems, a deeper understanding of the necessary and sufficient conditions of application would be timely. Such mechanisms have application in self-organizing adaptive peer-2-peer networks (Hales & Edmonds, in press) and distributed and spontaneously self-organizing mobile agent-based applications (where issues of trust and cooperation are paramount but can not easily be dealt with using traditional techniques).

SOME PREVIOUS TAG MODELS

There have been a number of tag (simulation) models implemented and each demonstrates how higher-than-expected levels of cooperation and altruism are produced when tags are employed. In all cases, the models implement evolutionary systems with assumptions along the lines of replicator dynamics (i.e., reproduction into the next generation proportional to utility in the current generation and no "genetic-style" cross-over operations, but low probability mutations on tags and strategies).

Riolo (1997) gave results of studies applying tags in a scenario where agents played dyadic (pairwise) Iterated Prisoner's Dilemma games (IPD). Tags (represented as a single real number) allowed agents to bias their partner selection to those with similar tags (probabilistically). He found that even small biases stimulated high levels of cooperation when there were enough iterations of the game with each pairing.

In Hales (2000), a tag model was applied to a single round PD, one where pairings resulted in a single game of PD. Tags were represented as binary strings. Pairing was strongly biased by tag identity (rather than probabilistic similarity). In this model, very high levels of cooperation were produced between strangers in the single-round game if the binary tag strings were long enough.

In Riolo et al. (2001) a tag model was applied to a resource-sharing scenario in which altruistic giving was shown to emerge. Agents were randomly paired (some number of times) and decided if to give resources or not. The decision to give was based on tag similarity mediated by a "tolerance gene" as well as the "tag gene" (both represented by real numbers). The utility to the receiving agent of any given resource was greater than that of the giving agent. It was shown that if each agent was paired enough times in each generation and the cost/benefit ratio was low enough, then high levels of cooperation were found.

In Hales and Edmonds (2003), tags were applied to a simulated robot coordination scenario, originally given by Kalenka and Jennings (1999), producing high levels of cooperative help giving.

MUTATION IN THE MODELS

We will now describe in a little detail how mutation was applied to the agents in each of the above models. We will not discuss the specific details of the reproduction process since we do not consider this relevant to the focus of this chapter—in all cases it is safe to assume that variants of "roulette wheel" selection and "tournament selection" were used. These produce probabilistic selection into the next generation following the replicator dynamics assumptions stated earlier. Neither will we focus on the interactions or specific payoffs applied in each model, suffice it to say all models capture some kind of collective coordination/cooperation problem in which cheating or free riding is possible under certain conditions.

In order to examine and compare mutation schemes, we make a distinction between the mutation rate applied to the tag and that applied to the strategy. In all cases agents are represented in the models using sets of artificial "genes" (some set of data types) that are mutated when copied into the next generation.

The published descriptions of the models all explicitly state that the mutation rate applied to

Table 1. Examples of the representations of tags and strategies in various tag models. For details see the text.

<Tag type> [range]	Strategy	Examples	Reference
<R> [0..1]	<R R R>	<0.05><1,1,1>	Riolo (1997)
<B B B B> [0	1]	< B >	<0 1 1 0><0>	Hales (2000)
< I > [1..500]	< B B >	<324><0 1>	Hales & Edmonds (2003)
< R > [0..1]	< R >	<0.6><0.5>	Riolo, et al. (2001)

the tag and the strategy is the same (some probability). We label this rate m. However, models vary in the mutation *operation* applied with probability m and in the way they represent tags and strategies. Here it is claimed that this variation of mutation operation and tag/strategy representation can *hide* what is best understood as a variation in *mutation rate*.

In Hales (2000) tags are represented as fixed length bit strings (experiments were conducted using various lengths of strings–in Table 1 we show the four bit case only) and strategies as a single bit (either to cooperate or to defect). The mutation rate was $m = 0.001$ and the population size was $p = 100$. Since each agent is completely represented by a binary string, the mutation operation is simply to flip each bit with probability m (both tag and strategy bits). It would superficially appear that strategy and tag are therefore mutated at the same rate and in the same way. However, the results given in Hales (2000) show that high cooperation only occurred when the number of tag bits L was large (L $\geq$ 32). In these cases the tag is more prone to mutation than the strategy. Any mutation in the tag creates a new distinct tag because pairing in the model is based on tag *identity* not *similarity*. The effective mutation rate on the tag as a whole is $1-(1-m)^L$, so for L = 32 bits the mutation rate on the tag is 32 times that on the strategy.

In Riolo et al. (2001), each agent is composed of two *real* numbers (see Table 1)—one representing its tag and one representing a so-called "tolerance." The tolerance is a kind of "proxy strategy." Essentially (simplifying) a smaller tolerance value means a less cooperative agent. Mutation is applied to both the tag and tolerance with probability $m = 0.1$. Again, superficially, it appears that both are being mutated at the same rate. However, the mutation *operation* applied to the tag and tolerance is not the same. When mutation is applied to the tag, it is replaced with a new random value drawn uniformly from the range but when the tolerance is mutated it has

Gaussian noise (of mean 0 and standard deviation 0.01) added to it. So tags, when mutated, get *new* values but tolerances get *modified* by small values. We would expect the absolute average tag change amount[3] to be one third when mutation is applied. Since $m = 0.1$ we might characterize the average overall tag change amount to be $\approx$ 0.0333. In the case of tolerance, the absolute average change would be almost two orders of magnitude lower ($\approx$ 0.0008).

In both Riolo (1997) and Hales and Edmonds (2003), our analysis becomes slightly less straightforward. In both cases strategies are composed of multiple "genes" which do not simply relate to unconditional cooperation or selfish behavior. This is in part due to the scenarios. In Riolo (1997), agents play the IPD with agents having similar tags for a number of rounds. The level of cooperation produced is not high and constant but fluctuates with periods of high and low cooperation. Tags are represented by single real values [0..1], strategies by triples of real values $<i, p, q>$ (see Table 1) capturing a probabilistic IPD strategy space (i is the probability of cooperation for the first round, p the probability of cooperation if in the previous round the other agent cooperated, and q the probability of cooperation if the other agent defected on the previous round). So a space comprising tit-for-tat as well as pure defection and pure cooperation is formed (along with probabilistic variants). The mutation rate $m = 0.1$ is the same for each trait as is the operation (adding Gaussian noise with mean 0 and standard deviation 0.5). Here we have an interesting counter-point to the previous model (Hales, 2000) where we stated (above) that because the tag was split into several parts, the effective mutation rate was higher than the strategy that was specified as a single "gene." Here, we have the reverse, so surely this suggests that the mutation rate applied to the tag is lower than that applied to the strategy? In one sense this is true. However, what is important is not the mutation of the representation as such, the stored value, but *how that value relates to behavior.* Since the strategy is a triple, in which pure cooperation is represented as all values being 1 and pure defection all values being 0, the relationship between mutation and the resultant change in strategy is not simple. However, we can note that the probability of going from a triple of zeros to a triple of ones (from pure defection to pure cooperation) in a single (or even multiple) mutation event is approaching zero. However, since we are talking about IPD, not single round PD, the situation is more complex and we leave detailed treatment to a future work[4].

In Hales and Edmonds (2003), simulated robots work in teams to unload trucks in a warehouse. Here again we have a strategy composed of multiple parts. In the model, tags are represented as single cardinal values [1..500] and strategies as pairs of binary values. Again, the way the strategy affects behavior is complex and moderated by the scenario. A strategy represented by bit values "11" represents full cooperation whereas a value of "00" represents completely selfish behavior. Mutation is applied to the triple of traits with rate $m = 0.1$. The mutation operation is to replace the existing value with another value chosen uniformly and randomly over the space. Again simplifying things a little, we can say that the probability of a strategy changing from 11 to 00 (or vice versa) is the probability that two bits are replaced with their complement $0.25(m^2) = 0.0025$. The probability of a completely new tag (tags are distinct integers, matching is based on identity) is $0.998(m) = 0.0998$.

So, our analysis of these existing models shows that tags mutate more quickly than strategies under algorithms that present a uniform *mutation rate*. Of importance (as stated before) is the *representation* of tags and strategies and *mutation operators* taken together with the mutation rate. Only by considering all these factors can an underlying average relative rate of change be determined between the two entities (tag and strategy). In

each case when we do this we find that the tag changes much more quickly than the strategy. Now we advance a hypothesis based on this.

HYPOTHESIS AND THEORY

From our analysis of the mutation schemes in the previous tag models, we now advance a qualitative hypothesis concerning a necessary condition for tag models to produce high cooperation in one-time interactions: *For tag-based systems to support high levels of cooperation, tags must mutate faster than strategies.* We can also state a qualitative "mini-theory" to explain this: *Cooperative tag groups need to spread (by mutation of tags) before free-riders (by mutation on strategies) invade the group.*

We don't have a quantitative complement to these two statements. It would appear that in order to determine the specific numbers in a specific scenario (model), we would need to consider the nature of the tag space, strategy space, and the way agents specifically interacted (the game). This is an aspect of on-going work.

TESTING THE HYPOTHESIS

In order to test (at least partially) our hypothesis, we implemented a new (minimal) tag model in which agents play single rounds of PD. We consider the result of high cooperation in the single round PD the most significant result so far advanced for tags. Additionally, the scenario is well understood and there are many existing models that allow for comparison. The single-round PD captures, in a minimal way, many of the essential features of the problems of cooperation in collective interactions. In our tag model (described below) we varied the relative mutation rate between the tag and strategy to examine if this had an effect on the amount of cooperation produced. Firstly we describe the PD.

The Prisoner's Dilemma

The Prisoner's Dilemma (PD) game captures a scenario in which there is a contradiction between collective and self-interest. Two players interact by selecting one of two choices: Either to "cooperate" (C) or "defect" (D). For the four possible outcomes of the game, players receive specified payoffs. Both players receive a reward payoff (R) and a punishment payoff (P) for mutual cooperation and mutual defection, respectively. However, when individuals select different moves, differential payoffs of temptation (T) and sucker (S) are awarded respectively to the defector and the cooperator. Assuming that neither player can know in advance which move the other will make and wishes to maximise his or her own payoff, the dilemma is evident in the ranking of payoffs: $T > R > P > S$ and the constraint that $2R > T + S$. Although both players would prefer T, only one can attain it. No player wants S. No matter what the other player does, by selecting a D move a player ensures he or she gets a higher payoff than their partner. In this sense a D move can't be bettered, since playing D ensures that the defector cannot be suckered. This is the so-called "Nash" equilibrium for the single round game. It is also an evolutionary stable strategy for a population of randomly paired individuals playing the game where reproduction fitness is based on payoff. So the dilemma is that if both individuals selected a cooperative move they would both be better off but both evolutionary pressure and game theoretical "rationality" selected defection.

The TagWorld Model

The TagWorld model presented here is similar to Hales (2000). What is new is that we explicitly vary the mutation rate applied to the tag while keeping the rate constant for the strategy.

Agents are represented by a single binary digit (the strategy bit) and a single real number in the range [0..1] (the tag). The strategy bit represents a pure strategy: either unconditional cooperation or unconditional defection. Initially the population has their strategy and tag values set randomly with uniform probability over the space of all possible values. The following evolutionary algorithm is then applied.

In each generation, each agent (a) is selected from the population in turn. A game partner is then selected. Partner selection entails the random selection of another agent (b) from the population such that (a) $\neq$ (b) but the tags of (a) and (b) are identical. If no agent exists with identical tags to (a) then (b) is selected at random from the entire population regardless of tag value. Consequently, (a) will always find a partner even if its tag does not match any other agent in the population. During game interaction, (a) and (b) invoke their strategies and receive the appropriate PD payoff (T, R, P, or S). After all agents have been selected in turn and played a game, a new population is asexually reproduced. Reproductive success (fitness) is proportional to average payoff (i.e., the total score divided by the number of games played). The entire population of agents is replaced using a "roulette wheel" selection method (Davis, 1991).[5]

Parameters Used in the Model

For our initial experiments (presented below) we used the following parameter value: The population size was $N = 100$ and the number of generations for each run of the model was 1,000. The PD payoffs were $T = 1.1$, $R = 1$, and $P = S = 0.0001$. These values were selected to give a very high incentive to cheat (T is high and P and S are low). P and S were selected as a small value but greater than zero (indicating a very small chance for agents, with Sucker or Punishment payoffs, of reproduction). If a small value is added to P (enforcing $T > R > P > S$), results are not significantly changed.

For the strategy bit the mutation rate was fixed constant at $m = 0.001$ (a low value). But for the tag, a mutation factor f was applied to m changing the

73

mutation rate. We varied f from [0..10] in increments of two. Mutation of the strategy involved flipping the bit value. Mutation of the tag involved replacing the tag value with another uniformly and randomly selected tag from the range [0..1]. To summarize, when an agent is selected for reproduction into the next generation, mutation is applied to the strategy bit (resulting in the bit being flipped with probability m) and to the tag (resulting in it being replaced with a new randomly selected tag with probability mf).

Results

The results are given in Figure 1. Cooperation increases as the mutation factor is increased. For each value of the mutation factor (f) given on the x-axis, 20 points are plotted from 20 individual runs (to 1,000 generations). Cooperation given on the y-axis represents the proportion of all game interactions in a run that were mutually cooperative. Since we have 100 agents, with one game each per generation and 1,000 generations per run, each point represents a proportion of mutual cooperation over 10^5 games. Each run had the same parameters but was initialized with different pseudo-random number seeds. The (smoothed) line joins the plotted average of the 20 points. The average is therefore over 2×10^6 individual games.

To improve readability noise has been added to the x-coordinate of each point (+/-0.5).

There are a number of interesting characteristics presented in Figure 1. First, we do indeed see an increase (on average) of cooperation when we increase the relative mutation rate of the tag with respect to the strategy. Given this, we have a little more confidence that our hypothesis may be correct since it allowed us to predict this properly. The increase is nonlinear, the average curve approximating a sigmoid shape with a threshold that would appear to be around f = 5. Notice that above f = 6 we see no results below 0.8 cooperation and below f = 4 we see no results above 0.2 cooperation.[6] Around the threshold we get high variance of results–indicating both high and low cooperation outcomes. So it would appear that at the threshold things become unpredictable and chaotic (i.e., the initial random variations of the runs send the model into different cooperation regimes) but that on either side of the threshold the outcome is predictable.

Further Results

Our initial results are encouraging and appear to indicate that applying a high mutation rate to the tag relative to the strategy produces high levels of cooperation (at least in the PD game). However,

Figure 1. Results from simulations plotting mutation factor (f) against cooperation

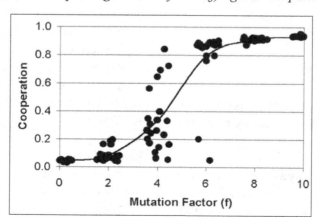

does this explain the cooperation demonstrated in those other models described previously? Also, we have only tested our hypothesis with one kind of

tag (a real number) and one kind of task (playing the PD). In order to begin to address these issues, we re-implemented the Hales (2000) model[7]. In

Figure 2. Results given in Hales (2000). T = PD temptation payoff and L is the tag length in bits. Runs were to 100,000 generations.

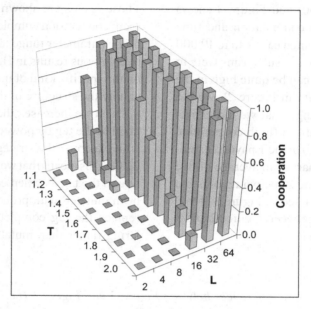

Figure 3. Reproduction of results using the same parameters as in Figure 2 (except that here runs were to only 10,000 generations). The main differences are where L = 8 and 16.

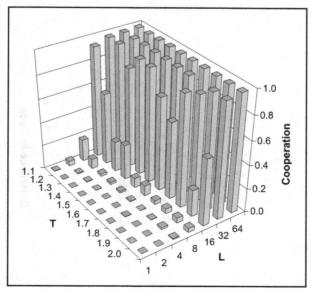

order to do this we extended the TagWorld model to incorporate tags represented as strings of binary digits with mutation being applied to *each bit in the string* with the same probability (m = 0.001) as the strategy bit.

First we docked the model with the results previously reported. Figure 2 shows the original results from Hales (2000) and Figure 3 shows the new results. Due to computation and time limitations, we only executed each run to 10,000 generations. In the original results, runs were to 100,000. Since variance can be quite high in the mid range of L (as shown in Figure 2), we did not expect exact matching–what we did expect was the same overall pattern (high cooperation where L >= 32 bits over all of the T payoffs examined). Each bar in the chart is an average of five independent runs with the same parameters but different random number seeds. Figure 3 shows the absolute difference between Figures 2 and 3 for comparison purposes.

Next we changed the model such that mutation was applied to the tag *as a whole* with the same probability as the strategy (m = 0.001). This was achieved by replacing the entire binary tag string with a new binary tag string randomly selected from the set of possible tag strings (i.e., replacing each bit with a randomly selected one). Those results are shown in Figure 5. As can be seen, cooperation completely disappears over all of the parameter range tested–this indicates that the previous results in Hales (2000) were related on the specific kind of mutation used rather than simply the structure of the tag (a binary string).

Next we increased the mutation factor (f) applied to the tag by powers of 2 (f = 1, 2, 4, 8..64) while keeping the strategy mutation rate at m = 0.001. This means that we apply the same mutation rate to the tag as when each bit in the string has been mutated with probability m but we simply replace the tag completely with a new binary string rather than mutating each bit separately.

Figure 4. Shows the absolute differences between Figure 2 and Figure 3 (i.e., the docking errors). As stated previously, we consider this to be due to the difference in generations—but we need to test this.

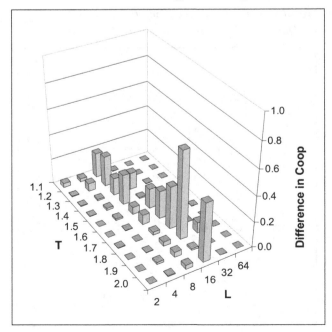

Figure 5. Results when the same mutation rate is applied equally to the tag and strategy. T is the PD temptation payoff and L is the tag length in bits.

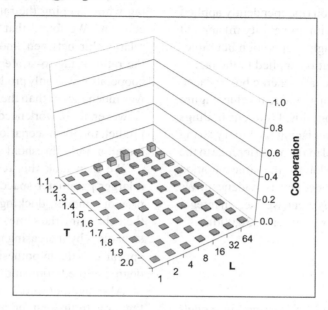

Figure 6. Results when mutation is increased by the tag length L such that the mutation factor f = L in all cases. Cooperation is restored.

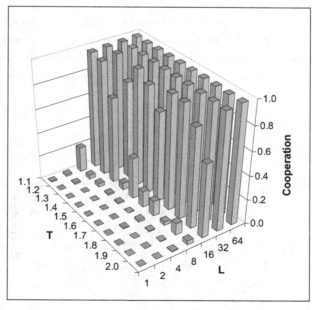

The results can be seen in Figure 6—cooperation reappears. This result indicates that it is not the specific kind of mutation (independently applied to each bit of the tag with probability m) applied that is necessary for high cooperation but rather the probability of mutation applied to the tag.

Finally, we kept the last scheme but replaced the binary string with a single real value. Figure 7 shows the results from this. From our findings we would expect that replacing the binary string with a real value should make no difference to the level of cooperation so long as the same mutation values are used and indeed this is evidenced. We also got the same results when we used an integer for the tag (with values between 0..30,000).

CONCLUSION

From a detailed analysis of existing tag models we identified an implicit assumption–the mutation rate of the tags was higher than that applied to the strategies. We tested this hypothesis in a new tag model by varying the mutation rate of the tag while keeping the rate applied to strategies constant. We found that there was a nonlinear relationship between amount of cooperation and the ratio of tag-to-strategy mutation rate. High cooperation was only produced when tag mutation was much higher than the strategy mutation rate. However, more work needs to be done in order to predict, for given scenarios, what the tag/strategy mutation ratio threshold value would be[8].

We then took this result and tested it over a larger parameter space by re-implementing a previous model, docking with that model, and then obtaining the same results with changed tag structures by increasing mutation rates. It would appear that the hypothesis holds, allowing for a degree of prediction and control.

Although our initial motivation for exploring tags was to understand aspects of human social phenomena, our current motivation for this work is to understand how to program artificial systems

Figure 7. The tag is replaced with a single real number but the mutation factor applied to tags (f) is increased by the same values as the binary tag length was increased previously. The tag mutation factor (f) appears to be the necessary condition to produce cooperation in these scenarios.

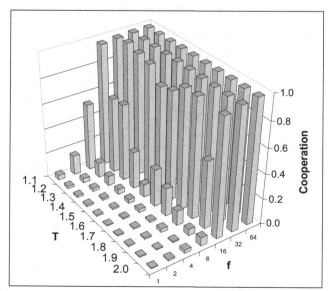

such as truly decentralized (i.e., serverless, where there is no central server but rather a collection of cooperating peer nodes), P2P self-organizing networks (Jelasity et al., in press). In these systems each node or "peer" needs to offer bandwidth and processing capacity to other nodes without necessarily getting a payback from those nodes. Additionally, each node has partial and often changing views of node members meaning that storage of reputation information becomes unwieldy and nonscalable. In on-going work we are attempting to import ideas such as tags developed in the complex system and social simulation communities into the engineering realm.

We believe that the single-round PD captures *one kind* of P2P engineering problem. If we can get nodes to cooperate in the PD, then we believe we can engineer them to share bandwidth and processing time, altruistically, in real systems. We have already demonstrated that the lessons learned here can be used in P2P file-sharing scenarios using simulation (Hales, 2004a, 2004b). We have therefore practically shown how results from PD type simulations can be applied to engineering problems. However we still have *many* issues to address, such as how systems can be engineered in which agents (nodes) can not "whitewash" a system (that is, simply defect all the time while never adapting–i.e., not acting in a boundly rational way) or how to stop agents from presenting different tags to different agents. Our next step is to apply these techniques to more realistic P2P simulations.

ACKNOWLEDGMENT

Thanks go to David Chavalarias for thoughtful and substantial comments on this work. We hope to address and incorporate these suggestions in future work.

REFERENCES

Davis, L. (1991) Handbook of genetic algorithms. New York: Van Nostrand Reinhold.

Edmonds, B., & Hales, D. (2003) Replication, replication and replication—Some hard lessons from model alignment. *Journal of Artificial Societies and Social Simulation, 6*(4).

Hales, D. (2000). Cooperation without space or memory: Tags, groups and the prisoner's dilemma. In S. oss. &, P. Davidsson (Eds.), *Multi-agent-based simulation. Lecture notes in artificial intelligence, 1979* (pp. 157-166). Berlin: Springer-Verlag.

Hales, D. (2001). *Tag based cooperation in artificial societies.* Ph.D. Thesis (Department Of Computer Science, University of Essex, UK.

Hales, D. (2002). Evolving specialisation, altruism and group-level optimisation using tags. In J.S. Sichman, F. Bousquet, & P. Davidsson (Eds.), Multi-agent-based simulation II. *Lecture Notes in Artificial Intelligence, 2581* (pp. 26-35). Berlin: Springer Verlag.

Hales, D., & Edmonds, B. (2003, July). Evolving social rationality for MAS using "Tags." In J. S. Rosenschein, et al. (Eds.) *Proceedings of the 2nd International Conference on Autonomous Agents and Multi-agent Systems (AAMAS03)* (pp. 497-503), Melbourne. ACM Press, 497-503.

Hales, D. (2004a). Self-organising, open and cooperative P2P societies—From tags to networks. Presented at the *2nd Workshop on Engineering Self-Organsing Applications* (ESOA 2004) located with the AAMAS 2004 Conference, NY, July 2004. To be published by Springer.

Hales, D. (2004b, August 25-27). From selfish nodes to cooperative networks—Emergent link-based incentives in peer-to-peer networks. To be presented at *The Fourth IEEE International Conference on Peer-to-Peer Computing (P2P2004)*, 2004, Zurich, Switzerland. To be published by IEEE press.

Hamilton, W.D. (1964). The genetical evolution of social behaviours. *Journal of Theoretical Biology, 7*, 1-52.

Holland, J. (1993). *The effect of labels (tags) on social interactions*. Santa Fe Institute Working Paper 93-10-064. Santa Fe, NM.

Jelasity, M., Montresor, A., & Babaoglu, O. (2004). A modular paradigm for building self-organizing peer-to-peer applications. *Proceedings of the 1st International Workshop on Engineering Self-Organising Applications (ESOA 2003)*. Springer.

Kalenka, S., & Jennings, N.R. (1999) Socially responsible decision making by autonomous agents. In K. Korta et al. (Eds.), *Cognition, agency and rationality* (pp. 135-149). Kluwer.

Nowak, M., & May, R. (1992). Evolutionary games and spatial chaos. *Nature, 359*, 532-554.

Nowak, M., & Sigmund, K. (1998). Evolution of indirect reciprocity by image scoring. *Nature, 393*, 573-557.

Riolo, R. (1997). *The effects of tag-mediated selection of partners in evolving populations playing the iterated prisoner's dilemma*. SFI Working Paper 97-02-016, Santa Fe, NM.

Riolo, R.L., Cohen, M.D., & Axelrod, R. (2001). Evolution of cooperation without reciprocity. *Nature, 414*, 441-443.

Roberts, G., & Sherratt, T.N. (2002). *Nature 418*, 449-500.

Sigmund, K., & Nowak, A.M. (2001). Tides of tolerance. *Nature, 414*, 403-405.

Trivers, R. (1971). The evolution of reciprocal altruism. *Quarterly Review of Biology, 46*, 35-57.

ENDNOTES

[1] This work partially supported by the EU within the 6th Framework Programme under contract 001907 (DELIS).

[2] It should be noted that the conclusions of these further studies have been questioned (Roberts and Sherrat 2002, Edmonds and Hales 2003). Essentially the scenarios do not bear too close a comparison to a PD because there is no dilemma.

[3] Here (and in the following examples) we make a few simplifying assumptions (namely that tags are treated as random variables).

[4] It is worth noting that the cooperation found in the paper (Riolo, 1997) was not of the "strong" single interaction kind given in Hales (2000) and Riolo et al. (2001). Indeed one of the findings of the paper was that tags did not produce cooperation in the single round game.

[5] Using this method the probability that an agent will be reproduced into the next generation is probabilistically proportional to average payoff.

[6] Points that appear to violate this are a result of the added noise.

[7] The code for the original model has long since gone to the big hard disk in the sky.

[8] This will depend on a number of factors and a discussion is beyond the scope of, and space allowed for, this paper. See Hales (2000, 2001) for a little more on this.

Chapter VII
Effects of Land Markets on Competition Between Innovators and Imitators in Land Use:
Results from FEARLUS–ELMM

J. Gary Polhill
Macaulay Institute, UK

Dawn C. Parker
George Mason University, USA

Nicholas M. Gotts
Macaulay Institute, UK

ABSTRACT

This chapter explores the effects of a more realistic agent-based land exchange mechanism on the relative competitive success of innovative and imitative strategies for selecting land uses, using the FEAR-LUS-ELMM model. A key question in our investigation is whether land use decision strategies can be studied in isolation from land-market exchange decision strategies. Results derived via computational experiments show that land-market modelling decisions do affect outcomes, improving to an extent the relative success of innovators. We also conclude that further additions are needed to our model, and finally, we question whether a "big bang" strategy may have been more effective than our step-by-step evolution to the land-market model, which was chosen to facilitate comparison to results derived from the original FEARLUS.

INTRODUCTION

This chapter is about spatially explicit agent-based social simulation of processes underlying land use change, in which both space and human agency are represented in rather simple and abstract ways. The work described forms part of the framework for the evaluation and assessment of regional land use scenarios (FEARLUS) project. We are interested in how various aspects of human decision-making processes related to land management interact to affect the competitive advantage of some groups over others, and how these interactions shape land-use change, particularly at the regional scale and in the medium to long term. Here, we focus on decisions to change land use and to acquire land. However, some of the issues discussed are relevant in a range of contexts involving systems of interacting, territory-holding agents—see Cioffi-Revilla and Gotts (2003).

Development of FEARLUS is motivated by the limitations of models that forecast land-use change solely on the basis of biophysical properties and economic returns. Earlier approaches to rural land use change (Benson, 1995; Parry, 1996) have assumed that land managers are driven purely by profit maximisation and have unlimited computational capabilities. There is a growing current of opinion within the land use research community that to model the drivers of land use change successfully, "Simulation of decisions by and competition between multiple actors and land managers is required" (Veldkamp & Lambin, 2001, p.2).

Those making land use decisions may be influenced in various ways by their neighbours (as well as wider social influences); the most obvious include imitation based on the success of innovative land uses or techniques (and conversely, avoidance of innovations seen to fail). The success of land managers may also be influenced by the successes and failures of neighbours, which affect managers' ability to acquire new land and diversify production. The original FEARLUS model was designed to specifically address the first point. The endogenous land market model (ELMM) expansion to FEARLUS discussed here is designed to address the second point. This chapter begins to explore how the addition of the more market-oriented land exchange mechanism in ELMM affects previously derived results on the relative competitive success of innovative and imitative land use selection strategies.

Our approach to simulation modelling makes considerable use of experiments. Simulations may be used simply to show that a model system can demonstrate a particular form of behaviour. However, if the model has any stochastic elements (including the selection of initial parameters), it is desirable to use experimental and statistical techniques to discover how the model *usually* behaves. Without such analysis, we cannot be sure an observed behaviour is robust. Moreover, comparing how a simulation model behaves under different parameter settings is central to understanding it, and this demands the ability to test whether apparent differences hold reliably.

The FEARLUS Model

The key constituents of the FEARLUS model used here, and how they interrelate, are shown in Figure 1. We adopt the convention of using capital letters to indicate entities in FEARLUS, italicised on first use.

A FEARLUS model consists of a set of *Land Managers* (representing households, not individuals), and their *Environment*, which includes a grid of square *Land Parcels*, and a set of possible *Land Uses*. Every *Year*, Land Managers select a Land Use for each Land Parcel they own, update their *Account* according to the *Yield* from the Land Uses selected, after which Land Parcels pass from Land Managers with a negative Account to their solvent *Neighbours* or new Land Managers at a fixed *Land Parcel Price*.

The definition of Neighbour may be varied within FEARLUS, but in this chapter two Land Managers are Neighbours if and only if they currently manage Parcels sharing a boundary or boundary point. A Land Parcel's *Grid Neighbours* are the eight Parcels orthogonally or diagonally adjacent to it. The set of Land Parcels owned by Land Managers owning Grid Neighbouring

Parcels of a Land Manager's Parcels is the *Social Neighbourhood* of that Land Manager.

The parameters of a FEARLUS model also specify how to determine the *External Conditions*, representing a combination of economic and climatic factors, and encoded as a bitstring, the length of which is a model parameter. The bitstring can vary from Year to Year but applies across the whole grid. The initial bitstring is determined randomly, and each subsequent bitstring is produced from its predecessor as illustrated in Figure 2 (b) by applying a predetermined *Flip Probability* (f) to each bit independently: If $f = 0$ the initial bitstring will be retained throughout; if $f = \frac{1}{2}$, each Year's bitstring is independent of its predecessors and the External Conditions are temporally uncorrelated. If $0 < f < \frac{1}{2}$, the External Conditions change, but are temporally correlated. Each Land Parcel has a set of *Biophysical Characteristics*, encoded as a bitstring and fixed for

the direction of a simulation run (again, the length of these bitstrings is a model parameter, the same for all Land Parcels). Both parameters affect *Yield* at the parcel level as per Figure 2 (c). There are also two numerical parameters unvarying over space or time: a *Break Even Threshold* (BET), specifying how much Yield must be gained from a Land Parcel to break even, and in the original FEARLUS model prior to ELMM, the *Land Parcel Price* (LPP).

The following sequence of actions occurs in the original (nonland market) FEARLUS model. In *Year Zero*, Land Parcels are assigned to Land Managers, and there is a random allocation of Land Uses to Land Parcels. (A specified number of Land Uses is created at random or loaded from a file.) Land Managers have an Account, initially set to zero (the Year Zero Yield does not affect this, but is available as information in Year 1).

Figure 1. UML class diagram showing the main entities in the FEARLUS model used here and how they inter-relate

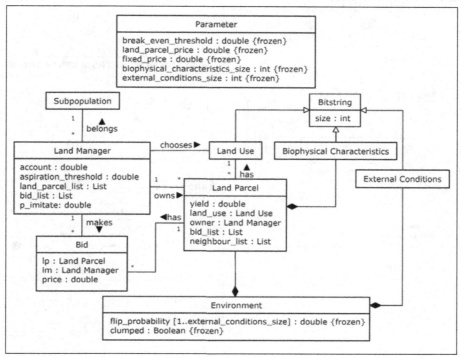

Figure 2. Depiction of the activities that take place each Year in FEARLUS, in order of occurrence: (a) Land Managers choose Land Uses; (b) External Conditions are calculated; (c) Yields are computed; (d) Land Managers update Accounts; (e) Land Parcels are put up for sale; (f) insolvent Land Managers retire; (g) Land Parcels for sale are given new owners. With the exception of (b) and (c), the activities are described using UML activity diagrams.

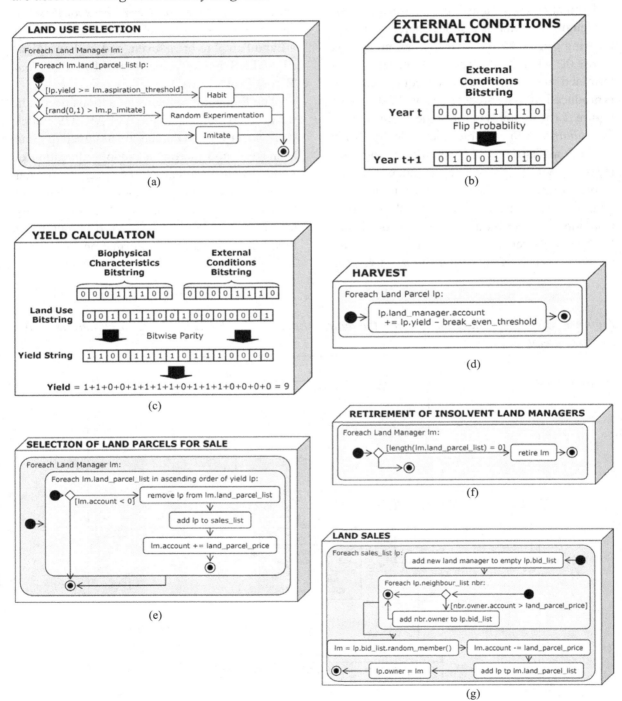

The rest of the run repeats the annual cycle shown in Figure 2.

A fuller description of FEARLUS models may be found in Polhill, Gotts and Law (2001), Gotts, Polhill, and Law (2003), and the FEARLUS user manual (http://www.macaulay.ac.uk/fearlus/). Typically, FEARLUS is used to investigate the relative success of Land Managers with various *Land Use Selection Algorithms* determined by the *Subpopulation* to which they belong. The proportion of *Land Parcels* collectively owned by *Land Managers* following competing approaches is used as the measure of those approaches' competitive success. (Note this is a population level, and not an individual, success measure.)

Improving FEARLUS's Land Market Representation

The Land transfer procedure in Figure 2 is very unrealistic: The Land Parcel Price is a global constant, and Neighbouring Managers have no choice about "buying" a Land Parcel for sale. We hypothesize that these restrictions may affect the success of Land Managers following different Land Use Selection Algorithms, since a relatively successful Land Manager forced to invest a fixed amount of capital in a Land Parcel without assessing its value may be more vulnerable to bankruptcy, diluting the potential success of their Algorithm. Alternatively, if a Land Manager is able to decide whether and how much to bid on a parcel, that Manager's Land Market transactions can reflect their overall decision-making strategy, and may themselves contribute to differential success and failure. Note that addition of these two decisions (as well as others, outlined below) adds new dimensions to the Land Manager's strategy. These nontrivial changes to the FEARLUS framework deserve careful analysis in order to determine: (a) whether the dynamics produced by the implemented changes correctly reflect the greater realism that we seek, and (b) whether that greater realism leads to changes in model outcomes.

Land is usually a scarce commodity; more is demanded than is available. Institutionally, markets serve to balance competition for scarce resources among competing agents. In theory, a well-functioning market will allocate scarce resources to their highest-valued use. (In practice, true equilibria are never reached.) If a model allows land to be allocated to the bidder valuing it most highly, the land rental rate should reflect the scarcity or shadow value of that land—the amount by which it would increase the profits of the agent with the winning bid. A functioning land market model will provide information on these shadow values of land at different points in space, allowing the modeller to explore the drivers of spatially heterogeneous returns.

Further, a functioning land market model might better reflect real-world incentives faced by agents. If more successful agents can bid on land of insolvent or less successful agents, it may allow faster consolidation of wealth and land holdings. Also, if the market for land becomes saturated, due perhaps to decreasing profitability of agricultural outputs, endogenously falling land prices may lead to land fallowing and/or abandonment, an important observed empirical phenomenon. Note that (as is clear from our implementation) a functioning land market simulation need not assume that land managers are economically rational profit maximisers.

ELMM replaces steps (e) and (g) in Figure 2 with a new process that allows Managers to choose which Parcels to buy, and creates their own bid for them. How this new process affects the interaction between innovators and imitators from earlier work with FEARLUS is explored in what follows. The following section briefly summarises the most relevant parts of the literature on innovation and imitation in agriculture, and results concerning the competitive performance of innovators and imitators using the pre-ELMM version of FEARLUS. We then describe ELMM and experimental work to explore its effect on these results, before a discussion and conclusion.

INNOVATE OR IMITATE?

The dynamics of imitation have been a consistent theme of work with FEARLUS (Polhill, Gotts, & Law, 2001; Gotts, Polhill, & Adam, 2003). Various forms of imitation have been both contrasted and used in combination with a very simple form of innovation—*Random Experimentation*—involving a uniform random choice among all the possible Land Uses. Both Random Experimentation and imitation have generally been used in combination with an *Aspiration Threshold* as per Figure 2 (a), where "Habit" means not changing Land Use. An Aspiration Threshold of zero will lead to no land-use change; conversely, a very high Aspiration Threshold means the Manager will always select the Land Use for that Land Parcel anew.

In the Selection Algorithms focused on here, imitation involves selecting the Land Use from those used by either the Land Manager themselves, or one of their Social Neighbours in the preceding Year.

Several different forms of Imitation have been investigated. Those relevant here are *Selective Simple Imitation* (SSI) and *Selective Best-mean Imitation* (SBI). In both of these, a score is calculated for each Land Use employed in the previous Year within the Social Neighbourhood, and a choice is made among those scoring highest; if one scores higher than all the rest, it is selected; if two or more share the highest score, each has an equal probability of being selected. In SSI, the score is the number of Parcels assigned to the Land Use in the most recent Year, in SBI, it is the mean Yield from those Parcels in the Social Neighbourhood assigned to that Land Use in the most recent Year.

We have also tried combining each form of imitation with a small amount of Random Ex-perimentation (specifically, a 1/16 probability of applying Random Experimentation rather than imitation if the threshold was not met). In general, adding this small amount of Random Experimentation made a big difference only when two Subpopulations using imitation were set in competition with each other, rather than with one using Random Experimentation. If all Land Managers are complete noninnovators (in the current context, never use Random Experimentation), there is a strong tendency towards monoculture—since once a Land Use happens to fall out of employment throughout the Environment, it will never be used again. Figure 3 demonstrates this, contrasting the Land Use pattern generated by various (combinations of) Land Use Selection Algorithms. Monoculture becomes a problem when the External Conditions change and the dominant Land Use is no longer profitable. In this sense, imitating Land Managers with no Random Experimentation depend on innovators to re-introduce Land Uses and under some conditions can exploit the risk taken by the innovators when experimenting, and are more successful.

Extensive experimentation, both published (Polhill, Gotts, & Law, 2001; Gotts, Polhill, & Law, 2003; Gotts, Polhill, & Adam, 2003; Gotts, Polhill, Law, & Izquierdo, 2003) and unpublished, has yielded some general conclusions concerning the competitive properties of these families of Land Use Selection Algorithms across a range of FEARLUS Environments. Those relevant here are:

- The HR family of Land Use Selection Algorithms (Random Experimentation combined with an appropriate Aspiration Threshold) is remarkably robust, given its seeming crudeness.
- In most Environments, at least some Land Use Selection Algorithms using imitation outperform HR with any Aspiration Threshold. This is more likely with increasing spa-

Figure 3. Illustration of the differences between innovation and pure imitation. Land Use patterns are shown from three simulation runs, each using three rather than eight Land Uses, as in the experiments with Land Uses represented in a shade of grey. (a) A run featuring agents with just the innovating Land Use Selection Algorithm, HR, generating a much more diverse landscape than (b), which features an imitator subpopulation (HSSI) converging to a monoculture. In (c) HR and HSBI compete, and the landscape shifts from one of mostly (though not completely) dominant Land Use to another in response to changes in the External Conditions.

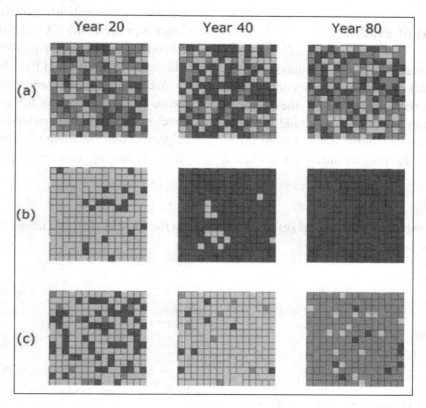

tial homogeneity of the Environment—particularly over short distances. With regard to temporal heterogeneity, intermediate degrees of autocorrelation appear to favour imitation most.

• Among the imitative strategies tried, SBI appears to be best or equally best across all Environments investigated, other than the most uncertain, where a variant which sometimes allows a lower-scoring Land Use to be selected does better (presumably because it leads to more diversity). Land Use

Selection Algorithms using SBI also beat HR in all but the most uncertain environments, where the advantages of diversity become important.

The question of the robustness of these findings naturally arises, since the competitive performance of various Land Use Selection Algorithms depends to a considerable extent on spatio-temporal heterogeneity. A full investigation of these results' robustness as the land market model changes is beyond our scope here: Our purpose is only to show that changes in land market models can affect the relative competitive advantage of Land Use Selection Algorithms.

THE EFFECT OF LAND MARKET MODELLING

Description of ELMM

Other agent-based land use models, such as Berger's (2001), already contain endogenised land rental markets. In this model, the decisions of which parcels to bid on and the bid for those parcels are simultaneously derived from farm-level mathematical programming models based

on optimisation behaviour, with bids reflecting shadow prices of land. Happe's (2000) AgriPoliS model also bases pricing for land rental on the shadow price. As with Berger's model, it assumes that transportation costs and exploitation of economies of scale result in farmers bidding for land parcels nearest to the farmstead. These cost advantages are explicitly modelled in the bidding function, whereas in FEARLUS they are implicitly embedded by only allowing Neighbouring Land Managers to buy a Land Parcel for sale.

We take a different approach to the optimization-based approach of Berger and Happe. As much of our work has been based on the acknowledgement that "satisficing" (Simon, 1957) rather than optimising is a more prevalent decision

Figure 4. Changes to steps (e) and (g) in Figure 2 made for ELMM, depicted using UML activity diagrams

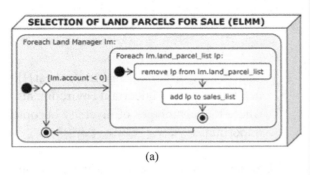

(a)

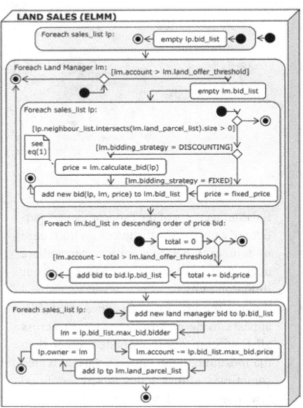

(b)

strategy among real-world actors, our land-market algorithms are designed accordingly. Regardless of decision-making assumptions, various aspects of land markets require algorithms or assumptions to specify how they will work. These are discussed in greater detail in Polhill, Parker, and Gotts (2005). Here, since we are interested in comparing original FEARLUS with FEARLUS-ELMM, we minimise modifications, attempting to isolate key components that make a difference. Below, we summarise the assumptions and algorithms of this early version of ELMM. The alterations to the model in Figure 2 to create FEARLUS-ELMM are shown in Figure 4.

a. *Decision to sell land.* Land Managers sell all Land Parcels when their Account is less than zero. See Figure 4 (a).
b. *Which land parcels to sell.* See (a).
c. *Selecting the reserve price.* The reserve price is the minimum a Land Manager will accept for a Land Parcel. It is not applicable in this version since Land Managers selling parcels are bankrupt.
d. *Decision to buy land.* Land Managers will try to buy land when they reach a threshold Account, the *Land Offer Threshold*. All such Land Managers generate a bid price (see (e) below) for the Parcels for sale in their Neighbourhood using a *Land Parcel Bidding Strategy*. They then use a *Land Parcel Selection Strategy* (see (f) below) to choose which of those bids they actually make.
e. *Deciding a bid price.* The following Land Parcel Bidding Strategies are used:
    • **Discounting bidding strategy:** The bid price is given by a discounted *Weighted* sum of the average profit the Land Manager has made per Land Parcel within the *Land Purchase Profit Window* time period of the Land Manager, and the last Profit of the Parcel for sale:

$$b = \frac{(1-w)\overline{p}_n - w(y - T)}{r}, \qquad (1)$$

where b is the bid price, w is the Weight, y is the last Yield of the Parcel, T is the BET, r is the interest rate that the Land Manager could earn on an exogenous investment opportunity, and if n is the Land Purchase Profit Window, Y the current Year, and p_i the Profit the Land Manager made per Land Parcel in Year i:

$$\overline{p}_n = \frac{1}{n} \sum_{i=(Y-n)+1,Y} p_i \qquad (2)$$

The denominator r in (1) reflects discounting over an infinite time horizon, on the basis that the time to bankruptcy of a Land Manager in FEARLUS is unknown and potentially unbounded. The higher the available interest rate, the lower the total expected return. The interest rate can alternatively be interpreted as a measure of the uncertainty of future returns: the higher the interest rate, the higher the perceived risk.

• **Fixed price bidding strategy:** A constant *Fixed Price* is offered by the Land Manager for all Land Parcels, to provide a comparison with original FEARLUS.

f. *Which land parcels to buy.* A *Buy Dearest Selection Strategy* is used, see Figure 4 (b).
g. *Determination of the final sale price.* Wooldridge (2002) discusses various kinds of auctions. Here, ELMM uses a first price sealed-bid (highest bidder wins) auction, adding to the set of bids generated by existing Land Managers a bid from a potential incoming Land Manager sampled from a distribution termed the *In-migrant Offer Price Distribution*.
h. *What to do with land that no-one wants to buy.* Land that no Neighbours wish to buy is automatically transferred to a new Land Manager, as per original FEARLUS.

i.   *Localisation of land sales.* Land Parcels are exchanged only between neighbouring Land Managers, as per original FEARLUS.

j.   *Handling debt.* Not applicable here.

Experiments with ELMM

In all models considered in this section, the Land Parcels are arranged in a 15×15 grid, with opposite sides joined to produce a toroidal topology. The bitstrings defining Land Uses' preferred conditions always contain a total of 16 bits. Environments differ in the division of these bits between biophysical characteristics (variable across space, but fixed over time) and external conditions (uniform across space but variable over time). External conditions may be either correlated or uncorrelated from Year to Year: In the former case, the flip probability is below 1/2 (values of 1/8, ¼, and 3/8 have been used); in the latter, 1/2. Similarly, the biophysical characteristics of Land Parcels may be either clumped or unclumped. In either case, each bit is initially independently set to 0 or 1 with equal probability for every Land Parcel. In the "clumping" process used here, which is carried out on each bit-position in turn during initialisation, adjacent Land Parcels are selected at random to swap nonmatching bit-values for as long as there is a swap that will increase the number of Grid Neighbouring Land Parcel pairs having the same value. The Environments used are detailed in Table 1.

Aside from the parameters specifying the amount and distribution of spatial and temporal variation in conditions affecting Yield, and the Selection and Bidding Algorithms followed by Land Managers (discussed below), the only model parameter varying over the experiments reported here is the Land Parcel Price (LPP)—and this parameter only applies in the case of experiments involving the pre-ELMM version of FEARLUS. In all cases, the BET is set at eight.

The experiments have been conducted with a view to seeing what effect, if any, more realistic land market models have on the relationship between innovators and imitators as represented by Habit-Random (HR) on the one hand, and Habit-Selective-Best-mean-Imitation (HSBI) and Habit-Selective-Simple-Imitation (HSSI) on the other; all using an Aspiration Threshold of 8. When studying the relationship between such strategies for land use decision making, is it possible that consideration needs also to be given to strategies for land parcel exchange? That is, can the land use decision making part of land managers' behaviour be studied in isolation from other strategic aspects of their business?

So far in FEARLUS, we have used three kinds of experiment to study land managers' strategies, dubbed Type 1, Type 2, and Type 3 experiments. A Type 1 experiment tests the hypothesis that "Subpopulation P does better than Subpopulation Q in Environment E," where "does better" means "owns a larger proportion of the Land Parcels at the time the simulation terminates" (see Polhill, Gotts, & Law, 2001 for more details on this, and on Type 2 and 3 experiments, which are not used here). In this chapter, we also present a new kind of experiment, dubbed Type 4, to compare differences in performance as various aspects of the Land Managers' behaviour is changed. A Type 4 experiment tests the following hypothesis using paired replicate runs with a sign test:

"Subpopulation A.X does better against Subpopulation B.X than Subpopulation A.Y does against B.Y in Environment E," where A and B refer to different Land Use Selection Algorithms (i.e., HR, HSBI, or HSSI) and X and Y to different market strategies and models (i.e., no bidding (N), fixed price (F), or discounting (D) with rate $r = 1$ and weight $w = 1/2$.). (An interest rate of one implies that managers only anticipate next year's rather than future returns. This simplification was done to facilitate comparison to fixed price bidding.) This hypothesis does not entail a complete reversal in the fate of A against B using market model X rather than Y, merely an improvement in performance.

Table 1. The Environments used in the experiments and preliminary exploration. The "label" is how they are referred to in the chapter. The "BC bits" column says how many bits are used to describe the Biophysical Characteristics in the run, with "BC Clumped?" stating whether or not these bits are spatially correlated using the clumping algorithm described in the text. The "EC bits" column is the number of bits used for the External Conditions, and their temporal correlation is described in "EC Correlated?": an entry of "No" indicates a Flip Probability of 1/2, an entry of "Yes" is followed by a description of the number of bits given a Flip Probability of less than 1/2. The last four columns indicate which formal experiments each Environment is used in. Those not used in a formal experiment (Env-H, -I, -J, -K, -L, and -P) were used in initial exploratory runs.

Env. label	BC bits	BC Clumped?	EC bits	EC Correlated?	Type 1 HSSI	Type 1 HSBI	Type 4 HSSI	Type 4 HSBI
Env-A	0	N/A	16	No	-	Yes	-	-
Env-B	0	N/A	16	Yes: 4 bits 1/8	-	Yes	-	-
Env-C	0	N/A	16	Yes: 8 bits 1/8	-	Yes	-	-
Env-D	0	N/A	16	Yes: 12 bits 1/8	-	Yes	-	-
Env-E	0	N/A	16	Yes: all 1/8	-	Yes	-	-
Env-F	0	N/A	16	Yes: all 1/4	-	Yes	-	-
Env-G	0	N/A	16	Yes: all 3/8	-	Yes	-	-
Env-H	1	No	15	No	-	-	-	-
Env-I	1	No	15	Yes: 5 bits 1/8	-	-	-	-
Env-J	1	Yes	15	Yes: 5 bits 1/8	-	-	-	-
Env-K	1	No	15	Yes: 10 bits 1/8	-	-	-	-
Env-L	1	Yes	15	Yes: 10 bits 1/8	-	-	-	-
Env-M	1	No	15	Yes: all 1/4	Yes	Yes	Yes	Yes
Env-N	1	Yes	15	Yes: all 1/4	Yes	-	Yes	-
Env-O	1	No	15	Yes: all 3/8	Yes	Yes	-	Yes
Env-P	1	Yes	15	Yes: all 3/8	-	-	-	-
Env-Q	4	No	12	Yes: all 1/4	Yes	Yes	-	Yes
Env-R	4	No	12	Yes: all 3/8	Yes	Yes	-	Yes
Env-S	8	No	8	Yes: all 1/4	Yes	Yes	Yes	Yes
Env-T	8	Yes	8	Yes: all 1/4	Yes	-	Yes	-
Env-U	8	No	8	Yes: all 3/8	Yes	Yes	-	Yes

Type 1 Experiments

A series of Type 1 experiments were conducted to test whether the changes made to FEARLUS to incorporate ELMM would cause us to change the results we would report. There are three possibilities:

a.   A significant result in favour of one Subpopulation in the original FEARLUS becomes a significant result in favour of the other in FEARLUS with ELMM.

b. A significant result in the original FEARLUS is no longer significant in FEARLUS with ELMM.

c. A result that is not significant in the original FEARLUS is significant in FEARLUS with ELMM.

Since there are many experiments being conducted (each experiment consisting of a single contest in one Environment involving 60 or 120 runs), we set the significance level at 0.01 to avoid false positives.

The experiments were conducted in three stages:

1. A control, in which the original FEAR-LUS, and FEARLUS with ELMM, were configured so that existing Land Managers can never afford to buy Land Parcels, so no land transfers occur. This is achieved in the original FEARLUS by setting the LPP to a number greater than the maximum Account it is possible to accrue within the time period of the simulation, and in FEARLUS with ELMM by setting the Land Offer Threshold to such a number.

2. A comparison of results bidding at a fixed price using the LPP in the original FEAR-LUS, and bidding using the Fixed Price Bidding Strategy and an In-migrant Offer Price always equal to this Fixed Price (so In-migrants bid the same as established Land Managers) in FEARLUS with ELMM.

3. Finally, we used FEARLUS with ELMM to compare results using a Fixed Price Bidding Strategy with a Discounting Bidding Strategy to see if the different Land Market models would alter previous results.

For all stages, we used the Environments and HR/HSBI and HR/HSSI contests noted in Table 1. For stages 2 and 3, we tried Land Parcel Price (or

equivalent in ELMM where appropriate) values of 4 and 16.

In the control, we expected there to be no difference between the results reported in this case, as in each model all Land Parcels are sold to new Land Managers, which proved to be the case. In stage 2, the key difference is that in original FEARLUS, Land Managers with a negative Account can sell their Parcels one at a time and are only bankrupt when they have no more Parcels to sell, whereas in FEARLUS with ELMM, Land Managers are bankrupt as soon as their Account is negative, selling all Parcels. Here, and in stage 3, differences in the results are possible. A summary of the differences found in stages 2 and 3 is depicted in Figure 5. The stage 2 results show that there is scope for the simple modelling decision about the arrangements when the Account is below 0 to affect the results that would be reported. The stage 3 results show effects due to changes in the bankruptcy arrangements in the Fixed Price case disappearing when Discounting is used. These results in Env-U and Env-N suggest a sensitivity to differences in the Land Market Model that, in general, could not be known beforehand.

Though the number of cases in which it occurred were relatively few, it is clear that changes to the mechanism by which Land is exchanged can affect the reported results of the competitiveness of strategies for choosing Land Uses.

Type 4 Experiments

Although the Type 1 experiments show that there is the potential for Land Market modelling decisions to change model results, only Type 4 experiments can statistically confirm that difference. There is a further motivation for conducting Type 4 experiments: In cases where the Type 1 results seem not to have been affected, the Type 4 experiments can show where there has nevertheless been a consistent difference in the performance of a Land Use Selection Strategy attributable to the change in the Bidding Strategy. Fewer Environments

Figure 5. Summary of Type 1 significant results. The small boxes show the Environment and winning Land Use Selection Algorithm of a significant result, which are joined by a line labelled with the Fixed Price and losing Land Use Selection to a black circle representing no significant result. Stage two comparisons are on the left hand side, and stage three on the right.

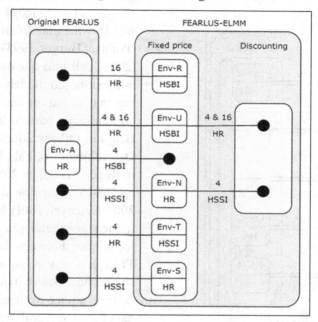

were studied using Type 4 experiments: six for HR/HSBI and four for HR/HSSI (see Table 1). The results are summarised in Figure 6.

Though these results show quite clearly that Land Markets have made a difference, further analysis and visual inspection of reruns in Env-N, Env-Q, Env-S, and Env-T at Price 4 indicates that an In-migrant effect is responsible for *all* differences observed between the Fixed Price and Discounting Land Market models. In-migrants affect the results in two ways. First, the probability of an In-migrant belonging to either Subpopulation is exactly 1/2, whereas the population of non In-migrant bids will be biased according to which of the Subpopulations is doing better. Second, In-migrant bids were set at a specific value, which, if high enough, will result in the great majority of Land Parcels being sold to In-migrants, leading in the extreme case to the same effective behaviour as when no bids are made

at all. Thus, a Subpopulation using a Land Use Selection Algorithm that performs badly in the Fixed Price case can gain when Land Markets are used by increasing the likelihood of occupying Land through the In-migrant mechanism. This is a possible explanation for the result in Env-M in Figure 6. HSSI loses in all Type 1 contests, and the high Price means that In-migrants often outbid others. In this case HSSI is performing more successfully in Discounting, but not because the Land Market model is better at rewarding good Land Use decision making. This may not be the only means by which In-migrants affect the results. Further experiments with different parameters are needed to explore this more thoroughly.

The important lesson here is that making Land Markets more realistic by allowing Land Managers to bid for Parcels rather than setting a Fixed Price cannot be done in isolation from consideration of other influences on Land Mar-

Figure 6. Summary of significant results from the Type 4 experiments, showing the Environment, Price, and Land Market models under which a Land Use Selection Algorithm performed better.

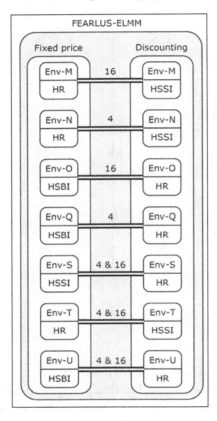

DISCUSSION

Imitation is one means of economising on computational resources and/or compensating for an absence of knowledge, and is known to be one way in which land managers choose what to do (Pomp & Burger, 1995). Schmidt and Rounsevell (2006) call into question the study of imitation in agent-based models of land use change, finding that imitation leaves little noticeable trace on landscape pattern in a case study in central Belgium. Other studies (e.g., Ryan & Cross, 1943; Deutschmann & Fals Borda, 1962, as reported in Rogers, 2003, pp.268-271; Hägerstrand, 1967, pp.158-163; Lansing & Kremer, 1994; Berger, 2001; Letenyei, 2001) do claim evidence of direct influence on the adoption of particular agricultural techniques between farmers within a locality. Though it may be significant that most of these studies have been carried out in areas where agricultural advice from nonlocal sources is likely to have been less readily available than in present-day Belgium, they do establish a case that the imitation of neighbours is important. Questions about imitation procedures (e.g., how imitators select their models, how far they are influenced by the simple popularity of an innovation among those models, and how far they require evidence of its success) are then clearly significant. These questions have not been much investigated empirically (the usual assumption being that adoption takes place, or at least is considered, when a threshold is passed in the proportion of adopters within some population). The work by Pomp and Burger (1995) is an exception, suggesting that farmers may imitate those most similar to themselves, or those they believe to have most information. They also suggest that successful adoption by a farmer *without* a prior history of successful innovation might be particularly influential: If the innovation succeeds in their hands, it must be highly advantageous! However, their econometric models do not

kets. Our efforts to maintain similarity with FEARLUS have been partly responsible for the distorting effect of In-migrants (Price 16 was that used in earlier work), and though exploring still lower values for Price than 4 may permit the desired comparison, more radical alterations to the model may be necessary to explore the effects of implementing land bidding. Our step-by-step model modification strategy may not be sufficient to test our hypotheses regarding the effects of land markets.

examine the consequences of these different types of imitation as we can with FEARLUS.

In the real world, innovators play an important and persistent role in agricultural environments. If they were not doing "better" than imitators in certain contexts, and according to certain metrics, they would not persist in the rural economy. In the real world also, in contrast to FEARLUS, land managers may choose not only land uses, but particular decision strategies, and these choices may also be based on imitation. Through innovation and intelligent imitation of decision strategies, a balance of decision makers of various types may evolve over time. These "decision ecologies" may evolve so as to ensure stability or long-run survival at the scale of the rural system. Whatever the properties of the rural system, at the scale of the land manager, the chosen strategy should have some attractiveness that motivates its selection. In short, there must be some reason to be an innovator, rather than an imitator.

Innovators as currently modelled in FEARLUS may experience too little success. Imitators seem to consistently capture a higher proportion of parcels, having, in the language of game theory, a second-mover advantage. It is possible that innovators are currently experiencing success in FEARLUS according to other individual rather than population scale metrics: From a "decision ecology" point of view, a viable landscape-scale system may in any case only need so many innovators. We have yet to examine metrics such as the number of parcels, average wealth, and average longevity of innovator land managers. Such metrics may still show that innovators experience relative success in particular environments.

If such analysis still indicates that innovators do relatively poorly, options exist for increasing the chance of success for innovation. In the real world, a choice to innovate into a new land use may be based on years of experience that translate into specialized knowledge of what land outputs are likely to succeed in the marketplace. Such experience could be captured in a modelling framework by giving managers who have innovated into profitable crops in the past greater knowledge regarding the potential profitability of new land uses than other agents. Innovators would also then need the ability to choose among potential new land uses. Innovators with such characteristics may earn early profits by being first to market with a desirable good, which demands a high price when supply is relatively low. To reflect these opportunities, the model would need to implement output prices for land uses that depend (in a decreasing fashion) on their total supply.

What we have begun to show here is that the strategy for choosing land uses cannot be considered in isolation from wider aspects of farm business management. Since the way the land market works can affect the outcome of the model, it is likely that differences in land acquisition strategy will affect the relative performance of different kinds of land managers.

Discussions among the LUCC modelling community have highlighted the importance of model validation and the need for a variety of spatial and a-spatial validation techniques (Veldkamp & Lambin, 2001; Parker et al., 2002). While the model enhancements described in this chapter are designed for theoretical exploration, our conjecture that a model with a functioning land market may perform better should ultimately be subject to empirical testing.

CONCLUSION

Various aspects of the way in which Land Markets are implemented can affect the relative performance of the Land Use Selection Algorithms. Referring back to the Type 1 experiments, the comparison between the original FEARLUS and FEARLUS-ELMM using Fixed Price shows that the different land market modelling decisions (a) and (b) in the list above (decision to sell and which Parcels to sell) can affect results. We also observe that In-migrant Land Managers can skew the outcome, relevant to decisions (g) and (h) (determination of final sale price and what to do with land no one wants to buy). Since In-migrants are a feature of real-world land markets, decisions on how to handle them merit separate consideration. Results comparing the Fixed Price with the Discounting Bidding Strategy have not conclusively shown that decisions (e) and (f) (how much to bid and which Parcels to buy) affect results in isolation from In-migrant bids, though this will be the subject of future work. Thus, at least some of the decisions outlined for simulating land markets are non-neutral with respect to other aspects of a model of land use change. We hope in future to study these effects in more detail, as well as to explore the influence of other aspects of land market modelling decisions on model behaviour.

ACKNOWLEDGMENT

This work was funded by the Scottish Executive Environment and Rural Affairs Department. We also thank the reviewers for some helpful comments on an earlier draft.

REFERENCES

Benson, J.F. (Ed.). (1995). *Journal of Environmental Planning and Management 38*(1). *Special Issue: The NERC/ESRC Land Use Modeling Programme.*

Berger, T. (2001). Agent-based spatial models applied to agriculture: A simulation tool for technology diffusion, resource use changes, and policy analysis. *Agricultural Economics, 25*(2-3), 245-260.

Cioffi-Revilla, C., & Gotts, N.M. (2003). Comparative analysis of agent-based social simulations: GeoSim and FEARLUS models. *Journal of Artificial Societies and Social Simulation, 6*(4). (http://jasss.soc.surrey.ac.uk/JASSS6-4.html as at 22/12/2003).

Deutschmann, P.J., & Fals Borda, O. (1962). *La Communicacion de las ideas entre los campesinos Colombianos.* Monografías Sociológicas 14, Universidad Nacional de Colombia, Bogotá.

Gotts, N.M., Polhill, J.G., & Adam, W.J. (2003). Simulation and analysis in agent-based modelling of land use change. *First Conference of the European Social Simulation Association, SIMSOC VI Workshop.* Retrieved January 5, 2004 from, http://www.uni-koblenz.de/~kgt/ESSA/ESSA

Gotts, N.M., Polhill, J.G., & Law, A.N.R. (2003). Aspiration levels in a land use simulation. *Cybernetics and Systems 34*, 663-683.

Gotts, N.M., Polhill, J.G., Law, A.N.R., & Izquierdo, L.R. (2003, April 7-11). Dynamics of imitation in a land use simulation. In *Proceedings of the Second International Symposium on Imitation in Animals and Artefacts,* University of Wales, Aberystwyth (pp. 39-46).

Hägerstrand, T. (1967). *Innovation diffusion as a spatial process.* Translated by Allan Pred with the assistance of Greta Haag. University of Chicago Press.

Happe, K. (2000). *The agricultural policy simulator (AgriPolis)—Version 1.0. discussion paper.* Institute of Agricultural Development in Central and Eastern Europe IAMO, Theodor-Lieser-Strasse 2, D-06120 Halle, Germany.

Lansing, J.S., & Kremer, J.N. (1994). Emergent properties of Balinese water temple networks: Coadaptation on a rugged fitness landscape. In C. G. Langton (Ed.). *Artificial life III* (pp. 201-223). Addison-Wesley.

Letenyei, I. (2001). Rural innovation chains: Two examples for the diffusion of rural innovations. *Hungarian Review of Sociology, 7*(1), 85-100.

Parker, D.C., Berger, T., & Manson, S.M. (2002). Agent-based models of land-use/land-cover change: Report and review of an international workshop. *Report No. 6. LUCC Focus 1*, Bloomington, IN.

Parry, M. L. (1996). Integrating global and regional analyses of the effects of climate change: A case study of land use in England and Wales. *Climate Change, 32*, 185-198.

Polhill, J.G., Gotts, N.M., & Law, A.N.R. (2001). Imitative versus nonimitative strategies in a land use simulation. *Cybernetics and Systems, 32*(1-2), 285-307.

Polhill, J.G., Parker, D.C., & Gotts, N.M. (2005, September 5-9) Introducing land markets to an agent based model of land use change: A design. In K.G. Troitzsch (Ed.), *Representing social reality: Pre-proceedings of the third conference of the European social simulation association, Koblenz* (pp. 150-157). Koblenz: Verlag Dietmar Völbach.

Pomp, M., & Burger, K. (1995). Innovation and imitation: Adoption of cocoa by Indonesian smallholders. *World Development, 23*(3), 423-431.

Rogers, E.M. (2003). *Diffusion of innovations* (5th edition). Free Press.

Ryan, B., & Gross, N.C. (1943). The diffusion of hybrid corn in two Iowa communities. *Rural Sociology, 8*, 15-24.

Schmidt, C., & Rounsevell, M.D.A. (2006) Are agricultural land use patterns influenced by farmer imitation? *Agriculture, Ecosystems & Environment, 115*(1-4), 113-127.

Simon, H.A. (1957). *Models of man, social and rational: Mathematical essays on rational human behaviour in a social setting.* New York: John Wiley & Sons.

Veldkamp, A., & Lambin, E.F. (2001). Predicting land-use change. *Agriculture, Ecosystems, & Environment, 85*, 1-6.

Wooldridge, M. (2002). *An introduction to multi-agent systems.* Chichester, UK: John Wiley.

Chapter VIII
Introducing Social Issues into a Minority Game by Using an Agent Based Model

Marco Remondino
University of Turin, Italy

Alessandro Cappellini
University of Turin, ISI Foundation, Italy

ABSTRACT

In this chapter, the authors perturb a minority game (MG) with some sociological issues, first by implementing a social network among the involved agents, through which they can somehow communicate their decision to a group of "friends," a local subset of those participating the game. Thus, the emergent aggregate behaviour will be very far from that of the original MG; the stress here is on the possibility of an agent changing his or her own decision, after getting the information from other n agents. Two different communication protocols among the agents will be examined: a synchronous one and the more realistic asynchronous one. Additionally, in some experiments a memory is introduced, acting as a selection mechanism. Last, some special agents, called Opinion Leaders, whose influence over the others is higher than normal, are implemented in order to study how this can change the aggregate results.

INTRODUCTION

Game theory (GT) is a distinct and interdisciplinary approach to the study of strategic behaviour. The disciplines most involved in game theory are mathematics, economics, and the other social and behavioural sciences. GT was founded by the great mathematician John von Neumann.

The key link between neoclassical economics and game theory is rationality. Neoclassical economics is based on the assumption that human beings are absolutely rational in their economic choices. The kind of rationality which is usually assumed in economics—perfect, logical, deductive rationality—is extremely useful in generating solutions to theoretical problems, but it fails to account for situations in which rationality is bounded (because agents can not cope with the complexity of the situation) or when ignorance about other agents' ability and willingness to apply perfect rationally leads to subjective beliefs about the situation. Even in those situations, agents are not completely irrational: They adjust their behaviour based on what they think other agents are going to do, and these expectations are generated endogenously by information about what other agents have done in the past. On the basis of these expectations, the agent takes an action, which in turn becomes a precedent that influences the behaviour of future agents. This creates a feedback loop: Expectations arise from precedents and then create the actions which, in turn, constitute the precedents for the next step.

GT was intended to confront just this problem: to provide a theory of economic and strategic behaviour when people interact directly, rather than through the market. In game theory, "games" have always been a metaphor for more serious interactions in human society.

The minority game (MG) is a simple, generalized framework, belonging to the GT field, which represents the collective behaviour of agents in an idealized situation where they have to compete through adaptation for some finite resource.

While the MG was born as the mathematical formulation of the "El Farol Bar" problem considered by Arthur (1994), it goes beyond this one, since it generalizes the study of how many individuals may reach a collective solution to a problem under adaptation of each one's expectations about the future. In Arthur (1994), the "El Farol Bar" problem was posed as an example of inductive reasoning in scenarios of bounded rationality.

The original formulation of this problem is as follows: N people, at every step, take an individual decision among two possibilities. Number one is to stay at home, number two is to go to a bar. Since the space in the bar is limited (finite resource), the time there is enjoyable if and only if the number of the people there is less than a fixed threshold (aN, where $a<1$). Every agent has his or her own expectation of the number of people in the bar, and according to their forecast decides whether to go or not. The only information available to the agents is the number of people attending the bar in the recent past; this means that there is no deductively rational solution to this problem, but there can be plenty of models trying to infer the future number according to the past ones.

An interesting aspect of the problem is that if most agents think that the number of people going to the bar is $> aN$, then they won't go, thus invalidating their own prevision. Computer simulations of this model shows that the attendance fluctuates around aN in a ($aN,(1-a)N$) structure of people attending/not attending. The bar problem has been applied to some proto-market models: At each time step agents can buy (go to the bar) or sell an asset and after each time step, the price of the asset is determined by a simple supply-demand rule.

The MG has been first described in Challet and Zhang (1997) as a mathematical formalization and generalization of the bar problem. It is assumed that an odd number of players take a decision at each step of the simulation; the agents that take the minority decision win, while the others loose. Stepping back to the bar problem, we can see it as a MG with two possible actions: $a1 = 1$ (to go to the bar) and $a2 = -1$ (not to go to the bar). After each round, the cumulative action value $A(t)$ is calculated as the sum of each value given to the single actions. The minority rule sets the comfort level at $A(t) = 0$, so that agent is given a payoff $-ai(t)g[A(t)]$ at each time step with g being an odd function of $A(t)$.

The MG has been chosen in this work since it's a model that could be used as a metaphor in many fields—it's intrinsically interdisciplinary (see Cappellini and Lamieri,2007 for an economic application on the dynamism of industrial sectors)and its structure is well known and quite straightforward enough to be described through an agent-based model. The perturbations to the original model described in this chapter, cover different sides. In order to extend the MG it would be possible to change:

- Topology (from regular mono/bi-dimensional to a social network).
- Cognitively the rules of reward and learning (evolutionary MG).
- How the information and feedbacks are spread and received (local information).
- The regime of interactions (global or local minorities).

By relaxing the original hypotheses, a model is obtained with local interactions and information, approaching somehow certain physical models more oriented to the Social Sciences, e.g., the Ising model and, in particular, the Sznajd model.

The purpose of the Ising model is that of imitating a phenomenon where individual elements modify their individual behaviour in order to conform to the behaviour of other individuals nearby. This happens for many phenomena in nature, e.g., cardiac thin filament activation with nearest-neighbour cooperative interactions (Rice et al., 2003). The Sznajd model (see Sznajd-Weron & Sznajd, 2000; Sznajd-Weron, 2005; Stauffer et al., 2000; Stauffer, 2001 for numerical implementation) is a sociophysics model of opinion formation, which is based on the Ising model. As an example, each spin can simulate a voter. Their opinions vary according to a trade union maxim: "United we Stand, Divided we Fall."

The main differences among those models and the one presented here are that the Sznajd model uses majority rule (here minority rule is applied) and, above all, that the model presented here uses a random topology, while the Sznajd model uses a regular one.

INTRODUCING COMMUNICATION: SOCIAL NETWORKS AND GRAPHS

The bar problem, as well as the MG in its original formulation, state that there is no communication among the agents involved in the simulation; the first idea presented here is to introduce a sort of a social network into the model, in order to see how the links among certain agents can change the aggregate results. A social network is defined as "a set of nodes—e.g., persons, organizations—linked by a set of social relationship—e.g., friendship, transfer of funds, overlapping membership—of a specific type" (Laumann et al., 1978).

Here, the minority rule will be very easy: A set of N agents chooses between (-1) and (1). Those in the minority (denoted with $n < N$) win and get a payoff equal to N/n: the fewer agents that stay in the minority, the higher the payoff. Also, the social network involved will be quite simple, just linking an agent to others with a relation limited to the possibility of asking a question: "Will you choose (−1) or (1)?" Not all the agents will be connected, though, so that some of them will have to make a prevision just considering the past few results, exactly like in the original MG.

In the example shown in Table 1, there are five agents involved in the simulation: Agent 1 can ask agents 2, 3, and 4, while agent 2 can ask agent 3, and number 3 can ask numbers 1 and 5; agent 4 can then ask numbers 1 and 5, while number 5 is a lonely agent (he or she can't ask anyone, even if two other agents can ask what he or she will do).

Any kind of network can be described in terms of a graph, composed of nodes and a set of lines, with edges joining the nodes. In a mathematician's terminology, a graph is a collection of points and lines connecting some (possibly empty) subset of them. The points of a graph are most commonly known as graph vertices, but may also be called nodes or simply points. Similarly, the lines connecting the vertices of a graph are most commonly known as graph edges, but may also be called arcs

Table 1. Definition of relations among agents

	1	2	3	4	5
1		x	x	x	
2				x	
3	x				x
4	x				x
5					

or lines. The study of graphs is known as graph theory, and was first systematically investigated by König in the 1930s (Gardner, 1984). Graphs come in a wide variety, withthe most common type beingthose with at most one edge (i.e., either one edge or no edges) that may connect any two vertices. Such graphs are called simple graphs and are the ones used in the present analysis. The edges of graphs may also be imbued with directedness. A normal graph in which edges are undirected is said to be undirected. Otherwise, if arrows may be placed on one or both endpoints of the edges of a graph to indicate directedness, the graph is said to be directed.

In this work, the graph used to represent the social network linking the agents together is bidirected, i.e., each edge points in both directions as once. This seems realistic, since this network can be thought of as a group of friends, or, in general, people who know each other. If A knows B, then it's quite obvious that B knows A in turn; those situations in which a subject disseminates his or her opinion to others and isn't touched by their decisions (e.g., advertisement, political campaigns, and so forth) is voluntarily not considered. That's because we suppose that this sort of dissemination comes "a priori," i.e., before this analysis starts; the interest here is in studying how a set of agents mutually connected into a network can influence one another and come to a final overall result. In Figure 1, an example of a network used in the model is shown. It's possible to notice that

some nodes (agents) can be left totally unlinked, thus having to take their decision just basing on their own forecasts.

THE SIMULATION FRAMEWORK

A community of reactive agents that must take a decision is used; the decision could be simply binary (e.g., to sell or to buy in a stock market, to go or not to go to a pub, and so forth) or more complex (e.g., choosing whom to vote for at the next election, choosing the colour for a car, and so on). While the mechanism behind the constitution of an opinion in human beings is beyond the purpose of this work, we'll analyze how a social network interconnecting a community of agents can influence their choices and, in particular, how it could determine changes of their own opinions. That's why simple, reactive agents have been used: No plans are required to carry out the initial decision that could even be randomly generated, and the only action they have to perform is to evaluate the opinions of their "friends," who are the other agents linked with them, and choose whether or not to be influenced by them.

Among the many toolkits and frameworks that can be used to build agent based simulations, JAS (http://jaslibrary.sourceforge.net) was selected for

Figure 1. Agents communicating over a network

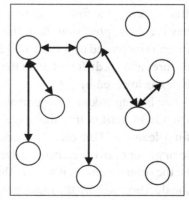

this work, since it includes graphical support for Social Network Analysis.

At the beginning of the simulation during the setup, a simple world is created, populated by N agents. These agents can be considered as the vertexes of a social network and the links among them (relations) as the edges. The network is directed and every arc is composed of two edges with opposite directions. Every agent has a list of F (friends) other agents, whom she/he can ask. This list is composed of the neighbours, i.e., the vertexes linked to the examined vertex (the agent). The nodes are randomly generated, and the links are created one by one.

The neighbourhood is intended as having sociological, as well as physical closeness. According to Laumann et al. (1978), the relations between the involved agents are considered as friendship. This social relationship is characterized by a random creation but is also very stable in short/medium term. The links in this simulation are directed and bi-directional, as is the friendship.

Here follows a brief description of the simulation process:

- At the beginning of each simulation step, every agent has its own forecast. The forecast is absolutely random between two choices —1 and +1.

- The decision taken by each agent (before communicating with others) is denoted with a "certainty index" equal to 1 (100%).

- Now an agent is randomly chosen. She/He starts asking the first in the list; if this one has the same prevision, then the certainty index is increased by a value of $1/F$, while if the prevision is different, than the certainty index is lowered by $1/F$.

- After having asked a statement to all the friends in her/his list, the agent takes the final decision: If the certainty index is equal to or greater than one, then the decision will be the original one. If it's lower than 1, then the decision will be the other possible one

- Another agent is then randomly chosen, and so on (the same agent can't be chosen twice during the same turn). Note that an agent that's been asked can still change his or her mind, based on the agents he or she will ask in turn

Before starting the simulation, two core parameters can be changed: the number of agents involved and the number of links among the agents. Three runs of the simulation are examined: one with 1,000 agents and 500 total links (an average of one link every two agents), another with 100 agents and 500 links (an average of five links for every agent), and the last one with 100 agents and 5,000 links (fifty links for every agent). In every run the MG is iterated 1,000 times.

ASYNCHRONOUS COMMUNICATION

Two communication protocols are implemented in the model. In the asynchronous protocol, agents act sequentially. So the first agents which act take their decision, and from then on they reply to the other agents with the new decision taken. The synchronous protocol states that the agents always communicate their original opinion to the others: They broadcast their opinion to all the agents who are linked to them. Finally, after having collected all the opinions of their friends, they reconsider their choice. The difference among the two protocols is studied by using the same starting parameters in the simulation (*ceteris paribus*).

The asynchronous case is examined first, where the agents act sequentially. So the first agents to act take a decision, and from then on they reply to the other agents with the new decision taken. As an example, we can think of a group of people using the phone two by two to communicate; in this way the last agent to speak already has complete information about the definitive choices of all the others to whom she spoke before.

In the output graph time can be read on the x-axis (1,000 iterations of the game), and two lines are plotted: The red one (the lower one in the graphs) depicts the decisions that changed while the blue one (the upper one) is for unchanged decisions. On the y-axis the number of decisions is shown (changed or not); the scale (10^1, 10^2, and 10^3) depends on the agents number.

The standard example is a world of 100 agents and 500 relations (Figure 2), in which an average of 65 out of 100 preserve their original decisions.

In a second run a different situation is depicted, in which the agents have many more relations among themselves: An average of fifty for every inhabitant (Figure 3).

A simple, common sense rule states that the more relations, the higher the probability to change opinion. This example proves the rule to be right and the presented model to be consistent with real world results; a counter example can now be given, i.e., a poor relations world, such as the one in Figure 4 with one thousand inhabitants and a total of just five hundred relations.

Here, less than 20 percent of the agents changed their opinion. In order to test the extreme situation,

Figure 2. 100 agents and 500 relations

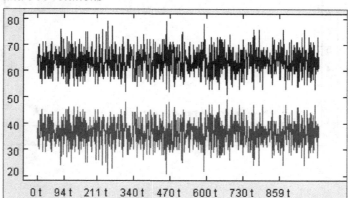

Figure 3. 100 agents and 5,000 relations

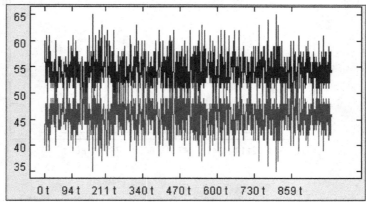

a world with no relations among the agents has been imagined (like in the original MG).

Obviously, in a world with one thousand unlinked agents no opinions change (Figure 5).

SYNCHRONOUS COMMUNICATION

The synchronous communication process is now explored, which can be compared to a situation in which a group of friends are physically in the main square of a small village, deciding what to do in the evening. They are speaking loud, all together, and so communication is "instantaneously" broadcasted and decisions are taken at the same time.

Now the agents always communicate to the others their original opinion: they broadcast their opinion to all the agents which are linked to them. Finally, after they collect all the opinions of their friends, they evaluate the certainty index and reconsider their choice.

Figure 4. 1000 agents and 500 relations

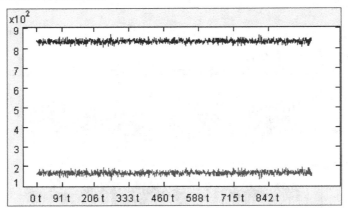

Figure 5. 1000 agents and zero relations

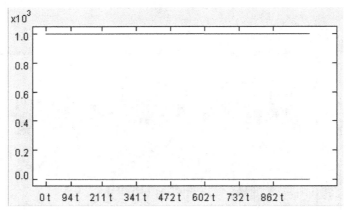

The simulation was executed with the new rule but with all the other parameters same as before (*ceteris paribus*).

In the first example (Figure 6) there are ten percent more opinion changes compared to the sequential model.

The best result is in the second run (Figure 7): the world rich of relations. The two lines overlap (even if there is a high variance in data).

A second simple rule coming from this analysis can be expressed: A synchronous communication among the agents increases their attitude to change opinion, which is at least ten percent higher.

The proof is the third run, in which again there is a higher result when compared to the asynchronous case.

MEMORY AND REWARDING

In this section the stress is on how the introduction of a simple kind of memory, based on past turns, can change the previous results This is one of the most simple strategies implemented in the original MG, though the aim is not the final result, be it win or lose, but the way the agents behave, i.e., change their original opinion, when their "mind" changes somehow.

Here a payoff system to reward the players in the minority is introduced. The memory is a list of length N (technically the same length can be used for all the agents or randomized, by using a range from 1 to 20). In each "box," the last cumulative

Figure 6. 100 agents and 500 relations

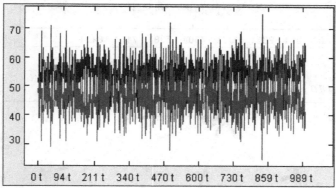

Figure 7. 100 agents and 5000 relations

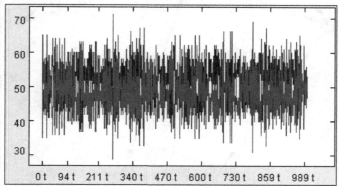

choice of the group to which the agent belongs is added. The value is normalized and is +1 if the sum of choices is higher than zero, or -1 if the sum is less than zero. The agent uses her/his memory by reading the list, and summing the last group choices. The agent choice will be +1 if the sum is lower than 0, meaning that the mode of the group is —1 and —1 in the opposite situation, or it can be random if there is no prevailing result.

A network graph is also introduced, in which the topology can be observed as the agents change their colours, red for "+1" and green for "-1".The relations (links) among the agents are bi-directional ones, and represented by the black arrows

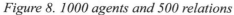

Figure 8. 1000 agents and 500 relations

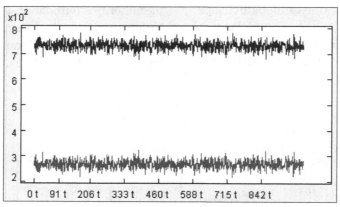

Figure 9. 10 agents and 10 relations topology

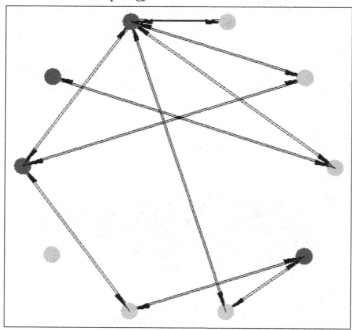

connecting the nodes. This means that if A can ask B, then B can, in turn, ask A. An example of this can be observed in Figure 9.

This figure depicts an interesting experiment composed of 10 agents and 10 relations, using memory and sequential communication.

Looking at the graph, we can observe that every group is in equilibrium. In fact, according to bounded rationality, each agent knows only the information about his own neighbours. Observing each agent's point of view, there are triplets Green-Red-Green or Red-Green-Red in perfect equilibrium, in which every agent respects the minority rule. The agents reach an elevated global optimum (Figure 10) of eight out of ten.

The stability of the system is strengthened by the steady distribution observed in Figure 11. In fact, the node that changes opinion is usually the isolated one.

The rewarding system counts one point for every agent that chooses a (local) minority option.

OPINION LEADERS: DECISIONAL POWER

In the attempt to create a more realistic situation, some special agents are introduced in the simulation. Normal agents change their mind according

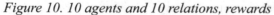

Figure 10. 10 agents and 10 relations, rewards

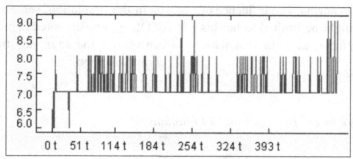

Figure 11. 10 agents and 10 relations, changed choices

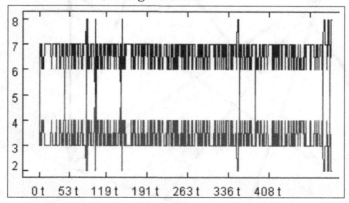

to a simple percentage rule, by computing how many of their neighbours have the same opinion. They then can influence in turn the others with the same system. Opinion Leaders (OLs) have a stronger influence and are less likely to change their own mind.

An OL is a person who is considered a credible source of information for others on a specific topic and who is sought out for that information. OLs are influential because they have certain characteristics which make them attractive to others. Whatever the reasons, OLs play a very important role in the community because their behaviours and values are emulated by others and they may be viewed as representing his/her community in many fields.

The key characteristic of an OL is that he or she is trusted to evaluate new information in the context of (local) group norms. The influence of each opinion leader might be limited to her/his own social network, or it may extend across many

networks. The other main features of an OL are that she/he must be:

- Sensitive to local environment and group norms
- Approachable and have good listening skills
- Perceived as clinically competent and caring
- Perceived as excellent evaluators

OLs are not necessarily are in official positions, early adopters or even innovators in their choices. That's why usually it's necessary to use *sociogram* techniques and surveys to identify them. It's therefore evident that OLs play a very important role in the formation of trends and decisions in a society.

In the simulation, some agents with the role of OL are implemented in order to see how they can change the aggregate trend in a MG with communication.

Figure 12. The network layer: 10 agents and 14 relations

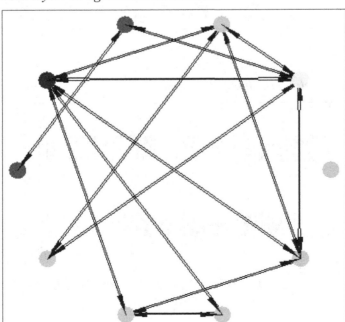

In the model, the OL is a minority agent with different thresholds. The basic idea is that OLs influence more people, and besides they must be quite sure about their decision. We can imagine she/he as an advocate or a supporter of a certain social or political cause. During agent creation, the two with the maximum number of links are selected. Their opinions are forced to be opposite, so that they become advocates for the two opposite causes in the game (binary choice). The weight related to OL ideas is also different; it's twice or ten times the original value.

An OL can change her/his own opinion, but usually this should be less frequent than for "normal" agents. At every step, she/he can randomly change opinion with a probability of 5 percent or if 87.5 percent (certainty index > 1,75) or more if his/her "friends" have taken his/her same decision

(this is a higher value when compared to the 50% + 1 of the normal agents, certainty index > 1).

RESULTS WITH OL

An example of results with OL is represented in a network layer of ten vertexes and fourteen edges, as shown in Figure 4. The minority agents are represented by red and green, as described before, in blue as the OL that chose —1, and the greens and in yellow the other one.

The OL opinion has a weight double that of the others. It's extremely interesting to observe the graphs of total opinions (Figure 13) and of OLs' opinions (Figure 14).

Both the minority rule (except for the very high boundary) and a very rare random event are

Figure 13. 10 agents and 14 relations: Agents choices

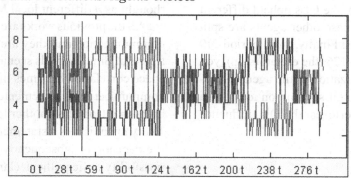

Figure 14. 10 agents and 14 relations: OLs choices

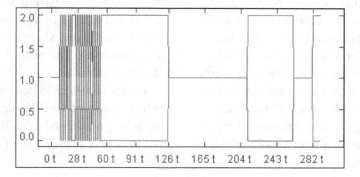

preserved. The initial paradigm is then conserved, while giving more realism to the model, e.g., in politics a common situation can be imagined with two main parties, of which OLs are supporters with different ideas. But in a dictatorship or in a period of "revolution," during which political positions aren't emerging, you can have that all the OLs support the same ideas, or that both continually change their opinions.

The correlation of the two series is 90.6%. So, in a small community, a person with many relations can change the aggregate "mood." This correlation could be an effective measure of OLs' influence on the population.

There are three main stylized structures/behaviours:From period 10 to 50 (the revolution/anarchy) you have a highly coordinated situation in which both OLs and almost 80 percent of the agents (8 out of 10) adopt the same idea. That implies an opinion switch the next turn.

On the other hand, from period 126 to 210 (the plain democracy), the OLs upheld different opinions, and in this case other agents are split between the two ideas. Finally, from period 210 to 260 and from 50 to 126 (the dictatorship), you can observe the polarization of the agents at opposite extremes of the OLs' common ideas. In a network with more vertexes, the Ols' influence decreases quickly.

LOCAL MINORITIES

Kauffman (1969), first described a disordered dynamical system that consists of N Boolean variables or spins in stable relation to each other (Kauffman Networks), used by gene regulatory systems (but also for spin glasses, evolution, social sciences, economics, and finance). Each gene changes its status (active or not) depending on some signals. Paczuski, et al. (2000) used that structure introducing a MG with personal limited information resources, but with a global reward mechanism.

Kalinowski, et al. (2000) describe a model in which agents who are placed in a circle are able to cooperate due to self-organization.

The term "Local" was introduced by Moelbert and Los Rios (2002). They depicted a one-dimensional, or square, lattice with communities of three or five individuals, each one interacting with two (four) nearest neighbours.

In Chau et al. (2004), a new model was introduced, called the Networked MG (NMG). It is a modified MG model in which all players can make use of not only global information but also local information from their neighbours that are disseminated through a network. The local information of a player is based on the choices of this player and his/her nearest neighbours on the ring.

In the model presented here, a more complex topology is used (not a simple ring); besides, the reward mechanism is not the same for all the agents involved; metaphorically this could be thought as n different local MGs.

All the previous works are based on a bounded communication and they are generally closer to a type of Small Worlds scenario. They show that space correlation becomes important. This local communication is implemented among the agents, but also introduces another level of information: Every agent issues a statement before acting and the decision is subsequently based on that. The possibility to lie in the declaration is not considered in this case.

Johnson, et al. (1999), while describing an evolutionary version of the MG (EMG), found that the introduction of partial information instead of global and diffuse news forced agents to take a decision based on inductive—rather than deductive—thinking. The result is a self-segregation of individuals.

Kirley (2004) extended this research in order to introduce small world connections in it. This spatial approach, and a small degree of disorder, lead to an improvement of system efficiency:

The agents can more effectively coordinate their behaviour.

Local evolutionary minority games (LEMG, Burgos et al., 2004) used an approach similar to Moelbert and Los Rios (2002) by introducing a Local perspective in global EMG model. It also found a dependence on network structure and a likeness with particular spin systems.

Finally, Namatame and Sato (2004) found coherent and systematic behaviours and a macroscopic pattern arising the strategic interaction of local rules.

In the literature there is a distinction between local and global models. A local model contains the global one as a particular case, where the neighbourhood is composed of all individuals (Burgos et al., 2004).

The greater advantage in using agent-based models is to examine the dynamics of a system at a microlevel, while the behaviour at the macrolevel is the aggregation of the micros.

The concept of local minority (LM) is introduced; the same concept was referred to as "relative minority" in a previous work (Remondino & Cappellini 2004). A LM is a group of individuals in the minority within a (partially) closed subset of the population. They also may not represent a global minority.

In Figure 15, a population splited into a chain of triplets (subsets of three individuals) can be observed. Their rewards depend on choices of neighbours only. In this configuration every agent could potentially be in one of the minorities. In fact five out seven agents are in different local minorities.

As a metaphor for local minorities, we can go back to a particular case of the MG—the bar problem quoted before. In that framework, local minorities can be represented by imagining that in the same pub there are many different rooms, with different features. For instance, one of them could have live music, the other one could be a smoking room, while the last one can be a no-smoking area. Of course, each room has a limited capacity so that the time spent there is enjoyable up to a certain threshold. So, it's advisable that the total amount of people is divided into local minorities (rooms), to make the time enjoyable for [an optimum number] many of them.

This perspective drives us towards some important considerations:

- The centrality of an exam at micro (meso) level of agent communities, instead of one of the total population, in order to understand the system dynamics.
- The representation of a bounded (partial) knowledge of the world. Is this an egoistic view? Is it important to be happier than my neighbours?
- Could this be an useful framework to study "word of mouth" or NIMBY (Not In My Backyard!) problems?

Figure 15. local minorities

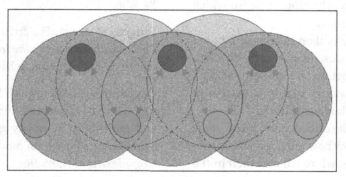

- The cumulative rewards for the individuals in the minority (minorities) could be greater than half of the number of agents: this means than more than one half of the population (the majority) is included in the local minorities.

CONCLUSION

While the original MG states that the agents involved must take a decision based on the historical data, their own experience and the forecasts about what the others will choose, in this chapter a form of communication of individual statements among them is introduced in order to see how the decision process would change. The stress here is not on the decision taken, be it the best or the worst, but on how the agents can change their decision when they are linked into a social network; in particular, this could be an empiric proof to a common sense rule: With a fixed number of agents, the more the links, the higher the probability to change opinion. An agent-based simulation was built, some real world parameters were tested, and the obtained results have been analyzed.

Two different communication protocols were employed among the agents: asynchronous and the more realistic synchronous, in order to see how this could affect the way the agents changed their opinions. Using the synchronous communication, the one in which an agent communicates with all others linked with him or her at the same time, the attitude to change opinion is at least 10 percent higher than in the asynchronous case, in which the agents act sequentially.

A sort of memory is then introduced, based on the past experiences, to act as a selection mechanism. In conjunction with communication, the thus composed simple cognitive system of agents creates local stable equilibria.

The framework described here gives some interesting results about how a network of connections among the agents who exchange their initial statement about a binary decision can change the way the aggregate behaves. In addition, other communication protocols can be analyzed using this framework.

Some specific agents were introduced lastly, called "Opinion Leaders" (OL), whose influence is higher than that of normal entities. In the real world an OL is a person who is considered a credible source of information for others on a specific topic and is sought out for that information. In this model, the agents defined as OLs are somehow special, in the sense that their opinion is "stronger" than the others', and is less subject to external influences. From the results, it emerges that in a small community, a person with many relations can change the aggregate "mood." This correlation could be an effective measure of an OL's influence on the population. By observing the results, a stylized political metaphor was introduced by identifying periods of "revolution/anarchy," "democracy," and "dictatorship" in the aggregate trend of decision making. This is, of course, just one of the many possible interpretations of the model presented model; for instance, the OLs can be thought of as the testimonials for some advertising campaign or advocates for a social cause, and so on.

REFERENCES

Arthur, W.B. (1994). Inductive reasoning, bounded rationality and the bar problem. *American Economics Association Papers and Proceedings 84*, 406.

Burgos, E., Ceva, H., & Perazzo, R.P.J. (2004). *Order and disorder in the local evolutionary minority game,* preprint, arXiv:cond-mat/0401363

Cappellini, A., & Lamieri, M. (2007). Industrial sectors dynamic study through a multichoice and multi-layer minority game formalism: An agent based simulation model. *Journal of Social Complexity, 3*(1), 85-96.

Challet, D., & Zhang, Y.C. (1997). Emergence of cooperation and organization in an evolutionary game, *Physica* A,*246*, 407.

Chau, H.F., Chow, F.K., Ho, H. (2004). Minority game with peer pressure. *Physica A*, Volume 332, 483-495, preprint, http://arxiv.org/PS_cache/cond-mat/pdf/0307/0307556.pdf

Gilbert, N.,& Terna, P. (2000). How to build and use agent-based models in social science, *Mind & Society, 1*, 57-72.

Johnson, N.F., Hui, P.M., Jonson, R., & Lo, T.S. (1999). Self-organized segregation within an evolving population. *Physical Review Letters, 82*(16), 3360.

Kalinowski, T., Schuklz, H.-J., & Briese, M. (2000). Cooperation in the minority game with local information. *Physica A, 277*, 502-508.

Kauffman, S.A. (1969), Metabolic stability and epigenesis in randomly constructed genetic nets. *Journal of Theoretical Biology, 22*, 434-467.

Kirley. M. (2004). Evolutionary minority games with small-world interactions. In D.G. Green, et al. (Eds.), *Proceedings of the 8th Asia Pacific Symposium on Intelligent and Evolutionary Systems* (to appear).

Laumann, E.O., et al. (1978). Community structure of interorganizational linkages. *Annual Review of Sociology, 4*, 455-484.

Mataric, M.J. (1995). Issues and approaches in the design of collective autonomous agents. *Robotics and Autonomous Systems, 16*(2-4), 321-331.

Moelbert, S., & De Los Rios, P. (2002). The local minority game. *Physica A, 302*, 217-227.

Morgenstern, O., & von Neumann, J. (1944). *Theory of games and economic behavior.* Princeton University Press.

Namatame, A., & Sato, H. (2004). Localized minority games and emergence of efficient dynamic order. *Lecture notes in economics and mathematical systems* (Vol. 550, pp. 71-86). Springer.

Ostrom, T. (1988). Computer simulation: The third symbol system. *Journal of Experimental Social Psychology*, 24, 381-392.

Paczuski, M., & Bassler, K.E. (2000). Self-organized networks of competing Boolean agents. *Physical Review Letters, 84*(14).

Rice, J.J., Stolovitzky, G., Tu, Y., & de Tombe, P.P. (2003). Ising model of cardiac thin filament activation with nearest-neighbor cooperative interactions. *Biophysical Journal, 84*, 897-909.

Remondino, M. (2003). Emergence of self organization and search for optimal enterprise structure: *AI evolutionary methods applied to ABPS, ESS03 proceedings*, SCS Europ. Publishing House.

Remondino, M., & Cappellini, A. (2004). Minority rule applied to multiple agents linked into a social network with communication and memory. *Wild@ACE 2004 proceedings*.

Remondino, M., & Cappellini, A. (2004). *Minority game with communication: An agent based model*. In SCS European Publishing House, editor, Simulation in Industry 2004, pages 155-160.

Remondino, M., & Cappellini, A. (2005). Influence of opinion leadership and communication in a minority game: An agent based simulation. In *ESSA 2005 proceedings* (pp. 239-246).

Sonnessa, M. (2004). *JAS 1.0: New features*. Oral presentation at the SwarmFest2004 conference, May 9-11.

Stauffer, D., Sousa, A.O., & Moss De Oliveira, S. (2000). Generalization to square lattice of Sznajd sociophysics model. *International Journal of Modern Physics C, 11*(6), 1239-1245. Available at http://www.ica1.uni-stuttgart.de/~sousa/papers/sznajd1.pdf

Stauffer, D. (2001). Monte Carlo simulations of Sznajd models. *Journal of Artificial Societies and*

Social Simulation 5(1). http://www.soc.surrey.ac.uk/JASSS/5/1/4.html

Sznajd-Weron, K., & Sznajd, J. (2000). Opinion evolution in closed community.*International Journal of Modern Physics, 11*(6), 1157-1165.

Sznajd-Weron, K. (2005). Sznajd model and its applications.*Acta Physica Polonica B*, 36(8), 2537-2547. http://arxiv.org/abs/physics/0503239

Troitzsch, K.G. (1996). Multilevel simulation. In K.G.Troitzsch, U. Mueller, G.N. Gilbert, & J.E. Doran (Eds.), *Social science microsimulation.* Berlin: Springer.

Woolridge, M., & Jennings, N.R. (1995). Intelligent agents: Theory and practice. *Knowledge Engineering Review, 10*(2), 115-152.

Chapter IX
Probabalistic Inference for Actor Centered Models

Gero Schwenk
University of Marburg, Germany

ABSTRACT

The analysis of relations between different levels of a system is a key issue in social science simulation. Here, I discuss the contribution of different modelling methodologies relative to this. Special emphasis is given to the formalism of "probabilistic graphical models," or "Bayesian networks," which are both advantageous for level transitory inference and integration of empirical data. Furthermore, issues of practicability and areas of application are considered. The argumentation is exemplified by the demonstration of a toy-application for which explicit level-transitory statements are inferred.

WHERE ARE WE NOW?
MODELLING ACROSS LEVELS

During the past years, agent-based modelling (compare Brassel, et al., 1997 and Weiss, 2000) has become the key methodology in the field of social simulation. Its success has been far reaching; my colleagues who do not engage in computational methods tend to use the words agent-based modelling (ABM) and social simulation synonymously.

In this chapter, I will be concur with at least some of the reasons for this tremendous success.

I usually do not forewarn the reader, but I will not discuss ABM's possibilities of informal, qualitative modelling. Rather, I will focus on examining how models can be set up to show emergent *global* behavior that is not coded in their *local* components.

Multi-agent systems (MAS) certainly do belong to this class of models. However, the modeler's toolbox can be stocked with a method which allows for more explicit theorizing in the micro-macro gap's domain. With the theory of probabilistic graphical models (compare Baldi & Brunak, 2001; Lauritzen, 1996; Pearl, 1988,

2000), I will introduce a formal calculus which may be employed to analyze the relation between the *component and system levels* of conception. A more extensive account on the metatheoretical aspects of this approach can be found in Schwenk (2004b).

It should be noted that acquaintance with the essential concepts of probabilistic micro-macro-modelling may be of considerable benefit for analysis of multi-agent systems, even if its formal apparatus is not employed.

THE SYSTEM'S ELEMENTS

As stated, the task is to find a formulation for the *relation of levels* of a given system. The first step is to define notions which allow us to tackle the problem effectively. I have chosen the concept of *identity of objects* to be the basis of my argument. Instead of directly asking for the nature of emergent properties, I start by examining how an object is *isolated* from its environment and is thus *identified*[1] as such.

Isolation by Causation

Interestingly, but maybe not surprisingly, *structural isolation* is the core idea of object-oriented and agent-based modelling. (I will touch on ABM's key aspect of autonomy shortly, after I have made the point on isolation clearer.) In both concepts, isolation of objects as containers of properties is accomplished by *information hiding*. As we know, this means that exogenously induced change of an object can only take place via a set of specific mechanisms, subsumed as its *interface*. With some refinement, this idea may serve as a foundation of a general ontology which is able to solve our problem, at least for practical purposes. What needs to be examined in more detail is the concept of *isolating mechanisms*. For example, in object-oriented modelling, these mechanisms are

allowed to be arbitrary functions, while in agent-based modelling, the set of isolating mechanisms is explicitly requested to map the autonomy of the agent's (more or less strictly defined) preimage.

Relating to the general problem, my choice of characteristics of the mechanisms in question is based on the following considerations: Since the concept of autonomy reflects the isolation of an object's properties from a certain set of *causal influences*, I will propose the notion of *causation* to be the constituting aspect of isolating mechanisms. *Manipulation* will serve as means to identify a mechanism's existence and genetic principle, which accords to a pragmatic epistemological conviction, so to speak.

Because of the importance of these considerations, I will give a short summary: Objects are isolated from their environment by a bundle of primitive causal mechanisms, with causality being understood in a manipulative sense.

The Concepts of Level and Autonomy

Now, having a definition of identity of objects, one can turn toward compounds of those. A first step is to decide on a definition of level. In accordance with the causal approach to identity, I will understand a *level* as the *set of all objects which contain properties that are connected by causal mechanisms*.

To locate a level's position in a specific *hierarchy*, it becomes necessary to refine the above criterion of identity in order to cover *composite objects*. This is accomplished by invoking the concept of *autonomy*: Given that a set of lower-level objects has a structure which exhibits relative environmental autonomy, aggregated *joint mechanisms* may be observed in it. As a result, a higher-level object may be identified by virtue of these higher-level mechanisms. It should be noted that within this scheme the *granularity* of mechanisms (and thus objects) is ultimately determined by what manipulations one is able to imagine and perform. Certainly a description of one type of granularity may be better than another.

In most applications, autonomy is fed into the model *ex ante*. Normally, the modeler has predefined ideas about the preimages of both element and system levels. However, subsets of the system may exhibit autonomy which can be identified by analyzing the *functionality* of the subsystems state-space.[2]

Level-transitory statements are at the core of interest in analysis of complex systems. However, it is important to note that those statements *must not be considered as causal*, since in this case the notion of level would be rendered meaningless. It is more appropriate to say that certain local states result from the dynamics of the system, which can be summarized *phenomenologically* by a level-transitory formulation.

Due to the setting of this article, the treatment of the above subjects can only be a sketchy one. For a more elaborate philosophical discussion, the reader is again referred to Schwenk (2006) and especially to Bischof (1998), Bunge (1979), Kim (1998), Pearl (2000), Sosa and Tooley (1993), and Stegmueller (1983).

GLOBAL BEHAVIOR IN LOCAL TERMS

After having introduced the ontology of the approach, I will discuss how it can be implemented using a formal calculus. As a first step, let's have a look at how *identity* and *aggregation* are handled in a selection of methods.

Agent-Based Modelling

As has been said, in an ABM determination of identity, or in reverse formulation, *system decomposition* is achieved by both information hiding and bundling of properties, with the latter being aimed at devising self-contained entities.

Aggregation, or *system synthesis*, is achieved by synchronized execution of the program formed by the set of coupled agents. Naturally, program execution is the default mode of inference and thus system synthesis in computer simulation. Examination of the model's trajectory, or it's behavior in state space, is the standard mode of discussing system behavior.

System Theory

Another major paradigm is *system theory*[3], which can be regarded as a variety of the theory of differential equations (compare Bischof, 1998 for an introduction for social scientists). Here, the systems components are *operators*, functions which transform input functions into output functions.

System decomposition in system theory takes place by formulating a system of equations. Usually, one ought to begin modelling the system by declaring a *black box*, with only gross input and output variables known. The black box is replaced by incrementally complex systems of explicit operator functions until a satisfactory granularity is reached. It should be noted that "object" is not a genuine term of systems theory, nor is causality: This allows for coupling of variables regardless of considerations about their location within a hierarchy of levels.[4]

The key strength of systems theory is that it provides tools for systems synthesis. Certainly the systems trajectory as a response to input can be computed by simulation. Moreover, the component operators can be aggregated algebraically in order to yield the system operator. Eventually, analytic propositions about system stability may be accessed by employing Laplace- or Z-transforms.

Probabilistic Graphical Models

The formalism I am most interested in is that of *probabilistic graphical models*, which is also known as *Bayesian networks*[5]. It is a variety of probability theory (compare Jaynes, 1974), which enables decomposed formulation of joint probability distributions. Graphical models are currently popular in artificial intelligence, bioinformatics, and epidemiology. I will postpone more detailed treatment until the next section and continue the comparison.

In graphical models, component properties are isolated by their structure of *conditional statistical independence*, which is encoded in a special kind of network, a *directed acyclic graph*. Most important is that *causal operators* for such independent structures exist (compare Pearl, 2000), connecting the above considerations on identity and level to formal inference.

The information stored in the components of the independence graph (the statistical associations between variables) can be considered *local* and may be aggregated to yield a *global* joint probability distribution (which is accomplished by the so called *chain rule for Bayesian networks*, as introduced below).

Perhaps the most significant logical aspect of probability theory is that it encodes *abductive* or *likelihood reasoning*. Abduction is the inversion of deduction: $A \Rightarrow B$, B is there, therefore A is more plausible; how plausible is coded in terms of probability. It can be interpreted that it is the possibility of *multiple causation* which corresponds to the use of probability in abduction. Thus, with joint probability distributions expressed by independence graphs, it is now feasible to employ abduction for reasoning about multicausality in structured systems.

One should note that a joint probability model represents the *local* dependence information *simultaneously*, and both abduction and deduction are employed to access the stored information in elementary or aggregated form.

A Sketch of Graphical Models

Now I want introduce the graphical model formalism in slightly more depth. The aim is to show how it can be used for level transitory inference in social science modelling. The starting point is a short description of the calculus.

Formalities

First, I will briefly review some basic concepts of Probability Theory. Then I will give a cursory introduction to the concepts necessary for building Bayesian network models. For reasons of brevity I will spare many details and especially the treatment of inference algorithms.

Decomposition of Joint Probability Distributions

The first concept to introduce is the concept of *joint probability distribution*. This is a mathematical structure where for every joint occurrence a statement is attributed a probability. Presumably you are familiar with the *fundamental theorem of probability theory*, which shows the equivalence of joint probability with a product of a conditional and a marginal probability:

$$P(a,b) = P(a|b)P(b)$$

This formula can certainly be extended for a joining of more than two variables, which leads to the *chain rule*:

$$P(x_1, ..., x_n) = \prod_j P(x_j \mid x_1, ..., x_{j-1})$$

Applying the chain rule allows for the decomposition of a joint probability distribution into a product of conditional and marginal distributions.

This immediately results in the following semantic advantage: The system of variables in scope can be described by their marginal distributions (as elementary properties) and their relationships in terms of conditional probabilities. *Thus, global probabilistic propositions can be decomposed into local ones.*

Graphs and Conditional Independence

Within the chain rule, indirect relationships between variables are represented explicitly. This prohibits the design of a network model of the system, since it would contain unnecessary connections between the marginal distributions. This can be avoided by accounting for *conditional independence*[6] of the considered variables: Two variables X and Y are said to be conditionally independent given Z if:

$$P(x|y, z) = P(x|z) \text{ whenever } P(y, z) > 0$$

Given that our network model should map the directions of the relations[7] and should furthermore contain no cycles (which is imperative since the elementary relations are to be represented simultaneously), we can find the set of prior variables in this network which makes a certain variable x_j independent of all its other predecessors. This set is called *parents of x_j or pa_j*. To eliminate all indirect connections towards x_j out of the directed and acyclic network, the *parents of x_j* need to satisfy the following condition:

$$P(x_j|pa_j) = P(x_j|x_1,..., x_{j-1}) \text{ for all } x_1,..., x_{j-1}$$
prior to x_j

This is the *Markov-parentship-criterion* for *directed acyclic graphs*. It is exactly this criterion which is employed to define the autonomy, or isolatability of an object with respect to certain *a priori* known properties.

The parentship-criterion can easily be applied to the chain rule. This allows for the decomposition necessary for local representation of a joint probability distribution by a directed acyclic graph invoking the *chain rule for Bayesian networks*:

$$P(x_1,...,x_n) = \prod_i P(x_i|pa(x_i))$$

This equation, together with the prerequisite of the representation of the conditional independence-relations between the marginal distributions via a directed acyclic graph, defines a Bayesian network.

Inference in Graphical Models

Reasoning in probability calculus consists basically of *projecting* a joint probability distribution down to subsets, which may be joints, marginals, or conditional probabilities. So the joint probability of two variables $(Y;X)$ can be projected towards the probability of the occurrence of a certain value y_i of the variable Y by summing over the values of X:

$$P(y_i) = \sum_{j=1}^{m} P(y_i, x_j)$$

This is also called *marginalization* and is denoted the following way, if applied to distributions:

$$P(Y) = \sum_X P(Y, X)$$

Conditional probabilities can be accessed by employing both fundamental theorems and marginalization:

$$P(y|x) = \frac{\sum_s P(y,x,s)}{\sum_{y,s} P(y,x,s)}$$

As outlined before, the strength of probability calculus can be seen in its natural ability to performing *abductive or likelihood reasoning* efficiently. The inversion of a conditional probability is accomplished by *Bayes' theorem*:

$$P(y|x) = \frac{P(x|y)P(y)}{P(x)} = L(x|y)$$

But as mentioned, a necessary prerequisite for all computations except abductive reasoning is access to the joint probability distribution. This may only be the case in the most seldom cases, since it grows exponentially with the number of variable values. Consequently, the local representation by a Bayesian network allows for the employment of local computations in order to gain results which may be intractable by common methods. This is accomplished by the various *inference algorithms*. For more information on this topic, the reader is referred to Baldi / Brunak (2001), Gilks, et.al. (1995), Jensen (2001), and Pearl (1988, 2000).

System Interpretation

With respect to application, systemic interpretation of probability models represents the core of this approach. It consists of a classification of possible statements with respect to the methodological considerations made above.

In short, the systemic semantics associated with graphical models can be summarized as follows:

- *Objects* are mapped on sets of random variables.
- *Causal mechanisms* are mapped on conditional statements.
- Expressions (conditional statements included) which contain only marginal terms are defined as *local*.
- Expressions (conditional statements included) which contain joint terms are defined as *global*.

Application of these semantics to level transitory analysis will be demonstrated subsequently. It is noteworthy that such a semantic could be in principle ported to a different calculus, with some function of *single variables* designating *local* statements and some function of a *set of variables* designating *global* statements. What would need to be examined is the syntactical basis of the notion of "causal mechanism" (as it is connected to the notion of identity) and the according mechanism of inference.

I do not present such a porting at this point. However, the reader may consider the idea when he or she is analyzing a model of their own, which is not a probabilistic one. To me, the above methodological ideas seem quite fertile, even if they are not implemented using the most powerful tool.[8]

Operationalization and Parameter Learning

It is unavoidable to mention another core strength of probability theory, namely its capability of modelling real world data. The reader may be familiar with the ubiquitous statistical methodology which is used for this task.

With *stochastic measurement theories* (compare van der Linden / Hambleton, 1997), however, there exist tools which are explicitly designed to parameterize social science models. A key aspect of those tools is the employment of maximum likelihood, or maximum *a posterori* methods, for inference of hidden parameters. Obviously these tools go hand in hand with a probabilistic approach to system representation, resulting in the possibility of very sophisticated operationalizations, which is normally not paralleled in agent-based modelling.

A TOY EXAMPLE

Now I will give a brief example in form of a reproduction of the so called *"Kirk-Coleman-Model"* (see Kirk / Coleman, 1967 and Schwenk, 2004b), which is nonoperational and simulates the dynamics of interaction and liking in a three-person group.

Brief Model Description

The theoretical basis of the original model are the "social behaviorist" works of Homans (1961), while the actual version is modified in direction of expected utility—theory and social impact theory. The qualitative structure of the model is like this.

Within every "agent" A_i there exist three types of (local) random variables:

- Its *Attitude*$_i$
- Its *Trust*$_{ij}$ to the other "agents" A_j
- The communicative *Action*$_i$ it will chose

The structure of functional dependencies B_{Ai} attributed to the variables of a single "agent" A_i is the following:

$$B_{Ai} = \{(\Delta Attitude_{ij}, Trust_{ij} \rightarrow Action_i),$$
$$n(Neighbours)*(Attitude_j, Action_j \rightarrow Attitude_i),$$
$$(Action_j, Trustj_i \rightarrow Trust_{ji})\}$$

For reasons of brevity, I will abstain from giving a detailed description of these functions, the reader may be referred to Schwenk (2004a), p. 45. However, it should be noted that these functions are implemented as discrete probability tables.[9]

If those dependencies variables are coupled over the agents, the graph of a timeframe of the model looks as depicted in Figure 1.

Higher Level

Subsequently, I will demonstrate an instance of level-transitory analysis, with the levels being defined *a priori*. (The reason for this is that the model has only a single attractor which is actor's indifference, or a joint uniform distribution over all variables. Being a constant property, it cannot supply a meaningful partition of the system's-state space.)

One possible definition of the system's global *property space* is given by Heider's (1958) *theory of structural balance*. The theory can be summarized in metaphorical terms as follows: If within a three-person group (a triad)[10] relations like "the friend of my friend is my friend" and "the enemy of my friend is my enemy" are fulfilled, the triad is said to be *balanced*. Otherwise, the triad is unbalanced, which leads to *cognitive*

Figure 1. The top line of nodes represents the systems composition at time t, the bottom line at time t + 1. The first three nodes in a line represent the action variables of the respective "agents" (indexed i = {1; 2; 3}), the following six are the trust variables for every possible interaction (indexed ij = {12; 13; 21; 23; 31; 32}), while the last three nodes in a line represent the "agents" attitude variables (indexed i = {1; 2; 3}).

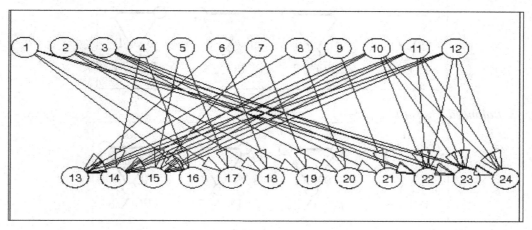

dissonance and consequently instability of the configuration.[11]

Within the model at hand, differences between "agents" attitudes have been mapped towards an evaluation variable. If this difference lower than a certain threshold, the evaluation of the respective other agent is positive (+), otherwise it is negative (−). Thus, the attitude space of the model has been mapped onto an evaluation space which is partitioned by balance theory into *balance states* and their *realizing configurations* (commonly called P-O-X triples), as depicted in Figures 2 and 3.

Level Transition

With this as starting point, one could arbitrarily ask how the immediate choice of an interaction partner (a *local* property) might depend on the balance state of the system, or on its realizing triad configuration (both being *global* properties).[12] As showcased, I chose agent 2 as a target of "top-down influences". This results in the computation of the following quantity over the possible configurations of its conditions:

$P(Action_{2,t+1} = x | Attitude_{1,t} = w, Attitude_{2,t} = y,$
$Attitude_{3,t} = z)$

The probability distributions have been aggregated to be mapped on balance states, according to their respective definition. This yields the following table, which describes the phenomenological top-down dependencies between balanced and interaction choice of "agent" 2, which is now labeled "O," according to balance theory schematics.

For interpretation the reader is referred to Schwenk (2004a), p.68. The eason for sparing the interpretation is the arbitrariness in choice of the threshold of the evaluation variable mentioned. Large parts of the interpretation are determined by this, which is one of the reasons to call it a "toy model." However, what is important for this demonstration is the *logical structure* of these level-transitory inferences.

PROSPECTS: EMPLOYING THE METHODOLOGY

I will conclude this article with a remark concerning advantages and handicaps of a probabilistic approach to actor-centered modelling. The key issue is the following:

Figure 2. Balanced triads (0 ≡ −, 1 ≡ +)

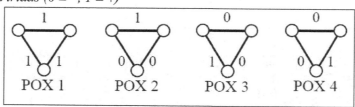

Figure 3. Balanced triads (0 ≡ −, 1 ≡ +)

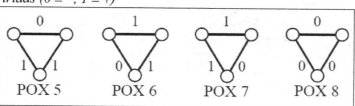

Table 1.

Class	$P_{mu}(Action_O=P)$	$P_{mu}(Action_O=X)$	$SD_{Pmu}(Action_O)$
P-O-X 1	0.5000	0.5000	0.0490
P-O-X 2	0.7273	0.2727	0.1080
P-O-X 3	0.5000	0.5000	0.2031
P-O-X 4	0.2727	0.7273	0.1080
P-O-X 5	0.3954	0.6046	0.0344
P-O-X 6	0.5000	0.5000	0.0421
P-O-X 7	0.6046	0.3954	0.0344
P-O-X 8	0.5000	0.5000	0.3674
Balanced	0.5000	0.5000	0.1887
Unbalanced	0.5000	0.5000	0.0714

Coherent higher level and level-transitory inference is not a matter of course in the analysis of structured systems. However, this inference is necessary since *comprehension of complex processes is always accompanied by the introduction of functional higher levels*. As shown, Graphical Models can be supplied with a precise interpretation which allows exactly for this.

Returning to the application, it may not be advantageous to employ a probabilistic approach under some circumstances. This may be the case if the model has a large number of components and/or has a long-range focus. Here, probabilistic inference may be simply too time consuming. On the other hand, the project may rely heavily on intuitive model formulation as, for example, a participatory modelling enterprise. In this case, a probability model may be harder to communicate than some alternative, e.g., a rule-based model.

The most frequent case may simply be that component theories of a model are formulated in deterministic language. Maybe an effort to reformulate those probabilistically is feasible, or alternatively a *post hoc* probabilistic model can be set up on simulation data. Even if this is not the case, I still encourage the reader to keep the above methodological considerations (and especially systemic semantics) in mind, while he or she is inferring conclusions from their own model.

REFERENCES

Baldi, P., & Brunak, S. (2001). *Bioinformatics: The machine learning approach.* Cambridge, MA: MIT Press.

Bischof, N. (1998) *Struktur und bedeutung: Eine ein fuehrung in die Systemtheorie.* Bern: Verlag Hans Huber.

Brassel, K., Moehring, M., Schumacher, E., & Troitzsch, K.G. (1997). Can agents cover all the world? In R. Conte, R. Hegselsman, & P. Terna (Eds.), *Simulating social phenomena* (pp. 122-138). Berlin/Heidelberg: Springer Verlag.

Bunge, M. (1979). *Treatise on basic philosophy Vol. IV, Ontololgy II: A world ofsSystems.* Dortecht: D. Reidel Publishing Company.

Gilbert, N., & Troitzsch, K. G. (1999). *Simulation for the social scientist,* Buckingham: Open University Press.

Gilks, W.R., Richardson, S., & Spiegelhalter, D.J. (Eds). (1995). *Markov chain Monte Carlo in practice.* Boca Raton: CRC Press.

Heider, F. (1958). *The psychology of interpersonal relations.* New York: Wiley

Homans, G.C. (1961). *Social behaviour: Its elementary forms*. New York: Harcourt, Brace and World, Inc.

Jaynes, E.T. (1974). *Probability theory with applications in science and engineering: A series of informal lectures*. Retrieved April 18, 2002 from, http://bayes.wustl.edu/etj/articles/mobil.pdf

Jensen, F. (2001). *Introduction to Bayesian networks und decision graphs*. Berlin/Heidelberg/New York: Springer Verlag.

Kim, J. (1998). *Mind in a physical world: An essay on the mind-body problem and mental causation*. Cambridge, MA: MIT Press

Kirk, J., & Coleman, J. (1967). Formalisierung und simulation von interaktionen in einer drei-personen-gruppe. In R. Mayntz (Ed.), *Formalisierte modelle in der soziologie*. Neuwied/Berlin: Luchterhand.

Lauritzen, S. L. (1996). *Graphical models*. Oxford: Clarendon Press.

van der Linden, W.J. & Hambleton, R.K. (Eds.). (1997). *Handbook of modern item response theory*. New York/Heidelberg: Springer Verlag.

Muehlenbein, H. (2002). *Towards a theory of organisms and evolving automata: Open problems and ways to explore*. Retrieved August 22, 2003 from, http://www.ais.fraunhofer.de/ muehlen/publications/Mue02a.ps.gz

Pearl, J. (1988). *Probabilistic reasoning in intelligent systems*. San Francisco: Morgan Kaufmann Publishers.

Pearl, J. (2000). *Causality*. Cambridge: Cambridge University Press

Schwenk, G. (2004). *Micro-macro relations in the Kirk-Coleman model*. Retrieved January 4, 2007 from, http://geb.uni-giessen.de/geb/volltexte/2004/1726/

Schwenk, G. (2006). Interlevel relations and manipulative causality. *Journal for General Philosophy of Science, 37*(1), 99-110.

Sosa, E. & Tooley, M. (Eds.). (1993). *Causation*. Oxford: Oxford University Press.

Stegmueller, W. (1983) *Probleme und Resultate der Wissenschaftstheorie und analytischen Philosphie; Band I: Erklaerung, Begruendung, Kausalitaet; Teil E: Teleologische Erklaerung, funktionalanalyse und Selbstregulation*. Berlin/Heidelberg: Springer Verlag.

Weiss, G. (Ed.). (2000) *Multiagent systems*. Cambridge Massachusetts: MIT Press.

ENDNOTES

[1] The reader may ask himself if this identification is meant to be a feature of "perception" or of "reality." This question cannot be answered with certainty. Of course some of our beliefs may prove more valuable than others and possibly be closer to "reality."

[2] Undertaking parameter studies in order to examine its attractor structure would be an example.

[3] It seems that, depending on the scientific community, "Cybernetics," "Control Theory," or "Signal Processing" would have also been good choices.

[4] If I remember correctly, this was something which astonished me when first looking at the design diagram of Jay Forrester's well known WORLD I model.

[5] I will use both terms interchangeably: I made contact with the topic over the AI radition of reasoning under uncertainty, in which the term "Bayesian Network" is common. "Graphical Model" is a rather statistical term which has grown faster in popularity.

6 More implications of conditional independence can be found at Pearl (2000), p.11, "Graphoid Axioms."

7 Usually one has to decide on the ordering of the variables by causal intuition. Nevertheless there exist methods to extract causal orderings form data as is introduced at Pearl (2000).

8 Admittedly, there may be pragmatic reasons to abstain from direct probability formulations, as lack of computing power or convenience of formulation.

9 A major reason for this has been restrictions on the availability of inference engines (compare the previous section) in line with project schedule.

10 Generalization to sets of triads is both feasible and common.

11 A memory hook for this rule may be that it parallels multiplication of signs in elementary algebra. "The enemy of my enemy is my friend" can be modeled by $(-) * (-) = (+)$

12 As stated before, it is very important to note that such top-down-influences *must not* be called causal, since in this case the notion of level would be rendered meaningless. It is a better formulation, that the top-down formulation aggregates over the processes of the system. Compare Schwenk (2004b).

Chapter X
Learning to be Altruistic

Gennaro Di Tosto
Institute of Cognitive Science and Technology, Italy

Mario Paolucci
Institute of Cognitive Science and Technology, Italy

Rosaria Conte
Institute of Cognitive Science and Technology, Italy

ABSTRACT

Evolutionary studies account for cooperation under the shadow of the future. But how can altruism spread without direct reciprocity? Learning from punishment, including criticism, is impossible in harsh environments where agents do not survive the rejections received. Imitation is indispensable, but what to imitate? Frequent behaviors are not necessarily socially desirable, nor is their fitness observable. In this chapter, agents meeting with infrequent but lethal food scarcity survive thanks to food sharing. Saving recipients from certain death, donations reduce altruists' lifespans. Results show that prudent donors, helping only when [they are] above the starvation point, are exploited by cheaters and are soon extinguished. The same happens with agents taking reciprocity into account, and helping only when their credits are turned off. Instead, agents endowed with dynamic goals (survival versus giving help) learn even the most unconditioned form of altruism, thus avoiding extinction. Tentative conclusions are discussed. Among others, dynamic goal-directed agents are autonomous entities learning even the most generous forms of altruism. Moreover, prudence is not necessarily more adaptive than unconditioned altruism; indeed, it may be self-defeating under the given conditions.

THE PROBLEM

The multi-agent systems literature (Shoham & Tennenholtz, 1992) and that of the social scientific realm point to the role of social learning in the establishment of useful social behaviors and laws. Agents learn to cooperate (Axelrod, 1997) in dyadic repeated interactions by mirroring each other's behavior. Consider as an example Axelrod's highly influential experiments with strategies of the family of Tit-for-Tat, TFT. Under the "shadow of the future" (future interaction) and in a mild environment in which one can learn from experience, an altruistic behavior (a behavior with a cost for the performing agent, whose benefits are addressed to some other agent) can be an evolutionary fit, if reciprocated; but what about harsh environments in which help denied leads to a certain death? Learning from direct experience, e.g., from distributed social control and punishment based on reputation, is not always possible. In really harsh environments, agents that are denied vital help may not survive long enough to change their behavior. In such a case, direct reciprocity makes no sense: altruistic strategies cannot evolve through natural selection because altruistic agents die, if they are not reciprocated.

On the other hand, how about really open environments in which future interaction is unpredictable? Altruism is often the fittest strategy even without a shadow of the future, i.e., when agents cannot expect to be reciprocated. Often, in social life, a really generous, unconditioned form of altruism is needed (cf. the notion of strong reciprocity put forward by Bowles & Gintis, 2001). How can it be learned? Observing others and imitating their behaviors is not always a good solution to the questions: whom, and what, to imitate? The most frequent behaviors are not necessarily desirable and the fittest are not transparent (Chattoe, 1998).

Finally, the necessity of altruism, even of an unconditioned form, raises two questions: How and who can learn it? and Can it be learned? Is it compatible with autonomous agents, especially if these are meant as rational entities, maximizing their utility function? Or, does it require another model of autonomous agency, goal-directed rather than utility-maximizing (Vanberg, 2003)?

In this chapter, properties of individual members favoring the diffusion of altruism in artificial societies are examined. The main results of a theoretical and multi-agent simulation work aimed at answering the questions above are presented and discussed.

We took inspiration from food sharing among vampire bats as an example of altruism evolved in a really harsh environment where animals have no time for learning from punishment. Ethological data (Wilkinson, 1984), in fact, show that these animals are affected by infrequent but lethal food scarcity (death inevitably follows two consecutive episodes of an unsuccessful hunt). Since vampires are allowed no resource accumulation, they avoid extinction by sharing food. While reducing the donors' lifetime, donations save recipients from a certain death.

THE TARGET PHENOMENON

Vampire bats puzzled ethologists for decades, while at the same time providing evidence for the theory of reciprocal altruism.

This species evolved a rather unique form of food sharing, consisting of successful hunters regurgitating a portion of the blood ingested in favor of unlucky fellows. Apparently, the rationale of this behavior cannot be found in kin selection, since the average rate of relatedness among individuals living in the same roosts is rather low (around six percent). Instead, simulation findings showed that altruism allows the rate of survivors to rise up to about 80 percent of the initial population in one year, as opposed to the bare 20 percent obtained in simulated roosts where individuals do not help one another (Wilkinson, 1990). Sociobiologists interpreted vampire bats' food-sharing as supporting the reciprocal altruism theory (Dawkins, 1976). Simulations supporting an alternative interpretation—based upon group selection theory—have recently been run (Paolucci et al., 2003).

Whatever the biological rationale of vampire bats, this species offers a good target for modelling altruism because its survival is strongly interdependent with the evolution of altruistic behavior. However, our study was aimed neither at contributing to the sociobiological debate around altruism nor at promoting ethological simulation, however fascinating such an interdisciplinary enterprise may appear. We intended to explore altruism at an abstract level, and discover its underlying mental ingredients. Far from addressing the question as to what the real vampire bat mind is like, we address the question as to what type of agent model is required for altruism to occur, and, in particular, whether autonomous agents can learn to be altruist.

In nature, vampire bats live in roosts (cavities of trees), where they return after hunting and in which they reproduce and perform other social activities (nursing, grooming, and sharing food).

As shown by Wilkinson, bats ask for help when starving. Will they always receive it?

With perfectly rational agents, which maximize the difference between benefits and costs, this type of help should never be received because donations reduce the life expectancies of helpers. On the other hand, vampire bats that do not share food are bound to extinguish in a couple of years.

Observational evidence shows that what vampire bats give to their fellows is much more useful for recipients than it is detrimental for donors. For example, according to Wilkinson's data, even a donation leading to a small reduction of the donor's life expectancy (six hours autonomy), which is almost inconsequential for its fitness, saves the recipient from certain death.

This sheds light on a weakly rational, or prudent form of altruism, which is performed without taking too much risk. Prudent agents should donate only when they are far above the starving point, and can therefore afford a loss of autonomy.

According to a prudent algorithm for food-sharing, agents help fellows asking for help if (a) recipients are starving, and (b) donors have at least two days' autonomy. Otherwise, they will deny help. In fact, it would be thoroughly irrational for them to give more than they keep.

THE SIMULATION MODEL

Our simulations are based on the *Repast* platform. Bats and roosts are modeled as objects. In-roosts are allowed to share food and groom one another. No other social activity has been modeled.

Each simulation cycle includes one daily and one nightly stage. During the daily stage, the simulated animals perform social activities (grooming and food sharing). In the night, they hunt. Hunting is modeled by the chance of success; in accordance with real-world data, its default value is set to 93 percent. In substance, each night 93 percent of the population will find food to survive; success in hunting will give the bats two days autonomy. The remaining seven percent will not find food; two days of unsuccessful hunting in a row are enough to starve a bat to death unless it receives help (in the form of regurgitated blood). Vampires cannot accumulate food. Although the average lifespan of these animals lasts around ten years, starvation and death are a constant menace to them (Wilkinson, 1984).

As to daily activities, grooming has at least two effects in nature: Thanks to and during it, animals familiarize and check their respective physical shape. Since satiation causes body volume inflation, a lucky hunter may grow to almost 50 percent more than its normal size, as can be easily detected by any grooming partner. Likewise, a starving bat is also likely to be recognized. Bluffing would immediately be found out.

Animals are immersed in grooming networks, which are randomly activated at the onset of the simulation. The network nodes represent potential partners for grooming interaction. Each day pairs are formed by each animal choosing one partner among the in-roosts.

As in the real world, in our model grooming has the effect of increasing the probability of food-sharing among in-roosts: A starving bat will turn to grooming partners for help, and will avoid death if any of them is found to be full (having had a good hunt).

Actions

In the model, the following actions can be performed:

- **Groom:** The condition for this action is that two agents are sorted out from the same grooming network. Grooming allows for help requests.
- **Ask for help:** The condition for the application of this action is that the postulant be starving. The request will be addressed to one agent in the same grooming network, if any. Otherwise, other in-roosts may be addressed as well. The effect of a request will be either donation or denial. In the first case, the postulant will ingest some blood and gain some hours of autonomy. In the second, it is bound to die.
- **Donate:** The condition for applying this action is that recipient is starving. The effect is that donor's autonomy is reduced and the recipient's is increased. Donating, in accord with ethological data, is a nonzero-sum interaction: The receiver gains more than the donor loses.
- **Deny help:** The condition is that agent received a request for help by someone. The effect is the latter's death. In the prudent strategy, help is denied if the agent is not coming from a successful hunt. Cheaters always deny help.

Figure 1. Prudent strategy. Boxplot, number of living agents at simulation's end by cheating rate. Two hundred runs for each value of cheating percentage.

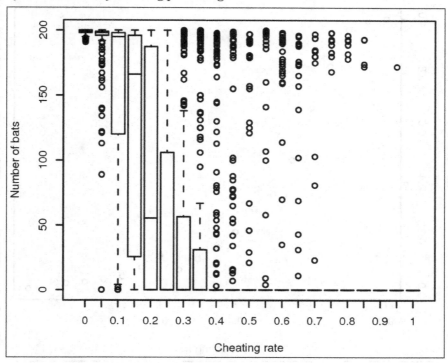

Robustness Against Cheaters

Wilkinson (1990) compared artificial data, drawn from his own simulations (without food-sharing), and found the rate of mortality among artificial bats inflated up to 82 percent, from a bare 24 percent, which occurs in nature. Our initial experiments reproduced these results (Paolucci et al., 2003). Apparently, then, altruism is vital for vampire bats.

The follow-up question then is, How about cheaters? What happens if some bats apply a strategy of systematically refusing help? Altruism is adaptive if altruists meet altruists. But what happens if they meet nonaltruists? Analytical models, e.g., the haystack models (Maynard-Smith, 1964), suggest that random assortment of altruists and nonaltruists lead groups to collapse.

Our simulations confirmed analytical conclusions. We simulated a population of prudent bats, with a variable percentage of cheaters (bats that never donate food). All simulations presented in this article are run on a single roost (all bats can interact with each other), starting with populations of 150 bats. The carrying capacity (maximum population) of the world is of 200 agents. Agents have lifespans of ten years and reproduce every 10 months, in accordance with etholgical data.

In Figures 1 and 2, the effect of a variable number of initial cheaters over global survival rate is shown. Figure 1 shows the boxplot of the number of living agents at the end of the simulation for 20 different values of the initial cheater/prudent ratio; for each value we run 200 simulations for about 30 years. In Figure 2, we show the success rate for the same set of simulations, defined as

Figure 2. Prudent strategy. Successful runs (number of simulations where population does not extinguish), by cheating rate.

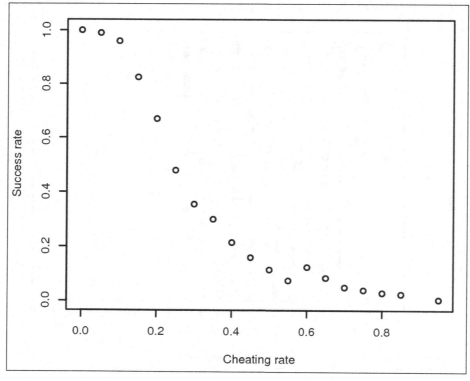

the percentage of the 200 runs in which at least one agent survives to the end.

Apparently, even a small number of cheaters leads the population to collapse. The population starts to decline as soon as the number of cheaters grows over a bare 10 percent, and extinguishes before these reach 40 percent. Sooner or later, depending on the initial number of cheaters, a mixed population is bound to extinguish. It is easy to see why: In isolation, cheating is a self-defeating strategy. Cheaters reproduce more than altruists, as long as they find any to exploit. As these die out, cheaters fall back in a no food sharing condition. Consequently, they will also extinguish in a couple of years.

Which ingredient is then needed for altruism to spread despite cheaters?

FIRST STUDY: CALCULATING RECIPROCITY

Reciprocity is considered the main factor in the evolution of cooperation. However, of the two forms of reciprocity—direct and indirect—direct reciprocity was argued above to be inapplicable to the present context. How about indirect reciprocity, then?

The abundant literature on this issue (Bowles & Gintis, 2001; Boyd & Richerson, 1992; Nowak & Sigmund, 1998) points to the effect of punishment, possibly based on reputation, on the emergence of indirect reciprocity. According to these studies, altruism spreads conditional to agents learning to reciprocate. Is this applicable to our scenario? Let us see.

When one thinks of it, the grooming network creates a familiarity as well as a reciprocity basin: Help giving allows animals to achieve credits, which will be extinguished if and when help is returned. A lucky hunt may last the short space of one night, and a fat hunter may soon shrink in starvation. Hence, it will be urged to go out for grooming in the hope to meet with a luckier

(and fatter) debtor. In less metaphorical terms, the grooming network facilitates re-encounters and therefore the extinguishing of credits.

Consequently, a question arises: What if animals are endowed with a memory of past grooming and food-sharing interactions, and of consequent credits?

Credit Network

We implemented a credit network by recording the number of animals that expired, the number of altruistic acts performed, and the number of credits turned on or off after each simulation.

Reciprocity is implemented thanks to this network. At any donation this is updated. In fact, either a previous donor is refunded—in which case its credit is extinguished and one link removed—or a new credit is formed and a new link is activated between current donors and their recipients. Whenever donors are reciprocated, their corresponding credits are canceled.

This credit network is investigated any time a request of help is received. In a more restrictive condition, only if no credit link is already active with the postulant, the agent will give help. Otherwise, help is denied. We found that this condition is too restrictive, and does not allow for population survival. In a less restrictive condition, shown in this chapter, help is denied only when the same postulant asks for help more than two times consecutively.

Agents search for potential donors within the grooming network. Only one trial is available. If help is denied, the postulant is bound to die.

One interesting thing about the credit network is that it can be passed on to one's offspring, which inherit parents' features and credits. Consequently, a given credit can be extinguished during the donor's life or after its death to the benefit of its offspring. Obviously, the more credits passed on to future generations, the higher the probability of survival of one's offspring.

Findings

As shown in Figure 3, the credit network does not improve things. Indeed, to investigate one's own credits when deciding whether or not to donate leads to a comparable number of cheaters in the population, with the same reduction of the global survival rate.

Apparently, these findings are nonintuitive: Turning off credits before donating again appears as a quite rational strategy. Looking at what effectively happens within the simulations, however, is rather instructive. The credit network has one main effect: It allows for lesser donations. Agents more often deny help. But this punishment is unfair,

as it penalizes not only cheaters but also unlucky altruists. Moreover, it is rather extreme: Postulants will die out and those among them who cheat will have no time to learn a more edifying conduct. Learning to reciprocate requires time, but in such harsh life conditions time is not available.

Should we conclude that learning is unfeasible? Or, perhaps, should we turn to a different form of learning leading to milder rather than tougher criteria for donations, including unconditioned altruism? Is it possible to learn such a form of altruism? Is it compatible with an autonomous agent?

We turned our attention to these questions in the successive study, which will be described below.

Figure 3. Prudent Strategies with and without credit network. Successful runs (number of simulations where population does not extinguish) by cheating rate.

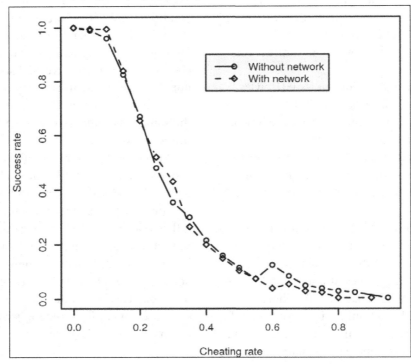

SECOND STUDY: DYNAMIC GOAL-DIRECTED AGENTS

In our previous study, altruists were invaded by cheaters, apparently because donations are discouraged in the credits network. Altruism conditioned to reciprocity is inapplicable to the present context where "cheaters stay, donors change" for the worse (help less). How to get cheaters to change? How to protect altruists, without discouraging donations? Rather than altruism conditioned to reciprocity, reciprocity ought to emerge from unconditioned altruism. Is this possible?

In this second study, we modeled autonomous (i.e., goal-directed) agents who learn to behave in an altruistic way.

We started with autonomous agents, endowed with altruistic motivations of variable intensity. Agents then range from the most to the least altruistic.

We then designed a learning mechanism so that agents become more or less altruistic depending upon internal rules. Noticeably here, autonomy is other than weak rationality. Unlike rational ones, goal-directed agents do not necessarily care about costs (Conte & Pedone, 1998). Whereas the prudent algorithm is a subversion of the rational model (performing an altruistic action at the minimum cost), the goal-directed one is not. However, both are autonomous.

Our agents are dynamic goal-directed entities, i.e., systems endowed not only with autonomous goals, but also with a mechanism for getting such goals to vary both quantitatively and qualitatively as a function of internal rules or heuristics.

Dynamic goal-directed action is an essential aspect of cognition (Castelfranchi, 1997; Conte, 2000). In a cognitive architecture, a goal is a highly dynamic mental construct which, thanks to beliefs, may be generated, abandoned, worked out, suspended, interrupted, achieved, compromised, etc. as an effect of its varying intensity.

In the simulation model at the present stage of development, the process of goal-dynamics was only partially implemented: Goals change with respect to their motivational force, rather than their representational content. Future extensions of this work will investigate qualitative goal-dynamics.

Agents are then modeled as goal-based systems, endowed with two goals of varying intensity—give help and stay alive—while their repertoire of actions (give blood or deny help) is kept constant.

Five plausible cases are derived. In the following table, the outputs of this motivational interplay as agents actions are given, together with mnemonic names for the five strategies; actions are characterized by the amount of autonomy sufficient to activate donation in hours (a full hunt gives 60 hours autonomy).

We then endowed agents with rules for modifying the values of their goals. For simplicity, we considered only those affecting the altruistic goal.

In particular two heuristics have been explored:

- **Action-based learning:** The value of altruistic goals increases or decreases as an effect

Table 1. Actions as outputs of motivations' interplay between goals (NG, SG). Each output is associated with a different strategy.

ACTIONS	NG	STRATEGY
Deny	< -2	Cheaters
Donate 6 at 48 deny at 24	-1	Prudents
Donate 12 at 48 6 at 24	0	Fair
Donate 24 at 48 12 at 24	1 or 2	Generous
Donate even at 12	> 3	Martyrs

of one's and others' actions. If one receives help, the force of the altruistic motivation increases, whereas it decreases if one gives help. This heuristic is apparently fair, but in fact is biased toward altruism. Independently from the agents' strategy, their altruistic motivations can intensify as long as everybody receives help. But only altruistic agents can see their motivations decreasing, because only such agents can give help. Therefore, we turned to more symmetric rules.

- **Credit-based learning:** After a given time interval (the average time in which at least one unsuccessful hunt can occur per agent, that is, about two hundred days), the agent's own credits are investigated. If help has been received within that period, the normative goal increases its strength; in the opposite case, its strength decreases.

What happens under the two circumstances? What are the effects of goal-dynamics on altruism, and more specifically on the fitness of the whole population?

Simulations have been initialized either by setting agents' goals to equal values (one strategy at the onset), or to all values (all strategies at the onset), or finally to extreme values, cheaters, and altruists (either martyr, fair, or prudent).

Findings

Simulations showed that different strategies—corresponding to different patterns of relationships among agents' goals (see Figures 4 and 5)—emerge, and their difference increases over time.

What is more interesting is that the most successful strategy appears to be the most altruistic.

Figure 4. Strategy differentiation with Action-based Learning. Averages of population divided by strategy. From left to right, initial populations of all Prudents, all Fairs, and all Martyrs.

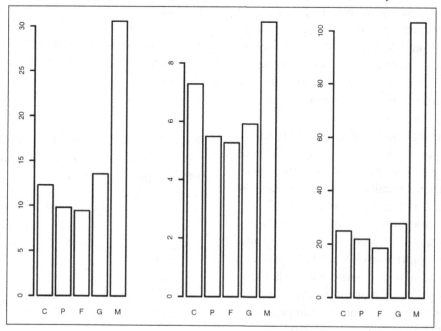

Whatever the initial strategy, agents learn to be more altruistic than anything else, and the population prospers.

The results of the different models explored are shown to be nontrivial. Indeed, prudent agents do better when they are modeled as rigid rather than dynamic systems: Comparing the results for 20 percent cheaters, given in Table 2, with the results obtained above, we observe that prudent rigid agents have a success rate of 0.67 without credit network, and a success rate of 0.655 with credit network. The opposite is true for unconditioned altruists. However, in general, the more altruistic strategies are always dominant and lead the population to an exponential growth, which is controlled in our simulations by means of a carrying capacity of 200 agents.

As expected, the comparison between the two heuristics for learning shows that credit-based learning is more symmetric than the other, which is instead slightly biased in favor of altruism. As a consequence, it is no surprise that altruistic strategies are less dominant with credit-based learning than with the other rule. Still, in both

cases, the majority of agents learn to exhibit an unconditioned form of altruism.

Obviously, the more altruistic the winning strategy, the more the population grows, which confirms the well-known law that altruistic populations do better than nonaltruistic ones. The question addressed in this chapter is whether unconditioned altruism can be learned and whether it can be learned by autonomous intelligent agents. Our findings seem to provide a tentatively positive answer to this question.

In short, altruism emerges and spreads in populations of dynamic goal-based systems, at least in populations with a relatively small number of agents where everybody can change either for better or worse. Under these conditions, agents learn to be altruistic more than anything else.

CONCLUSION

In artificial populations where food-sharing is indispensable to avoid extinction, the agent properties required for the spreading of altruistic

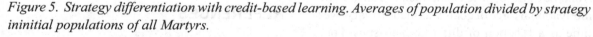

Figure 5. Strategy differentiation with credit-based learning. Averages of population divided by strategy ininitial populations of all Martyrs.

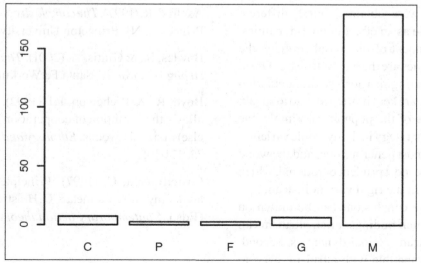

Table 2. Success rate per heuristic and initial population (20 percent cheaters). Initial populations of Martyrs (M), Prudents (P), and All five strategies in equal proportion (A).

HEURISTIC	M	P	A
Action-based	0,98	0,03	0,36
Credit-based	0,14	0,312	0,0

behavior have been explored by means of multi-agent simulation-based experiments.

Following ethological data, agents modeled as prudent donors, helping when far above the point of starvation, were found to survive and reproduce in absence of cheaters, but were unfit when assorted even with a minority of cheaters.

In a first battery of experiments, altruism conditioned to reciprocity was implemented on the prudent algorithm through a credit network. The poor performance of donors indicated the necessity to neutralize cheaters without discouraging donations.

Such a possibility was envisaged in a goal-based model of the autonomous agent, where this acts to achieve goals (either survival or helping) of varying intensity. Between-goals interrelationships give rise to different categories of agents, from the most to the least inclined to donate. The motivational force of goals was made to vary over time as a function of different heuristics. Four major findings were obtained. First, different strategies emerge as an effect of goal-dynamics. Second, independent of the initial strategy, the dominant strategies are the most altruistic. Third, cheaters do not extinguish nor lead the population to collapse: They are kept inoffensive, so to speak, by the dynamics of the population. Finally, the best performing strategy in the dynamic variant is found to be the most generous one, and the worst performing is the most prudent or rational, which performs better in the rigid variant instead.

Four tentative conclusions can be drawn on the grounds of such findings. First, altruism can be learned by means of goal-dynamics. Second, autonomy is compatible with altruism, even in

the most extreme form, provided it is modeled as a goal-directed agency. Third, prudence is not necessarily more rational than unconditioned altruism; indeed, it may be self-defeating under given conditions. Fourth, altruism conditioned to reciprocity does not necessarily contribute to the spreading of altruism. In the present scenario, it actually discourages donations. On the contrary, unconditioned altruism makes proselytes, thereby inducing reciprocity. Indeed, apparently the most altruistic strategies are also highly proselytizing. Consequently, they are learned easily or, otherwise stated, they are sensitive to dynamic mechanisms. Punishing cheaters is perhaps equally contagious, but it is bound to produce a world of cheaters. Donating, instead, will cause other agents, including cheaters, to change for better.

REFERENCES

Axelrod, R. (1997). *The complexity of cooperation.* Princeton, NJ: Princeton University Press.

Bowles, S., & Gintis, H. (2001). *The evolution of strong reciprocity.* Santa Fe Working Paper.

Boyd, R., & Richerson, P.J. (1992). Punishment allows the evolution of cooperation (or anything else) in sizable groups. *Ethology and Sociobiolgy, 13,* 171-195.

Castelfranchi, C. (1997). Principles of limited autonomy. In R. Tuomela & G. Holstrom-Hintikka (Eds.), *Contemporary action theory.* Kluwer.

Chattoe, E. (1998). Just how (un)realistic are evolutionary algorithms as representations of social processes? *Journal of Artificial Societies and Social Simulation, 1*(3). Retrived January 10, 2007, from http://www.soc.surrey.ac.uk/JASSS/1/3/2.html

Conte, R. (2000). Memes through (social) minds. In R. Auger (Ed.), *Darwinizing culture: The status of memetics as a science.* Oxford University Press.

Conte, R., & Pedone, R. (1998). Finding the best partner: The part-net system. In N. Gilbert, J. S. Sichman, & R. Conte (Eds.), *Multi-agent systems and agent-based simulation.* Berlin: Springer, 156-168).

Dawkins, R. (1976). *The selfish gene.* Oxford University Press.

Maynard-Smith, J. (1964). Group selection and kin selection. *Nature, 201*, 1145-1147.

Nowak, M.A., & Sigmund, K. (1998). Evolution of indirect reciprocity by image scoring. *Nature, 393*, 573-577.

Paolucci, M., Di Tosto, G., & Conte, R. (2003, October 3-4). Reciprocal vs group altruism among vampires. In *Proceedings of the Agent2003 Conference,* University of Chicago (pp. 543-554).

Shoham, Y., & Tennenholtz, M. (1992). On the synthesis of useful social laws in artificial societies. In *Proceedings of the 10ᵗʰ National Conference on Artificial Intelligence,* San Mateo, CA: Kaufmann (pp. 276-282).

Vanberg, V. J. (2003). The rationality postulate in economics: Its ambiguity, its deficiency and its evolutionary alternative. *Frieburg Discussion Papers on Constitutional Economics, 3.*

Wilkinson, G. S. (1984). Reciprocal food sharing in the vampire bat. *Nature, 308*, 181-184.

Wilkinson, G. S. (1990). Food sharing in vampire bats. *Scientific American, 2*, 64-70.

Chapter XI
Modelling of Water Use Decisions in a Large, Spacially Explicit, Coupled Simulation System

Andreas Ernst
University of Kassel, Germany

Carsten Schulz
University of Kassel, Germany

Nina Schwarz
Helmholtz Centre for Environmental Research, Germany

Stephan Janisch
Lugwig-Maximilians-Universität München, Germany

ABSTRACT

This chapter presents the purpose, the basic concepts, the implementation, and a scenario run of the agent-based part of a large decision support system for the water resources management of the Upper Danube basin, Western Europe. Sixteen process models from 11 disciplines in the natural and social sciences are integrated in the system. They use common spatial and temporal concepts to communicate with each other at run time. A variety of agents based on large scale empirical evidence serves to model the drinking water use of households. An example scenario run under global warming conditions shows the interplay between modelled water supply companies, households, climate, and groundwater resources.

INTRODUCTION

A Comprehensive Model of Social and Natural Aspects of a River Basin: The DANUBIA System

One of the problems of environmental decision making is the lack of a sound, coherent, and dynamic representation of social and environmental processes and the integrated projection of possible developments into the future. It is widely accepted that computer based decision support systems (DSS) can provide a useful basis to advance environmental decision making. However, such a DSS does rely heavily on a valid "core engine" which integrates the implementations of domain-relevant processes from the different fields and disciplines and their interactions. The GLOWA-Danube project, sponsored by the German Ministry of Education and Research since the year 2000, aims at providing such an integrated, spatially explicit DSS to enhance water-related decision making in the Upper Danube river basin under conditions of global environmental change (Mauser & the GLOWA-DANUBE project group, 2000, 2002; Ernst, 2002).

The river basin considered here has an extension of approx. 75.000 km², ranging from the Alps to the Bavarian lower plains, and includes parts of southern Germany, Austria, and Switzerland. About 10 million people are living there, and the basin includes high mountains, agricultural regions, as well as big cities such as Munich.

The DANUBIA system acts as the DSS's core engine and integrates 16 fully coupled process models from 11 scientific disciplines, ranging from hydrology to environmental psychology and from meteorology to tourism research (for a description of DANUBIA from a computer science perspective, see Barth, Hennicker, Kraus, & Ludwig, 2004). The system structure follows the structure of the domain: There are five components (Landsurface, Atmosphere, Groundwater, Rivernetwork, and Actor) as represented in Figure 1. Each component encompasses up to six models. For example, the actor component,

Figure 1. The five DANUBIA components as a UML diagram. The components Landsurface, Atmosphere, and Actor each encompass multiple models which are coupled among each other analogously to DANUBIA main components.

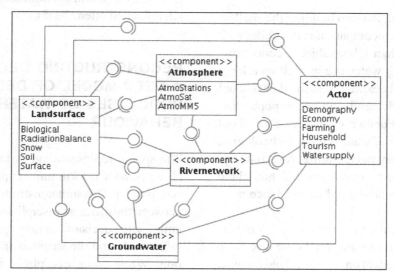

which gathers process models from the social sciences, is comprised of implementations of the household, demography, economy, watersupply, and tourism models. The components and their models are interconnected via a simulation framework which assures the communication linkage through interfaces, the setup and monitoring of simulation runs, the logging of model states, etc. Agent-based modelling plays a central role in the actor component.

In the following, the Household model will serve as an example to describe agent-based and spatially explicit modelling relating to domestic water use and water related satisfaction in the DANUBIA system. First, the empirical characteristics of domestic drinking water use will be sketched, followed by the description of a shallow model implementing the empirically observed relationships. Then, a more advanced, deep, decision making agent model will be presented together with its validation and a scenario run and its results. Finally, conclusions will be drawn and an outlook on the further research steps in the GLOWA-Danube project will be given.

CHARACTERISTICS OF DOMESTIC DRINKING WATER USE

The empirical data fed into building the shallow Household model encompass survey studies with up to now more than 1,400 subjects, concerning habits of drinking water use as well as a large amount of spatially explicit statistical data about drinking water demand and other population characteristics. Further evidence, e.g., about technical features of water-saving technologies, were extracted from the literature. As a first step, the data were used to configure 25 household types, differing in household size and income in a 5×5 matrix.

Some empirical characteristics of domestic drinking water usage are: (1) Water use is to some extent dependent on the household income.

Wealthier households have a tendency toward a higher per capita water demand, probably also due to a larger number of water using appliances, i.e., former investments; (2) Drinking water seems to be price elastic only to a small extent; (3) The larger the household, the smaller the per capita water demand. Our data show, e.g., savings through the more efficient use of dishwashers resulting in relatively less dish washing by hand; (4) There are clear seasonal dynamics, resulting in a higher water demand in summer due to more showering and garden watering; (5) There has been a steady decline in household water use since the 1970s because of technological innovations (use of more water-saving washing machines, toilets, and dish washers); and (6) The larger the agglomeration where the household is located, the higher its per capita water demand. This might be due to a relative difference in household structure (i.e., the age of its members) and subsequently to a different lifestyle.

In a second step we empirically investigated the water use behaviour of sociological lifestyles, using the ten Sinus-Milieus® (provided by Sinus Sociovision) and the corresponding spatially explicit data of Microm® (Micromarketing Systeme und Consult GmbH). The Sinus-Milieus® are not only commonly used in commercial market research, but also in environmental research (e.g., Kleinhückelkotten, 2005).

RECONSTRUCTING DECISIONS: A DEEP MODEL OF DECISION PROCESSES OF WATER-RELATED BEHAVIOUR

The spatial representation in DANUBIA is realised using a 1×1 km unit, a "proxel" (for "process pixel"). This unit constitutes a compromise between the different disciplines participating in building the decision support system with regard to the scale and the shape of spatial representation. While some disciplines have difficulties in downscaling their results to the 1×1 km unit, others have to upscale, and yet others (the behavioural sciences) have to translate from and to data that are usually oriented towards administrative boundaries.

From more than 75,000 proxels representing the size of the Danube river basin, 9,115 are inhabited. All of the model computations and all data exchange between models relate to specific proxels (refer to Kneer, Ernst, Eisentraut, Nethe, & Mauser, 2003). The Household model receives input data from the demography, economy, watersupply, and meteorology models during run time. Its output is mainly connected to the WaterSupply (water demand) and the RiverNetwork component (waste water), and to the user interface when providing data that are not used as inputs for further model computations but are presented to the end user (like household satisfaction).

In order to allow for the implementation of more complex decision processes within the agents of the actor component in DANUBIA, a generic framework for all actor models has been conceptualised, designed, and implemented. The most important elements of the so-called "DeepActor" framework are depicted by the UML diagram in Figure 2. Specific sensors relating to proxel information, to other actors, and also to simulated legal constraints, lay the groundwork for the decision algorithms to be defined by the specific actor model reifying the abstract base classes as provided by the framework. Decisions are made about the choice and instantiation of plans, themselves being chains of more specific actions.

The *DeepHousehold* model, as one of the implementations of a specific actor model, reconstructs domestic, water related decisions. Domestic water use has strong habitual components (much of the day-to-day water use of people is not, or no more triggered by conscious decision making), while there also are important conscious, deliberate decisions, e.g., when adopting water saving technological innovations or changing

Figure 2. A UML structure diagram showing the object classes in the DeepActor framework of DANUBIA. The DeepActor framework is an extension of the DANUBIA developer framework. The framework refines and adds (abstract) base classes aimed to provide a common conceptual and architectural basis for the development of agent-based social simulation models in GLOWA-Danube. Actual agent-based models are derived from this framework.

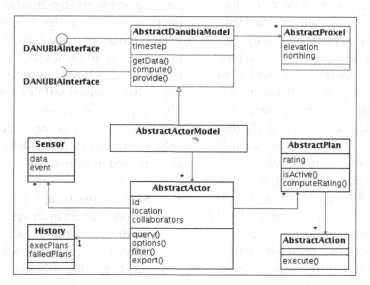

one's habits. The *DeepHousehold* model thus provides representations for both processes: a bounded rationality-based deliberate decision making mechanism together with an integrated habit component. Relevant decision parameters include the behaviour of other actors in the agent's network, the water price, weather conditions, environmental consequences of the behaviour, habits, and the individual history of the agent.

DeepActor models can be particularly useful if a realistic typology can be implemented that leads to a large variety of different behaviours. For example, households can be classified according to size, income, age range, or lifestyles. Within the DeepActor model concept, the actor type determines a set of core attributes, and preferences, possible plans comprising different actions to respond to changing conditions, to enable highly differentiated agent behaviour. All *DeepHousehold* agent types have different core attributes, but share the same set of plans.

Our typology introduces the household's attitude towards progress and modernization as an additional important dimension. The *DeepHousehold* agents are clustered in Sinus-Milieus®. The distribution of the ten milieus of the *DeepHousehold* agents is represented for each inhabited proxel.

As shown above, actors decide based on their inner state and the state of their environment, determined by physical parameters and by conditions resulting from decisions of other actors. Communication both between actors within an actor model and between actors of different models is essential for relaying information concerning the social and physical environment. Within the DeepActor models, this communication is achieved by means of data transmitted via sensors. In the current *DeepHousehold* model, the communication between different *DeepHousehold* agents triggers the diffusion of water-related technologies: Actors base their decision regarding these technologies upon their respective utility. The behaviour of peers within the social network

of an actor is part of the underlying utility function: The more peers within the network that currently have installed some technology A, the higher the utility for that technology A is. The relative weight of the behaviour of peers in the utility function depends on the agent type, with modern and educated agents paying less attention to the behaviour of their peers than actors with more traditional values.

In the *DeepHousehold* model, (conscious) decision making is implemented by calculating the subjective expected utility (SEU) of all the alternatives, which are plans in the set of known plans. In the case of habitual behaviour without any occurrence of special events (see below), no SEU calculation needs to be done and the basic habit plan is chosen. In the following paragraphs, the process of decision making in the *DeepHousehold* model is described.

DECISION MAKING

The different *DeepHousehold* agents possess individual profiles, which they obtain during the *initialising* step (Step 1). In the *DeepHousehold* model, the rational choice approach is refined by a situated component in every decision. In the *sensor query* step (Step 2), an agent perceives it's physical, social, and legal environment, which allows it to adapt to the current situation. In *options* (Step 3), an agent selects the plan set which can be relied on during the decision process. The subjective expected utilities are calculated in a *filter* step (Step 4), before the actions associated with the chosen plans are executed and the new values are *exported* (Step 5). Each step will now be explained in more detail:

- **Step 1 (*initialising*):** Decisions depend on the preferences in an agent's profile. There are different profiles for each of the implemented milieus, which are initialised at the very beginning of the model run. Every actor is assigned an ID, a location, and a set of collaborators (i.e., the agents in an agent's network). There is also information on the agent's age, its income, and the number of persons in the household (since agents in the model represent households).

The milieus differ with respect to the perceived importance of the environment, of prices, and of the behaviour or opinion of peers or significant others in the acquaintance or family networks. These values are inherited from the milieus and represent the individual components of the rational-choice decisions.

- **Step 2 (*sensor query*):** For the situated component of the decision, an import of data of the current environmental state is necessary, which is realised through the sensors (see Figure 2). The sensors also signal the occurrence of special events which may trigger further, more in-depth calculations. The agent processes data about air temperature, population, water price, and drinking water flags produced by the WaterSupply model (see Section 6). Events triggering a thorough decision making process are, e.g., a high air temperature or a drinking water quantity flag being calculated and set by the water supply model. A quantity flag can have four levels, where level 1 means "no shortage," level 2 means "news in print media or radio about a water shortage," level 3 means "specific appeals from a community official to save water," and level 4 is "manifest water scarcity and supply by tank vehicles." For the rational-choice calculations, the temperature, drinking water quantity flag value, etc. have to be transformed into index values between 0 and 1. For the quantity flag, the index calculation takes not only into account the current level of the flag but the also the duration of it having been shown on a specific proxel. A level 1 flag is transformed in an index of 0.0 while a level 4 flag is the upper

range of "no water" and therefore 1.0. Since people do not pay too much attention to a single newspaper article, the index value for the first occurrence of flag 2 starts with 0.10 and increases with the second occurrence to 0.12 and 0.15. Announcements from town officials like a major, or through loudspeakers from cars driving through the streets, are taken more seriously and therefore the index value starts with 0.3 and increases over the time to 0.4 and 0.5.

- **Step 3 (*options*):** Depending on the events that occurred, the set of active plans is generated as a subset of the plans known to the agent. Every plan defines an option concerning one kind of water use and its quantity or intensity. For example, the water use "shower" is calculated through the multiplication of the shower length, the shower frequency, and the shower flow of the household's shower head. In the current implementation, the shower length is set to six minutes as a mean that has been suggested by our empirical data.

In the following, we give some examples for the selection of active plans: The plan "shower frequency" becomes the goal of a thorough decision process if the water price is raised by five percent or more, if there is a drinking water quantity flag, or if the average daily temperature raises above 10°C.

Shower heads are appliances which, from time to time, have to be replaced by newer, most probably more efficient ones, so 1 percent of the agents decide every month about the acquisition of a new shower head.

Conscious decisions about the frequency of taking baths occur if the water price is raised, a drinking water quantity flag appears, or the temperature is very low (i.e., people like to take baths when its cold outside).

- **Step 4 (*filter*):** Every agent calculates its decision under consideration of its individual preferences, the situational circumstances, and the plan alternatives. For example, the shower frequency plan group consists of five plans (to shower twice a day, once a day, every second day, once a week, and not at all). These subplans differ in the values of their attributes entering the calculation. These attributes are the costs of executing the plan, its impact on the environment, and the fit of this plan to the milieu the agent belongs to.

These attribute values are multiplied with a corresponding factor, which is the sum of the individual preferences (e.g., the importance of the environment), and the situational circumstances (e.g., the numerical index of the drinking water quantity flag event).

• **Step 5 (*export*):** The actions of the chosen plans are executed and the consequential

state changes are exported to the proxel. The execution of multiple plans within one decision step is possible. Their aggregated individual consumption decisions define the dynamically changing water demand on the proxel level and as such, the micro-oundation of the macrophenomenon to be modelled. The total water demand for one proxel is computed as the result of the individual water demands of each of the lifestyle type agents multiplied by the number of agents of each type per proxel. After Step 5, a new cycle can start with a sensor query.

Besides the drinking water demand (and subsequently the waste water quantity produced by the households), the model currently derives the domestic water-related satisfaction from the drink-

Figure 3. A map of the drinking water demand in the Upper Danube river basin for one month as modelled by the DeepHousehold model in DANUBIA. The spatial resolution of the model is 1 km². One can distinguish the only sparsely populated region of the Alps with the Inn river valley in the South of the basin, and the larger cities further North, e.g., Munich in the middle.

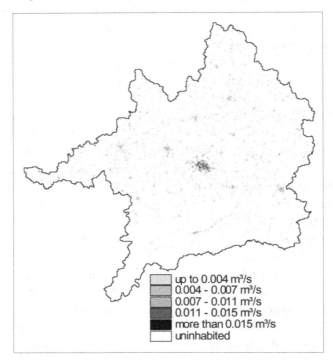

ing water allocated for household use in relation to its water demand. It is calculated as one minus the quantity flag index as described above.

VALIDATION OF THE MODEL

For the validation of the model, a threefold approach was chosen, relating to: (1) the comparison of the model's performance to the overall water consumption, (2) the consumption of the specific water use types, and (3) seasonal changes in temperature, respectively.

First, the modelled drinking water demand was compared to the statistical water demand. A snapshot of the resulting modelled drinking water demand in one month for all agents can be seen in Figure 3. The area with the highest water consumption per km² is the Munich region, located in the middle of the basin. In sum, the model produces, with 17.4 m³/s, a slight water demand overestimation of approximately one percent compared to the detailed reference statistic of the year 2001, including all inhabited proxels.

Second, the modelled fractions of the different types of water uses were compared to statistical data. The results indicate that the model on the one hand overestimates the water demand for personal hygiene: Our household actors consume about 65 litres per person a day for showering, bathing, teeth brushing, and hand washing, while statistical data (Abke, 2001) indicate a water demand of around 46 litres. On the other hand, the water demand for dish washing (model: six litres, statistical data: eight litres) and cleaning (model: one litre, statistical data: eight litres) is underestimated. Modelled water demands for washing machine, toilet use, and food preparation closely match statistical data.

Finally, due to a lack of monthly disaggregated statistical data for water consumption in Germany, the evaluation of seasonal changes in the water demand on a monthly basis is made on the grounds of a graphical analysis. The *Deep-*

Household model shows reasonable reactions to the modelled air temperature.

A SCENARIO RUN OF THE DEEPHOUSEHOLD MODEL

The following example and its first results draw upon two prototype DeepActor models, Water-Supply and Household, which were implemented using the DeepActor framework developed by the computer science group of GLOWA-Danube. These two models represent a crucial link between natural and social processes of water use via groundwater availability, groundwater extraction, distribution, and its use in the households.

Test simulations have been run and will be presented here for a 35-year (2000 – 2035), dry climate scenario[1]. Its aim is to test the functioning and interplay of the two models on the basis of a powerful climatic driving force. The scenario contains rather extreme climatic conditions: Based on a trend of increasing temperature of 4°C per 100 years (which conforms to the IPCC A2 scenario), observed meteorological data from the eight driest years between 1970 and 2003 were taken to provide the weather conditions.

The central function of the WaterSupply model is to continuously compare developments on the demand side with the present state of supply infrastructure and of water resources in order to satisfy the consumers, while respecting technical, economical, and ecological constraints. To this end, the WaterSupply actor model comprises 1,717 supply agents, which draw from over 8,000 sources. WaterSupply agents, as well as sources, are located on the proxels which represent their correct geographical location.

For the example scenario run presented here, only two contrasting milieus (post-materialists and traditionals) have been taken into account for the *DeepHousehold* model. The results of the run are depicted in Figures 4 and 5.

Figure 4. Driving forces (above) and modelled results (below) of the 35-year scenario run on the aggregated level. When considering the three main driving forces of air temperature, population, and quantity flags, the quantity flags show a clear shift towards water scarcity in some regions, while the air temperature shows corresponding seasonal changes, and the population decreases to a small extend. The water demand also shows seasonal changes. The water-related satisfaction is correlated to the level and the duration of quantity flags and therefore decreases during the scenario run.

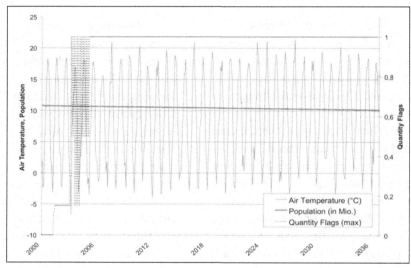

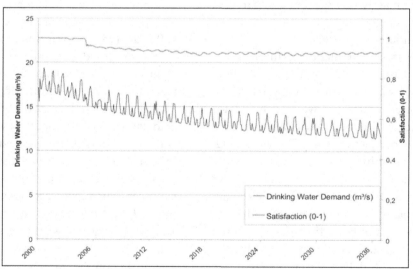

A typical signal in the water supply–domestic water demand chain passed between the Water-Supply and the Household models—are the so-called quantity flags, which are set by the suppliers and seen by the users. The flags inform about the quantitative and (in a later implementation version) qualitative state of water resources. The Household actors interpret these flags as if they were press reports or appeals to save water and react in accordance with them. The drinking water

Figure 5. Drinking water flags as produced by the deep WaterSupply actor model (above) and drinking water demand from the DeepHousehold model (below) toward the end of the 35-year hot and dry scenario run (shown here: June 2030). The domestic water consumers represented in the figure are those with post-materialist orientation. Areas of water shortage can be identified in the upper map (grey and black flags). They indicate the spatial extent and the growth over time of areas which will likely suffer water use conflicts in a dry Danube future, given a water supply infrastructure not radically different from today's. In these regions, domestic water consumption is reduced as a reaction to the shortages.

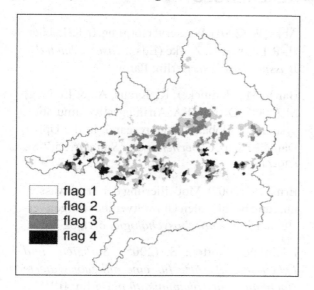

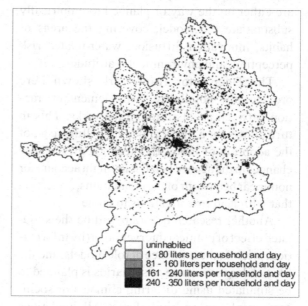

quantity flag levels used in the model are: (1) No problems reported, (2) multiple reports in the local newspaper about water supply problems, (3) a first public appeal to save water issued by the mayor, and (4) official restrictions for water use.

CONCLUSION

Rising temperatures, reduced precipitation, and shrinking groundwater aquifers: If this scenario is the Danube's tomorrow, it is necessary to have more precise ideas about the interplay between natural and social factors in the water cycle. How will a changing hydrological regime and water demand changes reciprocally affect each other in both space and time? Can more be known about

the probabilities of conflicts and their possible locations and causes? Tackling such questions is made possible in GLOWA-Danube through the integration of the socioeconomic components by means of DeepActor models of domestic, industrial, agricultural, and tourist water use and water supply. The scenario reported here is one step in this direction.

The model is able to reflect–beyond an estimation of future behaviour–phenomena such as agents' learning and changes in their habits, or deliberate decision making with regard to water shortage scenarios and the purchase of new appliances. Even upcoming technologies could be integrated with some knowledge about their characteristics.

According to our empirical findings, the Household model is being extended using all Sinus-Milieus® and thus integrating all our empirical data for habits and plan evaluation. The aim is to reach a high degree of precision of backcasting while having a sufficient theoretical depth and explanatory power. Thus, several studies are either on the way or planned to empirically substantiate the model, covering the areas of habits, innovation diffusion, water-related risk perception, and environmental attitudes.

The DeepActor framework shown here provides the possibility to implement interaction between agents through networks. This in turn allows for a fine-grained modelling, e.g., of the adoption of innovative technologies. Those changes in the agents' behaviour might account for nonlinear behaviour of the populations, a question that will lead investigations to come.

Another research question will be the simulated effect of political interventions (by information, pricing, the influence of role models, and the like). A large variance of scenarios is planned to be simulated using differing climates or socio-economic factors as driving forces. All simulations will take place with the coupled models within the DANUBIA system. The simulation results will be discussed with experts from the field and other stakeholders, in order to make adjustment and refinement to the modelled processes, e.g., flag calculation, plans, and actions. Discussions could also be fruitful with respect to defining and testing rules of allocation in case of dramatic water shortages.

It will be important to know how such modelled interventions will interact with quantitative and qualitative demographic changes that are to be expected in the region, i.e., a slightly shrinking and clearly ageing population. The model will be used to tackle questions of social sustainability, embedded in the framework of sustainability of the water cycle under conditions of global climatic change.

REFERENCES

Abke, W. (2001). Wasserversorgung. In K. Lecher, H.-P. Lühr, & U. Zanke (Eds.), *Taschenbuch der Wasserwirtschaft*. Berlin: Parey.

Barth, M., Hennicker, R., Kraus, A., & Ludwig, M. (2004). DANUBIA: An integrative simulation system for global change research in the Upper Danube basin. *Cybernetics and Systems, 35*(7-8), 639-666.

Ernst, A. (2002). Modellierung der Trinkwasser-nutzung bei globalen Umweltveränderungen–erste Schritte. *Umweltpsychologie, 6*(1), 62-76.

Kleinhückelkotten, S. (2005). *Suffizienz und Lebensstile. Ansätze für eine milieuorientierte Nachhaltigkeitskommunikation*. Berlin: BWV.

Kneer, J., Ernst, A., Eisentraut, R., Nethe, M., & Mauser, W. (2003). Interdisziplinäre Modellbildung: Das Beispiel GLOWA-Danube. *Umweltpsychologie, 7*(2), 54-70.

Mauser, W., et al. (2000). *GLOWA-DANUBE—Integrative techniques, scenarios and strategies regarding global changes of the water cycle (phase I)*. Proposal to the German Ministry of Education and Research. München: Ludwig-Maximilians-Universität.

Mauser, W., et al. (2002). *GLOWA-DANUBE –InTegrative techniken, Szenarien und Strategien zum globalen Wandel des Wasserkreislaufs (Phase II). Antrag auf förderung an das BMBF*. München: Ludwig-Maximilians-Universität.

ENDNOTE

[1] The run has been realised with the special efforts of the GLOWA-Danube groups from the geography department at the Ludwig-Maximilians-University, München (especially Wolfram Mauser) and from the University of Stuttgart (Roland Barthel and Darla Nickel).

Section II
The Empirically-Oriented

Chapter XII
Mechanisms of Automated Formation and Evolution of Social-Groups:
A Multi-Agent System to Model the Intra-Urban Mobilities of Bogotá City

Javier Gil-Quijano
Institut de Recherche pour le Développement, France

Marie Piron
Institut de Recherche pour le Développement, France

Alexis Drogoul
Institut de Recherche pour le Développement, France

ABSTRACT

In this chapter, we present a multi-agent system that models and simulates the dynamics of intra-urban mobility through the automated formation and evolution of both groups of households and groups of housing-units. We consider global rules of evolution instead of individual events to represent the evolution of both the population and the housing-stock. The moving mechanism is modelled by interactions between groups and urban-sector agents in a simulated housing market. We have tested this system on the basis of several census datasets of Bogotá city. The evolution of groups has been simulated over 20 years and compared to real data. The results of group formation and evolution mechanisms have been compared to classes produced by classical classification methods. Very good correlations have been found. The simulated population has been compared to real distributions of several Bogotá districts and appears to be close for an important number of them.

INTRODUCTION

Modelling a social system implies the intervention of dynamics at different space and time scales.

Unlike most multi-agent simulation examples, where only two levels of analysis are considered (the microscopic level where agents are located and simulated, and the macroscopic level where structures or emergent properties are analysed: Portugali & Benenson, 1995; Bura et al., 1996; Holm & Sanders, 2001; Bonnefoy, 2003), in social simulation, it is often necessary to consider actors at various levels with different temporalities and points of view. In the urban case, inhabitants, developers, and institutions have different points of view (space scales of analysis or action) about both what the city is and what phenomena are to be considered in a city. Their actions in what they consider as their environment generate consequences on various space and temporal scales. Consequently, when these types of systems are studied, it is generally necessary to consider more than two modelling levels, with heterogeneous agents interacting between them at different space and temporal scales. In certain cases, even more "artificial" objects are to be introduced, for instance abstractions (such as categories of individuals, social-groups, types of habitat, etc.) used to reduce the complexity of the simulation. These objects normally operate on scales located somewhere between micro and macroscales.

At this prospect, C. Mullon and M. Piron (Mullon et al., 2001; Piron et al., 2003), developed a model formalized within the framework of the game theory. They evaluate the evolution and redistribution of households, which change their housing inside the city. They adopt a synthetic approach: to establish intermediate levels of modelling localized between the geographical unit and the household. Thus, they used some multivariate structures of both social and habitat compositions on the scale of the city. But the model is not adapted to fluctuant structures. To work with that kind of structures, it is necessary to consider entities that can evolve, interact, appear, or disappear.

In this context, we are interested in implementing an automated constitution, evolution and behaviour (nature of their interactions) of agents which represent abstractions of reality. We call these agents, "abstract composed agents." Composed because the approach used to model their

formation is similar to the formation of groups or coalitions of agents: They are composed by a significant number of agents which are localized at a lower modelling level. Abstract, because they represent abstractions of reality. The composed agents act between them but also with agents at lower levels. Thus, there are interactions at several levels but also between several levels.

On this basis, the system presented here implements two complementary models: The first one allows the passage from microscopic level to an intermediate, or mesoscopic, level by the simulation of formation and evolution of groups of households and housing-units; the second one acts at the mesoscopic level and models the moving house process by the simulation of interactions between groups. In the first model, the evolution of groups is a consequence of evolution of both the population of households and housing-stock. We adopt a global approach to represent this evolution using general rules of evolution. Unlike traditional individual approach, used in particular in microsimulation (Orcutt et al., 1976; Clarke, 1996; Holm & Sanders, 2001; Antcliff, 1993), we do not consider individual events such as birth, ageing, marriage, or death. On the contrary, we consider global tendencies which describe the evolution of population and housing-stock in a synthetic way. Finally, interaction between the two models makes it possible to simulate the evolution of spatial distribution of a city's population over a given period of time.

GENERAL DESCRIPTION OF THE MODELS

At the microscopic level, we consider two types of micro-agents: households and housing-units. At the mesoscopic level, we also consider two types of meso-agents: groups of micro-agents and urban-sectors.

Groups are formed by similar micro-agents with respect to their sociodemographical characteristics. There are two types of groups: social-groups made up of households and groups-of-habitat made up of housing-units. Both households and housing-units are located in urban-sectors, spatial structures characterized by various functions (residential, commercial, industrial, etc.), their socioeconomical infrastructure (access roads, schools, hospitals, etc.), and their neighbourhood.

The macroscopic level refers to both levels: that of the city (set of urban-sectors) and that of the city planner who can control the flows of households, the habitat, and the relationships between places.

Our objective is to model the residential mobility in Bogotá city during a given period of time: from 1973 to 1993, dates of general censuses of population. To do it, we consider two complementary models:

- The first model, which allows the passage from microscopic level to mesoscopic level, models both the formation and the evolution of groups using two main mechanisms. The

first mechanism is based on a measure of difference between micro-agents. The second mechanism is based on the definition of evolution rules. This mechanism models the changes in the composition of population of households and housing-units.

- The second model represents spatial mobility as an exchange of groups of housing-units between social-groups and urban-sectors. This exchange is done via an auction mechanism.

Figure 1 depicts a simulation flow where the three fundamental mechanisms are presented. A more detailed description of these mechanisms is presented below.

FIRST MODEL: PASSAGE FROM MICROSCOPIC TO MESOSCOPIC LEVEL

The passage from microscopic to mesoscopic level is then done by the formation of groups of similar

Figure 1. Main simulation flow

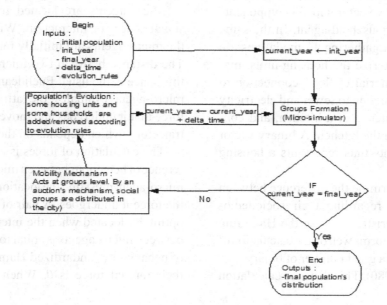

micro-agents. The micro-agents that we consider are reactive agents (Drogoul & Ferber, 1994). They represent either households or housing-units. They are characterized by p sociodemographical modalities. Micro-agents live in a two-dimensional interaction space. They move within this space under the influence of attraction/repulsion forces. These forces depend on a measurement of the difference between micro-agents. Each micro-agent modifies its location in the interaction space according to the attraction/repulsion force that it undergoes. Thorough explanations of the algorithms of group formation and group constitution as well as some optimisations are presented in Gil-Quijano and Piron (2007).

Difference of Behaviours Between Micro-Agents

Criteria selected to characterize households are: sex, age, birthplace, place of residence five years before the survey, level of literacy, activity, activity status of the householder, as well as the housing occupancy status and the number of people in the household. The nine criteria are considered as nominal variables (continuous variables are cut out into classes of variables values) that gather 34 modalities. A binary vector with 34 components thus represents a household-agent. In the same way, seven criteria gathering 16 modalities are selected to characterize the housing-units: material of walls, material of floor, connection to water supply, connection to sewer and electricity networks, the existence of a kitchen, and connection of water in the kitchen. A binary vector with 16 components thus represents a housing unit-agent.

In order to determine the difference between two micro-agents regarding their sociodemographical characteristics, we use the Hamming distance, which performs well on the calculation of distances between a great number of binary vectors (Hamming, 1980). This distance calculation

also allows the progressive introduction of new micro-agents within a simulation. We standardize the Hamming distance by dividing it by the number p of modalities. As standardized Hamming distance varies from *0* to *1*, it is possible to design a simple algorithm of group formation and to explicitly know the borderline cases of calculation. Different micro-agents have a value of *1* and similar micro-agents have a value close to *0*.

Attraction/Repulsion Force

There are several algorithms of group formation which implement an attraction/repulsion approach to represent interactions between agents. Most of them are based on social animals' behaviour, such as the work of Monmarché et al. (2002), where the formation of clouds of insects is adapted to data classification; or the work of Renault (2001), which uses the diffusion of pheromones to sort e-mails. Our algorithm is also based on an attraction/repulsion mechanism, but our approach is nearer to physical approaches than to social or ethological ones. We thus consider attraction/repulsion forces between micro-agents. These forces can be assimilated to electromagnetic fields. Micro-agents undergo these forces and move consequently.

Micro-agents are located in a two-dimensional space for interaction. Within this space, the micro-agents are initially randomly located. The distance between two micro-agents within this space is the usual Euclidean distance. Each micro-agent evaluates the attraction/repulsion force that it undergoes and moves according to a trajectory, which depends on the force.

The calculation of forces is based on the difference of behaviour between micro-agents. Each micro-agent must find the location that minimizes the force it undergoes. A pair of micro-agents is optimally located when the interaction distance between micro-agents is equal to their difference of behaviour (standardized Hamming distance); their mutual force is *0*. When the distance is greater than the difference of behaviour, agents attract each other. When the distance is smaller than the difference of behaviour, agents repel each other. At each simulation step, every agent determines the forces that it undergoes compared to every other agent. As simulation is executed, forces diminish until reaching a minimal value. In order to measure the global evolution of forces we calculate the average value of forces. We call this measurement the *energy of the system*.

Algorithm of Group Formation

Automated formation of groups of agents is not really studied in the multi-agent literature. Work rather refers to physical or biological objects (for example: hydrological structures built from drops of water (Servat, 2000), multicellular beings made up of single cells (Bonté, 2005) or e-mails sorting systems (Renault, 2001). In all of these works, the formation and evolution of groups

Figure 2. Group formation algorithm

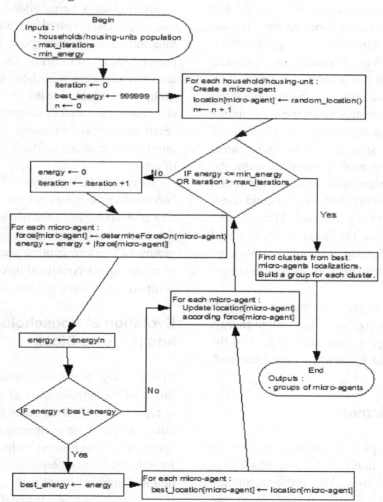

are performed starting from well-defined rules (physical or biological laws, keyword grouping). When groups represent abstract objects (like social-groups or groups-of-habitat), the conditions/rules of formation are difficult to define. We are interested in the definition of a mechanism of formation of this type of groups. In this way, we propose a mechanism of automated detection of structures which emerge as a consequence of interactions between micro-agents. Indeed, in traditional multi-agent systems, it is the observer who decides which are the emergent structures and studies them *a posteriori*. In our case, emergent structures are detected and agentified (reificated and instantiated) in an automated way. In this way, emergent structures become group-agents. These groups intervene thereafter in a dynamic way in evolution of the system.

We consider two stages in the group constitution process: formation of clusters of micro-agents, and creation of groups starting from these clusters. In the first stage, micro-agents form clusters as a consequence of their displacements. Displacements are the consequence of the action of attraction/repulsion forces. In the second stage, detection of clusters is performed. Then clusters become group-agents. The last stage is carried out by an algorithm of group detection that takes the distribution of micro-agents in interaction space into account.

The algorithm of group formation (Figure 2) is founded on minimization of the system energy. Minimizing energy is equivalent to finding the set of locations which minimizes the force each agent undergoes.

Evolution of Groups

Evolution of groups is a consequence of the changes of population and housing-stock over a given period of time. The group formation algorithm must take the evolution of groups into account. Population and housing-stock changes must be also taken into account. These changes are represented using evolution rules. To simulate the evolution of groups over a given period, we divide this period into years. At the beginning of the simulation, the algorithm of group formation is carried out on the initial population. At each time step, the population is modified by execution of the evolution rules. Groups are then updated to take these changes into account. Two situations are considered: on the one hand, disappearance of certain micro-agents which correspond to households and housing-units being removed by the evolution rules, on the other hand, creation of new micro-agents corresponding to households or housing-units being added by the evolution rules. The newly created micro-agents are located randomly in interaction space. Old micro-agents preserve their last location. Thereafter, the entire set of micro-agents update their location and groups are detected using the group formation algorithm. The number of iterations necessary to reach minimal system energy is smaller than the number of iterations used in the initial formation of groups.

To recall the evolution of groups between two consecutive years, we carry out a comparative analysis between the two sets of groups. We determine correspondences between a pair of groups of two consecutive years by comparison of micro-agents contained by each group and by comparison of each group's average profile.

Evolution of Household-Population and Housing-Stock

Traditionally, in micro-simulation models evolution of the population and the housing-stock is represented by local rules (Boman & Holm, 2004). In this type of approach each household and each housing unit evolve in an individual way. Evolution follows probabilities-based rules which define changes of state (birth, ageing, death, etc.). In a general way, the construction of these types of rules requires a great quantity of data. In our case, we have only data from two censuses. The construction of local rules starting from these two sets of data is inaccurate. Thus, we privilege a global approach. We do not consider local events, such as the household ageing. On the contrary, household population and housing-stock evolve in a global way following the execution of general rules of evolution. This approach introduces a simplification to model evolution of the population and the housing-stock. On the other hand, general rules of evolution perform better than locally-based systems to model complex dynamics of evolution of the housing-stock (role of the urban policies, economic dynamics like property speculation, practices of inhabitants like self-help housing, invasions of plots, illegal plot allotments, etc.). These rules are based on quotas of households and housing-units. Execution of each rule has as consequence the addition or suppression of households and housing-units corresponding to a certain profile. The user using several logical and genetic operators defines the profile and the quantity of households/housing-units to be added/removed. The additions/suppressions can be considered as disturbances that make the system evolve as a whole.

Description of Evolution Rules

Each rule is made up of four main parts: its *type* (addition/suppression), the *quantity* (*q*) of micro-agents to be created/removed, the *number of times* (*t*) which the rule will be carried out, and the *profile description*. Moreover, it is also possible to define the urban-sector, where the rule must be carried out. Since the housing-units are spatial entities, the rules, which operate on them, are necessarily defined in an urban-sector. The quantity *q* is an integer greater than *0*. The rule's type defines the action which is carried out, i.e., the removal or the addition of micro-agents. When action is "to add," a number *q* of new micro-agents corresponding to the rule's profile is created and added to the system. When the action is "to remove," *q* old micro-agents are selected according to their

difference (standardized Hamming distance) to the rule's profile. The *q* micro-agents whose difference to the rule's profile is lowest are then removed.

The number of times (*t*), which the rule will be executed, is equal to the number of simulation steps. A rule will be executed once by simulation step. By default, a simulation step represents one year. At each execution, the number of micro-agents that are created/removed is equal to *q/t*. If *q* is not a multiple of *t*, the number of processed micro-agents is rounded to the integer immediately lower than *q/t*. Because of this rounding, some micro-agents will not be created/removed in intermediate years. These micro-agents will be deferred to the final year; in this manner, exactly *q* micro-agents are processed by a given rule over the entire simulation period. There is an special case when *q/t*<1. In this case, instead of deferring the processing of all *q* micro-agents to the final simulation year, the rule will be carried out at each simulation step according to an execution probability. The addition/removal of the micro-agents is thus made in a gradual way over the entire simulated period.

The rule's profile is a set of criterion/modality couples. Following criteria and modalities shown in Table 1, a possible household profile is: [age = "26–45 years", sex = "male", activity status = "employed"].

There are three types of rules according to the profile's definition method:

- **Quota rules:** A profile is defined by an expression that is built using three logical operators (AND, OR, NOT). An expression combines modalities with logical operators.

- **Pseudo-random rules:** Profiles are built by the combination of descriptions of old micro-agents, using genetic operators. We use two genetic operators: the mutation operator and the crossover operator (Koza,

Table 1. Example of household description into three criteria and eight modalities

Criteria	Modalities		Criteria	Modalities
Age			Sex	
	< 25 years			Male
	26 – 45 years			Female
	45 – 60 years		Activity status	Employed
	> 60 years			Unemployed

1992). The user must define the mutation and crossover probabilities.

- **Mixed rules:** A portion of micro-agents is removed/added by execution of quota rules and another part by execution of pseudo-random rules. The use of pseudo-random rules can induce the creation of inconsistent micro-agents. To avoid these inconsistencies, the user defines integrity rules that prohibit certain configurations (for example: The householders older than 70 years should not be employed). These rules are created using the logical operators in the same way as the profiles of quota rules. Invalid profiles are not considered.

Automated Construction of the Evolution Rules

In order to validate the mechanism of group evolution, a simulated population's evolution must be as close as possible to real evolution. Thus, we conceived an automated system of generation of evolution rules. This system is based on real distributions of population and housing-stock of two different years. This system builds rules, which allows for the passing gradually from initial real distribution to the final one. Thus, suppression rules are built in order to make the initial distribution disappear, and addition rules are built in order to make the final distribution appear. The rules profiles are built starting from the real distributions. To do it, initially, every set of identical households/housing-units is detected within each distribution. A rule is built by set of identical households/housing-units. The profile of this rule corresponds to the description of the households/housing-units in the set. The quantity (*q*) of micro-agents to be processed by the rule is equal to the number of households/housing-units within the set.

Computer Model

The classes that represent the described model are depicted in Figures 3 to 5. Figure 3 depicts the various components, as well as the modelling levels. At the microscopic level, there are the *HousingUnit* and *Household* classes (specializations of the *MicroAgent* class). The calculation of the difference between agents is implemented in the *MicroAgent* class. At the mesoscopic level, there are the *SocialGroup* and *GroupOfHabitats* classes (specializations of the *Group* class), at the same level there is also the *UrbanArea* class. The group formation mechanism intervenes in the *GroupsBuilder* class.

Figure 4 depicts the group formation mechanism. We implemented the *AttractionGroupsBuilder* that is a specialisation of the *GroupsBuilder* class, the *ClustersDetector* class, and the *InteractionSpace* class. These three main classes implement the attraction/repulsion mechanism and the automated cluster detection process.

Figure 5 depicts the set of classes that implements the mechanism of evolution of population and housing-stock.

SECOND MODEL: PASSAGE FROM MESOSCOPIC TO MACROSCOPIC LEVEL

The group formation and evolution mechanisms act at the microscopic level. They model the automated constitution and evolution of social-groups and groups-of-habitats. These mechanisms make it possible to pass from the microscopic to the mesoscopic level. On the other hand, the passage from mesoscopic to macroscopic level is done by a meso-simulator, which models interactions between social-groups (groups of households), groups-of-habitats (groups of housing-units), and urban-sectors. The main objective of this meso-simulator is to model the mobility of households while localizing the decision to move at the group's level. Mobilities are defined starting from the housing supply and demand. Each urban-sector has vacant housing-units and sells them to social-groups. The main assumption on a household's mobility is: households search for housing according to a system of located preferences. The preference system depends on the social-group: Social-groups have a matrix of preferences by habitat and urban-sector, and a matrix of cost-of-moving between urban-sectors (Piron et al., 2003).

The meso-simulator implements an auction-based mechanism to simulate interactions between social-groups, groups-of-habitats, and urban-sectors. The social-groups and the groups-of-habitats are generated by the micro-simulator. In the meso-simulator, social-groups are buyers, urban-sectors are sellers, and the exchanged goods are sets of housing-units of a certain group-of-habitat. This system was originally presented in Gil-Quijano (2002). It was used to model residential mobility of Bogotá city. Unlike the original work, here the preferences matrices, the social-groups, and groups-of-habitats are built by an automated system: the micro-simulator.

Figure 3. Computer model: Main components and modelling levels

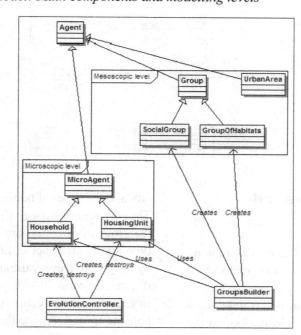

Figure 4. Computer model: Group formation mechanism

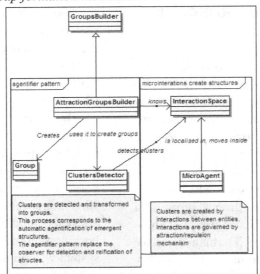

Figure 5. Computer model: Evolution of population and housing-stock mechanism

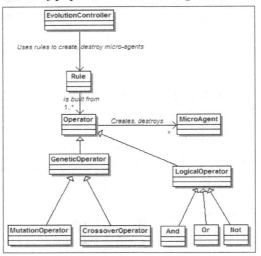

Matrices of Preferences and Cost-of-Moving

The user provides the matrix of cost-of-moving (cost-of-moving between two urban-sectors varies from *0* to *1*).

The preference matrices are determined starting from the distribution of the social-groups in the city and the types of housing which they occupy. The preference matrices of a social-group towards the groups-of-habitats are built according to the type and the number of housing-units occupied by the group in every urban-sector. For example, if a given group G1 occupies 50 housing-unitss in a given urban-sector A1, and if 30 of those housing-units belong to the T1 group-of-habitats and 20 to the T2 group-of-habitats,.then G1 has a 60 percent preference level (30/50) towards the T1 group and 40 percent (20/50) towards the T2 group in the A1 urban-sector.

Multihousing Auction System

In our system we consider global phenomena, consequently we are not interested in local moves-of-house, but in general moves-of-house for sets of households belonging to the same social-group. These general moves can be considered as flows of households (Piron et al., 2003) between the various urban-sectors, or as exchanges of sets of housing-units between the social-groups and the urban-sectors (Gil-Quijano et al., 2007). We present here a mechanism based on this type of exchange and which takes the housing supply and demand, as well as matrices of preferences and the cost-of-moving, into account.

To represent the mechanisms of the housing market, we use English multiobject auctions. Houssein et al. (2001) have studied this type of auction. In that type of auction, stocks of objects are proposed at the same time for sale. For this reason, this type of auction adapts very well to exchange sets of housing-units. We propose to model the dynamics of residential mobilities with a multi-agent system where the agents interact through English multiobjects auctions (moa) in a market of housing. We consider two main types of agents: social-groups (sets of homogeneous households) and urban-sectors (where social-groups are located). They exchange sets of housing-units of a given group-of-habitats through *moa* auctions. In that system, social-groups are buyers and urban-sectors are sellers. The urban-sectors propose sets of vacant housing-units of a certain group-of-habitats. The behaviour of buyers depends on demand and preference-matrices. Social-groups can subscribe to several auctions at the same time. The evolution of a given auction depends on both buyer and seller behaviours.

Calculation of the Demand for Housing

Demand for housing has two components: households without housing, and households that want to improve their current housing unit. The second component is calculated by each social-group. Each social-group tries to change the housing-units with the lowest preference level in each urban-sector with housing-units with a higher preference level.

Buyer Behaviour (Social-Group)

The choice of auctions to be considered by a social-group (a social-group subscribes only to auctions which propose advantageous housing-units) and its strategy (augmentation rate of submitted prices) depend on three criteria: the matrix of preferences, the matrix of cost-of-moving, and the level-of-need. The level-of-need represents the urgency (taking values from 0 to 1) of the demand. It is proportional to the group's demand. The level-of-need grows through time until the demand is satisfied. Each social-group chooses auctions which maximize its levels of preferences and minimize the costs of moving. As the level-of-need grows, the speed of price submission augmentations of the buyer is larger (thus the strategy is more aggressive).

In a given auction, at each turn a buyer has two possibilities: If the unit price that it proposes is the best among those submitted to the auction, it does not carry out new submissions, otherwise it increases the submitted unit price.

Seller Behaviour (Urban-Sector)

Each urban-sector creates a *moa* auction by group of vacant housing-units of a certain group-of-habitats. Each auction keeps a list of potential buyers with their required quantity and their suggested unit price. The seller opens an auction when at least two buyers have subscribed. New buyers can subscribe during the auction. The seller stops the auction when only one buyer is still submitting. Then the seller distributes the goods.

Migration

A migration takes place when a part of the households of a given social-group is relocated in a different urban-sector than it occupied before.

Computer Model

The mobility mechanism is implemented at the mesoscopic level. Relations and classes that intervene in this mechanism are depicted in Figure 6.

APPLICATIONS

Group Formation

We executed an optimized version of the algorithm of group formation (Gil-Quijano & Piron, 2007) on the 9,996 households residing in the central district "La Candelaria" of Bogotá city in 1973. This execution produced 11 social-groups.

Visual Evaluation of the Group Formation Mechanism

The sequence of images (see Figure 7) is the result of the execution of the group formation algorithm. It depicts the evolution of the distribution of households-agents in the interaction space. Each point represents a household. Initially, the households are distributed at random within the interaction space. As the algorithm of group formation is carried out, groups of households appear increasingly clear. The lower energy level is reached in iteration *296*.

The group constitution algorithm was executed on the configuration with the best energy level. This algorithm detected 11 groups of micro-agents that are depicted in Figure 8. Visually it is noted that some of groups (groups 3 and 4 for example) consist of several clusters instead of only one. Nevertheless, the algorithm found independent and well differentiated groups.

Group Evolution

In order to facilitate the evaluation of the group evolution mechanism, we utilized automated evolution rules. For this purpose, we used the

Figure 6. Computer model: Mobility mechanism

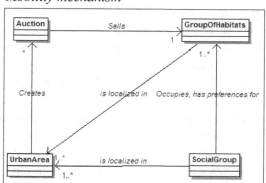

9,996 households of "La Candelaria" in 1973 as well as the *6,415* households of the same district in 1993. From these two populations, we built *,3058* suppression rules to reproduce gradual disappearance (over 20 years) of the household population of 1973. We also built *2,265* addition rules to reproduce the gradual appearance of population of 1993.

Figure 9 depicts the groups detected for the 1993 year. The distribution of household-agents has been produced from the execution of the evolution algorithm presented in Section 2. The starting point is the distribution in 1973 (Figure 8); household population evolves in 20 time steps. In Figure 9, groups have the same name as their correspondents in Figure 8. A new group appeared: Group 12. This group is the product of the detachment of a set of micro-agents from Group 3.

Description and Validity of the Groups

In this section we present a description of the social-groups. The clustering interpretation methods are generally founded on comparisons between percentages inside the clusters and the percentages obtained on the totality of elements to be classified. We measure the variance between the modalities of every cluster and the global modalities distribution. This serves to select the most characteristic criterion of each cluster.

Figure 7. Cluster formation in the interaction space– (micro-agents are household-agents)

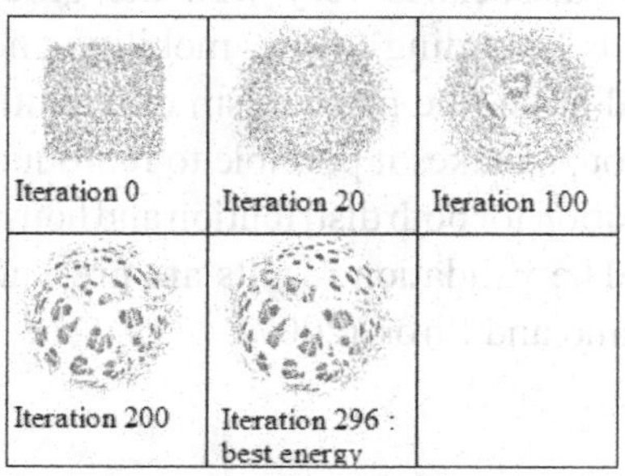

These statistics are converted into test-values that indicate the most characteristic modalities (Lebart et al., 2006).

Table 4 shows the most significant modalities of each of the 11 groups detected in the population of 1973.

Figure 8. Visualisation of detected groups (see Figure 7) Source: 1973 census data– CEDE Bogotá

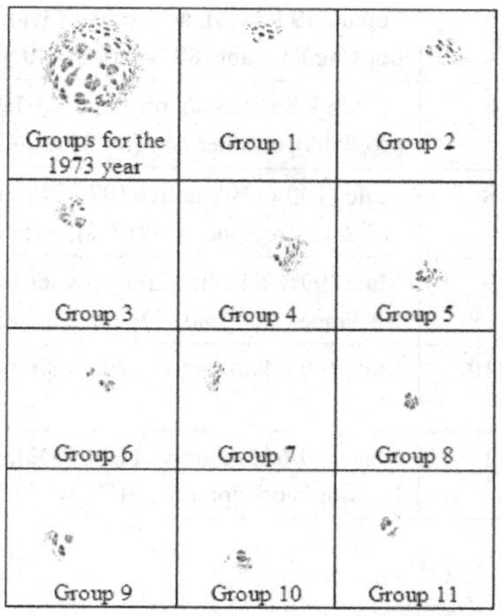

Figure 9. Visualisation of detected groups–1993 simulated data

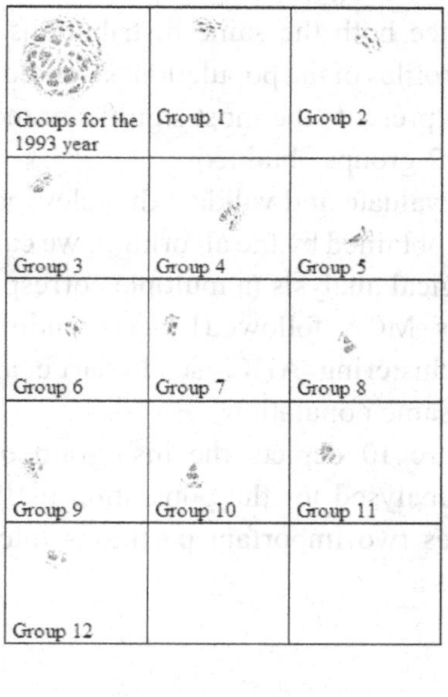

Table 4. Description of the 11 groups detected by the group formation algorithm according the sociode-mographical modalities of households in 1973 at "La Candelaria"

Group73 1 (7%)	Female (83/34%)[1], unemployed (98/22%), housing's owner (60/15%), another housing's occupancy (39/21%), +50 years (53/24%)
Group73 2 (13.3%)	Female (74/34%) , unemployed (97/22%), illiterate (10/4%), housing's tenant (98/64%), +60 years (19/11%)
Group73 3 (6.9%)	Another housing's occupancy (82/21%), Female (66/34%), 1-2 people/housing (53/36%) unemployed (33/22%)
Group73 4 (7.2%)	Female (92/34%), domestic worker (19/6%), migrant (36/19%), illiterate (18/4%), native (43/25%), housing's tenant (92/64%)
Group73 5 (8.6%)	Migrant (83/19%), search job (18/5%), male (100/66%), employee-worker (59/46%), domestic worker (13/6%), no native (95/75%), housing's tenant (99/64%), -25 years (32/18%)
Group73 6 (7.6%)	Female (99/34%), active (98/73%), no migrant (100/81%), employee-worker (66/46%), no native (99/75%), housing's tenant (88/64%), 30-40 years (35/25%)
Group73 7 (4.5%)	Search job (25/5%), migrant (78/19%), male (100/66%), employee-worker (69/46%), 1pers (35/19%), no native (96/75%), another act. (86/21%), -25 years (33/18%)
Group73 8 (19.2%)	Male (100/66%), active (99/73%), no migrant (100/81%), no native (100/75%), housing's tenant (100/64%), boss (13/8%), freelance (30/17%), +7peop. (21/15%)
Group73 9 (7.6%)	Male (99%/64), housing's owner (61/15%), native (72/25%), active (98/73%), no migrant (95/81%), boss (19/8%), freelance (34/17%), +7peop. (23/15%)
Group 7310 (9.9%)	Male (99/64%), active (96/73%), no migrant (96/81%), native (99/25%), housing's tenant (97/64%)
Group73 11 (8.2%)	Male (99/66%), active (100/73%), no migrant (100%/81), employee-worker (75/46%), no native (99/75%), another housing's occupancy (74/21%)

We proceed in the same manner to describe the 12 groups of households obtained after simulation of the evolution of groups. Simulation must reproduce both the same distributions and the same profiles of the population observed in 1993. Table 5 presents the most significant modalities of the 12 groups obtained.

To evaluate and validate the relevance of the groups obtained by the algorithm, we carry out a typological analysis (a multiple correspondence analysis–MCA–followed by an ascending hierarchical clustering–AHC– see Lebart et al., 2006) on the same population.

Figure 10 depicts the histogram of indice levels analysed for the population in 1973 that proposes two important partitions into 11 and five classes.

In the same manner, the AHC carried out on the population of 1993 proposes three partitions structured into seven, nine and 12 classes (Figure 11).

For 1973 and 1993, the algorithm produces, a number of classes and groups of agents quasi-similar to the classes obtained with typological analysis but offers weaker life-cycle related structures (Piron, 2005). On the other hand, the algorithm dissociates very well the groups of households according to sex, mobility, and origin. In addition, the mechanism of evolution of social-groups makes it possible to reproduce the 1993 situation for both distribution and household profiles. The validation results are presented in Gil-Quijano and Piron (2007).

Table 5. Description of the 11 groups detected by the group formation algorithm according the sociode-mographical modalities of households of 1993 at "La Candelaria"

Group93-1 (10%)	Female (67/34%), unemployed (96/22%), housing's owner (90/36%), +60 years (60/19%),
Group93-2 (10%)	Female (67/34%), unemployed (95/22%), illiterate (6/2%), housing's tenant (98/58%), +60 years (41/19%)
Group93-3 (5.4%)	Native (91/36%), housing's owner (89/36%), Female (66/34%), another housing's occupancy (10/6%), unemployed (33/22%)
Group93-4 (6%)	Domestic worker (10/1%), illiterate (18/4%), Female (87/34%), migrant (41/13%), search job (12/4%), no native (79/64%), housing's tenant (96/66%)
Group93-5 (6.5%)	Migrant (85/13%), search job (13/4%), male (99/66%), employee-worker (57/42%), no native (97/64%), housing's tenant (99/58%), -30 years (34/16%)
Group93-6 (7.8%)	Female (93/34%), active (99/75%), no migrant (100/86%), employee-worker (77/42%), housing's tenant (100/56%)
Group93-7 (7.8%)	Active (92/75%), search job (8/4%), male (100/66%), no migrant (96/86%), boss (15/8%), employee-worker (58/42%), native (92/36%), housing's owner (96/36%),
Group93-8 (15.8%)	Male (100/66%), active (100/75%), no migrant (100/86%), no native (98/64%), housing's tenant (100/58%), freelance (40/24%)
Group93-9 (4.3%)	Male (99%/64), another housing's occupancy (45/6%), housing's owner (55/36%), native (61/36%), active (98/75%), migrant (29/13%), freelance (55/24%), +7peop. (10/6%), 35-45 years (49/25%)
Group93-10 (12.7%)	Male (100/64%), active (97/753%), no migrant (92/86%), native (96/36%), housing's tenant (96/58%), -35 years (52/30%)
Group93-11 (9.7%)	Male (100/66%), housing's owner (89/36%), active (100/75%), no migrant (100/86%)), no native (100/64%), another housing's occupancy (17/6%)
Group93-12 (4.2%)	Female (95/34%), active (100/75%), illiterate (18/4%), no migrant (100/86%), no native (100/64%), housing's owner (85/36%), another housing's occupancy (15/6%)

Simulation Results for the Mobility Mechanism

A simulation was carried out with the first version of the "market based" system (preferences, matrices, social groups, and groups-of-habitats are static). The inputs of the simulations were: the census data of 1973 in Bogotá, the matrices of cost of moving, and the matrices of evolution of the population and the housing-stock. The simulation was carried out over 20 years. Comparing these inputs with the distribution of real population in 1993, the results of the population's distribution were validated. In a great number of districts, although the sizes of the populations are not exactly identical, the distribution of the simulated populations follows the distribution of the real ones. Figure 12 depicts the comparison between the simulated and the real populations for the "Puente Aranda" urban-sector for the group-of-habitats "housing in an unequipped zone." The distribution of the simulated population (white bars) follows the form of the distribution of the real population (black bars).

Figure 10. Histogram of the levels indices (AHC) from households of "La Candelaria" in 1973

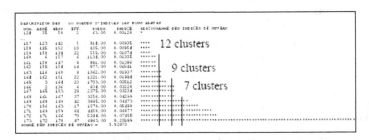

Figure 11. Histogram of the levels indices (AHC) from households of "La Candelaria" in 1993

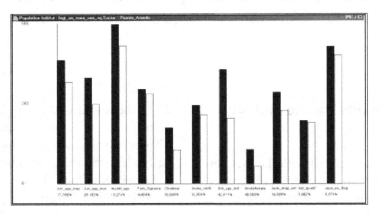

Figure 12. Example of mobility simulation results (Comparative graphic between the simulated (white bars) and real populations (black bars) for the habitat type "housing in an unequipped zone"

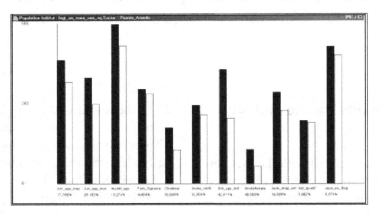

DISCUSSION AND CONCLUSION

The relevance of the obtained groups, their number, and their description, compared to the results of typological analysis, is satisfactory and encouraging. However, we do not have enough results to decide about the stability of the al-gorithm. Rather, it seems that the algorithm is sensitive to light fluctuations of the data (intro-duction of other variables and households). We are currently working to test its stability using a bootstrap method.

The market-based multi-agent system consti-tutes a good approach to model the interactions between groups. It allows building a simple and intuitive model. Some satisfactory results were obtained (Gil-Quijano et al., 2007). However, it is probable that it will be necessary to model new interaction rules, including the automated generation of rules starting from the results of the micro-simulator (the first step being the creation and determination of the evolution of the matrices as described in this chapter). This subject is in at the heart of our current research work.

Various optimizations were carried out in order to process a significant number of households. We thus hope to be able to use the algorithm to constitute groups of households and housing-units on the scale of the Bogotá city (it should be noted that the total population of Bogotá was 1/2 million households in 1973 and 1.5 million in 1993). Finally, we will carry out simulations taking the interactions between groups into account, in order to model the dynamics of residential mobility on the whole city over the period of analysis.

REFERENCES

Antcliff, S. (1993). *An introduction to DY-NAMOD–A dynamic population microsimulation model*. Canberra, Australia: National Centre for Social and Economic Modelling.

Bonnefoy, J.L. (2003). From households to urban structures: Space representations as an engine of dynamics in multi-agent simulations. *Cybergeo, 234*, 11.

Bonté, L. (2005). *Représentation multi-échelle pour plateformes à grands nombres d'agents*. Unpublished Master's degree report. Université de Lille, France.

Boman, M., & Holm, E. (2004). Multiagent systems, time geography and microsimulations. In M.O. Olson, & G. Sjöstedt (Eds.), *Systems approaches and their application: Examples from Sweden* (pp. 95-118). Kluwer International

Publishers, London: Kluwer International Publishers.

Bura, S., Guérin-Pace, F., Mathian, H., Pumain D., & Sanders, L. (1996). Multi-agent systems and the dynamics of a settlement system. *Geographical Analysis, 2*, 161-178.

Clarke, G.P. (Ed). (1996). Microsimulation for urban and regional policy analysis. *European Research in Regional Science, 6*, 88-116.

Drogoul, A., & Ferber J. (1994). Multi-agent simulation as a tool for studying emergent processes in societies. In N. Gilbert & J. Doran (Eds.), *Simulating societies: The computer simulation of social phenomena* (pp. 127-142). London: UCL Press.

Gil-Quijano, J. (2002). *Modélisation des mobilités résidentielles intra-urbaines par systèmes multi-agents à Bogotá: Système « market based » et système auto-organisé*. Unpublished master's degree report. LIP6-Université Paris VI. Retrieved January 12, 2007 from, http://www.ur079.ird.fr/equipe/fichiers/javier_Bogotá.pdf

Gil-Quijano, J., & Piron, M. (2007). Formation automatique de groupes d'agents sociaux par techniques d'apprentissage non supervise. In *Proceedings of Atelier Fouille de données et Algorithmes biomimétiques—EGC'07*, Namur, Belgium.

Gil-Quijano, J., Piron M., & Drogoul, A. (2007). Vers une simulation multi-agent de groups d'individus pour modéliser les mobilités résidentielles intra-urbaines. In *Revue Internationale de Géomatique* (Special number: *Dynamiques Urbaines et Mobilités*), 20.

Hamming, R. (1980). *Coding and information theory*. Prentice-Hall.

Houssein B., Chaib-draa, B., & Kropf, P. (2001). Multiagent auctions for multiple items. In *Proceedings of the Third International Bi-Conference Workshop on AOIS*, 2001, Montreal.

Koza, J. R. (1992). *Genetic programming: On the programming of computers by means of natural selection* (Fifth Printing), The MIT Press.

Lebart, L., Piron M., & Morineau, A. (2006). *Statistique exploratoire multidimensionnelle: Visualisation et inférence en fouilles de données.* Dunod, p. 480.

Monmarché, N., Guinot C., & Venturini, G. (2002). Fouille visuelle et classification de données par nouage d'insectes volants. In RSTI-RIA-ECA: *Méthodes d'optimisation pour l'extraction de connaissances et l'apprentissage,* (6), 729-752.

Mullon C., Piron, M., & Treuil, J.-P. (2001). An agent-based approach of urban migration flows. In *Proceedings of 13th European Simulation Symposium* (pp. 380-385), Marseille.

Orcutt, G.H., Caldwell, S., & Wertheimer II, R. (1976). *Policy exploration through microanalytic simulation.* Washington, DC: Urban Institute.

Piron, M., Dureau, F., & Mullon, C. (2003). Vers un modèle dynamique des mobilités résidentielles: développement sur Bogotá. In C. Tannier, H. Houot, & S. Chardonnel (Eds.), *Proceedings of 6th Rencontres de Théo Quant,* Université de Franche-Comté, p. 10.

Piron M., (2005). Comment évaluer et représenter le changement de la structure sociale de Bogotá? Les niveaux d'observation dans l'analyse du changement. In C. Tannier, H. Houot, & S. Chardonnel (Eds.). *Proceedings of 7th Rencontres de Théo Quant,* Université de Franche-Comté, p. 10.

Portugali, J., & Benenson, I. (1995). Artificial planning experience by means of a heuristic sell-space model: Simulating international migration in the urban process. *Environment and Planning A, 27,* 1647-1665.

Renault, V. (2001). Computation for metaphors, analogy and agents. In C. Nehaniv (Ed.), *The Journal of Artificial Societies and Social Simulation, 4*(1).

Servat, D. (2000). *Agent-based vs. PDE modeling of runoff dynamics:Simulation experiments.* Paper presented at the International Symposium on Soil Sructure, Water and Solute Transport at the IRD, Bondy, France.

ENDNOTE

[1] The percentage allocated to each modality corresponds to the number of households answering to this modality in the totality of households of the class. It must be compared with the percentage of the same modality in the entire population studied. For example, 83 percent of the heads of household of the first group are women, compared to 34 percent for the households of Candelaria in 1973.

Chapter XIII
The Role of Risk Aversion and Technical Trading in the Behaviour of Financial Markets

José Antonio Pascual
University of Valladolid, Spain

Javier Pajares
University of Valladolid, Spain

ABSTRACT

In this chapter we show how agent based social simulation helps us to improve some of the traditional models and theories in financial economics. In particular, we explore the links between the microbehaviour of investors and the aggregated behaviour of stock markets. First, we build an agent based model of an artificial financial market, populated only with rational investors. We observe that the statistical features of this market are in agreement with the theoretical markets suggested by mainstream financial economics, but far away from the features shown by real financial markets, like the Spanish Ibex-35, the Spanish stock market main Index. In order to fill the gap, we introduce heterogeneity in the model. We add psychological investors, as suggested by Kahnemen and Tversky (1979), and we are able to reproduce nonnormality, excess kurtosis, excess volatility, and volatility clustering. Then, we introduce technical traders, and we also get from the model higher levels of excess volatility and unit roots. In other words, psychological dealers seem to be responsible for volatility clustering, whereas technical traders trend to introduce unit roots into the process. All these "financial patterns" are a common feature not only for Spanish Ibex-35, also the most important stock markets. We conclude that agent based social simulation helps us to fill the gap between economic theory and real markets, as we explain the statistical features of financial time series from the bottom-up.

INTRODUCTION

Within the framework suggested by mainstream finance, investors take trading decisions in order to maximise constant absolute risk aversion utility functions. Markets are supposed to be efficient, so investors are able to form rational expectations about future value of the relevant variables by means of analysing all the available information. As markets are efficient, the role of technical trading is usually ignored, as prices include all the relevant information, so they cannot be forecasted by means of historical data analysis

Although a lot of stylised, elegant and rigorous models have been built under strong hypothesis about the rationality of investors, there are still some empirical statistical properties that cannot be properly explained. Among others, excess volatility, nonnormality of returns, excess kurtosis, volatility clusters, unit roots, etc. As a consequence, financial models should be improved to catch up these empirical facts.

As suggested in LeBaron et al. (1999) and Pajares et al. (2003, 2005), agent based social simulation can help us to explain why these anomalies take place. But we know from our common experience in real stock markets that investors are not as unbounded rational as supposed. Emotions play an important role in trading decisions and risk aversion changes over time. The proportion of technical dealers is extremely high in modern stock markets, so the influence of their behaviours cannot be ignored.

In this chapter, we explore the links between the microbehaviour of investors and the aggregated macrobehaviour of the market, filling the gap between the mainstream financial theories and the behaviour of real markets, so we use behavior modelling. In particular, we introduce different kind of investors, with different proportions and different trading rules, and we explore the statistical features of the historical series of prices, returns, etc. that emerge in our artificial financial model. We compare these features with the statistical properties of IBEX-35.

First, we build a basic model grounded on the artificial stock market by LeBaron et al. (op. cit). One stock is traded in the market, and it is also possible to lend or borrow at the risk free interest rate. Price emerges as a consequence of the bids and offers of shares.

In a first stage of our research, the model is only populated with rational agents who behave in a similar way to the "fundamental investors", in the sense that they process all the available information and form expectations about future prices and dividends. They decide to buy or sell depending on the disagreement of these expectations with real prices.

We have validated this model with LeBaron's, and we have checked that our model produces series of prices with the same statistical features: levels of standard deviation, kurtosis, trading volumes, prices; cross-correlation between squared returns and volume for different lags, etc.

Once we have validated our model, we investigate the financial properties and we see that the output of this "rational market" is nearly in agreement with the "ideal market" suggested by the literature.

But then, we have analysed the features of the Spanish stock index IBEX-35 and we have realised that the distribution of both prices and returns are not normal with strong tails and high kurtosis; there is a unit root in price series; returns are uncorrelated for different lags; and we can see volatility clusters, so the autocorrelations of squared returns are significantly positive even for high lags.

We want to fill the gap between these facts in IBEX-35 and the "ideal market" that emerges from the simple model above. In order to understand the financial concepts underlying the problem, we have broken down the problem into two steps.

First we have introduced psychological investors whose risk aversion changes over time depending on their previous performance in the market, as suggested by Kanheman and Tversky (op.cit). Doing that, the market becomes closer to the IBEX-35 because: volatility is greater than in the "rational market"; kurtosis increases as the proportion of psychological traders is higher; and volatility clusters emerge. We also see how the autocorrelations of squared returns become positive. However, we do not get a unit root in the series of prices.

Second, we run a market populated with both rational investors and technical dealers who buy or sell depending on trading signals concerning moving average crosses. In this case, excess volatility increases, kurtosis is also increased to the IBEX-35 levels; historical series are not normal and we get unit roots in the series of prices. However, although we also get volatility clusters, their weight is not as important as in the previous case, suggesting that volatility clusters may be caused by dynamic risk aversion, whereas the existence of unit roots has more to do with technical trading.

The rest of the chapter has been organised as follows. First, we explain the limitations of mainstream financial models, and we suggest how behavioural finance and social simulations might be useful to overcome some of these limitations. Then, in the second section, we review the main features of the basic model, populated only with rational investors. We also validate this basic model comparing it with LeBaron's. In the third section, we show the main features of the Spanish Index IBEX-35 and we compare them with the simulations of the "rational market". In fourth section we introduce psychological investors, and in the fifth section we show the influence of technical trading. We finish with the main conclusions of the chapter.

BEHAVIOURAL FINANCE AND SOCIAL SIMULATION

Mainstream finance (mainly neoclassical based finance) is grounded on simple and widely accepted assumptions, as the efficient market hypothesis, the expected utility theory and the strong level or rationality exhibited by investors. These hypotheses are so strong that they can be easily translated into mathematical models.

Markets are supposed to be efficient, so prices include all the relevant information about the mar-

ket. As a consequence, it is on average impossible to beat the market on the basis of public information: prices reflect accurately the future payments to which the particular asset gives title.

Within this framework, dealers process all the relevant available information in order to form rational expectations about the future value of the returns of all the stocks, and about their risks. The financial dealers want to form portfolios of stocks and they have to decide the proportion x_i invested in stock i. Investors process efficiently all the available information, so they are able to estimate the expected return of each stock ($E(r_i)$). They try to maximise the expected return of the portfolio for a given level of risk:

$$\max \ E(r_p) = \sum_i x_i \, E(r_i)$$
$$constr. \qquad \sigma_p^2 = \sigma_o^2 \qquad\qquad (1)$$

The solution of this optimisation problem gives us the popular capital asset pricing model (CAPM) equation, which shows how much return a dealer must demand for the level of systematic risk he/she takes.

$$E(r_i) = r_f + \beta_i [E(r_M) - r_f] \qquad\qquad (2)$$

Where β_i is a measure of the covariance of stock i with the average market index. The model is still quite popular within both academics and professionals; brokerage leading companies compute "accurate" levels of betas and offer them to their customers as an added value service.

However, real markets exhibit some empirical behaviour which has not been properly explained within this stylised framework. Sometimes, these empirical facts are called "anomalies" within the financial literature. Among others, real market usually exhibit over and under-reaction bubbles, excess volatility, unit roots, excess kurtosis, volatility clusters, etc. For instance, excess volatility means that the levels volatility observed in real markets are much higher than the theoretical levels suggested by the efficient market hypothesis.

As a consequence, financial researchers should find new approaches beyond the traditional market efficiency hypothesis and the capital asset pricing model, in order to formalise richer financial theories and models.

At a theoretical level, behavioural finance is one of the most promising approaches to overcome the limitations of the traditional paradigm. In broad terms, it argues that some financial empirical phenomena can be better understood by means of models in which some agents are not fully rational. In this way, agents real behaviour, agents psychology and emotions are taken into account, so that we could explain market aggregated behaviour. Behavioural finance takes ideas from psychology, and from the Kahneman and Tversky's (1979) prospect theory.

Furthermore, in real markets, investors do not exhibit similar and constant aversion to risk, and technical traders are usually very active in the market. Following the ideas from behavioural finance, in Pajares et al (2003), we suggest to include more realistic investors, taking into account their psychology, emotions and risk aversion; in our understanding, the role of technical trading is quite important in order to explain the behaviour of financial markets.

But if we do this, mathematical models become intractable: How can we model emotions and psychological behaviour by means of mathematical equations? How can we solve those set of equations to catch up the behaviour of the market? We need to move to a bottom-up approach, so that we could model the agents behaviour by means of rules.

So, at a methodological level, a generative approach allows (by means of computer simulation) to model real behaviours of human bounded rational investors, so we can build stylised agent based models which can reproduce the behaviour of real financial markets. By means of agent based simulation, we should get deeper understanding of the relations between the microbehaviour of the financial dealers and the aggregated behaviour of the market.

This is particularly important in financial markets, where the market efficiency hypothesis has never been completely refused, and prices are supposed to include all the relevant information about the traded stocks. Of course, it is known that not all the agents behave with full rationality; it simply means that, under some general conditions, the diversity of non fully rational behaviours cancels out at the macrolevel, so that, although dealers are not rational, they act "as if" they were. And market efficiency still holds at the macro (observed) level. In some sense, one of the purposes of our research is to find under what market conditions the "as if" hypothesis still holds.

THE "BASIC MODEL" WITH RATIONAL AGENTS

This starting model has been widely inspired in the model by LeBaron et at (1999). Their pioneering model has become a reference to study financial markets, and a lot of models in the literature have also been based on it, so that we can compare our results with previous works.

A single risky stock is traded and it is also possible to borrow or lend money at the risk free interest rate. For the purpose of this chapter, the amount of dividends paid by the risky stock follows a first-order auto-regressive model, but we can use any kind of dividend structure. Anyway, dealers do not know, ex-ante, the future value of dividends, but they can build models in order to forecast the underlying structure. Prices emerge endogenously as a consequence of bids and offers.

Dealers in this basic model behave as "fundamental investors" as they process all the relevant information about the market in order to form expectations about future prices and dividends.

In particular, each agent is endowed with a set of rules that translates information about the market into expectations. These rules are improved by mean of a genetic algorithm. The particular issues concerning this learning mechanism can be seen in Pascual (2006).

Agents compare the expectations about prices plus dividends (p_t+d_t) with current prices, and buy or sell in consequence. They buy when their expectation is higher than the money they would receive if they were to lend the money at the free interest rate (r_f); otherwise they sell. The buying or selling demand also depends on the risk aversion (λ) and the forecast variance (σ^2). Following LeBaron et al. (*op.cit*):

$$x_{i,t} = \frac{E_{i,t}(p_{t+1} + d_{t+1}) - p_t(1 + r_f)}{\lambda \sigma^2_{i,t,p+d}} \qquad (3)$$

where E means expectation and $x_{i,t}$ is the demand of shares for agent i at time t. The risk aversion λ is constant and the higher the value of λ, the lower the demand; in this way, agents behaving with less risk aversion will try to form portfolios with a higher proportion of risky assets (stocks) than risk-free assets (risk free interest rate).

The model has been programmed in JAVA, as we think it is a widely used language, so that other colleges engaged in social simulation could use and extend the model.

Validation of the Model Based on LeBaron's Results

Before any other kind of research, we should validate our model. We have used the model by LeBaron for this purpose. In concrete, following LeBaron, we have simulated the modes of fast and slow learning. In the case of fast learning, agents update their decisions rules by means of the genetic algorithm each 250 periods, whereas in the slow learning case, agents need 1,000 periods to update their rules.

In Table 1, we show the main statistical data for typical simulations in both models. The standard deviation of the returns is over 2, and there is some excess kurtosis (it should be 0 under the normal distribution). Anyway, the fast learning mode exhibits more excess kurtosis than the slow mode. Something similar happens with the excess return over the risk free interest rate and the trading volume.

Table 1. Statistical data in LeBaron model and our model

	Fast Learning		Slow Learning	
	SF-ASM	Our	SF-ASM	Our
Std. Dev.	2.147	2.095	2.135	2.081
Ex. Kurtosis	0.320	0.229	0.072	0.098
ρ	0.007	0.012	0.036	0.051
Ex. Return	3.062	2.315	2.891	2.183
Trading Volume	0.706	0.434	0.255	0.209

Figure 1. Volume autocorrelations

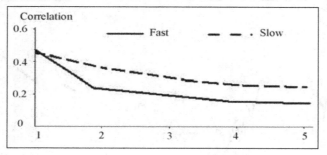

Following LeBaron et al. (op.cit) we have also computed the autocorrelation of the returns ($\rho(r_{t+j}, r_t)$) for different lags (j) and the cross-correlations of the squared returns with trading volume ($\rho(r^2_{t+j}, V_t)$). Our results are completely similar to the ones by LeBaron: autocorrelations quickly tend to zero and the cross-correlations with trading volume have a peak for lags between -1 and 2 (see Figures 1 and 2).

THE SPANISH STOCK MARKET

The Ibex-35 is the most relevant index in the Spanish market. It is built with the 35 most important companies (in terms of trading volume and assets) trading in the "Mercado Continuo", the main stock exchange Spanish market. Ibex-35 is an arithmetic weighted average index, and the weights depend on both trading volume and assets.

In Figure 3 we show the evolutions of this index, we analyse 1000 closing price from June 1 to June 5.

We are interested in the stylised facts observed in the most important financial markets and summarised in Cont (2001), such as absence of autocorrelations, excess kurtosis, volatility clustering, excess volatility, positive autocorrelations of squared returns, etc.

We have performed normality tests. When working with time series, it is usually advisable to look at the histogram or to study certain descriptive statistics (like skewness (S) and kurtosis(K)) in more detail. More formally, we have tested normality by means of the Jarque-Bera test $JB = \frac{n}{6}[S^2 + \frac{1}{4}(K-3)^2]$ and $P(JB) = \int_{JB}^{\infty} \chi^2_{\nu=2}(x)dx$. The hypothesis that the distribution is normally distributed is rejected at a confidence level $(1-a)$ if $JB >=$ ChiSquare-Distr$[2, 1-a]$.

We reject the hypothesis of normality for both the series of prices and returns. In particular, kurtosis of returns is 4.892, so Ibex-35 has heavy tails. The autocorrelation function of returns is not significant at all, even for small lags. We have performed stationarity tests (Augmented Dickey Fuller and Phillips Perron), and the null of a unit

Figure 2. Correlation of squared returns with volume

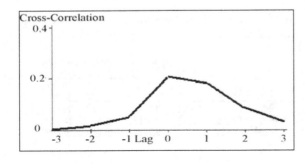

Figure 3. Evolution of Ibex 35

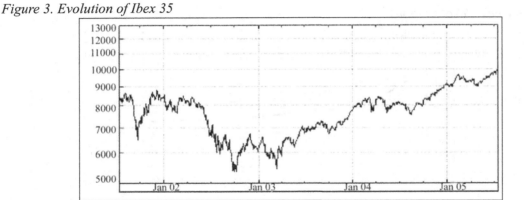

root in the series of prices could not be rejected at the 10% level.

In Figure 4, we show the variance, so we can appreciate some volatility clustering. In Figure 5, we see the autocorrelations of the squared returns: they are positive even for high lags. This is a measure of volatility clustering (Cont (op.cit)).

According to these data, our first conclusion is that the Spanish market is not different to the most important stock markets all over the world.

The Gap Between the IBEX-35 and the "Basic Model"

Now we compare the statistical properties of the IBEX-35 with the basic model, a market populated only with "fundamental investors" who form expectations about futures prices and dividends. In Figures 6 (nonspecific simulation), we show a typical simulation. We have run thousands of simulations, obtaining similar features in all of them.

As it happens in the real markets, both prices and returns are not normally distributed, and the autocorrelation function of returns becomes insignificant even for small lags (Figure 7).

However, kurtosis is 3.723, far away from the levels exhibited by IBEX-35, and volatility levels are much lower than the levels of the Spanish stock markets. Furthermore, volatility clusters, very common in the Spanish market, do not appear at all in the "rational market" as we do not see significant autocorrelations of squared returns (see Figure 7, right).

We also do not appreciate unit roots, on the augmented Dickey-Fuller, or Phillips-Perron tests.

The main conclusion of these results is that the market populated only with rational agents has an output which is closer to the theoretical models proposed in mainstream financial literature than to the real Spanish Stock Market.

Figure 4. Returns of Ibex 35

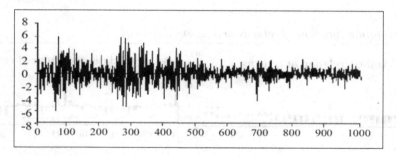

Figure 5. Autocorrelations of the squared returns

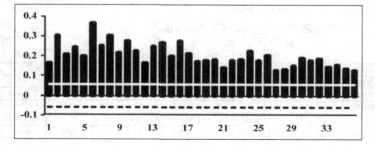

THE ROLE OF RISK AVERSION AND PSYCHOLOGICAL INVESTORS

Kahneman and Tversky (op. cit) explored the real behaviour of human beings facing risk. Their contributions have been extremely relevant to understanding a lot of economic happenstance. In particular, the fields of "Behavioural Economics" and "Behavioural Finance" are strongly grounded in their research. For the purposes of this chapter,

we have to realize that, according to Kahneman and Tversky's experiments, the aversion against risk is not independent from the wealth of the investor.

In the model populated only with rational agents, the investors had constant risk aversion in equation (3). Now, we introduce agents that form expectations of future prices and dividends using all the relevant information, but their risk aversion is changed depending on the evolution of their wealth, that is, depending on the perform-

Figure 6. Typical price and return evolution

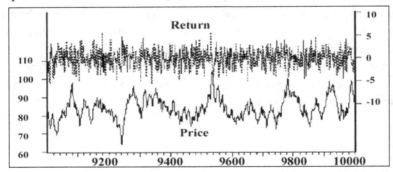

Figure 7. Autocorrelation function of returns and squared returns

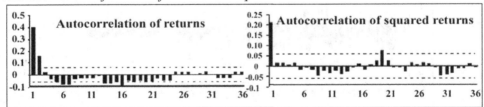

Table 2. Average figures for 10 simulations

	20BF		15BF5KT		10BF10KT		5BF15KT		20KT	
	P	R	P	R	P	R	P	R	P	R
Mean	81.929	0.000	81.399	-0.004	81.347	-0.001	79.703	-0.002	78.910	-0.002
Std. Dev.	7.367	1.956	7.367	1.977	7.519	2.024	8.978	2.256	9.950	2.462
Exc.Var.%	81.543		88.532		108.048		169.059		231.946	
Skewness	-0.275	-0.004	-0.141	-0.016	-0.281	0.099	-0.652	-0.038	-0.764	-0.085
Kurtosis	4.166	3.431	3.903	3.625	3.782	4.047	4.034	4.625	4.689	6.374
J-B	69.208	7.746	37.373	16.339	38.608	47.326	115.706	110.250	216.147	475.671
Prob.	0.000	0.021	0.000	0.000	0.00	0.000	0.000	0.000	0.000	0.000

ance of their previous deals. In particular, the risk aversion coefficient could take two values. If an agent's actual wealth is higher than the average that she/he enjoyed during the 10 previous periods, then her/his risk aversion is reduced. In this way, the denominator in equation (3) becomes lower and the agent will demand more shares in the next period.

In Table 2, we can see the average figures for 10 simulations, for different proportions of rational agents (BF) and psychological agents (KT). For instance, 15bf5kt means that the market is populated with 15 fundamental investors and 5 psychological agents (KT from Kahneman and Tversky).

Kurtosis increases as the number of psychological investors gets higher; the levels are now closer to the numbers exhibited by IBEX-35. The same is true for the excess volatility. The series are also not normally distributed (the probability of being normal equals zero).

The autocorrelations of squared returns begin to be significant whenever the proportion of KT agents becomes important (see Figure 8), which means that volatility clustering appears in markets with high proportion of psychological investors. However, we have not detected a unit root in the series of prices, as it happened for IBEX-35.

TECHNICAL TRADING

Now we build a model populated with fundamental investors and technical investors. Everyday thousands of dealers around the world study charts involving price and volume, looking for trends, stylised patterns, etc. Most of them compute moving averages of prices (usually using excel-based software) and they buy or sell shares depending on the movements of those moving averages. The number of dealers whose behaviour follow these rules is so high that, in our understanding,

Figure 8. Autocorrelations of squared returns with 15bf5kt, 10bf10kt and 5bf15kt (typical simulation)

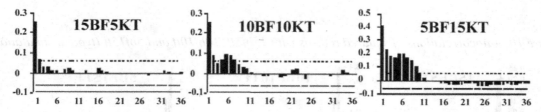

Figure 9. Bids-Offers depending on MA

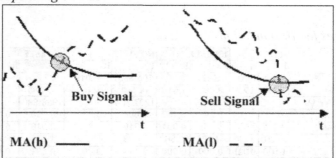

technical trading cannot be ignored if we want to develop realistic theories in finance.

In our model, we have introduced technical traders who compute a low order ($MA(l)$) and a high order moving average ($MA(h)$) of prices; they buy shares when the $MA(l)$ crosses from down to up to the $MA(h)$ and sell stocks if $MA(l)$ crosses the other one from top to down (see Figure 9).

In Table 3, we show numbers for different proportions of technical traders (TFagents). When the number of them increases, both excess volatility and prices increase significantly. Normality of both individual series of prices and returns is rejected, although the probability computed with mean S and mean K is different from 0 in some case. Kurtosis also evolves to the levels exhibited by Ibex-35, and the higher the proportion of technical traders, the greater the excess kurtosis. However, although we have got evidence of volatility clusters, this evidence is not as strong as it was in the previous case or as it is in the real Spanish Market (see Figure 10).

On the other hand, the market reproduces the existence of unit roots in the series of prices. This

evidence is higher whenever the proportion of technical traders increases.

CONCLUSION

We show how agent based social simulation allows us to build financial models which are able to catch up some of the statistical properties of real financial markets. We conclude that orthodox models from financial economics could be improved by means of agent based modelling and behavioural finance.

To this aim, we have built an artificial stock market that includes fundamental, psychological and technical dealers. Fundamental investors process all the available information and form expectations about the value of future prices and dividends. They buy or sell comparing these expectations with present data. Psychological dealers update their risk aversion according with their past performance, and technical traders use the crosses of moving averages as buying/selling signals. Our purpose is to understand the relations

Figure 10. Autocorrelations of squared returns with 15bf5tf, 10bf10tf and 5bf15tf (typical simulation)

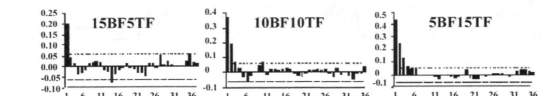

Table 3. Average figures for 10 simulations

	20BF		15BF5TF		10BF10TF		5BF15TF	
	P	R	P	R	P	R	P	R
Mean	81.929	0.000	99.027	-0.005	105.969	-0.016	107.234	-0.012
Std. Dev.	7.367	1.956	9.363	1.610	18.581	1.456	20.985	1.301
Exc. Var. %	81.543		215.857		1207.224		1398.980	
Skewness	-0.275	-0.004	0.246	0.162	0.006	0.131	0.098	0.354
Kurtosis	4.166	3.431	3.862	4.091	2.710	4.036	2.918	5.538
J-B	69.208	7.746	41.105	53.962	3.509	47.568	1.877	289.241
Prob.	0.000	0.021	0.000	0.000	0.173	0.000	0.391	0.000

between the micro-behaviour of the investors and the macrobehaviour of the market, filling the gap between financial theories and the statistical properties of real financial time series.

We concentrate on the Spanish Stock Market. According to our simulations, we find that the presence of rational investors alone does not explain properly the statistical properties of the real Spanish Stock Market. Moreover, the output of this "ideal market" reminds us of the theoretical markets suggested by the mainstream financial paradigm.

In order to fill the gap, we have included psychological investors and technical traders. In both cases, excess volatility and kurtosis are closer to the numbers we see in the Spanish IBEX-35 index.

Furthermore, we have learnt from our simulations that psychological trading helps us to understand the emergence of volatility clustering, whereas technical trading has more to do with higher levels of kurtosis and the existence of unit roots in the series of returns. In other words, psychological dealers are related to the emergence of bubbles, and technical trading makes the system stationary.

REFERENCES

Cont, R. (2001) Empirical properties of asset returns: Stylised facts and statistical issues. *Quantitative Finance, 1,* 223-236.

LeBaron, B., Arthur, W.B., & Palmer, R. (1999). Time series properties of an artificial stock market. *Journal of Economic Dynamics and Control, 23,* 1487-1516.

Kahneman, D., & Tversky, A. (1979). Prospect theory: An analysis of decisions under risk. *Econometrica, 47,* 313-327.

Pajares, J., Pascual, J.A., Hernández, C., & López-Paredes, A. (2003). *A behavioural, evolutionary and generative approach for modelling financial markets.* Paper presented at the First Conference of the European Social Simulation Association (ESSA). Groningen. The Netherlands.

Pajares, J., Pascual, J.A., Hernández, C., & López-Paredes, A. (2005). *The role of risk aversion and technical trading in the behaviour of financial markets.* Paper presented at the Third Conference of the European Social Simulation Association (ESSA). Koblenz. Germany.

Pascual, J. A. (2006). *Modelado Multiagente de Mercados Financieros: Un Enfoque Basado en el Comportamiento Individual de los Inversores.* Unpublished doctoral thesis. Departamento de Organización de Empresas y C.I.M. ETS de Ingenieros Industriales. Universidad Del Valladolid. Spain.

Chapter XIV
Emissions Permits Auctions:
An Agent Based Model Analysis

Marta Posada
INSISOC University of Valladolid, Spain

Cesáreo Hernández
INSISOC University of Valladolid, Spain

Adolfo López-Paredes
INSISOC University of Valladolid, Spain

ABSTRACT

In this chapter the authors demonstrate with three relevant issues that agent-based modelling (ABM) is very useful to design emissions permits auctions and to forecast emission permits prices. They argue that ABM offers a more efficient approach to auction design than the usual mechanistic models. The authors set up the essential components of any market institution far beyond supply and demand. They build an ABM for the emissions permits auction of the Environment Protection Agency (EPA) and demonstrate why the EPA failed. In the second experiment they show that in a competitive and efficient auction, the continuous double auction, there is room for traders' learning and strategic behavior, thus clearing the perfect market paradox. In the third experiment they build an ABM of the Spanish electricity market to get CO_2 emissions price forecasts that are more accurate than those obtained with econometric or mechanistic models.

INTRODUCTION

Emission trading (ET) and the role of externalities rights in protecting the commons. The Kyoto Protocol of 1997 brought climate policy onto the national and international agendas. Is it possible to solve the air quality problem while allowing economic growth? It is doubtful that the goals of climate protection can be achieved within a "win-win" scenario, with gains in both economic growth and the environment, without any additional cost for the society. As no environmental policy provides a free lunch, the control of greenhouse effects is associated with costs. Therefore, it is crucial to find cost-effective policies. The closest to a free lunch is a market of permits, since it just involves an exchange of rights. Emissions trading has the potential to control greenhouse gas emissions at the lowest economic costs. Several books and recent papers have dealt with emission trading in general: Tietenberg (2006 for a review of the literature), Hansjürgens (2005), and Posada (2006a).

It is generally agreed that a free market is more efficient than central planning, and so, emission trading is superior to *command and control* regulations. The market will discipline the pollutant firms. The emissions cap safeguards the global environmental goals, while trading is a flexible and dynamic solution. It is also easily enforceable at the firm level: The monitoring and the enforcement of the emissions-trading scheme guarantees total compliance. In summary, emissions trading is a natural case for climate policy, and if there ever was an environmental problem designed for emissions trading, it is global warming. But this brings the issue of ET design to the forefront.

The need to go beyond experimental economics. Mechanistic models used by economists in general equilibrium theory are of little relevance for the designers of real-world emissions trading auctions because they are drastically simplified for the purposes of analytical tractability. To allow for strategic behaviour among the traders, game theory has been extensively used. But the dynamic nature of auctions defies mathematical game theory and asks for computational and laboratory experiments with soft agents, where we could calibrate for learning and strategic behaviour (López et al., 2002).

Analysis and diagnosis of ET institutions: The failure of the EPA auction. In 1990, the first emissions trading auction was introduced in the US by the Environmental Protection Agency (EPA). It has been applied to the SO_2 emissions of electric utilities since 1993. The way in which the EPA auction was organized was quite peculiar, and was not mandatory in the Clean Air Act Amendments. The aim of these peculiar trading rules to be described later on was intended for the benefit of clean firms. However, they have brought the auction failure. After some years, most of the trade was private and the EPA auction sold 2.8 percent of the total amount of allowances.

There have been analytical efforts to understand the very poor results of the EPA emissions trading mechanism even under extreme simplifying assumptions about trader's nonstrategic behaviour (Cason, 1993) or about complete information of the valuations (Kline & Menezes, 1999). We will show in the following that we could have predicted the EPA's failure using an ABM approach (Posada et al., 2004).

We demonstrate that the EPA auction's failure was due to an explicit rule intended for the benefit of clean firms. The rule caused just the contrary effects: It created strong incentives for sellers to under-offer their marginal cost. This fact indicates that institutions matter in terms of market efficiency and raises the issue of auction design.

The design of emissions permits (EP) auctions. We know from experimental economics with human agents that the continuous double auction (CDA) is efficient (Smith, 1989). But since we cannot control for agents' learning and behaviour in this setting, the following major question was not addressed: To which extent is the institution robust against agents learning and strategic behavior?

The first experiment with artificial agents in the continuous double auction (CDA) by Gode and Sunder (1993) produced surprising results.

They claimed that the allocative efficiency of a double auction derives largely from institutional rules and was independent of traders' motivation, intelligence, or learning. Several papers followed to check that institutions matter but so does agents' learning as far as price dynamics and efficiency is concerned: Cliff and Bruten (1997); Gjestard and Dickhaut (1998); Tesauro and Das (2001); Walsh et al. (2002); Li and Smith (2004). In Posada (2006b) we extend these works in several relevant ways and show that strategic agent behaviour can take place in a CDA for the benefit of active agents without affecting the global auction efficiency.

The electricity market and CO_2 ET. Forecasting dynamic prices of EP. To assess the impact of CO_2 ET on the electricity market we need to estimate permit prices and a link between the two markets: the spot power market and the CO_2 market. The resulting forecasts from top-down models are very poor (Springer, 2003). The chapter, following Posada et al. (2005), ends up with an ABM analysis of the Spanish CO_2 market as a CDA, to forecast permit prices for alternative firm behaviors. We satisfactory reproduce recent price data from the European ET. To our knowledge, no other research has used behavioral modelling for the CO_2 forecast but the POWERACE model (Weidlich et al., 2005).

EXPLAINING THE FAILURE OF THE EPA AUCTION

Following Smith (1989), there are three essential dimensions (ExIxA) in market design. E: *the environment* (initial endorsements, preferences, and transaction costs), I: *the institution* (the actual exchange rules and the way the contract is closed), and A: *the agents' behaviour.*

Institution (I): EPA

The EPA institution waits for all traders to place offers before clearing the market. It ranks the bids, from high to low, and the offers, from low to high. The lower asking price is matched with the highest remaining bidder by the institution, as long as the asking price is below a bid price. The transaction price is at the bid price.

Environment (E)

The supply and demand functions are built by the aggregations of sellers and buyers' private valuations, respectively. Seller i has n_i units to trade, but only one is trading in each period. He or she has a vector of marginal costs $(MaC_{i1}, MaC_{i2},..., MaC_{ini})$ for the corresponding units. Here MaC_{i1} is the marginal cost to seller i of the first unit, MaC_{i2} is the cost of the second unit, and so on. Similarly, Buyer j has m_j units to trade and he or she has a vector of reserve prices $(RP_{j1}, RP_{j2},..., RP_{jmj})$ for the corresponding units. Here RP_{j1} is the reserve price to buyer j of the first unit, RP_{j2} is the reserve price of the second unit, and so on.

In an emission permits market, the traders are the firms. Firms may not emit more emissions than the number of rights they hold. The pollutant firms will be buyers and the clean firms will be sellers. If a firm has more emissions than assigned rights, it has to purchase emission rights in order to cover the emission overshoot with emission rights. If a firm has an excess of rights, it may sell them.

Agents' Behaviour and Learning

Each trader is either a buyer (pollutant firm) or a seller (clean firm). The assumption of fixed roles conforms to extensive prior studies, including experiments involving human subjects. Each agent only faces the following decision: *to make an order either to buy or to sell an emission permit.*

In the works referred to earlier on (Cason, 1993; Kline & Menezes, 1999), the strategic behaviour of the agents *to make an order* was far too simple. In our model, buyers and sellers behave strategically under incomplete information. They try to maximize expected surplus, defined as the product of the gain from trade and the probability for a bid/offer to be accepted. The Zero Intelligence Unconstrained (ZIU) strategy developed by Gode and Sunder (1993) allows a training strategy in the first period. A ZIU agent generates random order prices ignoring the state of the market and it is free to engage in money-losing transactions.

Each buyer chooses the bid b that maximizes expected surplus, defined as the product of the gain from trade (equal to the reservation price minus the price p) and the probability for a bid b to be accepted Π_b. The price p is equal to the bid b. The idea behind the strategy is that low bids will achieve high gains but they have low probability to be accepted while high bids will achieve lower profits but the probability to be accepted is higher:

$$\max \hat{B}(b) = \max \Pi_b (PR - b) \qquad (1)$$

Each seller chooses the offer a that maximizes expected surplus, defined as the product of the gain from trade (equal to the estimated price $\hat{p}$ minus the marginal Cost MaC) and the probability for an offer a to be accepted Π_a:

$$\max \hat{B}(a) = \max \Pi_a (\hat{p} - MaC) \qquad (2)$$

We estimate the transaction price as the average transaction price in HM for each offer a because the transaction price takes place at the bid price of the buyer to whom the seller is matched. Interpolation is used for prices at which no traders are registered in HM.

To calculate the buyers' belief function Π_b, we use the belief function developed by Gjerstad and Dickhaut (1998). This probability was originally developed for a continuous double auction. Each GD agent forms a subjective belief that some agent will accept his order. GD agents use the history HM of the recent market activity (the orders leading to the last M traders: *ABL* accepted bids that are less than b, *AL* both accepted and rejected offers that are less than b, and *RBG* rejected bids that are greater than b; *AAG* accepted offers that are greater than a, *BG* both accepted and rejected bids that are greater than a, and *RAL* rejected offers that are less than (a) to calculate this belief. Interpolation is used for prices at which no orders or traders are registered in HM to calculate the belief function:

For buyers: $\hat{q}(b) = \dfrac{ABL(b) + AL(b)}{ABL(b) + AL(b) + RBG(b)}$

$$(3)$$

For sellers: $\hat{q}(a) = \dfrac{AAG(a) + BG(a)}{AAG(a) + BG(a) + RAL(a)}$

$$(4)$$

THE SIMULATIONS AND SOME SELECTED RESULTS

All the simulations were run with SDML, a strictly declarative model language developed and maintained by the Center for Policy Modelling of the Manchester University (http://www.cpm.mmu.ac.uk/sdml). For a brief and clear introduction to social simulation tools, see Gilbert and Troitzsch (2005) and Galán et al. (2003) for rigour and reliability in agent-based social simulation multiagent models.

Twenty firms, with ten units to trade for each firm, were used in the simulations of thirty runs and 10 periods per run. Note that all the firms have the same units to trade. Therefore, the number of agents in each side of the market determines the excess of demand (supply). Each player only knows his own valuations. Valuations are independently distributed. The seller's valuations are uniformly distributed on the interval

[0,10] and the buyer's valuations are uniformly distributed on the interval [20,30]. Each ZIU agent generates orders uniformly distributed on the interval [0,40]. We focus on the transaction prices and the under-offered behaviour in three following scenarios:

* A **balanced industry** where there are the same number of buyers (clean firms) and sellers (pollution firms): 10 buyers and 10 sellers.
* A **pollutant industry** where there are more sellers than buyers.
* A **clean industry** where there are more buyers than sellers.

In the **balanced industry** case, the average transaction prices (□) are below the average competitive equilibrium price (see Figure 1.b). Moreover, most of the transaction prices are in the sellers' support, i.e., in the range [0,10].

In the **clean industry,** the average competitive equilibrium prices go down (see Figure 1.c). The bids tend to slightly lower values than in the balanced industry. Competition amongst sellers force all final prices to be in the sellers' support. When we compare two clean industries, one (with 16 sellers and four buyers) cleaner than the other (with 13 sellers and seven buyers) we find that the value of excess supply does not affect the results or the conclusions.

In the **pollutant industry,** the average competitive equilibrium prices go up (see Figure 1.a). We obtain higher bids (and higher prices) than in a balanced industry. We compare two pollutant industries, one (with 16 buyers and four sellers) more contaminant than the other (with 13 buyers and seven sellers). Given the results in clean industries, one might be tempted to conjecture that competition amongst buyers forces all final prices to be in the buyers' support if there is excess demand. However, this is not true. The reason stems from the different treatment of buyers and sellers in the EPA auction. Intuitively, if buyers submit bid prices above the sellers' support, all sellers will compete for the highest price by asking zero. However, in pollutant industries we reject Kline's conjecture that if an equilibrium exists it will involve nonuniform price bids that all lie in the sellers' support. However it is true that price bids in the buyers' support cannot be an equilibrium since buyers would also have an incentive to bid zero, as the last periods of the transaction prices show.

The trading rules of EPA auction create strong incentives for sellers to under-offer their marginal cost. We observe under-offer behaviour in all types of industries. We can conclude that the EPA design was wrong and this could have been forecasted should the mechanistic proposal have been tested with ABM simulations.

Figure 1. Transaction prices in EPA auctions: (a) pollutant, (b) balanced, and (c) clean industries

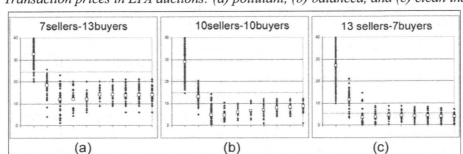

INSTITUTIONS MATTER AND SO DOES AGENTS' STRATEGIC BEHAVIOUR

The main conclusion of the real EPA experience is that the institution matters. Looking for an appropriate CO_2 emission market design, we choose the continuous double auction (CDA), since there is evidence of the robustness of the CDA in terms of efficiency from experimental economics (Smith, 1989). The subtle question is: To what extent go agents' learning and strategic behaviour affect agents' surplus under global auction efficiency? We summarize the main findings from Posada et al. (2004, 2006a, 2006b) in relation with this issue.

The Institution: CDA

In a CDA market, a trader may make a bid or an offer at any time during the trading period, but once it is made it will persist until the trader chooses to alter it, remove it, or it is accepted. Trades are executed as new offers arrive. We use one form of CDA—with order queue—because the convergence to equilibrium is faster.

Learning and Strategic Behaviour in CDA

In the EPA auction, the traders face only one decision: *How much should they offer?* While in CDA markets, traders face three decisions: *How much should they offer? How soon should they place a bid or offer? Under what circumstances should they accept an outstanding bid or offer of some other trader?*

To answer these questions, Rust et al. (1993), Cliff and Bruten (1997), and Gjestard and Dickhaut (1998) developed different agents' learning capabilities (K, ZIP, and GD, respectively). We focus on the interactions between software bidding strategies. Tesauro and Das (2001) tested agents' performance in homogeneous populations and in two specific heterogeneous settings. Accordingly, we extend their experiments for interactions among heterogeneous agents in all the strategy space. But the relevant extension of the works referred to above is that we allow the agents to choose a strategy from a set of three alternatives (K, ZIP, and GD) looking for the best bidding strategy. To take this decision, each agent only knows their own reservation prices and the information generated in the market, but he or she doesn't know the bidding strategy or the profit achieved in a market session by the other agents.

The Main Findings

We evaluated fixed strategy behaviour versus strategic behaviour under different environments with the ABM model of a CDA. The environment can be static or dynamic, and supply and demand of emissions permits can be symmetric or not. Due to space limitation, we only include sample graphics of the full results. The interested reader may consult the references and/or write to the authors.

Under static and symmetric environments (Figure 2.a). For *homogeneous populations* (fixed strategies), efficiency is always achieved even if the agents are ZI. Convergence needs at least ZIP agents. With GD agents we obtain the highest efficiency. For *heterogeneous populations* (fixed strategies),: when the K agents are at least 50 percent, efficiency decreases and convergence is not achieved if one side is populated with only (opportunist) K agents (Figure 2.b). K agents draw from the other side's surplus. Efficiency is achieved and there is convergence in the remaining space of strategies. For *agents with strategic choice* (Figure 2.c), there are no Nash equilibriums but there are stable regions in the percentage of selected strategies. Efficiency and convergence is achieved. But those who end up as K agents get higher surplus (free riding behaviour).

Under static and asymmetric environments
(Figure 3a). For *homogeneous populations* (fixed strategies), convergence is achieved with prices just towards the rigid side of the market. The highest efficiency is achieved with GD agents. For *heterogeneous populations* (fixed strategies), when K agents are at least 50 percent, convergence can be achieved if they are on the rigid side (Figure 3b). K agents again draw from the other side's surplus. There is some loss in efficiency. For *agents with strategic choice* (Figure 3c), the ZIP agents do worse than in the symmetric case. The final population is composed mainly of GD and K agents. Convergence is achieved and there is no significant loss of efficiency. K agents populate the rigid side and again get more surplus than the others.

Under dynamic environments with gradual elasticity change. Efficiency is not achieved and there is no convergence except with GD agents for *homogeneous/heterogeneous populations*

with fixed strategies. For *strategic choic,*: there is convergence, and efficiency is achieved. There are more GD agents than ZIP or K, but they coexist with other agents.

EMISSIONS PERMITS PRICE FORECASTS FOR THE SPANISH CO$_2$ ET

In Posada et al. (2005), we presented a model to investigate the effects of CO$_2$ ET on the electricity market. This is a direct application of the model from Section 3 and provides a forecast of EP prices that could allow us to measure their impact on the merit order of power plants and the change in the power generation mix.

In this section we are only concerned with the dependence of the CO$_2$ market on the electricity market as a first step of ongoing research with the full electricity market model.

Figure 2. Fixed strategy behaviour versus strategic behaviour under a static and symmetric environment: (a) Environment, (b) Fixed Strategies (50% K-50% GD), and (c) Strategic choice.

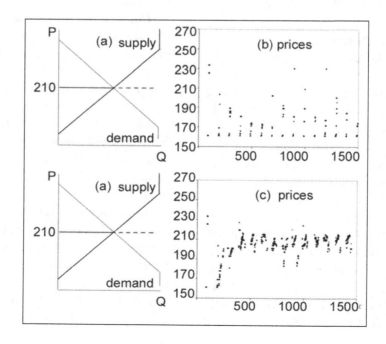

The Model

The components of the model are those in Figure 4. There are two types of agents in the electricity market: *Producer agents* (that sell electricity) and *distributor agents* (that buy electricity). We have considered the seventeen largest Spanish electricity plants that are owned by the four main firms (Endesa, Iberdrola, Unión Fenosa, and Hidroeléctrica del Cantábrico) in our model. These plants include fuel, hydro, and nuclear technologies to generate electricity. Notice that only some electricity plants (those with fuel combustible) can be sellers or buyers in the emission permits market. The National Allocation Permits (*NPAs*) has fixed the number of emission permits among installations in six key industrial sectors (electricity production, oil refineries, coke ovens and steel mills, cement, glass and ceramics manufacturing, and paper pulp and board mills) from 2005-2007.

The Spanish electricity producers with combustible fuel technologies have received 54 percent of the NAP emission permits in this period.

The Institution (I) for the Spanish CO_2 ET is assumed to be a CDA for all the previous reasons about efficiency.

The agents' behaviour (A). The agents have to decide on three alternatives: going to the auction, paying a fee, or investing in abetment. They are assumed to be GD agents, although as we found, this does not much affecteither the final convergence prices or auction efficiency. We further assume that there are no explicit oligopoly agreements out of the market.

The environment (E). The annual emission quantity of the fuel plants depends on both the specific emission rate (SER) and the annual electricity quantity traded (EQT) in the electricity market, in the following way:

Annual emission quantity =SER*EQT,

Figure 3. Fixed strategy behaviour versus strategic behaviour under static and asymmetric environment: (a) Environment, (b) Fixed Strategies (50% K-50% GD), and (c) Strategic choice.

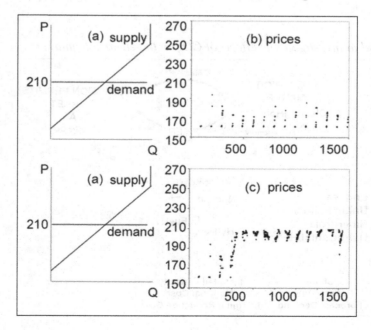

where SER depends on the production—mix of the generating firms (Table 3).

To forecast CO_2 prices we need the estimates of the annual quantity of emissions and the reservation prices of the agents (selling or buying permits) that are obtained from the emissions marginal reduction cost of the generating firms. An agent will buy emissions permits, invest in cleaning technology, or pay a fine if his or her allowance is less than the annual quantity of emissions. The decision will be determined by the emission marginal reduction cost (MRC) and by the amount of the fine, 40 €/tm.

Results of the CO_2 EP Price Dynamics Simulations

In the starting year (2005), only one of the ten fuel plants had a permit to sell and the resulting price was very high (25 €/Tn). With this high price as a reference, two plants endogenously decided to invest in cleaning technology for the year 2006. The resulting CO_2 permit price settled down within the [18-22 €/Tn] range (Figure 5), quite close to the observed European market price (Figure 6).

Thus, even with very few selling and buying firms, a competitive price comes up, as advanced by standard economic theory. This behavioural bottom-up model can be adapted with simple reprogramming effort to cope with more realistic forthcoming scenarios (more participant countries and sectors and alternative permits allowances).

CONCLUSION

Emissions permits trading has the potential to control greenhouse gas emissions at the lowest economic costs and is possibly superior to, and at least a complement of, command and control

Table 3. Marginal reduction cost and specific emission rate of the main Spanish electricity firms

Firm	MRC	SER
Endesa	18	1,200
Iberdrola	10	0.950
Unión Fenosa	22	0.999
Hidro del Cantábrico	25	1,117

Figure 4. Our model to investigate the effects of CO_2 on the electricity market

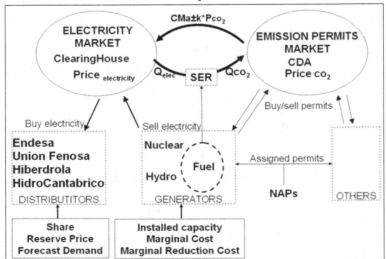

regulations. If there ever was an environmental problem designed for emissions trading, it is global warming. This makes imperative the issue of ET design.

The EPA failure has demonstrated that the institution matters and auction engineering is necessary. Subsequent research from game theory on the causes of this failure proved the scan value of mechanistic design to help the regulators decide on a proper emission trading auction. Experimental benchmarking simulation is now the companion of any mechanistic design when defining auction institutions in practice. Experimental economics with soft agents allows us to control the agents' strategic behaviour. A proper experiment should always specify the triplet IxExA (Institution, Environment, and Agents' behaviour).

We have provided an answer to an open question: Why did the first emissions permits auction of the EPA fail? Theoretical economics and game theory (mechanistic design) were unable to explain the failure. Looking for an answer, we built an ABM model of agents' behavior under incomplete information of the valuations and strategic behaviour from both market perspectives. The simulations have revealed that the trading rules of EPA auction create strong incentives for sellers to under-offer their marginal cost. We observe under-offer behaviour in all types of industries (balanced, clean, and pollutant). The aim of the peculiar EPA trading rules was for the benefit of clean firms (sellers). However, the results were against the aim of the rules. The average transaction prices are below the average competitive equilibrium price and the transaction prices are in the sellers support in both balanced and pollutant industries.

The failure of the EPA auction and our simulations show that institutions matter. Experimental economics results with humans have shown that

Figure 5. Prices for three sellers and seven buyers for the simulated Spanish CO_2 market

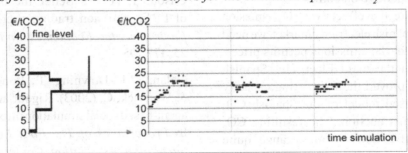

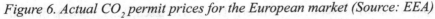

Figure 6. Actual CO_2 permit prices for the European market (Source: EEA)

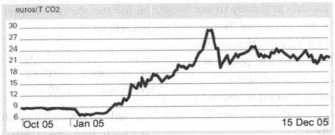

the CDA is efficient. To which extent is this efficiency robust against agents' learning and strategic behavior? Since we have to control for agent behavior, we have to go beyond experimental economics and use artificial agent models. The first experiments in auction design with artificial agents (Gode & Sunder, 1993) were seen as an indication of the robustness of institutional rules against agents' learning and strategic behavior. We have extended previous results against this claim in terms of market efficiency, price convergence, and Nash equilibrium. We have shown that the institution matters but so does agent behaviour. We have contributed to solve the "paradox of competition" as put forward by Gjerstad (2006). In fact, the simulations of CO_2 emission trading on the Spanish electricity market show that a lot of competition and strategy may go on within a CDA, resulting in high efficiency and convergence, but not necessarily in the ratio of buyers and seller or alternative strategic behaviour surplus. A substantial deviation from equilibrium earnings is compatible with price convergence and almost full efficiency. There is room for strategic behaviour even under competitive outcomes.

To investigate the effects of CO_2 emission trading on the Spanish electricity market, we need good forecasts for the emissions permits prices. With data from the main Electricity Spanish firms, we have proved the forecasting capacity of our agent-based model of the Spanish CO_2 emissions permits auction. The resulting CO_2 permit price settles down within a range, quite close to the observed European market price. The accuracy of this bottom-up forecast is quite remarkable and certainly outperforms any of those obtained with top-down models presently in use (Springer, 2003). But the most relevant feature is the behavioural focus of the model that allows ex ante analysis, not only ex post and projective forecasts. The behavioural forecasts are part of a greater project and ongoing applied research to model the electricity market and to measure the effects of the ET on the sector.

In essence, simulation tools (bottom-up multiagent modelling) as those used here are available for auction engineering, and this fact will have deep consequences for regulating the access to the commons in general and for climate policy in particular. Even more, since auctions are a mechanism for dealing with scarcity and allocation, our findings may be relevant in production and management engineering as well (market-oriented programming). Thus, there is a lot of interesting, future research to be conducted in and out the scope of this chapter.

ACKNOWLEDGMENT

We gratefully acknowledge financial support from the Spanish MEC, n° 2005-05676. We wish to thank the anonymous referees for their helpful comments.

REFERENCES

Cason, T. (1993). Seller incentive properties of EPA's emission trading auction. *Journal of Environmental Economics and Management, 25*, 177-195.

Galan, J.M., Downing, T., López-Paredes, A., & Warwick, C. (2003). Rigour and reliability in agent-based social simulation through replication. In *Proceedings of The First European Social Simulation Association Conference, ESSA'03*, Groningen, The Netherlands.

Gilbert, N., & Troitzsch, K.G. (2005). *Simulation for the social scientist* (2nd ed.). UK: Open Univerisity Press.

Gjerstad, S., & Dickhaut, J. (1998). Price formation in double auctions. *Games and Economic Behaviour, 22*, 1-29.

Gjerstad, S. (2006). The competitive market paradox (Tech. Rep. No. 1180). Purdue University.

Gode, D., & Sunder, S. (1993). Allocative efficiency of market with zero-intelligent traders: Market as a partial substitute for individual rationality. *Journal of Political Economy, 101,* 119-137.

Hansjürgens, B. (Ed.). (2005). *Emissions trading for climate policy: US and European perspectives.* UK: Cambridge University.

Kline, J.J., & Menezes, F.M. (1999). A simple analysis of the US emission permits auctions. *Economic Letters, 65,* 183-189.

Li, L., & Smith, S. (2004). Speculation agents for dynamic, multi-period continuous double auctions in B2B exchanges. In *Proceedings of the 37th Hawaii International Conference on System Sciences.*

López-Paredes, A., Hernández C., & Pajares, J. (2002). Towards a new experimental socio-economics: Complex behaviour in bargaining. *Journal of Socioeconomics, 31,* 423-429.

Posada, M. (2006a). *Emission permits for climate policy: Agent based modelling in natural resources management.* Pearson Education.

Posada, M. (2006b). Strategic software agents in continuous double auction under dynamics environments. In *Proceedings of IDEAL 2006.* Spain

Posada, M., Hernández, C., & López, A. (2004). Emission permits auctions: An agent based modelling approach. In *proceedings of the 2nd International Conference of the ESSA.* Spain.

Posada, M., Hernández, C., & López, A. (2005). Electricity and emission permits auctions in Spain: An agent based modelling approach. In *Proceedings* of the *3rd International Conference of the ESSA.* Germany.

Posada, M., Hernández, C., & López, A. (2006a). Learning in a continuous double auction market. In P. Mathieu, B. Beaufils, &O. Brandouy (Eds.), *Artificial economics—Lecture notes in economics and mathematical systems 564.* Springer.

Posada, M., Hernández, C., & López, A. (2006b). Strategic behaviour in a continuous double auction market. In *Proceedings* of *Artificial Economics.* Denmark.

Rust, J., Miller, J., & Palmer, R. (1992). Behaviour of trading automata in a computerized double auction market. In D. Friedman & J. Rust (Eds.), *The double auction market: Institutions, theories, and evidence* (pp. 155-198). Addison-Wesley.

Weidlich, A., Sensfuß, F., Genoese, M., & Veit, D. (2005). Studying the effects of CO_2 emissions trading on the electricity market–A multi-agent-based approach. In *Proceedings of the 2nd Joint Research Workshop:Business and emissions trading.* Springer.

Springer, U. (2003). The market for GHG permits under the Kyoto protocol—A survey of model studies. *Energy Economics 25,* 527-551.

Smith, V. (1989). Theory, experiment and economics. *Journal of Economic Perspectives,* 783-801.

Tesauro, G., & Das, R. (2001). High-performance bidding agents for the continuous double auction. *Proceedings of the Third ACM Conference on Electronic Commerce.*

Tietenberg, T.H. (2006). *Tradable permits bibliography.* Retrieved December 31, 2006 from, http://www.colby.edu/personal/t/thtieten/trade.html

Chapter XV
Intergovernmental Negotiations:
Peer Coordination in Intergovernmental Policy Networks

Nicole J. Saam
University of Erfurt, Germany

David Sumpter
Uppsala University, Sweden

ABSTRACT

Concession behavior is typically seen in bargaining processes, e.g., in intergovernmental negotiations. In traditional bargaining theory, especially in game-theoretic models, concessions to opponents are interpreted as actions in which the conceding party loses face. In this article, we propose a new approach to bargaining: peer coordination. Rather than losing face on conceding to opponents, focal governments will increase their reputation among peers when adjusting to the present positions of the peers. Relying on a data set on the EU Intergovernmental Conference of 1996, which led to the Amsterdam treaty, we test and corroborate the hypothesis that a peer coordination model which assumes peer coordination in intergovernmental policy networks makes better predictions for negotiation outcomes than a random model which we interpret as a kind of null model.

INTRODUCTION

How can states economize on transaction costs in intergovernmental negotiations that span months and years and include many governments? Reaching a decision becomes harder the more agents are involved. Once we move out of the bilateral setting, many different constellations with many negotiation parties can be considered: (a) a group of separate, individual negotiators, (b) bilateral negotiations with multiple participants on each side, (c) a group of advisers preparing one side for negotiations, (d) a permanent decision-making or advisory group, or (e) an ad hoc decision-making or advisory group (Raiffa, Richardson, & Metcalfe, 2002, p. 385).

Coalition formation is one way to economize on transaction costs. It is an emergent phenomenon which is often observed in multilateral intergovernmental negotiations. There is a well-established tradition in political science of studying coalition formation from a game-theoretic point of view (Riker, 1962; Axelrod, 1970; De Swaan, 1973; Peleg, 1980, 1981; Deemen, 1997; Saam,Thurner, & Arndt, 2004). Coalition formation is the extreme type of coordinated action in bargaining processes. At the other limit, there is uncoordinated action in which governments have only very limited opportunities to economize on transaction costs.

In between, there is a type of coordinated action that does not automatically imply coalition formation but that nevertheless economizes on transaction costs: peer coordination in intergovernmental policy networks. It is the charm of the peer coordination approach in intergovernmental policy networks that concessions to opponents are not interpreted as actions in which the conceding party loses face. Rather, focal governments will increase their reputation among peers when adjusting to their present positions (Section 2). In this article, *we test and corroborate* (Section 5) *the hypothesis that a peer coordination model*

which assumes peer coordination in ex ante *intergovernmental policy networks* (Section 4) *makes better predictions for negotiation outcomes than a random model which we interpret as a kind of null model*. We rely on a data set from the EU Intergovernmental Conference of 1996 which led to the Amsterdam Treaty (Section 3).

THEORY

Negotiations Involving Multiple Parties

Governments that want to bring about a certain prefered outcome need not necessarily form coalitions. Their concession behavior need not be based on an agreement on the part of two or more players to coordinate their actions. Particularly, in multilateral negotiations with many issues, it seems implausible that multiple coalitions form in an explicit way. Either there would be overlapping memberships in many issue-specific coalitions, or there would be only a few coalitions that spread over several issues with several governments outside the coalitions. Both alternatives make bargaining rather more than less difficult.This argument has been expecially emphasized for our empirical case with negotiations in the European Union. Nugent stresses the fluidity and weakness of coalition structures in the EU: "cohesive and fixed alliances ... between particular governmentts do not exist. Rather, governments tend to

Figure 1. Uncoordinated and coordinated action in multilateral bargaining

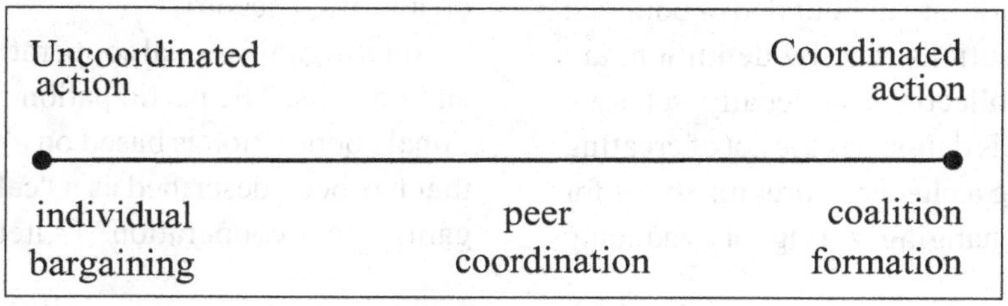

Uncoordinated action		Coordinated action
individual bargaining	peer coordination	coalition formation

come together in different combinations on different issues" (Nugent, 1999, 474). Wright (1996, 152) and Hayes-Renshaw and Wallace (1997, 227) point to the unpredictability and complexity of coalitions' structures. Thomson, Boerefijn, and Stokman (2004) do not find evidence for a coalition structure in actor alignments in European Union decision making. Therefore, we have suggested an alternative approach (Saam & Sumpter, forthcoming a) in which coalitions may emerge or not. Coalition formation is conceived as one extreme type of coordinated action in bargaining processes. At the other extreme, there is uncoordinated action. However, in between there is a type of coordinated action that does not imply coalition formation (see Figure 1): peer coordination in intergovernmental policy networks.

Peer Coordination in Intergovernmental Policy Networks

The peer coordination type of multilateral bargaining relies on two lines of theory: (1) theories of interorganizational network formation, particularly the concepts of interorganizational network, networking, mutual adjustment type of coordination, calculus of interorganizatonal cooperation, and the concept of peers; (2) concepts in the policy network line of argument in political science.

Theories of interorganizational network formation. Relying on the sociology of organizations, we perceive policy networks as a special type of interorganizational network (Alter & Hage, 1993). Alter and Hage define networks as the basic social form that permits interorganizational interactions in exchange, concerted action, and joint production. Networks are unbounded or bounded clusters of organizations that, by definition, are nonhierarchical collectives of legally separate units. Networking is defined as the act of creating and/or maintaining a cluster of organizations for the purpose of exchanging, acting, or producing

among the member organizations (Alter & Hage, 1993, 46).

Whetton (1987) has classified the extremely broad concept of coordination that ranges from simple ad hoc agreements to participation in formally organized coordination councils into three types: mutual adjustment, corporate, and alliance. They vary in intensity, form of social power, formalization, and scope of coordination activity. Mutual adjustment is the weakest form of coordination, while corporate is the strongest. Coalitions are an example of the alliance type of coordination. We will focus our attention on the mutual adjustment type of coordination. This type–which may also be interpreted as a strategy of interaction–provides the narrowest range of benefits but also the fewest costs. Complete authority is retained by the participating organizations. Interaction rules are developed as the need arises in the process of interaction. Their violation is not regarded as severely as in other coordination strategies, nor are the types of sanctions for violation as severe. There is no central unit to monitor or detect violations. As a consequence, there are almost no sanctions. The group of organizations that interact in a mutual adjustment type of coordination is referred to as a system of peers (Whetton, 1987, 244). Attempts to change the balance of power among organizations tend to be resisted. Social power is based on influence and coordination is achieved by mutual adjustment. Differences of opinions regarding goals can be resolved only through negotiation between participants. The main difference from the alliance type of coordination is that in the latter, power is exercised both by the system and by the members. Alliances are based on a written accord.

Interorganizational cooperation has both costs and benefits. The participation in interorganizational cooperation is based on a rational decision that has been described as a "calculus of interorganizatonal cooperation" (Alter & Hage, 1993,

35ff.). Organizations calculate that the benefits outweigh the losses before they combine their efforts with others. Examples of costs are: loss of resources–e.g., time, money, information—loss of reputation, loss of autonomy and ability to unilaterally control outcomes, conflict over goals, and delays in solutions due to problems in coordination. Examples of benefits are: opportunities to learn and adapt, gain of resources, gain of influence over domain, and gain of mutual support.

Policy networks. Following Pappi and Henning (1998), we refer to policy networks as social choice systems. Policy networks among member states prior to negotiations are interpreted ex-post as influence networks. Influence is conceptualized as an exchange of resources. Participation in policy networks presupposes the possession of resources on the side of the actors. Exchanges of resources are continuous in policy domain networks. It is the goal of the actors to bring specific policy decisions closer to their preferred outcome. It is important to note that not all network members are mobilized for all decisions.

An integrated perspective. Perceiving policy networks as a special type of interorganizational networks, we relate both lines of theory. Peer coordination in intergovernmental policy networks is reconstructed as a mutual adjustment type of coordination in which governments which belong to a policy domain interact in exchange, concerted action, or joint production. Here we use the broader network definition of Alter and Hage (1993) in order to allow the specification of different types of networks, e.g., with respect to the mechanism of peer selection. Peer coordination is a behavioural strategy of rational governments which are involved in multilateral bargaining. A focal government is defined as a government that actively (not only passively) engages in peer coordination. It selects peers, exchanges information on the bargaining positions and opinions on the ongoing negotiations, and adjusts to the

positions of the peers. Information on bargaining positions and opinions on ongoing negotiations does not spread passively. Rather, it is a sensitive kind of knowledge, where the latest position and opinion of a government will often be private knowledge. So, information is exchanged because during the interaction, the focal as well as the peer government describes and explains her view and discusses and tries to convince the other. Governments that do not declare a preference for a position at the beginning of the negotiations never act as a focal government with respect to that issue. Many peers cause high transaction costs to the focal government. They also bring cognitive overload. As a consequence, focal governments have to economize on peers.

Peer selection and homophily. Originally, the concept of peers refered to a group of people of the same age. People of the same age were assumed to be exposed to and influenced by the same socioeconomic and sociocultural situations, as opposed to people of another age. This concept has been generalized and transferred. Today, it applies to individuals as well as organizations or governments. Government peer selection has to be explained by several determinants, notably different forms of of homophily between governments. Homophily is the selection of peers on the basis of some similarity to the self. For governments this can be a shared preference for the same negotiation outcome, political ideology of the political party in government, socioeconomic and sociocultural situation of the society, historical ties that relate to common historical experiences, etc.

McPherson, Smith-Lovin, and Cook (2001) describe how the homophily principle structures social network ties of every type, including marriage, friendship, work, advice, support, information transfer, exchange, comembership, and other types of relationships that have been of interest to social scientists since the classical article that introduced that principle (Lazarsfeld & Merton,

1954). Durrett and Levin (2005) have shown in a theoretical model how homophily can lead to stable co-operating groups, i.e., stable peer groups. These groups can persist even if the peers share only some of the above determinants. The key factor that gives rise to such co-operation is that peers adjust their position to one closer to that of others. In terms of social mechanisms, such an approach can also be thought of as rational imitation (Hedström & Svedberg, 1998, Chapter XII; Hedström, 2005). There exists a wealth of formal modelling tools for investigating such social imitation (Sumpter, 2006).

The bargaining positions change throughout the negotiation process due to concessions of the governments. However, as concessions need not be declared in public, they may be private knowledge. We assume that the focal government is not forced by the peer governments to move to the positions of the peers. Within the mutual adjustment type of coordination, they do not have the power to induce concessions. Rather, focal governments describe and explain their view, and discuss and try to convince their peers. Concessions depend on the peers' positions and on the national interest of a focal government with respect to an issue under negotiation (see salience in Coleman, 1966). The greater the national interest, the less likely the nation is to be swayed by the opinion of others.

Each of these peers is also a focal government with specific peers. Altogether, in intergovernmental negotiations, governments interact in partial networks of focal government and peer governments, which we call peer networks. The peer networks overlap. For analytical reasons, we distinguish *issue-specific systems of peer networks* from *the whole system of peer networks*. The latter refers to all peer networks of a multiple issue negotiation system. Particularly in multilateral, multiple issue, multi-stage, and multi-level negotiation systems, it is very improbable that there is any peer network that does not overlap with at least one other peer network. Concession behaviour in these overlapping peer networks is described as mutual adjustment. Focal governments adjust to their peers (and only to them). Adjusting to peers may be reconstructed as rational behaviour. *Rather than losing face in conceding to opponents, focal governments will increase their reputation among peers when adjusting to the present positions of the peers.* The overall outcome of such a system of overlapping peer networks results from many incremental adjustment processes within the peer networks. An agreement is achieved when these incremental adjustment processes finally converge as a result of overlapping memberships of governments in many peer networks. If they do not converge, the negotiations have failed. In this subsection, we just hinted at the theoretical action foundation of our approach. It has to be further elaborated.

Although from the analytical point of view, individual bargaining, peer coordination, and coalition formation may be looked upon as ideal types, from an empirical perspective the dichotomy between uncoordinated and coordinated action in multilateral bargaining may be interpreted as a continuum. Then, individual bargaining may develop into peer coordination when focal governments start to realize that they have (or once have had) peers, and peer coordination may develop into coalition formation when governments realize that they and their peers have exceedingly overlapping memberships and that they could benefit from binding themselves into a more formalized mode of coordination, namely coalitions. In other words, coalitions may emerge out of peer cooperation. However, they need not do so. This is the charm of the peer coordination model in intergovernmental policy networks.

Mechanisms of Peer Selection

What are the reasons for a focal government to select another government as a peer? We propose several alternatives, e.g., ex ante transnational coordination, preference, salience, power, neighbourship, and random (Saam & Sumpter, forthcoming b). In this chapter, we concentrate on two of these mechanisms: ex ante transnational coordination and random coordination.

The motivation for *ex ante transnational coordination* is functional collaboration of ministries in their respective policy domains (Andreae & Kaiser, 1998, 43ff.). We assume that the more ministries of a country *B* that have been contacted during ex ante transnational coordination by ministries of country *A*, the more often will the government of *B* be selected as a peer by the government of *A* during the real negotiations. Rather than losing face in conceding to opponents, focal governments will increase their reputation among peers and other political actors, like national ministries, when adjusting to the present positions of the peers. This mechanism of peer selection is suited to establish reputation beyond single issues and may have a long-term effect. Ex ante transnational coordination may also be based on homophily.

A second mechanism is *uniform random peer selection*. This mechanism is not based on homophily; instead, governments are selected from the pool of all governments uniformly at random. The uniform random model provides us with a null model to test networks based on homophily against. There is also, however, theoretical justification for uniform random selections that can be made in two diffent ways. The first is that governments sample a few positions of other governments at random without respect to issue or the other governments' positions. A completely random sampling network may be difficult to motivate in terms of the actions of governments, since governments may well bias their peer selection in some manner. An alternative explanation–which we prefer—therefore, is that uniform peer selection reflects the hypothesis that decisions are made through some approximate knowledge of what positions are held on average by the governments. This is a highly plausible mechanism: Uniform random sampling reflects

the fact that governments make decisions based on their perception of the position of other governments, weighting each government equally. In order to reduce transaction costs, only a subsection of peers are sampled. This mechanism is not suited to establish reputation among governments because each government knows that it has the same chance of being selected as a peer as all the other governments. Relations are unreciprocated and highly transient.

Note that we have described all selection mechanisms as stochastic. In order to reduce transaction costs, a focal government will only poll the opinion of a number of peers—a sample—at any point in time. If governments apply the selection mechanisms in a stochastic way, each potential peer has the chance of being selected as a peer. Throughout the whole negotiation process, focal governments will be able to describe and explain their view, and discuss and try to convince all potential peers. This has some influence on the overlap of peer networks: Peers will change more often than in the case where governments apply the selection mechanisms in a deterministic way. Thus, governments are able to establish and use more weak ties. As Granovetter (1974) has shown, it is through the relatively weak ties of less frequent contacts that new and different information is likely to become available. However, governments that have not declared a preference for a position at the beginning of the negotiations are not selected as peers.

THE EU INTERGOVERNMENTAL CONFERENCE 1996

The Intergovernmental Conference of 1996 constituted another step–like Maastricht or Nice–of an institutional reform contributing to the constitutionalization of European integration. Hitherto, EU constitution building proceeded gradually, i.e., member states consented on voluntarily incomplete contracts. The Amsterdam conference took place from April 1996 to June 16/17, 1997. The Intergovernmental Conference of 1996 had the purpose of fulfilling Political Union, of (re-) balancing the division of power, but especially of preparing the institutional setting for an EU enlargement. The Maastricht Treaty already contained provisions for the amendment of the constitutional framework of the EU. These provisions included the date of reconvening as well as particular issues to be negotiated.

During prenegotiations within the so-called Westendorp reflection group, an intergovernmental preparation of the Intergovernmental Conference of 1996 took place from June 1995 to December 1995. This group of delegates of the member states reached an agreement on the agenda, i.e., with regard to the issues to be negotiated. The report of the Westendorp group provided a set of roughly formulated issues, i.e., it delivered broad political goals and guidelines. The Service Juridique of the Council of the European Union processed these global issues into 30 precise issues with hard legal options. Each issue included an explicit status quo with indications on its legal status. Legal options were ordinally arrayed, going from the least integrationist to the most far-reaching option. This prestructuring of issues and options demonstrates the enormous institutionalization of this negotiation system.

National delegations negotiated during 16 months in Brussels. They tried to find out each other's ranges of maneuver and their discretionary leeways in order to maximize their own governments' expected utility of a negotiated outcome taking into account the implied internal and intergovernmental transaction costs. Through bilateral and multilateral communication, negotiators tried to find out simultaneously their domestic as well as their external restrictions (Thurner, et al., 2003; Thurner, 2004). This process led to a preliminary settlement of a part of the issues in the Dublin II report (December 1996). The final game reached its climax at the Amsterdam Summit. The resulting Amsterdam Treaty was formally implemented through a ratification process under specific constitutional provisions in each member state (an exhaustive identification of formal ex-post ratification requirements as well as discretionary agenda setting powers of all involved EU member states is provided by Stoiber &Thurner, 2004).

Further Backgrounds of Theorizing

Our empirical example requires that we consider another branch of theory. In order to identify the players we need a theory that describes who these players are. It turns out that the players are determined by the decision rule on constitutional reforms of the European Union.

Intergovernmental Negotiations under unanimity rule. Negotiations involving multiple parties take place under different decision rules. Parliamentary negotiations are often governed by voting rules, with simple majorities, two-thirds majorities, or even more complicated double-criteria. In intergovernmental negotiations, simple majority rule may apply. However, we also find unanimity rule very often. For example, in the European Union unanimity is necessary for decisions on constitutional reforms. Unanimous decisions are supposed to be efficient and lead to an optimal aggregation of preferences (Buchanan &Tullock, 1997; Rae, 1975). However, with an increasing number of agents, the process of decision-making becomes more and more difficult. In recent years, the efficiency of unanimity rule has been questioned (Colomer, 1999; Guttman, 1998).

Liberal intergovernmentalism. Following liberal intergovernmentalism (Moravcsik & Nikolaïdis, 1999), we view European integration as a sequence of intergovernmental bargains or treaties with the governments continuing to be the "Masters of the Treaty." We do not rely on the multi-level governance approach (Hooghe &

Marks, 2001) that proposes to take into account both domestic interests and institutions as well as international and supranational constellations. Our basic argument is that only the member states have a right to vote on constitutional reforms of the European Union.

Empirical Data

We use a data set from the EU Intergovernmental Conference of 1996 (Thurner, Pappi, & Stoiber, 2002; many thanks to Paul W. Thurner for allowing us to use some of this data). Data collection combined analysis of documents and standardized interviews of top-level bureaucrats in EU member states. The survey is centered around 30 documents, so-called fiches (CONF 3801/96 to CONF 3830/96) as prepared by top lawyers in the Council's Service Juridique. The documents are conceived as constituting a multi-dimensional issue space. Each of these issues is considered to constitute a one-dimensional negotiation space with ordinally arrayed options.

The data set includes quantitative data on preferences of the involved governmental actors prior to negotiations, transnational networks among governmental actors, as well as negotiation outcomes. We use data especially on: (1) the status quo, negotiation options, and empirical negotiation outcome on each issue; (2) the national interest of each member state with respect to each issue (derived from the answers of the ministry of foreign affairs); (3) weights that measure the connectedness of each member state with each other during the pre-negotiation phase based on how often actors of one member state have addressed actors of another member state (see Thurner, Pappi, & Stoiber, 2002, 149-158). Policy networks among member states prior to negotiations are ex-post interpreted as influence networks.

STRUCTURE OF THE MODEL

Our formal model of peer coordination is based on the theoretical model which we have outlined above. In particular, we emphasise exchange of information through local interactions. This leads us to an opinion formation model (Weidlich, 1994) that is capable of modelling the dynamics of interacting populations with discrete attitudes. In order to give our approach grounding in the rationalist approach to negotiation, we also frame our model in terms of the adaptive play framework (Young, 1993a,b, 1998) that is capable of modelling peer selection.

Basic Model

We assume an international negotiation system consisting of 15 governments $i \in \{1, \ldots, 15\}$ negotiating over 46 issues $k \in \{1, \ldots, 46\}$. Let $O_k = \{1, \ldots, m_k\}$ be the set of possible outcomes for each issue k, where m_k is the number of negotiation options. Each issue's negotiation options are discrete, ordinally scaled, and located in a Euclidian negotiation space. The options are known from empirical data (see Section 3). Define the legally defined status quo in the k-th issue $SQ_k \in O_k$ and the Amsterdam negotiation result in the j-th issue $AO_k \in O_k$. Call the announced ideal point of a government i in issue k $w_{ik*} \in O_k$. Governmental preferences over the outcomes can be characterized by the following von Neumann-Morgenstein utility function $U_i(o_k, w_{ik*}) = 1 - |w_{ik*} - o_k|$. We assume issue-by-issue negotiations, i.e., each issue is negotiated separately. Negotiations take place during a time span of 16 months.

For a particular issue, each individual government i, starts with a negotiation position, $w_{ik}(0) = w_{ik*}$, at negotiation step 0. This position is known from empirical data (see Section 3). Our assumption is that the greater the national interest of a government with respect to an issue, the less likely the government is to be swayed by the opinion of peers. Or, seen from the perspective of concession behaviour, the less often it will consider making a concession. Therefore, we use the empirical data on the national interest to initialize action probabilities of each government with respect to each issue. Whenever a government will be chosen as a focal government of that time step, it will consider a concession. Initially, we set a parameter λ_i to be proportional to the national interest with respect to that issue; λ_i is the average time between opinion polling. Then, each government selects a random time $\tau(i)$, according to an exponential distribution with parameter λ_i, at which to "poll the opinion" of other governments and consider a concession. Thus, governments to which an issue is important will poll opinion, and thus change opinion, less often than those to which an issue is less important. Governments with no position, i.e., governments that have not declared a preference for a position at the beginning of the negotiations, never poll or affect opinion.

The simulation is then run in discrete time steps as follows: Start with $t=0$.

1. **Selecting the focal government:** The government with lowest value of $\tau(i)$ is selected to be the focal government for this time step.

2. **Peer selection:** Focal government i picks a set S, of size s, of other governments randomly according to mechanism of peer selection. This set of governments are those that have been polled by the focal government. During the interaction with each peer, the focal government receives information on each peer's actual bargaining position.

3. **Concession behavior:** We assume that governments make incremental concessions. From their present bargaining position they move either one position to the left or to the right. The probability that the focal government moves its position to the left increases

with the number of polled governments with a position to the left, and likewise, the probability it moves right increases with the number of polled governments with a position to the right. Specifically, we note that $R=|\{j \in S, : w_{jk}(t) > w_{ik}(t)\}|$, respectively $L=|\{j \in S, : w_{jk}(t) < w_{ik}(t)\}|$, is the number of polled governments with a position to the right, respectively left of the focal government. In a single time step a government can only move left or right or stay still. If $L=R$, the government does not move position. If $R>L$, then the probability that the focal government moves right is:

$$\frac{\exp(\alpha R)}{\exp(\alpha R) + \exp(\alpha q)} \quad (1)$$

where q is the threshold at which the probability that the government moves right equals $\frac{1}{2}$ and α determines the steepness of this threshold. Figure 2 plots this threshold function for various values of α. As can be seen from Figure 2, α dramatically changes the probability that a focal government moves. Whereas there is a smooth increase in the probability to move when α is small (e.g., $\alpha=1$), there is an abrupt increase when α is high (e.g., $\alpha=10$).

We thus select a uniformly distributed number between 0 and 1, and if it is less than eqn 1, the focal government moves one step to the right, i.e., $w_{ik}(t+\tau(i))=w_{ik}(t)+1$. Similarly, if $L>R$ then:

$$\frac{\exp(\alpha L)}{\exp(\alpha L) + \exp(\alpha q)} \quad (2)$$

is the probability that the focal government moves one position left.

4. We update $w_{ik}(t+\tau(i))=w_{ik}(t)$ for all governments, j, not equal to i; $t=t+ \tau(i)$ and $\tau(i) = \tau(i)+\lambda_i$ and return to stage one.

For an overview on all variables and parameters of the model see Table 1.

Figure 2. Examples of equation (1), plotted for various values of α, with q=3

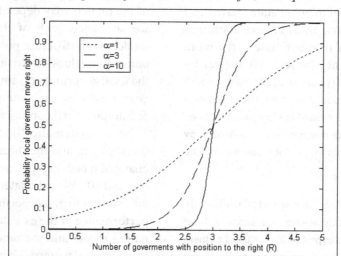

The simulation ends when all governments have adopted the same position or if no unanimous decision is reached after 16 simulated months have passed, then the status quo option is adopted (i.e., the negotiations have failed). The mean value of λ_i over all issues was 0.1616 polls per month.

Mechanisms of Peer Selection

We implement two alternative mechanisms of peer selection: ex ante transnational coordination and random.

Table 1. Variables and parameters of the formal model

Variable	Interpretation	Initialization
w_{ikt}	**bargaining position** of government i with respect to issue k at t ($t > 1$)	-
parameter		
k_k	**issues** (k = 1 to 46)	empirical data
m_k	**number of different declared positions** with respect to issue k	empirical data
g_i	**national government** (i = 1 to 15)	empirical data
w_{ik*}	**declared initial bargaining position** of government i with respect to issue k	empirical data
λ_{ik}	**salience** of issue k for government i	empirical data
s	**sample size:** Number of governments that a government polls the opinion of	$s = 5$
q	**quorum:** Threshold value at which the probability that a government moves equal 50%	varied in experiments: $1.0 \leq q \leq 4.5$
α	**steepness of threshold value**	varied in experiments: $1 \leq \alpha \leq 10$

Ex ante transnational coordination model. The more ministries of member state *j* have been contacted during ex ante transnational coordination by ministries of member state *I,* the more often will government *j* be selected as peer by focal government *i* (pseudo-code: pick nonself players randomly with probabilities $p_1 = p_{ij}$ calculated from the number of ministries of member state *j* that had been contacted during ex ante transnational coordination by ministries of member state *i;* allow the same nation to be picked more than once).

Random model. Peers are selected uniformly at random (pseudo-code: each peer is a nonself player randomly chosen, each with probability $p_2 = 1/14$;i.e., there are 15 players in total. The same nation can be picked more than once).

MODEL RESULTS

We have implemented this model, run experiments, and finally checked for the robustness of the simulation results. Because the performance of the models may depend on parameter values, we simulated each of the two peer selection models with different possible combinations of parameter values. In particular, we assumed that the focal governments sampled the opinion of s=5 goverments on each sampling occasion (Saam & Sumpter, forthcoming a) and investigated the effect of systematically changing the quorum threshold, q, and the threshold steepness, α (we changed q between one and four, and α between one and 10). We calculated Pearson's correlation coefficients to guage performance (Table 2). The performance of the ex ante transnational coordination model and the random model follow the same general pattern. There is a global minimum of performance at $q=1$ and $\alpha=1$. Starting from this global minimum, incrementing either *q* or *α* leads to a quick increase in model performance. For all combinations of *q* and *α* with both $q \geq 2$ and $\alpha \geq 2$, correlation coefficient r is located between 0.66 and 0.74, which is quite good.

Table 2. *Results of sensitivity analysis. Model performance as a function of parameters, q and α (s=5). The table shows the correlation between simu-lated negotiation outcome (mode of predicted model outcomes over 500* or 1000** simulation runs) and empirical Amsterdam negotiation outcome (Pearson's correlation coefficient).*

Ex ante transnational coordination model*

alpha / q	1	2	3	4	5	6	7	8	9	10
1	0,16	0,12	0,48	0,64	0,66	0,65	0,69	0,68	0,66	0,67
2	0,35	0,70	0,72	0,72	0,73	0,72	0,71	0,72	0,72	0,70
3	0,69	0,72	0,73	0,71	0,73	0,74	0,73	0,72	0,72	0,73
4	0,73	0,71	0,73	0,72	0,72	0,73	0,73	0,73	0,71	0,72

Random model**

alpha / q	1	2	3	4	5	6	7	8	9	10
1	0,09	0,14	0,37	0,53	0,57	0,62	0,61	0,62	0,62	0,61
2	0,36	0,66	0,70	0,72	0,71	0,72	0,71	0,71	0,71	0,72
3	0,67	0,71	0,70	0,71	0,70	0,72	0,72	0,71	0,71	0,70
4	0,73	0,73	0,72	0,73	0,72	0,72	0,72	0,72	0,72	0,72

Table 3 presents descriptive statistics of the performance of the two models. Table 3 shows that the ex ante transnational coordination model has the best overall performance (mean correlation coefficient of 0.67). However, most interestingly, the performance of the random model does not differ that much (mean correlation coefficient of 0.64). The Kruskal-Wallis Test is highly significant at the 0.001 level. The mean rank of each of the models is located at 84.0 (random model) and 101.0 (ex ante transnational coordination model). This indicates that the results of the random and the ex ante transnational coordination models may not differ significantly. We apply the Wilcoxon-Test that compares the models' performances against each other. The test is based on the number of times the performance of one model is greater than, equal to, or less than that of the other. We find that the ex ante transnational coordination model's performance is different from the random model's (asymptotic significance 0.000; Z=-3.76 based on positive ranks) which allows us to refute the null model.

DISCUSSION

In research on multilateral, multi-issue negotiations, descriptive case studies still prevail. In this chapter, we have contributed to positive bargaining theory on negotiations involving multiple parties. In this setting, the social relations between policy domain actors are crucial for explaining policy outcomes. We have presented and tested a theoretical approach to peer coordination in intergovernmental policy networks, in which the formation of coalitions is no longer a strict consequence of the model assumptions. Coalition formation is conceived as one extreme type of coordinated action in bargaining processes. At the other extreme, there is uncoordinated action. However, in between there is a type of coordinated action that does not automatically imply coalition formation: peer coordination in intergovernmental policy networks.

Relying on a data set on the EU Intergovernmental Conference of 1996 which led to the Amsterdam treaty, we compared the performance of two alternative mechanisms of peer selection. The random model was used as a kind of null model. We found that the ex ante transnational coordination model has the better performance, and it is significantly different from the random model. Therefore, as long as we have no further data on our empirical case (with respect to q and α), we should prefer the ex ante transnational coordination model.

This result implies that peer coordination during negotiations is a promising approach to explain the outcome of intergovernmental negotiations. It may now be applied to further examples of multi-party, multi-issue negotiations.

We conclude with suggestions for further research: The peer coordination approach still

Table 3. Descriptive statistics of the performance (Pearson's correlation coefficient) of the models of peer selection

Model of peer selection	N	Mean	Std. Dev.	Minimum	Maximum	Mean Rank
Ex ante transnational coordination	40	.67	.14	.12	.74	101.0
Random	40	.64	.15	.09	.73	84.0

needs some conceptional clarifications. In its present form, parameter α has not yet been given a sociological interpretation. Is it a behavior of a focal government? Is it a situational constraint? Beyond this, alternative mechanisms of peer selection may be tested (see Saam & Sumpter, forthcoming b).

ACKNOWLEDGMENT

DS is funded by the Royal Society.

REFERENCES

Alter, C., & Hage, J. (1993). *Organizations working together*. Newbury Park, CA: Sage.

Andreae, L., & Kaiser, K. (1998). Die "Außenpolitik" der fachministerien. In W.Eberwein, & K. Kaiser (Eds.). *Deutschlands neue außenpolitik, 4*, 29-46. München: Oldenbourg.

Axelrod, R. (1970). *Conflict of interest*. Chicago: Markham.

Black, D. (1958). *The theory of committees and elections*. Cambridge: Cambridge University Press.

Buchanan, J. M., & Tullock, G. (1997). *The calculus of consent: Logical foundations of constitutional democracy*. Ann Arbor: The University of Michigan Press.

Coleman, J.S. (1966). The possibility of a social welfare function. *American Economic Review, 56*, 1105-1122.

Colomer, J.M. (1999). On the geometry of unanimity rule. *Journal of Theoretical Politics, 11*, 543-553.

De Swaan, A. (1973). *Coalition theories and cabinet formations*. Amsterdam: North Holland.

Durrett, R., & Levin, S.A. (2005). Can stable social groups be maintained by homophilous imitation alone? *Journal of Economic Behavior and Organization, 57*, 267-286.

Felsenthal, D.S., & Machover, M. (1998). *The measurement of voting power*. Cheltenham: Edward Elgar.

Granovetter, M. (1974). *Getting a job*. Cambridge, Mass.: Harvard University Press.

Guttman, J.M. (1998). Unanimity and majority Rule: The calculus of consent reconsidered. *European Journal of Political Economy, 14*, 189-207.

Hayes-Renshaw, F., & Wallace, H. (1997). *The council of ministers*. London: Macmillan.

Hedstrom, P., & Swedberg, R. (Eds.). (1998). *Social mechanisms: An analytical approach to social theory*. Cambridge: Cambridge University Press.

Hedstrom, P. (2005). *Dissecting the social: On the principles of analytical sociology*. Cambridge: Cambridge University Press.

Hooghe, L., & Marks, G.W. (2001). *Multi-level governance and European integration*. Lanham: Rowman & Littlefield.

Lazarsfeld, P., & Merton, R.K. (1954). Friendship as a social process: A substantive and methodological analysis. In M. Berger, T. Abel, & Ch. H. Page (Eds.), *Freedom and control in modern society* (pp. 18-66). New York: Van Nostrand.

McPherson, M., Smith-Lovin, L., & Cook, J.M. (2001). Birds of a feather: Homophily in social networks. *Annual Review of Sociology, 27*, 415-44.

Moravcsik, A., & Nikolaïdis, K. (1999). Explaining the \treaty of Amsterdam: Interests, influence, institutions. *Journal of Common Market Studies, 37*, 59-85.

Nugent, N. (1999). *The government and politics of the European union*. London: Macmillan.

Pappi, F.U., & Henning, C.H.C.A. (1998). Policy networks: More than a metaphor? *Journal of Theoretical Politics, 10*, 553-575.

Peleg, B. (1980). A theory of coalition formation in committees. *Journal of Mathematical Economics, 7*, 115-134.

Peleg, B. (1981). Coalition formation in simple games with dominant players. *International Journal of Game Theory, 10*, 11-33.

Putnam, R.D. (1988). Diplomacy and domestic politics: The logic of two-level games. *International Organization, 42*, 427-460.

Rae, D.W. (1975). The limits of consensual decision. *The American Political Science Review, 69*, 1270-1294.

Raiffa, H., Richardson, J., & Metcalfe, D. (2002). *Negotiation analysis: The science and art of collaborative decision making*. Cambridge, MA.: The Belknap Press of Harvard University Press.

Riker, W. (1962). *The theory of political coalitions*. New Haven: Yale Univ. Press.

Saam, N.J., & Sumpter, D. (forthcoming). Intergovernmental negotiations: Peer selection in intergovernmental policy networks.

Saam, N.J., & Sumpter, D. (forthcoming a). Coalition formation as emergent phenomenon in intergovernmental negotiations. *Journal of Policy Modeling*.

Saam, N. J., Thurner, P. W., & Arndt, F. (forthcoming b). Zeuthen-Harsanyi reconsidered: Modeling negotiation dynamics with Boudedly rational agents.

Saam, N. J., Thurner, P. W., & Arndt, F. (2004). Dynamics of international negotiations. A simulation of EU intergovernmental conferences. *Mannhei-mer Zentrum für Europäische Sozialforschung: Arbeitspapiere–Working Papers* No. 78.

Saam, N.J., Thurner, P.W., & Arndt, F. (2004). Dynamics of international negotiations: A simulation of EU intergovernmental conferences. In C. van Dijkum, J. Blasius, H. Kleijer, & B. van Hilten. (Eds.). *Recent developments and applications in social research methodology. Proceedings of the Sixth International Conference on Logic and Methodology*. August 17-20, Amsterdam, The Netherlands.

Shapley, L.S., & Shubik, M. (1954). A measure of evaluating a distribution of power in a committee system. *American Political Science Review, 48*, 787-792.

Stoiber, M., & Thurner, P.W. (2004). Die ratifikation intergouvernementaler verträge: Konstitutionelle erfordernisse und akteursspezifische agendakontrolle. In F.U. Pappi, E. Riedel, P.W. Thurner, & R. Vaubel. (Eds.), *Die institutionalisierung internationaler verhandlungen* (pp. 173-204) Frankfurt/Main.

Sumpter, D.J.T. (2006). The principles of collective animal behaviour. *Philosophical Transactions of the Royal Society of London: Series B, 361*, 5-22.

Thomson, R., Boerefijn, J., & Stokman, F. (2004). Actor alignments in European Union decision making. *European Journal of Political Research, 43*, 237-261.

Thurner, P.W. (2004). *Die graduelle konstitutionalisierung der Europäischen Union. Eine quantitative fallstudie am beispiel der regierungskonferenz 1996*. Habilitation thesis: Univ. of Mannheim.

Thurner, P.W., Kroneberg, C., & Stoiber, M. (2003). Strategisches signalisieren bei internationalen verhandlungen. Eine quantitative analyse am beispiel der regierungskonferenz 1996. *Zeitschrift für Internationale Beziehungen, 10*, 287-320.

Thurner, P.W., Pappi, F.U., & Stoiber, M. (2002). EU Intergovernmental conferences: A quantitative analytical reconstruction and data-handbook of domestic preference formation, transnational networks and dynamics of compromise during the Amsterdam Treaty negotiations. *Mannheimer Zentrum für Europäische Sozialforschung: Arbeitspapiere–Working Papers* No. 60, *IINS Research Paper* No. 15.

Van Deemen, A.M. (1997). *Coalition formation and social choice*. Boston: Kluwer Academic Publishers.

Walker, J.L. (1969). The diffusion of innovation among the American states. *American Political Science Review, 63*, 880-899.

Weidlich, W. (1994). Synergetic modelling concepts for sociodynamics with application to collective political opinion formation. *Journal of Mathematical Sociology, 18*, 267-291.

Whetton, D.A. (1987). Interorganizational relations. In J. Lorsch (Ed.), *Handbook of organizational behavior* (pp. 238-253). Englewood Cliffs, NJ: Prentice-Hall.

Wright, V. (1996). The national coordination of European policy making. In J. Richardson (Ed.), *European Union: Power and policy making*. London: Routledge, pp. 238-253.

Young, H.P. (1993a). The evolution of conventions. *Econometrica, 61*, 57-84.

Young, H.P. (1993b). An evolutionary model of bargaining. *Journal of Economic Theory, 59*, 145-168.

Young, H.P. (1998). *Individual strategy and social structure*. Princeton, NJ: Princeton University Press.

Chapter XVI
Regional Policy Hints from Heterogeneous Agents Simulation

M. Salzano
Università di Salerno, Italy

ABSTRACT

Following the traditional approach to decision theory it is very difficult to obtain policy hints for complex systems. On the other hand, the study of complex systems supplies powerful instruments that capture useful information on the behaviour of economic systems. This difficulty is enhanced when we are interested in differential regional effects. In fact, for complex systems, even for aggregate analysis, results will differ deeply for each simulation. The literature has shown how we could obtain policy hints for these kinds of systems. Here, we will extend this methodology to the case of differential regional effects. The analysis will be based on a New-Keynesian microfounded model with heterogeneous agents proposed by Salzano (2005). It will be developed in two directions: (a) obtaining better models of differential regional policy effect; (b) obtaining policy suggestions for differential regional effects. We will compare the results of our scheme against traditional results.

INTRODUCTION

In this work, we consider the differential effects of economic policy it is possible to obtain for regional economic areas where economic agents each are heterogeneous in their preferences. We will analyse how it is possible to choose the correct policy tool for obtaining a required regional differential effect.

During the last decade, in the policy agenda of national governments and international organizations, there has emerged the design of policies that seek to reduce spatial disparities in economic well-being - Regional policy.[1]

As noted by Puga, "Despite large regional policy expenditures, regional inequalities in Europe have not narrowed substantially over the last two decades, and by some measures have even widened. Income differences across States have fallen, but inequalities between regions within each State have risen."[2]

A possible explanation could be that, apart from specific regional policy interventions, the general implemented policy could have specific differential effects on different areas.

The idea that both fiscal and monetary policies could have regional differential effects is well diffused in the literature. On the other hand, these kinds of effects are not always correctly considered. "In reality, the nation is made up of diverse regions that are linked but that respond differently to changing economic circumstances. For example, the large declines in crude oil prices in the mid-1980s affected energy-producing regions very differently from energy-consuming regions."[3] Each area has "different resource potentials and confronts different obstacles to growth." Of course, the regional differential effects of a policy are difficult to be studied. In fact, the single effect in each region is subject to a complex behaviour and therefore to a certain degree of uncertainty. This uncertainty will grow when differential effects are of interest.

The analysis of these types of policy effects is usually based on some outcome measure about spatial disparities in aggregate output or consumption. Some models *emphasize* the dynamics of technology-related-variables, others the medium term variables as work, production, and consumption. Critical assumptions within the former kind of models are based on the dynamics of technology-related variables[4], while they are mainly related to the utility maximization of *representative* economic agents in the latter group.

The use of representative economic agents implies the impossibility of considering social and information interaction.[5]

Ignoring social interactions and learning is understandable in order to keep macroeconomic models manageable. If modelling these processes does not contribute significantly to a better representation of the economy, there is not justification to bear the cost of building and simulating more complicated models. .... [However] social interactions are the source of externalities that when ignored may generate policy recommendations which are seriously biased (Robalino, 2000).

A good understanding of differential effects of an economic policy must be based on the mechanism at the basis of its operability.

Generally, economic systems are considered complex. Many theoretical analyses highlight that the mechanisms at the basis of the operability of the complex systems differ from traditional ones. In fact, for the modelization of complex systems, we must take into account the characteristics of such systems and highlight a two-way tie between macro and micro–the problem of microfoundation. It is well known that it is not possible to set up analytical models for complex systems. In fact, these systems can be defined as systems for which no model less complex than the system itself can forecast their behaviour exactly and in detail. No crisp analytical models and solutions are possible.

To deal with the microfoundation question correctly, the possibility of using heterogeneous agents simulation has been emphasized[6]. The side-effect is that, following the traditional approach to decision theory, there is difficulty in the application of results obtained from the agents simulation of complex systems to the analyses of economic policies effects and then to obtain policy hints. In fact, as each simulation will cause a different result, the traditional approach to decision theory based on global or local optimization cannot be applied any more. As consequence, it is unusual that such kinds of analysis are conducive to economic policy suggestions. In fact, complex systems need both a different method of modelling and an alternative approach to the theory of decisions.

Salzano (2005) has demonstrated how policy suggestions could be obtained in the case of economic complex systems, starting from heterogeneous agent simulations.[7] Here, we will try to show how it is possible to obtain economic policy suggestions for complex systems for the case in which we are interested—differential regional effects.

We will start with a summary regarding the main results already obtained and we will summarize the basic model. Then, we will addresses the difficulties that appear when we are interested in differential regional effects and the how it is possible to obtain regional economic policy suggestions from heterogeneous agent simulations.

After having considered the state of the art, we will explicitly start from a New-Keynesian model based on the hypothesis of microeconomic rationing (fixed price and salary in the short period), and heterogeneous agent.[8] Then, we introduce the explicit consideration of heterogeneity and imperfect information.

We will consider our economy divided in two areas with some variables characterizing their agents.

We will use a "bottom-up," "top-down" mix approach. For the simulation, we used one of the simpler and powerful "shells": *NetLogo*.[9]

First, the macroproperties that emerge from the interactions between heterogeneous individuals localized in the two areas are analyzed without considering the public sector (bottom-up approach). Moreover, the modifications caused by such emergent properties on the individuals' preferences through the communication process will be considered (evolutionary "top-down" approach). Then, we will consider the effect of the increase of public expenditure and the differential effects in the two areas.

The comparison with traditional results and the motivations of the differences will close the job.

THE STATE OF ART: RELATIONSHIP WITH THE EXISTING WORKS

The economic analysis is developed by building models of social phenomena. By a model, we mean a *simplified* representation of reality. According to Varian, the efficacy of a model derives from the elimination of irrelevant details, which allows the economist to concentrate on the essential elements of economic reality that he or she tries to understand. Of course, in this "reduction," the problem is how to choose which elements are essential. We consider that at least the sign of results must not change. "A complete reduction would be hopeless and interminable. ... Reduction is necessary to some extent, but it can never be complete."[10]

Until the 70s, a large part of Keynesian economics was only interested in macroeconomic aggregates like inflation, unemployment, and gross domestic product, never considering what the relationship could be between them and the choices made by the different agents in the economy.

The macrolevel properties of an economic system are normally synthesized in the Walrasian, Keynesian, Neoclassical, etc. equilibriums. They rest on equilibrium-based analytical models and, generally, imply a separation between the macro and microlevels (problems of aggregation) or, at best, on a unidirectional relationship between the former and the latter level through aggregated variables (often monetary) such as unemployment, inflation, interest rate, and level of prices or salaries.

Many studies have shown the insufficient realism of macromodellization because of the lack of microeconomic foundations. This is a usual question in science. In fact, as Jon Elster (1983) wrote: "Generally speaking, the scientific practice is to seek an explanation at a lower level than the explanandum."[11] The lack of both such a micro-foundation and of a theoretical basis of general equilibrium has been one of the main reasons for a substantial abandoning of macroeconomic theories, above all the Keynesian ones.[12]

The more recent attempt of mainstream economics to base macroeconomics on "sound microeconomic foundations," or to reduce macroeconomics to microeconomics, has been "motivated by a specific form of reductionism, based on the use of the individual as the given and fundamental use of analysis. ...[It] ... has now run into the sand."[13] Both the hypothesis that all individuals have an *identical* utility function, and individual utility maximisation have devastating consequences for the microfoundations project. As Hodgson (1999) noted: "We have no theoretical basis to assume that real-world market systems can ... [be based on] ... the interactions of atomistic individuals."

Arrow (1986, p. S390) declares: "... [I]t is widely assumed that all individuals have an *identical* utility function. Apart from ignoring obvious differences in individual tastes, this denies the possibility of gains from trade arising from individual differences." Starting from the assumption of individual utility maximisation, Sonnenschein (1972, 1973a, 1973b), Mantel (1974), and Debreu (1974) showed that ,"[T]here is no basis for the assumption that excess demand functions in an exchange economy are downward sloping." The consequences for neoclassical general equilibrium theory are devastating (see Kirman,1989). In fact, "[T]he assumption of rationality or utility maximisation ... gives no guidance to an analysis of macro-level phenomena" (Rizvi,1994a, p. 363). "[T]he uniqueness and stability of general equilibria .... may be indeterminate and unstable unless very strong assumptions are made ... [society behaves as a single individual]. The idea that we should start at the level of the isolated individual is one which we may well have to abandon" (Kirman, 1989, p. 138).[14]

This was the end of the microfoundations project in general equilibrium theory or attempts to base macroeconomics on neoclassical micro-foundations.

As Rizvi (1994b)[15] pointed out, "it was this partially-hushed-up-crisis in general equilibrium theory in the 1970s that led to the adoption of game theory in the 1980s.[T]heoretical work in game theory has raised questions about the very meaning of 'hard core' notions such as rationality. ... [The effect of this crisis has been] ... to turn economics into a branch of applied mathematics, where the aim is not to explain real processes and outcomes in the economic world, but to explore problems of mathematical technique for their own sake. .... Economics thus is becoming a mathematical game to be played in its own terms, with arbitrary rules chosen by the players themselves, unconstrained by questions of descriptive adequacy or references to reality. ... Anti-reductionists often emphasise emergent properties at higher levels of analysis that cannot be [completely] reduced ...."[16] to or explained wholly in terms of another level.

Many attempts to overcome this limit are present in the literature: fundamental market imperfections (Fokke & Folkerts-Landau, 1982; Nishimura, 1998), incomplete and asymmetric information, competition (Ng, 1980), rationing[17] (Muellbauer & Portes, 1978; Clower, 1965; Leijonhufud, 1968) and agents' coordination (Gallegati, 1999a). Obviously, when information is incomplete and the markets do not clear instantaneously, the learning behaviour of the individual determines the system's dynamics. This has opened the path to several explanatory models of economy, more or less microfounded.

The New-Keynesian model (Salzano, 1993; Gallegati, 1999b) constitutes an interesting example of partial microfoundation. It is a micro-founded, macromodel based on the hypothesis of the Representative Agent. In it, the consumer agent works with the purpose of acquiring assets.

If he or she is rationed on one of the markets (assets or work), he or she changes their choices also based on the other market. The trouble was that, given the technical tools available at the time, an effective microfoundation of the macroeconomic model was difficult to obtain. Of course, "The philosophical basis of ... [policy decisions] ... must make use of the concept of emergence."[18]

Some efforts have been made in the direction of our interest for obtaining: (a) better models of aggregated or regional policy effect; and (b) policy suggestions.

Better Models of Aggregated or Regional Policy Effect

a. **The role of social interactions for growth: The case of technology-related variables.** An example of the first case is Robalino (2000). Centering his analysis on technology-related variables, he develops "an agent-based macroeconometric model for the developing world that endogenizes the process of technology diffusion by formalizing the role of social interactions. In this model, macrobehavior emerges from microeconomic decisions made by decentralized heterogeneous agents who are organized in networks. These networks influence agents' information flows, their expectations about the dynamics of the economic environment, and ultimately their technology adoption decisions. The model is used to address the question of how to allocate aggregate income to the creation of human and produced capital, and how to distribute over time the consumption of natural resources and environmental services, in order to generate a sustainable growth path that maximize inter-temporal social welfare."[19]
    Another example, based on heterogeneous agents Simulation, is Salzano (2005).

b. **A New-Keynesian microfounded model based on heterogeneous agents:** Some first steps, versus the solution of microfoundation which we will follow in this work, have been proposed. At least a partial overcoming of the main limits of this sort of model has been tried with a New-Keynesian model based on heterogeneous agents. Salzano (2005) has extended a New-Keynesian model to specific considerations of interacting heterogeneous agents. In this model—a model of rationing with fixed prices[20]—it is possible to compare the results obtained with both Representative and heterogeneous agents. The shell of simulation is of a hybrid kind. In fact, it has aspects of both equation and agent simulation. Obviously, if there is only one individual and one firm the microeconomic and macroeconomic models coincide.

The Case of Representative Agents (RA)

The representative agents have perfect knowledge about the offers and demands of other agents. On this basis, they set their optimal behaviour in every market. All the individuals (who buy goods for consumption and who work) have the same preferences. Analogous hypotheses hold for the firms (that produce and sell). "Government" is an agent that modifies economic policy (public expenditure—taxes). The public expenditure for "goods and services" is subject to preferential satisfaction.

Different equilibriums—of Keynesian, Neoclassical, Repressed Inflation, and Under-Consumption type—can be caught up according to the kind of rationing met by agents on the market. Of course, in this case the model could also be solved analytically, causing results that are compatible—even if in some way different because they are more general—with those obtainable on the basis of the traditional approach.

The agents possess a very simple and economically based personal equation: They manifest demand for goods if they think they are able to find work and vice versa, while the firms have an analogous function of supply and demand.

The exchange is held at the intersection point of these functions.

According with the type of rationing, we could reach various types of equilibriums. In Figure 1, the main types of equilibrium or regimes are depicted. The case in which no agent is rationed—the Walrasian case (Figure 1a); classic unemployment (Figure 1b)—is manifest when the consumer agent is rationed in both markets, while the firm does not assume more workers in order to satisfy the greater demand since the wages are too high. If the consumer agent is rationed in the work market and the firm is rationed on that of goods, there is a Keynesian equilibrium (Figure 1c).[21] The regimes are the same for all agents of the same type. Here, the usual effects of public expenditure are obtained in each topical case. Shifting from one "regime" to the other is possible.

Obviously, we assume the number of firms to be smaller or equal to that of individuals. Moreover, as aggregated individuals must be considered "analytically manipulable" both vertically and horizontally, each agent will manifest an equal part of demand or offer with respect to the aggregated values.

The Case of Heterogeneous Agents (HA)

The literature has considered various kinds of heterogeneity, but not all increases the model's realism (Mirowski & Somefun, 1998). Often, it has been limited to making a partition of the reality into two or more subsets.[22] The RA model allows interrelations only among agents of different kinds, for example, consumers and producers (Gallegati & Kirman, 1999; Salzano, 2005). Here we will consider the heterogeneity of an individual's preferences that does not show such a limit.

We can complete the New-Keynesian model with the heterogeneity of the agents' preferences without losing its original characteristics. However, macroeconomic properties can emerge, such as a "bottom-up" approach. Of course, acquired knowledge about the behaviour of other agents could modify these preferences. During consumption time, they encounter other individuals with whom they exchange information on the goods and the work of each firm. On this basis, they can change their preferences. The individual could obtain information by meeting others (particularly friends) and can modify his or her choice of firm from which to buy or where to work. Individuals receive information only by a restricted group of friends; the past level of macroeconomic activity could modify individual preferences in personalized ways according to personal history.

The consequences of this direct interaction among agents are very important. There are different scenarios for each agent. Moreover, we will introduce the possibility that the individuals can exchange information about the situation experienced by each agent and that this can modify their preferences. This micromechanism introduces feedback effects from the macro to the microlevel ("top-down"). This feedback is the effect of rules that must be valid only in aggregate. When we introduce the hypothesis of heterogeneity in the agents' preferences, we need one behavioural equation for each agent. This means that we must resort to simulations. For heterogeneous agents, the punctual effect depends on the situation of rationing met by each single agent and the total equilibrium of the exchanges is obtained as a sum of the single effects. This is different from the equilibrium that we could forecast based on the aggregated demand and offer. Therefore, the result based on the aggregated demand and offer is different from the sum of the single results.[23]

The aggregation of the various equilibriums ("bottom-up") can provoke a total equilibrium which is different from the hypothetical one we can reach if the markets are aggregated before the exchange (complex dynamics). A corollary of this is that for each couple of agents that exchange on the market —individual and firm—economic policy can have different effects.

Figure 1. Different new-Keynesian scenarios

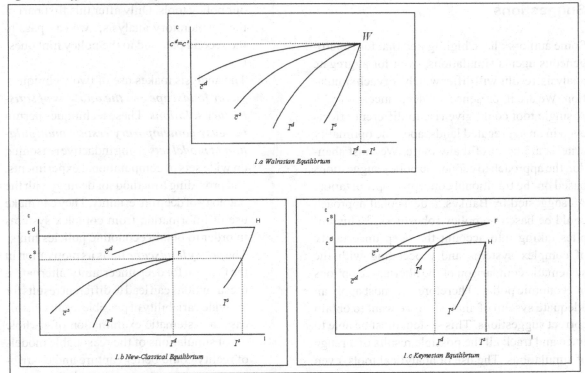

The Phase Modifications and the "Top-Down" Approach

In many economic models based on agents, the macroeconomic aspects mainly play a role of emergent property. On the other hand, in real economic systems some of the emergent property (originating from the bottom-up approach) must be considered as a phase change, the consequence of which modifies the behaviour of agents (top-down approach). Often, the simulation literature uses a simple Ising model for analysing the consequences of phase modifications.[24] The contemporary consideration of these aspects implies the use of a model that is a mix of the "bottom-up" and "top-down" approaches.[25]

At the economic level, the effect of the phase change can be seen by the fact that the economic agent modifies his or her behaviour because of the economic scenery in which they are or think it to be. This implies a macrofoundation of the microeconomic behaviour.[26] In the model, if a certain number of individuals "are satisfied" or "not satisfied" by their exchanges, and pass this information to others, the preferences of the latter would be modified and, therefore, new emergencies would emerge. In this way, the level of the micro- and macro interrelations is not hierarchical, but circular.

Obviously, the model considers only the points most widely considered in the literature; understanding their influence on the economic mechanisms provides a good starting point in order to elaborate more realistic regional policy models.

The Effect of HA and Policy Suggestions

Some authors[27] have highlighted that for Heterogeneous agents simulations, even for aggregate analysis, results will differ widely for each simulation. We are in presence of "deep uncertainty."[28] A single tool could give rise to different effects even in an aggregated landscape. The optimality criteria are not useful any more. We must abandon the approach to economic policy suggestions based on the traditional concept of optimization. As suggested by Bankes, a decisional approach could be based on policy robustness.[29] This implies taking into account the deep uncertainty of complex systems and proceeding with the systematic comparison of the alternative options of economic policy. Therefore, we must apply an adequate system of analysis if we want to obtain correct suggestions. This system must be able to trace and track all the possible results of a range of simulations. The use of analytical tools, even if it is still possible in some cases, does not seem to be adequate any more and we must abandon it. A way is through a visual analysis tracing all the results in a single diagram.[30]

In order to obtain policy suggestions based on a principle of "robustness," it seems possible to use the approaches of "exploratory modelling"[31] and "adaptive strategies." Here, we will highlight only the first approach. It implies two tools: The "policy landscape" and the "analysis of satisfactory solutions." While such tools are important independently from the more or less aggregated level of our analysis, in the case of regional policy they face some different and peculiar questions, especially if economic policies are intended for obtaining a differential in regional effects.

a.   **The exploratory analysis:** "Exploratory modelling" is an approach to decision-making under conditions of deep uncertainty.[32] The point of the exploratory analysis is that of being aware of the range of possible results that we could obtain with the use of our policy tools. Only after this first part of the "exploratory analysis," we can pass to the second part and to the policy hint question.

The analysis makes use of two techniques: *policy landscape* and *the analysis of satisfactory solutions*. These techniques permit *the easy contemporary results manipulation of model sets*, using inductive reasoning on wide sets of computational experiments, and providing a method for dealing with the ontology of deep uncertainty. They can make use of information from complex systems in order to obtain economic policies hints. The *policy landscape* finds its motivation in the fact that for deep uncertainty, alternative presumptions can lead to different results for the wide variability of possible results. In this case, a systematic examination of a whole set of simulations of the reasonable models of reality could better capture and contribute to represent the necessary information. The landscape allows for the calculation of the effects of economic policies to be subordinated to a robustness test. On the other hand, the *analysis of satisfactory solutions* is necessary because no recommendation of economic policy, obtained as a result of an optimisation in regard to a single model, can take account of all the knowledge that can be available for a complex adaptive system. In scenarios that could easily vary like the complex system, an alternative to the suggestion of a single set of economic policies is to give the decision makers some sets of options that operate satisfactorily or reach one minimal threshold of effectiveness. Given the multidimensionality of the problem and, the judgment difficulties it creates, there is a preference for a graphical tool that can show many possible alternatives all at once.

b. **Differential regional policies effects:** In the case of regional analysis for RA, we obtain equal results for each simulation. The consideration of agents' heterogeneity contrasts with such results. In fact, supposing we have only two regions, each couple within the two groups of agents of each region will find a different equilibrium and the aggregated equilibrium will be different still in each region for the different interrelations that will manifest, caused by its diverse socioeconomic structure. The aggregated equilibrium we reach (income, work, and so on for region 1 + Region 2) on the basis of a traditional macroeconomic model, will be different from that we obtain on the basis of a microfounded model with heterogeneous agents. The same is true for "each" regional equilibrium. Such an equilibrium is not necessary coincident with the aggregated ones.[33] "The sum is more [or different] than the parts."

An analogue, and more ample difference, is obtained for the effect of economic policy (public expenditure (PE)).

Of course, the question is worse when we deal with regional differential effects in the hypothesis of HA. In this case large problems exist. In fact, in the traditional approach we could obtain diverse differential results only by using different tools or modifying the level of the used tool. On the other hand, in the complex approach we obtain them even when we use the same tool at the same level. This is the effect of heterogeneous agent interrelation.

There is a dimensional question here, because for each point that is a possible solution of a first system (or region), we have to calculate its possible difference with respect to all the points of a possible solution for the other system. This means that we obtain a different solution for each possible value of our second system.[34] In fact, the dimensions for each solution's value of the second

system, provides a new system. Therefore, there is an increase of dimensional space in the solution of the complete system.

We need to proceed to a policy choice based on ample dimensional space, than that usually considered for aggregated complex systems. Thus, even if the starting methodology remains the same, for the appraisal of the regional differential effect of economic policy we must validate, and even modify the methodology already proposed for complex aggregated systems. Therefore, even in this case, we must apply an adequate system of analysis if we want to obtain suggestions that are more correct.

THE SIMULATION CONTEXT

On the basis of the model delineated before, we considered the differential effect of the same levels of public expenditure (PE) on two regions. For the sake of simplicity: (a) the whole economy is constituted by only two regions whose agents have different characteristics; (b) economic agents operate in a New-Keynesian scenerario with rationing; (c) each agent can only have interrelations with other agents of its area;[35] (d) we studied only the level of production of the two regions; (e) only the individuals were considered different in the two regions; and (f) individuals were different only in the elasticity of aggregate demand to work possibility.

The Analysis of the Simulations' Results

We will concentrate on: (a) The implication of HA-emergence of macroeconomic characteristics—the volatility of results and the insurgence of endogenous fluctuations (b) the implications of HA on regional differential effects of a simple economic policy—public expenditure; and (c) how closely attention must be paid to choosing the more robust policy when we make use of agent simulations, and the modification of methods necessary–if any–for the analysis of differential effects.

a. **The implication of HA-emergence of macroeconomic characteristics: The volatility of results and the insurgence of endogenous fluctuations.**

    The main implication of the HA hypothesis regards the emergence of macroeconomic characteristics that are not present in the case of RA. This is evident if we compare two graphs, both obtained with the same economic structure for the production in the two regions, with and without the HA hypothesis (Figure 2). In the graphs, we report only one level of PE. Without it, the two levels of income are equal and remain so for every different simulation (we run each simulation at time 1; of course, the same is valid even with time simulations); in the case of HA, we obtained a different result each time. Therefore, HA caused the emergence of volatility in the results.

    Of course, if considered with respect to time, this fact implies the emergence of endogenous fluctuations.

b. **The implications of HA on regional differential effect of a simple economic policy: Public expenditure.**

On the basis of the proposed regional model, we have carried out many simulations. We obtained the level of production for each region and its differences for each level of public expenditure (Figure 3 a, b, and c). Here, for clarity, we reported only the first 30 runs. Each line indicates a different level of PE. From the graph, it is easy to see how for each level of PE we obtained many different differential effects. The values are the ones obtained in each simulation. Moreover, the levels of their variations (Min & Max) are different and not monotonically increasing with the level of PE.

Therefore, suppose a government would like to obtain a certain level XX (indicated by the relative level in Figure 3c) of differential effect between the two regions. It could choose every value of PE. In fact, each of them could have the desired effect, but also every other effect. This is the problem and why an "Exploratory Analysis" seems necessary.

c. **How closely attention must be paid to choosing the more robust policy when we make use of agent simulations–tools for analysing the effect of policies.**

The use of the information obtained by the study of complex systems for the formation of economic decisions and policy sugges-

Figure 2. Income effects of public expenditures in the two regions

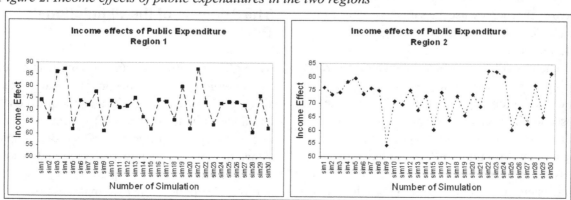

tions is not strongly diffused. On the other hand, the study of complex systems supplies powerful instruments which capture useful information on the behaviour of economic systems (agent simulations are an example of this). This seems due to the fact that the approach generally used to suggest economic policy is intended for policy creation that must operate well on some "single" forecast of the future course of economy.[36]

This traditional methodology is in strong contrast with the complexity concept itself. In fact, every system where behaviour can be captured from a precise model, does not give origin to any "emergence" and therefore cannot be defined as complex. Conversely, the behaviour of complex adaptive systems cannot be captured from a precise model and thus exactly forecasted because ***deep uncertainty*** characterizes them.

In order to formulate credible economic policy suggestions for complex adaptive systems, we must find strategies that operate reasonably well (that are robust) for a large range of reasonable scenarios rather than indicate an "optimal policy."[37] They must be robust for the range of

Figure 3a. Income effect of public expenditure–Region 1

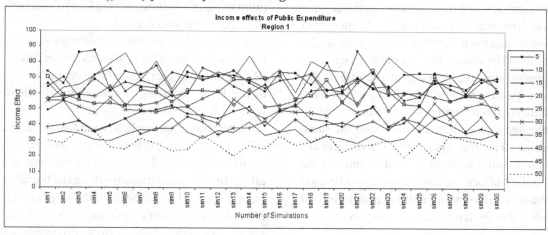

Figure 3b. Income effect of public expenditure–Region 2

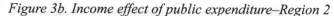
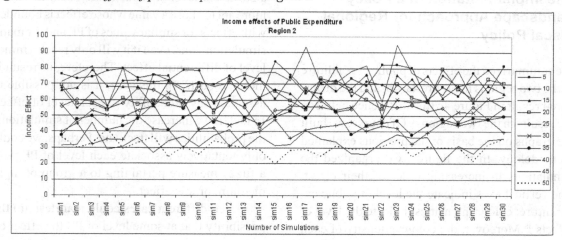

Figure 3c. Differential income effect of public expenditure

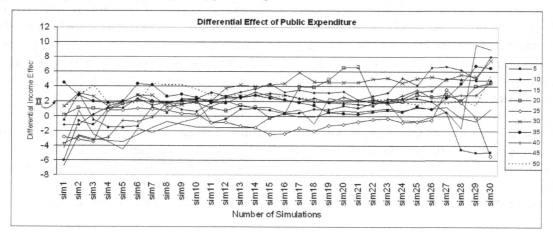

possible behaviours of a complex and adaptive system. Therefore, we must not use the models to forecast results but to supply knowledge about the direction of the effects of possible policies.

Suppose we take account of the effect of a public expenditure. For simplicity, and for the possibility of comparing our results, we could hypothesize that both areas start with the same industrial structure. Then, only the differences in the individual preferences will influence the fiscal policy effect. Of course, we hypothesized that the same amount of public expenditure will be directed to each productive structure.

The Implementation of a Policy Landscape Approach for Regional Fiscal Policy

We summarized the effects of public expenditure in the two regions in Figure 4a-4b, and the differential result in Figure 4c (the difference between the results in the two regions). Of course, we built the graphs on the basis of the previous explained methodology. In the figures, we organized the simulations in increasing order of their effect. The vertical axes indicate the level of public expenditure; colour intensities indicate the level of effects.[38] Moreover, the colour intensity of each

point of Figure 4c indicates the level of difference of effect in the two regions.

On the basis of Figure 4c, it seems evident that we should choose a level of public expenditure of S1, S3, or S7. In fact, these levels could allow us to reach the highest differential effect. Clearly, level S7 is more robust.

Alternatively, it could happen that the highest effect is not robust; this case will manifest when we find very low values near the level chosen for all the line of simulations (0-30 on the horizontal axis). This is what happens for the level S1. Here, it would be necessary to choose the level of PE giving rise to the highest effect compatible with a sufficient level of robustness. Then, it will be more apt to chose a value whose effect is bounded with effects for similar values of PE and for many simulation-runs, even if it will only reach a minor level of differential effect. Therefore, its result is more "robust." In this case, it is not possible to associate any probability to each level of effect. In fact, if we increase the number of simulations, the probabilities will fluctuate. Perhaps, we could only tentatively associate each level of PE with a fuzzy measure pertaining to a group of high, medium, or low effect.

Other, different cases could manifest: (a) the possibility that at some level of PE the effect on

Figure 4a. Effects of public expenditure in the first region

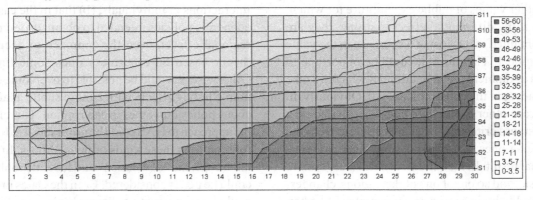

Figure 4b. Effects of public expenditure in the second region

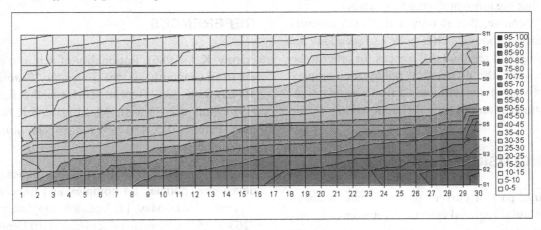

Figure 4c. Differential effects of public expenditure

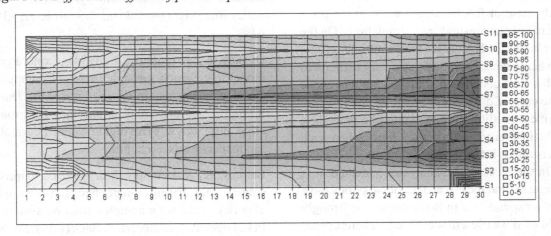

the region 1 could be negative. Conversely, there are other values of public expenditure for which, even if the differential effect is strong, they are not obtained at the cost of a decrease in the value of region 1. Therefore, it could be opportune to build agraphical representation in which we take into account the constraint R1>=0. Obviously, in this case other choices are possible—based on a robustness criterion—that are different from the previous ones; (b) It is possibly some counterfactual result. In fact, if the scenario (Keynesian, Classic, and so on) of one of the regions changes, we could obtain a strong differential effect when the public expenditure devoted to this region is less that the amount devoted to another.

Of course, this is only a first step towards the formulation of better policy suggestions for dealing with regional differences. In order to be successful, the differential policy for complex adaptive systems will itself have to be adaptive, but this is reserved for a different work.

CONCLUSION

A large part of current policy debate is about differential regional effects. As it is easy to understand, for evaluating the differential effect of a public policy, we have to subtract the effect on a country from that of another. The fact is easy for the case of RA because we are in the presence of only one result for all simulations. On the other hand, for HA, as we have multiple results, each being equally possible, it is very difficult to reach a firm conclusion. This situation is worse in the case of differential effect for the increase of dimensionality. Here, we suggest a procedure to obtain more certain policy hints when such effects are of interest.

On the basis of the analysis conducted, it is evident: (a) that the effect of regional policy tools (public expenditure in this example) is strongly modified if we use a model based on heterogeneous agent simulation that takes into account the interactions of individuals; (b) that in the case of economic policies intended to obtain differential regional effects, even the approach to decision theory based on robustness finds some limits. Otherwise, it would be possible to overcome economic policy effects with a more subtle analysis about policy outcomes in each region. Therefore, the approach to HAS could be profitably used even for obtaining these kinds of policy hint-s. In this landscape, the "devolution" and federal problems could be better considered. Even the Oates model could be revisited on a firmer basis.

REFERENCES

Arrow, K.J. (1986). Rationality of self and others in an economic system. *Journal of Business*, *59*(4.2), S385-S399. Reprinted in Hogarth & Reder (1987) and in J. Eatwell, M. Milgate, &P. Newman, Peter (Eds.), *The new palgravedictionary of economics*,

Bankes, S. (2002). Tools and techniques for developing policies for complex and uncertain systems. *PNAS*-May 14, Vol. 99, supplment 3, 7263-7266; www.pnas.org/cgi/doi/10.1073/pnas. 092081399

Bankes, S. (1993). Exploratory modelling for policy analysis. *Operational Research*, *41*, 435-449.

Bankes, S., & Gillogly, J. (1994). Exploratory modelling: Search through spaces of computational experiments. In *Proceedings of the Third Annual Conference on Evolutionary Programming*. http://www. evolvinglogic.com/Learn/absandpapers/explsearch. html

Bankes, S., & Lempert, R.J. (1996). Adaptive strategies for abating climate change: An example of policy analysis for aomplex adaptive systems. In L. Fogel, P. Angeline, & T. Back (Eds.), *Evolu-*

tionary programming V: Proceedings of the fifth annual conference on evolutionary programming, (pp. 17-25). Cambridge, MA: MIT Press.

Bohm, V. (1983). Quantity rationing vs. IS-LM: A synthesis. *Discussion Paper.* N. 252-83, University at Mannheim.

Carlino, G.A., & DeFina, R. (1996). Does monetary policy have differential regional effects? *Federal Reserve Bank of Philadelphia Business Review Articles.*

Clower, R.W. (1965). The Keynesian counter-revolution: A theoretical appraisal. In F. Hahn & F. P. R. Brechling (Eds.), *The theory of interest rates.* London: MacMillan.

Elster, J. (1983). *Explaining technical change.* Cambridge: Cambridge University Press.

Fokke, D., & Folkerts-Landau, I. (1982). *Intertemporal planning, exchange and macroeconomics.* Cambridge University Press.

Gallegati, M., DelliGatti, D., & Mignacca D. (1999a). Agents heterogeneity and coordination failure: An experiment. In M. Gallegati & A. P. Kirman (Eds.), *Beyond the representative agent* (pp. 165-82). Cheltenham: Elgar.

Gallegati, M, Ardeni P.G., Boitani A., & Delli Gatti, D. (1999b). The new Keynesian economics: A survey. In M. Messori (Ed.), *Financial constraints and Mmrket failures.*Cheltenham: Elgard.

Gallegati, M. & Kirman, A.P. (Eds.).(1999) *Beyond the representative agent.* Cheltehnam: Elgar.

Hodgson, G. M. (1999). *Institutions and the viability of macroeconomics: Some perspectives on the transformation process in post-communist economies* http://graphics.stanford.edu/projects/rivet/

Kanbur, R., & Keen, M. (1993). Jeux sans frontieres: Tax competition and tax coordination when countries differ in size. *American Economic Review,* 880-85.

Kirman, A. (1992). Whom or what does the representative individual represent? *Journal of Economic Perspectives, 6,* 117-36.

Kirman, A.P. (1989). The intrinsic limits of modern economic theory: The emperor has no clothes. *Economic Journal (Conference Papers), 99,* 126-139.

Lane, D.A. (1998). Is what is good for each good for all? In B. Arthur, S. Durlauf & D. Lane (Eds.), *Economy as a complex, evolving system II.* Reading, MA: Addison-Wesley.

Lane, D.A. (2002). Complessità: Modelli e inferenza. In P. M. Biava (Ed.). *Complessità e biologia,* Bruno Mondadori Editori, 13-42.

Lempert, R.J. (2002). A new decision sciences for complex systems. In *Colloquium Paper Platforms and Methodologies for Enhancing the Social Sciences through Agent-Based Simulation,* PNAS, 99 (3), 7309-7313.

Mintz, J., & Tulkens, H. (1986). Commodity tax competition between member states of a federation: Equilibrium and efficiency. *Journal of Public Economics,* 149-56.

Muellbauer, J., & Portes R. (1978). Macroeconomic models with quantity rationing. *The Economic Journal,* 788-821.

Nishimura, K. (1998). Expectation heterogeneity and price sensitivity. *European Economic Review, 42,* 619-629.

Puga, D. (2002). European regional policies in light of recent location theories. *Journal of Economic Geography* 2(4), 372-406.

Robalino, D.A. (2000). *Social capital, technology diffusion and sustainable growth in the developing world.* Ph.D. dissertation, RAND Graduate School of Policy Studies.

Ruby, A. (2003). http://www. digitaleconomist. com/intro_4020. html

Salzano, M. (1993). *Le variabili fiscali nei modelli Neo-Keynesiani*. Napoli: Liguori Editore.

Salzano, M. (2005). Una simulazione neo-keynesiana ad agenti eterogenei. In P.Terna, R. Boero, M. Morini, & M. Sonnessa (Eds.). *Simulazione, modelli ad agenti e scienze sociali*. Mulino.

Schelling, T. (1978). *Micromotives and macrobehavior*. New York: Norton.

Shneiderman, B. (2004). Foreword. In Chen. *Information visualization: Beyond the horizon*. http://www.cs.umd.edu/users/ben/Chen-InfoViz-book-foreword.pdf

ENDNOTES

[1] See en.wikipedia.org/wiki/Regional_policy. The argument for regional policy is that it is both an instrument of financial solidarity and a powerful force for economic integration.

[2] Puga (2002).

[3] Carlino and DeFina (1996).

[4] These are defined exogenously, or endogenized by formalizing the effects of changes in input prices or R&D investments. For the critics of this kind of models, See Robalino (2000), whoe notes that the fact that "decentralized heterogeneous economic agents interact and share information about the dynamics of the economy and the characteristics of new technologies, has been always ignored. Yet, it is this process which is behind the diffusion of new technologies and ultimately the dynamics of macro variables ...".

[5] For a summary on this point see Salzano (2005).

[6] Is has been pointed out by Salzano (2005) that not all kinds of heterogeneity has the same effect. We will consider here heterogeneity in preferences.

[7] In these Agent-based models (ABM), the real world mechanisms are reproduced for obtaining a qualitative comprehension about the agents' behaviour. One avoids quantitative forecasts. Of course, the traditional tools for the analysis of effects of economic policy, based on optimality concept, cannot be used.

[8] For a critics of the Representative Agent and the concept of Heterogeneity, see Kirman (1992).

[9] For the shells, see: http://ccl.northwestern.edu/netlogo/. For the proposed simulation, see: http://www.ecople.org/ in "New Keynesian Simulation."

[10] Hodgson (1999)

[11] Elster (1983, pp. 20-4) cited by Hodgson (1999).

[12] See Ruby (2003).

[13] Hodgson (1999).

[14] Hodgson (1999).

[15] Cited in Hodgson (1999).

[16] Hodgson (1999).

[17] See the large but dated survey by Salzano (1993).

[18] Hodgson (1999).

[19] Robalino, D. A. (2000).

[20] Following Bohm (1983), we could explicitly introduce price and wage modification based on demand and offer. This could be combined with incremental expectations or with "cost push terms."

[21] For other cases and a wider esposition, see Salzano (2005).

[22] See Gallegati and Kirman (1999).

[23] Of course, in the case of RA, the effect of economic policy is identical for each agent while this must be considered only a specific case for heterogeneous agents.

[24] Perhaps the most known among these simplified models is the bi-dimensional Ising. It can be used for simulating the behaviour of simple magnets. For an elementary exposition, see: http://www.phy.syr.edu/courses/ijmp_c/Ising.html It seems, there are some differences between the "macroeconomic"

local scenary and the Ising Model. In fact, the first could assume different "levels" that the latter cannot assume.

25 This is not new. See the references cited in Salzano (2005).

26 The importance of which has been emphasized both by Schelling (1978) and by Lane (1998 & 2002).

27 See Salzano (2005) and Bankes (2002).

28 See the definition by Bankes (2002).

29 See Bankes (2002) and references reported there.

30 Information visualization is a compelling technique for the exploration and analysis of the large, complex data sets generated by these tools. Visualization takes advantage of the immense power, bandwidth, and pattern recognition capabilities of the human visual system. It enables analysts to see large amounts of data in a single display, and to discover patterns, trends, and outliers within the data.http://graphics.stanford.edu/projects/rivet/ For the relevance and usability of Visual Analysis in the case of complex systems, see Shneiderman (2004). He said "I believe that the essence of information visualization ... is to accelerate human thinking with tools that amplify human intelligence. ... The payoffs to users of information visualization tools will be in the significant insights that enable them to solve vital problems at the frontiers of their fields. ... The process of information visualization is to take data available to many people and to enable users to gain insights that lead to significant discoveries."

31 See Bankes (1993).

32 This approach could also be called "Computer-Assisted Reasoning" (CAR). See Bankes and Gillogly (1994).

33 For a demonstration, see Salzano (2000).

34 Of course, this could mean an increase in the "dimension" of the solution. This is similar to the question faced in none-zero-sum games if we do not know what the sum of the real results is, but only the percentage of one competitor with respect to the other.

35 Many kinds of interrelation between the agents of the two regions could be considered. Different hypotheses could be of interest for more sophisticated models. For example, the hypothesis of nonzero transport costs when agents can exchange and relate with all the other agents of the economy could be of interest for a heterogeneous agent version of Kanbur-Keen or similar model of fiscal competition (see Kanbur & Keen, 1993); Mintz & Tulkens (1986).

36 For this part see Bankes (op. cit.) and Bankes and Lempert (1996).

37 Lempert (2002).

38 Of course, when modelling a concrete economy, in order to try to highlight the effects of economic policy we must start from the effective value of the transactions or from some other known aggregated value. Thus, after having obtained a wide set of simulations we must only take into consideration the parameters that at time zero (the present time) could give rise to values of our aggregate variable similar to those effectively observed. In our case, applying the methodology of the "Reasonable Scenery of Economic Policy," it would be possible to choose a subset of our simulations and concentrate further study exclusively on these values. This successive study can consist both in a deepening of implications of the single variables and in an analysis based on the "Set of the Level of the Satisfactory Solutions."

Chapter XVII
Analyzing the Influences of Passive Investment Strategies on Financial Markets via Agent–Based Modeling

Hiroshi Takahashi
Okayama University, Japan

Satoru Takahashi
Mitsui Asset Trust and Banking, Japan

Takao Terano
Tokyo Institute of Technology, Japan

ABSTRACT

This chapter develops an agent-based model to analyze microscopic and macroscopic links between investor behaviors and price fluctuations in a financial market. This analysis focusses on the effects of passive investment strategy in a financial market. From the extensive analyses, we have found that (1) passive investment strategy is valid in a realistic efficient market, however, it could have bad influences such as market instability and inadequate asset pricing deviations, and (2) under certain assumptions, passive investment strategy and active investment strategy could coexist in a financial market.

INTRODUCTION

Financial economics researchers have become active since 1950s and many prominent theories regarding asset pricing and corporate finance have been proposed (Markowitz, 1952; Modigliani & Miller, 1958; Sharpe, 1964; Shleifer, 2000). The assumption of the efficiency of financial markets plays an important role in the literature in traditional financial theory and much research have been conducted based on that assumption (Friedman, 1953; Fama, 1970). For example, capital asset pricing model (CAPM), one of the most popular asset pricing theories in the traditional financial literature, is derived based on the assumptions of the efficient market and rational investors. CAPM indicates that the optimal investment strategy is to hold market portfolio (Sharpe, 1964).

Conventional investment methods are classified into two types: One is active investment strategy and the other is passive investment strategy. The objective of active investment strategy is for an investor to get an excess return better than they would have done if they simply accepted average market returns. However, these strategies sometimes fail because of unpredictable phenomena in the financial markets. On the other hand, passive invest management tries to maintain an average return using benchmarks based on market indices. Passive investors invest their assets in company stock in proportion to market weights and maintain it throughout investment periods. Since it is very difficult for investors to get an excess return in an efficient market, passive investment strategy is considered to be an effective investment method.

Recently, researchers in behavioral finance have raised some doubts about the efficient market assumption, by arguing that an irrational trader could influence asset prices (Shiller, 2000; Shleifer, 2000; Kahneman & Tversky, 1979; Kahneman & Tversky, 1992). Therefore, if the inefficient market exists, the passive investment strategy might not be effective. Moreover, we have various other questions: What would happen in a macrolevel when a very large number of investors employed the passive strategy.

To address these problems, we employ an agent-based model (Arthur, 1997; Axelrod, 1997) in order to analyze the relation between microrules and macrobehavior (Axtell, 2000; Russell, 1995).

In the literature, it has frequently been reported that a variety of macrobehavior emerges bottom-up from local microrules (Epstein, 1996; Levy, 2000; Terano, 2001; Terano, 2003; Arthur, 1997; Tesfatsion, 2002). We have developed an artificial financial market model with decision-making agents. So far, we have reported on micro-macro links among agents and markets, investors' behaviors with various mental models, and risk management strategies of firms (Takahashi, 2003; Takahashi, 2004; Takahashi, 2006). In this chapter, in enhancing the agent-based simulator we have developed, we will uncover the effects of passive investment strategies in a financial market. The objective of the research is to investigate: (1) the influences of micro and macrolevels of passive investment strategies, (2) roles of the evaluation method, and (3) financial behaviors, when there are so many investors with different strategies.

The next section of this chapter describes the model utilized for this analysis, then analysis results are discussed in Section Three. Section Four contains a summary and conclusion.

DESCRIPTION OF AN AGENT-BASED FINANCIAL MARKET MODEL

A computer simulation of the financial market involving 1,000 investors was used as the model for this research; shares and risk-free assets being the two possible transaction methods. Several types of investors exist in the market, each undertaking transactions based on their own stock calculations. This market is composed of three major steps: (1) generation of corporate earnings, (2) formation of investor forecasts, and (3) setting transaction prices. The market will be moving through the repetition of these steps. Regarding the parameters of the model, please refer to the appendix (1).

Assets Traded in the Market

This market consists of both risk-free and risky assets. There is a financial security (as risky assets) in which all profits gained during each term are distributed to the shareholders. Corporate earnings (y_t) are expressed as ($y_t = y_{t-1} \cdot (1 + \varepsilon_t)$), however they are generated according to the process $\varepsilon_t \sim N(0, \sigma_y^2)$ with shares trading after the public announcement of profit for the term. Each investor is given common asset holdings at the start of the term with no limit placed on debit and credit transactions.

Modeling of Passive Investors

Passive investors of the simulation model invest their assets with the same ratio as the market benchmarks. This means that: (1) each passive investor keeps one volume stock during the investment periods, (2) the investment ratio to stocks is automatically determined, and (3) the trade strategy follows buy-and-hold of initial interests.

Modeling of Active Investors

Active investors make decisions based on expected utility maximization (Black & Litterman, 1992). Contrary to passive investors, active investors forecast the stock price. In the following section, we will explain the forecasting models of active investors.

Forecasting Models of Active Investors

a. **Fundamentalists:** We will refer to the investors who make investment decisions based on fundamental values as "fundamentalists." We adopt the dividend discount model, which is the most basic derivation model for the fundamental value of stocks.

The fundamentalists are assumed to know that profit accrues according to Brownian motion. They forecast the stock price P_{t+1}^f and the profit y_{t+1}^f from the profit of the current period (y_t) and the discount rate of the stock, (δ) as $P_{t+1}^f = y_t / \delta$ and $y_{t+1}^f = y_t$, respectively.

b. **Trend predictors:** We formulate a model of the investor who finds out the trends from randomly fluctuating stock prices. This type of investor predicts the stock price of the next period by extrapolating the latest stock trends (10 days). The trend predictors forecast the stock price and the profit from the trend at period $t-1$ (a_{t-1}) as $P_{t+1}^f = P_{t-1} \cdot (1 + a_{t-1})^2$ and $y_{t+1}^f = y_t \cdot (1 + a_{t-1})$, where $a_{t-1} = (1/10) \cdot \sum_{i=1}^{10} (P_{t-i} / P_{t-i-1} - 1)$. Predicted price ($P_{t+1}^f$) and profit ($y_{t+1}^f$) are different when the trend measurement period is different.

c. **Loss over estimation investors:** We formulate a model in which the investor doubles the loss estimates from the reference stock price. In the model, the reference stock price is one of 10 periods beforehand. When the most recent price (P_{t-1}) is lower than the price at the reference point (P_t^{ref}), the "Loss over estimation investors" forecast the stock price (P_{t+1}^f) by converting the original predicted price ($P_{t+1}^{bef\ f}$) using the formula $P_{t+1}^f = 2.25 \cdot P_{t+1}^{bef\ f} - 1.25 \cdot P_t^{ref}$. As for the original predicted price ($P_{t+1}^{bef\ f}$), we use the dividend discount model.

d. **Overconfident investors:** Bazerman reported that human beings tend to be overconfident in their own abilities (Bazerman, 1998). In the area of behavioral finance, Kyle analyzed the influence of overconfident investment behavior on the markets with the analytical method (Kyle, 1997). Also in a real market, we often find that each investor talks about different future prospects with confidence. It seems that all investors tend to have overconfidence in varying degrees.

We formulate the model of investors who are overconfident in their own predictions by assuming that they underestimate the risk of the stock. The risk of the stock estimated by an overconfident investor (σ^s) is calculated from the historical volatility (σ^h) and the adjustment factor to determine the degree of overconfidence constant value k (k=0.6) as $(\sigma^s)^2 = k (\sigma^h)^2$.

Calculation Method for Expected Rate of Return on Stock

The investors in this virtual market predict the stock price and the corporate profit at the term t+1(P_{t+1}^f *and* y_{t+1}^f) based on the corporate profit at the term t (y_t) and the stock prices at and before the term t−1 ($p_{t-1}, P_{t-2}, P_{t-3},...$). In the following, we represent the predicted values of the stock price and the corporate profit by the investor i (i=1,2,3...) as $P_{t+1}^{y,i}$ *and* $y_{t+1}^{f,i}$, respectively. The expected rate of return on the stock for the investor i ($r_{t+1}^{\text{int},i}$) is calculated as:

$$r_{t+1}^{\text{int},i} = (r_t^{im} \cdot c^{-1} \cdot (\sigma_{t-1}^s)^{-2}$$

$$+ r_{t+1}^{f,i} \cdot (\sigma_{t-1}^s)^{-2}) \cdot (c^{-1} \cdot (\sigma_{t-1}^s)^{-2} + (\sigma_{t-1}^s)^{-2})^{-1},$$

where $r_{t+1}^{f,i} = ((P_{t+1}^{f,i} + y_{t+1}^{f,i})/P_t - 1) \cdot (1+\varepsilon_t^i)$ and $r_t^{im} = 2\lambda(\sigma_{t-1}^s)^2 W_{t-1} + r_f$ (Black & Litterman, 1992).

Determination of Traded Price

The traded price of the stock is determined at the price the demand meets the supply (Arthur, 1997). Both the investment ratio (w_t^i) and the amount of the stock held by investors ($\sum_{i=1}^{M}(F_t^i \cdot w_{t_i}^i)/P_t$) are a decreasing function of the stock price, when the total amount of the stock issued in the market (N) is constant. We derive the traded price as $\sum_{i=1}^{M}(F_t^i \cdot w_{t_i}^i)/P_t = N$ by calculating the price

(P_t) where the total amount of the stock retained by investors (($F_t^i \cdot w_{t_i}^i$)$/P_t$) meets the total market value of the stock.

EXPERIMENTS AND DISCUSSIONS

The series of our experiments is divided into the two parts: First, we have fundamentalist agents and passive-investment agents in the market to investigate the influences of the two strategies. Next, in order to analyze the effects, we introduce the other investors, such as trend chasers, loss-over-estimation investors, and overconfidant investors.

Trading with Fundamentalist and Passive Investors

Figures 1 and 2 illustrate the case where there exist the same 500 numbers of the two kinds of investors (Case 0). Figure 1 shows the histories of stock prices. The solid line in Figure 1 represents the traded price and the line with x represents the fundamental value. Figure 2 depicts the histories of cumulative excess returns for each investor. This graph shows that the fluctuation of the traded price agrees with that of fundamental value. The line with x mark in Figure 2 shows the performance of passive investment strategies and the dotted line shows the fundamentalist ones. The performances of fundamentalists are slightly different among them, because each fundamentalist respectively has a predicting error. As the traditional asset pricing theory suggests, the trading prices coincide with fundamental values and fundamentalist and passive investors can get the same profit on average.

Next, using natural selection principles of Genetic algorithms (see Appendix 2 for details), let the investor agents change their strategies when: (1) the excess returns are under target (e.g., over 10%), (2) the excess returns are under 0%, and (3) the excess returns are too bad (e.g., under 10%).

Figure 1. Price transition(Case 0)

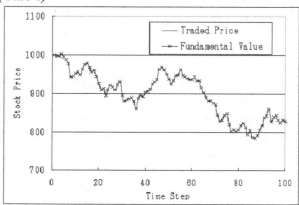

Figure 2. Cumulative excess returns(Case 0)

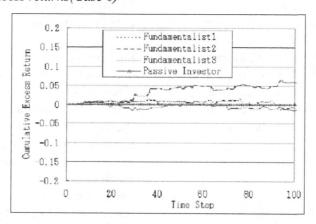

Figure 3. Price transition (Case 1)

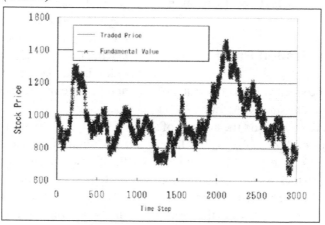

Figure 4. Transition of number of investors (Case 1)

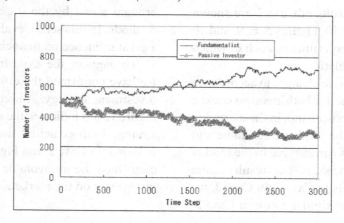

Figure 5. Distribution of fundamentalists (Case 1, 100 Steps)

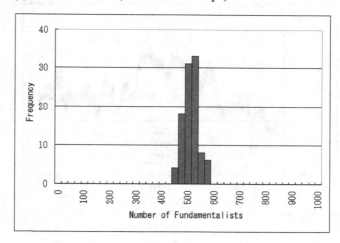

Figure 6. Distribution of fundamentalists (Case 1, 1500 Steps)

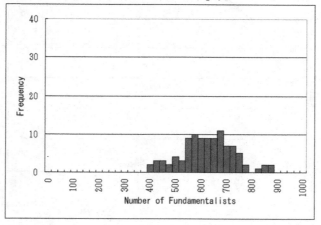

The results of Case 1 are shown in Figures 3, 4, 5, and 6. The results of Case 2 are shown in Figures 7, 8, 9, and 10. Figures 5, 6, 9, and 10 are obtained by 100 experiments, each of which consists of 3,000 simulation steps.

In Case 1, traded price changes in accordance with fundamental value and both investors coexist in the market. On the other hand, in Case 2 traded price doesn't reflect the fundamental value and only passive investors can survive in the market after around 1,600 time steps. This result is quite different from the ones in Case 1. In Case 3, we have obtained results similar those in Case 2.

These differences among each experiment are brought about by the difference in evaluation methods. In this sense, evaluation methods have a great influence on financial markets.

Throughout the experiments shown above, we have confirmed the effectiveness of passive investment strategy. Among them, the result in Figure 12 has indicated the superiority of passive strategy in more actual situations. However, as is shown in Case 2 and Figure 11, we have also confirmed the unfavorable influence of passive investment on the market.

Figure 7. Price transition (Case 2)

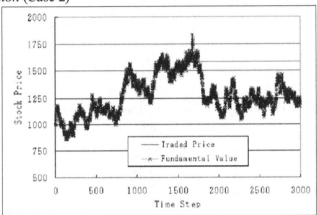

Figure 8. Transition of number of investors (Case 2)

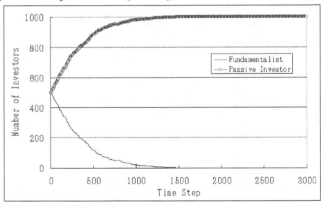

Figure 9. Distribution of fundamentalists (Case 2, 100 Steps)

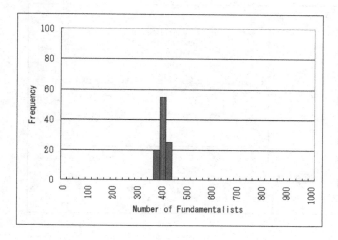

Figure 10. Distribution of fundamentalists (Case 2, 400 Steps)

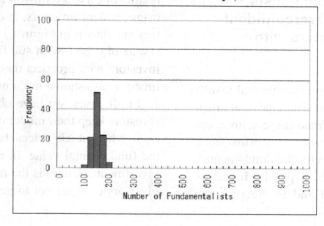

Figure 11. Price transition

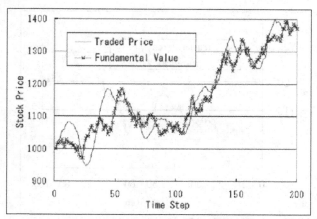

Figure 12. Cumulative excess returns

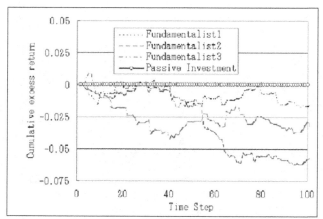

Trading with Fundamentalists, Passive Investors, Overconfident Investors, and Investors with Prospect Theory

This section describes the experimental results with the five different investor agents: fundamentalists, passive investors, trend chasers, investors with prospect theory, and overconfident investors. First, the results of Case 4 with 400 Fundamentalists, 400 trend chasers, and 200 passive investors are shown in Figures 13 and 14. Second, the

results of Case 5 with 400 fundamentalists, 400 overconfident investors, and 200 passive investors are shown in Figures 15 and 16. Third, the results of Case 6 with 400 fundamentalists, 400 investors with prospect theory, and 200 passive investors are shown in Figures 17 and 18.

In all cases, we have observed that passive investors keep their moderate positions positive, even when stock prices largely deviate from the fundamental value. In other words, passive investment strategy is the most effective way if investors do want not to get the worst result in

Figure 13.Price transition (Case 4)

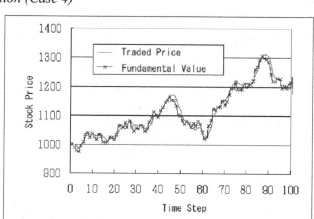

Figure 14. Cumulative excess returns (Case 4)

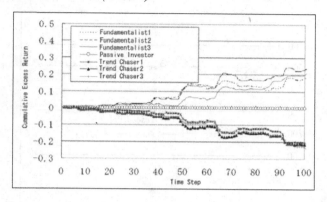

Figure 15. Price transition (Case 5)

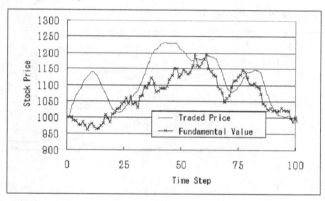

Figure 16. Cumulative excess returns (Case 5)

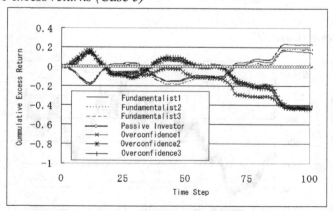

Figure 17. Price transition (Case 6)

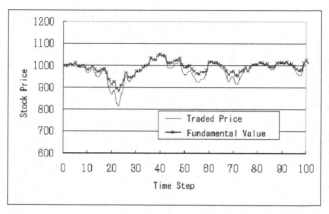

Figure 18. Cumulative excess returns (Case 6)

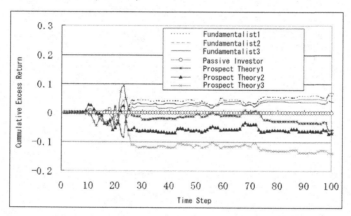

Figure 19. Price transition (Case 7)

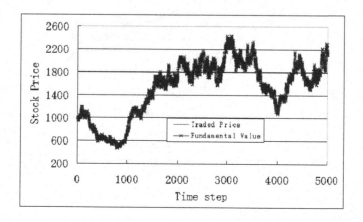

Figure 20. Transition of number of investors (Case 7)

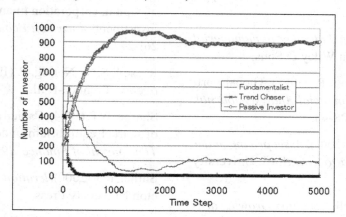

any cases, even if they have failed to get the best result. In the asset management business, some investors adopt the passive investment approach to avoid getting the worst performance.

Figures 19 and 20 show the results where the agents are able to change their strategy when the excess returns are less than 0. In this experiment, we have slightly modified the natural selection rule as described in the previous section. In the following experiments, investors change their strategy depending on their recent performance as in previous section; after that, investors change their strategy randomly by a small possibility (0.01%) which corresponds to mutation in genetic algorithms. The result shown in Figure 20 suggests that there remain both fundamentalist and passive investors in the market and that they keep the market stable. The results shown in Figures 19 and 20 are quite different from the ones in Case 2. These results suggest that even slight differences in the market conditions and investors behavior could cause large changes in the markets. In this sense, these results are thought-provoking.

SUMMARY AND CONCLUSION

This chapter utilizes the agent-based model to analyze both microscopic and macroscopic as-

sociations in the financial market. In the process, it has been found that: (1) passive investment is usually effective, however, it has had a bad influence on the market, such as when market prices do not reflect fundamental values and become unstable, and when their number becomes too large, (2) the variety of investors is dramatically changed, according to the evaluation criteria of investment, and (3) active and passive investors can coexist when there are so many investors with different strategies in the market. Future issues include market modeling, which takes more realistic conditions into account.

REFERENCES

Arthur, W. B., Holland, J.H., LeBaron, B., Palmer, R.G., & Taylor, P. (1997). Asset pricing under endogenous expectations in an artificial stock market. In *The Economy as an Evolving Complex System II* (pp.15-44). Addison-Wesley.

Axelrod, R. (1997). *The complexity of cooperation—Agent-based model of competition and collaboration.* Princeton University Press.

Axtell, R. (2000). Why agents? On the varied motivation for agent computing in the social sciences, *The Brookings Institution Center on*

Social and Economic Dynamics Working Paper, November, No.17.

Bazerman, M. (1998), *Judgment in managerial decision making.* John Wiley & Sons.

Black, F., & Litterman, R. (1992). Global portfolio optimization, *Financial Analysts Journal*, September-October, 28-43.

Brunnermeier, M.K. (2001). *Asset pricing under asymmetric information.* Oxford University Press.

Epstein, J.M., & Axtell, R. (1996). *Growing artificial societies social science from the the bottom up.* MIT Press.

Fama, E. (1970). Efficient capital markets: A review of theory and empirical work. *Journal of Finance*, 25, 383-417.

Friedman, M. (1953). *Essays in positive economics.* Chicago: University of Chicago Press.

Goldberg, D. (1989). *Genetic algorithms in search, optimization, and machine learning.* Addison-Wesley.

Kahneman, D., & Tversky, A. (1979). Prospect theory of decisions under risk. *Econometrica*, 47, 263-291.

Kahneman, D., & Tversky, A. (1992). Advances in prospect theory: Cumulative representation of uncertainty. *Journal of Risk and Uncertainty, 5.*

Kyle, A.S., & Wang, A. (1997). Speculation duopoly with agreement to disagree: Can overconfidence survive the market test? *Journal of Finance*, 52, 2073-2090.

Levy, M., Levy, H., & Solomon, S. (2000). *Microscopic simulation of financial markets.* Academic Press.

Markowitz, H. (1952). Portfolio selection. *Journal of Finance*, 7, 77-91.

Modigliani, F., & Miller, M.H. (1958). The cost of capital, corporation finance and the theory of investment. *American Economic Review*, 48, 3, 261-297.

Russell, S., & Norvig, P. (1995). *Artificial Intelligence*, Prentice-Hall.

Sharpe, W.F. (1964), Capital asset prices: A theory of market equilibrium under condition of risk, *The Journal of Finance*, 19, 425-442.

Shiller, R.J. (2000). *Irrational exuberance.* Princeton University Press.

Shleifer, A. (2000). *Inefficient markets.* Oxford University Press.

Takahashi, H., & Terano, T. (2003). An agent-based approach to investors' behavior and asset price fluctuation in financial markets. *Journal of Artificial Societies and Social Simulation, 6, 3.*

Takahashi, H., & Terano, T. (2004). Analysis of micro-macro structure of financial markets via an agent-based model: Risk management and dynamics of asset pricing. *Electronics and Communications in Japan*, 87, 7, 38-48.

Takahashi, H., & Terano, T. (2006). Emergence of overconfidence investors in financial markets. *Fifth International Conference on Computational Intelligence in Economics and Finance.*

Terano, T., Nishida, T., Namatame, A., Tsumoto, S., Ohsawa, Y., & Washio, T. (Eds.). (2001). *New frontiers in artificial intelligence.* Springer Verlag.

Terano, T., Deguchi, H., & Takadama, K. (Eds.). (2003). Meeting the challenge of social Ppoblems via agent-based simulation. *Post Proceedings of The Second International Workshop on Agent-Based Approaches in Economic and Social Complex Systems*, Springer Verlag.

Tesfatsion, L. (2002). Agent-based computational economics. *Economics Working Paper*, No.1, Iowa Sate University.

APPENDICES

1. List of Parameters of the Proposed Model

The parameters used in the proposed model are summarized as follows:

M: The number of investors (1,000)

N: The number of issued stocks (1,000)

F_t^i: The total amount of assets of the investor i at the term t (F_0^i=2,000:common)

W_t: The stock ratio in the market at the term t (W_0 =0.5)

w_t^i: The investment ratio of the stock of the investor i at the term t (w_0^i =0.5:constant)

σ_y: The standard deviation of the profit fluctuation ($0.2/\sqrt{200}$:constant)

δ: The discount rate of the stock (0.1/200:constant)

λ: The degree of risk aversion of the investor (1.25:common,constant)

c: The adjustment coefficient for variance (0.01)

σ_t^h: The historical volatility of the stock (for the recent 100 terms)

σ_n: The standard deviation of the dispersion of the short term expected rate of return on the stock (0.01: common)

k: The adjustment coefficient for confidence (0.6)

2. Rules of Natural Selection Principle

This section explains the rules of natural selection principle. The principle used in this chapter is composed of two steps: (1) selection of investors who change their investment strategies, and (2) selection of a new strategy. Each step is described in the following sections:

Selection of Investors who Change Their Investment Strategies

After 25 terms have passed since the market has started, each investor makes decision at a regular interval (every five terms) whether he/she changes the strategy. The decision is made depending on the cumulative excess return during the recent five terms and the investors who obtain smaller return changes the strategy at higher probability. To be more precise, the investors who obtain negative cumulative excess return change the strategy at the following probability:

$$p_i = \max(0.3 - a \cdot e^{r_i^{cum}}, 0),$$

p_i: Probability at which investor i changes its own strategy,

r_i^{cum}: Cumulative return of investor i during the recent five terms,

a: The coefficient for the evaluation criteria (0.2,0.3,0.4).

Selection of New Strategy

We apply the method of genetic algorithm (Goldberg,(1989) to the selection rule of new strategy. The investors who change the strategy tend to select the strategy that has brought positive cumulative excess return. The probability to select s_i as new strategy is given as: $p_i = e^{r_i^{cum}} / \sum_{j=1}^{M} e^{r_j^{cum}}$, where r_i^{cum} is the cumulative excess return of each investor.

Chapter XVIII
Exploring the Effects of Campaigning Strategies for the Organisation of Collective Action Using Empirical Data

Robert Tobias
Swiss Federal Institute of Aquatic Science and Technology, Switzerland

Hans-Joachim Mosler
Swiss Federal Institute of Aquatic Science and Technology, Switzerland

ABSTRACT

In a collective action, people act together with the intention of producing public goods. Public, or collective, goods are states or objects that benefit the many but only emerge if a sufficient number of persons make contributions. The present study explains the dynamics of participation in collective action campaigns by considering the interaction of different processes. With the resulting model, it is possible to determine the optimal combination of diffusion measures for such a campaign. Before using the model for experimenting, we calibrate its parameters using data from a real world collective action. We find this to be a most important step in order to demonstrate that the model can be grounded empirically and to demonstrate the practical usefulness of simulation for consulting and design of real world processes. Finally, some "what if" scenarios reveal the model's power of explanation and prediction.

INTRODUCTION

States or objects that benefit many but arise only from the contributions of a large enough number of people are called collective goods. Collective goods can range from the joint purchase of an office coffee machine to political agreements on fishing quotas, for example. Collective goods are created through collective actions. That means that a number of people must act together collectively with the intention to produce a collective good. For example, a contribution to the collective goods "clean air" or "traffic security" would be to reduce one's own driving speed. The focus of the research in this area is investigation of the conditions under which individuals will participate in collective action and contribute towards the collective good.

Our assumption is that the dynamics of the development of the number of participants in collective actions are determined by three processes:

a. Internal processes of the factors in individuals (individual-internal processes)
b. Processes that arise from social influence among individuals (social influence processes)
c. Processes that are triggered by the implementation of diffusion measures for recruiting participants (diffusion processes)

Individual-Internal Processes

Following Klandermans' model (1984), we assume that individual participation is dependent upon the following variables:

- *Attitude* towards participation in the collective action, meaning a person's opinion that participating is good or bad.
- The *return* that a person expects to receive through participation, meaning whether the person finds participation in the action rewarding
- The person's *subjective social norms*, meaning the degree to which the person feels that he or she is under social pressure to participate or not participate.
- Perceived and actual *difficulties and barriers* that hinder participation.

Only if in the interaction of these four factors a specific threshold can be exceeded, will the person participate. The factors are not static; they can change over time and thus exhibit their own dynamics.

Social Influence Processes

The individual-internal factors, such as attitude and subjective social norm, change when the individual interacts with other persons. Attitude change is caused by quite complex persuasion processes, which prompted our use of the elaboration likelihood model (ELM) from Petty and Cacioppo (1986).

Diffusion Processes

We distinguish among three fundamental types of diffusion techniques:

- **"Self-serve" diffusion:** People are given the opportunity to decide on their own to participate in a collective action. For example, information materials and sign-up sheets (commitment forms) are placed in dispensers in public places, where they are freely accessible to everybody.
- **Centralized diffusion:** With this technique, people are recruited actively by the promoters of a collective action from a central geographic location or a center of social activity. Campaign promoters speak to people and give them the information materials and sign-up sheets needed for decision-making on participation. For example, a diffusion event can be staged by setting up information booths at central public locations in a community. At the booths, passers-by are actively encouraged to take part, and they can make a formal commitment to participate.
- **Diffusion via the social network:** This technique utilizes the social network in a community in order to elicit participation in

a collective action. For example, to stimulate word-of-mouth promotion of a program, written requests are sent to all persons known to be participating at a certain point in time, asking them to encourage others to become participants.

There are significant differences among these three diffusion techniques with respect to their characteristics and the dynamics that they engender.

The present study aims to answer the following general research questions:

Taking under consideration the three interlocking processes described above, how can we explain the dynamics of collective action?

What combination of diffusion measures is the best for eliciting participation?

The focus of this chapter will be on the interaction of the different processes (individual-internal processes, social influence processes, and diffusion processes) in order to explain the dynamics of collective actions.

THE SIMULATION MODEL OF THE DYNAMICS OF COLLECTIVE ACTION

In defining an agent-based simulation, the different aspects have to be distinguished.

The Agent Model

The model of how agents make the decision to participate or not participate in a collective action is represented in Figure 1 (see Mosler & Tobias, 2000; Mosler & Tobias, 2001).

Whether or not an agent will participate depends first of all on his or her intention to do so, the threshold that must be overcome in order to realize participation, and the difficulties that may hinder formal participation in the campaign. If intention minus difficulty is greater than threshold, the agent will participate; otherwise, the agent will not. Difficulty is dependent upon the diffusion technique that is implemented and the social position of an individual, as we will discuss further below.

Intention is the mean of attitude, return, and subjective social norm (we based attitude and

Figure 1. Model of individual decision-making on participation. The arrows are variables; the blocks are transition functions.

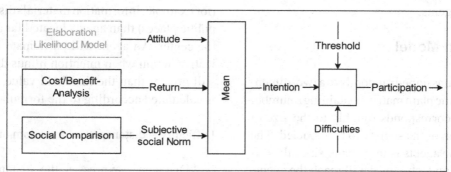

subjective social norm on the theory of planned behavior from Ajzen, 1988). All three factors are conceived as dynamic factors. However, for reasons of simplicity, attitude is shown here as a static variable, since we have left out the elaboration likelihood model for the present study (for a simulation of the ELM, see Mosler, Schwarz, Ammann, & Gutscher, 2001).

To calculate the return, we chose the simplest approach and simply subtract the subjectively perceived costs of participation from the subjectively perceived benefit of the collective good. However, the benefit is 0 if the expected and actual number of participants lie below the number of participants held to be necessary by the agent for creation of the collective good (success limit). The model also allows simulating all-or-none contracts as proposed by Marwell and Oliver (1993). In this case, people only have to make contributions, if a certain number of people could be found that are willing to contribute. This number is called here the contract-base. When modelling a collective campaign that uses an all-or-none contract, the number of expected participants always corresponds to the contract base.

Calculation of the subjective social norm was done by calculating the mean of the intentions of contact persons of each agent.

The model now contains a number of agents that function according to the rules outlined. The next step is to construct a population structure out of such agents.

Population Model

The agents are assigned randomly to a two-dimensional quadratic plain matrix containing a number of cells that corresponds roughly to the size of the population of the society to be modeled. The position of the agents is important, since the different diffusion techniques will reach the agents more or less well dependent upon their location within the matrix. However, it is important not to think of position as a geographic location. In-

stead, position represents the agent's relation to the society, the agent's proximity in social space. If, for example, a city is modeled, an agent in the center of the matrix represents a person that is strongly oriented towards this city and spends a lot of time here. An agent far from the center of the matrix, in contrast, represents a person, that is more oriented towards another place and only spends little time in the city.

Connecting the agents within the network proceeds on the assumption that relations between agents are reciprocal. This means that if Agent 1 is influencing Agent 2, then Agent 2 is also influencing Agent 1. Every agent is connected to a certain number of other agents that can be located anywhere in the matrix. This network represents a close circle of acquaintances.

Modelling the Diffusion Techniques

For modelling *self-serve diffusion*, the only thing we need to establish is the degree of difficulty that agents will experience once they have decided on their own to participate in a collective action. Although we assume that the degree of difficulty will be subject to some random variations, the following tendency holds: Agents located at or near the center of the matrix will experience fewer obstacles to formal participation in the campaign because, through their social activities, they are more likely to come into contact with the campaign (for example, information materials dispensers in public places) than agents located far away from the center. An agent will participate in the collective action when intention minus difficulty is still greater than the threshold value. Difficulty is calculated according to the formula:

$$\text{Difficulty} = \text{distance}_s \times a_1 + \text{random number} \times z_1$$

"Distance$_s$" expresses the distance of the agent from the center of the matrix. Parameter a_1 determines how much more difficult it is for an agent far from the center to participate in the campaign on his or her own accord, while z_1 sets the strength of the random influencing factor. This random number ranges from 0 to 1; it is reset for every agent on each time step of the simulated campaign. The two parameters a_1 and z_1, in contrast, are constant values for every agent over all runs of the simulation. Distance$_s$ varies between agents but is constant over time.

With self-serve diffusion, each agent has basically the same chance of participating (though different difficulties to do so). When modelling *centralized diffusion* techniques, however, we have to establish what agents will be reached by the diffusion event. Here again, chance and the positions of the agents play a role. But this time, it is not the agent's distance from the center of the matrix that is decisive, but rather the agent's distance from the center of the diffusion event, which can be placed anywhere within the matrix. In order to determine whether an agent will be reached by the campaign event, the following equation was calculated for each:

"Reachability" = 1 − distance$_c$ × a_2 + (random number − 0.5) × z_2

Here, "distance$_c$" is the agent's distance from the centralized diffusion event. The other parameters correspond to those in the formula for the difficulty in self-serve diffusion. If reachability is greater than 0, the campaign reaches the agent, otherwise, it does not. The random number is reset for each agent and each event, while a_2 and z_2 remain constant over the entire course of the simulation and are the same for each agent. Again, distance$_c$ varies between agents but is constant over time.

For *diffusion via the social network*, we have to establish whether an agent encourages others to participate in the campaign or not. We assume that here basically the same processes occur as in the decision to participate, but that the limit that must be exceeded is higher. How much higher

the limit lies is kept constant for all agents over all runs of the simulation.

Note: Self-serve diffusion depends on the activity of the individuals and so is "active" anytime, whereas the other forms of diffusion must be organized and so only take effect in specific moments of time.

The Course of the Simulation

In each time step of the simulation, one diffusion event as self-serve, centralized, or network diffusion takes place. This means that one time step can be usually interpreted as one day. The order in which the three types of diffusion measures are implemented is either given by the events of a real-world campaign (see empirical section) or chosen freely by the experimenter. Within each diffusion event, the participation model is calculated for all agents or for all agents that are reached by the event. Calculating the model means that all dynamic values of the variables are calculated anew, including the variable that expresses whether the agent participates or not.

Interdependent values (i.e., the subjective social norm and the return) are calculated at the beginning of a day, or of a diffusion event, for all agents. The values remain constant until the next day. This is a plausible assumption when considering that, as a rule, the current number of participants is announced at most once a day and that it is hardly likely that agents will talk about the collective action more than once a day (to assess their acquaintances' intentions).

METHOD OF THE EMPIRICAL INVESTIGATION

The data were collected in the Swiss municipality of Muensingen near Bern, the capital of Switzerland. Muensingen is a city with a population of 10,000 inhabitants; due to its size, it forms a regional center. The city of Muensingen is experiencing ever-heavier traffic throughout the city, even in residential areas. In an attempt to resolve the problems that the traffic burden is causing, a collective action campaign was launched in 1998 by our research team in cooperation with the public authorities of Muensingen (see Mosler, Gutscher, & Artho, 2001).

Procedures and Subjects

The data for this investigation were collected by means of questionnaires sent to the same 1,411 persons before and shortly after the end of the complete campaign. The samples were drawn randomly from the total population of 18 to 65-year-old residents. The response rate, at 49% for the first survey and 30% for the second, was good, but for the present investigation only 185 cases could be used. However, this reduced set of cases is still sufficiently representative of the demographic structure of Muensingen.

The questionnaire surveys provided individual subjective data at specific time points. In addition, we had access to the aggregated behavior measure: the number of new participants (self-commitments) gained per day throughout the course of the campaign. The present investigation focuses on these "objective" data.

Data for the Agent Model

With the exception of threshold value, the values of the individual variables of the agents are grounded completely empirically for our investigation. Attitude was tapped following Ajzen (1988). Two items, which formed a sum scale, asked respondents whether they saw participation in the campaign as necessary/not necessary or senseless/meaningful or somewhere in-between (there were six answer choices for each). These items were included in both the pre- and post-questionnaire. To calculate return, the post-questionnaire asked about benefit, costs, and success limit. The expected number of participants was

tapped by both questionnaires. Costs and benefit were measured by direct questions on how much personal effort participation in the campaign required (cost) and how much personal benefit would result if everyone in Muensingen drove more slowly (benefit of the collective good). Both items had 0 to 9 answer choices. The success limit was assessed by asking how many participants would be required in order for the "slow-down" campaign to show noticeable effects. Here respondents chose from twenty answer choices, ranging from 200 to 4,000 persons signed-up to participate (in increments of 200). For the expected number of participants on the pre-questionnaire, respondents chose from 0 to 8,000 persons in seven increments. The post-questionnaire asked about the number of participants in the same way that the success limit had been assessed.

Data for Constructing the Population

To project the results of the sample to the population, we utilized official census statistics for age groups sorted by gender and the official number of participants as the projection base. From this we derived the multiplication factor, times which an agent representing a person in the sample was copied. The sample was based on the population of persons between 18 and 65 years, 6,878 in total. So this amount of agents was generated. Since no data were collected that would allow the agents to be positioned as they would be in real-life Muensingen, they were assigned randomly to an 83 X 83 matrix, leaving 11 spaces empty.

Data for the Diffusion Measures and Simulation Runs

The most important information on the diffusion measures is *when* (point in time) the diffusion measures were implemented during the campaign. We can also estimate the number of persons that were reached by the first, centralized diffusion event (this was at least 1,500) based on a questionnaire item that asked people what had first alerted them to the campaign. The position of the information booths in the model was determined by plausible assumptions, based on the fact that in Muensingen we staged centralized diffusion events twice, once at the annual Christmas Fair and once in front of two large stores. Both centralized diffusion events reached mainly those persons who tend to spend more of their time in Muensingen. The event at the Christmas Fair was therefore placed at the center of the matrix (coordinates 40, 40). The event at the stores reached mainly persons who shop in Muensingen, but spend less time in the center of the city. Therefore, for the model we placed this event within the greater central area, but somewhat outside the exact center of the matrix (coordinates 45, 45). The data on the number of participants gained at the two information booths and the number of persons reached through the first centralized diffusion event at the fair allow estimation of the three parameters of participation threshold, a_2, and z_2 (a_2 is the distance parameter and z_2 the weighting of the random number in the equation for reachability; see the section on modelling diffusion techniques). This means that for the centralized diffusion measures, the data allow complete calibration of the model. The following values resulted from calibration: $a_2 = 0.055$, $z_2 = 1.5$, and participation threshold = 0.4, with 1,565 agents reached at the first centralized diffusion event.

The parameters of self-serve diffusion are determined on the basis of the number of newly recruited persons on days with no other diffusion event. Because of the frequency of these days, the data allow not only calibration of the model, but also testing. To calibrate the parameters a_1 and z_1 of the equation for difficulty, the numbers of participants over three days are necessary, though 59 are available. The following values resulted from calibration: $a_1 = 0.007$, $z_1 = 2$.

The single parameter for diffusion among members of a social network was set according to the information on the number of participants that were gained through the sending out of letters. For this diffusion event, all known participants at a specific point in time were sent a letter asking them to encourage others to participate in the campaign. Calibration yielded a threshold for activating acquaintances of 0.83.

Because the simulation runs directly on the basis of days, the events could be taken over 1:1. Only Saturdays and Sundays were cut out of the simulation, since formal participation was not possible on these days. One exception was the two information booth events, which were both staged on weekends. At the start of the simulation, the 93 agents having the highest value on intention were designated as participants. This corresponds to the 93 persons who were already participating in the real Muensingen campaign even prior to the official start of the campaign. Most of these persons were the organizers of the campaign. Then, for each of the 63 days of the campaign, a diffusion event was calculated. In Muensingen, the first event was a centralized diffusion event (information booth at the Christmas Fair), followed by a 30-day period during which self-serve diffusion (material in dispensers) provided information that allowed people to make their own decision to participate. The next event was the second centralized event (information booths at two large stores), followed by four more days of self-serve diffusion up until the letter event. The letters, sent to known participants two days after the second centralized event, took mostly two days to reach their recipients. Finally, there was a period of 25 more days until the diffusion phase was ended. Now the behavioral phase began, and people were supposed to begin driving more slowly through the city. Figure 2 provides an overview of the increase in the number of participants in dependency upon the various diffusion measures during the 63 days of the campaign.

RESULTS

First, the parameters of the diffusion measures were calibrated on the basis of the empirical data. This provided the empirical grounding, the basis for conducting the exploration and the "what if" scenarios.

Calibration and Exploration of the Simulation Model

Figure 2 shows the empirical course and the course of the model, which was calculated with optimally set parameters. Large portions of the two curves exhibit practically perfect correspondence. The only thing that the model did not replicate were the "steps" between the first and second information booth events.

In order to investigate the extent to which the dynamics arise due to individual-internal and/or through social influence processes, return and subjective social norm were set at their starting values. Figure 2 reveals that keeping these factors static does not alter the qualitative course, but the curve as a whole becomes flatter. The two factors result in a speeding up of the campaign starting at about Day 15. After the second information booth event, keeping the value of return fixed results in a greater flattening of the curve than fixing the value of subjective social norm. All together, we can say that the dynamic course of the number of participants is dominated by the diffusion processes, whereas this development comes under the increasing influence of individual-internal and social influence processes when the number of participants is high.

"What if" Scenarios

Having calibrated the model and conducted exploratory analyses, we can now investigate alternative measures for collective action campaigns in the hope of learning some lessons for future campaigns. The present study examines three modifications of the real campaign that we conducted in Muensingen:

Figure 2. Graphical representation of the increase in number of participants during the days of the campaign: calibrated model, calibrated model with fixed values for subjective social norm (SSN), and calibrated model with fixed values for return. IB1 is the first information booth event, IB2 the second information booth event, and L is the letter event.

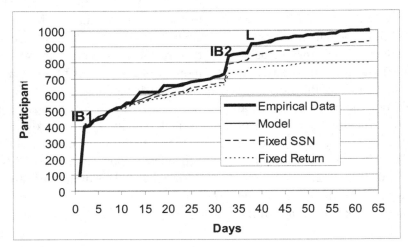

- **Restructuring:** What are the effects of the positioning and number of centralized diffusion measures or network diffusion?
- **Duration of the campaign:** Can more participants be gained if we extend the length of the campaign or if we conduct another centralized diffusion event during the extension in time?
- **All-or-none contracts:** What is the effect of an all-or-none contract, and what is the best contract basis?
- **Combination:** How many participants can be recruited by means of a campaign with centralized diffusion events every 20 days and network diffusion towards the end of the campaign? What effect would an all-or-none contract have in this case?

Figure 3 presents the results of restructuring and lengthening the duration of the campaign.

Figure 3 reveals that the events can be moved back and forth along the time axis without causing any significant change to the final number of participants. This means that whereas the diffusion measures do indeed significantly influence the dynamics and also the final number of participants in collective actions, their sequence within the course of the campaign does not play a role when it comes to the final results.

Figure 3 demonstrates that extending the duration of the campaign increases the number of participants considerably. The strong flattening of the curve showing the development of the number of participants towards the end of a campaign can be misleading. If many persons have a specific success limit (in Muensingen this was a success limit of 1,000 persons), there is a rapid increase in the number of participants once the limit is reached. Even without staging any further diffusion events, 10 percent more participants are gained. If an additional diffusion event is staged, this increases to 25 percent more participants.

The next experiment analyzes the effect on development of the number of participants if the campaign uses an all-or-none contract, as proposed by Marwell and Oliver (1993), with various con-

Figure 3. Graphical representation of the effects of staging the second centralized diffusion event earlier in time, staging the network diffusion earlier in time, both together, and extending the campaign by 25 days with and without adding another centralized diffusion event.

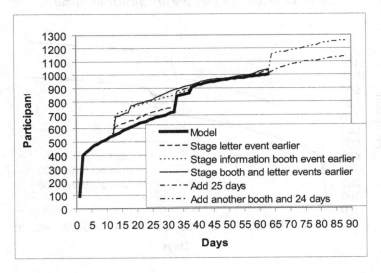

tract bases. With an all-or-none contract, persons asked to participate in collective action are told from the start the minimum number of people that must sign up before the action can take place. The results are shown in Figure 4.

Depending on the contract basis, the number of participants mobilized can be noticeably raised or reduced; indeed, the campaign can even fail utterly. If relatively many people have a success expectation that corresponds to the contract basis, a large part of the population will see the benefit of the action from the start and will result in a strong acceleration of the action. In Muensingen, about 60 percent of the population expected the action to succeed with less than 1,200 participants, and this led to the acceleration. Moreover, the contract basis is indeed achieved, or even exceeded. This means that the contract becomes valid, and the participants must now make good on their pledges. With this contract, 20 percent more participants could be gained.

Nevertheless, the implementation of an all-or-none contract entails considerable risk. If the contract basis selected is too low, as shown by the example contract basis of 900, too many persons now expect a lower number of participants, and at the same time, only a few additional persons consider the benefit of the proposed action, since the basis lies below the critical limit, in this case 1,000 persons. This poorly-chosen contract basis would have led to 20 percent *fewer* participants than the results without an all-or-none contract. Figure 4 shows that a contract basis of 1,500 would not have raised the number of participants. No participants are lost if the contract basis is too high, but if the contract basis is not met at the end, the conditions of the contract have not been fulfilled and participants do not have to make good on their pledges. This spells the total failure of the entire campaign.

As a final experiment, we investigated combinations of the diffusion measures discussed above: lengthening the duration of a campaign that used an all-or-none contract, changing the timing of the centralized diffusion events, increasing the number of these events while at the same time lengthening the duration of the campaign, and the latter scenario combined with an all-or-none contract. Figure 5 presents the results.

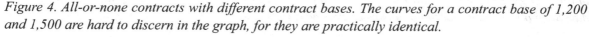

Figure 4. All-or-none contracts with different contract bases. The curves for a contract base of 1,200 and 1,500 are hard to discern in the graph, for they are practically identical.

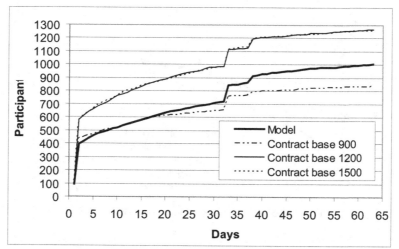

Figure 5. Extending the duration of a campaign that uses an all-or-none contract (contract basis = 1,200 participants), both with and without an additional centralized diffusion event; and a new campaign concept with four centralized diffusion events at intervals of 20 days and a network diffusion event at the end, both with and without using an all-or-none contract (basis = 1,200).

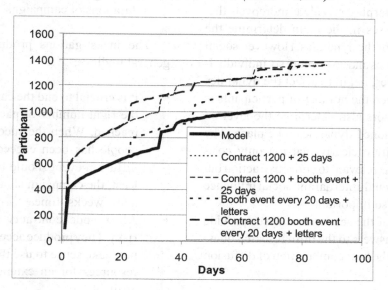

Figure 5 reveals that extending the time period of the campaign in combination with an all-or-none contract would have produced practically no additional participants. Even the addition of an additional centralized diffusion event brings little improvement. This shows that since an all-or-none contract results in a considerable acceleration in the number of participants at the start of a campaign, the duration of the campaign can also be shortened.

The last two scenarios can be seen as "maximum" solutions. A campaign period of four months is already very lengthy, and four centralized diffusion events and a network diffusion event make the campaign expensive and work-intensive. Still, those scenarios produce a gain of almost 40 percent more participants.

It is interesting to observe that implementing an all-or-none contract hardly affects the final number of participants gained for the action. The contract does, however, accelerate the development of this number at the start of the campaign. The milestone of 1,200 participants, for instance, is reached about one month earlier with an all-or-none contract. However, if there is enough time available to conduct a campaign, the risks of introducing an all-or-none contract can be eliminated by simply choosing instead a sufficiently long time period for the campaign. Even with the most effort-intensive campaign using an all-or-none contract, 794 potential participants were not reached, but 64 percent of the persons having an intention higher then the participation-threshold could be activated.

DISCUSSION

The first research question addressed was the extent to which the three processes (and which of these processes in particular) explain the dynamics of a collective action. The results yield the following answer: A complex interaction of individual-internal, social influence, and diffusion processes seem to be responsible for the dynamics of collective action. Exploration of this complex interplay revealed, moreover, that diffusion processes in the main determine the rough structure of the dynamics. However, social influence processes and, even more so, individual-internal processes, begin to affect the dynamics significantly when the number of participants is high. These factors also determine the level on which the mentioned dynamics take place. The results demonstrate clearly that not only cost-benefit analysis is relevant to collective action but that other individual-internal and social influence processes are also important.

The results of the scenario analyses provide the following answers to the third research question, regarding the best combination of diffusion measures:

a.   The positioning of the diffusion measures along the time axis had no significant effect on the ultimate success of the collective action campaign.

b.   Extending the duration of the campaign, particularly in combination with additional diffusion events, is effective if the number of participants reached corresponds to a number that many people believe will lead to success.

c.   All-or-none contracts can bring a collective action campaign to greater success if the contract basis is slightly larger than the number of participants that many people believe will lead to success of the action. If the contract basis is lower, the number of participants gained is lower than the number of participants gained without using a contract. If the contract basis is much higher, the conditions of the contract might not be met, and the collective action cannot be launched at all.

d.   All-or-none contracts can accelerate an action campaign, but in the end effect they contribute no more than do multiple implementations of diffusion measures or longer durations of campaigns.

The investigations produce the following general findings:

• It is crucial to end the campaign only when the right number of participants has been reached. When the success limit of many people has been exceeded, an additional diffusion event should be staged, or at the least, the campaign should be extended by a few weeks' time.

• All-or-none contracts are powerful, but risky. They produce acceleration, but it does not make sense to use them if the time and resources for an extensive campaign are available.

• The intention to participate is only one factor in participation. Besides intention, it is crucial that the people who would be willing to participate are in fact reached by the campaign.

These findings show once again that the interaction of the three types of processes determines the dynamics of collective action. The simulation model can provide support: Simulation can produce an estimate of the required length of time for the campaign, show the efforts that would be required, and evaluate whether an all-or-none contract would, after all, be more efficient.

REFERENCES

Ajzen, I. (1988). *Attitudes, personality, and behavior*. Chicago: Dorsey Press.

Klandermans, B. (1984). Mobilization and participation: Social-psychological expansions of resource mobilization theory. *American Sociological Review, 49,* 583-600.

Marwell, G., & Oliver, P.E. (1993). *The critical mass in collective action.* Cambridge: Press Syndicate of the University of Cambridge.

Mosler, H.-J. (2002). Agent-based simulation of an environmental action campaign: Changing people's behaviour via their inner contradictions. In A.E. Rizzoli, & A.J. Jakeman (Eds.). Integrated assessment and decision support. *Proceedings of the 1st biennial meeting of the International Environmental Modelling and Software Society.* Como: iEMSS, 2, 202-207.

Mosler, H.-J., Gutscher, H., & Artho, J. (2001). Wie können viele Personen für eine kommunale Umweltaktion gewonnen werden? [How to gain many participants for communal environmental action?] *Umweltpsychologie,* 5(2), 122-140.

Mosler, H.-J., & Tobias, R. (2000). Die Organisation kollektiver Aktionen durch Beeinflussung der individuellen Teilnahmeentscheidung. Eine Simulationsstudie [Organizing collective action through influencing the individual's decision to participate. A computer simulation]. *Kölner Zeitschrift für Soziologie und Sozialpsychologie, 52,* 264-290.

Mosler, H.-J., & Tobias, R. (2001). Who participates in a collective action? A psychologically based simulation with 10,000 agents. In C. Urban (Ed.), Second *Workshop on Agent-Based Simulation* (pp. 77-82). Ghent, SCS-Europe.

Mosler, H.-J., Schwarz, K., Ammann, F., & Gutscher, H. (2001). Computer simulation as a method of further developing a theory: Simulating the elaboration likelihood model (ELM). *Personality and Social Psychology Review,* 201-215.

Petty, R. E., & Cacioppo, J. T. (1986). The elaboration likelihood model of persuasion. In L. Berkowitz (Ed.), *Advances in experimental social psychology,* 9, 123-205. New York: Academic Press.

Chapter XIX
Examining the Myth of Money with Agent–Based Modelling

Satoru Yamadera
Tokyo Institute of Technology, Japan

Takao Terano
Tokyo Institute of Technology, Japan

ABSTRACT

This chapter presents an agent-based computational model of the emergence of money. It is based on classical economic theories of money, advocating that money is a symbol of credibility. The most interesting and mysterious feature of money is the divergence of its face value from its intrinsic value. People accept and appreciate a piece of chapter because it is believed as money. The model examines how such belief creates money in a society. Furthermore, by incorporating spatial activities of agents into the simulations, the model can examine various hypotheses which were difficult to examine in previous approaches. The simulation results show that parameters such as credibility and communication between agents will affect the outcomes. The model not only provides the foundation for a more generalized theory of money, but also demonstrates that agent-based modelling can be an effective tool to examine various hypotheses of social sciences.

INTRODUCTION

Why do people use money? Why do people accept sheer paper in exchange for goods? How has money emerged? These are long-lasting questions which annoyed ancient philosophers such as Aristotle as well as modern economists. Karl Polanyi, a great philosopher of economic thoughts, compares money to a symbol such as language, alphabet, and measurement (Polanyi, 1957). According to his idea, money is a symbol of brief to be accepted in exchange for everything by everyone. In other words, the credibility to be generally accepted as a means of payment is the key to becoming money. Therefore, by incorporating Polanyi's theory into an agent-based computational model, we can shed light on the "myth" of money. The model in this chapter shows the process of certain goods gaining credibility within a community, then, the process eventually leads to the emergence of money. This model overcomes deficiencies of previous studies and models of the emergence of money by incorporating spatial activities of agents. Historical evidence show that many currencies were created locally. In other words, the emergence and use of money was affected by geographic or social boundaries. In addition, this model is flexible enough to compare the impact of changes in parameters; it can examine which parameter has a greater affecton the emergence of money and how the parameter affects the emergence of money. As a result, the model can demonstrate various outcomes. The outcomes show that difference in credibility of goods, constraints on agent movements, and a communication strategy, will significantly affect results in which goods emerge as money.

The model in this chapter not only provides the foundation for establishing a more general theory of money, but also demonstrates the effectiveness of agent-based modelling as a tool to analyze social sciences. Agent-base modelling can be a new methodology to expand the scope of social sciences.

RELATED WORK

Classical Theories of Money

There are many definitions and thoughts concerning money. The most common approach is to divide money into three functions. Nobel Prize laureate Sir John Hicks (1967) defined money as a unit of account, a means of payment, and a store of values. Others have focused on trade or social interactions. Carl Menger (1892) claimed in *On the Origins of Money*, that the most saleable goods become money. From a legalists' perspective, Georg Knapp claimed the State theory of money,

in which whatever was recognized by the State as money becomes legal tender and the only effective means of payment (Mann, 1992). Alan Greenspan (2002), the former Federal Reserve Chairman, said in a speech that "the history of money is the history of civilization or, more exactly, of some important civilizing values. Its form at any particular period of history reflects the degree of confidence, or the degree of trust, that market participants have in the institutions that govern every market system, whether centrally planned or free."

Though the definitions and thoughts are varied, there is a common notion: The value of money needs to be detached from its intrinsic value. It may sound tautological but the value of money is given because it is money. More importantly, the value must be recognized and accepted by everyone within a community, otherwise it cannot be used as money. A great fan of Michael Jackson may accept his autograph in exchange for a Mercedes. But, normally people will not accept it. In this context, Polanyi's view on money seems more plausible and comprehensive as the definition of money. Polanyi (1957) claimed that money is a symbol of brief to be accepted by everyone. Therefore, money is defined in the social context. In other words, anything can serve as money as it gains the credibility of the society.

Historical evidence, even recently, clearly shows that credibility is the key to the establishment of money. Tenino, a small town in Washington Sate, U.S., faced a shortage of money caused by the failure of the Citizen's Bank of Tenino during the Great Depression[1]. The Tenino Chamber of Commerce solved this problem by issuing wooden scrip. The issuance relieved the shortage, and the scrip was circulated in the town. This was possible because people in the town agreed to accept it as money. Of course, this recognition was only effective in Tenino; no other town accepted the scrip as money. This episode clearly shows that once goods are recognized as a means of exchange by everyone, they become money. The process of the emergence of money depends on how fast the credibility emerges. In the case of Tenino, it was very quick.

Formalization of the Classical Theories

Economists have been trying to formalize classical theories of money. The most influential work is Kiyotaki and Wright (1989). They studied how the existence of a medium of exchange increases welfare compared to the world of barter. They showed that welfare is maximized if one of three goods becomes as a medium of exchange, i.e., money. In the model, storability of goods is the key determinant to becoming money. Another work is Luo (1999), which showed an evolutionary model of money in which agents imitate the more successful strategies, and eventually one strategy is selected to produce generally accepted media of exchange.

There is another approach to objectify classical theories: it is a simulation. Marimon, McGrattan, and Sargent (1990) constructed an intelligent agent model and examined Kiyotaki and Wright (1999). Yasutomi (2000) demonstrated the emergence of money by modelling Menger's theory in which saleability of goods is the key determinant to becoming money. Sasaki et al. (2002) expanded the Yasutomi model to analyze the emergence of international currency through transactions of goods and exchanges of currency. Arifovic (2001) analyzed competition between two currencies as the emergence of international currency. Another interesting work is Duffy (2001), in which he examined Kiyotaki and Wright (1989) by modelling simulations of artificial agents and real agents.

THE FRAMEWORK OF THIS MODEL

The model in this chapter is designed to overcome deficiencies of the previous studies in two ways. First, the model is designed to utilize local in-

formation and rules only. The agent models in the previous studies often incorporated a market mechanism inside to compare the value of all goods in the model. This is inappropriate. The agent models are designed to produce outcomes by micro-interaction of agents, but if agents act based on macro-information, the outcomes cannot be regarded as purely derived from the microinteractions. For example, in Yasutomi's (2000) model, the agents buy a good if the "marketability" of the good is higher than its threshold. Decisions by the agents are based on the information of the ranking of "saleability" of goods calculated by the centralized system which monitors all transactions. However, in the early period of human history, it is more natural to presume that we did not have such a centralized system. To simulate the early history of money, it is important to build a model which only utilizes information from the bottom, not from the top down.

Second, the model in this chapter incorporates agents' movements and spatial constraints on agents' action in the process of the emergence of money. It is reasonable to assume from the history of money that factors such as geography, distance, and communication affected the process of the emergence of money. In addition, the model is constructed flexibly to examine the impact of changes in parameters such as credibility and distance in communication. In order to incorporate spatial activities of agents, KK-MAS[2] was chosen as a multi-agent simulator.

Basic Concept of Modelling (No.1 Model)

The emergence of money in this model is defined as the situation where one good is believed to be the most credible by every agent in the community. As mentioned above, in this model agents act locally and decide locally. Agents exchange information with neighboring agents regarding which good is the most credible (Figure 1).

Figure 1. Basic image of the model

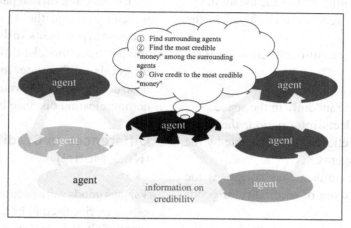

Then, agents move around within the space and communicate with each other. As this process continues, the information of the credibility of the goods is shared by the agents, and the most credible good is expected to emerge.

In this simulation, five goods are to be compared and chosen as money by the agents: Red, Blue, Black, Yellow, and Green. The number of goods can be increased or reduced. Historically speaking, the goods notably used as money seem to be several, not hundreds; these are metal, stone, salt, shells, rice, and domestic livestock. The color of the agents will change as

the process of exchanging information proceeds. Once all agents turn the same color, the good of the color is believed by the all agents as the most credible good, i.e., money (Figure 2).

The number of agents in this simulation is one hundred. The number of agents can be increased, though the simulation will require more time to get results. At the beginning, the agents are equally divided into five colors, thus, there are twenty agents for each color.

Agents are deployed in the space. The initial location of agents in the space is very important because the process of the emergence of money

Figure 2. Emergence of money

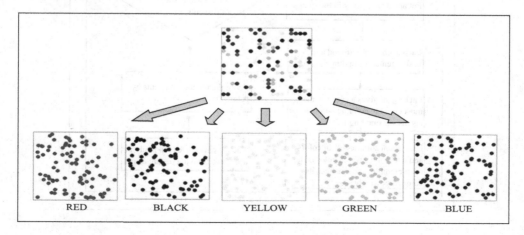

will be affected significantly by the location. As the default setting, agents are deployed in the space randomly.

The simulation goes through following steps (Figure 3):

1. Agents are put randomly in the space.
2. An agent collects information, the value of which is believed to be credible by the neighboring agents.
3. Based on the information collected, the agent adds a score of credibility of goods respectively.
4. By sorting the scores, the agent chooses the most credible good.
5. The agent turns into the color of the most credible good.
6. The agent moves randomly in the space.
7. This will continue until the all agents believe one color as the most credible good.

By changing various parameters in this model, we can examine the emergence of money in various environments. In this chapter, we examine another three models: differences in credibility of goods, difference in spatial constraints obstructing agents' movement, and difference in communication distance between agents.

Differences in Credibility of Goods (No.2 Model)

Various goods were used as money in history. For example, rice used to be a means of exchange in Japan. Salt, fish, and even a big stone were used as money (Davis, 2002). Among all goods, gold has the longest history; it was used as money until recently. Even these days, gold is still regarded as a safe haven by some investors. Governments hold gold as foreign reserves even though the gold standard was abolished. So, what makes gold so credible? Why do people put high value on gold

Figure 3. Flowchart of the No.1 model

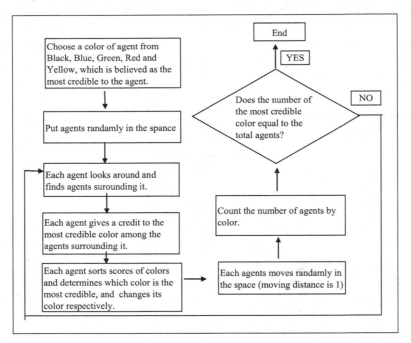

compared to other metals? Karl Marx said that gold and silver are, in their nature, money. Gold is chosen as money probably because it does not corrode, i.e., it can serve as a very good store of value. In other words, a good which can perfectly maintain its value is expected to emerge as money. To examine this hypothesis, the No.2 model makes a modification from the No.1 model by changing weights of the previous information of credibility. The red color maintains the previous score of the credibility as 100 percent and the other goods, i.e., Blue, Green, Yellow, and Black, reduce their score of credibility by 1 percent.

Spatial Constraints Obstructing the Movement of Agents (No.3 Model)

The history of money tells us that different places had different money. People in the Yap Islands used stone money (Davis, 2002). Salt was a common instrument of commerce in Abyssinia, currently Ethiopia (Kurlansky, 2003). Even today, there are as many currencies as countries. In the No.3 model, we examine the impact of spatial boundaries on the emergence of money. In the model, the space is divided into several areas (Figure 4). The movements of agents are constrained by the boundaries. This modification in the No.3 model enables us to

examine the emergence of local currencies. The model also examines the impact of restrictiveness of the boundary on the emergence of money. One case is more restrictive; the space is completely segregated into two areas, and the movements of agents are confined within the segregated area. The other case is less restrictive; though the space is segregated, agents can exchange information through the wall. Thus, the agents can be affected by the information from the outside of the boundaries.

Difference in Communication Distance between Agents (No.4 Model)

How is credibility built in a society? How does communication between agents affect the credibility and the process of the emergence of money? Although communication between agents is a very important factor which influences the process of the emergence of money, the previous studies could not examine the impact of communication. In order to assess the impact, the moving distance of agents is changed in the No. 4 model. In the models from No.1 to No.3, agents move randomly but at the same distance. In the No.4 model, the Red agents move shorter

Figure 4. Division of initial space in No. 3 model

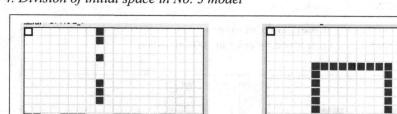

distances than the others, i.e., Blue, Black, Green, and Yellow. This means that the Red agents are expected to communicate with neighboring agents who are much closer than other agents. On the other hand, the other agents are expected to send their information to more distanced agents. Red agents might create a small community within a short distance, while the other agents are expected to create a larger community. However, it is an open question as to which strategy is superior. It needs to be examined by the simulation.

SIMULATION RESULTS

The Emergence of Money (No.1 Model)

Though agents are put and move randomly in the space, eventually one color is chosen as the most credible by all agents in the simulation. The model demonstrated the emergence of money as Figure 5 shows. The simulation results show that each of five goods is likely to become money with probability of 20 percent, respectively (Figure 6),

Figure 5. The emergence of money

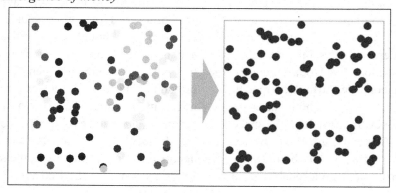

Figure 6. Frequency of emergence by color

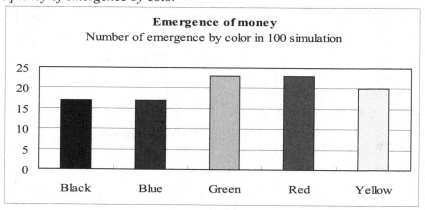

which is consistent with the expectation since there is no difference in characteristics among the five colors.

Figure 7 is one example in which the Blue emerged as money. Although the chance to emerge as money is equal for every color, none of the emergence paths was the same. Even among results of the same color, the path to become money was totally different from one another.

Besides, the variance of the number of simulation steps to finish the simulation is large (Figure 8). These results clearly show that the emergence of money is a complex adaptive system, in which a slight difference at the beginning will create very different consequences. In this case, the initial location of agents creates different emerging paths and outcome.

Figure 7. The path to become money

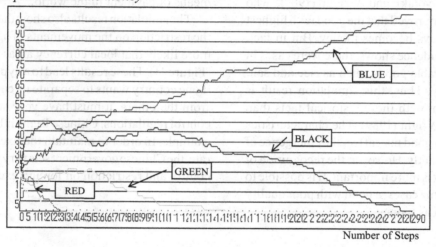

Figure 8. Variance of the number of steps to finish the simulation

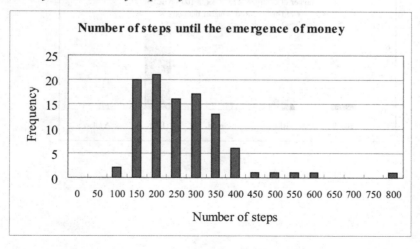

Impact of Difference in Credibility on the Emergence of Money (No.2 Model)

As expected, the No. 2 model demonstrated results that the Red, which is the most credible among the five colors, became money much more often than the other colors (Figure 9).

Although the results were as expected, it is interesting to see there were some cases where the rest of colors could become money, even though the probability was very small. This is contrary to Kiyotaki and Wright (1989), who mathematically proved that the good with highest storability always becomes money. But in fact, as historical evidence shows, there were cases in which less storable goods, such as rice and salt, became money. Thus, this simulation result is more consistent with these historical facts than Kiyotaki and Wright (1989). The characteristics and quality of a good may affect the emergence of money significantly. However, the recognition of the community is more important. Ii is possible to presume, in some cases, a good with poor quality may be chosen as money.

Impact of the Spatial Constraint on the Emergence of Money (No.3 Model)

In the No. 3 model, the boundaries to obstruct agents' movements created local currencies. The simulation results show that local currencies emerged in different areas (Figure 10) though one color eventually dominated the whole space. This result is consistent with the history of money. Local currencies had emerged in various areas, but gold eventually became the most pervasive means of payment in the world.

The simulation results also show that the higher the restriction on the movements of agents is, the more likely that local currency areas are created (Figure 11). These results lead to a hypothesis that if one country wants to separate its currency area from the others, it must have very strict capital control regulations. Chinese Renminbi is such an example. In order to maintain the fixed exchange rate, the Chinese government sets very tight capital control and restriction on foreign exchange.

Figure 9. Results in which credibility of the Red is high

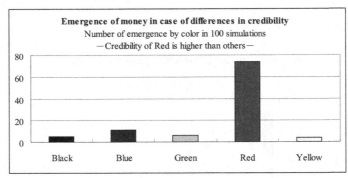

Figure 10. Emergence of different currency areas

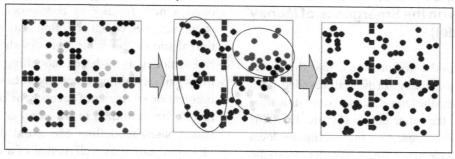

Figure 11. Emergence of money in more restricted areas

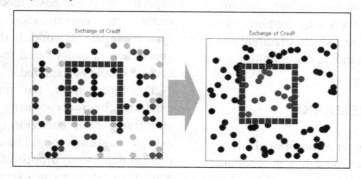

Figure 12. Results with differences in moving distance

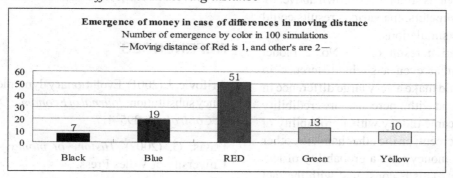

Impact of the Different Communication Strategies on the Emergence of Money (No.4 Model)

The No. 4 model demonstrated that the closer communication strategy of the Red prevailed much more often than the long-distance communication strategies of the other colors (Figure 12). This result brings an interesting implication for local currency and electric money. In order to expand the use of these new means of payment, the means should start from a smaller community, instead of starting from a large community. The closer communication strategy emphasizes high credibility in a local area. Once the strong credibility in a small community is created, the credibility can expand over the surrounding communities.

CONCLUDING REMARKS

The model in this chapter demonstrated promising uses of agent-based modelling in economics and other social sciences. The model could not only simulate the emergence of money but also compare the emergence of money in different environments. Such comparisons were not possible in the previous studies. As shown above, by modifying parameters, the various results could be obtained by simulations.

The simulation result of the No. 2 model demonstrated that even a slight difference in credibility would make a very large difference in outcomes. A good with 1 percent more credibility than others became money with a probability of more than 70 percent; on the other hand, the other goods became money with a probability of less than 10 percent. This is consistent with the fact that gold, which hardly erodes, is more likely to become money. Also the result is consistent with the fact that certain goods such as rice and salt, which are less credible than gold, can be money, though the probability is much smaller.

Agent-based computational modelling can open a new frontier of economics and other social sciences which are often criticized as too unrealistic or too subjective. As shown in the No. 4 model, agent-based modelling provides a means of examining a new hypothesis of communication strategies of agents, which was never able to be examined in the previous approach. Agent-based modelling can avoid deficiencies of formalization as well as that of a conceptual approach. As shown in this chapter, by using agent-based modelling, various hypotheses can be created and examined without having real experiments. Agent-based modelling can provide methods to answer questions of complex social systems of the real world. In this regard, further application of agent-based modelling in social science should be explored.

For future work, the model needs to be expanded by incorporating research results and findings of behavioral psychology and experimental economics. The modelling based on more in-depth study of positive analysis of human behavior enables us to examine and simulate the emergence of money more realistically, contributing to, for example, calculating the probability of the emergence of a local currency system in a society.

REFERENCES

Arifovic, J. (2001). Evolutionary dynamics of currency substitution. *Journal of Economic Dynamics & Control, 25*, 395-417.

Davis, G. (2002). *History of money.* Cardiff: University of Wales Press.

Duffy, J. (2001). Learning to speculate: Experiments with artificial and real agents. *Journal of Economic Dynamics and Control, 25*, 295-319.

Greenspan, A. (2002). *The history of money.* Speech at the opening of an American numismatic society exhibition. New York: Federal Reserve Bank of New York.

Hicks, J. (1967). *Critical essays in monetary theory*. Oxford: Clarendon Press.

Kiyotaki, N., & Wright, R. (1989). On money as a medium of exchange. *Journal of Political Economy, 97*, 927-54.

Kurlansky, M. (2003). *Salt*. New York: Penguin Group.

Luo, G. (1999). The evolution of money as a medium of exchange. *Journal of Economic Dynamics & Control, 23*, 415-458.

Mann, F.A. (1992). *Legal aspects of money* (5th ed.). London: Clarendon Press.

Marimon, R., McGrattan, E., & Sargent, T. (1990). Money as a medium of exchange in an economy with artificially intelligent agents. *Journal of Economic Dynamics and Control*, 14, 329-373.

Menger, C. (1892). On the origin of money. *Economic Journal, 2*, 239-255.

Polanyi, K., (1957). *The semantics of money-use: Explorations*. Toronto: University of Toronto.

Sasaki, Y., Yamashita, T., Kawamura, H., Kurumatani, K., & Ohuchi, A. (2002). Emergence of key currency in international trade by production and trader agents. In H.J. Caulfield & S-H. Chen et al. (Eds.), *Proceeding Of the Sixth Joint Conference on Information Sciences, Association for Intelligent Machinery* (pp. 1073-1076).

Yasutomi, A. (2000). The emergence and collapse of money. *Physica, D82*, 180-194.

Section III
The Participant and Experimentally–Oriented

Chapter XX
Friends and Buffaloes:
One Game, Two Modelling Processes

Stanislas Boissau
Wageningen University and Ecole des Hautes Etudes en Sciences Sociales (EHESS), Vietnam

François Sempé
Institut de la Francophonie pour l'Informatique (IFI), Vietnam

Alain Boucher
Institut de la Francophonie pour l'Informatique (IFI), Vietnam

Alexis Drogoul
Institut de Recherche pour le Développement (IRD), France

François Bousquet
*Centre de Coopération Internationale en Recherche Agronomique
pour le Développement (CIRAD), France*

ABSTRACT

Starting from a simple gaming-simulation experiment about the management of a common resource, two modelling experiments were conducted in different settings. In the first experiment, the game was played by farmers and the modeller subsequently inferred a model from behaviour observed during the game. In order to address the validation problems underlying this type of modelling, a new experiment was conducted, in which computer science students played the game and then "self-modelled" their behaviour. We shall present, compare, and discuss both these modelling processes. We show that self-modelling facilitated a better understanding of the players' behaviours, although it is not a complete solution.

INTRODUCTION

In the past few years, a new approach to modelling, called companion modelling (ComMod), has been developed by a group of researchers (Barreteau et al., 2003). This approach often describes a combination of gaming simulation and multi-agent modelling. The companion modelling approach pursues two interrelated objectives: understanding complex systems and supporting collective decision-making. In practice, the different experiments carried out by ComMod researchers have led to different combinations of gaming-simulation and multi-agent modelling, depending on the objective the research question and the problem to be tackled (Bousquet et al., 2002; Barreteau, 2003). One issue of particular interest in these various experiments has been the involvement of stakeholders in the modelling process itself, which may lead to participatory modelling or participatory simulations. One way of involving stakeholders is to have them participate in a gaming simulation. Observed behaviours and outputs of the gaming-simulation can then be used as a starting point for multi-agent modelling. In this chapter, we present two interrelated experiences involving the stakeholders in the modelling process and draw relevant methodological conclusions.

The first part of this article presents the Game of Buffaloes: This gaming simulation about the management of dwindling grazing land, which was conducted with farmers of Northern Vietnam, led to a multi-agent model aiming to reproduce the players' behaviour. In order to overcome validation problems, a hypothesis is formulated according to which players may be able to self-model their own behaviour. This hypothesis and the subsequent "Game of Friends" are presented in the second part. The third, and final, part presents an analysis of our findings and of difficulties encountered.

THE GAME OF BUFFALOES

The Context

The first experiment was conducted in the mountainous areas of northern Vietnam as part of a more global project aimed at understanding how farmers in this region deal with increasing land scarcity (Boissau, 2005). It took place in two villages of Duc Van commune (Ngan Son district, Bac Kan province) inhabited by two different ethnic groups, namely Tay and Dao. In these villages, farmers rely mainly on irrigated rice cultivation, especially since sloping land has been allocated to individual households. They also rear buffaloes, which are an essential part of their livelihood, especially for ploughing fields. Buffaloes graze on sloping land surrounding the village. Sloping land was also allocated to households in order to protect the forest. Villagers consider grazing land as a common resource, and so any household is able to graze its buffaloes on any grass-covered land, regardless of its owner[1]. Over the past few years, the World Food Program organised the planting of pine trees as part of a reforestation program. Trees were mainly planted on grassland, which led to a decrease in grazing area after a few years. The gaming-simulation has been designed to understand how local farmers deal with this issue.

The Game

Each game session was organized for five players. The players were selected among villagers on the basis of the socioeconomic characteristics of their household, the main factors being the surface area of paddy fields and the number of buffaloes. Each game was organized so that the five players would represent a panel of families ranging from rich to poor.

The players were placed around a game board designed as a 5×5 cell grid representing the grazing land (Figure 1). Each cell had a resource level that could evolve from zero to three. At the beginning of the game, the resource level was set to 3 on each cell and the players were randomly allocated between one and six buffaloes.

At each turn, players had to place their buffaloes on the game board knowing that each buffalo had to "eat" one unit's worth of resources. If there were more buffaloes than resources on

Figure 1. Game settings

a specific cell, the facilitator drew at random to decide which buffaloes would "eat" the resources, and which buffaloes would not. "Starving" buffaloes were identified and "died" after starving for three rounds. At the end of each turn, resources were renewed and increased by one point, with a maximum level of three. At the end of the round, players could also buy or sell buffaloes.

At the beginning of the fourth, sixth, and eighth rounds, five randomly chosen cells were declared unsuitable for pasture and could not be accessed anymore, so that, at the eighth round, only 10 cells remained accessible to the players. This decrease in the amount of resources available in the game corresponds in real-life to the planting of pine trees and/or to a decrease in fallow land following the ban on swidden cultivation.

After having played the game four times, we observed that although no actual negotiation took place among the players, they could manage the resource scarcity by decreasing the size of their individual herds while restricting the number of starving buffaloes. The graphics (Figure 2) show that the players managed to reduce the size of their herd while the number of starving buffaloes stayed generally quite low, and the "crisis" never lasted more than three turns. One could especially observe that, throughout the games, the players never discussed the "crisis" and how to solve it

as one could have expected. The players also did not try to count the total amount of resources available in order to calculate how many buffaloes it could support. Instead, it seemed that players took individual decisions, but in such a way that the collective goal—not exceeding the carrying capacity of the resources—was achieved.

One may also notice that the number of buffaloes for each player generally did not exceed seven, even if the players had enough points to buy more buffaloes, as is shown in Figure 3. By comparing Figures 2 and 3, one can see that generally, players who start out with the biggest herds tend to stop buying buffaloes first, whereas players with a smaller herd try to accumulate points to buy new buffaloes.

The Model

The development and outcomes of the games were recorded through handwritten notes and audio-video recording. Analysis of this material has enabled us to formulate the hypothesis that the main motivation for players' behaviour was avoiding conflict with other players. We observed that during the game, whenever a player was "forced" to put its buffaloes on a cell already occupied by the buffaloes of another player because all the cells were already occupied by

Figure 2. Evolution of the number of buffaloes per player over the four games

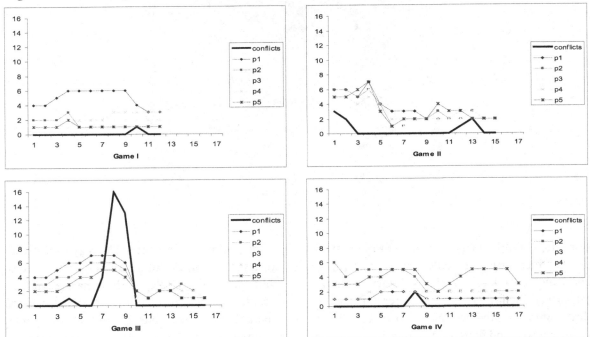

Figure 3. Evolution of the number of buffaloes available, i.e., the number of buffaloes a player can buy

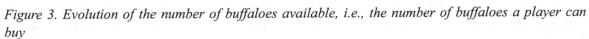

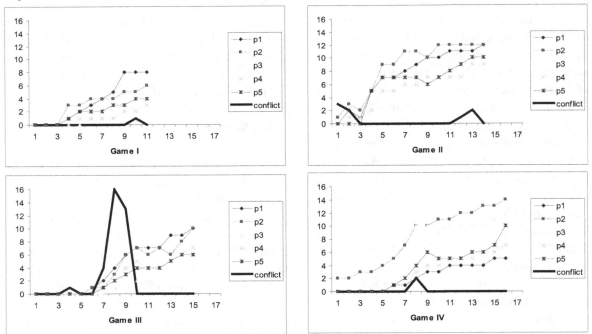

at least one buffalo, at the end of the round, one or both players with buffaloes on the same cell tended to reduce the size of their herd, even if none of the buffaloes was "starving," i.e., there were enough resources to feed all the buffaloes. We interpreted such behaviour as a willingness to avoid potential conflict, while the increasing proximity between buffaloes acted as a warning of potential conflict.

Figure 4. The model environment

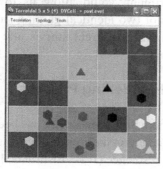

In order to test this hypothesis, a computerised multi-agent model has been developed using the Cormas platform (Bousquet et al., 1998). The environment is very similar to a game board (Figure 4), with different colours representing the level of resources.

In the model, agents do not take into account the level of resources when making decisions about increasing or decreasing the size of their herd. Instead, they base their decisions on the avoidance of potential conflict. For this purpose, we introduced a variable called "representation" for each agent, which may be described as a combination of the number of buffaloes an agent would desire, and the number of buffaloes he thinks is suitable. At the beginning of the simulation, the level of this variable may be quite high (maybe more than five) as resources are abundant and raising many buffaloes may be an additional source of income. But at each turn, the agent compares his

Figure 5. Examples of simulation outputs

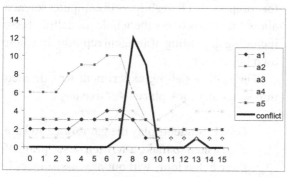

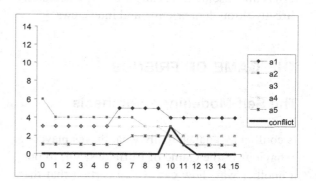

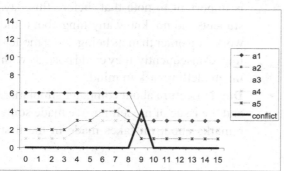

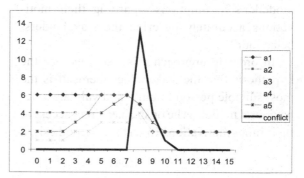

"representation" with the number of buffaloes he actually owns and may revise his "representation" depending on whether or not he detects potential conflict (i.e., his buffaloes sharing a cell with the buffaloes of other agents). For example, an agent who has more buffaloes than his "representation" but does not detect any conflict may "increase his representation," while, on the other hand, an agent with fewer buffaloes than his "representation" who encounters potential conflict may "decrease his representation." After this stage of "updating agents' representation," the agents try to "even out their representation," i.e., buying buffaloes if they have fewer than their "representation" or selling them in the opposite case.

Figure 5 presents the outcome of some simulations.

Even if this model allows us to reproduce outcomes similar to those of the board game, the issue of validation remains. How can we be certain that the players' behaviour really is motivated by conflict avoidance? This matter is particularly delicate, as such a behavioural pattern is unconscious and can hardly be elucidated directly through debriefing and interviews.

THE GAME OF FRIENDS

The Self-Modelling Hypothesis

Is conflict avoidance really what drives players' behaviour in the Game of Buffaloes? Or, to put it another way, how can we be certain that the modeller's assumptions regarding their motivations accurately describe the stakeholders' behaviour?

In order to approach this issue, we use the hypothesis that the stakeholder themself is the most suitable person to build and validate a behavioural model, as he or she has direct access to their inner motivation. To test this hypothesis, a self-modelling experiment has been conducted. A group of computer science students were asked to play a game similar to the Game of Buffaloes then build a model of their own behaviour.

Self-modelling is only a working hypothesis: We are aware that introspection is neither easy nor reliable. In addition to testing this hypothesis, the self-modelling experiment would provide us with material (i.e., writing by students during their work) to evaluate the gap between a behavioural model and underlying motivations. Moreover, this experiment would allow us to compare the results of two identical gaming simulations conducted with different stories and different stakeholders.

The Self-Modelling Process

The self modelling experiment has been carried out with students of the French-speaking Institute of computer science (IFI—Institut de la Francophonie pour l'Informatique) in Hanoi, Vietnam. These students are graduate computer engineers, some of whom teach at university level or work for companies. Their abilities in computer science allow them to process the whole modelling task, including the coding of an agent reproducing their own behaviour.

The self modelling experiment was divided into steps that took place over five days:

- **Day 1:** Students play the game once and are then asked to make a written description of their behaviour, without any assistance. It is important to note that, before this day, students did not know anything about the workshop other than its being about modelling. Consequently, they could not play with the modelling task in mind.

- **Day 2:** Lecture about computer simulation and the issue of modelling. We made some remarks about mistakes made in the first descriptions. Students could then correct them, this time with the help of the game log, which they used as a memory-jog for their own actions.

- **Days 3 to 5:** From the previous descriptions, each student had to build a computational model through the writing of the pseudocode and then of the code for an agent who would reproduce their behaviour during the game. A computerized simulation of the game was available for the students to test their agent. Finally, the students had to evaluate their model, comparing the real game and a simulation of the game running with the agents they coded. During these days, we assisted them in building the model, but we tried not to interfere with their approach.

Thus, at the end of the workshop, we could use the following material:

- First "spontaneous" written description of their behaviour.
- Second written description with the help of a game log.
- Pseudo code of the agent.
- Code of the agent.
- Evaluation of the model.

It is worth mentioning that this workshop was part of the students' regular curriculum and was being marked. This may have given the students a proper motivation to complete the modelling work. Also, they had to write their final report in French, rather than in Vietnamese. Describing actions and motivations with precision in a foreign language often proved to be a difficult task, as most of the students had only been studying French for two years.

The Game of Friends

The Story

We changed the scenario of the Game of Buffaloes because students are not familiar with the life of a farmer and an unfamiliar situation could lead to fanciful behaviour. However, the Game of Friends reproduces exactly the same structure as the Game of Buffaloes, only within a different story. In the Game of Friends, each player starts out with a certain amount of friends. Each time a player takes a turn, he or she has to download a movie on the internet for each of his friends in order to keep them satisfied. Internet sites are shared and resources are limited. Unsatisfied friends get angry and may leave the player. The player can make new friends (spending "free time" currency) or leave some old friends. The structure of both games is exactly the same (i.e., number and evolution of resources), only the vocabulary has

Figure 6. Player interface. The squares of the grid stand for Internet sites. The numbers on each square represent the maximum number of possible movie downloads for a given Internet site. Small circles represent downloads carried out, with each player tagged by colour. Dark grey squares are overused sites (for the yellow player) which can create unsatisfied friends.

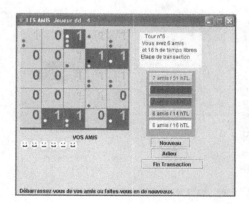

changed: friends instead of buffalos and Internet sites instead of grazing land.

The Game Board

Instead of a game board, the Game of Friends has been implemented as a client/server application. One client is an interface for a human player (Figure 6) or an agent that acts like a human player. This architecture allows us to:

- Save a game log
- Replay a game from a game log
- Make a simulation of the game where players are agents
- Mix agent players and human players in the same game
- Change the information displayed by the client interface

Different Games

Nineteen students took part in the experiments. Each game was played by five players, both human and artificial, and lasted 23 turns. One game included an artificial player. All games took place

at the same time, in the same room, but players did not know who they were playing with.

We wanted to take advantage of the computerized game board in two ways:

1. Each game offered the players four different levels of information. We wanted to identify which information can influence behaviour, such as the amount of information about the environment or about other players.

2. One artificial greedy player (AGP) was introduced in one game. We wanted to see if the behaviour of a particular player would influence the other players. Our AGP had a very simple behaviour: It made new friends as soon as it had enough free time and never left its existing friends.

Two types of information could change:

- **Player information (PI). Full PI:** The player has access to information about other players, such as the number of their friends, their amount of free time, and which Internet site they chose. Reduced PI: the above information is hidden.

Figure 7.1. Game type I—Full PI, full EI, no AGP

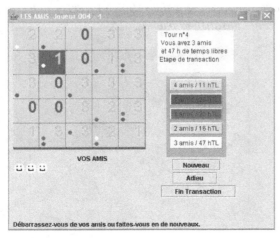

Figure 7.2. Game type II—Full PI, reduced EI, no AGP

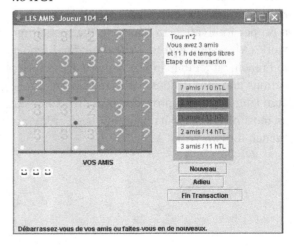

Figure 7.3. Game type III—Reduced PI, Full EI, no AGP

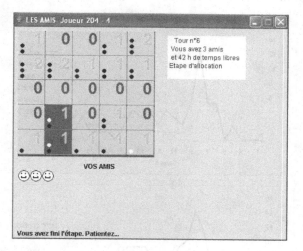

Figure 7.4. Game type IV—Reduced PI, reduced EI, one AGP

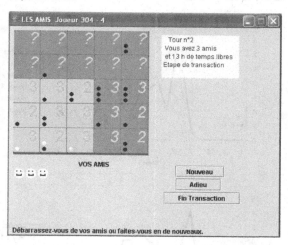

- **Environment information (EI). Full EI:** One player knows the exact number of downloads allowed for each Internet site. Reduced EI: At the beginning of his or her turn, when the player chooses a site, the number of downloads for this site and the surrounding ones is displayed. The number of downloads is not updated for the other sites.

The client interfaces for the four games are presented in Figure 7.

First, we started by explaining the rules of the game, insisting on one important factor: There is no defined goal, no good or bad behaviour. The students then played a few rounds to make sure everybody understood the principle of the game. We then started the game proper.

Results

Overuse of Resources

The charts in Figure 8 show the evolution of the number of friends over the four games. We first notice that in all games conflict for resources (i.e., the number of Internet sites where demand exceeds supply) stays above zero, sometimes at a low level (Figure 8, Game II), sometimes at a high level (Figure 8, Games III and IV).

Second, we can observe different types of evolution in the number of friends:

1. **Increase-decrease:** A decrease begins when the resources get scarce. (Game I, player 1)
2. **Increase-no decrease.** (Game III player 4)
3. **Chaotic.** (Game III, player 1)

We would like to emphasise the fact that a chaotic Number of Friends curve does not necessarily imply chaotic behaviour. The number of friends may drop suddenly because a large number of friends become angry and leave the player. A good example of this phenomenon is the very simple behaviour of the AGP in game IV that produces a complex curve for the number of friends.

Moderate Behaviour

The "available friends" charts (Figure 9) show the number of new friends that a player could

Figure 8. Evolution of the number of friends for each player during the four games. The bold curve represents the number of conflicts, i.e., the number of Internet sites where demand exceeds supply.

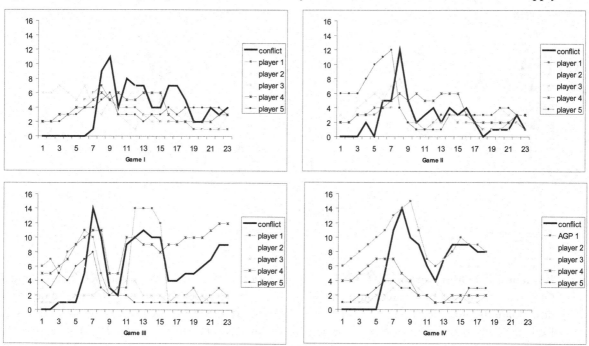

Figure 9. Evolution of the number of friends available, i.e., the number of new friends one player could make

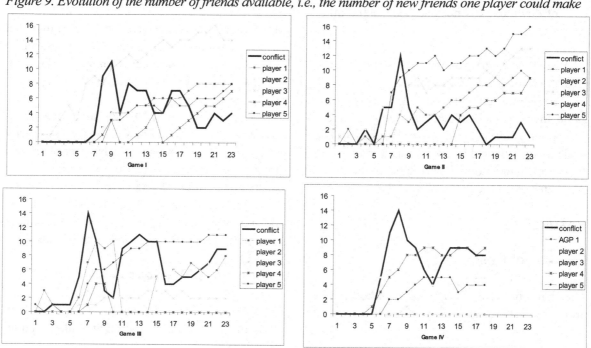

make but chooses not to. Although resources are always overused, most players reduce or restrict the number of their friends. Only two of them adopted a greedy behaviour: player 4 in game III and, surprisingly, player 3 in game IV. This last player started with only one friend, then became quite unlucky (out of a total 28 conflicts his friends suffered, 21 of them became unsatisfied). It would therefore not be accurate to describe the behaviour of this player as "greedy."

We can also observe from these charts that most of the players (16 out of 19) start out with a greedy behaviour which they later abandon (14 of 16) when resources get scarce.

No Noticeable Information Factor

It is not possible to identify a difference in behaviour linked to the information available to players from previous charts. Moderate behaviour can be found in all the games represented. This does not mean that what one player can perceive has no influence at all, but that this influence–if it does exist—is tiny and would require a larger population in order to be observable. Another explanation is possible : The mood of one's friends—which is the only information common to all games—has a major influence on behaviour.

Influence Between Players

It is worth mentioning that the presence of players who keep a lot of friends did not influence more moderate players to change their behaviour (games II and IV). It seems that "unfairness" just stays unnoticed.

What are the Motivations?

One could say that avoiding conflict remains the main motivation for most players in the Game of Friends, as was the case in the Game of Buffaloes. Two factors can explain why conflicts remain above zero: first, the rarity of greedy behaviour

and second, the fact that players tend to react late to resource scarcity.

Differences Between the Two Games

Three major differences are apparent when comparing the results of the two games:

- In the Game of Friends, the number of conflicts stays positive whereas in the Game of Buffaloes, the number of conflicts quickly drops to zero.
- In the Game of Friends, the number of friends for each player does not stabilize, even after more than 20 rounds, whereas in the Game of Buffaloes, the number of buffaloes for each player stabilises after less than 15 rounds: Whenever the total number of buffaloes becomes adapted to the level of resources, players stop buying and selling buffaloes (typically, at the end of the game, 10 buffaloes for 10 points of resources).
- In the Game of Friends, more varied and complex behaviours can be observed, such as chaotic and greedy behaviour. Consequently, suggesting a single behavioural model is not an option.

We interpreted the aforementioned differences in the results of the two games according to three factors.

The Story Behind the Game

Changing the game's storyline in order to avoid fanciful behaviour might have induced further differences, as the attitude of farmers towards buffaloes and grazing land may be quite different from the attitude of students towards friends and bandwidth. Game theory literature calls the consequences of changing the way of presenting an experiment "framing effect" (Kahneman & Tversky, 1979). Van Dijk and Wilke (1997) consider that "framing effects may be one of the key factors that determine what norms people use." In game theory, framing generally refers to presenting the issue as a gain or as a loss. In our case, the framing difference was even more substantial as the entire story was changed. It is thus highly plausible that underlying behavioural norms at work in both games may be different and lead to different results. Beside their role in rice cultivation, buffaloes represent a lot of money for farmers. Buffaloes are often used as a kind of "savings account" and the loss of a buffalo would be a blow for farmers. Even if students often said that they disliked having unsatisfied friends, having an unsatisfied friend may not be as tragic as losing a buffalo.

The Setting of the Game

The first issue is the anonymity of players in the Game of Friends. Comparison between different settings within economic experiments, and more specifically in common pool games, has shown that the level of cooperation tends to drop when the subjects play anonymously (Liebrand et al., 1992; Ostrom et al., 1994).

Another related issue is that in the Game of Friends, players were only facing a computer, whereas in the Game of Buffaloes, all the players were sitting together around the game board and were able to observe each others' actions directly. Even if no real verbal negotiation took place during the Game of Buffaloes, the setting was more favourable to cooperation among the players and one can imagine that nobody would have dared to create conflict by maintaining a large herd.

The Stakeholders

Obviously, farmers and students may not share the same references, even if they are from the same country—especially as computer students are experienced computer gamers (games in

Vietnam are very cheap and popular) and probably experienced playing such games in a very different way from a farmer.

Students may also have considered the game as a theoretical exercise. They participated in the context of a workshop as part of their regular university curriculum. For farmers, on the other hand, the game was an opportunity to discuss a real issue with the potential to change the household's economic situation.

Moreover, social relationships between players may be very different. On the one hand, in each session of the Game of Buffaloes, the players came from the same village. This means that they may have all kind of kin, social, and economical relationships. Also, in these mountainous villages, mutual help for agricultural work is commonplace. Conflict avoidance is therefore quite understandable. On the other hand, computer science students are in a much more competitive environment, and a few players openly admitted that they were trying to create conflicts with certain other players.

Important Similarities

These different factors may explain why the level of cooperation is higher in the Game of Buffaloes than in the Game of Friends. However, it must be pointed out that behaviours are not all that different overall: moderation is characteristic. Except for two students who adopted a greedy behaviour, all others restrained the number of their friends, and this self-restraint becomes apparent when resources get scarce. The major difference lies in the perception of the problem: Conflicts are a problem for farmers, but for students, the problem arises later, when too many of their friends become angry.

The analysis of the self-modelling experiment by students may also help us to understand the differences between the two games.

ANALYSIS OF THE SELF-MODELLING EXPERIMENT

Poor Models

The self-modelling process has revealed several interesting points:

- Written descriptions usually lacked precision or, conversely, concision: Getting an adequate level of information for modelling proved difficult. Students also referred to actions as random (e.g., "I chose an Internet site at random") which in actual fact were not. The term "random" is often used when a player cannot explain why he acts in a certain way.

- As pseudo-code contains the logic of a program (tests and loops), this step stands for a hidden modelling process. It had a focusing effect: Students were forced to transform their imprecise—or excessively elaborate—written description into a computational model of their behaviour.

- Many actions remained unexplained and some students had to model "from outside," i.e., they had to infer their behaviour from the game log.

- Because they had discovered some weaknesses or contradictions in their strategy during the game, students tended to "improve" their behaviour in the model. They wanted a consistent behaviour for their agent, although they were told that in the Game of Friends there are no "good" or "bad" behaviours.

It seems that models built by the students are not very useful in themselves. An expert in modelling could probably make better models just by analyzing the game logs. The main reasons for the poor quality of the models lie in the persistence of nonconscious action—which is difficult to grasp and model—in the tendency to idealise that which biases the model, and finally, the difficulty of the modelling task itself.

Rich Materials

However, self-modelling materials show that players refer mainly to their friends' unpleasant mood when explaining why they reduce the number of their friends (two thirds of the students). Those references can be found both in the written descriptions ("I left angry friends because I did not want them to leave me at the next turn," and "I dislike having angry friends") and in the models ("I left all my angry friends" and "if more than one friend was unsatisfied, I did not make new friends."...)

The amount of resources is also present in descriptions and models (five times). But this information is often computed in such a complex way that it is hard to believe that it represents a real perception during the experiment: "if the amount of resources is more than five times the number of my friends…." In fact, one student who used this kind of test says explicitly that it came from the analysis of the game log because they could not remember the motivations for their actions. Finally, the number of conflicts rarely seems to be involved in the decision making process: Only one student used this information in their code.

CONCLUSION

Two gaming simulations with the same underlying structure but different scenarios and stakeholders were conducted in Vietnam. In the Game of Buffaloes, the farmers' behaviour seems to match the behavioural model based on conflict avoidance. In the Game of Friends, less moderate behaviour can be explained by the stakeholders' different perception of the situation: Students react to their friends' mood while farmers tend to react to conflict.

The self-modelling experiment conducted with the Game of Friends was an attempt to go further into participatory design: While a modeller can only interpret the behaviour observed, a stakeholder has direct access to his/her own motivation. In fact, we observed that introspection is no easy task, even in simple situations. Very often, students were not able to explain why they behaved the way they did. Additionally, if the tendency to idealise is a common problem in the traditional modelling process, the resulting bias may be stronger with modelling apprentices.

However, such self-modelling experiments are a tool to improve our understanding and modelling of the players' behaviour. For instance, we could see that the students generally focused on their friends' mood in order to make a decision. They disliked having angry friends and tried several ways of avoiding this.

Self-modelling is probably not a comprehensive solution to the issue of behaviour validation but it brings very useful information to the modelling expert because the "self-modeller" has to question his/her own behaviour in a situated way. It might be worth developing this situated questioning in traditional modelling processes, for instance with the help of assistant agents during participatory simulation sessions. Such situated questioning used to complement traditional interviews has already been applied to air traffic management in order to elicit expert knowledge (Sempé et al., 2005).

REFERENCES

Barreteau, O. (2003). The joint use of role-playing games and models regarding negotiation processes: Characterization of associations. *Journal of Artificial Societies and Social Simulation, 6*(2). http://jasss.soc.surrey.ac.uk/6/2/3.html

Barreteau, O. et al. (2003). Our companion modelling approach. *Journal of Artificial Societies and Social Simulation, 6*(2). http://jasss.soc.surrey.ac.uk/6/2/1.html

Boissau, S. (2005). Co-evolution of a research question and methodological development: an example of companion modelling in northern Vietnam. In F. Bousquet, G. Trebuil, & B. Hardy (Eds.), *Companion modelling and multi-agent systems for integrated natural resource management in Asia.* Los Banos, Philippines: IRRI.

Bousquet, F., Bakam, I., Proton, H., & Le Page, C. (1998). Cormas: Common-pool resources and multi-agent systems. *Lecture Notes in Artificial Intelligence, 1416*, 826-838.

Bousquet, F., Barreteau, O., d'Aquino, P., Etienne, M., Boissau, S., Aubert, S. et al. (2002). Multi-agent systems and role games : Collective learning processes for ecosystem management. In M. Janssen (Ed.), *Complexity and ecosystem management: The theory and practice of multi-agent approaches.* Edward Elgar Publishers.

Castella, J.C., Boissau, S., Nguyên, H.T., & Novosad, P. (2006). Impact of forestland allocation on land use in a mountainous province of Vietnam. *Land Use Policy, 23*(2), 147-160.

Kahneman, D., & Tversky, A. (1979). Prospect theory. *Econometrica, 47*, 263-291.

Liebrand, W., Messick, D., & Wilke, H. (1992). *Social dilemmas: Theoretical issues and research findings.* New York: Pergamon Press.

Ostrom, E., Gardner, R., & Walker, J. (1994). *Rules, games, and common-pool resources.* University of Michigan Press.

Sempé, F., Nguyen, D.M., Boissau, S., Boucher, A., & Drogoul, A. (2005). *An artificial maieutic approach for eliciting expert's knowledge in multi-agent simulation.* Paper presented at the Sixth International Workshop on Multi-Agent-Based Simulation (MABS), July 2005, Utrecht (Netherlands).

Van Dijk, E., & Wilke, H. (1997). Is it mine or is it yours? Framing property rights and decision making in social dilemmas. *Organizational Behavior and Human Decision Processes, 71*(2), 195-209.

ENDNOTE

[1]   In fact, a household does not actually own land but has a land use right for a period of 50 years (Castella et al., 2006).

Chapter XXI
The Evolution of Coworker Networks:
An Experimental and Computational Approach

Arianna Dal Forno
University of Torino, Italy

Ugo Merlone
University of Torino, Italy

ABSTRACT

When selecting work team members, several behavioral components concur. In this chapter we are interested in investigating the effects of these components in terms of team selection, agent aggregation, and performance of groups. A computational model, together with a theoretical approach and the results of two human experiments where subjects interact in a similar game, allow us to identify some of the most important determinants. Our results suggest that the occurrence of two factors is crucial: the presence of leaders as aggregators of knowledge and agents being able to expand and improve their higher profit projects. It is particularly evident that leaders have a threefold role. First, they increase the social network of other agents, making possible projects otherwise impossible. Second, they state the pace of a balanced growth in terms of social network, while taming the otherwise combinatorial explosion. Finally, they help in selecting one of the theoretically possible equilibria.

INTRODUCTION

In firms and organizations most employees belong to some formal work groups. Since one of the determinants of work group performance is the group composition, the ability to understand how people choose their group members is a crucial step in understanding what leads to the creation of successful groups. These factors may be extremely important for managers when assembling formal work groups.

Our purpose is to analyze, through a formal model, how group composition evolves as the result of the repeated interaction of individuals. In particular, we want to consider how the individual behavior, in terms of partner selection, exerted effort, and leadership may influence the social network and the team composition, as summarized in Figure 1.

In our model we describe the interactions between agents as networks evolving over time. A model of evolution of a friendship network is presented in Zeggelink (1995); in this model, the dynamics of the network structure are considered as the result of individual characteristics and behavioral rules, such as preferences for similar friends. Banks and Carley (1996) provide a description of the mathematical models for network evolution when ties are directed and the node set is fixed. They show that many of these models tend asymptotically towards equilibrium distributions where all individuals are equally likely to be connected to all other individuals.

An empirical study on group composition is presented in Hinds, et al. (2000). Their findings show that, when selecting group members, people are biased towards others of the same race, others who have a reputation for being competent and hard working, and others with whom they have developed a strong working relationship in the past. Human interaction and team formation is a complex phenomenon, almost intractable by formal analysis. We consider both an experiment with human subjects and an agent-based modelling (ABM) computer simulation where agents have different behavioral rules. Our purpose is not to replicate the observed human behavior in experiments. Rather, it is to use the empirical data to infer some of the not directly observed behaviors that generated them and model them in our artificial agents.

To identify the relevant components in team formation, we introduce and compare different behavioral rules in the computational model of interaction among artificial agents we consider. This way we are able to break down the agents' behavior in microphases. We study the relative importance of each of these individual aspects of behavior when leading towards the emergence of some macrobehaviors in the artificial society we consider. Our agents are all utility maximizers but, at the same time, they are heterogeneous in terms of behavioral rules. This is not a contradiction: They try to maximize their utility given the fact that, for example, they may or may not free ride. We want to study how heterogeneity (in our sense individual attributes at the microlevel) affects, at the macrolevel, the network structure and its dynamics. Finally, the task our agents are asked to perform incorporates both intragroup and intergroup levels of conflict and, for this reason, may be interpreted as a sort of generalized team game as studied in Bornstein (2003).

Figure 1. Team composition as the result of individual behavior

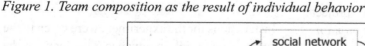
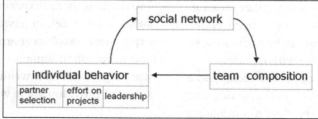

The Theoretical Model

The organization consists of n agents univocally identified by an index $i \in N = \{1,2,\dots,n\}$. Agents interact forming teams to work on some unspecified project in which at most m members can participate. Both in the artificial simulations and the human subjects experiments, we fixed $m = 7$ (for an empirical motivation of this choice see chapter II in Miller & Rice, 1967).

Each agent can choose its partners from a subset $M \in N$ of known people. Knowledge of agents in the organization is described using a sociomatrix $\mathbf{K}$. Each element k_{ij} of the sociomatrix $\mathbf{K}$ indicates whether agent i knows agent j: zero indicates that i does not know j; conversely, value one indicates that i knows j. We assume that each agent knows itself; as a consequence all diagonal entries are set to one. $\mathbf{K}$ is not necessarily a symmetric $n \times n$ matrix.

Agents can participate in at most two projects; in each of them their decision is twofold:

1. They must specify the designated members of the team.
2. They must specify the effort they will exert in each team.

When all participating agents agree on the team composition, this, together with their efforts, constitute an *implemented project* and is univocally determined.

The relation "*i* works with *j* in an implemented project" defines a nondichotomous symmetric matrix $\mathbf{W}$ where element $w_{ij} \in \{0,1,2\}$ is defined by the number of projects in which agents i and j work together. Matrix $\mathbf{W}$ defines the project network; when n agents work together on an n-member project we say they form a *size n clique* since in the graphical representation of matrix $\mathbf{W}$ they are depicted as a clique with n nodes.

Within each implemented project agents play a public goods game. The efforts of the participants are aggregated and used to produce a commodity with a production function f; the output is shared among the members of the team. We denote c_i, agent i's cost of effort, and assume that greater effort means greater cost to the agent and increasing marginal cost. The profit of agent i in project p can be formalized as follows:

$$\pi_{i,p} = \frac{f\left(\sum_{j \in T_p(i)} e_j\right)}{n} - c_i(e_i) \qquad (1)$$

where e_i is agent i's effort and $T_p(i)$ is the set of partners of agent i in project p. We assume: (1) there exists a unique level of effort maximizing the agent's profit; (2) there exists a unique Nash equilibrium e^N; (3) when all the agents exert the same effort, both the optimal effort e^N and the optimal profit increases with the number of members participating in the project.

In order to keep the math simple we considered in our experiments and simulations the following profit formulation:

$$\pi_{i,p} = \frac{\left(\sum_{j \in T_p(i)} e_j\right)^2}{n} - e_i^3 \qquad (2)$$

In this case it is easy to prove that $e^N = 2/3$, and that the socially optimal effort for a n member project is $e_n^S = 2n/3$. With this profit formulation, when everybody exerts the socially optimal effort, the individual profit increases with the number of agents in the project.

EXPERIMENTAL DESIGN

Instructions for the experiment were given to the subjects one week in advance. Our focus in the experiment was observing patterns in aggregation and cooperation among subjects. Our first step was to give detailed written instructions to the subjects, providing them with the profit formulation, answering their questions and discussing several examples.

Motivating subjects in experiments is a well-known problem in the experimental economics literature. While the experiment was framed as a learning experience (Bergstrom & Miller, 2000), we encouraged active participation in our subjects, giving them up to one mark in addition to whatever their grade would be in the final exam of the Math class (the maximum available grade is 30/30 and the passing grade is 18/30). Subjects were also told that their reward depended on their performance, that is, the total aggregate profit over the whole experiment (reward = ranked performance normalized in [0,1]).

Here we report the data from students who were first year undergraduates in the Math class of Business Administration at the University of Torino. Subjects were told that the experiment would last five minutes plus preliminary discussion in each session.

We ran two series of experiments. The first series consisted of 21 sessions, each including about 93 individuals while the second one consisted of 12 sessions with about 48 individuals.

In each session subjects were asked to provide two project proposals, each consisting of the list of project participants and the individual effort the subject was willing to exert. Before the begin-

ning of each session students were given about fifteen minutes to coordinate, and at the end of each session subjects were asked to fill in and return the form in Figure 2.

Successively, before any new session of the experiment, profits and profits aggregated over time for each individual were publicly posted.

THE COMPUTATIONAL MODEL

In the agent-based simulation we consider, each turn is divided into three phases. First, the agents propose and discuss the team composition for projects. Then, agents under some conditions try to expand the sociomatrix in order to increase the probability of obtaining a larger consistent project. Finally, agents propose the two best projects that emerged in the discussion and the game is played.

Communication and Discussion Among Agents

We could observe in the human subjects of our experiments that some individuals performed an essential role in terms of coordination of partners: Often they suggested both the effort and the team composition. Some of these subjects were able to

Figure 2. Report form

Last name: _____ Name: _____ Turn: _____

Project 1

Last name of members (no more than 7, always include yourself)
1 _____ 2 _____ 3 _____ 4 _____
5 _____ 6 _____ 7 _____
Effort exerted in this project: _____

Project 2

Last name of members (no more than 7, always include yourself)
1 _____ 2 _____ 3 _____ 4 _____
5 _____ 6 _____ 7 _____
Effort exerted in this project: _____

find the socially optimal effort as a function of the number of project members, and suggested it to their teammates. Replicating the optimal effort in the following turn was something that spread quite immediately among the subjects. By contrast, the process of selecting the team composition was more complex. We could observe before each session of the experiment some subjects spending a considerable amount of time selecting their teammates.

The first approach considered artificial agents who randomly chose their project compositions, but the results were quite different from what we observed in human subjects. In fact when agents choose their project compositions randomly, the probability of obtaining a seven-member project is very low, because they must know each other and the number of possible projects each subject may propose is very high. Assume a population of n individuals knowing each other. We denote with r the number of team members. If $r \leq n$, then teams of different dimension can be formed, up to r-member teams. For the sake of simplicity we

call an r-member team a *size r clique*. Therefore, the number of projects that can be obtained with exactly r individuals (i.e., the number of r-cliques) is equal to the binomial coefficient $C_{n-1,r-1}$. In Table 1 we show how many size r cliques, with $r=2,\ldots,$ 7, are possible in a population of n individuals.

Comparing the figures in Table 1 allows us to understand how the sociomatrix can play an important role. In fact, in an n-agent society where all the agents know each other, the probability of obtaining size seven cliques is very low; for example, in the case of a seven-agent society, the probability that the seven-agent project is implemented is $(1/64)^7 = 1/2^{42}$.

In our model we implemented the discussion and proposal of projects, allowing each agent to propose up to 50 projects and had agents choose the best feasible common project. This is a sort of brainstorming process in which agents propose whatever comes into their mind. The agents rank their feasible projects assuming that they exert the socially optimal effort.

Table 1. The number of possible projects in a population consisting of n individuals.

n	Size 2 cliques	Size 3 cliques	Size 4 cliques	Size 5 cliques	Size 6 cliques	Size 7 cliques	Total
7	6	15	20	15	6	1	64
8	7	21	35	35	21	7	127
9	8	28	56	70	56	28	247
10	9	36	84	126	126	84	466
11	10	45	120	210	252	210	848
12	11	55	165	330	462	462	1486
13	12	66	220	495	792	924	2510
14	13	78	286	715	1287	1716	4096
15	14	91	364	1001	2002	3003	6476
16	15	105	455	1365	3003	5005	9949
17	16	120	560	1820	4368	8008	14893
18	17	136	680	2380	6188	12376	21778
19	18	153	816	3060	8568	18564	31180
20	19	171	969	3876	11628	27132	43796

Individual Diversity in Social Interaction and Leadership

According to their behavioral class and to the feasible projects that emerged during the discussion among agents, some of them may decide to act on the sociomatrix. In other words, we consider agents that may decide to introduce their acquaintances to others and/or expand the sociomatrix including all the agents known by their acquaintances. The social interactions have an effect on the following turn. At the moment, we do not consider situations in which a leader may bargain with other agents about the team composition, because even with the simple kinds of social interaction so far implemented, the model is rather interesting.

Game Interaction

According to the results that emerged in the communication phase, each agent proposes the two best projects. In this phase agents may decide whether to play the socially optimal effort as in the communication phase. Then profits are computed and payoffs are given to agents.

Classes of Behavior and Structural Properties of the Sociomatrix

Given the complexity of the model, the behavior of artificial populations depends on four dimensions, namely: the *initial sociomatrix* form, the *team selection behavior*, the *effort determination behavior*, and the *social leadership behavior*.

Initial Sociomatrix

As discussed previously, the number of known agents is crucial in terms of the ability to select work groups with several agents. This has been modeled using the dichotomous sociomatrix **K**, describing the knowledge relation between agents.

Our agents are assumed to be located on a circle graph where all nodes are interchangeable. At the beginning of each simulation the mutual knowledge between agents may assume different forms. Specifically, we consider the following cases:

- **Total mutual knowledge:** Every agent knows each other. In this case sociomatrix **K** is unitary.
- ***n*-neighbor knowledge:** This graph generalizes the circle graph we discussed above. While in the circle graph each agent knows just one agent on each side, in the *n*-neighbor knowledge graph each agent knows *n* neighbors on each side. For one-neighbor knowledge, that is, the circle graph, only size two cliques are possible, while, in order to have size seven cliques, we need six-neighbor knowledge. In this case each agent knows 13 individuals.
- **Previously observed sociomatrix:** It is possible to assume as an initial sociomatrix any previously saved one. For example, it is possible to start with the final sociomatrix that emerged during another simulation.

Team Selection Behavior

Since, as we saw previously, the combinatorial aspects of the team selection process must be carefully considered in order to have agents converging towards large projects, we developed different approaches in modelling this aspect of behavior. The most interesting were:

1. Considering the project with the largest number of members and expanding it, keeping the same agents and adding one more new agent.
2. Considering the two best projects and expanding the second one either by adding one more subject or proposing a new project with at least one agent more than the second-best project.

Since in the game played with our human subjects they were allowed to propose at most two projects, in our artificial agents we have them consider their two most profitable projects that emerged in the discussion.

The behavioral rules allowing agents to keep their best projects and to expand them proved to be extremely important in the simulations. These kinds of rules allowed, for example, the emergence of strong connections between agents.

Effort Selection Behavior

The behaviors we implemented in terms of effort selection are, at the moment, extremely unsophisticated:

1. Playing the Nash effort, i.e., free riding when the number of team members is greater than one
2. Playing the socially optimal effort

These behaviors can be justified, recalling the structure of the game the participants are called to play. In fact, since the game bears the structure of a public goods game, effort selections behaviors one and two can be interpreted as the two strategies of a multiplayer Prisoner's Dilemma, where playing the social Nash effort stands for "defecting," and playing the socially optimal effort stands for "cooperating." In the experiments we observed, the human subjects almost always exerted the socially optimal effort; this can be explained by assuming that players' behavior is driven by considerations of fairness and equity (e.g., Fehr & Schmidt, 1999). As a consequence, we consider agents belonging to class two for what concerns the effort selection; this choice allows for separating the free rider issue from the choice of the teammates.

Social Leadership Behavior

Leadership is a topic that has been of interest to different disciplines such as organizational psychology, management, and sociology for several decades, yet many other authors, ranging from business executives to collegiate athletic coaches, have approached this topic. Given the simple structure of our model, we consider leadership as a form of influence (Yukl, 1989) and, citing Jex (2002), "…acknowledge that *the essence of leadership is influencing other people's behavior*" (p.267). As a result, when modelling social leadership behaviors we are interested in considering only quite simple behaviors. Assuming that agents are located on a circle graph, all the agents are interchangeable and know just their closest neighbors; in this case only size two clique projects are possible. In addition, some of them may wish to act in the social network in order to allow the selection of larger projects; we call these agents *social leaders*. Specifically, for these agents we considered several actions in order to expand the sociomatrix; the most interesting were the following:

2. Provided that the leader knows less than the thirteen agents, when the first best project is not a size seven clique, or the first best project is a size seven clique but the second project is not, then the agent introduces all the agents it knows to each other.
3. When the leader knows less than seven agents and the best project is not a size seven clique, or the agent knows less than eight agents and the best project is a size seven clique but the second best project is not, the leader expands the vector of its known agents in order to include all the agents in the sociomatrix that have a geodesic distance smaller than three; in a friendship relation

this would simply mean that "the friends of my friends become my friends."

These combined procedures were the most effective for the emergence of connected clusters similar to those we observed in the human subjects experiment. In fact, the social leaders expand the sociomatrix only when it is necessary to improve the size of projects. While the first procedure acts on the other agents, the second one increases the number of agents the social leader may contact. Given the combinatorial intractability of the project selection process, it is important to balance carefully the sociomatrix expansion with the number of members of implemented projects. Finally, the effect of these combined procedures is similar to what we observed in the human subject experiment, that is, the presence of agents looking for people to be included in their projects who suggested the team composition; since we do not consider explicitly communication in our model, what we obtain seems to be a good approximation of these behaviors.

Results

Comparing the human subjects experiments and the first computer simulations we performed, several important aspects emerged.

While human subjects exhibited a tendency to aggregate and form size seven cliques, the artificial agents had great difficulty in forming even size four cliques. In a situation with a population consisting of more than twenty agents where all agents know each other, the combinatorial problem discussed previously can prevent the emergence of size seven cliques: "To know everyone is to know no one." For these reasons the initial sociomatrix is rather important.

Another important aspect to be considered is that agents must be able to remember the projects that were more profitable and in some way try to improve them.

Expanding Project Agents Population

The results obtained from populations entirely consisting of class 1 team selection behavior are quite interesting. While at first sight, a population in which agents implement this behavioral strategy and do not free ride should reach the situation in which agents have projects with as many members as possible, our simulation does not show this result. To understand why this does not happen, it is sufficient to consider a population consisting of just five agents. Assume that for three of them the most profitable project is to work together, while the remaining two agents form a size two clique as illustrated in Figure 3.

Then for the size three clique agents, the only way to expand their project is to include the same agent selected from the remaining two agents, and have this one propose a project in which it includes all of the size 3 clique agents. This is impossible since each agent's strategy is just to expand its best project by one.

Nevertheless, a population consisting entirely of agents with this team selection behavior displayed interesting properties in terms of

Figure 3. Final project configuration in a five-agent population

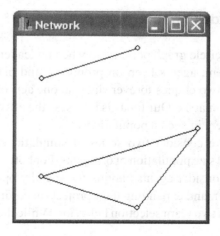

random graphs. Recall that given a fixed set of n distinguishable vertices, random graphs theory considers the space G^n of sequences of random graphs. Any element of G^n is a graph process, that is a nested sequence of graphs $G_0 \subset G_1 \subset ... \subset G_{n^*}$, with $n^* = \binom{n}{2}$ and G_t having precisely t edges (for details see Bollobás, 1998). With this population we obtain a sequence of graphs such that the subsequence at times $t \equiv 2(\mathrm{mod}\,3)$ is nondecreasing, that is:

$$G_2 \subseteq G_5 \subseteq G_8 \subseteq ... \subseteq G_{3k+2} \subseteq ... \subseteq G_T$$

While this behavior is interesting as being related to the theoretical literature on random graphs, it is quite different from what we observed in the human experiments.

The agents' inability to improve the projects efficiently seemed to be the main problem. One successful strategy for agents consisted of the parallel implementation of two phases: the expansion of the best project by adding one more member, and the proposal of a brand new project with at least one agent.Furthermore, another problem seemed to rely on the static nature of the knowledge sociomatrix $\mathbf{K}$; one solution could be to assume this matrix evolving over time, for this reason we also introduced agents with a socially active role.

Leader Effects

In a circle graph population when no leaders are present, agents keep on proposing and playing size two cliques forever since no one acts on the sociomatrix. Our focus is to assess the effects of leaders in such a population.

We consider two series of simulations in a fixed size population of 63 agents. For both series we consider agents playing the socially optimal effort, and expanding their projects according to class two team selection behavior. While the first

series analyzes the optimal number of leaders and their positioning, the second assesses the social leadership effects when the number of leaders is optimal.

For both series we describe the experiment, the variables we observe, and discuss the results. The artificial population data are the mean of five independent replications; we decided not to consider many more replications since the results were quite stable and the time for each replication was quite long (about five hours on a Pentium 4 CPU 2.80 GHz, Ram 512 MB). Specifically we observe evolution at turns 1, 2, 3, 4, 5, 6, 10, 20, 30, 40, 50, 60, 100, 200, 300, 400, 500, 600, 1,000, 2,000, 3,000, 4,000, 5,000, 6,000, and 10,000. This time choice allows observation of both the short and long term evolution. Finally, we compare the artificial population results with human experiment.

Optimal Number and Positioning of Leaders

In the first experiment we introduced agents assuming social leadership behaviors in different proportions. In the following figures we report the network evolution in terms of number of links and components for the different experiments we considered: six, seven, and eight-interval leaders, no leaders, and randomly located leaders in the proportion of one out of seven.

Social Leadership Effects

In the second experiment we first observe the final sociomatrix in a seven-interval leader population. Then we start another simulation with no leaders, taking as initial the final sociomatrix obtained at the end of the previous simulation instead of the circle graph. This way one of the effects of having leaders in the population has been already incorporated: The sociomatrix is already expanded. While theoretically this sociomatrix is necessary to obtain the same outcome of the simulation with leaders, the results were quite different.

Result Discussion

The relations analyzed with the model we consider may be described as valued graphs with several network components. Since the density of a graph—which is a recommended measure of group cohesion (see Blau, 1977)—is proportional to the number of links, this statistic together with the number of components seems to be appropriate for our analyses. This way, the different situations can be described as follows:

- Several links and several components indicate the presence of isolated *size n cliques*.
- Several links and few components indicate the presence of several connected *size n cliques*.
- Few links and several components indicate the presence of several isolated agents.
- Few links and few components indicate the presence of simple structure such as the circle graph or chains of agents.

While we could observe **chains of agents connected to size *n* cliques** only in the computer simulations, both in our simulations and human subjects experiments we observed **weakly con-nected clusters** (different size *n* cliques with one or two connections) and **strongly connected clusters** (different size *n* cliques with several connections). The occurrence of these structures gives a qualitative idea of the network evolution. For example, in both human subject experiments and computer simulation, the occurrence of a few strongly connected clusters indicates that agents are cooperating in large projects.

Considering the first series of experiments, refer to Figures 4, 5, and 6 without the "no-leader" data. Both in terms of links (Figure 4) and nontrivial network components (Figure 5), seven-interval leaders seems to be the best configuration for leaders, even if at the beginning, having eight-interval leaders seems slightly more effective. Furthermore, we can observe that the number of links, even with the optimal number of leaders, remains slightly less than 549, which is the number of links where each agent participates in two seven-member projects. This may be explained considering how leaders act in expanding the sociomatrix of the population. Having too many leaders at the beginning can hamper large group formation; as a consequence, the optimal number of leaders is not constant over time. These results are interesting since they clearly suggest that in the long run, one and only one social leader is needed for each group of seven agents.

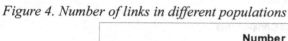

Figure 4. Number of links in different populations

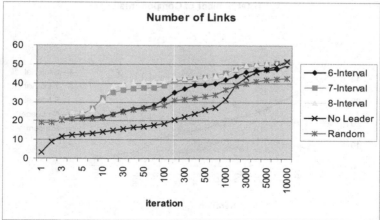

Considering the number of components in the network, it is possible to observe the role played by leaders. This is evident, including also the trivial components, i.e., the isolated agents, as shown in Figure 6.

Observing the final form of the sociomatrix, we found that leaders were not the agents with more connections. By contrast, the agents in the "influence area" of two leaders were those with more connections. As it concerns the second se-

ries of experiments, while evolution with leader is presented in Figure 7 and evolution with no leader is presented in Figure 8, numerical data are respectively labeled "seven-Interval" and "No Leader" in Figures 4, 5, and 6.

Comparing Figures 7 and 8, we can see that even on the first turns the situation is completely different as the result of the initial sociomatrix. While given a circle initial sociomatrix, agents start implementing projects with their neighbors;

Figure 5. Number of nontrivial components in different populations

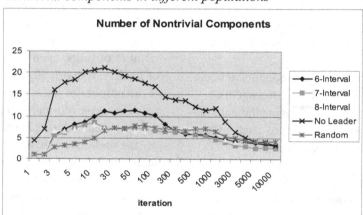

Figure 6. Total number of components in different populations

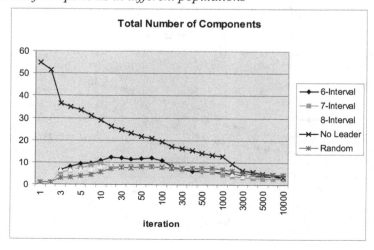

Figure 7. Project network evolution in populations with seven-interval leaders and circle graph initial sociomatrix

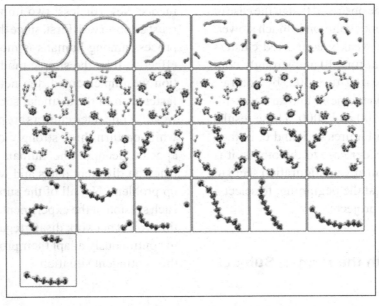

Figure 8. Project network evolution in populations with no leader and previous case final sociomatrix as the initial one

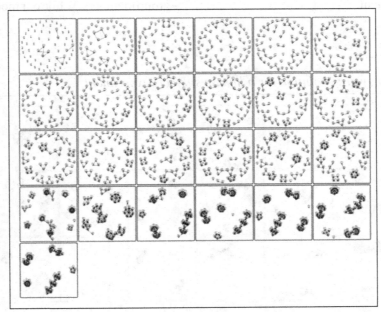

in the other case, many agents are isolated due to the large number of agents they already know. Furthermore, it can be observed that in the case of no leaders the network evolution is much slower: In Figure 7 size six weakly connected clusters appear consistently at turn 10 and strongly connected clusters appear at turn 100, by contrast in Figure 8 these phenomena appear later, respectively on turns 600 and 2000. These results find confirmation in Figures 4, 5, and 6, in fact, comparing the no leader case to the others, it is evident that leaders in any configuration seem to be essential, at least at the beginning, to select a number of effective projects.

Comparison with the Human Subject Results

Finally, in Figure 9, the project network evolution is reported for one of the human subject experiments we considered. In this case the reported turns are consecutive from the first one to the end of the experiment.

We found the same tendency to aggregation with human subjects as in the artificial experiments. Nevertheless, two important differences must be observed. First, since the project selection process among humans is more interactive and effective than the simple model of communication we implemented, the network evolution is faster than in the artificial society; here size six weakly connected clusters are present on turn two while on turn three strongly connected clusters appear. Second, the human experiment took place on different dates and we had the no-turn up problem: Not all of the subjects turned up at each session of the experiment. This may explain the project network disaggregation: Subjects had to continuously adapt their projects according to the contingent situation.

CONCLUSION

A first important aspect is the role of communication and mutual knowledge between potential group members. While our model was not intended

Figure 9. Project network evolution for a human subjects experiment

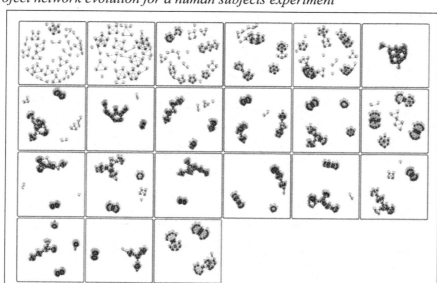

to capture the individual communication between subjects, even in the much simpler model of project discussion we considered, the importance of mutual knowledge and agent coordination in choosing the project to implement is relevant. For example, our model explains both the difficulties in large groups with no leaders and the problems emerging when too many leaders are present. In fact, we compared the effectiveness of leaders in terms of number of links in the organization. According to our findings, the number of leaders and their relative location is extremely important. In this sense, the leadership role is necessary for a sort of implicit coordination of agents. In our model, leaders do not suggest projects, rather they act on the social network and they may help the emergence of projects in the discussion phase. That is, social leaders are cardinal in stating the pace of a balanced expansion of the social matrix; essentially they tame the combinatorial explosion while fostering mutual knowledge among agents. Given the role of social leaders in group formation, it is interesting to consider the model of group development by Tuckman (1965). This model in its original form consists of four stages: forming, storming, norming, and performing. While our model was not meant to replicate Tuckman's model, some considerations are in order. First we can interpret the role of social leader in sharing members' mutual knowledge as a way to reduce uncertainty in the forming stage when importance is placed on making acquaintances, sharing information, and testing each other. Second, we can also observe a sort of norming stage as the group members exert the effort which is optimal to the group and do not free ride. As a final point, it must be observed that since in our model the leaders are those agents that incentivize knowledge among the others, they are not those with the most connections.

REFERENCES

Banks, D.L., & Carley, K.M. (1996). Models for network evolution. *Journal of Mathematical Sociology, 21*(1-2), 173-196.

Blau, P. M. (1977). *Inequality and heterogeneity.* New York: Free Press.

Bergstrom, T.C., & Miller, J.H. (1977). *Experiments with economic principles: Microeconomics.* New York: McGraw-Hill.

Bollobás, B. (1998). *Modern graph theory.* New York: Springer-Verlag.

Bornstein, G. (2003). Intergroup conflict; Individual, group and collective interests. *Personality and Social Psychology Review, 7*(2), 129-145.

Fehr, E., & Schmidt, K.M. (1999). A theory of fairness, competition and cooperation. *Quarterly Journal of Economics, 114*, 817-868.

Hinds, P.J., Carley, K.M., Krackhardt, D., & Wholey, D. (2000). Choosing work group members: Balancing similarity, competence, and familiarity. *Organizational Behavior and Human Decision Processes, 81*(2), 226-251. Jex, S.M. (2002). *Organizational psychology: A scientist-practitioner approach.* New York: John Wiley & Sons.

Miller, E.J., & Rice, A.K. (1967). *Systems of organization:The control of task and sentient boundaries.* London: Tavistock Publications.

Tuckman, B. W. (1965). Developmental sequences in small groups. *Psychological Bulletin, 63*, 384-399.

Yukl, G. (1989). *Leadership in organizations.* Englewood Cliffs, NJ: Prentice-Hall.

Zeggelink, E. (1995). Evolving friendship networks: An individual-oriented approach implementing similarity. *Social Networks, 17*, 83-110.

Chapter XXII
Modelling Knowledge Production and Integration in Working Environments

Piergiuseppe Morone
University of Foggia, Italy

Richard Taylor
Manchester Metropolitan University, UK

ABSTRACT

This chapter introduces a formal model of a complex knowledge integration process named "thinking along." Here, the firm is modelled as a working environment consisting of agents arranged into work-practices, which provide the context for their interactions. The objective of the simulations reported here is to compare two different practice structures and test their effectiveness for solving problems by thinking along. To do so, we will also introduce the notion of problem complexity as the basis for different experiments. From such a comparison, it emerged that complex problems are better tackled when practices group together agents with disparate skills (i.e., divisional practices) whereas simple problems can be more effectively addressed by organisational practices composed of agents with similar skills (i.e., functional practices). In either case, the simulated knowledge integration process played the dominant role.

INTRODUCTION

Enterprises are increasingly seen as complex systems within which learning processes take place individually as well as through the dynamic interaction of peers. From a descriptive point of view, it has been observed how organisational learning requires both (1) specialisation as a means to acquire high expertise and (2) differentiation as a viable way of broadening the scope of possessed knowledge. From an analytical point of view, on the other hand, emphasis is placed on how knowledge is acquired individually (individual learning) as much as on how it is integrated by means of peers' interactions (interactive learning).

High complexity of work processes such as problem-solving, R&D, etc., typically faced by knowledge workers suggests the importance of knowledge integration in such environments. This could be facilitated or it could be impaired by the organisational structure of the workplace.

It seems straightforward to envisage a nexus between the complexity of problems to be addressed in a working environment and the kind of skills required for their solution. For instance, firms producing a standardised product face a low level of uncertainty[1] and therefore can *ex-ante* define the set of skills necessary to perform the required routines and easily integrate them. However, increasing the complexity of the task performed by firms might increase uncertainty and as a result require a broader spectrum of knowledge to address *ex-post* unpredictable problems which might arise over the production process. This, in turn, might have significant effects over workplace organisation as grouping skilled workers endowed with different expertise becomes crucial to promote effective knowledge-integration processes.

Knowledge transfer has been widely considered a dominant mechanism of knowledge integration. Once transferred, knowledge is mastered and subsequently integrated with personal knowledge. However, the mechanism of knowledge integration presents a dilemma: Tacit knowledge is difficult, and also inefficient, to transfer. Moreover, knowledge transfer counters the specialisation argument previously introduced as it assumes that individuals absorb diverse specialised knowledge by means of face-to-face encounters. As put by Berends et al. (2004): How is it possible to integrate knowledge without actually transferring it? In a recent study, the authors suggested a solution to such a dilemma; their core idea is that peers'

interactions might be useful in solving problems, without aiming at transferring knowledge. Such a mechanism has been labelled *"thinking along,"* meaning that two (or more) individuals combine their specialised knowledge to solve a problem; nonetheless, at the end of the interaction they do not share that knowledge (Berends et al., 2004).

However largely debated, few efforts to model such complex learning mechanisms have been made so far. Building our work on the *thinking along* concept and on the empirical analysis of Berends et al. (2004), we present an agent-based model which attempts to capture the overall complexity of knowledge integration in an industrial research setting. We shall model a working environment (e.g., R&D department) within which individuals aim at solving problems. Agents are arranged into *practices* (i.e., working groups). They can solve problems individually (if they posses all the knowledge required to do so) or jointly with one or more colleagues working in the same practice.

The objective of the simulation experiments reported here is to compare two different practice structures and test their effectiveness for solving problems by thinking along. To do so we will also introduce the notion of problem complexity as the basis for different model scenarios.

KNOWLEDGE INTEGRATION AND LEARNING IN WORKING ENVIRONMENTS

Knowledge is an essential ingredient needed for the initiation of innovation processes, and the ability to acquire it is considered as an indispensable skill for innovative firms. At the same time, the capacity of firms to innovate is determined not only by the individual ability of their employees to integrate new pieces of knowledge into the production system (individual learning) but also by the ability of the organisation itself to absorb knowledge produced externally and translate it into the production processes (interactive learning). In addition, firms' learning requires an effective management of two separate processes: *speciali-sation*, as a means to acquire high expertise, and *differentiation*, as a viable way of broadening the scope of possessed knowledge (Galunic & Rodan, 1998; Garud & Nayyar, 1994; Grant, 1996a, 1996b; Huang & Newell, 2003; Kogut & Zander, 1992, 1996; Okhuyzen & Eisenhardt, 2002; Purvis et al., 2001; Spender, 1996).

This organisational capacity opens up a range of new possibilities for firms that wish to innovate, considering the limits of individual learning, such as the need to constantly specialise or to be actively engaged in relevant work processes (see Simon, 1991; Lave & Wenger, 1991). Another constraint associated with individual learning in firms is the dispersion of knowledge, i.e., the information needed to realise an innovative production processes is fragmented and distributed among a large number of employees. Within a context of a growing need for specialisation and differentiation of the learning processes enters the importance of the role played by the firm as a system of disseminating, co-ordinating, and, finally, integrating knowledge (Tsoukas, 1996).

The process by which knowledge is integrated into production processes consists of two main elements: transfer and integration. *Knowledge integration* combines dispersed bits of knowledge held by individuals to be applied in a coordinated way. *Knowledge transfer* denotes a process in which bits of information are transferred from one individual to another such that the recipient can absorb it into his or her already existent personal knowledge (i.e., some previously acquired related knowledge is required). This knowledge diffusion mechanism (transfer) is the one most cited by both academic literature and firm management literature (see, for instance, Morone & Taylor, 2004; van der Bij et al., 2003; Cabrera & Cabrera, 2002; Hansen, 1999; Szulanski, 1996). Nevertheless, this mechanism does present some disadvantages: It is expensive and often time-consuming; it is difficult to apply in the case of tacit knowledge (Collins, 1974; Kogut & Zander, 1992) or in the case of two different practices (Brown & Duguid, 1991); and it off-sets the specialisation of employees needed for innovation as it assumes that individuals absorb diverse specialised knowledge by means of face-to-face encounters (Demsetz, 1991). Such critiques would apply to any integrating mechanism based upon knowledge diffusion.

As pointed out by a new stream of literature, the possibility to *integrate knowledge* without having to transfer it might provide a solution to these drawbacks. In this regard, worth noting is the work of Grant (1996a; 1996b; 1997; 2001) who identified three other knowledge-integration mechanisms: (a) rules and directives, (b) sequencing and routines, and (c) group problem-solving, where the two former mechanisms allow the firm concerned to maintain specialisation and at the same time save on knowledge transfer. However relevant the theoretical work of Grant (as well as of Demsetz, 1991) on knowledge integration processes is, it lacks a solid empirical basis and requires further exploration. As mentioned in the introduction, an attempt in this direction was carried out by Berends et al. (2004), who examined knowledge integration in an industrial context. In this work we shall refer to their definition of knowledge integration as dominated by the *thinking along* framework. As put by the authors, *thinking along* is a mechanism that allows for knowledge integration without the need for transfer. The following example will clarify what exactly the authors meant in their original definition of thinking along:

"Consider the following interaction. [...] Luke comes to Jason, a colleague within the Group Buijs. Luke tells Jason that he wants to use an infrared camera to gain images of the heat distribution in an optical disc. This camera needs a filter to measure at a particular depth. Luke had used the camera before to measure the heat distribution in glass, but he wants to employ it for the measurement of polycarbonate now. This requires a different filter. He has purchased a filter but got distorted pictures. He wondered whether the noise in the pictures was caused by characteristics of the filter. The supplier yielded a graph of the characteristics of the filter. "*It is possible to draw conclusions from such a graph, but I lack the expertise to do so*" says Luke. Therefore, he goes to Jason, who works at the same corridor. Jason is an expert in optics and optical filters. Luke shows Jason the graph and asks: "*If you look at that, do you believe that the filter has a reasonable performance? Do you think that it has enough layers?*" Using his knowledge of optics in general and filters in particular, Jason concludes that the filter seems to be of sufficient quality. For Luke this is a reason to believe that his unsatisfactory results were not caused by a bad filter: "*Now I am pretty sure that I am not fooled by the supplier.*" In this episode, Jason offers an answer that was new to him. Jason did not know in advance about the filter that Luke wanted to use, let alone have an opinion about the quality of the filter. His evaluation was developed during the interaction. [...] we called this type of interaction "thinking along with somebody." Thinking along is quite common in industrial research." (Berends et al., 2004, 11-12).

The authors formed their analysis upon ethnographic studies (i.e., close observation of work practices in their natural context using the methods of work-shadowing as well as interviewing) and named it after an expression adopted by some of the group members. To put it concisely, thinking along is the process whereby an actor applies knowledge temporarily to someone else's problem and communicates the generated ideas to that other person.

According to the authors, there are three ways in which thinking along contributes to the practices of researchers: (1) enhancing creativity by generating possible solutions, (2) enhancing reliability by evaluating proposed solutions, and (3) stimulating reflection by asking questions. The thinking along mechanism may initiate a multiplicity of approaches to problem-solving and the results can be highly unpredictable. It is therefore useful in situations of great uncertainty and/or intellectual standstill, by enhancing practices capabilities to tackle and solve problems.

Along this line of reasoning, it is worth investigating the relation existing between knowledge integration processes and workplace organisation. As broadly acknowledged, workplace structure and re-organisation is a driving source for increases in productivity and innovation potential. Changes in workplace organisation have driven the recent increase in labour productivity observed through most western countries and in most sectors. This has attracted the attention of several authors, attempting both to categorise the different practices' structures (e.g., Lave & Wenger, 1991; Wenger, 1998, 2000; Lindkvist, 2005) as well as to study the impact of workplace organisation or human resources management on labour productivity (Black & Lynch, 1996; Eriksson, 2003; Huselid, 1995; Ichniowski et al., 1997; Milgrom & Roberts, 1990).

AN AGENT-BASED MODEL OF KNOWLEDGE INTEGRATION

Defining Agents' Knowledge Profiles and System Knowledge Profile

We assume a population of N agents allocated into practices. Each agent is endowed with a *knowledge profile* (KP), defining the competencies or expertise possessed. Agents' KPs are defined as subsets of the *system knowledge profile* (SKP), which is generated at the beginning of the execution (simulation) of the model and represents the overall knowledge present in the system. The SKP is represented by a network of nodes and links: Nodes in the SKP can be thought of as skills or units of knowledge. Directed links connect each unit of superior knowledge (*in-edges*) to one or more units of inferior knowledge *(out edges)*[2], indicating that knowledge depends upon the prior acquisition of other knowledge. Using graph notation we can write: *SKP* (Σ, Ψ), where $\Sigma = \{N_0, N_1,..., N_{MAX}\}$ is the set of units of knowledge, and $\Psi = \{\Psi(i), i \in \Sigma\}$ gives the list of requirements to go from one node to another.

Figure 1 below shows an example of an SKP graph composed of 80 nodes (units of knowledge) plus the root node. The algorithm which generates the SKP also groups the nodes into clusters that we interpret as *fields of expertise* (fields) or focused areas of competence.

To clarify the notion of directed relations and of fields of expertise it is useful to refer by example to a description of Figure 1. The algorithm mentioned above involves the definition of parent lists and child nodes. An initial parent list consists of the root skill (number one) plus the initial skills (those numbered two through six). Through an iteration process subsequent child nodes are created and associated with a randomly chosen parent list, from which a number of parent nodes are drawn. When the child node is added to the SKP, for each parent a directed link is made from parent to child. Acquisition of the child node as a learnt unit of skill depends upon the prior acquisition of all parents (given by the existence of directed relations).

There are two additional transformations which are applied to the chosen parent list before

Figure 1. System knowledge profile

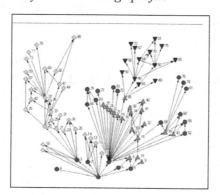

the current child is added to it: (1) for each parent with a small probability, that parent is deleted from the list, and (2) with a small probability, the element list is split into two parent lists. The algorithm shall not be documented fully here[3]; what is important to note is that because parent lists are allowed to split, the system can generate several independent areas of knowledge, representing fields of expertise in which different agents can specialise.

Fields must consist of a minimum number of skill nodes to be recognised as forming a focused area of inquiry. In Figure 1 there are three fields of expertise: one denoted by triangles (19 skills), one by diamonds (29 skills), and one by inverted triangles (13 skills). Circular nodes are not associated to particular fields. As can be seen from the figure, some fields are more specialised than others. For large SKPs there can be many independent fields defined, including a large number of highly specialised ones. Some skills may become the basis for development of an entire field (e.g., node 45); other skills may be important due to their having many out-edges (e.g., nodes 3, 7, and 37).

Each agent performs a depth-first search to construct his or her individual KP. This occurs at the initial stage of the simulation and represents the *individual learning* process. Starting from the root node, the agent subsequently selects (randomly) more specialised nodes from the SKP[4].

Again it is useful to refer by example to Figure 1. Suppose the SKP is being used to build a knowledge profile for Agent0. The agent has obtained skills 1, 5, 8, and 11. A target node is selected, say, skill 15 (child of skill 11). However, by the dependence rule of directed links, Agent0 has to obtain all of the parents of 15 before acquiring it. The network shows that 7 is a parent of 15, and therefore becomes the next skill to be obtained (a subtarget in the search algorithm). Node 7 can be obtained directly because the only parent of 7 is the root node itself. The algorithm will then continue with 15 being the next skill to be learnt, followed by one of the children of 15 (i.e., 30, 32, 34, or 40) as the next target.

This *individual learning* algorithm generates heterogeneous agents endowed with different specialisations of knowledge. We can then allocate them to practices accordingly.

Defining Agents' Working Environment

We shall define two possible business organisational structures:

1. **Functional structure:** Agents with similar skills and expertise are grouped together (i.e., departmentation). Such structure allows task specialisation and expertise to develop and avoids redundancy of functions across

groups that occurs in divisional design.

2. **Divisional structure:** Grouping of agents is structured according to specific projects, products, customers, locations, topics, etc. Therefore, agents with different skills are grouped together.

In our model, interactions will happen within practices but not amongst them. Figures 2a and 2b clarify, through an example, how these two alternative structures look.

Agents are allocated into practices according to their knowledge profiles as follows: First, we count the number of possessed skills that are associated with each field of expertise. Accordingly, we declare them as experts in a particular field. However, this is carried out under the constraint that a limited number of expert individuals of each

Figure 2a. Functional structure of R&D department of a pharmaceutical enterprise

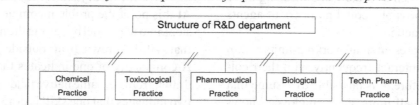

Figure 2b. Divisional structure of R&D department of a pharmaceutical enterprise

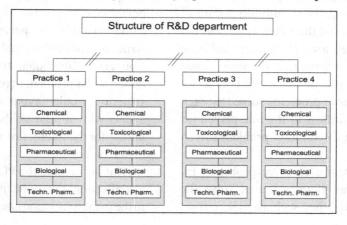

field is allowed. To set this maximum number, we divide the total number of agents in the system by the total number of fields and round this value up to the nearest integer.

During the set up phase, if and when this maximum is reached, we set the field as "closed." Subsequently, allocated agents will not have the possibility of association with a closed field but will be allocated to the remaining "open" field for which their count of possessed skills is the highest. If, at time of allocation, there are two fields for which an agent has an equal count, then the field of expertise will be allocated by random selection.

In the case of functional structure, it is relatively straightforward to put the agents into practices in which they have a common field, the number of practices equalling the number of fields. In order to make comparable simulations, in the case of divisional structures we specify that the number of practices should be equal to the number of fields, and we then allocate them ensuring there are, as far as possible, equal numbers of agents within each practice.

Practices represent small working-units within which agents interact frequently with their colleagues. Therefore, it is plausible to assume that within such small units, each employee knows quite well what other employees know and how well they know it. We capture this characteristic by defining a *practice memory* (PM) that acts as a repository of information. Specifically, in our model we assume agents are initially aware of the field of expertise of their colleagues but not of how capable they are. The system collects, for each practice, information on who solved the problems. The practice memory contains a count of the number of problems solved by each of its members regardless of the role played (as individual problem solver, joint problem solver, or partner).

Agents first attempt to solve problems individually. However, if they cannot solve the problem individually, they seek assistance from their network of acquaintances. Hence, the emergence of a new problem drives the agents' search for solutions and motivates them to contact and interact with other agents.

Defining Problems

The system is endowed with an ex-ante determined *problems list* (PL), which represents all the possible problems an agent might face over the simulation. All problems are generated in the initialisation phase of the simulation, at the same time as the SKP is created.

Each problem is associated with a set s of skills: $s = \{k_1, ..., k_z\}$ and an associated *complexity*. Problem complexity is a parameter that is fixed for each simulation (all problems within a simulation have the same complexity value). Problems are generated by first selecting any skill at random from the SKP, but we specify that the chosen skill must be attached to a field of expertise. We call this field the *local field* for the current problem. At this point the problem complexity parameter steps into the model by setting the number of skills that will be drawn from outside the local field. A complexity of one indicates that all skills are drawn from the same native field; a complexity of two indicates that one skill is drawn from outside the local field; a complexity of three indicates two from outside, etc.[5]

It is worth noting that by changing problem complexity different workplace structures will perform differently. Specifically, we expect to observe a better performance for divisional structures when the problem complexity is high. Conversely, functional structures should perform better when problems are field specific, as such structure would favour the interaction among agents with similar skills and could represent a hurdle for the interaction of agents specialised in different areas.

Having created the PL and the agents' KPs at initialisation, the model is now ready to proceed to the main simulation phase where agents attempt to solve problems. The single objective of agents is to integrate all of the skills necessary to solve the problem.

Agent Problem-Solving Step

As mentioned earlier, agents aim at solving problems which they face while carrying out their working activities. Problems are unique: They each require a different combination or set of skills. If these skills can be accessed, then we assume that the problem will always be solved. In the model it is assumed that skills are atomised components of knowledge that contribute to problem-solving in a way that follows an additive law (i.e., Agent0 possesses node 15 and Agent2 possesses node 26 and by integrating their knowl-

Figure 3. Program flow for agent problem-solving routine

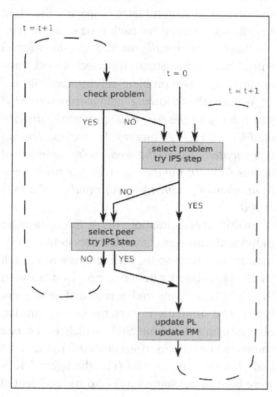

edge they can solve the problem uniquely defined by 15, 26). This is a simplification of the Berends et al. (2004) study which actually proposed a number of subprocesses of knowledge integration which can be distinguished as "see," "evaluate," and "discuss" processes (discussed earlier). Our model is a simplification which allows a very basic conceptualisation of problem-solving and interaction among peers.

The agent problem-solving routine (illustrated in Figure 3) starts with selection of the problem. Problem selection is done in accordance with the number of skills possessed by the agent, i.e., the higher the number of skills possessed by the agent and associated with the problem, the higher the probability of his or her selecting that problem from the problems list PL. The agent then attempts to solve the problem individually (IPS). If this step fails, then we turn to the joint problem-solving (JPS) step and the *thinking along* mechanism. JPS involves selecting a peer "intelligently," for which there are two criteria. First, the specialisation of the peer should correspond to the nature of the expertise required. Second, the number of problems solved by the peer should be the highest.

In this step (labelled "select peer" in Figure 3) the agent may contact *one* additional peer from within the same practice. This is where the *thinking along*[6] mechanism steps into the model: If the contacted peer possesses some knowledge required to solve the problem, he or she will contribute, although no knowledge transfer will take place. If, on the contrary, the contacted agent is not able to help in solving the problem, the agent who initiated the interaction will record that the peer was contacted. In all of the experiments reported here, it is assumed that agents are *perseverant* in their approach to problem-solving. That is, if they fail to solve a problem during cycle *t* they continue with the same problem at cycle *t + 1* contacting a different peer.

However, there is an important problem-checking step that occurs whenever a problem-solving cycle fails. As shown at the top of Figure 3, "check problem" will initiate a new selection if the current problem was solved by another agent or group of agents. Not shown in Figure 3 is that the agent also records to the common practice memory if the problem was found to be *unsolvable*, that is, all of the peers were contacted and no solution was found. In this case, there is no further reason to select that problem (the practice as a unit does not possess the skills).

As the left-hand loop of Figure 3 executes, the *perseverant* problem solver will make a list of those agents who contributed expertise helping to solve the problem faced. These peers will appear as *partners* if the attempt subsequently succeeds. If the problem-solving step is successful (right-hand loop of Figure 3) then the practice memory is updated and the problem is declared solved and removed from the PL. Whether the agent completed an individual problem-solving (IPS) or a joint problem-solving (JPS) step or was contacted as a partner by another agent, the score of problems for that agent is incremented by one unit. This information on who solved the problems is accessible to all members of the practice, and hence the awareness of colleagues' level of expertise improves over time and becomes the basis for "intelligent" partner selection.

SIMULATION EXPERIMENTS WITH THE MODEL

In this section we present the results of several batches of experimental runs which will allow us to compare the performance of different workplace organisations in accordance with the kind of task faced by the firm (i.e., the complexity of the problem met by simulated agents).

The JAVA platform with the RePast libraries (North et al., 2006) was used in implementation.

Experimental Set-Up

We ran three sets of simulations, varying peers' selection strategies. In the first set of simulations we defined *intelligent agents* that select peers intelligently and according to the routine described earlier. Subsequently, we ran two new sets of simulations assuming: (1) that agents select peers for interaction grounding their decision only on the prior knowledge they have on their colleagues' field of expertise, and (2) a completely random peer-selection process. We label these types of agents respectively *semi-intelligent agents* and *zero-intelligent agents* and compare their performance, investigating the effectiveness of these types of metaknowledge for problem-solving.

For each set of simulations we ran several repetitions (each repetition is composed by a batch of 100 runs), keeping constant all fixed parameters while varying the problem complexity (pc) as integer values drawn from the set {1,2,3,4} and the practice structure (contrasting functional and divisional structures). Comparing the eight repetitions obtained for each type of agent (i.e., *intelligent, semi-intelligent,* and *zero-intelligent*) will allow us to investigate the effect of workplace organisation upon problem-solving capabilities.

We used the following fixed parameters: *SKP size = 80 (plus the root node); normally distributed KP with* $\mu = 20$ *and* $\sigma = 2$— *the distribution is truncated around the mean value; number of agents (N)=20; number of skills per problem = 6; number of problems = 40; number of cycles = 100.*

In this set of simulations the difference among individual runs was controlled very deliberately, in order to minimise the differences within each batch. This allows a better comparison between the eight repetitions and across different agent types. The simulations were made very similar, always using the same SKP, which is the one shown in Figure 1 (indifferent for *all* simulations) and also the same agents (i.e., the agents' KPs were built in the same way) who were allocated always into the same practices (according to the type of organisational structure). As discussed above, the number of practices is endogenously determined, and in this case we had three practices. Also, the same PL was defined (according to the *pc* parameter). The only part which varied, apart from the problem complexity and the practice structure (as already discussed), was the agent step order, i.e., the order in which the agents carried out the problem-solving step (Figure 3). The (sequential) ordering of agents carrying out this step was randomised differently for each simulation within the batch, and is therefore the only source of variation within batches.[7]

Findings and Interpretations

In Table 1 we report the general system statistics collected at the end of the simulations. These statistics are calculated as an average over batches of one hundred runs. We can observe several regularities in this table: (1) practices never manage to solve all 40 problems (by investigating individual knowledge profiles we discovered that skills 58, 67, and 72—a closely related subset of the field marked with inverted triangles in Figure 1—were not possessed by any agent); (2) divisional structure is always over-performing vis-à-vis the functional structure in terms of overall number of problems solved when problem complexity is set higher than 1; (3) the share of problems solved jointly is always higher than that of problems solved individually; moreover, when introducing a degree of complexity into the problem structure, the relative

importance of individual problem-solving drops significantly; (4) the average number of partners involved in the thinking along process increases with the complexity of the problem.

As predicted, this finding implies that the more complex a problem is, the more relevant becomes co-operation in order to solve it. At the same time, note that this result does not hold when *pc=3* in the case of functional practices; this could be due to the specific artefacts of the simulation or to some intrinsic properties of the model. We shall investigate this issue more thoroughly in the next section when we will present the sensitivity analysis. It is worth noting that (with the exception of functional practices and *pc = 3*) the architecture of the practice does not appear to have an effect on the relative share of problems solved individually or by thinking along. Note also that *all* problems are solved jointly when *pc=4*, a finding independent of the practice architecture.

Table 1 shows that, in general, an increase in the problem complexity is always matched by an increase in the relevance of knowledge integration as a means of problem-solving. This finding is corroborated by the time series data. We observe a statistically significant difference between the two series as the functional practice performs steadily better than the divisional one when simple problems are considered.[8] The trend is reversed when problem complexity is greater than one.

We shall now investigate (for different practices architectures) the evolution of the problem-solving process while introducing different degrees of

Table 1. General statistics of system performance

Practice structure	Problem complexity	Total problems solved	JPS	IPS	Avgerage number of partners
DIVISIONAL	1	26	84.00%	16.00%	2.38
DIVISIONAL	2	19	97.42%	2.58%	2.85
DIVISIONAL	3	17	94.76%	5.24%	2.88
DIVISIONAL	4	12	100.00%	0.00%	3.37
FUNCTIONAL	1	29	87.72%	12.28%	2.41
FUNCTIONAL	2	13	96.31%	3.69%	3.09
FUNCTIONAL	3	6	79.33%	20.67%	2.64
FUNCTIONAL	4	3	100.00%	0.00%	3.27

complexity into the problem structure. Looking at Figures 4a and b, we can see that with increasing problem complexity firm performance decreases monotonically in both functional as well as divisional cases. Note that the performance declines both in terms of number of problems solved and the speed at which this happens.

This result implies that firms' practices become less effective when problems faced by employees are of growing complexity. If this finding is predictable for functional practices, where homogeneously specialised agents might encounter serious difficulties in solving complex problems, it is somehow surprising in the case of divisional practices, where diversely specialised agents should make the most out of thinking along in solving complex problems.

Possibly, the explanation to this puzzle lies in the specific combination of knowledge profiles and the problems list. In fact, such a combination determines the "solving space," i.e., the theoretical maximum number of problems which each practice can *ex-ante* solve. Note that the solving space is also determined by the way agents are allocated into practices, as it acts as a constraint to the possibilities of knowledge integration. The solving space coincides with the steady state level of our model and is exogenously determined through the initial parameterisation. It coincides with the unification of the problems that can be solved in each practice.

On the contrary, the speed of convergence depends crucially upon the problem-solving ability both individually and in partnership. The effectiveness of thinking along is, in turn, affected by networking opportunities (i.e., with whom each agent has the opportunity to interact) and by the individual perception of these relationships (i.e., how well does each agent know his or her peers). In order to investigate the relevance of model parameterisation to system performance, we shall now conduct a sensitivity analysis.

Sensitivity Analysis

In this section we will conduct a sensitivity analysis, aimed at corroborating the earlier results. If we obtain similar findings, then we shall confidently be able to extend our results to a broader set of situations (i.e., different problems to be solved, different agents allocated in different ways, and endowed with different KPs). We again ran batches of one hundred simulations and for each simulation we defined different PL, KPs, Practice allocations, and step order; we kept the SKP constant. As before, we ran eight batches, varying problem complexity and practice structure. In Table 2 we summarise the average results of each batch. Note that individual runs now have different convergence values so the entries in the third column of Table 2 are nonintegers.

Figure 4. Speed of "problem- solving" by structure and problem complexity

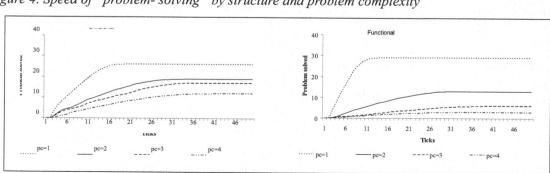

| 4a. Divisional architecture | 4b. Functional architecture |

Confronting these results with those reported in Table 1, we can immediately observe that the sensitivity analysis confirms that functional structure over-performs vis-à-vis divisional structure when simple problems are considered; on the other hand, divisional practices over-perform vis-à-vis functional structure when we consider complex problems. A second result that is confirmed by this sensitivity analysis is that an increase in problem complexity is matched by an increase in the number of agents involved in thinking along processes (and this is true for all cases, hence casting away the peculiar result observed earlier in the case of functional practices dealing with problems of complexity degree 3). Moreover, we can also observe in this case a very similar increase in problems solved jointly when shifting from $pc=1$ to $pc \geq 2$.

Looking at the convergence dynamic, we observe (Figure 5) again a monotonic decrease in firms' performance while increasing problem complexity, and again this result is independent from practices' structure. As mentioned earlier, this was predictable for firms organised into functional practices but was counterintuitive for divisional organisations.

Peer Selection Strategies and System Performance

As mentioned earlier, each practice is endowed with a practice memory which helps agents in selecting "intelligently" the best peers for interaction. Specifically, each agent is initially aware of his or her colleagues' fields of expertise, and over time gathers information on their performance in

Table 2. General statistics of system performance—sensitivity analysis

Practice structure	Problem complexity	Total problems solved	JPS	IPS	Avgerage number of partners
DIVISIONAL	1	25.76	82.84%	17.16%	2.38
DIVISIONAL	2	22.8	97.24%	2.76%	2.76
DIVISIONAL	3	20.46	99.56%	0.44%	3.11
DIVISIONAL	4	18.76	99.79%	0.21%	3.29
FUNCTIONAL	1	27.46	85.91%	14.09%	2.45
FUNCTIONAL	2	15.63	96.10%	3.90%	2.71
FUNCTIONAL	3	11.49	99.30%	0.70%	2.95
FUNCTIONAL	4	8.87	99.77%	0.23%	3.12

Figure 5. Speed of "problem-solving" by structure and problem complexity—sensitivity analysis

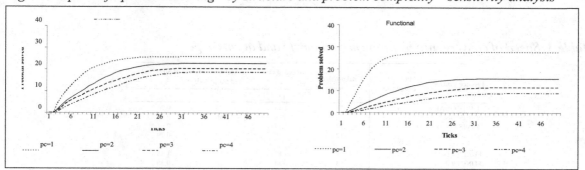

5a. Divisional architecture   5b. Functional architecture

solving problems. In this section we shall compare system performances while varying peers' selection strategies; we will compare *intelligent agents* (IAs) examined earlier with *semi-intelligent agents* (SIAs) and *zero-intelligent agents* (ZIAs).

Since in this simulation we vary only peers' selection strategies, we expect the system to converge to the same levels observed earlier for intelligent agents. What might change is the speed of convergence, as IAs should be more efficient in solving problems when compared to SIAs and ZIAs. Hence, by comparing the speed of convergence of different types of agents we should get a measure of the efficiency of practice memory as well as a measure of the relevance of prior knowledge of peers' fields of expertise.

In Table 3 we compare speeds of convergence, calculated as the average number of problems solved per period until the steady state is reached; it can immediately be observed that there is not a sizeable difference in convergence speed between intelligent and semi-intelligent agents. Surprisingly enough, semi-intelligent agents solve problems faster than intelligent agents in several cases. In divisional practices, for example, SIAs are faster than IAs when *pc*=1 and 4, slower when *pc*=3, and have the same speed when *pc*=2. As far as functional practices are concerned, SIAs overperform IAs only when *pc=4*; in all other cases they display a lower speed of convergence.

This finding comes as a surprise; in fact, we can infer that practice memory is not as effective

as was foreseen while developing the model. As clearly emerges from results presented in this section, agents selecting peers using the information stored in the practice memory sometimes perform worse than agents selecting peers using solely prior information on fields of expertise. We can thus conclude that, in some cases (e.g., divisional practices dealing with simple problems), an excess of information might lead the system to a worse performance.

Finally, we shall mention that zero-intelligent agents performed much better than expected, specifically when dealing with complex problems. In fact, if being intelligent or semi-intelligent speeds up the convergence when simple problems are considered, this advantage disappears almost completely when shifting to complex problems. One factor to consider in relation to peer-selection strategies is the scope of possible interactions: In this model we have restricted both the size of practices (to a relatively small scale) and the ability to select outside one's own practice (not permitted). Under less restrictive circumstances, the relevance of agents' metaknowledge and strategies could be highly significant.

CONCLUSION

This chapter presented an agent-based model of knowledge integration processes for the industrial research sector. We carried out simulation experiments to test the effectiveness of different work

Table 3. Speed of convergence by problem complexity and agents' type

Practice structure	Problem complexity	Total problems solved	Speed of convergence (average number of problems' solved per period)		
			IA	SI	ZI
DIVISIONAL	1	26	1.18	1.24	0.93
DIVISIONAL	2	19	0.56	0.56	0.54
DIVISIONAL	3	17	0.47	0.46	0.41
DIVISIONAL	4	12	0.29	0.30	0.29
FUNCTIONAL	1	29	1.81	1.71	1.45
FUNCTIONAL	2	13	0.38	0.36	0.35
FUNCTIONAL	3	6	0.15	0.15	0.15
FUNCTIONAL	4	3	0.08	0.09	0.06

practice arrangements with regard to problem-solving activities of a firm.

The mechanism that was labelled *"thinking along"*—a type of knowledge integration without transfer—by Berends et al. (2004) and which was represented in our model as joint problem-solving (JPS) behaviour was found to be dominant over individual problem-solving (IPS) in all simulations reported here (Tables 1 and 2). This finding was obtained despite the fact that IPS preceded JPS in the simulation cycle (Figure 3); on the other hand, it should be noted that individuals had relatively small KPs compared to the size of the SKP.

The first experiment directly compared functional and divisional architectures for working practices by using identical SKP, PL, and agent KPs. As we expected, divisional architecture outperformed functional structure in the cases of more complex problems (*pc=2, 3, 4*). However, the functional structure prevailed in the case of *pc=1* (where all skills are drawn from the same field): this is another intuitive result since it can be maintained that, if all problems are narrowly defined, then the firm may benefit most from focused interactions. It follows from this result that, in order to achieve maximum efficiency, firms should be arranged into work practices according to the nature of the problems faced: If normally confronted by predictable, focused problems, the most effective arrangement for the firm would be functional, whereas if challenged by unpredictable, complex problems, it would be divisional.

Sensitivity analysis of the first case supported these conclusions and allowed us to dispose of artefacts introduced by the random aspect of simulation set up. Specifically, it showed that IPS was monotonically decreasing with problem complexity.

As reported above, analysis of the agents' KPs showed that a few skills were not possessed by any agent. This accounts for the failure of the system to solve all 40 problems, and it also explains why in this case the "solving space" decreases with problem complexity. The reason is that for higher values of *pc*, construction of the PL involves drawing more frequently from the "triangle" field (as this field is smaller and therefore less likely to be selected as local in the first instance). It follows that the not-possessed skills are then more likely to be selected.

Solving space is, of course, completely determined from the beginning of a simulation. While it offers a way to compare functional and divisional practices, it complicates comparison of performance across different values of problem complexity.

In addition to solving space (or steady state level), percentages of IPS and JPS, and average number of partners, we used time series data (Figures 4 and 5) and calculations of the *rate of problem-solving* (Table 3).

A final interesting conclusion comes from the comparison of different peer selection strategies. We compared *intelligent agents* (that select peers using information stored in the Practice Memory) with *semi-intelligent agents* (selecting peers for interaction grounding their decision only on the prior knowledge they have on their colleagues' field of expertise) and *zero-intelligent agents* (applying a completely random selection process). We found that peer selection strategies were not sizably affecting agents' performance and that, in some cases, following an intelligent strategy was affecting negatively the overall system performance.

Further research could investigate possibilities for initiating knowledge integration across practices by relaxing the constraints we have imposed on the system. The thinking along phenomenon refers to such events and their relative frequency compared to interactions within a practice has been measured (Berends et al., 2004). Whilst less frequent, such cross-practice interactions could be disproportionately influential because they offer a solution to the limiting solving space.

A further idea to be pursued is adaptive practices with endogenous selection of members. This approach would be highly suited to address questions concerning working environments with changing skill requirements.

REFERENCES

Berends, J.J., Debackere, K., Garud, R., & Weggeman, M.P.C.D. (2004). *Knowledge integration by thinking along* (Working Paper 04.05). Nedlands, Eindhoven Centre for Innovation Studies.

Black, S., & Lynch, L.M. (1996). Human capital investments and productivity. *American Economic Review, 86*(2), 263-267.

Brown, J.S., & Duguid, P. (1991). Organizational learning and communities of practice: Toward a unified view of working, learning and innovation. *Organization Science, 2*, 40-57.

Cabrera, A., & Cabrera, E.F. (2002). Knowledge-sharing dilemmas. *Organization Studies, 23*, 687-710.

Camerer, C., & Weber, M. (1992). Recent developments in modelling preferences: Uncertainty and ambiguity. *Journal of Risk and Uncertainty, 5*(4), 325-370.

Collins, H.M. (1974). The TEA set: Tacit knowledge and scientific networks. *Science Studies, 4*, 165-86.

Demsetz, H. (1991). The theory of the firm revisited. In O. E. Williamson, S.G. Winter, & R.H. Coase (Eds.), *The nature of the firm* (pp. 159-178). New York: Oxford University Press.

Eriksson, T. (2003). The effects of new work practices: Evidence from employer-employee data. In T. Kato, & J. Pliskin (Eds.), *The determinants of the incidence and the effects of participatory organizations:. Advances in the economic analysis of participatory and labor-managed firms* (Vol. 7, pp. 159-178). New York: Elsevier.

Galunic, D.C., & Rodan, S. (1998). Resource combinations in the firm: Knowledge structures and the potential for Schumpeterian innovation. *Strategic Management Journal, 19*, 1193-1201.

Garud, R., & Nayyar, P. (1994). Transformative capacity: Continual structuring by inter-temporal technology transfer. *Strategic Management Journal, 15*, 365-385.

Grant, R.M. (1996a). Prospering in dynamically-competitive environments: Organizational capability as knowledge integration. *Organization Science, 7*, 375-387.

Grant, R.M. (1996b). Toward a knowledge-based theory of the firm. *Strategic Management Journal, 17* (Winter Special Issue), 109-122.

Grant, R.M. (1997). The knowledge-based view of the firm: Implications for management practice. *Long Range Planning, 30*, 450-454.

Grant, R.M. (2001). Knowledge and organization. In I. Nonaka, & D. J. Teece (Eds.), *Managing industrial knowledge* (pp. 145-169). London: Sage.

Halbwachs, M. (1950). *La mémoire collective.* Paris: Les Presses universitaires de France.

Hansen, M.T. (1999). The search-transfer problem. *Administrative Science Quarterly, 44*, 82-111.

Huang, J.C., & Newell, S. (2003). Knowledge integration processes and dynamics within the context of cross-functional projects. *International Journal of Project Management, 21*, 167-176.

Huselid, M.A. (1995). The impact of human resource management practices on turnover, productivity, and corporate financial performance. *Academic Management Journal, 38*(3), 635-672.

Ichniowski, C., Shaw, K., & Prennushi, G. (1997). The effects of human resource management practices on productivity: A study of steel finishing lines. *American Economic Review, 87*(3), 291-313.

Knight, F.H. (1921). *Risk, uncertainty and profit.* Boston: Houghton Mifflin Company.

Kogut, B., & Zander, U. (1992). Knowledge of the firm, combinative capabilities, and the replication of technology. *Organization Science, 3,* 383-397.

Kogut, B., & Zander, U. (1996). What firms do? Coordination, identity and learning. *Organization Science, 7,* 502-518.

Lave, J., & Wenger, E. (1991). *Situated learning.* Cambridge: Cambridge University Press.

Lindkvist, L. (2005). Knowledge communities and knowledge collectivities: A typology of knowledge work in groups. *Journal of Management Studies, 42*(6), 1189-1210.

Milgrom, P., & Roberts, J. (1990). The economics of modern manufacturing: Technology, strategy, and organization. *American Economic Review, 80*(3), 511-528.

Morone, P., & Taylor, R. (2004). Knowledge diffusion dynamics of face-to-face interactions. *Journal of Evolutionary Economics, 14,* 327-351.

North, M.J., Collier, N.T., & Vos, J.R. (2006). Experiences creating three implementations of the repast agent modeling toolkit. *ACM Transactions on Modeling and Computer Simulation, 16*(1), 1-25.

Okhuyzen, G.A., & Eisenhardt, K.M. (2002). Integrating knowledge in groups. *Organization Science, 13,* 370-386.

Purvis, R.L., Sambamurthy, V., & Zmud, R.W. (2001). The assimilation of knowledge platforms in organizations: An empirical investigation. *Organization Science, 12,* 117-135.

Simon, H.A. (1991). Bounded rationality and organizational learning. *Organization Science, 2,* 125-134.

Spender, J.C. (1996). Making knowledge the basis of a dynamic theory of the firm. *Strategic Management Journal, 17* (Winter Special Issue), 45-62.

Szulanski, G. (1996). Exploring internal stickiness: Impediments to the transfer of best practice within a firm. *Strategic Management Journal, 17,* 27-44.

Tsoukas, H. (1996). The firm as a distributed knowledge system. *Strategic Management Journal, 17* (Winter Special Issue), 11-25.

van der Bij, H., Song, X. M., & Weggeman, M. (2003). An empirical investigation into the antecedents of knowledge dissemination at the strategic business unit level. *Journal of Product Innovation Management, 20,* 163-179.

Wenger, E.C. (2000). Communities of practice and social learning systems. *Organization 7*(2), 225-246.

ENDNOTES

[1]   We refer to *Knightian uncertainty* (Knight, 1921).

[2]   Here we refer to superior and inferior knowledge as, respectively, more and less specialised knowledge.

[3]   However, the algorithms used to create the *SKP* and the search process to generate *KP* are available from the authors upon request.

[4]   Note that we do not assume that agents possess full information on knowledge profiles, nor that they carry out a goal-directed search process. Simply, they target any (randomly chosen) child node of the previously learnt node.

[5]   "Outside" of the local field includes both skills associated with another field and those that are unassociated.

[6]   We reported a brief description of this dynamic, described by Berends et al. (2004), in the previous section.

[7]   This approach could result in very specific and atypical results and will therefore be supported by a thorough sensitivity analysis in which several other parameters are tested.

[8]   Note that we can reject the null hypothesis that the data from the divisional and the functional simulations have the same mean distribution in favour of the alternative hypothesis that most of the values of the functional series tend to be higher, at the 0.0001 level of statistical significance, according to a standard t-test. This result holds for the whole series as well as for the restricted converging series (i.e., the subsample of the series which encompasses only the ticks required to reach the steady state).

Chapter XXIII
Stress and Expectation in Double–Auction Market:
Simulations to Study Models Deduced from Experimental Economics

Juliette Rouchier
GREQAM, France

Stephane Robin
GATE, France

ABSTRACT

This chapter describes a multi-agent model of a double-auction market in which simulations are led. In our market study, we focus on information processing and hence make assumptions about the cognitive use that agents make of this information. For some years now, experiments have been used to study auctions and now resulting data are used to make hypotheses about learning. We propose simulations here that are organised on the same model as experiments, as a succession of auction sessions where each agent is either seller or buyer and has to exchange before the end. Communication is made of bids and asks that can be accepted by the others and lead to transactions. Our main result is the fact that we actually obtain convergence although agents have no knowledge of others' limit prices and only interact through a completely impersonal market. This corresponds to experimental data, which is a positive result in our search of the representation for economic rationality and is discussed methodologically in the chapter.

INTRODUCTION

Trading institutions, such as markets, are at the centre of economics preoccupation. However, their rules and how they are interpreted by individuals are rarely discussed in the economic literature. The fact that a small variation in the market institution can have a large effect on behaviours and as a result affect prices and efficiency has been clearly demonstrated by experimental studies of markets (Plott, 1989). These experiments are often interpreted in terms of information use: Markets are seen as structures that enable the aggregation of information into prices (Hayek, 1945, p. 526). To understand the formation of price in a diverse institutional context, one needs to represent markets as decentralised co-ordination mechanisms where emergence takes place, and create a better view of their aggregation properties. The first thing to study is the use that individuals make of the market—how they interpret the signals and act according to the communication channels they can use. We propose to combine the experimental method and a simulation technique to study price formation and market efficiency through the understanding of individual behaviour and learning.

There exist a lot of different market institutions, each of which display different properties and performance measures. We are interested in studying the Double-Auction mechanism because it is recognised as being one of the most efficient market structures (Holt, 1995). When a market is organised with this institution, prices converge quickly towards the Walrasian equilibrium price and allocation is Pareto efficient.

The joint use of experimental results and building of artificial societies is an exercise that is now spreading in economics, certainly due to the fact that in both fields, researchers are keen to identify, model, and test the actual behaviour of individuals when faced with some economic choices (Duffy, 2001). At the moment, both approaches viewing social systems as emergent structures based on dynamical interactions of learning agents are interested in the coherence and applicability of theories more than their exactness in an abstract setting (Smith, 2002). Although the double auction (DA) has been studied intensively in the laboratory, only recently have tools started to become available to provide a behavioural theory of the DA market. To participate in the development of such a theory, we want to test a set of hypotheses regarding behaviours of agents in the context of this market, and hence we created a multi-agent platform that allows the testing of several types of cognition. In this chapter we explore different cognitive processes of artificial agents, varying how much information the agent gets from the environment and how it uses its memory. By comparing results of simulations and results of experiments we would like to see if it's possible to evaluate our learning models according to the relative proximity to actual human behaviours. This can help us understand what humans actually learn when they are faced with that type of exchange institution, and hence build artificial agents that might adapt to closely related institutions.

In the following section we present the DA institution and the main results observed in an experimental DA market, and explore literature on the joint use of experiments and simulations. Then we describe the multi-agent system we built following the framework of a DA auction and include several proposals for agent cognition. Our first results consist of a set of observed data from artificial market sessions, based on some usual indicators like the existence of a convergence towards equilibrium or the efficiency globally attained that enable us to assess some aspects of our model as well as correct others. Eventually, we propose the methodology we want to use to carry on in our research.

DA INSTITUTION AND EXPERIMENTAL MARKET

Double Auction Markets Rules

The continuous double auction (DA) is a two-sided progressive auction. To represent this mechanism, we use a framework that is considered as typical in experimental economics, and which was proposed by Friedman (Friedman, 1993). Agents are divided in two groups: buyers and sellers who cannot change roles. Both have limit prices for the commodities traded: Buyers cannot spend more and sellers get less than this private value. All limit values are known only to the agent that is characterised by it. Only one type of good is exchanged, each agent possesses or must get one unit of that good. At any moment, buyers can submit a bid and similarly, sellers can submit and ask, both being an offer expressed as a price. Buyers and sellers may propose an offer or accept the offer made by agents on the other side of the market. If a bid or ask is accepted, a transaction occurs at the offer price. An improvement rule is typically imposed on new offers entering the market: Submitted bids (asks) must exceed (be less than) the standing bid (ask). Each time an offer is satisfying for one of the participants, he/she announces that they accept the trade at the given price, and the transaction is completed. Once a transaction is completed, the market is cleared (there is no standing bid or ask anymore) and the agents who have traded go out of the market. Then, as at the opening of the market, the first offer can take any value and imposes a constraint on any following offer. After a fixed time, or when all goods have been sold, the market closes. If some agents have not traded yet, they cannot do it anymore. Studying auctions with artificial agents, we consider that they must exchange. In

Figure 1. Bids, asks and transaction prices as a function of time for an experiment with four sellers and four buyers trading for 15 periods. Vertical lines represent opening and closing time and the horizontal black line represents the equilibrium value. Each dot is a bid or an ask. Red circles linked together indicate the prices of transactions. The convergence towards the equilibrium price within each market opening and along the time is visible (experiments by Robin, students of the ENSGI in Grenoble, 1999).

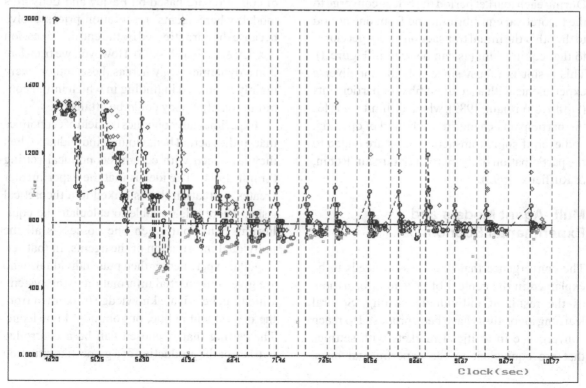

experiments, participants get no reward if they don't exchange but get some otherwise.

Usually, an experiment on a double auction market is organised as a succession of market periods. Here, we are interested in markets where the same situation applies at the beginning of each market, agents being given exactly the same limit value. In the laboratory, price patterns, volume, distribution, and market efficiency are the observed variables. Efficiency measures how well the system reaches the efficient Pareto allocation: The surplus made by agents is compared to the best possible surplus with ideal matching (Plott & Smith, 1978). When the market is repeated, the evolution of prices of transactions in time can be considered as an indication of how well participants adapt to the opportunities offered by the market setting.

In experiments, DA institution is a very good market institution because a high efficiency is quickly attained (Holt, 1995; Plott, 1989). There is a global "learning" taking place at two levels: During each market period the prices converge to the theoretical equilibrium, and from one period to the other the initial transaction prices get closer to that equilibrium (as can be seen in Figure 1). This result is robust since it holds for diverse experiments with a small number of participants (Smith & William, 1989), when the limit value for the participants change at each market opening, and even if some transaction costs are added to the participation of the market (Noussair, Robin, & Ruffieux, 1998).

Multi-Agent Models and Experimental Economics

The convergence that is witnessed needs to be explained in the context of private information, as the result of individual learning. Several learning algorithms have been proposed to reach convergence in artificial markets with settings that are equivalent to the experimental ones.

One important result is that this institution puts such a large constraint on possible proposals that even Zero-Intelligence agents (acting randomly but following the rules of behaviour defined by the institution) are quite good participants in such a simulated environment (Gode & Sunder 1993, 1994). What Brewer et al. (2002) showed, however, is that this convergence would only be attained if the limit prices of the agents were staying the same (see the next section as to why this is a special case of the double auction), and that it is an intra-period convergence, with no convergence from one time-step to another. From this they conclude that no simple algorithm could help attain a good representation of global behaviour or the system, not to mention the imperfection of the represented individual cognition. The assessment of the cognition then has to be based on experimental data, treated through a precise protocol of econometric comparison to evaluate the likeliness of the convergence.

Our main assumptions in the representation of cognition are based on Easley and Ledyard's model, where agents' reservation prices evolve because they are stressed by the end of the session (Easley & Ledyard, 1993). However, we translate it in a dynamic way, whereas these authors were mainly interested in finding in which initial configuration efficiency could be attained.

Experimental economics is a field of economics that studies actual behaviour of individuals when they are faced with certain economical setting (Smith, 1994). The idea is that the experimenter creates a situation that is linked to a theoretical issue, where it is possible to calculate the equilibrium behaviour when one possesses all the individual information of the agents. In that setting, the experimenter then puts individuals who are given only partial information in the system, which can be private knowledge (unknown from the others) and public, or common, knowledge. The setting that is chosen can be a controlled market, or the production of a game-like situation ("game" understood as in "game theory"): It is always an archetypical setting in which the role, ability to act, and communication rules for each actor are very clear, quite limited, and very easy to observe. Differences between human actions and theoretical behaviour can be interpreted as alternate motivational aspects from the classical approach or as signs of limited cognitive ability when an optimal calculus is too difficult. By varying the information that the individual gets during an experiment and analysing the different results that are globally produced, it is possible to formulate positive assumptions about the decision process of individuals.

The comparison between experimental results and the building of an artificial society is an exercise that is now spreading in economics, certainly because in both fields researchers are keen to identify, model, and test the actual behaviour of individuals in some economic setting (Duffy, 2001). For most researchers, experiments and simulations are not used to destroy theories but to ask new questions or identify situations where theory cannot help anticipate results (Smith, 2002; Rouchier, 2006). This enables them to specify the limits of existence of phenomena and find alternative explanations to individual actions, revealing sometimes contradictive rationalities (Bousquet et al., 2002); it also leads to the appearance of new ways to describe and consider scientific results, with issues being not solely focused on positive results, but also on applicability in systems (Barreteau & Bousquet, 2000; Smith, 2002).

Experimental economists have started to use artificial agents to complement their experiments. Some simulations are used to roughly calibrate parameters of experiments (which they call "experiments with artificial agents"). A more elaborate approach consists in proposing cognitive algorithms for the agents and then calibrating them with results of human participants playing in an equivalent setting. This is what Gode and Sunder propose about a double-auction market (1994). Duffy (2001) describes this process on the topic of speculation, and he even proposes some mixed simulations where humans exchange with other humans as well as with artificial agents. Eventually, Janssen and Ahn propose a very precise calibration work to compare two models of rationality in a common-good provision game: the Experience-Weighted Attraction by Camerer (EWA) and the Best Response with Signalling (BRS) (Janssen & Ahn, 2003). Our work is related to these research programs.

MODEL AND SIMULATIONS OF DA MARKET

Artificial Setting And Agents' Learning

In our market, there are thus buyers and sellers who are given limit prices at the beginning of the simulation. The simulation is organised as a succession of market *sessions* made up of a certain number of *steps*. It is important to make this number relatively high compared to the number of participating agents so that all can make proposals. At each step the market is defined by either a couple of outstanding bids and offers, which constrain the agents' proposals, or by a clear situation, with any proposal being acceptable. Stress times (as explained below) and limit values are randomly attributed to agents at the beginning of the simulation.

To structure the learning of our agents, we took as a reference the chapter by Easley and Ledyard (1993). They propose to structure the individual decision-making process around two elements: reservation price and stress. The reservation price is the price that is proposed by an agent and evolves in time; for a seller, it is the minimal price for a transaction at a given moment: It thus has to be higher than or equal to the limit price and can decrease along the time. For a buyer, it is the maximum price for a transaction and thus is always less than or equal to the limit price and can increase in time. Stress is the time-pressure that is perceived by the agent: It expresses the fact that the agents know they have to exchange before the end of the market period.

An agent is defined by their attributes: *Type* (seller or buyer), *Limit price*, *Stress time*, *Memory* (either "global" and the agent remembers all transactions that take place or "local" and the agent only remembers its own transactions), *Memory length* (the number of past transactions remembered), and Reservation price.

Here we keep the same conditions for each successive market: Agents always keep the same role, either buyer or seller and have the same private limit price. The memory is a list that evolves each time a transaction occurs.

Memory. We test several ways to memorise past transactions. A "local" memory will only take into account transactions in which the agent was involved. A "global" memory is based on all transactions in the society. The memory length represents the number of transactions that are used to produce the averaging of reference value.

Reservation price. The reservation price is the maximum price a buyer is ready to pay or the minimum price a seller wants to get for their good. It evolves at each period, and within a period can change at each step following the stress time. The definition of the reservation price depends on initial values and on past transactions. At the beginning of the simulation, reservation prices are defined as functions of the limit values of the agent and the space of possible values, Diff:

Diff = minimum value for sellers − maximum value for buyers. (1)

Initial reservation price is randomly chosen.
Seller:

$$RP = U \ [\text{Limit value} ; \text{Limit value} + (\text{Diff} / 2)].$$
(2)

Buyer:

$$RP = \text{Max} \ (U \ [\text{Limit value} - (\text{Diff} / 2) ; \text{Limit value}] ; 0).$$
(3)

At the beginning of each session, the reservation price depends on the success of the agent in the previous session:

- If it succeeded to make a transaction then the price of exchange is the new reservation price.
- If it did not exchange, then its reservation price is unchanged.

The algorithm of revision for a seller:

- If the seller can calculate the average value of transactions and if its reservation price is higher than that value, then the new RP is the maximum of this Average and the Limit Value of the agent:

$$RP = \text{Max} \ (\text{Average}, \text{Limit value}). \quad (4)$$

- If the seller cannot calculate the average value of the transaction or if their reservation price is lower than the average value, then they reduces their reservation price to get to a value that is still higher than their limit value. The decrease is such that, if the agent revises at each step he or she would reach Limit Value at the end of the session if the agent was revising at each time-step:

$$De = (RP - LV) / (T - L)$$
$$RP = \text{Max} \ (LV ; RP - De). \quad (5)$$

The calculus is symmetrical for a buyer, provided the value stays positive. In any case, once the reservation price equals the Limit Value, the agent does not revise anymore. The reservation price is used by the agents to make offers and bids on the market as described in the following section.

Stress. The time pressure is defined by the individual stress-time of the agent, also used by Easley and Ledyard (1993). At any time-step after the stress time, the agent has a chance to revise his or her reservation price. This opportunity changes at each step T and results from a random test. An agent with stress time ST participating in a session of length L revises if:

$$U[0;1] > (L - T) / (L - ST). \qquad (6)$$

$U[a;b]$ is a random number following a uniform law in $[a;b]$. Hence the probability to revise gets greater as time passes.

The evolution of stress time takes place at the end of a session and depends on the success of the agent:

- If the agent made a transaction then the stress time occurs later in the session (ST = U [ST + 1; L-1]).

- If the agent fails to transact, stress time is lowered (ST = U [1 ; ST − 1]).

Simulations and Initialisation

Time-steps. A simulation is a succession of market sessions, organised as a succession of sets. At each odd step, buyers make a proposal and at each even step, sellers make a proposal. Each time a transaction is concluded, the market is cleared, which means that there is no outstanding bid or offer.

At each step, agents revise their reservation price. Then, one agent is randomly selected among those whose reservation price allows them to accept the offer. A seller can make a transaction if their reservation price is lower than the last bid made by a buyer. In that case, the transaction price is the one that had been proposed by

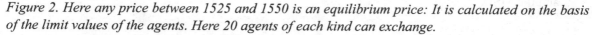

Figure 2. Here any price between 1525 and 1550 is an equilibrium price: It is calculated on the basis of the limit values of the agents. Here 20 agents of each kind can exchange.

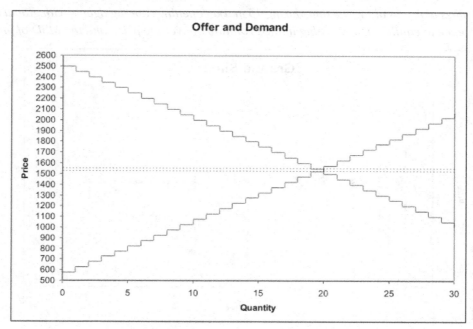

the buyer. If no one can exchange, one seller is chosen among those whose reservation price is lower than the outstanding offer. Then, one goes to the next step.

Initialisation. A simulation is defined by:

- A number of sellers and buyers (30; 30)
- The number of steps per session (200) and the number sessions per simulation (15)
- Limit prices are assigned to agents (see Figure 2)
- Type of memory: global (Sim1) or local (Sim2)
- Length of memory (10—the maximum number of transactions per period)
- Stress time is equal for all and randomly chosen from 1 to 199

Observations. The criteria that are used are:

- The average price of transaction on a market and the MSD.

- The number of deals that take place.
- The global surplus that is made over a session (sum of the difference between transaction price and limit price).
- The efficiency that compares this surplus to the ideal surplus.

RESULTS

We give here the results for one typical simulation of Sim1 and Sim2 and give a short interpretation of these data. Simulations are very similar in results.

When agents have information about all transactions that take place, and memorise 10 transactions, exchange prices get close to the equilibrium price quickly. However, there is still a marginal, but significant, inefficiency.

The representation of average price is common and converges quickly, being the basis of all agents' revision process. Hence, prices do converge to equilibrium price and the acceptable price for

Figure 3. Values of prices along the time during 15 market openings among agents with global memory. The convergence to equilibrium is visible in the evolution of average price and the MSD of prices.

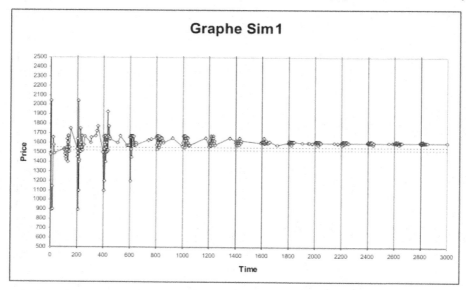

Table 1. In simulations with global perception, convergence to the equilibrium is quick. There is a reduction of dispersion along the time and a high efficiency for the system.

Period		1	2	3	4	5	6	7	8	9	10
Price	Average	1498	1555	1577	1602	1620	1620	1617	1607	1607	1604
	Stand. Dev.	238	212	164	106	45	41	34	20	15	10
Quantity		24	25	24	21	20	20	19	17	18	19
Surplus		18500	17825	17900	18825	18150	18950	17625	16825	17800	17575
Efficiency		95%	91%	92%	97%	93%	97%	90%	86%	91%	90%

Period		11	12	13	14	15
Price	Average	1603	1602	1602	1601	1602
	Stand. Dev.	9	9	7	6	5
Quantity		19	19	19	19	18
Surplus		18425	19225	19225	18175	18100
Efficiency		94%	99%	99%	93%	93%

Figure 4. Quick convergence of prices of transactions for the simulation with local perception for agents

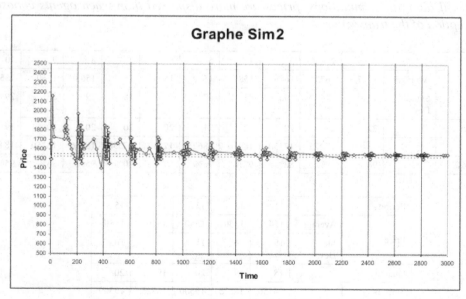

a transaction is close to it. Agents whose limit prices are too high (or low) are excluded from the transaction process, which is an expected result. The transactions mostly take place at the beginning of the period. This shows that agents have in memory the price that had been attained previously and that their reservation price has adapted to that value.

However, in our simulations some agents do not exchange although they could. At the end of each period, a high number of transactions takes place in a short time, but all agents who wish to do not have time to exchange. Apparently, the fact that the time is discrete has an impact here, which was unsuspected (because some authors announced that it didn't have any influence). This will have to be taken into account in the next research.

This dynamic is also biased because agents who trade in one session increase their stress time and hence want to trade later. They could exchange and some get the best surplus in trade, but the reduction of their stress because of previous success becomes a burden to action.

In Sim2, agents use their own transactions only to evaluate prices. Average transaction prices are quickly close to the equilibrium, but dispersion of prices is higher than in Sim1. Individual history can make us understand that. Even if the market gets close to equilibrium, agents who have transacted far from that value will store this data and use it as a new reservation price and as a reference of market price. Less agents are excluded from exchange because more have a false representation of market prices, thus a higher number of inefficient exchanges takes place. More goods are exchanged, but less efficiently, than with global knowledge of price.

Table 2. Average price converges quickly towards equilibrium when agents perceive only their own transactions. All along the simulations, prices are more dispersed than when agents choose with a general perception of the transaction.

Period		1	2	3	4	5	6	7	8	9	10
Price	Average	1727	1672	1639	1584	1579	1565	1571	1563	1560	1552
	Stand. Dev.	156	144	105	83	67	50	38	29	27	29
Quantity		22	23	22	22	21	20	20	20	20	19
Surplus		18400	17275	17150	18950	18675	17300	17550	18550	18750	18475
Efficiency		94%	89%	88%	97%	96%	89%	90%	95%	96%	95%

Period		11	12	13	14	15
Price	Average	1548	1550	1550	1550	1550
	Stand. Dev.	19	16	11	11	10
Quantity		18	19	20	19	20
Surplus		16750	18875	19500	18725	19500
Efficiency		86%	97%	100%	96%	100%

CONCLUSION

The reason why we started doing this work in the first place was to establish a new link between experimental economics and simulations and to try to see which kind of data could be used from one field to adapt to the other. Hence, we developed a model and a simulation platform to represent a double-auction setting to relate simulated data to experimental data that had been gathered by one of the authors.

The model is built on several types of knowledge: First we use some hypotheses enunciated by other researchers (Easley & Ledyard, 1993) on the cognitive abilities of agents when they are faced with this market situation; then the mechanisms of price revision were based on the expertise of the experiment specialist.

The cognition model we built enables us to represent convergence of the prices towards the equilibrium, and a reduction of deviation of prices in time. Moreover, we attain an inter-period convergence, showing that the agents actually learn some elements of their environment. However, we have not led enough simulations nor econometric tests to decide which of our algorithms gives results that would be reasonably close to humans behaviours. We thus have to progress in the methodological aspect of our work to relate simulations and experiments.

Even more worrying for our platform is the issue of time representation, which might have to be revised. For the moment, our artificial agents behave globally in a nonassessable manner. Indeed, although convergence is attained, the repartition of exchanges is clearly different from the one witnessed in experiments. The changing stress time which pushes the successful agents to stress later than they used to and the discrete time, create transaction jams at the end of the session. Strangely enough, the more successful the agent, the less chance it has to exchange at the next session.

This result made us look at simulations where stress time would be fixed during the whole simulation, and the first quick observations showed that the results seemed more reasonable than the one we had. This hypothesis that seemed reasonable (agents are less stressed when they succeed) and that we added to the Easley and Ledyard framework, seems to create trouble in the global functioning of the system. Further work will be done to refine the description of the cognition: Here the analysis of human data can be of clear help.

The next step in our work is to try to assess this cognition in a new way, using plainly the association between simulations and experiments. First we want to check behaviours on a step-by-step individual basis: giving our artificial agents the information of a human past actions at each step and see if they behave in the same way as humans. This evaluation brings us to an AI approach where individual cognition is studied.

To go back to a more distributed IA approach, we would have to integrate the represented humans in the assessment of the actions. We would like to make experiments mixing agents and humans in the same setting. First, humans could play with artificial agents as other potential transaction partners (Duffy, 2001), and the humans would be used as experts to spot strange phenomena and assess plausibility. Then artificial agents could be advisers for humans: We would evaluate how much this transforms the behaviour of humans. All these approaches rely a lot on our ability to build an econometric and precise evaluation of the data, now that our platform has been tested.

REFERENCES

Barreteau, O., & Bousquet, F. (2000). SHADOC: A multi-agent model to tackle viability of irrigated systems. *Annals of Operations Research, 94,* 139-162.

Bousquet, F., Barreteau, O., Mullon C., & Weber J. (1999). An environmental modelling approach: The use of multi-agents simulations. In F. Blasco, & A. Weill (Eds.), *Advances in environmental and ecological modelling* (pp. 113-122). Paris: Elsevier.

Brewer, P., Huang, M., Nelson, B., & Plott, C. (2002). On the behavioural foundations of the law of supply and demand: Human convergence and robot randomness. *Experimental economics, 5*, 179-208.

Duffy, J. (2001). Learning to speculate: Experiments with artificial and real agents. *Journal of Economic Dynamics and Control*, 25, 295-319.

Easley, D., & Ledyard, J. (1993). Theories of price formation and exchange in double-oral auction. In D. Friedman & J. Rust (Eds.), *The double auction market: Institutions, theories, and evidence* (pp. 63-97).Readin, MA: Addison-Wesley

Friedman, D. 1993. The double oral auction market institution: A survey. In D. Friedman & J. Rust (Eds.), *The double auction market: institutions, theories, and evidence* (pp. 3-26). Reading, MA: Addison-Wesley.

Gode, D., & Sunder, S. (1993). Allocative efficiency of markets with zero-intelligence traders: Markets as a partial substitute for individual rationality. *Journal of Political Economy, 101*, 119-137.

Gode, D., & Sunder, S. (1994). Human and artificially intelligent traders in a double auction market: Experimental evidence. In K. Carley & Prietula (Eds.), *Computational organization theory* (pp. 241-262). NJ: Lawrence Erlbaum Associates.

Hayek, F. A. (1945). The use of knowledge in society. *American Economic Review, 35*, 519-530.

Holt, C. (1995). Industrial organization: A survey of laboratory research. In J. H. Kagel & A.E. Roth (Eds.), *Handbook of experimental economics* (pp. 349-444). Princeton: Princeton University Press.

Noussair, C., Plott, C., & Riezman, R. (1995). An experimental investigation of the patterns of international trade. *The American Economic Review, 85*(3), 462-491.

Noussair, C., Robin, S., & Ruffieux, B. (1998). The effect of transactions costs on double auction markets. *Journal of Economic Behavior and Organization, 36*, 221-233.

Plott, C.R., & Smith V.L. (1978). An experimental examination of two exchange institutions. *The Review of Economic Studies, 45*, 133-153.

Plott, C.R. (1989). An updated review of industrial organization: Applications of experimental methods. In Schmalensee & Willig (Eds.), *Handbook of industrial organization*. North-Holland, pp 1109-1176.

Rouchier, J. (2006). Data gathering to build and validate small scale social models for simulation. In J.P. Rennard (Ed.), *Handbook of research on nature inspired computing for economics and management*. Hershey, PA: Idea Group Reference.

Smith, V. (1962). An experimental study of competitive market behavior. *Journal of Political Economy, 70*, 111-137.

Smith, V. & Williams V.A. (1989). The boundaries of competitive price theory: Convergence, expectations, and transaction costs. In L. Green & J. Kagel (Eds.), *Advances in behavioral economics, Vol. 2*. Norwood, NJ: Ablex Publishing.

Smith, V.L. (1994). Economics in the laboratory. *Journal of Economic Perspectives, 8*, 113-131.

Smith, V. (2002). Method in experiment: Rethoric and reality. *Experimental economics, 5*, 91-110.

Chapter XXIV
Stakeholder Participation in Investigating the Impact of E-Commerce Upon the Value Chain

Richard Taylor
Manchester Metropolitan University, UK

ABSTRACT

This chapter discusses qualitative and quantitative approaches to informing and validating ABMs. Research is introduced which addresses the question of how new e-commerce technology is leading to the restructuring of value chains. A case study was undertaken within a major international organisation, focusing on exploring those issues identified as interesting and important by a small stakeholder group working in the company and actively participating in the research. A central theme of this chapter is the interaction and relationship with stakeholders during the project, regarding the development of the ABM. The chapter concludes that a multi-methodological approach is appropriate to simulation-based projects, and identifies stakeholder participation as being useful in several ways, in particular because it facilitiates model validation.

INTRODUCTION

This chapter presents work which is both multi-method, uniting qualitative and quantitative approaches with agent-based modelling, and highly stakeholder-orientated, involving senior industry managers at different stages of the project. Whilst the latter point is going to be the main focus of this chapter, the first point remains important, particularly where it concerns stakeholder validation.

A detailed case study was undertaken within the power and automation division of a major international organisation. The research question concerns the nature of the impact that electronic commerce (or e-commerce, for short) technology is having upon the manufacturer, the downstream supply system, and the nature of relationships with distribution partners. The case study was carried out in 2001-2003 during a period of business process reengineering (BPR). The transformation programme was intended to develop "e-business" capability by integrating existing e-commerce systems with a new Internet-based electronic mall system specifically designed to improve links with customers. More precisely, it was thought that the transformation would improve information flow, customer service, and internal efficiency at the organisation. The paper describes managers' perceptions of the impacts of these changes upon the business and the implications for their traditional supply chain partners: the distributors.

Value chains and inter-organisational systems (IOS) have been shown to be a fruitful area for the application of agent-based techniques (Parunak & Vanderbok, 1998; Moss, Edmonds et al., 2000; Fioretti, 2001). The approach is well suited because the systems under investigation have certain properties (involvement of many heterogeneous actors, high interaction, decentralization, and communication infrastructure) that are typical of systems developed and studied by researchers in this field. Continuing along this line of investigation, the current work considers the introduction of a new ICT and models its impact upon the value chain. The research will be shown to illustrate that quantitative and qualitative methods can be usefully combined in formulating the model and that participation can help to target the objectives of simulation projects.

LITERATURE REVIEW

Essential to the creation and operation of supply systems is the provision of effective information flow between the various business processes: A frequent concern is that some of the links are not as good as others in this respect. Aimed at improving these networking aspects, one new information and communications technology (ICT) which appears to be impacting the supply chain is the Internet. The development of the Internet shows potential as a flexible "transportation layer" for a new generation of e-commerce applications.

Internet-based e-commerce was foreshadowed by earlier applications developed using Electronic Data Interchange (EDI) protocols for linking together large departments, providing propriety platforms for high-volume business data, in secure, yet relatively inflexible arrangements. Nowadays the Internet is seen as bringing a new set of characteristics to the e-commerce domain and there has been a take-off of interest in the technology. There has been a rapid commercialisation of the Internet as a new channel for providing product information and availability, marketing, ordering systems and order tracking, and powerful tools for handling customer-relations management.

Research has identified new organisational and market forms, and new opportunities and risks (Timmers, 1999; Turban, et al., 1999; Berryman, et al., 2000), as well as suggesting industries in which e-commerce may have a large impact, e.g., financial markets (Bakos et al., 2000), tourism and leisure (Chircu & Kauffman, 2000; McCubbrey, 1999), or car dealerships (Watson & McKeown, 1999; Marshall, et al., 2000). Notably, these are mainly the services industries involving a concentration of information processing activities which may be automated, decentralised, open to other potential improvements, or subject to competition from Internet-only companies, the so called "cybermediaries" (Jin & Robey, 1999).

The problem of disintermediation in the context of technological change has been studied closely by generations of researchers. More recently, in the early days of electronic networking technologies, researchers argued that we would see much disintermediation (Malone, et al., 1987; Tapscott, 1996) i.e., traditional intermediaries would be bypassed in the process of reshaping certain industrial sectors. Others have questioned whether this disintermediaton process is as universal as first suggested. For example, consider the more sophisticated model of Chircu and Kauffman (2000), who introduce the concept of the inter-mediation-disintermediation-reintermediation (IDR) framework which they argue applies to the introduction of new IT innovations that cause structural adjustments. The idea is that changing market conditions also bring new opportunities for intermediation to which the threatened intermediary should adapt, or reintermediate:

A disenfranchised traditional player is able to compete again by leveraging technological innovations with cospecialized assets. (Chircu & Kauffman, 2000)

Moreover, there are significant problems encountered by the initiators of technological transformations themselves. Experience with EDI implementaton suggested that the value of e-commerce depends upon how well it can be integrated with existing business systems and processes, and with those of partnering firms (Riggins & Mukhopadhyay, 1994). Comparing several case studies of trading partner uptake of EDI systems, Mukhodaphyay et al. (1995) conclude that the initiators of such systems have the most to gain from the network, but that they also carry the largest risks. Riggins and Mukhopadhyay (1999) identify two types of risk. Trading partners might not adopt the system (adoption risk), and even if they do, may not carry out satisfactory implementation, so the full benefits may not be realised (implementation risk). Adoption

risk might be due to a lack of organisational or technological readiness (Chau, 2001). Some of these problems have been solved by the ubiquity of the Internet, its flexibility, and perhaps above all its low cost, but some of them remain.

Fundamentally, the availability of new technological solutions creates a tension between the more technologically orientated companies wishing to coordinate more strongly, and their business partners, some of whom might be reluctant to change their existing processes.

Methodology

Case study research (Yin, 1994) was chosen for several reasons. First, it supplies real problems and issues to address. Second, it is likely to provide a good supply of qualitative and quantitative data with which to give empirical basis to the model. Third, it helps to establish stakeholders to evaluate the merit of ABM and research findings.

Large manufacturing companies based within the locality of the university were contacted based on prior links and stated interest in e-commerce. Initial contact was made through a telephone call, followed up by a letter of introduction containing a project overview. The procedure was to obtain the names of relevant people from administrators by asking to speak to e-commerce managers. The main problem that had not been anticipated was that the decision-making on e-commerce matters was often found to take place at a national or European level rather than with the local managers that were approached.

At Automata[1], initial meetings took place in February and March 2001 involving two managers, one of whom had been recently appointed as leader of the e-business team. The other manager was responsible for advising existing customers, many of whom he had a long established relationship with concerning the new opportunities available for e-commerce. These managers were self-selecting participants based on their having a special interest in the subject. They shall be referred to as the "stakeholders," since they occupy an important role in the research project, being co-investigators, domain experts, and project evaluators.[2] At this stage, their input was instructive in defining the problem, identifying research questions, and evaluating plausibility and practicality of the approach.

Later that year, semi-structured interviews took place with nine company employees. The interviewees were suggested by the stakeholders, and included people responsible for promoting e-commerce systems to business partners, and those using the EDI and Internet systems on a daily basis. Interview respondents were asked how they anticipated the impacts of Internet-based e-commerce on the function of the department and the likely benefits and problems associated with this transformation. Data were collected using a

tape recorder, and transcripts were made which were imported into ATLAS.ti for analysis.[3]

The model was programmed using the SDML (Wallis & Moss, 1994) platform. SDML is based on Smalltalk, which is a declarative, object oriented programming language. SDML was specifically designed for developing ABMs of social and economic scenarios, and has a large range of functionality that makes it highly suited to this task.

In order to improve the relevance and accuracy of the model, the findings were taken back into the field to involve the stakeholders in an iterative evaluation process. The objective is to create an interplay between data collection, model development, and validation. The arrow on the left of Figure 1 indicates the iteration of the redevelopment cycle.

Case studies allow a perspective that is fundamentally inclusive because they permit the collection of a wide spectrum of different data types. This study draws upon several different paradigms and combines individual methods, in particular integrating the qualitative with the quantitative. Integrative approaches are justified by the argument that flexibility in choice of research methods allows a richer understanding to develop of complex issues (such as the impact of technological change). This is what Mingers (2001) terms strong pluralism where *"all research situations are seen as inherently complex and multidimensional, and would thus benefit from a range of methods."*

The methods (outlined in Table 1) are listed with the corresponding research approach (un-

Figure 1. Methodology flow diagram

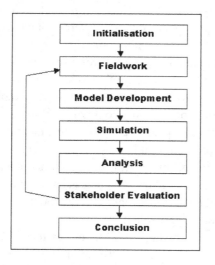

Table 1. Summary of the research methods

Method	Approach	Data Type
In-depth Interviews & Analysis	Interpretive	Qualitative (emergent findings)
Simulation Modelling	Formal	Qualitative & Quantitative
Stakeholder Evaluation	Interpretive	Qualitative
Mall Statistics	Positivist	Quantitative

derlying philosophical perspective) and the data types involved. Interviews and stakeholder evaluation generated qualitative inputs; quantitative data consisted of sales and marketing data. By the definition of Mingers (2001), this design is multi-method.

Both qualitative and quantitative data collection can be enhanced by stakeholder involvement. The role played by stakeholders is a type of participatory research method. Such methods involve other clients making significant contributions to the research process. Stakeholder involvement in ABM development is not entirely new, in particular it has been developed in natural resources and ecosystems management (see review by Bousquet & Le Page, 2004) where it has been well-received in a growing number of projects (Janssen, 2002; Barreteau et al., 2003) in particular, role-playing experiments. However, there is scarce literature concerning ABMs and participatory research within a *commercial* setting.

According to Easterby-Smith et al. (1991, p5-6), management research has three distinctive factors that must be taken into account: The practice of management is eclectic and cuts across technical, cultural, and functional boundaries, managers are powerful and busy people, and they are responsible for thought and decision-making and therefore capable of taking action based on new understandings or research results.

Both natural resources and commercial management research must be adaptable and sensitive to these three factors. Moreover, both endeavours are concerned with the existence of uncertainty (Simon, 1959; Cyert & March, 1963) having been influenced by formal modelling techniques in the field of decision theory. Meanwhile, there has been a parallel development of participatory or methods that combine experimental elements with cycles of learning and application to practice. Role-playing games, conceptual modelling, adaptive management research, and action research have become popular social science methods.

Participatory ABM-building issues are very similar for natural resources and organisational management and therefore so are the methodologies. The main difference could be related to, on the one hand, the strong commercial pressures on managers of firms and, on the other, managers' difficulties in satisfying conflicts over limited natural resources. It is not yet clear what, if any, differences this implies in the design of social simulation research. However, some insights gained from the current project will be discussed later.

Case Study Overview

As part of a large multinational based in the UK, the company manufactures a range of products to equip factories with industrial automation equipment. The market is exclusively business-to-business: Engineers work closely with customers, supplying technological expertise to help design new production facilities. The company has thousands of direct customers who are supplied directly from a central European store. There are also a large number of independent distributing companies (distributors) who hold stock locally, covering every region of the UK. Unlike the manufacturer, they provide for credit card purchases and are willing to take the financial risk of dealing with smaller customers. The distribution arrangement is shown in Figure 2.

The factory automation and power supply sector has some well developed systems for business-to-business e-commerce, and its market leaders demonstrate an organisational culture very supportive of the new technology. From the point of view of the organisation, which shall be known as Automata, e-commerce is seen as a critical set of opportunities to improve customer services provision in the short-term, and to provide key strategic advantages in the long-term.

The stakeholders' involvement helped to target the research towards relevant issues: Initial discussions established that it would be appro-

Figure 2. Market structure: Heavy lines show the flow of orders and normal lines show the market relationships presenting all other kinds of information flow.

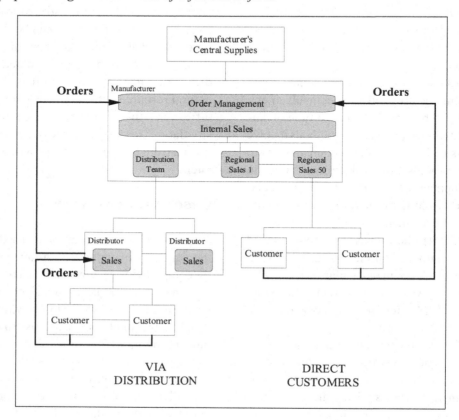

priate to focus on Customer Services (CS), the area that was estimated to be the most affected in the short-to-medium term by the introduction of the electronic mall. Moreover, there was some degree of uncertainty over policy-making options in this area.

At Automata, EDI is well-established and has been used with business partners (some distributors and some large customers) for a number of years. The focus now is on providing e-commerce to the remaining partners through the development of an Internet-based electronic mall tied into a gateway system, and operated in parallel with existing manual ordering systems. The proposed e-commerce system is shown in Figure 3. As the initiator, it is essential that the manufacturer set up processes to effectively manage the customer and distributor adoption of e-commerce. However, it appeared that the manufacturer was well aware of customer needs, carrying out customer readiness surveys, publicising and putting forward e-commerce to their distributors, and having a dedicated e-business team.

MODEL DESIGN

The research design intended three areas where the model could be compared with the target: (1) model assumptions are informed by interview data, (2) simulation results are compared with statistical logs from the mall, and (3) stakehold-

Figure 3. Proposed information infrastructure: Type of document is shown in a bold font and transmission medium is shown in italics.

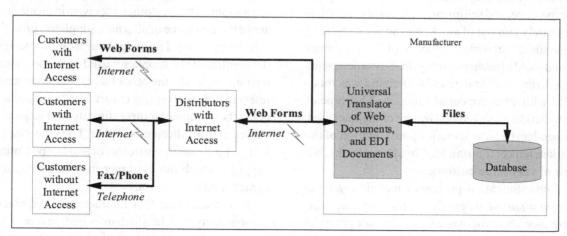

ers participate in an iterative evaluation and redevelopment process. Points (2) and (3) will be addressed in the discussion later. Because (1) does not concern stakeholder participation, it be covered only briefly here while introducing the model.

An ABM of the supply chain described in the previous section was developed, in which direct customers are supplied by a (single) manufacturer, and other customers are supplied by independent intermediaries. The model is simulated through discrete time-steps, called trading cycles, in which agents interact via market transactions and various communication interactions.

Customer and intermediary agents are located on a grid where the concept of "neighbourhood" is important in defining how interactions take place: A neighbourhood is defined as the area including eight squares in each of the cardinal directions (North, South, East, and West), and neighbours are all the agents lying within these squares. The geographical aspect is important because communication takes place exclusively amongst neighbouring agents. Second, local distribution services are highly valued by some customers.

It is assumed that technological competence of distributors varies:

Some of our distributors are much better than others: some are more technically competent. They employ the right people with the right backgrounds and training. At this moment in time I have some reservations about the ability of some of our distributors to serve our customers in the way we would like. (P4)

High, low, and medium levels of technical competence are modelled (by coding with the integer values 1, 2, and 3, respectively). By comparison, it is assumed that the technical competence of the manufacturer (in terms of knowledge of the products, and product areas in which they operate) is at the medium level.

Intermediaries make a profit on their sales because they buy at a discounted price and sell on to customers at a higher "selling price." Intermediaries that are not profitable, having zero profits over the trading cycle, (i.e., they do not achieve any sales) are removed from the simulation in subsequent cycles.

Intermediary agents are therefore distinguished by geographical location, technological competence, and selling price. In reality, distributors rarely run out of stock, and so for simplicity we assume that replenishment equals the number of units sold in each trading cycle. Customer agents also differ in their demands. Demand was modelled with an exponential function. This type of distribution was sketched by one of the interview respondents as a schematic approximation of the market: tens of thousands of small customers, but tens of very large customers.

Communication processes include *referrals communication*, where the customer receives information about the existence of alternate potential suppliers, and *"endorsements" communication,* or influence processes. Referrals communication appears in two varieties. "Customer referrals" is defined as the process where, in each trading cycle,

the customer has a "word of mouth" communication interaction with one of its neighbours, chosen at random. The customer receives information about the existence of alternate suppliers through this interaction: The neighbour communicates the identity of the supplier it used in the previous trading cycle. On the other hand, "manufacturer referrals" describes the case where a customer contacts the manufacturer directly and requests a referral to an alternate supplier. Then the manufacturer informs the customer of another potential supplier, which the customer may subsequently contact and order from.

It was assumed that interactions take place among customers, in which information is passed about the characteristics of the supplier and about the nature of the electronic mall. Fieldwork analysis identified several hypotheses about e-commerce (HEC) and about distributors (HINT)

Table 2. The HEC and the HINT

HEC
It is extra work for us to use the mall compared to a manual system
Almost everybody will soon be using Internet-EC: We should be doing it too
Instantaneous and quick access to information (compared to traditional channels) is a benefit to us
The 24-hour availability of access provided by the mall is of benefit to my company
The provision of up-to-date and accurate information on the mall is of benefit to us
The digitisation of product data sheets and the availability of software updates is a benefit
The reduced possibility of errors occurring in orders going through the mall is a benefit
The provision of more user-friendly ways of accessing account information on the mall is a benefit
It is expensive for us to set up and maintain Internet-based systems compared to manual ones
I am concerned about security issues with Internet-based systems compared to manual systems
I am receptive to Internet-based EC because I expect we shall receive extra discounts if we adopt
I am concerned about the lack of technical support and experience within the company of using EC
I am receptive to EC because I expect we will receive more customer referrals if we adopt
HINT
The supplier offers a good discount on the selling price of the product
I am concerned that the distributor may lack technical competence
The location (ability to offer a local service) of the supplier is a benefit

considered by the interview respondents to be influential in shaping attitudes (see Table 2).

This communicated information, which was labelled *statement* is one type of "endorsement": Agent reasoning is based on an "endorsements scheme" derived from the work of Cohen (1985). Endorsements can be viewed as reasons to believe or disbelieve a hypothesis. In the model, agents collate data relating to hypotheses about intermediary performance and about the benefits and disadvantages of using Internet-EC. Information is gathered through interactions with neighbouring agents, with the manufacturer, and through experience of using the Internet-EC system. The endorsements scheme uses a lexicographical ranking system whereby different beliefs are assigned a different level of importance: Those regarded as more important take precedence over lesser ones when agents take decisions. The advantage of an endorsements scheme is that it allows the use of qualitative data to initialise the model, and preserves the structure of that data throughout the course of the simulation.

Agents are endowed either with a manual-card-based or IT-computer-based systems. Two IOS also exist for placing orders—FAX-telephone or EDI. They can subsequently adopt the Internet mall system for ordering (direct customers) or for collecting information (intermediated customers).

Automata's e-commerce strategy is to ensure that customers and distributors are informed of new possibilities for doing business electronically and, moreover, to encourage and provide incentives to use their systems. These incentives would include offering financial support (funding and equipment) to help with setting up EC, technical support and training for use of EC systems, and a discount incentive, as became clear through the fieldwork:

We are starting to incentivise them by giving them an extra percent [of discount] if they can trade with us electronically. (P8)

It may be a case of getting somebody to get in his car and go round and see everybody and promote it and say 'this is how to do it' and get people in there and help customers set it up because they haven't always got the resources to put time into setting it up at their end. (P7)

SDML clauses were defined to represent EC Set-Up, EC Technical, and EC Discount support strategies, providing arguments for the amount of support and trading cycle when the offer is made. This permits flexibility for exploring the role of manufacturer interventions in shaping customer attitudes.

SIMULATION OF SCENARIOS

The scenarios presented here include different specifications of agent interaction and communication, with manufacturer strategies for the support of EC adoption. Taylor (2003) includes further results, including sensitivity analysis of model outcomes to initial conditions and different parameterisations of the model.

The first two scenarios, S1 and S2, compare two different communication processes. S1 explores customer referrals via "word of mouth" communication, whilst S2 explores manufacturer referrals. The addition of new links (i.e., possible choices of supplier) can be interpreted as a trend of increasing competition for customers. For illustration, Figures 4 and 5 show comparison of single runs initialised with the same random seed.

Examining intermediaries' market share (Figure 4a), large variation in the first few cycles of the simulation is noticable. Then, from around TC40, a group of four distributors having high sales volumes can be observed clearly separating from the rest. Whereas the largest distributor, intermediary-14, reaches 1,687 units at TC100, and the second, third, and fourth largest all manage sales of 900+ units, there is a clear cut-off point between these four and the rest of the distributors,

Figure 4. Manufacturer referrals scenario (S1) results showing time series of intermediary sales (a:top panel), intermediary profits (b:middle panel), and number of adopters/users (c:bottom panel)

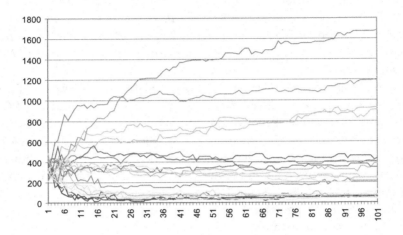

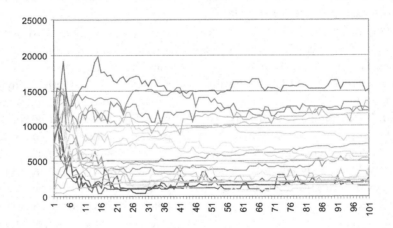

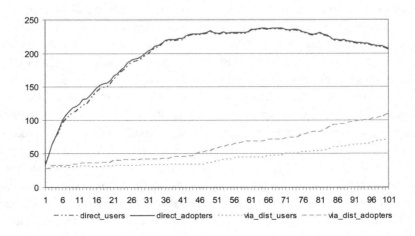

all of which manage sales of under 500 units per cycle, from TC 20 onwards. In fact, in the later stages of the simulation, the four larger distributors receive orders for more than twice as many units as the next largest distributor. Profits are more evenly distributed, however, with five large distributors sharing a similar amount of profits, at around 10-15,000 each, but also with a group of six medium-sized distributors making profits of 5-10,000, and the rest making between 1-5,000 profits. In this simulation, all intermediaries survive until TC100. Seventeen of them are consistent users of Internet-EC.

The number of users of EC is high for direct customers, reaching a maximum of 236 at TC64. As illustrated in Figure 4c, the number of users gradually drops after TC70. This is because the addition of new adopters is slower than the decline in total number of direct customers: Shifting direct customers to distributors was a parallel manufacturer policy being simulated. The graph also illustrates a notable gap between the number of adopters and the number of users via distribution, revealing that some customers, after having adopted the mall, subsequently stop using it.

In contrast to the first scenario, in S2 customer referrals are specified rather than manufacturer referrals. Figures 5a and b were obtained from the same simulation run, specifying customer referrals but no communication of endorsements. The results in Figure 5a show the domination of the intermediation function by a single intermediary, intermediary-14, obtaining more than twice the volume of sales of the second largest (2,685 units compared to 1,319 units). Although five intermediaries manage sales volumes of greater than 500 units, there is high inequality. The majority has sales of less than 200. This inequality is also reflected in the result that there is one intermediary casualty: Intermediary-2 survives only up until TC19. The largest intermediary also makes a profit of more than 18,795 in TC100 (an increase of 24 percent over S1). In fact, Figure 5b shows a sharp decline in profits for many

Figure 5. Time series of intermediary sales (top panel), intermediary profits (middle panel) of customer referrals scenario (S2), and number of adopters/users (bottom panel) of customer referrals with endorsements scenario (S3).

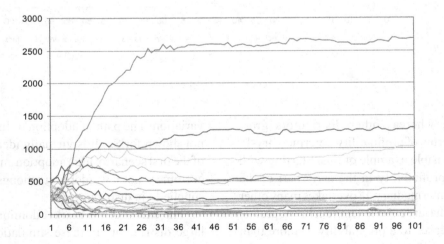

continued on next page

Figure 5 continued

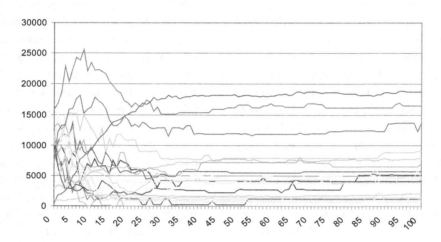

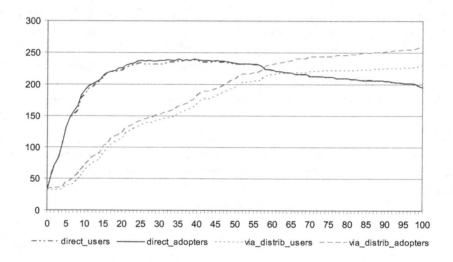

distributors, whereas other distributors grow quickly in terms of profitability. Intermediary-18 is the most visible example of this: Starting with a very low profitability in the early part of the simulation, Intermediary-18 overtakes many other distributors that are experiencing declining profits, rapidly increases to a profitability of more than 15,000 by cycle 20, and becomes the most profitable intermediary in TC27. Compared to S1, this simulation exhibits greater short-to-medium-term

variation. The path of adoption of Internet-EC is not shown for S2. It is virtually identical to that of the first scenario: high adoption amongst direct customers but low adoption amongst customers supplied via distribution.

The extent of the market domination by few large distributors in these simulations gives us an important result: It suggests that customer referrals, a local "word of mouth" customer-to-customer communication, leads to more distributor

Figure 6. Log of cumulative sales—customer referrals with communication of endorsements (S3)

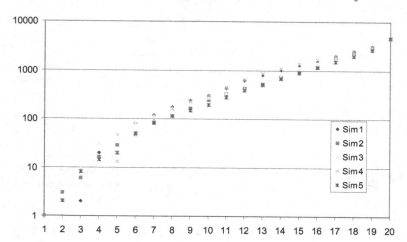

inequality compared to manufacturer referrals. It results in large majorities of customers choosing the same (few) suppliers.

In the simulation shown in Figure 5c, where agents collate endorsements, the number of customers via distribution reaches a maximum of 260 agents in TC100. This is approximately three times as many as in the case without endorsements (83) or in S1 (109), whilst the number of direct adopters is approximately the same. This suggests the increase in intermediated customers adopting must be attributed to the communication of endorsements during those interactions. Communication of endorsement drives the high level of adoption: Through customer-to-customer persuasion interactions, intermediated customers can collect information relating to the benefits (and disadvantages) of e-commerce. In this case, many of them are persuaded to adopt.

Finally, Figure 6 shows the results of a test for the existence of the Pareto Power Law distribution, which states that there is a logarithmic relationship between the cumulative frequency of events (in this case, number of units sold) and the smallest to largest ordering of objects to which those events are ascribed (in this case, intermediaries). The figure shows five plots for the small simulations[4] with customer referrals without endorsements communication. Excepting the first two or three data points, there appears to be a linear relationship.

The following simulation experiments consider manufacturer support strategies for Internet-based EC: support with EC set-up, with technical knowledge, and extra discounts. All of these simulations are carried out with customer referrals and endorsements communication without preferential referrals. Results of the four simulations are shown in Figure 7, where the number of users is plotted against time cycle on a single graph. It is clear that in the simulation runs where no support is offered to direct customers, usage is the lowest (43 customers in TC 100) whereas, offering some kind of support always results in a higher level of usage. This is not surprising since the model assumed that the customers always view these support interventions positively. In the "Set-Up Support Only" simulation there is a small increase to 56 customers, and in "Technical Support Only," there is an increase to 62 customers. The "Extra Discounts" incentive resulted in the largest increase in level of usage to 69 customers (a 60 percent increase over "No Support").

Figure 7. Time series of simulation of manufacturer support strategies (S3)

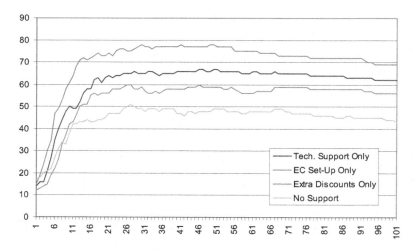

Figure 7 also demonstrates *s*-shaped adoption and usage curves, indicating a slow initial take-up, moving into a period of faster adoption, and gradually slowing to a saturation point after about thirty cycles. This is an important result because it shows that the model exhibits an outcome resembling a pattern identified in empirical studies of technology diffusion. Further model details and analysis of simulation experiments can be found in Taylor (2003).

DISCUSSION

The earlier section showed how the interview data were used to inform model assumptions. This section discusses the points (2) and (3) concerning model validation, reintroducing the stakeholders to do so.

Collaboration between the researcher and the stakeholders entailed frequent e-mail, telephone, and face-to-face discussions and presentations. The aim was to develop the partnership and an understanding of the project. The participation was organised to best fit into the agendas of the

stakeholders, according to the research needs at the time.

Consultation always took place at the headquarters of Automata, using their facilities. The model was not intended to be used directly in these sessions, although on one occasion a demonstration was given. This experience showed that it was quite difficult to explain, in one sitting, details of the implementation. Also, the set of input parameters were too large and the visualisations in this case, not particularly helpful. A simpler model, linked to some conceptual modelling beforehand, could have been more successful.

The stakeholders brought some statistical data detailing the recent performance of the Internet mall to one of these meetings. Figure 8, a chart produced by one of the stakeholders, shows the number of mall orders and the total number of order lines included in those orders.

Order lines specify type of product and number of units required. Orders therefore range from the very large (many units of many different types of product) to the very small (a single line requesting one unit) Mall statistics therefore only give an estimation of the value of Internet sales. The

Figure 8. Mall statistics chart produced by one of the stakeholders

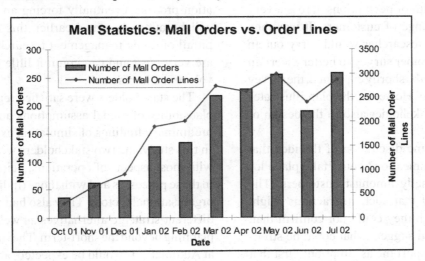

chart illustrates an increasing number of orders and order lines over the period October 2001 to July 2002. In addition, there were increasing numbers of customer adopters (i.e., registered users on the Web site) over this period. There were 35 customers submitting a total of 36 orders during the month of October 2001 (1.029 orders per customer) compared with 201 customers submitting 258 orders during July 2002 (1.284 orders per customer) which represents an increase of 25 percent in orders per customer. They submitted an increasing number of order lines: from 306 lines in 36 orders (an average 8.5 lines per order) to 2,882 lines in 258 orders (an average 11.17 lines per order), an increase of 31 percent. This represents a significant increase in transaction volumes and indicates that customers may feel increasingly at ease with the new system.

In the research design, point (2) marks the comparison between macro outputs of the model and empirical data of a similar nature. The mall statistics provided a general outline of what *macrolevel behaviour* the model should be capable of producing. Statistical testing, as exemplified in the cross-validation approach (Moss & Edmonds, 2005), cannot be carried out using such a dataset.

That the ABM generated textbook patterns of adoption and use of e-commerce does not constitute a strong validation of the simulation. It does, however, show that the simulation system behaves plausibly across different scenarios.

The more stringent test of validation is the qualitative validation of *microlevel behaviour*: point (3) mentioned earlier. This aspect relies upon the participation of the stakeholders in an iterative evaluation and redevelopment process. It involves assessing both the assumptions upon which the model is based and the microbehaviour of simulated agents in terms of their plausibility, as outlined in Downing et al. (2003).

In the participatory sessions, model assumptions were discussed, for example, the set of hypothesised drivers and inhibitors of Internet e-commerce (Table 2). During the fieldwork, some factors were more frequently or emphatically highlighted by a respondent. Responses guided an initial ranking of these hypotheses in terms of importance. Discussing these findings with the stakeholders and describing the model that was being developed then helped to refine the rankings used in the endorsements model. Whilst Automata thought they had identified many of these factors, they realised that they knew very little about breadth of perceptions across a very heterogeneous range of customers. It was then planned that the researcher would carry out an independent customer survey to better ascertain this. For reasons to be shortly explained, the survey did not take place. However, the plan illustrates the role of the stakeholder also in the design of the research.

There was some discussion of the idea that "referrals communication" could take place locally and informally amongst customers. The stakeholders said that such interactions might take place, though they could not confirm that. However, they did suggest what could be stronger reasons to support the assumption: First that customer-customer interactions might also take place indirectly through visits from members of the Regional Sales teams (i.e., the engineer might report what other customers are doing), and second through staff turnover (employees move from company to company, bringing new ideas with them). These discussions provided additional factual and nuanced information and demonstrated how stakeholder participation can improve and strengthen the process of model development.

The participation of the stakeholders enabled iteration of the evaluation loop described in Figure 1. However, there were some unforeseen difficulties related to the changing circumstances within the company, which hindered the redevelopment cycle. The imminent arrival of a new director and of the approaching retirement of one of the stakeholders would, it was anticipated, provoke changes both in the way the department was run and in the focus of development for the e-commerce team. After the initial high level of enthusiasm for the project, these factors led to a lessening of involvement in the project in the face of more pressing commitments. Stakeholder evaluation meetings were therefore shorter and fewer than had been expected. The consequences of this reduced involvement were: lack of access

to data, difficulties in completing the model evaluation process, eventually forcing an end to the collaboration. As stated earlier, this is a typical pitfall of doing management research: Contacts are very busy and can commit little time to involvement in research.

The stakeholders were satisfied regarding the plausibility of model assumptions and with the preliminary findings of simulation experiments. In this study, the two stakeholders were familiar with most aspects of operations, being involved in those processes and with those (individual and organisational) actors. They also had to consider different strategic alternatives as well as future planning beyond the short-term. The stakeholders at Automata, as would be expected, are sensitive to results that "do not look right," i.e., not like anything they have observed or, in the case of scenario development, believe to be plausible. The stakeholders did not understand the model in the fullest sense of tracing the microbehaviours of embedded agents and building up accounts of agents' perceptions, interactions, and decisions. Providing explanations for behavioural outcomes in this manner (see Taylor, 2003, 187 for an example) was the intended approach for the participatory sessions, but was not carried out. Method (3) of comparing the simulation model with the target was therefore only partially realised, in the iterative evaluation of model assumptions and agents' rules and preferences.

CONCLUSION

Methodological issues have been addressed about the nature of stakeholder involvement in agent-based simulation projects, and about the possible ways to validate a model with different kinds of empirical data. Questions arising from case study inquiry concerned the impact of Internet-EC on the supply chain, and in particular the implications for the traditional intermediaries: the distributors. Fieldwork analysis was supportive of a weak disintermediation hypothesis—that some limited disintermediation could be expected, and that this could form part of a manufacturer strategy to improve information flow throughout the value chain.

The approach used was base model development on qualitative and quantitative information provided by the stakeholders and interviews with respondents identifying the main units of agency and processes involved. Subsequently, the ABM was employed to explore the areas of uncertainty concerning the nature and effects of communication among customers. Automata knew very little about these processes, it being problematic to collect such information. Further uncertainty existed over the kind of support strategies that would need to be employed.

The model development cycle was reported, wherein the stakeholders also contributed to the evaluation of the research in several ways. These validation procedures were carried out in order to help establish confidence in the plausibility and relevance of the model to the case. It is worth noting that the number of stakeholders involved here was very small. This illustrates the fact that the success of a research project involving industrial partners depends critically upon getting the attention and interest of one or two key managers. Indeed, it may be difficult to get an initial "foot in the door" of the organisation. But once this can be secured, it can illustrate the principle described by Hammersley and Atkinson (1983, p. 60) as informal "sponsorship" that serves to validate the presence of the researcher and pave the way for access. Furthermore, as in this case study, the sponsoring individual(s) are likely to be willing to fulfill the stakeholder role. There are difficulties associated with this methodology which have also been seen: Obtaining required access to these people can be problematic and changing circumstances can curtail the research.

Whilst it should be emphasised that formal models cannot substitute for multiple case studies

informed by qualitative research, it appears that is much to be gained from using ABM in parallel. In essence, this is the argument for multimethodology: a debate which is attracting much attention in the area of management of information systems. On the basis of findings reported in this chapter in commercial or organisational research settings, ABM can be proposed as one such alternative.

ACKNOWLEDGMENT

The author would like to thank Professor Scott Moss, Dr. Bruce Edmonds, and Professor Ray Hackney for their guidance, and he would also like to thank his associates at Automata for their contributions to the project. He would like to thank colleagues at ESSA and the anonymous referee for helpful comments.

REFERENCES

Bakos, Y., Lucas, H.C. Jr., Oh, W., Simon, G., Viswanathan, S. & Weber, B. (2000). *The Impact of Electronic Commerce on the Retail Brokerage Industry*. New York, Stern School of Business: New York University.

Barreteau, O., Le Page, C., & D'Aquino, P. (2003). Role-playing games, models and negotiation processes. *Journal of Artificial Societies and Social Simulation, 6*(2). Retrieved January 13, 2007, from http://jasss.soc.surrey.ac.uk/6/2/10.html

Berryman, K., Harrington, L.F, Layton-Rodin, D. & ReRolle, V. (2000). Electronic commerce: Three emerging strategies. *The McKinsey Quarterly, 3,* 129-136.

Bousquet, F. &Le Page, C. (2004) Multi-agent simulations and ecosystem management: A review. *Ecological Modelling, 176,* 313-332.

Chau, P.Y.K. (2001). Inhibitors to EDI adoption in small businesses: An empirical investigation. *Journal of Electronic Commerce Research 2*(3).

Chircu, A.M., & Kauffman, R. (2000). Reintermediation strategies in business-to-business electronic commerce. *International Journal of Electronic Commerce, 4*(4), 7-42.

Cohen, P.R. (1985). *Heuristic reasoning about uncertainty: An artificial intelligence approach.* London: Pitman.

Cyert, R.H., & March, J.G. (1963). *A behavioural theory of the firm.* Prentice-Hall.

Downing, T.E., Moss, S., & Pahl-Wostl, C. (2003). Understanding climate policy using participatory agent-based social simulation. In S. Moss & P. Davidsson (Eds.), *Multi agent based social simulation.* Springer, 198-213.

Easterby-Smith, M., Thorpe, R., & Lowe, A. (1991). *Management research : An introduction.* London: Sage.

Fioretti, G. (2001). Information structure and behaviour of a textile industrial district. *Journal of Artificial Societies and Social Simulation (JASSS) 4*(4). Retrieved January 13, 2007 from, http:// jasss.soc.surrey.ac.uk/4/4/1.html

Janssen, M. (2002). *Complexity and ecosystem management: The theory and practice of multi-agent systems.* Cheltenham: Edward Elgar Publishing.

Jin, L., & Robey, D. (1999). ,Explaining cybermediation: An organizational analysis of electronic retailing. *International Journal of Electronic Commerce, 3*(4).

Hammersley, M., &. Atkinson, P. (1983). *Ethnography:Principles in practice.* London: Tavistock Publications.

Malone, T. W., Yates, J., & Benjamin, R. (1987). Electronic markets and electronic eierarchies. *Communications of the ACM , 30*(6), 484-497.

Marshall, P., Sor, R., & Mckay, J. (2000). An industry case study of the impacts of electronic commerce on car dealerships in Western Australia, *Journal of Electronic Commerce Research, 1*(1), 1-16.

McCubbrey, D. J. (1999). Disintermediation and reintermediation in the U.S. air travel distribution industry: A Delphi study. *Communications of the Association for Information Systems, 1.*

Mingers, J. (2001). Combining IS research methods: Towards a pluralist methodology. *Information Systems Research, 12*(3), 240-259.

Moss, S., Edmonds, B., & Wallis, S. (2000). *The power law and critical density in large multi agent systems.* CPM Report No. 71, Manchester Metropolitan University.

Moss, S., & Edmonds, B. (2005). Sociology and simulation: Statistical and qualitative cross-validation. *American Journal of Sociology, 110*(4).

Mukhodaphyay, T., Kekre, S., & Kalathur, S. (1995). Business value of information technology: A study of electronic data interchange, *MIS Quarterly, 19*(2), 137-156.

Parunak, V., & Vanderbok, R. (1998). *Modeling the extended sypply network.* ISA Tech'98, Houston, Texas.

Porter, M.E. (1985). *Competitive advantage: Creating and sustaining superior performance.* New York: Free Press.

Riggins, F.J., & Mukhopadhyay, T. (1994). Interpdependent benefits from interorganizational systems: Opportunities for business partner re-engineering. *Journal of Management Information Systems, 11*(2), 37-57.

Riggins, F.J., & Mukhopadhyay, T. (1999). Overcoming EDI adoption and implementation risks. *International Journal of Electronic Commerce, 3*(4), 103.

Simon, H. A. (1959). *Administrative behaviour* (2nd ed.). Macmillan.

Tapscott, D. (1996). *The digital economy: Promise and peril in the age of networked intelligence.* New York and London: McGraw-Hill.

Taylor, R.I. (2003). *Agent-based modelling incorporating qualitative and quantitative methods: A case study investigating the impact of e-commerce upon the value chain.* Unpublished PhD Thesis, Manchester Metropolitan University.

Timmers, P. (1999). *Electronic commerce: Strategies and models for business-to-business trading.* New York: Wiley.

Turban, E., Lee, J., King, D., & Chung, H.M. (1999). *Electronic commerce: A managerial perspective.* Prentice Hall.

Wallis, S., & Moss. S. (1994). Efficient forward chaining for declarative rules in a multi-agent modelling language, *CPM Report No.: 004,* Manchester Metropolitan University

Watson, R.T., & McKeown, P.G. (1999). Manheim auctions: Transforming interorganizational relationships with an extranet. *International Journal of Electronic Commerce, 3*(4), 29-46.

Yin, R.K. (1994). *Case study research: Design and methods.* London, Sage.

ENDNOTES

[1] For marketing reasons, the organisation did not wish their identity to be known, so the organisational pseudonym Automata has been adopted here.

[2] Stakeholders can be distinguished from other industry contacts by their participatory role in determining the scope, objectives, and methods of the research, as well as in its evaluation.

[3] Scientific Software Development's ATLAS. ti is widely used by researchers in the social and management sciences to organise their primary data and to facilitate the qualitative analysis. The main benefit of using ATLAS for model development lies in making explicit the mapping of case data to model assumptions.

[4] Large and small simulations were carried out, where the size of grid and number of agents differed. Unless noted otherwise, all simulations reported here refer to the large simulations.

Compilation of References

Abke, W. (2001). Wasserversorgung. In K. Lecher, H.-P. Lühr, & U. Zanke (Eds.), *Taschenbuch der Wasserwirtschaft*. Berlin: Parey.

Ahrweiler, P., Gilbert, N., & Pyka, A. (2001). Innovation networks—A simulation approach. *Journal of Artificial Societies and Social Simulation, 4*(3).

Ajzen, I. (1988). *Attitudes, personality, and behavior*. Chicago: Dorsey Press.

Allingham, M.G., & Sandmo, A. (1994). Income tax evasion: A theoretical analysis. *Journal of Public Economics, 1*, 323-338.

Alm, J., Jackson, B.R., & McKee, M. (2004). The effects of communication among taxpayers on compliance. *The IRS Research Bulletin*, 37-48.

Alter, C., & Hage, J. (1993). *Organizations working together*. Newbury Park, CA: Sage.

Amblard F., & Deffuant, G. (2004). The role of network topology on extremism propagation with relative agreement opinion dynamics. *Physica A., 343*, 725-738.

Andreae, L., & Kaiser, K. (1998). Die "Außenpolitik" der fachministerien. In W.Eberwein, & K. Kaiser (Eds.). *Deutschlands neue außenpolitik, 4*, 29-46. München: Oldenbourg.

Andreoni, J., Erard, B., & Feinstein, J.S. (1998). Tax compliance. *Journal of Economic Literature, 36*, 818-860.

Antcliff, S. (1993). *An introduction to DYNAMOD–A dynamic population microsimulation model*. Canberra, Australia: National Centre for Social and Economic Modelling.

Arifovic, J. (2001). Evolutionary dynamics of currency substitution. *Journal of Economic Dynamics & Control, 25*, 395-417.

Arrow, K.J. (1986). Rationality of self and others in an economic system. *Journal of Business, 59*(4.2), S385-S399. Reprinted in Hogarth & Reder (1987) and in J. Eatwell, M. Milgate, &P. Newman, Peter (Eds.), *The new palgravedictionary of economics*,

Arthur, B. (1994). Inductive reasoning and bounded rationality. *American Economic Association Papers, 84*, 406-411.

Arthur, W. B., Holland, J.H., LeBaron, B., Palmer, R.G., & Taylor, P. (1997). Asset pricing under endogenous expectations in an artificial stock market. In *The Economy as an Evolving Complex System II* (pp.15-44). Addison-Wesley.

Arthur, W.B. (1994). Inductive reasoning, bounded rationality and the bar problem. *American Economics Association Papers and Proceedings 84*, 406.

Arthur, W.B., Holland, J. H., LeBaron, B., Palmer, R., & Taylor, P. (1994). Artificial economic life: A simple model of a stock market. *Physica D 7*, 264-274.

Axelrod, R. (1970). *Conflict of interest*. Chicago: Markham.

Axelrod, R. (1984). *The evolution of cooperation*. Basic Books: New York.

Axelrod, R. (1997). *The complexity of cooperation—Agent-based model of competition and collaboration*. Princeton University Press.

Axelrod, R., & D'Ambrosio, L. (1994). *Annotated bibliography on the evolution of cooperation.* Retrieved from http://www.cscs.umich.edu/research/Publications/Evol_of_Coop_Bibliography.html

Axtell, R. (2000). Why agents? On the varied motivation for agent computing in the social sciences, T*he Brookings Institution Center on Social and Economic Dynamics Working Paper*, November, No.17.

Back, I., & Flache, A. (2006). The viability of cooperation based on interpersonal commitment. *Journal of Artificial Societies and Social Simulation*, 9(1) 12. http://www.soc.surrey.ac.uk./JASSS/

Bakos, Y., Lucas, H.C. Jr., Oh, W., Simon, G., Viswanathan, S. & Weber, B. (2000). *The Impact of Electronic Commerce on the Retail Brokerage Industry.* New York, Stern School of Business: New York University.

Baldi, P., & Brunak, S. (2001). *Bioinformatics: The machine learning approach.* Cambridge, MA: MIT Press.

Bankes, S. (1993). Exploratory modelling for policy analysis. *Operational Research, 41*, 435-449.

Bankes, S. (2002). Tools and techniques for developing policies for complex and uncertain systems. *PNAS*-May 14, Vol. 99, supplment 3, 7263-7266; www.pnas.org/cgi/doi/10.1073/pnas. 092081399

Bankes, S., & Gillogly, J. (1994). Exploratory modelling: Search through spaces of computational experiments. In *Proceedings of the Third Annual Conference on Evolutionary Programming.* http://www. evolvinglogic.com/Learn/absandpapers/explsearch. html

Bankes, S., & Lempert, R.J. (1996). Adaptive strategies for abating climate change: An example of policy analysis for aomplex adaptive systems. In L. Fogel, P. Angeline, & T. Back (Eds.), *Evolutionary programming V: Proceedings of the fifth annual conference on evolutionary programming*, (pp. 17-25). Cambridge, MA: MIT Press.

Banks, D.L., & Carley, K.M. (1996). Models for network evolution. *Journal of Mathematical Sociology, 21*(1-2), 173-196.

Barreteau, O. (2003). The joint use of role-playing games and models regarding negotiation processes: Characterization of associations. *Journal of Artificial Societies and Social Simulation, 6*(2). http://jasss.soc.surrey.ac.uk/6/2/3.html

Barreteau, O., et al. (2003). Our companion modelling approach. *Journal of Artificial Societies and Social Simulation, 6*(2). http://jasss.soc.surrey.ac.uk/6/2/1.html

Barreteau, O., & Bousquet, F. (2000). SHADOC: A multi-agent model to tackle viability of irrigated systems. *Annals of Operations Research, 94*, 139-162.

Barreteau, O., Le Page, C., & D'Aquino, P. (2003). Role-playing games, models and negotiation processes. *Journal of Artificial Societies and Social Simulation, 6*(2). Retrieved January 13, 2007, from http://jasss.soc.surrey.ac.uk/6/2/10.html

Barth, M., Hennicker, R., Kraus, A., & Ludwig, M. (2004). DANUBIA: An integrative simulation system for global change research in the Upper Danube basin. *Cybernetics and Systems, 35*(7-8), 639-666.

Bazerman, M. (1998), *Judgment in managerial decision making.* John Wiley & Sons.

Bendor, J., & Swistak, P. (2001). The evolution of norms. *American Journal of Sociology, 106*, 1493-545.

Ben-Naim, E., Krapivsky, P.L.,Vazquez, F., & Redner, S. (2003). Unity and discord in opinion dynamics. *Physica A., 330*(1-2), 99-106

Benson, J.F. (Ed.). (1995). *Journal of Environmental Planning and Management 38*(1). *Special Issue: The NERC/ESRC Land Use Modeling Programme.*

Berends, J.J., Debackere, K., Garud, R., & Weggeman, M.P.C.D. (2004). *Knowledge integration by thinking along* (Working Paper 04.05). Nedlands, Eindhoven Centre for Innovation Studies.

Berger, T. (2001). Agent-based spatial models applied to agriculture: A simulation tool for technology diffusion, resource use changes, and policy analysis. *Agricultural Economics, 25*(2-3), 245-260.

Bergstrom, T.C., & Miller, J.H. (1977). *Experiments with economic principles: Microeconomics*. New York: McGraw-Hill.

Bernasconi, M. (1998). Tax evasion and orders of risk aversion. *Journal of Public Economics*, 67, 123-134.

Berryman, K., Harrington, L.F., Layton-Rodin, D. & Re-Rolle, V. (2000). Electronic commerce: Three emerging strategies. *The McKinsey Quarterly*, *3*, 129-136.

Bischof, N. (1998) *Struktur und bedeutung: Eine einfuehrung in die Systemtheorie*. Bern: Verlag Hans Huber.

Black, D. (1958). *The theory of committees and elections*. Cambridge: Cambridge University Press.

Black, F., & Litterman, R. (1992). Global portfolio optimization, *Financial Analysts Journal*, September-October, 28-43.

Black, S., & Lynch, L.M. (1996). Human capital investments and productivity. *American Economic Review*, *86*(2), 263-267.

Blau, P. M. (1977). *Inequality and heterogeneity*. New York: Free Press.

Bloomquist, K.M. (2003). Trends as changes in variance: The case of tax noncompliance. *The IRS Research Bulletin*, 59-66.

Bloomquist, K.M. (2003). Tax evasion, income inequality and opportunity costs of compliance. *National Tax Association Proceedings*, 91-104.

Bloomquist, K.M. (2004, September). *A comparison of agent-based models of income tax evasion*. Paper presented at the 2nd Annual Conference of the European Social Simulation Association and Model-to-Model Workshop, Valladolid, Spain.

Bloomquist, K.M. (2004). Multi-agent based simulation of the deterrent effects of taxpayer audits. *National Tax Association Proceedings*, 159-173.

Bohm, V. (1983). Quantity rationing vs. IS-LM: A synthesis. *Discussion Paper*. N. 252-83, University at Mannheim.

Boissau, S. (2005). Co-evolution of a research question and methodological development: an example of companion modelling in northern Vietnam. In F. Bousquet, G. Trebuil, & B. Hardy (Eds.), *Companion modelling and multi-agent systems for integrated natural resource management in Asia*. Los Banos, Philippines: IRRI.

Bollobás, B. (1998). *Modern graph theory*. New York: Springer-Verlag.

Boman, M., & Holm, E. (2004). Multiagent systems, time geography and microsimulations. In M.O. Olson, & G. Sjöstedt (Eds.), *Systems approaches and their application: Examples from Sweden* (pp. 95-118). Kluwer International Publishers, London: Kluwer International Publishers.

Bonnefoy, J.L. (2003). From households to urban structures: Space representations as an engine of dynamics in multi-agent simulations. *Cybergeo, 234*, 11.

Bonté, L. (2005). *Représentation multi-échelle pour plateformes à grands nombres d'agents*. Unpublished Master's degree report. Université de Lille, France.

Bornstein, G. (2003). Intergroup conflict; Individual, group and collective interests. *Personality and Social Psychology Review, 7*(2), 129-145.

Bousquet, F., & Le Page, C. (2004) Multi-agent simulations and ecosystem management: A review. *Ecological Modelling, 176*, 313-332.

Bousquet, F., Bakam, I., Proton, H., & Le Page, C. (1998). Cormas: Common-pool resources and multi-agent systems. *Lecture Notes in Artificial Intelligence, 1416*, 826-838.

Bousquet, F., Barreteau, O., d'Aquino, P., Etienne, M., Boissau, S., Aubert, S. et al. (2002). Multi-agent systems and role games: Collective learning processes for ecosystem management. In M. Janssen (Ed.), *Complexity and ecosystem management: The theory and practice of multi-agent approaches*. Edward Elgar Publishers.

Bousquet, F., Barreteau, O., Mullon C., & Weber J. (1999). An environmental modelling approach: The use of multi-agents simulations. In F. Blasco, & A. Weill (Eds.),

Advances in environmental and ecological modelling (pp. 113-122). Paris: Elsevier.

Bowles, S., & Gintis, H. (2001). *The evolution of strong reciprocity*. Santa Fe Working Paper.

Boyd, R., & Richerson, P.J. (1992). Punishment allows the evolution of cooperation (or anything else) in sizable groups. *Ethology and Sociobiolgy, 13*, 171-195.

Boyle, J.,Lusk, E., Overleed, R., & Wos, L. (1984). *Automated reasoning: Introduction and applications.* Englewood Cliffs, NJ: Prentice-Hall.

Bradshaw, G.G., Langley, P., Simon, H.A., & Zytkow, J.M. (1987). *Scientific discovery: Computational explorations of the creative processes.* MIT Press.

Brassel, K., Moehring, M., Schumacher, E., & Troitzsch, K.G. (1997). Can agents cover all the world? In R. Conte, R. Hegselsman, & P. Terna (Eds.), *Simulating social phenomena* (pp. 122-138). Berlin/Heidelberg: Springer Verlag.

Brewer, P., Huang, M., Nelson, B., & Plott, C. (2002). On the behavioural foundations of the law of supply and demand: Human convergence and robot randomness. *Experimental economics, 5*, 179-208.

Brown, J.S., & Duguid, P. (1991). Organizational learning and communities of practice: Toward a unified view of working, learning and innovation. *Organization Science, 2*, 40-57.

Brunnermeier, M.K. (2001). *Asset pricing under asymmetric information.* Oxford University Press.

Buchanan, J. M., & Tullock, G. (1997). *The calculus of consent: Logical foundations of constitutional democracy.* Ann Arbor: The University of Michigan Press.

Bunge, M. (1979). *Treatise on basic philosophy Vol. IV, Ontololgy II: A world ofsSystems.* Dortecht: D. Reidel Publishing Company.

Bura, S., Guérin-Pace, F., Mathian, H., Pumain D., & Sanders, L. (1996). Multi-agent systems and the dynamics of a settlement system. *Geographical Analysis, 2*, 161-178.

Burgos, E., Ceva, H., & Perazzo, R.P.J. (2004). *Order and disorder in the local evolutionary minority game,* preprint, arXiv:cond-mat/0401363

Cabrera, A., & Cabrera, E.F. (2002). Knowledge-sharing dilemmas. *Organization Studies, 23,* 687-710.

Camerer, C., & Weber, M. (1992). Recent developments in modelling preferences: Uncertainty and ambiguity. *Journal of Risk and Uncertainty, 5*(4), 325-370.

Camerer, C.F., & Ho, T.H. (1994). Violations of the betweenness axiom and nonlinearity in probability. *Journal of Risk and Uncertainty, 8,* 167-196.

Cappellini, A., & Lamieri, M. (2007). Industrial sectors dynamic study through a multichoice and multi-layer minority game formalism: An agent based simulation model. *Journal of Social Complexity, 3*(1), 85-96.

Carlino, G.A., & DeFina, R. (1996). Does monetary policy have differential regional effects? *Federal Reserve Bank of Philadelphia Business Review Articles.*

Cason, T. (1993). Seller incentive properties of EPA's emission trading auction. *Journal of Environmental Economics and Management, 25,* 177-195.

Castelfranchi, C. (1997). Principles of limited autonomy. In R. Tuomela & G. Holstrom-Hintikka (Eds.), *Contemporary action theory.* Kluwer.

Castella, J.C., Boissau, S., Nguyên, H.T., & Novosad, P. (2006). Impact of forestland allocation on land use in a mountainous province of Vietnam. *Land Use Policy, 23*(2), 147-160.

Challet, D., & Zhang, Y.C. (1997). Emergence of co-operation and organization in an evolutionary game, *Physica A,246,* 407.

Chattoe, E. (1998). Just how (un)realistic are evolutionary algorithms as representations of social processes? *Journal of Artificial Societies and Social Simulation, 1*(3). Retrieved January 10, 2007, from http://www.soc.surrey.ac.uk/JASSS/1/3/2.html

Chau, H.F., Chow, F.K., Ho, H. (2004). Minority game with peer pressure. *Physica A*, Volume 332, 483-

495, preprint, http://arxiv.org/PS_cache/cond-mat/pdf/0307/0307556.pdf

Chau, P.Y.K. (2001). Inhibitors to EDI adoption in small businesses: An empirical investigation. *Journal of Electronic Commerce Research 2*(3).

Chavalarias, D. (2004). *Métadynamiques en cognition sociale–Quelle définition de meilleur est la meilleure?* Unpublished doctoral dissertation, Ecole Polytechnique, Paris, France.

Chavalarias, D. (2006). Metamimetic games: Modeling metadynamics in social cognition. *Journal of Artificial Societies and Social Simulations, 9*(2).

Chavalarias, D. (2007). La part mimetique des dynamiques de congition sociale: cle pour penser l' auto-transformation du social. *Novuvelles Perspectives en Sciences Sociales, 2*(2).

Chircu, A.M., & Kauffman, R. (2000). Reintermediation strategies in business-to-business electronic commerce. *International Journal of Electronic Commerce, 4*(4), 7-42.

Christian, C. (1993/1994). Voluntary compliance with the individual income tax: Results from the 1988 TCMP study. *The IRS Research Bulletin,* 35-42.

Cioffi-Revilla, C., & Gotts, N.M. (2003).Comparative analysis of agent-based social simulations: GeoSim and FEARLUS models. *Journal of Artificial Societies and Social Simulation, 6*(4). (http://jasss.soc.surrey.ac.uk/JASSS6-4.html as at 22/12/2003).

Clarke, G.P. (Ed) (1996). Microsimulation for urban and regional policy analysis. *European Research in Regional Science, 6*, 88-116.

Clower, R.W. (1965). The Keynesian counter-revolution: A theoretical appraisal. In F. Hahn & F. P. R. Brechling (Eds.), *The theory of interest rates.* London: MacMillan.

Cohen, P.R. (1985). *Heuristic reasoning about uncertainty: An artificial intelligence approach.* London: Pitman.

Coleman, J.S. (1966). The possibility of a social welfare function. *American Economic Review, 56,* 1105-1122.

Collins, H.M. (1974). The TEA set: Tacit knowledge and scientific networks. *Science Studies, 4,* 165-86.

Colomer, J.M. (1999). On the geometry of unanimity rule. *Journal of Theoretical Politics, 11,* 543-553.

Cont, R. (2001) Empirical properties of asset returns: Stylised facts and statistical issues. *Quantitative Finance, 1,* 223-236.

Conte, R. (2000). Memes through (social) minds. In R. Auger (Ed.), *Darwinizing culture: The status of memetics as a science.* Oxford University Press.

Conte, R., & Castelfranchi, C. (1995). Simulating multi-agent interdependencies. A two-way approach to the micro-macro link. In K.G.Troitzsch, U. Mueller, G.N. Gilbert, & J. Doran (Eds.), *Social science microsimulation* (pp. 394-415). Springer.

Conte, R., & Pedone, R. (1998). Finding the best partner: The part-net system. In N. Gilbert, J. S. Sichman, & R. Conte (Eds.), *Multi-agent systems and agent-based simulation.* Berlin: Springer, 156-168).

Cosmides, L. (1989). The logic of social exchange: Has natural section shaped how humans reason? Studies with the Watson selection task. *Cognition, 31,* 187-276.

Cosmides, L., & Tooby, J. (1993). Cognitive adaptations for social exchange. In J.H. Barkow, L. Cosmides, & J. Tooby (Eds.), *The adapted mind: Evolutionary psychology and the generation of culture* (pp. 163-228).

Cyert, R.H., & March, J.G. (1963). *A behavioural theory of the firm.* Prentice-Hall.

Davis, G. (2002). *History of money.* Cardiff: University of Wales Press.

Davis, J.S., Hecht, G., & Perkins, J.D. (2003). Social behaviors, enforcement and tax compliance dynamics. *The Accounting Review, 78*(1), 39-69.

Davis, L. (1991) Handbook of genetic algorithms. New York: Van Nostrand Reinhold.

Dawkins, R. (1976). *The selfish gene.* Oxford University Press.

De Swaan, A. (1973). *Coalition theories and cabinet formations.* Amsterdam: North Holland.

de Vos, H., & Zeggelink, E.P.H. (1997). Reciprocal altruism in human social evolution: The viability of reciprocal altruism with a preference for 'old-helping-partners.' *Evolution and Human Behavior, 18,* 261-78.

de Vos, H., Smaniotto, R., & Elsas, D.A. (2001). Reciprocal altruism under conditions of partner selection. *Rationality and Society, 13*(2), 139-183.

Deffuant G., & Huet, S. (2006). Collective reinforcement of first impression bias. *Proceedings of the 1st World Conference on Social Simulation.* Kyoto.

Deffuant, G. (2006). Comparing extremism propagation patterns in continuous opinion models. *Journal of Artificial Societies and Social Simulation, 9*(3). http://jasss.soc.surrey.ac.uk/9/3/8.html

Deffuant, G., Amblard, F., Weisbuch, G., & Faure, T. (2002). How can extremism prevail? A study based on the relative agreement interaction model. *Journal of Artificial Societies and Social Simulation, 5,4.* http://jasss.soc.surrey.ac.uk/5/4/1.html

Deffuant, G., Neau, D., Amblard, F., & Weisbuch, G. (2001). Mixing beliefs among interacting agents. *Advances in Complex Systems, 3,* 87-98.

Demsetz, H. (1991). The theory of the firm revisited. In O. E. Williamson, S.G. Winter, & R.H. Coase (Eds.), *The nature of the firm* (pp. 159-178). New York: Oxford University Press.

Dennett, D. (1989). *The intentional stance.* MIT Press; reprint edition.

Derrida, B., & Flyvbjerg, H. (1986). Multivalley structure in Kauffman's model: Analogy with spin glasses. *J. Phys. A*19, L1003-L1008.

Deutschmann, P.J., & Fals Borda, O. (1962). *La Communicación de las ideas entre los campesinos Colombianos.* Monografías Sociológicas 14, Universidad Nacional de Colombia, Bogotá.

Downing, T.E., Moss, S., & Pahl-Wostl, C. (2003). Understanding climate policy using participatory agent-based social simulation. In S. Moss & P. Davidsson (Eds.), *Multi agent based social simulation.* Springer, 198-213.

Drogoul, A., & Ferber J. (1994). Multi-agent simulation as a tool for studying emergent processes in societies. In N. Gilbert & J. Doran (Eds.), *Simulating societies: The computer simulation of social phenomena* (pp. 127-142). London: UCL Press.

Duffy, J. (2001). Learning to speculate: Experiments with artificial and real agents. *Journal of Economic Dynamics and Control, 25,* 295-319.

Durrett, R., & Levin, S.A. (2005). Can stable social groups be maintained by homophilous imitation alone? *Journal of Economic Behavior and Organization, 57,* 267-286.

Easley, D., & Ledyard, J. (1993). Theories of price formation and exchange in double-oral auction. In D. Friedman & J. Rust (Eds.), *The double auction market: Institutions, theories, and evidence* (pp. 63-97).Readin, MA: Addison-Wesley

Easterby-Smith, M., Thorpe, R., & Lowe, A. (1991). *Management research : An introduction.* London: Sage.

Edmonds, B. (2000). *The purpose and place of formal systems in the development of science.* CPM Report 00-75, MMU, UK. (http://cfpm.org/cpmrep75.html)

Edmonds, B. (2003). Against: A priori theory For: Descriptively adequate computational modelling. In E. Fullbrook (Ed.), *The crisis in economics: The post-autistic economics movement: The first 600 days* (pp. 175-179). Routledge.

Edmonds, B., & Hales, D. (2003) Replication, replication and replication—Some hard lessons from model alignment. *Journal of Artificial Societies and Social Simulation, 6*(4).

Edwards M., Huet, S., Goreaud F., &Deffuant, G. (2003). Comparing an individual-based model of behaviour diffusion with its mean field aggregate approximation. *Journal of Artificial Societies and Social Simulation,* *6*(40. http://jasss.soc.surrey.ac.uk/6/4/9.html

Elster, J. (1983). *Explaining technical change.* Cambridge: Cambridge University Press.

Epstein, J.M., & Axtell, R. (1996). *Growing artificial societies social science from the the bottom up.* MIT Press.

Eriksson, T. (2003). The effects of new work practices: Evidence from employer-employee data. In T. Kato, & J. Pliskin (Eds.), *The determinants of the incidence and the effects of participatory organizations:. Advances in the economic analysis of participatory and labor-managed firms* (Vol. 7, pp. 159-178). New York: Elsevier.

Ernst, A. (2002). Modellierung der Trinkwassernutzung bei globalen Umweltveränderungen–erste Schritte. *Umweltpsychologie, 6*(1), 62-76.

Fama, E. (1970). Efficient capital markets: A review of theory and empirical work. *Journal of Finance, 25,* 383-417.

Fehr, E., & Schmidt, K.M. (1999). A theory of fairness, competition and cooperation. *Quarterly Journal of Economics, 114,* 817-868.

Felsenthal, D.S., & Machover, M. (1998). *The measurement of voting power.* Cheltenham: Edward Elgar.

Fioretti, G. (2001). Information structure and behaviour of a textile industrial district. *Journal of Artificial Societies and Social Simulation (JASSS) 4*(4). Retrieved January 13, 2007 from, http:// jasss.soc.surrey.ac.uk/4/4/1.html

Fisher, M., & Wooldridge, M. (1977). Distributed problem-solving as concurrent theorem-proving. In Boman & van de Velde (Eds.), *Multi-agent rationality.* Springer-Verlag.

Flache, A. (2001). Individual risk preferences and collective outcomes in the evolution of exchange networks. *Rationality and Society, 13*(3), 304-348.

Flache, A., & Hegselmann, R. (1999a). Altruism vs. self-interest in social support. computer simulations of social support networks in cellular worlds.*Advances in Group Processes*, 16, 61-97.

Flache, A., & Hegselmann, R. (1999b). Rationality vs. learning in the evolution of solidarity networks: A theoretical comparison. *Computational and Mathematical Organization Theory, 5*(2), 97-127.

Fokke, D., & Folkerts-Landau, I. (1982). *Intertemporal planning, exchange and macroeconomics.* Cambridge University Press.

Foster, D., & Young, P. (1990). Stochastic evolutionary game theory. *Theoretical Population Biology, 38,* 219-232.

Friedman, D. (1993). The double oral auction market institution: A survey. In D. Friedman & J. Rust (Eds.), *The double auction market: institutions, theories, and evidence* (pp. 3-26). Reading, MA: Addison-Wesley.

Friedman, J. (1971). A non-cooperative equilibrium for supergames. *Review of Economic Studies, 38,* 1-12.

Friedman, M. (1953). *Essays in positive economics.* Chicago: University of Chicago Press.

Galan, J.M., Downing, T., López-Paredes, A., & Warwick, C. (2003). Rigour and reliability in agent-based social simulation through replication. In *Proceedings of The First European Social Simulation Association Conference, ESSA'03*, Groningen, The Netherlands.

Gallegati, M, Ardeni P.G., Boitani A., & Delli Gatti, D. (1999b). The new Keynesian economics: A survey. In M. Messori (Ed.), *Financial constraints and Mmrket failures.*Cheltenham: Elgard.

Gallegati, M. & Kirman, A.P. (Eds.).(1999) *Beyond the representative agent.* Cheltehnam: Elgar.

Gallegati, M., DelliGatti, D., & Mignacca D. (1999a). Agents heterogeneity and coordination failure: An experiment. In M. Gallegati & A. P. Kirman (Eds.), *Beyond the representative agent* (pp. 165-82). Cheltenham: Elgar.

Galunic, D.C., & Rodan, S. (1998). Resource combinations in the firm: Knowledge structures and the potential for Schumpeterian innovation. *Strategic Management Journal, 19*, 1193-1201.

Garud, R., & Nayyar, P. (1994). Transformative capacity: Continual structuring by inter-temporal technology transfer. *Strategic Management Journal, 15*, 365-385.

Giere, R.N. (1988). Explaining science: A cognitive approach. *Science and its conceptual foundations series.* Chicago; London: University of Chicago Press.

Gilbert, N., & Troitzsch, K.G. (2005). *Simulation for the social scientist* (2nd ed.). UK: Open Univerisity Press.

Gilbert, N.,& Terna, P. (2000). How to build and use agent-based models in social science, *Mind & Society, 1*, 57-72.

Gilks, W.R., Richardson, S., & Spiegelhalter, D.J. (Eds). (1995). *Markov chain Monte Carlo in practice.* Boca Raton: CRC Press.

Gil-Quijano, J. (2002). *Modélisation des mobilités résidentielles intra-urbaines par systèmes multi-agents à Bogotá: Système « market based » et système auto-organisé.* Unpublished master's degree report. LIP6-Université Paris VI. Retrieved January 12, 2007 from, http://www.ur079.ird.fr/equipe/fichiers/javier_Bogotá.pdf

Gil-Quijano, J., & Piron, M. (2007). Formation automatique de groupes d'agents sociaux par techniques d'apprentissage non supervise. In *Proceedings of Atelier Fouille de données et Algorithmes biomimétiques—EGC'07,* Namur, Belgium.

Gil-Quijano, J., Piron M., & Drogoul, A. (2007). Vers une simulation multi-agent de groups d'individus pour modéliser les mobilités résidentielles intra-urbaines. In *Revue Internationale de Géomatique* (Special number: *Dynamiques Urbaines et Mobilités),* 20.

Gjerstad, S. (2006). The competitive market paradox (Tech. Rep. No. 1180). Purdue University.

Gjerstad, S., & Dickhaut, J. (1998). Price formation in double auctions. *Games and Economic Behaviour, 22,* 1-29.

Gode, D., & Sunder, S. (1993). Allocative efficiency of market with zero-intelligent traders: Market as a partial substitute for individual rationality. *Journal of Political Economy, 101,* 119-137.

Gode, D., & Sunder, S. (1994). Human and artificially intelligent traders in a double auction market: Experimental evidence. In K. Carley & Prietula (Eds.), *Computational organization theory* (pp. 241-262). NJ: Lawrence Erlbaum Associates.

Goldberg, D. (1989). *Genetic algorithms in search, optimization, and machine learning.* Addison-Wesley.

Gotts, N.M., Polhill, J.G., & Adam, W.J. (2003). Simulation and analysis in agent-based modelling of land use change. *First Conference of the European Social Simulation Association, SIMSOC VI Workshop.* Retrieved January 5, 2004 from, http://www.uni-koblenz.de/~kgt/ESSA/ESSA

Gotts, N.M., Polhill, J.G., & Law, A.N.R. (2003). Aspiration levels in a land use simulation. *Cybernetics and Systems 34,* 663-683.

Gotts, N.M., Polhill, J.G., Law, A.N.R., & Izquierdo, L.R. (2003, April 7-11). Dynamics of imitation in a land use simulation. In *Proceedings of the Second International Symposium on Imitation in Animals and Artefacts,* University of Wales, Aberystwyth (pp. 39-46).

Granovetter, M. (1974). *Getting a job.* Cambridge, Mass.: Harvard University Press.

Granovetter, M. (1985). Economic-action and social-structure: The problem of embeddedness. *American Journal of Sociology, 91*(3), 481-510.

Grant, R.M. (1996). Prospering in dynamically-competitive environments: Organizational capability as knowledge integration. *Organization Science, 7,* 375-387.

Grant, R.M. (1996). Toward a knowledge-based theory of the firm. *Strategic Management Journal, 17* (Winter Special Issue), 109-122.

Grant, R.M. (1997). The knowledge-based view of the firm: Implications for management practice. *Long Range Planning, 30,* 450-454.

Grant, R.M. (2001). Knowledge and organization. In I. Nonaka, & D. J. Teece (Eds.), *Managing industrial knowledge* (pp. 145-169). London: Sage.

Greenspan, A. (2002). *The history of money*. Speech at the opening of an American numismatic society exhibition. New York: Federal Reserve Bank of New York.

Guttman, J.M. (1998). Unanimity and majority Rule: The calculus of consent reconsidered. *European Journal of Political Economy, 14*, 189-207.

Hägerstrand, T. (1967). *Innovation diffusion as a spatial process*. Translated by Allan Pred with the assistance of Greta Haag. University of Chicago Press.

Halbwachs, M. (1950). *La mémoire collective*. Paris: Les Presses universitaires de France.

Hales, D. (2000). Cooperation without space or memory: Tags, groups and the prisoner's dilemma. In S. oss. &, P. Davidsson (Eds.), *Multi-agent-based simulation. Lecture notes in artificial intelligence, 1979* (pp. 157-166). Berlin: Springer-Verlag.

Hales, D. (2001). *Tag based cooperation in artificial societies*. PhD Thesis (Department Of Computer Science, University of Essex, UK.

Hales, D. (2002). Evolving specialisation, altruism and group-level optimisation using tags. In J.S. Sichman, F. Bousquet, & P. Davidsson (Eds.), Multi-agent-based simulation II. *Lecture Notes in Artificial Intelligence, 2581* (pp. 26-35). Berlin: Springer Verlag.

Hales, D. (2004). Self-organising, open and cooperative P2P societies—From tags to networks. Presented at the *2nd Workshop on Engineering Self-Organsing Applications* (ESOA 2004) located with the AAMAS 2004 Conference, NY, July 2004. To be published by Springer.

Hales, D. (2004, August 25-27). From selfish nodes to cooperative networks—Emergent link-based incentives in peer-to-peer networks. To be presented at *The Fourth IEEE International Conference on Peer-to-Peer Computing (P2P2004)*, 2004, Zurich, Switzerland. To be published by IEEE press.

Hales, D., & Edmonds, B. (2003, July). Evolving social rationality for MAS using "Tags." In J. S. Rosenschein, et al. (Eds.) *Proceedings of the 2nd International Conference on Autonomous Agents and Multi-agent Systems (AAMAS03)* (pp. 497-503), Melbourne. ACM Press, 497-503.

Hamilton, W.D. (1964). The genetical evolution of social behaviours. *Journal of Theoretical Biology, 7*, 1-52.

Hammersley, M., &. Atkinson, P. (1983). *Ethnography: Principles in practice*. London: Tavistock Publications.

Hamming, R. (1980). *Coding and information theory*. Prentice-Hall.

Hansen, M.T. (1999). The search-transfer problem. *Administrative Science Quarterly, 44*, 82-111.

Hansjürgens, B. (Ed.). (2005). *Emissions trading for climate policy: US and European perspectives*. UK: Cambridge University.

Happe, K. (2000). *The agricultural policy simulator (AgriPolis)—Version 1.0. discussion paper*. Institute of Agricultural Development in Central and Eastern Europe IAMO, Theodor-Lieser-Strasse 2, D-06120 Halle, Germany.

Harris, Louis and Associates, Inc. (1988). *Taxpayer opinion survey*. Internal Revenue Service Document 7292 (1-88).

Hauert, C. (2001). Fundamental clusters in spatial 2 × 2 games. In *Proceedings of the Royal Society London B* (vol. 268, pp. 761-769.)

Hayashi, N., & Yamagishi, T. (1998). Selective play: Choosing partners in an uncertain world. *Personality and Social Psychology Review, 2*, 276-289.

Hayek, F. A. (1945). The use of knowledge in society. *American Economic Review, 35*, 519-530.

Hayek, F.A. (1978). *New studies in philosophy, politics, economics and history of ideas*. Chicago: Chicago University Press.

Hayes-Renshaw, F., & Wallace, H. (1997). *The council of ministers*. London: Macmillan.

Hedstrom, P. (2005). *Dissecting the social: On the principles of analytical sociology*. Cambridge: Cambridge University Press.

Hedstrom, P., & Swedberg, R. (Eds.). (1998). *Social mechanisms: An analytical approach to social theory*. Cambridge: Cambridge University Press.

Hegselmann, R. (1996). Solidarität unter ungleichen. In R. Hegselmann & H.-O. Peitgen (Eds.), *Modelle sozialer dynamiken—Ordnung, chaos und komplexität* (pp. 105-128). Wein: Hölder–Pichler–Tempsky.

Hegselmann, R. (1998). Experimental ethics–A computer simulation of classes, cliques and solidarity. In C. Fehige & U. Wessels (Eds.), *Preferences* (pp. 298-320). Berlin: De Gruyter.

Hegselmann, R., & Krause, U. (2002). Opinion dynamics and bounded confidence models, analysis and simulation. *Journal of Artificial Societies and Social Simulation, 5*(3). http://jasss.soc.surrey.ac.uk/5/3/2.html

Heider, F. (1958). *The psychology of interpersonal relations*. New York: Wiley

Hempel, C. G. (1966). *Philosophy of natural science*. Englewood Cliffs, NJ: Prentice-Hall.

Hicks, J. (1967). *Critical essays in monetary theory*. Oxford: Clarendon Press.

Hinds, P.J., Carley, K.M., Krackhardt, D., & Wholey, D. (2000). Choosing work group members: Balancing similarity, competence, and familiarity. *Organizational Behavior and Human Decision Processes, 81*(2), 226-251. Jex, S.M. (2002). *Organizational psychology: A scientist-practitioner approach*. New York: John Wiley & Sons.

Hodgson, G. M. (1999). *Institutions and the viability of macroeconomics: Some perspectives on the transformation process in post-communist economies* http://graphics.stanford.edu/projects/rivet/

Holland, J. (1993). *The effect of labels (tags) on social interactions*. Santa Fe Institute Working Paper 93-10-064. Santa Fe, NM.

Holt, C. (1995). Industrial organization: A survey of laboratory research. In J. H. Kagel & A.E. Roth (Eds.), *Handbook of experimental economics* (pp. 349-444). Princeton: Princeton University Press.

Homans, G.C. (1961). *Social behaviour: Its elementary forms*. New York: Harcourt, Brace and World, Inc.

Hooghe, L., & Marks, G.W. (2001). *Multi-level governance and European integration*. Lanham: Rowman & Littlefield.

Houssein B., Chaib-draa, B., & Kropf, P. (2001). Multiagent auctions for multiple items. In *Proceedings of the Third International Bi-Conference Workshop on AOIS, 2001*, Montreal.

Huang, J.C., & Newell, S. (2003). Knowledge integration processes and dynamics within the context of cross-functional projects. *International Journal of Project Management, 21*, 167-176.

Huselid, M.A. (1995). The impact of human resource management practices on turnover, productivity, and corporate financial performance. *Academic Management Journal, 38*(3), 635-672.

Ichniowski, C., Shaw, K., & Prennushi, G. (1997). The effects of human resource management practices on productivity: A study of steel finishing lines. *American Economic Review, 87*(3), 291-313.

Internal Revenue Service. (1996). *Federal tax compliance research: Individual income tax gap estimates for 1985, 1988, and 1992*. IRS Publication 1415 (Rev. 4-96), Washington, DC.

Janssen, M. (2002). *Complexity and ecosystem management: The theory and practice of multi-agent systems*. Cheltenham: Edward Elgar Publishing.

Jaynes, E.T. (1974). *Probability theory with applications in science and engineering: A series of informal lectures*. Retrieved April 18, 2002 from, http://bayes.wustl.edu/etj/articles/mobil.pdf

Jelasity, M., Montresor, A., & Babaoglu, O. (2004). A modular paradigm for building self-organizing peer-to-peer applications. *Proceedings of the 1st International Workshop on Engineering Self-Organising Applications (ESOA 2003)*. Springer.

Jensen, F. (2001). *Introduction to Bayesian networks und decision graphs*. Berlin/Heidelberg/New York: Springer Verlag.

Jin, L., & Robey, D. (1999). ,Explaining cybermediation: An organizational analysis of electronic retailing. *International Journal of Electronic Commerce, 3*(4).

Johnson, N.F., Hui, P.M., Jonson, R., & Lo, T.S. (1999). Self-organized segregation within an evolving population. *Physical Review Letters, 82*(16), 3360.

Kahneman, D., & Tversky, A. (1979). Prospect theory of decisions under risk. *Econometrica, 47*, 263-291.

Kahneman, D., & Tversky, A. (1992). Advances in prospect theory: Cumulative representation of uncertainty. *Journal of Risk and Uncertainty, 5*.

Kalenka, S., & Jennings, N.R. (1999) Socially responsible decision making by autonomous agents. In K. Korta et al. (Eds.), *Cognition, agency and rationality* (pp. 135-149). Kluwer.

Kalinowski, T., Schuklz, H.-J., & Briese, M. (2000). Cooperation in the minority game with local information. *Physica A, 277*, 502-508.

Kanbur, R., & Keen, M. (1993). Jeux sans frontieres: Tax competition and tax coordination when countries differ in size. *American Economic Review*, 880-85.

Kauffman, S.A. (1969), Metabolic stability and epigenesis in randomly constructed genetic nets. *Journal of Theoretical Biology, 22*, 434-467.

Kim, J. (1998). *Mind in a physical world: An essay on the mind-body problem and mental causation*. Cambridge, MA: MIT Press

Kirk, J., & Coleman, J. (1967). Formalisierung und simulation von interaktionen in einer drei-personen-gruppe. In R. Mayntz (Ed.), *Formalisierte modelle in der soziologie*. Neuwied/Berlin: Luchterhand.

Kirley, M. (2004). Evolutionary minority games with small-world interactions. In D.G. Green, et al. (Eds.), *Proceedings of the 8th Asia Pacific Symposium on Intelligent and Evolutionary Systems* (to appear).

Kirman, A. (1992). Whom or what does the representative individual represent? *Journal of Economic Perspectives, 6*, 117-36.

Kirman, A.P. (1989). The intrinsic limits of modern economic theory: The emperor has no clothes. *Economic Journal (Conference Papers), 99*, 126-139.

Kiyotaki, N., & Wright, R. (1989). On money as a medium of exchange. *Journal of Political Economy, 97*, 927-54.

Klandermans, B. (1984). Mobilization and participation: Social-psychological expansions of resource mobilization theory. *American Sociological Review, 49*, 583-600.

Kleinhückelkotten, S. (2005). *Suffizienz und Lebensstile. Ansätze für eine milieuorientierte Nachhaltigkeitskommunikation*. Berlin: BWV.

Kline, J.J., & Menezes, F.M. (1999). A simple analysis of the US emission permits auctions. *Economic Letters, 65*, 183-189.

Kneer, J., Ernst, A., Eisentraut, R., Nethe, M., & Mauser, W. (2003). Interdisziplinäre Modellbildung: Das Beispiel GLOWA-Danube. *Umweltpsychologie, 7*(2), 54-70.

Knight, F.H. (1921). *Risk, uncertainty and profit*. Boston: Houghton Mifflin Company.

Kogut, B., & Zander, U. (1992). Knowledge of the firm, combinative capabilities, and the replication of technology. *Organization Science, 3*, 383-397.

Kogut, B., & Zander, U. (1996). What firms do? Coordination, identity and learning. *Organization Science, 7*, 502-518.

Kollock, P. (1994). The emergence of exchange structures: An experimental study of uncertainty, commitment, and trust. *American Journal of Sociology, 100*(2), 313-45.

Koza, J. R. (1992). *Genetic programming: On the programming of computers by means of natural selection* (Fifth Printing), The MIT Press.

Kuhn, T. S. (1962). *The structure of scientific revolutions.* Chicago: University of Chicago Press.

Kurlansky, M. (2003). *Salt.* New York: Penguin Group.

Kyle, A.S., & Wang, A. (1997). Speculation duopoly with agreement to disagree: Can overconfidence survive the market test? *Journal of Finance, 52,* 2073-2090.

Lane, D.A. (2002). Complessità: Modelli e inferenza. In P. M. Biava (Ed.). *Complessità e biologia,* Bruno Mondadori Editori, 13-42.

Lane, D.A. (1998). Is what is good for each good for all? In B. Arthur, S. Durlauf & D. Lane (Eds.), *Economy as a complex, evolving system II.* Reading, MA: Addison-Wesley.

Lansing, J.S., & Kremer, J.N. (1994). Emergent properties of Balinese water temple networks: Coadaptation on a rugged fitness landscape. In C. G. Langton (Ed.). *Artificial life III* (pp. 201-223). Addison-Wesley.

Laumann, E.O., et al. (1978). Community structure of interorganizational linkages. *Annual Review of Sociology, 4,* 455-484.

Lauritzen, S. L. (1996). *Graphical models.* Oxford: Clarendon Press.

Lave, J., & Wenger, E. (1991). *Situated learning.* Cambridge: Cambridge University Press.

Lawler, E., & Yoon, J. (1993). Power and the emergence of commitment behavior in negotiated exchange. *American Sociological Review, 58*(4), 465-481.

Lawler, E., & Yoon, J. (1996). Commitment in exchange relations: Test of a theory of relational cohesion. *American Sociological Review, 61*(1), 89-108.

Lawler, E.J. (2001). An affect theory of social exchange. *American Journal of Sociology, 107*(2), 321-52.

Lazarsfeld, P., & Merton, R.K. (1954). Friendship as a social process: A substantive and methodological analysis. In M. Berger, T. Abel, & Ch. H. Page (Eds.), *Freedom and control in modern society* (pp. 18-66). New York: Van Nostrand.

LeBaron, B., Arthur, W.B., & Palmer, R. (1999).Time series properties of an artificial stock market. *Journal of Economic Dynamics and Control, 23,* 1487-1516.

Lebart, L., Piron M., & Morineau, A. (2006). *Statistique exploratoire multidimensionnelle: Visualisation et inférence en fouilles de données.* Dunod, p. 480.

Lempert, R.J. (2002). A new decision sciences for complex systems. In *Colloquium Paper Platforms and Methodologies for Enhancing the Social Sciences through Agent-Based Simulation,* PNAS,99 (3), 7309-7313.

Letenyei, I. (2001) . Rural innovation chains: Two examples for the diffusion of rural innovations. *Hungarian Review of Sociology, 7*(1), 85-100.

Levy, M., Levy, H., & Solomon, S. (2000). *Microscopic simulation of financial markets.* Academic Press.

Li, L., & Smith, S. (2004). Speculation agents for dynamic, multi-period continuous double auctions in B2B exchanges. In *Proceedings of the 37th Hawaii International Conference on System Sciences.*

Liebrand, W., Messick, D., & Wilke, H. (1992). *Social dilemmas: Theoretical issues and research findings.* New York: Pergamon Press.

Lindkvist, L. (2005). Knowledge communities and knowledge collectivities: A typology of knowledge work in groups. *Journal of Management Studies, 42*(6), 1189-1210.

Longino, H. (1990). *Science as social knowledge.* Princeton: Princeton University Press.

López-Paredes, A., Hernández C., & Pajares, J. (2002). Towards a new experimental socio-economics: Complex behaviour in bargaining. *Journal of Socioeconomics, 31,* 423-429.

Luce, R.D., & Raiffa, H. (1957). *Game and decision: Introduction and critical survey.*

Luo, G. (1999). The evolution of money as a medium of exchange. *Journal of Economic Dynamics & Control, 23,* 415-458.

Malone, T. W., Yates, J., & Benjamin, R. (1987). Electronic markets and electronic eierarchies. *Communications of the ACM, 30*(6), 484-497.

Mann, F.A. (1992). *Legal aspects of money* (5th ed.). London: Clarendon Press.

Marimon, R., McGrattan, E., & Sargent, T. (1990). Money as a medium of exchange in an economy with artificially intelligent agents. *Journal of Economic Dynamics and Control, 14,* 329-373.

Markowitz, H. (1952). Portfolio selection. *Journal of Finance, 7,* 77-91.

Marshall, P., Sor, R., & Mckay, J. (2000). An industry case study of the impacts of electronic commerce on car dealerships in Western Australia, *Journal of Electronic Commerce Research, 1*(1), 1-16.

Marwell, G., & Oliver, P.E. (1993). *The critical mass in collective action.* Cambridge: Press Syndicate of the University of Cambridge.

Mataric, M.J. (1995). Issues and approaches in the design of collective autonomous agents. *Robotics and Autonomous Systems, 16*(2-4), 321-331.

Mauser, W., et al. (2000). *GLOWA-DANUBE—Integrative techniques, scenarios and strategies regarding global changes of the water cycle (phase I).* Proposal to the German Ministry of Education and Research. München: Ludwig-Maximilians-Universität.

Mauser, W., et al. (2002). *GLOWA-DANUBE –InTegrative techniken, Szenarien und Strategien zum globalen Wandel des Wasserkreislaufs (Phase II).* Antrag auf förderung an das BMBF. München: Ludwig-Maximilians-Universität.

Maynard-Smith, J. (1964). Group selection and kin selection. *Nature, 201,* 1145-1147.

McCubbrey, D. J. (1999). Disintermediation and reintermediation in the U.S. air travel distribution industry: A Delphi study. *Communications of the Association for Information Systems, 1.*

McPherson, M., Smith-Lovin, L., & Cook, J.M. (2001). Birds of a feather: Homophily in social networks. *Annual Review of Sociology, 27,* 415-44.

Menger, C. (1892). On the origin of money. *Economic Journal, 2,* 239-255.

Milgrom, P., & Roberts, J. (1990). The economics of modern manufacturing: Technology, strategy, and organization. *American Economic Review, 80*(3), 511-528.

Miller, E.J., & Rice, A.K. (1967). *Systems of organization: The control of task and sentient boundaries.* London: Tavistock Publications.

Mingers, J. (2001). Combining IS research methods: Towards a pluralist methodology. *Information Systems Research, 12*(3), 240-259.

Mintz, J., & Tulkens, H. (1986). Commodity tax competition between member states of a federation: Equilibrium and efficiency. *Journal of Public Economics,* 149-56.

Mittone, L., & Patelli, P. (2000). Imitative behaviour in tax evasion. In B. Stefansson & F. Luna (Eds.), *Economic modelling with swarm.* Amsterdam: Kluwer.

Modigliani, F., & Miller, M.H. (1958). The cost of capital, corporation finance and the theory of investment. *American Economic Review, 48,* 3, 261-297.

Moelbert, S., & De Los Rios, P. (2002). The local minority game. *Physica A, 302,* 217-227.

Monmarché, N., Guinot C., & Venturini, G. (2002). Fouille visuelle et classification de données par nouage d'insectes volants. In RSTI-RIA-ECA: *Méthodes d'optimisation pour l'extraction de connaissances et l'apprentissage,* (6), 729-752.

Moravcsik, A., & Nikolaïdis, K. (1999). Explaining the \treaty of Amsterdam: Interests, influence, institutions. *Journal of Common Market Studies, 37,* 59-85.

Morgan, M., & Morrison, M. (Eds.). (1999). *Models as mediators: Perspectives on natural and social science.* Cambridge: CUP

Morgenstern, O., & von Neumann, J. (1944). *Theory of games and economic behavior.* Princeton University Press.

Morone, P., & Taylor, R. (2004). Knowledge diffusion dynamics of face-to-face interactions. *Journal of Evolutionary Economics, 14,* 327-351.

Mosler, H.-J. (2002). Agent-based simulation of an environmental action campaign: Changing people's behaviour via their inner contradictions. In A.E. Rizzoli, & A.J. Jakeman (Eds.). Integrated assessment and decision support. *Proceedings of the 1st biennial meeting of the International Environmental Modelling and Software Society.* Como: iEMSS, 2, 202-207.

Mosler, H.-J., & Tobias, R. (2000). Die Organisation kollektiver Aktionen durch Beeinflussung der individuellen Teilnahmeentscheidung. Eine Simulationsstudie [Organizing collective action through influencing the individual's decision to participate. A computer simulation]. *Kölner Zeitschrift für Soziologie und Sozialpsychologie, 52,* 264-290.

Mosler, H.-J., & Tobias, R. (2001). Who participates in a collective action? A psychologically based simulation with 10,000 agents. In C. Urban (Ed.), Second *Workshop on Agent-Based Simulation* (pp. 77-82). Ghent, SCS-Europe.

Mosler, H.-J., Gutscher, H., & Artho, J. (2001). Wie können viele Personen für eine kommunale Umweltaktion gewonnen werden? [How to gain many participants for communal environmental action?] *Umweltpsychologie, 5*(2), 122-140.

Mosler, H.-J., Schwarz, K., Ammann, F., & Gutscher, H. (2001). Computer simulation as a method of further developing a theory: Simulating the elaboration likelihood model (ELM). *Personality and Social Psychology Review,* 201-215.

Moss, S., & Edmonds, B. (2005). Sociology and simulation: Statistical and qualitative cross-validation. *American Journal of Sociology, 110*(4).

Moss, S., Edmonds, B., & Wallis, S. (2000). *The power law and critical density in large multi agent systems.* CPM Report No. 71, Manchester Metropolitan University.

Muehlenbein, H. (2002). *Towards a theory of organisms and evolving automata: Open problems and ways to explore.* Retreived August 22, 2003 from, http://www.ais.fraunhofer.de/ muehlen/publications/Mue02a.ps.gz

Muellbauer, J., & Portes R. (1978). Macroeconomic models with quantity rationing. *The Economic Journal,* 788-821.

Mukhodaphyay, T., Kekre, S., & Kalathur, S. (1995). Business value of information technology: A study of electronic data interchange, *MIS Quarterly, 19*(2), 137-156.

Mullon C., Piron, M., & Treuil, J.-P. (2001). An agent-based approach of urban migration flows. In *Proceedings of 13th European Simulation Symposium* (pp. 380-385), Marseille.

Myles, G.D., & Naylor, R.A. (1996). A model of tax evasion with group conformity and social customs. *European Journal of Political Economy, 12,* 49-66.

Namatame, A., & Sato, H. (2004). Localized minority games and emergence of efficient dynamic order. *Lecture notes in economics and mathematical systems* (Vol. 550, pp. 71-86). Springer.

Neilson, W. S. (2003). Probability transformations in the study of behavior toward risk. *Synthese, 135,* 171-192.

Nishimura, K. (1998). Expectation heterogeneity and price sensitivity. *European Economic Review, 42,* 619-629.

North, M.J., Collier, N.T., & Vos, J.R. (2006). Experiences creating three implementations of the repast agent modeling toolkit. *ACM Transactions on Modeling and Computer Simulation, 16*(1), 1-25.

Noussair, C., Plott, C., & Riezman, R. (1995). An experimental investigation of the patterns of international trade. *The American Economic Review, 85*(3), 462-491.

Noussair, C., Robin, S., & Ruffieux, B. (1998). The effect of transactions costs on double auction markets. *Journal of Economic Behavior and Organization, 36*, 221-233.

Nowak, M., & May, R.M. (1992). Evolutionary games and spatial chaos. *Nature, 359*, 826-829.

Nowak, M., & Sigmund, K. (1998). Evolution of indirect reciprocity by image scoring. *Nature, 393*, 573-557.

Nugent, N. (1999). *The government and politics of the European union*. London: Macmillan.

Okhuyzen, G.A., & Eisenhardt, K.M. (2002). Integrating knowledge in groups. *Organization Science, 13*, 370-386.

Orcutt, G.H., Caldwell, S., & Wertheimer II, R. (1976). *Policy exploration through microanalytic simulation*. Washington, DC: Urban Institute.

Ostrom, E., Gardner, R., & Walker, J. (1994). *Rules, games, and common-pool resources*. University of Michigan Press.

Ostrom, T. (1988). Computer simulation: The third symbol system. *Journal of Experimental Social Psychology, 24*, 381-392.

Paczuski, M., & Bassler, K.E. (2000). Self-organized networks of competing Boolean agents. *Physical Review Letters, 84*(14).

Pajares, J., Pascual, J.A., Hernández, C., & López-Paredes, A. (2003). *A behavioural, evolutionary and generative approach for modelling financial markets*. Paper presented at the First Conference of the European Social Simulation Association (ESSA). Groningen. The Netherlands.

Pajares, J., Pascual, J.A., Hernández, C., & López-Paredes, A. (2005). *The role of risk aversion and technical trading in the behaviour of financial markets*. Paper presented at the Third Conference of the European Social Simulation Association (ESSA). Koblenz. Germany.

Paolucci, M., Di Tosto, G., & Conte, R. (2003, October 3-4). Reciprocal vs group altruism among vampires. In *Proceedings of the Agent2003 Conference*, University of Chicago (pp. 543-554).

Pappi, F.U., & Henning, C.H.C.A. (1998). Policy networks: More than a metaphor? *Journal of Theoretical Politics, 10*, 553-575.

Parker, D.C., Berger, T., & Manson, S.M. (2002). Agent-based models of land-use/land-cover change: Report and review of an international workshop. *Report No. 6. LUCC Focus 1*, Bloomington, IN.

Parry, M. L. (1996). Integrating global and regional analyses of the effects of climate change: A case study of land use in England and Wales. *Climate Change, 32*, 185-198.

Parunak, V., & Vanderbok, R. (1998). *Modeling the extended sypply network*. ISA Tech'98, Houston, Texas.

Pascual, J. A. (2006). *Modelado Multiagente de Mercados Financieros: Un Enfoque Basado en el Comportamiento Individual de los Inversores*. Unpublished doctoral thesis. Departamento de Organización de Empresas y C.I.M. ETS de Ingenieros Industriales. Universidad Del Valladolid. Spain.

Pearl, J. (1988). *Probabilistic reasoning in intelligent systems*. San Francisco: Morgan Kaufmann Publishers.

Pearl, J. (2000). *Causality*. Cambridge: Cambridge University Press

Peleg, B. (1980). A theory of coalition formation in committees. *Journal of Mathematical Economics, 7*, 115-134.

Peleg, B. (1981). Coalition formation in simple games with dominant players. *International Journal of Game Theory, 10*, 11-33.

Petty, R. E., & Cacioppo, J. T. (1986). The elaboration likelihood model of persuasion. In L. Berkowitz (Ed.), *Advances in experimental social psychology, 9*, 123-205. New York: Academic Press.

Piron M., (2005). Comment évaluer et représenter le changement de la structure sociale de Bogotá? Les niveaux d'observation dans l'analyse du changement. In C. Tannier, H. Houot, & S. Chardonnel (Eds.). *Proceedings of 7th Rencontres de Théo Quant*, Université de Franche-Comté, p. 10.

Piron, M., Dureau, F., & Mullon, C. (2003). Vers un modèle dynamique des mobilités résidentielles: développement sur Bogotá. In C. Tannier, H. Houot, & S. Chardonnel (Eds.), *Proceedings of 6th Rencontres de Théo Quant*, Université de Franche-Comté, p. 10.

Plott, C.R. (1989). An updated review of industrial organization: Applications of experimental methods. In Schmalensee & Willig (Eds.), *Handbook of industrial organization*. North-Holland, pp 1109-1176.

Plott, C.R., & Smith V.L. (1978). An experimental examination of two exchange institutions. *The Review of Economic Studies, 45*, 133-153.

Polanyi, K., (1957). *The semantics of money-use: Explorations*. Toronto: University of Toronto.

Polhill, J.G., Gotts, N.M., & Law, A.N.R. (2001). Imitative versus nonimitative strategies in a land use simulation. *Cybernetics and Systems, 32*(1-2), 285-307.

Polhill, J.G., Parker, D.C., & Gotts, N.M. (2005, September 5-9) Introducing land markets to an agent based model of land use change: A design. In K.G. Troitzsch (Ed.), *Representing social reality: Pre-proceedings of the third conference of the European social simulation association, Koblenz* (pp. 150-157). Koblenz: Verlag Dietmar Völbach.

Pomp, M., & Burger, K. (1995). Innovation and imitation: Adoption of cocoa by Indonesian smallholders. *World Development, 23*(3), 423-431.

Porter, M.E. (1985). *Competitive advantage: Creating and sustaining superior performance*. New York: Free Press.

Portugali, J., & Benenson, I. (1995). Artificial planning experience by means of a heuristic sell-space model: Simulating international migration in the urban process. *Environment and Planning A, 27*, 1647-1665.

Posada, M. (2006). *Emission permits for climate policy: Agent based modelling in natural resources management*. Pearson Education.

Posada, M. (2006). Strategic software agents in continuous double auction under dynamics environments. In *Proceedings of IDEAL 2006*. Spain

Posada, M., Hernández, C., & López, A. (2004). Emission permits auctions: An agent based modelling approach. In *proceedings of the 2nd International Conference of the ESSA*. Spain.

Posada, M., Hernández, C., & López, A. (2005). Electricity and emission permits auctions in Spain: An agent based modelling approach. In *Proceedings of the 3rd International Conference of the ESSA*. Germany.

Posada, M., Hernández, C., & López, A. (2006a). Learning in a continuous double auction market. In P. Mathieu, B. Beaufils, & O. Brandouy (Eds.), *Artificial economics— Lecture notes in economics and mathematical systems 564*. Springer.

Posada, M., Hernández, C., & López, A. (2006b). Strategic behaviour in a continuous double auction market. In *Proceedings of Artificial Economics*. Denmark.

Puga, D. (2002). European regional policies in light of recent location theories. *Journal of Economic Geography 2*(4), 372-406.

Purvis, R.L., Sambamurthy, V., & Zmud, R.W. (2001). The assimilation of knowledge platforms in organizations: An empirical investigation. *Organization Science, 12*, 117-135.

Putnam, R.D. (1988). Diplomacy and domestic politics: The logic of two-level games. *International Organization, 42*, 427-460.

Rae, D.W. (1975). The limits of consensual decision. *The American Political Science Review, 69*, 1270-1294.

Raiffa, H., Richardson, J., & Metcalfe, D. (2002). *Negotiation analysis: The science and art of collaborative decision making*. Cambridge, MA.: The Belknap Press of Harvard University Press.

Remondino, M. (2003). Emergence of self organization and search for optimal enterprise structure: *AI evolutionary methods applied to ABPS, ESS03 proceedings*, SCS Europ. Publishing House.

Remondino, M., & Cappellini, A. (2004). *Minority game with communication: An agent based model.* In SCS European Publishing House, editor, Simulation in Industry 2004, pages 155-160.

Remondino, M., & Cappellini, A. (2005). Influence of opinion leadership and communication in a minority game: An agent based simulation. In *ESSA 2005 proceedings* (pp. 239-246).

Renault, V. (2001). Computation for metaphors, analogy and agents. In C. Nehaniv (Ed.), *The Journal of Artificial Societies and Social Simulation, 4*(1).

Rice, J.J., Stolovitzky, G., Tu, Y., & de Tombe, P.P. (2003). Ising model of cardiac thin filament activation with nearest-neighbor cooperative interactions. *Biophysical Journal, 84,* 897-909.

Riggins, F.J., & Mukhopadhyay, T. (1994). Interpdependent benefits from interorganizational systems: Opportunities for business partner re-engineering. *Journal of Management Information Systems, 11*(2), 37-57.

Riggins, F.J., & Mukhopadhyay, T. (1999). Overcoming EDI adoption and implementation risks. *International Journal of Electronic Commerce, 3*(4), 103.

Riker, W. (1962). *The theory of political coalitions.* New Haven: Yale Univ. Press.

Riolo, R. (1997). *The effects of tag-mediated selection of partners in evolving populations playing the iterated prisoner's dilemma.* SFI Working Paper 97-02-016, Santa Fe, NM.

Riolo, R.L., Cohen, M.D., & Axelrod, R. (2001). Evolution of cooperation without reciprocity. *Nature, 414,* 441-443.

Robalino, D.A. (2000). *Social capital, technology diffusion and sustainable growth in the developing world.* Ph.D. dissertation, RAND Graduate School of Policy Studies.

Roberts, G., & Sherratt, T.N. (2002). *Nature 418,* 449-500.

Rogers, E.M. (2003). *Diffusion of innovations* (5th edition). Free Press.

Rouchier, J. (2006). Data gathering to build and validate small scale social models for simulation. In J.P. Rennard (Ed.), *Handbook of research on nature inspired computing for economics and management.* Hershey, PA: Idea Group Reference.

Ruby, A. (2003). http://www. digitaleconomist. com/intro_4020. html

Russell, S., & Norvig, P. (1995). *Artificial Intelligence,* Prentice-Hall.

Rust, J., Miller, J., & Palmer, R. (1992). Behaviour of trading automata in a computerized double auction market. In D. Friedman & J. Rust (Eds.), *The double auction market: Institutions, theories, and evidence* (pp. 155-198). Addison-Wesley.

Ryan, B., & Gross, N.C. (1943). The diffusion of hybrid corn in two Iowa communities. *Rural Sociology, 8,* 15-24.

Saam, N. J., Thurner, P. W., & Arndt, F. (2004). Dynamics of international negotiations. A simulation of EU intergovernmental conferences. *Mannheimer Zentrum für Europäische Sozialforschung: Arbeitspapiere–Working Papers* No. 78.

Saam, N. J., Thurner, P. W., & Arndt, F. (forthcoming). Zeuthen-Harsanyi reconsidered: Modeling negotiation dynamics with Boudedly rational agents.

Saam, N.J., & Sumpter, D. (forthcoming). Coalition formation as emergent phenomenon in intergovernmental negotiations. *Journal of Policy Modeling.*

Saam, N.J., & Sumpter, D. (forthcoming). Intergovernmental negotiations: Peer selection in intergovernmental policy networks.

Saam, N.J., Thurner, P.W., & Arndt, F. (2004). Dynamics of international negotiations: A simulation of EU intergovernmental conferences. In C. van Dijkum, J.

Blasius, H. Kleijer, & B. van Hilten. (Eds.). *Recent developments and applications in social research methodology. Proceedings of the Sixth International Conference on Logic and Methodology.* August 17-20, Amsterdam, The Netherlands.

Sabater, J., Paolucci, M., & Conte, R. (2006). Repage: Reputation and image among limited autonomous partners. *Journal of Artificial Societies and Social Simulation, 9*(2), 3.

Salzano, M. (1993). *Le variabili fiscali nei modelli Neo-Keynesiani.* Napoli: Liguori Editore.

Salzano, M. (2005). Una simulazione neo-keynesiana ad agenti eterogenei. In P.Terna, R. Boero, M. Morini, & M. Sonnessa (Eds.). *Simulazione, modelli ad agenti e scienze sociali.* Mulino.

Sasaki, Y., Yamashita, T., Kawamura, H.,Kurumatani, K., &Ohuchi, A. (2002). Emergence of key currency in international trade by production and trader agents. In H.J. Caulfield & S-H. Chen et al. (Eds.), *Proceeding Of the Sixth Joint Conference on Information Sciences, Association for Intelligent Machinery* (pp. 1073-1076).

Schelling, T. (1978). *Micromotives and macrobehavior.* New York: Norton.

Schmidt, C., & Rounsevell, M.D.A. (2006) Are agricultural land use patterns influenced by farmer imitation? *Agriculture, Ecosystems & Environment, 115*(1-4), 113-127.

Schneider, F., & Enste, D.H. (2000). Shadow economies: Size, causes, and consequences. *Journal of Economic Literature, 38*(1), 77-114.

Schüssler, R. (1989). Exit threats and cooperation under anonimity. *The Journal of Conflict Resolution, 33,* 728-749.

Schüssler, R., & Sandten, U. (2000). Exit, anonymity and the chances of egoistical cooperation. *Analyse & Kritik, 22*(1), 114-129.

Schwenk, G. (2004). *Micro-macro relations in the Kirk-Coleman model.* Retreived January 4, 2007 from, http://geb.uni-giessen.de/geb/volltexte/2004/1726/

Schwenk, G. (2006). Interlevel relations and manipulative causality. *Journal for General Philosophy of Science, 37*(1), 99-110.

Sempé, F., Nguyen, D.M., Boissau, S., Boucher, A., & Drogoul, A. (2005). *An artificial maieutic approach for eliciting expert's knowledge in multi-agent simulation.* Paper presented at the Sixth International Workshop on Multi-Agent-Based Simulation (MABS), July 2005, Utrecht (Netherlands).

Servat, D. (2000). *Agent-based vs. PDE modeling of runoff dynamics:Simulation experiments.* Paper presented at the International Symposium on Soil Sructure, Water and Solute Transport at the IRD, Bondy, France.

Shapley, L.S., & Shubik, M. (1954). A measure of evaluating a distribution of power in a committee system. *American Political Science Review, 48,* 787-792.

Sharpe, W.F. (1964), Capital asset prices: A theory of market equilibrium under condition of risk, *The Journal of Finance, 19,* 425-442.

Shiller, R.J. (2000). *Irrational exuberance.* Princeton University Press.

Shleifer, A. (2000). *Inefficient markets.* Oxford University Press.

Shneiderman, B. (2004). Foreword. In Chen. *Information visualization: Beyond the horizon.* http://www.cs.umd.edu/users/ben/Chen-InfoViz-book-foreword.pdf

Shoham, Y., & Tennenholtz, M. (1992). On the synthesis of useful social laws in artificial societies. In *Proceedings of the 10th National Conference on Artificial Intelligence,* San Mateo, CA: Kaufmann (pp. 276-282).

Sigmund, K., & Nowak, A.M. (2001). Tides of tolerance. *Nature, 414,* 403-405.

Simon, H. A. (1959). *Administrative behaviour* (2nd ed.). Macmillan.

Simon, H.A. (1957). *Models of man, social and rational: Mathematical essays on rational human behaviour in a social setting.* New York: John Wiley & Sons.

Simon, H.A. (1991). Bounded rationality and organizational learning. *Organization Science, 2*, 125-134.

Smaniotto, R.C. (2004). *"You scratch my back and I scratch yours" versus "love thy neighbour": Two proximate mechanisms of reciprocal altruism.* PhD thesis, ICS/University of Groningen. Available online at http://irs.ub.rug.nl/ppn/269506969

Smith, V. & Williams V.A. (1989). The boundaries of competitive price theory: Convergence, expectations, and transaction costs. In L. Green & J. Kagel (Eds.), *Advances in behavioral economics, Vol. 2.* Norwood, NJ: Ablex Publishing.

Smith, V. (1962). An experimental study of competitive market behavior. *Journal of Political Economy, 70,* 111-137.

Smith, V. (1989). Theory, experiment and economics. *Journal of Economic Perspectives,* 783-801.

Smith, V. (2002). Method in experiment: Rethoric and reality. *Experimental economics, 5,* 91-110.

Smith, V.L. (1994). Economics in the laboratory. *Journal of Economic Perspectives, 8,* 113-131.

Sonnessa, M. (2004). *JAS 1.0: New features.* Oral presentation at the SwarmFest2004 conference, May 9-11.

Sosa, E. & Tooley, M. (Eds.). (1993). *Causation.* Oxford: Oxford University Press.

Spender, J.C. (1996). Making knowledge the basis of a dynamic theory of the firm. *Strategic Management Journal, 17* (Winter Special Issue), 45-62.

Springer, U. (2003). The market for GHG permits under the Kyoto protocol—A survey of model studies. *Energy Economics 25,* 527-551.

Stauffer, D. (2001). Monte Carlo simulations of Sznajd models. *Journal of Artificial Societies and Social Simulation* 5(1). http://www.soc.surrey.ac.uk/JASSS/5/1/4.html

Stauffer, D., Sousa, A., & Schulze, C. (2004). Discretized opinion dynamics of the Deffuant model on scale-free networks. *Journal of Artificial Societies and Social Simulation, 7*(3). http://jasss.soc.surrey.ac.uk/7/3/7.html

Stauffer, D., Sousa, A.O., & Moss De Oliveira, S. (2000). Generalization to square lattice of Sznajd sociophysics model. *International Journal of Modern Physics C, 11*(6), 1239-1245. Available at http://www.ica1.uni-stuttgart.de/~sousa/papers/sznajd1.pdf

Stegmueller, W. (1983) *Probleme und Resultate der Wissenschaftstheorie und analytischen Philosphie; Band I: Erklaerung, Begruendung, Kausalitaet; Teil E: Teleologische Erklaerung, funktionalanalyse und Selbstregulation.* Berlin/Heidelberg: Springer Verlag.

Stoiber, M., & Thurner, P.W. (2004). Die ratifikation intergouvernementaler verträge: Konstitutionelle erfordernisse und akteursspezifische agendakontrolle. In F.U. Pappi, E. Riedel, P.W. Thurner, & R. Vaubel. (Eds.), *Die institutionalisierung internationaler verhandlungen* (pp. 173-204) Frankfurt/Main.

Sumpter, D.J.T. (2006). The principles of collective animal behaviour. *Philosophical Transactions of the Royal Society of London: Series B, 361,* 5-22.

Suppes, P. (1962). Models of data Logic. In E. Nagel, P. Suppes, & A. Tarski (Eds.), *Methodology and the philosophy of science: Proceedings of the 1960 international congress* (pp. 252-261). Palo Alto, CA: Stanford University Press. Retrieved from http://suppes-corpus.stanford.edu/article.html?id=41

Sznajd-Weron, K. (2005). Sznajd model and its applications. *Acta Physica Polonica B,* 36(8), 2537-2547. http://arxiv.org/abs/physics/0503239

Sznajd-Weron, K., & Sznajd, J. (2000). Opinion evolution in closed community. *International Journal of Modern Physics, 11*(6), 1157-1165.

Szulanski, G. (1996). Exploring internal stickiness: Impediments to the transfer of best practice within a firm. *Strategic Management Journal, 17,* 27-44.

Takahashi, H., & Terano, T. (2003). An agent-based approach to investors' behavior and asset price fluctuation in financial markets. *Journal of Artificial Societies and Social Simulation, 6*, 3.

Takahashi, H., & Terano, T. (2004). Analysis of micro-macro structure of financial markets via an agent-based model: Risk management and dynamics of asset pricing. *Electronics and Communications in Japan, 87*, 7, 38-48.

Takahashi, H., & Terano, T. (2006). Emergence of overconfidence investors in financial markets. *Fifth International Conference on Computational Intelligence in Economics and Finance.*

Tapscott, D. (1996). *The digital economy: Promise and peril in the age of networked intelligence.* New York and London: McGraw-Hill.

Tarde, G. (1890). *Les lois de l'imitation.* Jean-Marie Tremblay (Ed.), Les classiques des Sciences Sociales.

Tarde, G. (1898). *Les lois sociales.* Esquisse d'une sociologie. Jean-Marie Tremblay (Ed.), Les classiques des Sciences Sociales.

Taylor, P.D., & Jonker, L.B. (1978). Evolutionary stable strategies and game dynamics. *Mathematical Biosciences, 40*, 145-156.

Taylor, R.I. (2003). *Agent-based modelling incorporating qualitative and quantitative methods: A case study investigating the impact of e-commerce upon the value chain.* Unpublished PhD Thesis, Manchester Metropolitan University.

Terano, T., Deguchi, H., & Takadama, K. (Eds.). (2003). Meeting the challenge of social Ppoblems via agent-based simulation. *Post Proceedings of The Second International Workshop on Agent-Based Approaches in Economic and Social Complex Systems*, Springer Verlag.

Terano, T., Nishida, T., Namatame, A., Tsumoto, S., Ohsawa, Y., & Washio, T. (Eds.). (2001). *New frontiers in artificial intelligence.* Springer Verlag.

Tesauro, G., & Das, R. (2001). High-performance bidding agents for the continuous double auction. *Proceedings of the Third ACM Conference on Electronic Commerce.*

Tesfatsion, L. (2002). Agent-based computational economics. *Economics Working Paper*, No.1, Iowa Sate University.

Thomson, R., Boerefijn, J., & Stokman, F. (2004). Actor alignments in European Union decision making. *European Journal of Political Research, 43*, 237-261.

Thurner, P.W. (2004). *Die graduelle konstitutionalisierung der Europäischen Union. Eine quantitative fallstudie am beispiel der regierungskonferenz 1996.* Habilitation thesis: Univ. of Mannheim.

Thurner, P.W., Kroneberg, C., & Stoiber, M. (2003). Strategisches signalisieren bei internationalen verhandlungen. Eine quantitative analyse am beispiel der regierungskonferenz 1996. *Zeitschrift für Internationale Beziehungen, 10*, 287-320.

Thurner, P.W., Pappi, F.U., & Stoiber, M. (2002). EU Intergovernmental conferences: A quantitative analytical reconstruction and data-handbook of domestic preference formation, transnational networks and dynamics of compromise during the Amsterdam Treaty negotiations. *Mannheimer Zentrum für Europäische Sozialforschung: Arbeitspapiere–Working Papers* No. 60, *IINS Research Paper* No. 15.

Tietenberg, T.H. (2006). *Tradable permits bibliography.* Retrieved December 31, 2006 from, http://www.colby.edu/personal/t/thtieten/trade.html

Timmers, P. (1999). *Electronic commerce: Strategies and models for business-to-business trading.* New York: Wiley.

Trivers, R. (1971). The evolution of reciprocal altruism. *Quarterly Review of Biology, 46*, 35-57.

Troitzsch, K.G. (1996). Multilevel simulation. In K.G.Troitzsch, U. Mueller, G.N. Gilbert, & J.E. Doran (Eds.), *Social science microsimulation.* Berlin: Springer.

Tsoukas, H. (1996). The firm as a distributed knowledge system. *Strategic Management Journal, 17* (Winter Special Issue), 11-25.

Tuckman, B. W. (1965). Developmental sequences in small groups. *Psychological Bulletin, 63*, 384-399.

Turban, E., Lee, J., King, D., & Chung, H.M. (1999). *Electronic commerce: A managerial perspective*. Prentice Hall.

Turkle, S. (1984). The second self, computers and the human spirit. London: Granada.

Tversky, A., & Kahneman, D. (1992). Advances in prospect theory: Cumulative representation of uncertainty. *Journal of Risk and Uncertainty, 5*, 297-323.

Urbig, D. (2003). Attitude dynamics with limited verbalisation capabilities. *Journal of Artificial Societies and Social Simulation, 6*(1). http://jasss.soc.surrey.ac.uk/6/1/2.html

Urbig, D., & Lorenz J. (2004, September 16-19). Communication regimes in opinion dynamics: Changing the number of communicating agents. In *Proceedings of the Second Conference of the European Social Simulation Association (ESSA)*, Valladolid, Spain.

Van Deemen, A.M. (1997). *Coalition formation and social choice*. Boston: Kluwer Academic Publishers.

van der Bij, H., Song, X. M., & Weggeman, M. (2003). An empirical investigation into the antecedents of knowledge dissemination at the strategic business unit level. *Journal of Product Innovation Management, 20*, 163-179.

van der Linden, W.J. & Hambleton, R.K. (Eds.). (1997). *Handbook of modern item response theory*. New York/Heidelberg: Springer Verlag.

Van Dijk, E., & Wilke, H. (1997). Is it mine or is it yours? Framing property rights and decision making in social dilemmas. *Organizational Behavior and Human Decision Processes, 71*(2), 195-209.

Vanberg, V. J. (2003). The rationality postulate in economics: Its ambiguity, its deficiency and its evolutionary alternative. *Frieburg Discussion Papers on Constitutional Economics, 3*.

Vanberg, V., & Congleton, R. (1992). Rationality, morality and exit. *American Political Science Review, 86*, 418-431.

Varela, F.J. (1989). *Autonomie et connaissance*. Seuil.

Veldkamp, A., & Lambin, E.F. (2001). Predicting landuse change. *Agriculture, Ecosystems, & Environment, 85*, 1-6.

Walker, J.L. (1969). The diffusion of innovation among the American states. *American Political Science Review, 63*, 880-899.

Wallis, S., & Moss. S. (1994). Efficient forward chaining for declarative rules in a multi-agent modelling language, *CPM Report No.: 004*, Manchester Metropolitan University

Wartofsky, M. W. (1979). *Models*. Boston Studies in the Philosophy of Science, Vol. 129. Dordrecht: Reidel.

Watson, R.T., & McKeown, P.G. (1999). Manheim auctions: Transforming interorganizational relationships with an extranet. *International Journal of Electronic Commerce, 3*(4), 29-46.

Weidlich, A., Sensfuß, F., Genoese, M., & Veit, D. (2005). Studying the effects of CO_2 emissions trading on the electricity market–A multi-agent-based approach. In *Proceedings of the 2nd Joint Research Workshop: Business and emissions trading*. Springer.

Weidlich, W. (1994). Synergetic modelling concepts for sociodynamics with application to collective political opinion formation. *Journal of Mathematical Sociology, 18*, 267-291.

Weidlich, W., & Haag, G.(1999). *An integrated model of transport and urban evolution*. Springer.

Weisbuch, G., Deffuant, G., Amblard, F., & Nadal, J.P. (2002). Meet, discuss and segregate! *Complexity, 7*(3), 55-63.

Weiss, G. (Ed.). (2000) *Multiagent systems*. Cambridge Massachusetts: MIT Press.

Wenger, E.C. (2000). Communities of practice and social learning systems. *Organization 7*(2), 225-246.

Whetton, D.A. (1987). Interorganizational relations. In J. Lorsch (Ed.), *Handbook of organizational behavior* (pp. 238-253). Englewood Cliffs, NJ: Prentice-Hall.

Wieselquist, J., Rusbult, C., Agnew, C., Foster, C., & Agnew, C. (1999). Commitment, pro-relationship behavior, and trust in close relationships. *Journal of Personality and Social Psychology, 77*(5), 942-66.

Wilensky, U. (1999). *NetLogo.* Center for Connected Learning and Computer-Based Modeling, Northwestern University. Evanston, IL.

Wilkinson, G. S. (1984). Reciprocal food sharing in the vampire bat. *Nature, 308,* 181-184.

Wilkinson, G. S. (1990). Food sharing in vampire bats. *Scientific American, 2,* 64-70.

Wooldridge, M. (2002). *An introduction to multi-agent systems.* Chichester, UK: John Wiley.

Woolridge, M., & Jennings, N.R. (1995). Intelligent agents: Theory and practice. *Knowledge Engineering Review, 10*(2), 115-152.

Wright, V. (1996). The national coordination of European policy making. In J. Richardson (Ed.), *European Union: Power and policy making.* London: Routledge, pp. 238-253.

Wu, G., & Gonzalez, R. (1996). Curvature of the probability weighting function. *Management Science, 42,* 1676-1690.

Yamagishi, T., Hayashi, N., & Jin, N. (1994). Prisoner's dilemma networks: Selection strategy versus action strategy. In U. Schulz, W. Albers, & U. Mueller (Eds.), *Social dilemmas and cooperation* (pp. 311-326). Heidelberg: Springer.

Yasutomi, A. (2000). The emergence and collapse of money. *Physica, D82,* 180-194.

Young, H.P. (1993a). The evolution of conventions. *Econometrica, 61,* 57-84.

Young, H.P. (1993b). An evolutionary model of bargaining. *Journal of Economic Theory, 59,* 145-168.

Young, H.P. (1998). *Individual strategy and social structure.* Princeton, NJ: Princeton University Press.

Yukl, G. (1989). *Leadership in organizations.* Englewood Cliffs, NJ: Prentice-Hall.

Zeggelink, E. (1995). Evolving friendship networks: An individual-oriented approach implementing similarity. *Social Networks, 17,* 83-110.

Zeggelink, E., de Vos, H., & Elsas, D. (2000). Reciprocal altruism and group formation: The degree of segmentation of reciprocal altruists who prefer old-helping-partners. *Journal of Artificial Societies and Social Simulation, 3*(3). http://www.soc.surrey.ac.uk/JASSS/3/3/1.html

About the Contributors

Bruce Edmonds is Director of the Centre for Policy Modelling at the Manchester Metropolitan University, and a Senior Research Fellow there. He gained his first degree in Mathematics and his Ph.D. in philosophy on *Measures of complexity*. His field is the intersection of sociology and computer science: both applying social mechanisms to the organisation of distributed computer science and the use of computational techniques to model aspects of society. For more information about him, see his Web site at http://bruce.edmonds.name

Cesáreo Hernández Iglesias is Professor of Business and Economics (B&E) and head of the Business and Economics Department at the University of Valladolid, Spain. He graduated from the University of Barcelona in Industrial Engineering (1970) and Economics (1974). He obtained his Ph.D. in 1975 on applications of Control Theory to Econometrics. He initially worked in time series analysis in econometric modelling as a postgraduate at the L.S.E. and Imperial College in London from 1971-74. His current research interests within the INSISOC Group (Engineering Social Systems Group) include economic methodology and social simulation.

Klaus G. Troitzsch has been a full professor of computer applications in the social sciences at the University of Koblenz-Landau since 1986. He took his PhD in political science from the University of Hamburg. From 1974 to 1978 he was a member of the Liberal Party Group in the Parliament of Hamburg. In 1979 he returned to academia as a senior researcher in an election research project. His main interests in teaching and research are social science methodology and, particularly, the simulation of social processes. He was among the founders of the Research Committee on Modelling and Simulation of the German Sociological Association (1988), of the SimSoc Consortium, which publishes the Journal of Artificial Societies and Social Simulation (JASSS, now in its tenth year), and of the European Social Simulation Association (ESSA). Most of his research projects were devoted to developing simulation tools for micro, multilevel, and agent-based simulation or to implement simulation courses for social scientists, part of which have been offered in annual summer and spring courses for nearly ten years. He is author, co-author, and co-editor of a number of books and articles on simulation, and he organised several national and international conferences in social simulation.

* * * * *

István Back is currently finishing his dissertation at the Department of Sociology at the University of Groningen, and is a member of the research school ICS (Interuniversity Center for Social Science Theory and Methodology). His main research interest is the study of social dilemmas from a combined emotional and rational choice perspective. He creates formal models and computer simulations of social phenomena and tests derived hypotheses using laboratory experiments with human subjects, scenario studies, and surveys. He has recently published his work in the *Journal of Artificial Societies and Social Simulation.*

Kim M. Bloomquist is a senior economist with the U.S. Internal Revenue Service's Office of Research. He has held that position for 11 years and has over 25 years experience as an economist for the U.S. government. Mr. Bloomquist also is a Ph.D. student in Computational Social Science at George Mason University, Fairfax, Virginia. His recent research has focused on tax compliance measurement, computational modeling of taxpayer compliance behavior, and empirical analysis of Pareto income distributions. Mr. Bloomquist is married and lives in Fairfax, Virginia.

Stanislas Boissau is a social scientist with a main interest in management of common-pool resources. He is currently writing his Ph.D. thesis on local institutional change in a context of increasing land scarcity. He has been doing extensive field work in Bac Kan province (Vietnam) where he conducted several gaming-simulation and participatory modelling experiments.

Alain Boucher graduated in computer engineering from the Ecole Polytechnique of Montreal (Canada) in 1994. He received his Ph.D. degree from the Joseph Fourier University (Grenoble, France) in 1999. He worked on a European research project (ASTHMA) for three years at INRIA Sophia-Antipolis (France) until 2002. He is currently Professor at the Francophone Institute for Computer Science (IFI-AUF) in Hanoi (Vietnam). His research interests are in computer vision (content-based indexing and retrieval, pattern recognition, and image interpretation) and artificial intelligence (multi-agent systems, machine learning, knowledge acquisition, and user modeling).

François Bousquet is a modeler based at CIRAD (French Agricultural Research Centre for International Development) in Montpellier France. He specializes in social simulation applied to the interactions between societies and resources. He develops specific research on participatory modeling, called companion modeling. He is involved in different research projects, several of them based on applications to companion modeling in South-East Asia. Publications can be found at: http://cormas.cirad.fr

Alessandro Cappellini was born in Turin, Italy. He studied Economics at the University of Turin, where he obtained his Masters Degree in July 2003, with a Thesis in Mathematical Economics concerning stock market simulation with artificial and natural agents. He holds a Ph.D. (obtained in 2006) in Economics simulation, obtained at the University of Turin, Italy. His main research interests are computer simulation and experiments applied to Finance, Economics and Social Sciences. He is also interested in behavioural finance, and is a founder of the Italian behavioural finance association (A.I.FIN. C). Nowadays he is a Research Associate at the Lagrange Interdisciplinary Laboratory for Excellence in Complexity–LIEC at ISI Foundation.

David Chavalarias is a researcher at the Ecole Polytechnique, Paris and the Paris Ile-de-France Institute for Complex Systems. He has a background in mathematics and computer sciences (Ecole Normale Supérieur—Cachan) and a Ph.D. in cognitive sciences at the Ecole Polytechnique. He focuses his research on social systems modeling and particularly social cognition, defined as the crossroad of cognitive sciences and complex systems sciences. Deeply involved in the promotion of complex systems sciences, he is member of the Complex Systems Society executive committee.

Rosaria Conte is head of the Laboratory of Agent Based Social Simulation at the Institute of Cognitive Science and Technology of the National Research Council, Italy. She teaches Social Psychology at the University of Siena. She is a member of the ESSA (European Association of Social Simulation) Management Committee. Her main background is in cognitive science, although her publications range from cognitive and interaction modeling to agent-based simulation, and from cultural evolution to the study of altruism, cooperation, and social norms. Her research interests include the formal computational study of coalition formation, social dependence, norms representation and reasoning, and the role of cognition in the propagation of norms. She has published more than 100 scientific works including international books, refereed journal articles, and book chapters.

Arianna Dal Forno, Ph.D. (University of Trieste, 2001) is a post-doctoral fellow at the department of Applied Mathematics at University of Turin. Her main research interests are mathematical modeling of organizations and microstructure of market architectures. She has been a visiting post-doctoral scholar at Harvard University. Her most recent publications have been published in *Journal of Economic Interaction and Coordination*, *Journal of Artificial Societies and Social Simulation*, *Nonlinear Dynamics, Psychology, and Life Sciences*, and *Decisions in Economics and Finance*.

Guillaume Deffuant has been head of the Laboratoire d'Ingénierie des Systèmes Complexes at Cemagref since 1997. He has been the leader of several projects in LISC, and coordinated the European project IMAGES from 1997 to 2001. His Ph.D. in cognitive science, supervised by F. Varela, was about self-organising geometrical structures and learning theory. His research interests are currently social and ecological modelling, and more particularly, understanding collective effects generated by individual interactions.

Gennaro Di Tosto is an associate researcher at the Institute of Cognitive Science and Technology of the National research Council, Italy. His main research interests are social behaviors, e.g., cooperation and altruism, their evolutionary basis, and their cognitive prerequisites. He has been applying agent-based models to the study of altruistic behavior, and is studying the factors that can promote cooperation in on-line reputation systems.

Alexis Drogoul graduated with a degree in artificial intelligence from the University of Paris 6 (France) in 1990. He received his Ph.D. degree (multi-agent systems for problem solving and simulation) from the same University in 1993. Recruited in 1995 as an associate professor, he became Full Professor in 2000 and joined the IRD in 2004. He is currently Senior Researcher in the IRD-GEODES research unit, in which he leads the multi-agent team, which focuses on multi-agent and individual-based simulations of complex systems. He is interested in the study, by modeling and simulation, of the emergence of spatial, temporal, behavioral, and/or social structures within natural systems. His research thus covers a wide range, from the simulation of animal societies to the design of multi-robots systems, problem-solving systems, and agent-oriented methodologies. He is a member of the program committee of the major conferences in these domains (IJCAI, AAMAS, SAB, etc.) and an expert for the NSF and EEC on agent-based technologies.

Andreas Ernst holds a chair in environmental systems analysis and is head of the SESAM (Socio-Environmental Systems Analysis and Modelling) research group at the Center for Environmental Systems Research (CESR) at the University of Kassel, Germany. His interests include, among others, phenomena of complexity, agent-based modelling of motivational and cognitive aspects of behaviour and learning, interdisciplinary approaches to environmental problems, the application of decision modelling to spatially explicit large-scale domains, psychological and economic aspects of innovation and innovative behaviour, and phenomena of social interaction, especially in resource conflicts. He is currently Chairman of the environmental psychology division of the German Psychological Association (DGPs).

Andreas Flache is an Associate Professor at the Department of Sociology of the University of Groningen, The Netherlands, and a member of the research school ICS (Interuniversity Center for Social Science Theory and Methodology). His research addresses mainly cooperation problems and social integration, social networks, and learning theory. He studies the application of computational and game theory modeling, laboratory experimentation, and survey research. Recent publications of his were included in *Journal of Conflict Resolution, Rationality and Society, Journal of Mathematical Sociology, Journal of Artificial Societies and Social Simulation*, and Proceedings of the National Academy of Sciences, among other journals. For more information see: http://www.ppsw.rug.nl/~flache

Javier Gil-Quijano is a Ph.D. student of computer science at the University Paris VI–LIP6 in collaboration with the IRD (Research Institute for Development, France) . His work concerns the use of multi-agent systems (MAS) in simulation of urban systems and automatic classification of huge volumes of data. Currently he is interested in applications of MAS to the automatic recognition of sequential data patterns in data warehouses and the Web. He was born in Colombia and went to France following a master of sciences on robotics and computer graphics at the University Los Andes in Bogotá. Currently, he is a temporary teacher of introduction to databases and programming languages at the University of Montpellier 1 (France).

Nick Gotts is a Senior Research Scientist in the Integrated Land Use Systems group at the Macaulay Institute. Until 1996, his research mainly concerned qualitative spatial representation and reasoning. Since then he has concentrated on complex systems dynamics, particularly on agent-based social simulation, but also on cellular automata. He is particularly interested in the origins of complexity, in the distinctive features of complex adaptive systems which include agents capable of modelling and criticising the systems to which they belong (i.e., human beings), and systematic approaches to comparing, validating, and combining agent-based models using formal ontologies and related formalisms.

David Hales. BSc (Honors) Computer Science (Aston University), 1991; MSc Artificial Intelligence (Essex University), 1995; Ph.D. (Essex University) 2001 on Tag-based cooperation in artificial societies. He is a Postdoctoral Researcher at the Dept. of Computer Science, University of Bologna, Italy. His research interests include: agent-based social simulation, self-organizing software, the application of social theories to computational systems, and P2P systems. A full list of his publications is available from his Web site at http://www.davidhales.com Dr. Hales is an elected officer and member of the European Social Simulation Association (ESSA).

Stephan Janisch received his Diploma in Computer Science (honors), with minors in physics from LMU München, Institute of Computer Science, , Germany (2003). Since 2003 he has been a Research Assistant at the Department of Programming and Software Engineering at the University. The working title of his Ph.D. is*Generic components for the implementation of socioeconomic models.*

Hans-Joachim Mosler is an associate professor of social and environmental psychology at the University of Zurich, Switzerland and head of the research group "Modelling Social Systems" at EAWAG (Swiss Federal Institute of Aquatic Science and Technology). His education and academic qualifications are as follows: Diploma (Master's Degree) in zoology with a thesis in ethology, University of Zurich (1980); Lizentiat (Master's Degree) in psychology with thesis in social psychology, University of Zurich (1986); Doctorate in psychology, Dr. phil. I, University of Zurich (1990). Postdoctoral thesis and qualification as university professor in psychology at the University of Zurich (1998). Visiting professor at the University of Kassel (Department of Psychology and Center for Environmental Systems Research) Summer 1997-1998. His current research is on behavioural change in large populations using agent-based simulations.

Dr. Adolfo Lopez is a lecturer in Business and Economics at the University of Valladolid. He graduated from the University of Oviedo in Industrial Engineering (1994) and obtained his Ph.D. in 2000 on applications of agent-based simulation to economic analysis, in the University of the Basque Country. His research interests within the INSISOC Group (Engineering Social Systems Group) include computer simulation of social and economic behaviour and industrial policy.

Ugo Merlone (Ph.D.,University of Trieste, 1998) is associate professor of Applied Mathematics at University of Turin. His main research interests are mathematical modeling of organizations and bounded rationality agent interaction dynamics. He has published several papers in peer reviewed journals and has been a visiting scholar at the University of Arizona, London School of Economics, and Harvard University. Further details are available from http://web.econ.unito.it/merloneugo/.

Piergiuseppe Morone is Associate Professor of Economics at the University of Foggia (Italy). He obtained an MA in Development Economics at the University of Sussex and a Ph.D. in Science and Technology Policy at SPRU (Science and Technology Policy Research–University of Sussex). He also obtained a Ph.D. from the University of Bari (Italy) in Policy for Sustainable Development. He teaches Economics of Innovation at the University of Foggia. His major fields of research include: evolutionary economics, economics of innovation, and cognitive economics.

Javier Pajares is Lecturer in Business and Economics at the University of Valladolid, Spain, within the research team InSiSoc, Ingeniería de los Sistemas Sociales (Social System Engineering Centre). He graduated from the University of Valladolid with a degree in Industrial Engineering (1991). He worked for the Spanish Oil Company Repsol (1991-96), at the Crude and Commodities Department. He obtained his Ph.D. in 2001, from the University of the Basque Country. His current research interests include innovation and R&D management, industrial policy design and assessment, valuation of R&D investments, and computer simulation of industry evolution.

Mario Paolucci is Technology Expert at LABSS (Laboratory of Agent Based Social Simulation, http://www.istc.cnr.it/lss/) in the ISTC/CNR (Institute for Cognitive Science and Technology), Rome. He has been teaching Fundamentals of Computer Science II at the University Of Perugia and of Databases at the University of Rome 1. His research interests include Social Artefacts, Norms, Reputation, Responsibility, and the Cultural Evolutionary Mechanisms that support them. He has been studying and applying Agent Theory and Multiagent-based Social Simulation to understand Social Artefacts. He has chaired the RASTA '02 and '03 workshops, the RAS '04 workshop, and the MABS '07 workshop; he is the coordinator for the eRep project in the FP6. His publications include a book on Reputation with Rosaria Conte and articles on JASSS and Adaptive Behavior.

Dawn Parker is Assistant Professor in the Department of Environmental Science and Policy and Center for Social Complexity, George Mason University. Previously, she completed a post-doctoral fellowship in modeling at CIPEC, Indiana University, following completion of her Ph.D. in Agricultural and Resource Economics from UC Davis. Her research interests center around the dynamics of human-environment interactions that result from humans' decisions regarding allocation of scarce resources, focusing on development of multi-agent system models of land-use and land-cover change (MAS/LUCC), including methodological issues and efforts to develop this new research area into a scientifically mature field.

Jose A. Pascual is Lecturer in Business and Economics at the University of Valladolid, Spain, within the research team InSiSoc, Ingeniería de los Sistemas Sociales (Social System Engineering Centre). He graduated from the University of Valladolid in Industrial Engineering (1999) and obtained his Ph.D. in 2006 from the University of Valladolid. His research interests within the INSISOC Group include computer simulation of social and economic behaviour and industrial policy.

Marie Piron is a researcher for the IRD (a unit of research 013). Her research work concerns modelling of the spatial dynamics and social structures in urban systems. She studies the evolution and formation of social structures by statistical techniques, in particular, by the multi-dimensional exploratory analysis. She is especially interested in the study of time-stable social structures. These last years she has worked mainly on the city of Bogota.

Gary Polhill is Senior Research Scientist in the Integrated Land Use Systems group at the Macaulay Institute, specialising in agent-based modelling of socioenvironmental systems and rigorous approaches to their design and interpretation. Prior to joining the Institute, he worked in industry as a professional programmer, following training in Artificial Intelligence and Neural Networks. His research interests are in coupled social and biophysical systems, looking at decisions and actions of actors in landscapes, and the use of semantic grid services to facilitate best practice in agent-based modelling, documentation, comparison, and design.

Marta Posada is lecturer in Environmental Economics and Management at the University of Valladolid where she graduated in Industrial Engineering. She obtained her Ph.D. in 2006 on applications of agent-based simulation to auctions. Her research interests within the INSISOC Group (Engineering Social Systems Group) include computer simulation of social and economic behaviour.

Marco Remondino was born in Asti, Italy, and studied Economics at the University of Turin, where he obtained his Master's Degree in March, 2001 with 110/110 cum Laude et Menzione and a Thesis in Economical Dynamics. He holds a Ph.D. in Computer Science, obtained at the University of Turin, Italy. His main research interests are computer simulation applied to social sciences, enterprise modeling, agent-based simulation, multi-agent systems and BDI agents. He has been part of the European team which defined a Unified Language for Enterprise Modeling (UEML). He is currently working on a grant from Lagrange Project on Complex Systems.

Stéphane Robin is a researcher in economics at GATE, CNRS, in Lyon, France. His main tool is experimental economics, which he uses to study different topics related to markets and cooperative behaviours. He first focused on reciprocity in cooperative games and coordination among firms, with a special interest in the role of emotions to induce reciprocal behaviours. He then studied markets and the influence of the institution, such as the type of auction, or ability to communicate, on the convergence of prices. More recently he has focused on the influence of the same institutions in the revelation of the willingness to pay in consumers. He is also interested in the relation between political opinion and behaviour for consumers on an individual level, and the influence of expressed public opinion on consumption. One of his fields of application is the consumption behaviour regarding GMO in France.

Juliette Rouchier is a researcher in economics at GREQAM, CNRS, in Marseille, France. She has a degree in mathematics, and started to use social simulation for her Master's, which she still uses as her main research tool. She focuses on the representations that individuals build through economic interactions: either images of each other or of the value of the good that is exchanged. This approach implies a focus on economic institutions and their evolution, such as markets, gift giving, consensus apparition, and network formation. On an individual level, she addresses the issues of learning and trust building. She was also involved in a project dealing with environmental management issues, such as water management or GMO dissemination in Europe. She participates in contemporary research on the validation and transmission of results obtained from multi-agent simulations. Her recent research deals with goods markets in theory but also through examples. She has studied the fruits and vegetables wholesale market of Marseille, France, and gained some insight into the organic market for vegetables in Japan.

Nicole J. Saam received her M.A. and Dr. Phil. in political science from the University of Stuttgart/ Germany. She obtained her habilitation in sociology from the University of Mannheim/Germany. From 1993 to 2001 she worked at the Institute of Sociology of the University of Munich/Germany. From 2001 to 2004 she was a temporary professor at the universities of Mannheim, Leipzig, and Marburg. Since 2005 she has been a professor of sociology at the University of Erfurt/Germany. Her research fields include: social theory, especially rational choice, social science methodology, especially social simulation, political sociology, sociology of organization, and sociology of economics.

Massimo Salzano is Professor of Public Finance, Regional Public Finance, Environmental Economics—University of Salerno. He is Coordinator of the International Master "Economics and Complexity" Project: "Scienza e Tecnologia nella Società della Conoscenza: Economia e complessità" FIRB. He is also General Editor, Economics & Complexity, and General Editor for the New Economics Windows, book series published by Springer-Verlag. His selected publications include: *The control of economics as a complex system: Economics & complexity* (Winter1997-98); *Economics: Complex windows* (edited with Alan Kirman),published by Springer-Verlag; *Complex hints in public finance* (edited with David Colander), published by Springer-Verlag; Globalization, complexity and holism—a new research strategy in globalisation and welfare (in *Globalisation and welfare* (2003/4), edited by by Greve and Jespersen, RUC.

Carsten Schulz studied psychology in Heidelberg, Germany (Diploma), and was a member of the SESAM research group at CESR until February 2007. His research interests are agent-based modelling and environmental behaviour. He co-developed the concept, design, and implementation of the DeepHousehold model.

Nina Schwarz studied environmental sciences in Lueneburg, Germany (Diploma). She was also a member of the SESAM research group at CESR. Her Ph.D. thesis in the GLOWA-Danube project was about the diffusion of water-related innovations among domestic households, integrating innovation characteristics, lifestyles, and theories of social psychology into an agent-based model. She is now working as a postdoctoral researcher at the Helmholtz Centre for Environmental Research–UFZ, Leipzig, Germany.

Gero Schwenk is a junior researcher at the DFG Research School on Group Focused Enmity at the University of Marburg, Germany. Being a sociologist by training, his general interest is in understanding how complex interaction of individuals results in global structures of behavior. In pursuit of this goal he is involved in the fields of science theory, empirical social research, machine learning, social networks, cognition, and computational modelling. His recent work covers aspects such as measurement of social influence and bounded rationality in complex networks.

François Sempé received his Ph.D. degree from the Pierre & Marie Curie University (Paris, France) in 2004. Since then he has worked as a researcher at the Francophone Institute for Computer Science (IFI-AUF) in Hanoi (Vietnam). His research focuses on multi-agent simulation and modeling in several domains: mobile robotics, emergent learning, and participative design.

Dr. David Sumpter received his Ph.D. in Mathematics from the University of Manchester. Since then he has worked at the Universities of Bath, Oxford (UK) and Umeå (Sweden). He is currently a Royal Society University Research Fellow at the Department of Zoology, Oxford. His research fields include: collective animal behaviour, mathematical biology, and group decision-making.

Takao Terano is Professor, Department of Computational Intelligence and Systems Science, Interdisciplinary Graduate School of Science and Engineering, Tokyo Institute of Technology, Tokyo. He received his BA degree in 1976 and M.A. in 1978, both from the University of Tokyo, Japan, and Doctor of Engineering in 1991 from Tokyo Institute of Technology, Japan. Between 1978 and 1989, he was research scientist at the Central Research Institute of the Electric Power Industry. His research interests include: genetic algorithm-based machine learning, case-based reasoning, analogical reasoning, distributed artificial intelligence, cooperative agents, computational organization theory, and knowledge system development methodology. He is a member of the editorial board of major AI-related academic societies in Japan and a member of IEEE, AAAI, and ACM.

Hiroshi Takahashi is Associate Professor, Graduate School of Humanities and Social Sciences, Okayama University, Japan. He received his BA degree in 1994 from the University of Tokyo, Japan, M.S. in 2000, and Ph.D. in 2002, both from the University of Tsukuba, Japan. Bwtween 1994 and 1997, he was a research scientist at Miyanodai Technology development center of Fuji Photo Film. From 1997 to 2005, he was Senior Researcher at Mitsui Asset Trust and Banking. His research interests include finance, behavioral economics, genetic algorithm-based machine learning, decision theory, data mining, and agent-based modeling. He is a member of the Nippon Finance Association, JSAI, and SICE, and a chartered member of the security analysts association of Japan.

Satoru Takahashi is a fund manager at Mitsui Asset Trust and Banking, Japan and a Ph. D. candidate, Graduate School of Business Management, University of Tsukuba.
He received his BS and MS degrees from Tokyo University of Science in 1996 and 1998, respectively, and received an MBA from the University of Tsukuba in 2004. He is a Ph. D. candidate in the Graduate School of Business Management, University of Tsukuba. Since 1998, he has been with Mitsui Asset Trust and Banking Co., Ltd. He is a member of The Information Processing Society of Japan.

Richard Taylor is a research associate at the Centre for Policy Modelling in the Business School of Manchester Metropolitan University. He obtained an MSc in Evolutionary and Adaptive Systems at the School of Cognitive and Computing Sciences, University of Sussex. He obtained a Ph.D. applying social simulation in the area of business-to-business e-commerce. His research interests include social simulation and agent-based social networks.

Robert Tobias studied civil engineering at the Swiss Federal Institute of Technology in Zurich, where he obtained his degree in 1989. After a couple of years working as geotechnical engineer, he went to the University of Zurich, where he studied psychology, informatics, and sociology. He obtained his degree in 2000 and his Ph.D. in 2006. Since 1998 he has been working in computer simulations of social scientific theories and intervention measures for communities at the Division of Social Psychology of the University of Zurich. Since 2002 he has also worked at the Swiss Federal Institute for Aquatic Science and Technology (EAWAG) in the division of Systems Analysis, Integrated Assessment and Modeling (SIAM). Main topics of his work are the development of formal models for application-oriented integration of theories, simulation based planning, and conducting of behaviour-change campaigns, and the development of instruments for data-gathering that allow repeated measuring of constructs used in simulation-models.

Gérard Weisbuch is a senior research associate (DR) at the CNRS and works at the Ecole Normale Supérieure in Paris. A physicist by education, he has been investigating social systems from the perspective of complex systems since 1992, working on sustainable development, markets, opinion propagation, and, more generally, institutions. He is presently the director of the French program on Complex Systems in the Human and Social Sciences. He collaborated on several European projects: Exystence, COSIN, GIACS, and the IMAGES project, on the occasion of which the bounded confidence model was developed (1997-2000).

Satoru Yamadera is a PhD candidate, Department of Computational Intelligence and Systems Science, Interdisciplinary Graduate School of Science and Engineering, Tokyo Institute of Technology, Tokyo. He has been working for the Bank of Japan since 1989. He received his BA in Law in 1989 from Keio University, Japan, his MSc in Public Administration and Public Policy in 1994 from London School of Economics, UK, and MA in Systems Management in 2005 from Tsukuba University, Japan. His research interests cover economic modeling with agent-based modeling and institutional economics.

Index